I0729553

The Male Nude

DAVID LEDDICK

The Male Nude

TASCHEN

Bibliotheca Universalis

Content

The Liberation of the Male Nude Image in the 20th Century

Five hundred and seventy-six pages of male nude images may sound impressive, but assembling that many photographs of naked men at the beginning of the 21st century is not as difficult as it may seem. There are many men and women taking photographs of the male body, publishing them in an assortment of magazines and selling them to collectors. Nowadays the sight of a male nude in a photograph is no longer exceptional. But this was not always the case.

At the end of the 19th century, the male nude was almost entirely absent from photography, with the exception of Sandow, a blond bodybuilder from Königsberg in what was then Prussia. A former artist's model, he became known as "the world's strongest man". Florenz Ziegfeld took him in hand after his first appearance in the United States and soon he became known as "the world's most perfect man." The popular cartes de visite, something like the postcards of today, featured Sandow in nothing but a fig leaf. But he seemed to be the only one who could get away with it. Male nudity was beyond the pale and could be permitted only rarely in painting or the occasional vaudeville performance. In the framework of art, male nudity regained respectability. The naked female body, in contrast, had never been lost to view since the days of antiquity.

In ancient Greece the nude male body was considered the ideal subject
for sculpture. The tunics and togas in which men dressed in any case left much
male flesh exposed. However, conducting sports competitions completely
nude was a conscious decision on the part of the Greeks. Previously the young
men had worn some kind of cover-up, but it was decided that they should run,
wrestle, throw javelins and the discus naked. This was perhaps because the form
of homo-sexuality the Greeks condoned – an interest by older men in younger
men – led the older men to want to see the younger men performing in a perfect
and unadorned state, as much like statuary as possible.

Quite obviously the male body was considered a sex object at that time.
More so than the female body, which was less often sculpted than the male and
frequently veiled in draperies.

The tradition of male nude sculpture for use in monuments and the beauti-
fication of wealthy men's villas continued into the Roman era, but with the rise
of Christianity the male nude disappeared. In fact, under the influence of the
Eastern church, which forbade images, all depictions of humans ceased. The
church did nonetheless allow iconic representations of the saints and important
figures, but these were two-dimensional and usually executed in chaste mosaic.

What a relief the Renaissance must have been for lovers of the human form.
The long years of waiting were well rewarded. Michelangelo led the way with his
David, and many tomb and decorative sculptures. The male nude forms on the
ceiling of the Sistine Chapel were in the same style as his sculpture: imposing,
noble and hearkening back to the past. Classical sculptures were recovered from
centuries of subterranean seclusion to reveal ancient ideals of beauty in the
form of the male body. Contemporary sculptors occasionally buried their work,
hoping to have it "uncovered" as an antiquity!

The male nude, as sculpted and cast in bronze by Donatello, Cellini, Michelangelo, and many others, became an accepted form of art in the Renaissance
and thereafter. The Renaissance, brought to France through the efforts of
François Premier in the 15th century, heralded the return of the male nude and
the female too, of course. The willowy, slim-hipped, long-legged females featured in the sculpture of the time are close to the models of today. Buxomness

was to come later. The male nude remained the stalwart, well-muscled warrior type that was predominant in Italy.

The art training of this time required students to draw their subjects nude, before painting them fully dressed; this led to a truer understanding of the human body and how it worked. Leonardo da Vinci had examined cadavers, and art and medicine advanced together in their exploration of the body. Even the Sun King Louis XIV was drawn nude before being painted with all his robes and scepter. Is it possible that the very well-built body in the drawing was the king's own? It seems unlikely that he would have had the patience to pose, but then again he was considered handsome in his youth.

Paintings of the gods and assorted mythological scenes continued to include the male nude through the 16th and 17th centuries in France, but less in Northern countries. Dürer was a handsome man and portrayed himself in the nude. He frequently painted male and female nudes, though he did not draw on the classic tradition; there was a certain realism about his male figures. The Northern climate would have discouraged any display of nudity: Clothes were essential there. In France and Italy, however, warmer weather gave a certain freedom to the body, and seeing it partially unclad was no novelty.

In the early 19th century, with the rise of Napoleon, art styles changed to some degree and were often used to the greater glory of the Emperor. Napoleon wanted to secure his shaky throne by welding it to solid traditions of the past. Painters like David obliged and naked men abounded in paintings like "The Oath of the Horatii," designed to ennoble war and warriors. The sculptor Antonio Canova was enormously successful in producing classical forms in pure white marble. His large and naked Napoleon was not much favored by the emperor, however, and finally found a home in Wellington's sumptuous town house in London, as a kind of war trophy after his defeat of Napoleon at Waterloo.

After Napoleon's fall, a more commercially oriented government headed by the "citizen king" Louis-Philippe, swept images of the nude male abruptly from the scene. Contemporary man, all buttoned-up in a black suit and top hat appeared incongruous beside his classical counterpart.

The first photographers, however, quickly developed a lucrative business copying models' poses and selling them to artists. Procuring live models was always expensive for struggling painters, and photographs of models in a series of classic poses were of great utility. This is how the photographic male nude came into being. Images of models squatting, bending, lifting, or struggling with another male nude, were copied and used as source material by a flood of artists, mainly in Paris.

In the United States in the latter part of the 19th century, the Philadelphian painter Thomas Eakins used photographic studies to create poses and scenes he would later put to canvas. These photographs were themselves works of art. There also seems to have been a voyeuristic side to his work. He obviously derived enjoyment from enticing good-looking young men to shed their garments and pose for a photograph – highly unusual behavior in prudish Victorian society.

One of the first steps away from using art as an excuse for looking at the male body was taken by Eadweard Muybridge. Fascinated by human and animal bodies in motion, he devised a technique for using a sequence of cameras to photograph movement. His male and female nudes ran, jumped, danced, shot-putted, and displayed how the body actually performs when moving. These photographs took a very long time to be published in the strait-laced American society of the 1870s and 1880s but science eventually prevailed, and photographic images of the male nude became available for the first time to the general public.

The first still photographs of the male nude were taken by Baron Wilhelm von Gloeden in Taormina, Sicily. The expatriate Baron was short of funds and photographed local boys, clad only in wreaths and sandals, and sometimes even less. These pictures supposedly recaptured the naked lifestyle of ancient Greece and were sold to tourists. The Baron's cousin, Guglielmo Plüschow, did similar work and, by the end of the century, male nudes not even pretending to be ancient Greek replicas were being shot by several photographers in Rome. At the same time in Germany, Theodor Hey was photographing less classical male nudes, mainly in sunlit outdoor settings.

Just before World War I Diaghilev's Ballet Russe, on tour from Russia, had an enormous impact on music, painting, fashion, and behavior in general. Its stars, among them Nijinsky and Pavlova, were frankly sexual on stage and their repertoire of ballets created an atmosphere of powerful emotion and dissolute movement. And what was more, you could clearly see the dancers' lithe and slender bodies.

The war brought an end to much Victorian hypocrisy and prudery, perhaps in part because clothing became less formal. Men in uniform and women engaged in war work couldn't afford to be constricted or spend time dressing elaborately. For women in particular, dress became much simpler, with corsets and full-length skirts being abandoned. War always brings a relaxed moral code with it and this livelier, more overtly sexy world welcomed new advances in art photography, including many nudes.

Art photographers, using plenty of soft focus, chose similar themes. Fred Holland Day had misty, wistful youths lounging around on large rocks and in sylvan pools, always nude. Imogen Cunningham later photographed her handsome husband Roi clambering about Mount Rainier in the buff. And the unfettered 1920s brought both male and female movie stars prepared to show unlimited amounts of flesh.

Rudolf Valentino and Ramón Navarro were two stars with an ambiguous sexuality whose bodies were their business. The motion picture industry saw that men as sex objects were good box office, and so proceeded to present the public with more. This was fertile ground, previously held by Sandow and his body beautiful alone. It represented a major step away from the formal Victorian male image, complete with beard and black three-piece suit.

Vaudeville regularly presented dancers like Ted Shawn of the Denishawn company, and circulated photographs for fans everywhere. These usually showed them in their stage attire, or lack of it.

The freeing of the body had been anticipated before the war by "naturalists" and nudists, who vacationed in the nude. Men, furthermore, had a growing interest in improving their physique, and once you had a fine physique, the tendency was to want to show it off. This became the subject matter for magazines that began to appear in the postwar period, increasing the visibility of the male nude image.

While nature and nudist magazines had their serious readers, they presented an opportunity for everyone to see naked men and women. Despite their innocent nature, these magazines were kept on top shelves or under the counter and the brave buyer had to ask for them.

The physique magazines began as equally innocent vehicles for the exchange of tips on weight-training and diet. But the accompanying pictures of the hale and hearty weight-lifters pleased a homosexual readership that never went near a gymnasium. The publishers were quick to comprehend this, and these magazines soon began to portray their bodybuilding stars in more sensually exciting ways.

Actors' and dancers' publicity stills, and photographs of nudists and bodybuilders, formed the sum total of material available to the average nudity-lover before World War II. Some photographers like George Platt Lynes in the United States, Angus McBean in England, and Raymond Voinquel in France were photographing the male nude, but this was largely for the pleasure of their friends. A male nude would occasionally appear in a photography exhibition but this was rare. Most men were still reluctant to see themselves as nature made them.

World War II loosened morals and dress codes even further and after the war physique magazines appeared in a brand-new format. This was "beefcake" for beefcake's sake, as practiced by Bruce of Los Angeles, Lon of New York and a number of others. Now there was a real plethora of images for those who wanted them.

But the male nude image was still under fire. The photographers and particularly Bob Mizer's "Physique Pictorial" magazine came under constant attack. The publisher of "Grecian Guild Pictorial", Lynn Womack, finally managed to get the Supreme Court to decide that nudity was not obscene. This represented a big step forward for the male nude and one that was quickly seized upon by photographers and magazines.

This was 1968. Attitudes toward "getting naked" were becoming relaxed but despite nude streakers featuring regularly in the newspapers, it still took a while for photography to catch up. While nude images spread rapidly in what was still the "under the counter" press, they had a tougher time being accepted into the art world.

Ten years after the Supreme Court decision, the first show devoted to male nudes at the Marcuse Pfeifer Gallery in New York met with a poor reception from male critics. They still saw the male nude as the province of homosexuals or women who wanted to view men in a reduced way, stripped of power. Only René Ricard caught what was bothering the critics. He wrote: "Don't men's genitals have a certain... decorative look, like an accessory thrown in to be amusing?" The penis was the problem. Men did not want their penises to be seen as amusing. And to avoid that response it was better to cover up.

Unfortunately for the critics, the tide was against them. Robert Mapplethorpe was already on the New York scene at the time of the exhibition, and was soon to be recognized as a major force in the art world. His flowers and pretty people and large penises were a heady combination for the financially flush public of the 1980s. It was the disco era; people were sexually active and AIDS had not yet hit. The male nude had won respectability. This was art and the public was buying it. Following Mapplethorpe into the arena were the commercial photographers Bruce Weber, Herb Ritts, Francesco Scavullo, Greg Gorman, and many others. Soon the male nude was selling underwear, fragrance, and women's wear.

Books, calendars, and postcards proliferated, along with gay porn films and their evanescent "stars," who became overnight celebrities. Jeff Stryker appeared in "Interview Magazine". He had no problem about telling his female interviewer which part of his anatomy set him apart from other porn stars.

Now we have entered a period where male frontal nudity is ubiquitous. Film stars like Bruce Willis and Tim Robbins openly permit us a glimpse of their genitalia. Movies about the making of porn movies have arrived on the scene.

Interestingly enough, with the male nude out of the closet, codes of dress are becoming even more relaxed. Business wear is becoming sporty. Even very serious businesses allow casual wear on Fridays. And many firms in warmer climates such as Los Angeles or Miami make no formal requirements at all. In

Miami Beach even the policeman wear shorts and ride bicycles. And they have
to have nice legs, too.

The patriarchal Victorian figure in his buttoned-up collar is gone. His
counterpart of our day is passé and only to be found lurking in the most rarefied
heights of executive offices. Younger men are working out at the gym. Their
wage-earning wives and girlfriends demand it.

It took two wars and a lot of determined men and women photographers to
get men out of their duds and back to the Classical and Renaissance view of what
a man was: beautiful, on a par with women. Now men and women share many of
the same kinds of jobs and responsibilities. It is no longer the man's job to bring
home the bacon and the woman's job to fry it and look beautiful at the same
time. Beauty is now as much a man's responsibility as a woman's.

Strangely enough, we're finding that those qualities homosexual men have
always admired in other men are exactly what women like too. It's just that
nobody ever asked them before. Dependent upon men, they kept their mouths
shut. Now they can admire a strong thigh, a broad back, or a rippling abdomen.
What has been demanded of women for centuries – "be beautiful" – is now
being demanded of men too. Men may be surrendering their Big Daddy image
by going naked, but they are also entering a more user-friendly mode.

Just as it is unlikely that women will return to the kitchen and give up their
freedom, there is little chance that the male nude will cover up again any time
soon. It took a century for the male body to fight its way clear of clothing. It feels
good. And what we have learned in this century is, if it feels good... do it.

Ein Buch von 576 Seiten über männliche Aktfotografie zusammenzustellen ist ganz schön viel, sollte man meinen. Allerdings ist es heute, zu Beginn des 21. Jahrhunderts, auch nicht allzu schwierig, eine so große Anzahl von Fotos nackter Männer zu finden. Viele Fotografen, Männer wie Frauen, machen Aufnahmen von nackten Männern, und es gibt ein breites Spektrum von Magazinen, die ihre Fotos veröffentlichen und zumeist an interessierte Sammler verkaufen. Der Anblick eines Männeraktes lässt heute keinen mehr erschauern.

Gegen Ende des vorletzten Jahrhunderts hingegen war der nackte Mann fast gänzlich aus der Öffentlichkeit verbannt. Eine der seltenen Ausnahmen war Eugene Sandow, ein blonder Hüne aus Königsberg im damaligen Preußen. Sandow, ursprünglich ein Aktmodell, hatte sich durch das, was wir heute Bodybuilding nennen und was damals schlicht Gewichtheben hieß, zum „stärksten Mann der Welt" gestählt und machte tatsächlich auch international Furore. Er ging in die Vereinigten Staaten und sicherte sich umgehend einen Platz in Florenz Ziegfelds legendärer Schauspieltruppe. Die beliebten „cartes de visite", vergleichbar den heutigen Starpostkarten, zeigten Sandow mit nichts als einem Feigenblatt bekleidet. Es werden wohl nicht nur weibliche Fans entzückt gewesen sein.

Wenn man will, kann man fern hinter Sandow die Statuen des antiken Griechenlands entdecken, die Verkörperungen des ewigen Kanons klassischer Schönheit. Doch fest geschlossen steht diese Ahnenreihe nicht. Während der weibliche Akt seit der Antike niemals dem Blick entschwunden ist, fehlt dem männlichen Pendant diese Kontinuität. Zumindest einem männlichen Akt, der Virilität, animalische Leidenschaft und Schönheit ausdrückte.

In der Antike war der nackte männliche Körper das häufigste Motiv in der Bildhauerei, was unter anderem sicher daran lag, dass z. B. im antiken Griechenland der körperliche Umgang unter Männern zwangloser war. So war es damals eine bewusste Entscheidung der Griechen, sportliche Wettkämpfe völlig nackt auszutragen. Anfangs bedeckten die jungen Männer noch ihre Scham, aber dann beschloss man, die olympischen Disziplinen nackt auszutragen. Der Grund hierfür mag in der Duldung einer besonderen Form der Homosexualität gelegen haben – der Hinwendung älterer Männer zu jüngeren Männern. Bei den Älteren hatte dies den Wunsch aufkommen lassen, die Jüngeren so, wie die Natur sie geschaffen hatte, antreten zu lassen, damit sie so statuengleich wie möglich wirkten.

Die Tradition, Statuen nackter Männer in öffentlichen Gebäuden, auf Plätzen oder in Privatvillen wohlhabender Bürger aufzustellen, setzte sich im antiken Rom fort. Mit dem Aufkommen des Christentums verschwanden die Darstellungen männlicher Akte. Der Einfluss der Ostkirche, die Bildnisse jeglicher Art verbot, reichte sogar so weit, dass auf Darstellungen alles Menschlichen überhaupt verzichtet wurde.

Was dem christlichen Mittelalter fremd bleiben musste, gelang erst der Renaissance: die Wiedervereinigung antiker Motive und antiker Themen. Michelangelos David, seine Grabdenkmäler und zahlreiche weitere Statuen lassen den stattlichen, edlen Mann der Antike wiederauferstehen und mit ihm den ewigen Kanon klassischer Schönheit. In der Sixtinischen Kapelle malte er den nackten männlichen Körper im Stil seiner Statuen: stattlich vornehm und der Vergangenheit zugewandt.

Als die Renaissance dank der Bemühungen François Premiers in Frankreich Einzug hielt, kam mit ihr auch die Aktdarstellung. Die gertenschlanken, schmalhüftigen und langbeinigen Frauen, die sich in der Bildhauerei der damaligen

Zeit finden, kommen dem weiblichen Idealtypus unserer Tage sehr nahe. Bei den männlichen Akten herrschte auch weiterhin der muskelbepackte kriegerische Typus vor, wie man ihn aus Italien kannte.

Von den Kunststudenten wurde im Zuge ihrer Ausbildung verlangt, dass sie ihre Modelle erst nackt zeichneten, bevor sie bekleidet gemalt wurden – eine gute Gelegenheit, die Kenntnisse über den menschlichen Körper zu vertiefen. Leonardo da Vinci untersuchte Leichen, um sein Wissen über die Anatomie zu verbessern. Fortan gingen Kunst und Medizin in der weiteren Erforschung des Körpers gemeinsame Wege. Sogar Ludwig XIV. wurde erst nackt gezeichnet, bevor er in vollem Ornat porträtiert wurde. Allerdings ist die Frage erlaubt, ob für den außerordentlich gut gebauten Körper auf dem Gemälde wirklich Ludwig XIV. Modell gestanden hat, da es unwahrscheinlich ist, dass der König hierzu die Geduld aufbrachte; andererseits galt er in seiner Jugend als eine Schönheit.

So wird uns über die Jahrhunderte nur selten ein Blick auf den männlichen Akt gewährt. Und er blieb zumeist auf Götterbildnisse, Darstellung mythologischer und allegorischer Szenen beschränkt. In nördlicheren Gefilden waren Aktdarstellungen grundsätzlich weniger verbreitet. Dürer, ein gutaussehender Mann, zeichnete sich nicht nur selbst nackt, sondern malte auch Männer und Frauen unbekleidet. Dabei ließ er sich nicht von klassischen Traditionen leiten, seine Männerakte scheinen eher dem alltäglichen Leben entsprungen zu sein. Das Klima im Norden verhinderte die Zurschaustellung von Nacktheit, Bekleidung war unerlässlich. Hingegen sorgte in Frankreich und Italien ein wärmeres Klima für eine gewisse Freizügigkeit.

Die Herrschaft Napoleons Anfang des 19. Jahrhunderts brachte eine Veränderung des künstlerischen Schaffens mit sich, der Kaiser vereinnahmte die Kunst häufig zu Propagandazwecken. Napoleon wollte die unsichere Monarchie unbedingt in der Tradition der Vergangenheit verankern, und Maler wie David unterwarfen sich diesem Ansinnen. In dem Gemälde „Der Schwur der Horatier" wimmelt es förmlich von nackten Männern, einzig zu dem Zweck, den Krieg zu verherrlichen. Der Bildhauer Canova wiederum war mit seiner Methode der „Aufweichung" klassischer Traditionen außerordentlich erfolgreich.

Und als das Bürgertum die alte Herrschaftsschicht ablöste, wurde der Hoffnung schnell ein Ende bereitet. Der Bürger, das heißt der um Macht, Einfluss und wirtschaftlichen Erfolg ringende Mann, hätte es nur als Verlust seiner Würde verstehen können, wenn man ihn in seiner Körperlichkeit bloßgestellt hätte. Den nackten Mann wollte er nicht sehen.

Erst mit dem Aufkommen der Fotografie im 19. Jahrhundert gewinnt der männliche Akt wieder an Bedeutung. Die Anfänge waren durchaus prosaischer Natur. Die ersten Aktaufnahmen von Männern sollten weniger gut betuchten Künstlern die teuren Aktmodelle ersetzen. Ihnen kamen Aktfotos in klassischen Posen sehr gelegen, und so hielt der nackte Mann Einzug in die Fotografie. In der Hocke, ein Gewicht stemmend, im Ringkampf mit einem anderen Mann – diese Posen wurden in großer Zahl fotografiert und dienten zahllosen Künstlern als Vorlage.

So machte sich in der zweiten Hälfte des 19. Jahrhunderts etwa auch der amerikanische Maler Thomas Eakins aus Philadelphia die Fotografie zunutze, um Posen und Szenen zu kreieren, die er dann in seinen Gemälden umsetzte. Eakins Arbeiten waren sicherlich nicht frei von einem voyeuristischen Motiv. Aus den Bildern spricht auch eine deutliche Begeisterung aller Beteiligten. In der steifen Atmosphäre seiner Epoche muss das etwas Ungewöhnliches gewesen sein.

Einer der ersten, dem nicht die Kunst den Vorwand lieferte, einen Blick auf den nackten männlichen Körper zu werfen, war Eadweard Muybridge. Muybridges Interesse galt dem Körper in Bewegung, und er entwickelte eine Technik, mit Hilfe mehrerer Kameras Bewegungsabläufe im Bild festzuhalten. Seine nackten Männer und Frauen sind beim Laufen, Springen, Tanzen oder Kugelstoßen zu sehen und veranschaulichen die tatsächlichen Bewegungsabläufe. Doch selbst diese wissenschaftlichen Studien konnten in der sittenstrengen amerikanischen Gesellschaft der 1870er und 1880er Jahre nur gegen hartnäckigen Widerstand veröffentlicht werden.

Die ersten Fotos nackter Männer, die nichts anderes als dies sein wollten, nahm Baron Wilhelm von Gloeden im sizilianischen Taormina auf. Der in Italien lebende Baron fotografierte die Jungen seiner Wahlheimat im Adamskostüm.

Gloeden wollte in seinen Bildern das freie, ungezwungene Leben im antiken Griechenland nachempfinden. Seine Kunden waren durchreisende Touristen. Zugleich betrieb er einen florierenden Versandhandel. Guglielmo Plüschow, ein Vetter des Barons, produzierte in Neapel auf dieselbe Art und Weise. Zusätzlich entstanden in Rom gegen Ende des Jahrhunderts Aktaufnahmen von Männern, ohne den Rückbezug auf ein fernes Arkadien. In Deutschland fotografierte zur selben Zeit Theodor Hey nackte Männer, zumeist im Freien, in der Sonne. Hey sollte seine Arbeit bis zum Ausbruch des Ersten Weltkrieges fortsetzen.

Ein neues Körperbewusstsein vermittelte auch das Diaghilev-Ballett aus Russland, das Europa im Sturm eroberte. Nijinsky und Pavlova, die Stars des Balletts, stellten sich auf der Bühne ungeniert zur Schau. In allen Stücken des Repertoires herrschte eine Atmosphäre starker Emotionalität: die Bewegungen waren raumgreifend, und die geschmeidigen, schlanken Körper der Tänzer zeichneten sich deutlich unter der Kleidung ab.

Nach dem Krieg, der schon immer auch eine Aufweichung moralischer und sittlicher Konventionen mit sich brachte, widmete sich die Fotografie verstärkt dem männlichen Akt, auch wenn man noch ausgiebig auf den Weichzeichner setzte. Fred Holland Day fotografierte seine wehmütig dreinschauenden Modelle zumeist vor großen Felsen und an Waldseen, Imogen Cunningham lichtete ihren Ehemann Roi im Adamskostüm beim Klettern im Gebirge ab.

Auch die Filmstars der goldenen zwanziger Jahre, Männer wie Frauen, hatten nichts dagegen, viel nacktes Fleisch sehen zu lassen. Ihre Fotografien wurden ebenso gerne gekauft wie die prominenter Tänzer des Vaudevilles, etwa eines Ted Shawn, der in äußerst knappen Bühnenkostümen aufzutreten pflegte.

Die Befreiung des Körpers war bereits vor dem Krieg von Naturfreunden und Nudisten propagiert worden. Unter den Männern wuchs das Interesse an körperlicher Ertüchtigung. Dem neuen Interesse am Körper verdankten die sogenannten „Physique-Magazine" ihr Entstehen. Sicher hatten diese Magazine auch ernsthaft interessierte Leser, aber sie boten auch allen denen die Gelegenheit, Männer und Frauen nackt zu betrachten, die den Mut aufbrachten, nach den trotz ihres harmlosen Charakters unter Ladentischen versteckten Heften zu fragen. Auch die reinen Bodybuilder-Zeitschriften fingen recht harmlos als

Informationsbörsen mit Tipps zur richtigen Ernährung etc. an. Die dazugehörigen Abbildungen gesunder und kräftiger Gewichtheber gefielen auch einer homosexuellen Leserschaft, die ein Sportstudio wohl niemals betreten hätte. Die Verleger stellten sich schnell auf diese Leserschicht ein und porträtierten ihre Bodybuildingstars zunehmend in aufreizenden Posen.

Die Nudisten- und Sportmagazine lieferten neben den Standfotos von Schauspielern und Tänzern das einzige Material, auf das der Liebhaber des Männeraktes Zugriff nehmen konnte. In „ernsthaften" Fotoausstellungen blieb der männliche Akt weiterhin die Ausnahme.

Nach dem Zweiten Weltkrieg erschienen die Bodybuilder-Magazine in selbstbewussterer Aufmachung. Endlich wurde „Männerfleisch" ohne Vorwand gezeigt. Bruce of Los Angeles, Lon of New York und viele andere zeigten den nackten Mann unverblümt als Lustobjekt.

Dennoch stießen Fotografen wie Herausgeber in der Öffentlichkeit auf geringe Akzeptanz. Vor allem Bob Mizer, der Herausgeber des legendären Magazins „Physique Pictorial", sah sich ständigen Attacken ausgesetzt. Und Lynn Womack vom „Grecian Guild Pictorials" musste noch 1968 vor den Obersten Gerichtshof ziehen. Dieser entschied, dass Nacktheit nicht per se obszön sei – ein gewaltiger Fortschritt, den sich Fotografen wie Zeitschriftenmacher umgehend zunutze machten.

In der etablierten Kunstszene fand der männliche Akt aber auch jetzt noch keine Anerkennung. Als zehn Jahre nach der Entscheidung des Obersten Gerichtshofes die Marcuse Pfeifer Gallery in New York erstmals eine Ausstellung ausschließlich mit Männerakten präsentierte, stieß sie in der Kritik auf Ablchnung. Männerakte galten immer noch als Domäne von Homosexuellen oder als boshafter Versuch weiblicher Künstlerinnen, Männer ihrer Würde zu berauben. Doch der Zeitgeist sollte sich rasant wandeln. Robert Mapplethorpe hatte zur Zeit der Ausstellung bereits die New Yorker Szene betreten und avancierte bald zum Star. In den hedonistischen 80ern waren seine Bilder von Blumen, attraktiven Menschen und großen Genitalien eine fulminante und erfolgreiche Mischung. Es war die Disco-Ära: Sex war zügellos, AIDS als Gefahr noch nicht erkannt, und der nackte Mann war nicht mehr verpönt. Der Männerakt war

Kunst, und er war kommerziell erfolgreich. Zu Mapplethorpe gesellten sich Werbefotografen wie Bruce Weber, Herb Ritts, Francesco Scavullo, Greg Gorman und viele andere. Fotos nackter Männer halfen Unterwäsche, Parfüms und Damenmode zu verkaufen.

Das Geschäft mit Büchern, Kalendern und Postkarten mit männlichen Akten florierte, und selbst die „Stars" schwuler Pornofilme avancierten zu wenn auch flüchtigen Berühmtheiten. Im „Interview Magazine" erschien ein Interview mit Jeff Stryker, in dem er der Interviewerin ohne Scheu verraten durfte, wieviel ihn von anderen Pornodarstellern unterschied.

Heute sind wir in einer Phase, in der der nackte Mann keine Besonderheit mehr ist. Renommierte Filmstars wie Bruce Willis oder Tim Robbins gestatten uns flüchtige Blicke auf ihre Männlichkeit, und durch die Städte radeln Polizisten in Shorts, und knackige Beine haben sie auch noch.

Viele Jahre und das Engagement zahlreicher Fotografinnen und Fotografen waren nötig, um den Mann von seinen Kleidern zu befreien, zu den Vorbildern der Antike und Renaissance zurückzukehren und den nackten Mann in seiner kreatürlichen Schönheit wiederzuentdecken. So unwahrscheinlich es ist, dass die moderne Frau sich wieder in ihre traditionelle Rolle zurückdrängen lässt, so unwahrscheinlich ist es, dass der nackte Mann sich wieder verhüllt. Es hat lange gedauert, das Kostüm abzulegen. Aber das fühlt sich gut an. Und wenn es sich gut anfühlt: tu es einfach.

Cinq cent soixante-seize pages de nus masculins. Ça peut paraître beaucoup !
Pourtant, réunir autant de photos d'hommes nus aujourd'hui en Europe et
aux Etats-Unis n'est pas aussi difficile que cela en a l'air. Il existe désormais
beaucoup d'hommes et de femmes qui photographient le corps masculin pour
tout un assortiment de revues ou de collectionneurs. La vue d'une photo
d'homme nu ne fait plus frémir personne.

Mais cela ne fut pas toujours le cas. A la fin du XIXᵉ siècle, il était quasiment
impossible de voir un homme nu, à l'exception de Sandow, un culturiste blond
de Königsberg (alors en Prusse orientale). Ancien modèle d'atelier, Sandow fut
surnommé « l'homme le plus fort du monde ». Lorsqu'il émigra aux Etats-Unis,
Florenz Ziegfeld le prit en main et le promut rapidement « l'homme le plus parfait du monde ». Les cartes postales d'alors, très populaires, le présentaient vêtu
d'une simple feuille de vigne. Toutefois, il était apparemment le seul à pouvoir
se le permettre car la nudité masculine se cachait soigneusement, ne faisant que
quelques rares apparitions fugitives dans les tableaux ou sur les scènes de vaudeville. Dans les deux cas, elle se devait de faire référence à la tradition artistique,
ce qui lui conférait un certain degré de respectabilité.

Dans la Grèce antique, le corps nu de l'homme était le sujet de prédilection
des sculpteurs. Cela s'explique certainement par le fait que les hommes se
promenaient partout en petite tunique ou en toge, et que le corps n'était pas
tabou. Néanmoins, que les athlètes participent aux compétitions sportives entièrement nus n'était pas tout à fait innocent de la part des Grecs. Les premiers
temps, les jeunes sportifs portaient bien un petit quelque chose, jusqu'à ce qu'il
soit décidé officiellement que, dorénavant, ils courraient, lutteraient, lance-
raient le javelot et le disque dans le plus simple appareil. Cela était dû sans doute
au fait que la forme d'homosexualité admise par les Grecs, à savoir l'attrait des
hommes mûrs pour les hommes plus jeunes, incitait les amateurs de compétitions sportives à vouloir admirer leurs protégés à l'œuvre dans toute leur perfec-
tion et simplicité.

De toute évidence, le corps de l'homme était alors considéré comme un objet
de désir ; plus que celui de la femme, qui était moins fréquemment sculpté et le
plus souvent drapé dans des étoffes.

La tradition qui consistait à embellir les monuments publics et les villas
de riches patriciens avec des sculptures d'hommes nus perdura dans la Rome
antique, puis disparut avec l'avènement du christianisme. De fait, sous l'influence de l'Eglise de rite oriental, qui interdisait les images, toute représen-
tation humaine disparut. Lorsque l'Eglise chrétienne finit par s'assouplir,
elle autorisa les icônes de saints et de personnages importants, mais sous la
forme de mosaïques.

Quel soulagement pour les amateurs de beauté charnelle lorsque survint la
Renaissance ! Michel-Ange ouvrit la voie avec son David et de nombreuses autres
sculptures destinées à orner les tombeaux et les palais. Ses fresques de la chapelle
Sixtine lui permirent d'appliquer le même style dans sa sculpture, créant des
hommes nus imposants, nobles et inspirés de l'art antique. On se mit à creuser
la terre pour déterrer les statues grecques et romaines, considérées comme le
summum de la beauté masculine.

Le nu masculin, sculpté et coulé dans le bronze par Michel-Ange, Donatello,
Cellini et bien d'autres encore, devint un genre artistique reconnu. Lorsque,
au début du XVIe siècle, la Renaissance se déplaça en France sous l'égide de

François Ier, le nu masculin la suivit. Les femmes idéalisées, longilignes, avec des hanches étroites et de longues jambes, étaient alors proches de nos canons de beauté actuels. Le nu masculin, lui, resta le vaillant guerrier bien bâti qui prédominait en Italie.

La formation artistique de l'époque requérait des étudiants qu'ils dessinent leurs sujets nus avant de les habiller, ce qui favorisa une grande connaissance de l'anatomie et du fonctionnement du corps humain. Léonard de Vinci fit de nombreuses esquisses de cadavres, et l'art et la médecine progressèrent ensemble dans leur étude du nu. Même Louis XIV fut dessiné nu avant d'être revêtu de ses somptueux vêtements de cour et de son sceptre. Est-il possible que le corps si bien fait qui apparaît dans les ébauches soit vraiment le sien ? Il n'avait probablement pas la patience de poser, mais d'un autre côté, on dit qu'il était très beau dans sa jeunesse. Petit, mais beau.

Tout au long des XVIe et XVIIe siècles en France, les dieux de l'Antiquité et les scènes mythologiques continuèrent à offrir de nombreux prétextes pour montrer des hommes nus. En Allemagne, Dürer, qui était fort bel homme, se dessina en tenue d'Adam et réalisa de nombreux nus masculins et féminins. Il ne s'inspirait pas de la tradition classique et ses corps d'hommes étaient plus réalistes. Ceci dit, les nus étaient moins courants dans les pays du Nord, dont les températures n'encourageaient guère la nudité. Rester couvert était une question de survie. En revanche, les climats plus cléments d'Italie et de France donnaient au corps une plus grande liberté. Voir celui-ci partiellement dévêtu n'y était pas une nouveauté.

Au début du XIXe siècle, l'arrivée au pouvoir de Napoléon entraîna un regain d'intérêt pour le classicisme, qui fut souvent exploité par l'Empereur comme un outil de propagande. Il tenait à conférer une légitimité à son trône chancelant en l'associant le plus possible aux traditions du passé. Des peintres tels que David relevèrent le défi. Les tableaux de ce dernier, comme « Le Serment des Horaces », n'étaient pas avares d'hommes nus et visaient à anoblir la guerre et les guerriers. Le sculpteur Antonio Canova parvint à merveille à réinterpréter les traditions classiques dans des formes pures et sensuelles en marbre blanc. Toutefois, son grand nu de Napoléon ne plut pas à l'Empereur. Il finit par trouver sa place dans le somptueux hôtel particulier du duc de Wellington à Londres, comme une sorte de trophée de guerre après sa victoire à Waterloo.

Après la chute de Napoléon et l'avènement d'un gouvernement plus orienté vers les affaires, incarné par Louis-Philippe, « le roi commerçant », les images d'hommes nus disparurent brusquement de la scène. Il semblait y avoir une contradiction entre l'image des bourgeois collet monté, engoncés dans des redingotes noires et des chapeaux haut de forme, et le nu masculin traditionnel.

Dès son apparition, la photographie découvrit l'intérêt de faire poser des modèles pour vendre leur image aux artistes. Les modèles vivants coûtaient cher pour les jeunes peintres qui pouvaient ainsi réaliser des études du corps humain à moindre frais. La photo de nu masculin venait de naître. Accroupi, corps fléchi, soulevant des poids, luttant avec un autre homme nu, toutes ces poses étaient reproduites et utilisées comme source d'inspiration par de nombreux artistes, surtout à Paris.

Dans la seconde moitié du siècle, à Philadelphie, le peintre Thomas Eakins photographiait des scènes et des modèles qu'il utilisait ensuite dans ses tableaux. Il alla au-delà de simples études pour créer des photographies qui étaient de l'art à part entière. Son travail avait également un léger parfum de voyeurisme. Il prenait manifestement un certain plaisir à convaincre de beaux jeunes hommes de se déshabiller devant son objectif, ce qui était très inhabituel en cette période de pruderie victorienne.

L'un des premiers à se démarquer de cette tendance, et à se servir du prétexte de l'art pour admirer des hommes nus, fut Eadweard Muybridge. Fasciné par l'appareil locomoteur humain et animal, il inventa un système photographique qui lui permettait de décomposer le mouvement. Il photographia des hommes et des femmes nus en train de courir, sauter, danser, lancer le poids, afin d'analyser la manière dont s'articulait le corps en action. Ces clichés attendirent longtemps avant d'être publiés dans l'Amérique puritaine des années 1870 et 1880, mais la science eut le dessus et certains privilégiés purent enfin voir des nus masculins.

Les premières photographies de nu masculin qui cherchaient à n'être rien d'autre que ce qu'elles étaient, furent prises par le baron Wilhelm von Gloeden à Taormina, en Sicile. Expatrié et ruiné, le baron photographiait des adolescents vêtus d'une simple couronne de fleurs, et encore ! Ces images, censées évoquer le quotidien de la Grèce antique, étaient vendues aux touristes. Le cousin du baron, Guglielmo Plüschow, concoctait des images similaires à Naples. Avant la fin du siècle, plusieurs autres photographes romains réalisaient des photos de nu masculin qui ne faisaient plus semblant d'imiter la Grèce antique. A la même époque, en Allemagne, Theodor Hey photographiait des hommes nus dans une veine moins classique et continua de le faire, le plus souvent dans des paysages ensoleillés, jusqu'à la Première Guerre mondiale.

Juste avant la guerre, les ballets russes de Diaghilev débarquèrent de Russie, révolutionnant la musique, la peinture et le comportement général. Leurs vedettes, dont Vaslav Nijinski et Anna Pavlova, avaient une attitude ouvertement érotique sur scène et le répertoire des ballets dégageait une puissante atmosphère d'émotion et d'abandon sensuels. En outre, les costumes des danseurs ne cachaient rien de leur corps souple et élancé.

La guerre asséna un coup rude à l'hypocrisie et la pruderie victoriennes, sans doute en partie parce que les vêtements devinrent moins formels. Les hommes en uniforme et les femmes, qui participaient à l'effort de guerre, ne pouvaient se permettre d'avoir leurs mouvements entravés par des tenues trop étriquées ou sophistiquées. Pour les femmes notamment, la mode devint plus pratique et abandonna les corsets et les jupes longues. Les guerres entraînent toujours un relâchement des mœurs. Une Europe plus assoiffée des plaisirs de la vie et plus ouverte sexuellement accueillit favorablement l'évolution de la photographie …et de ses nus masculins de plus en plus nombreux.

Des photographes d'art s'engagèrent dans cette voie, tout en travaillant avec des objectifs flous. Fred Holland Day montrait de jeunes éphèbes mélancoliques perchés sur de gros rochers ou allongés au bord d'étangs, toujours nus. Un peu plus tard, Imogen Cunningham photographia son beau mari Roi escaladant Mount Rainier dans le plus simple appareil. Dans les Années folles, les vedettes de cinéma, hommes et femmes, ne voyaient pas d'objections à être photographiés très légèrement vêtus.

Rudolf Valentino et Ramón Navarro étaient tous deux des vedettes à la sexualité ambiguë dont le corps était le principal outil de travail. L'industrie cinématographique se rendit bientôt compte que les hommes objets remplissaient les salles. Il y avait là un terrain fertile que seul Sandow avait exploré auparavant. Un nouveau pas venait d'être franchi.

Le vaudeville présentait régulièrement des danseurs tels que Ted Shawn, de la compagnie Denishawn, et les photographies destinées à leurs admirateurs les montraient généralement dans leur tenue de scène, à savoir pas grand-chose.

Avant la guerre, les nudistes et les naturistes, qui passaient leurs vacances nus, avaient anticipé la libération du corps. Les hommes cherchaient de plus en plus à améliorer leur physique. Cela ne nécessitait pas forcément d'être nu mais, après tant d'efforts pour se muscler, ils avaient généralement tendance à vouloir se montrer. Dans la période d'après-guerre, un nouveau genre de revues apparut, s'adressant à ceux qui s'intéressaient au corps humain.

Les magazines de nudisme et de naturisme avaient certes leurs lecteurs assidus, mais ils offraient surtout la possibilité à tous et à toutes de voir des hommes et des femmes nus, et ils ne s'en privèrent pas. En dépit de leur caractère innocent, ils étaient généralement rangés sur le rayon le plus élevé des kiosques à journaux ou sous le comptoir, et le client devait rassembler tout son courage pour les demander.

Les premiers temps, les magazines de culturisme étaient, eux aussi, d'innocents véhicules pour échanger des conseils de régime et de musculation. Mais leurs images de jeunes malabars sains et vigoureux séduisaient également un lectorat d'homosexuels qui ne mettaient jamais les pieds dans un gymnase. Les éditeurs le comprirent rapidement et commencèrent à présenter leurs champions de culturisme sous des formes plus affriolantes.

Avant la Seconde Guerre mondiale, les amateurs de nudité devaient se contenter de clichés d'acteurs, de danseurs, de nudistes et de culturistes. Il y avait bien des photos artistiques de nu masculin, réalisées par George Platt Lynes aux Etats-Unis, Angus McBean en Angleterre ou Raymond Voinquel en France, mais elles étaient généralement réservées à leurs amis. Il arrivait qu'un nu masculin parvienne jusque dans une exposition de photographies, mais c'était rare. La réticence des hommes à se voir tels que la nature les avait faits ne se dissipait pas facilement.

La Seconde Guerre mondiale fit encore se relâcher d'un cran les mœurs et les codes vestimentaires. A la fin des années 40, les magazines de culturisme réapparurent sous un format très différent. Cette fois, on montrait de beaux gosses pour le plaisir de voir de beaux gosses, comme ceux de Bruce of Los Angeles, de Lon of New York et de bien d'autres encore.

Toutefois, le nu masculin déclenchait encore les foudres de la censure. Les photographes, et notamment la revue de Bob Mizer, « Physique Pictorial », essuyaient le feu croisé des pudibonds. L'éditeur de « Grecian Guild Pictorial » se débattit jusque devant la Cour Suprême, qui décida enfin que la nudité n'était pas obscène. Un grand pas venait d'être franchi, et de nombreux photographes et magazines sautèrent sur l'occasion.

On était en 1968. Bien que l'atmosphère générale soit à la liberté des mœurs et que le mot d'ordre soit « nous n'avons rien à cacher », la photographie mit un certain temps à se mettre à la page, en dépit des streakers qui faisaient régulièrement la une des journaux.

Si les photos de nus se multiplièrent rapidement dans une presse toujours vendue sous le comptoir, elles avaient encore plus de mal à se faire accepter dans le monde des galeries d'art.

Dix ans après le jugement de la Cour Suprême, la première exposition consacrée au nu masculin s'ouvrit à la Marcuse Pfeifer Gallery à New York. Elle reçut un accueil glacial de la part des critiques hommes. Pour eux, le nu masculin appartenait au domaine des homosexuels et de féministes qui souhaitaient voir des images d'hommes rabaissés et vulnérables. Seul René Ricard osa déclarer : « ...vous ne trouvez pas que les organes génitaux de l'homme ont un certain aspect... décoratif ? Comme un accessoire qu'on aurait placé là en guise de détail amusant. » Ainsi donc, le problème, c'était le pénis. Les hommes ne voulaient pas que leur pénis prête à rire.

Malheureusement, les critiques n'étaient pas dans l'air du temps. Ou plutôt, heureusement. A l'époque de cette exposition, Robert Mapplethorpe était déjà sur la scène new-yorkaise. Il devait bientôt être reconnu comme une force artistique majeure grâce à sa savante utilisation du sex-appeal et son sens aigu des relations publiques. Ses fleurs, ses portraits de personnalités du beau monde et ses gros plans de sexes masculins offraient une combinaison enivrante pour les nouveaux riches des années 80. Le disco battait son plein, les libidos étaient galopantes et le sida n'était encore qu'une lointaine rumeur. Le nu masculin devint un art, et le public l'apprécia.

Des photographes de publicité emboîtèrent le pas à Mapplethorpe : Bruce Weber, Herb Ritts, Francesco Scavullo, Greg Gorman et bien d'autres encore. Bientôt, des hommes nus vendirent des sous-vêtements, des parfums et de la mode féminine.

Les livres, les calendriers, les cartes postales proliférèrent, tout comme l'industrie du porno gay dont les « stars » évanescentes devinrent des célébrités. Jeff Stryker fut interviewé pour le magazine « Interview ». Il n'eut aucune fausse pudeur à expliquer à la journaliste ce qui le différenciait des autres acteurs du porno.

Aujourd'hui, la nudité frontale, si elle n'est pas encore devenue banale, est partout. Des vedettes de cinéma comme Bruce Willis et Tim Robbins nous laissent entrevoir quelques fragments intimes de leur anatomie, suivant les traces de Sharon Stone. Une série de films sur l'industrie du porno se préparent.

Phénomène intéressant, à mesure que le nu masculin apparaît au grand jour, le costume étriqué tend à disparaître. Le vêtement de sport devient vêtement de travail. Même des sociétés très guindées autorisent leurs employés à s'habiller plus décontracté au bureau le vendredi. Dans des régions chaudes comme à Los Angeles ou Miami, il n'y a plus aucun code vestimentaire. A Miami Beach, même les policiers sont en short et se déplacent à vélo. Il faut dire qu'ils ont de très jolies cuisses.

L'homme d'affaires victorien collet monté et obsédé par les attributs du pouvoir n'est plus. Il ne subsiste qu'au travers de quelques dinosaures qui hantent les hauteurs étouffantes des bureaux de direction. Les hommes plus jeunes développent leurs pectoraux dans les clubs de gym. Leurs femmes et leurs petites amies l'exigent.

Il aura fallu deux guerres et la détermination de nombreux photographes, hommes et femmes, pour que l'homme baisse enfin son pantalon et renoue avec la vision de l'homme des artistes de l'Antiquité et de la Renaissance : celui-ci doit être beau. Aujourd'hui, hommes et femmes partagent les mêmes emplois et responsabilités, et être beau est autant la responsabilité de l'homme que celle de la femme.

Paradoxalement, les qualités que les homosexuels ont toujours admirées chez les hommes sont celles que les femmes apprécient. Personne ne leur avait auparavant demandé leur avis. Dépendantes des hommes, elles se taisaient. A présent, elles sont libres d'admirer une belle cuisse, un dos large, un abdomen en tablette de chocolat. Ce qu'on a exigé d'elles pendant des siècles, «Soit belle», on l'exige désormais aussi des hommes. Ces derniers y ont peut-être perdu leur image de protecteurs, mais ils y ont gagné le droit d'être tendres.

Tout comme il y a peu de chances que les femmes retournent un jour dans leur cuisine et abandonnent leurs libertés, il est peu probable que le nu masculin se couvrira à nouveau. Il lui aura fallu un siècle pour se dépêtrer de ses vêtements. Ça fait du bien. Or ce siècle nous a appris une chose: quand ça nous fait du bien... alors, il ne faut pas hésiter!

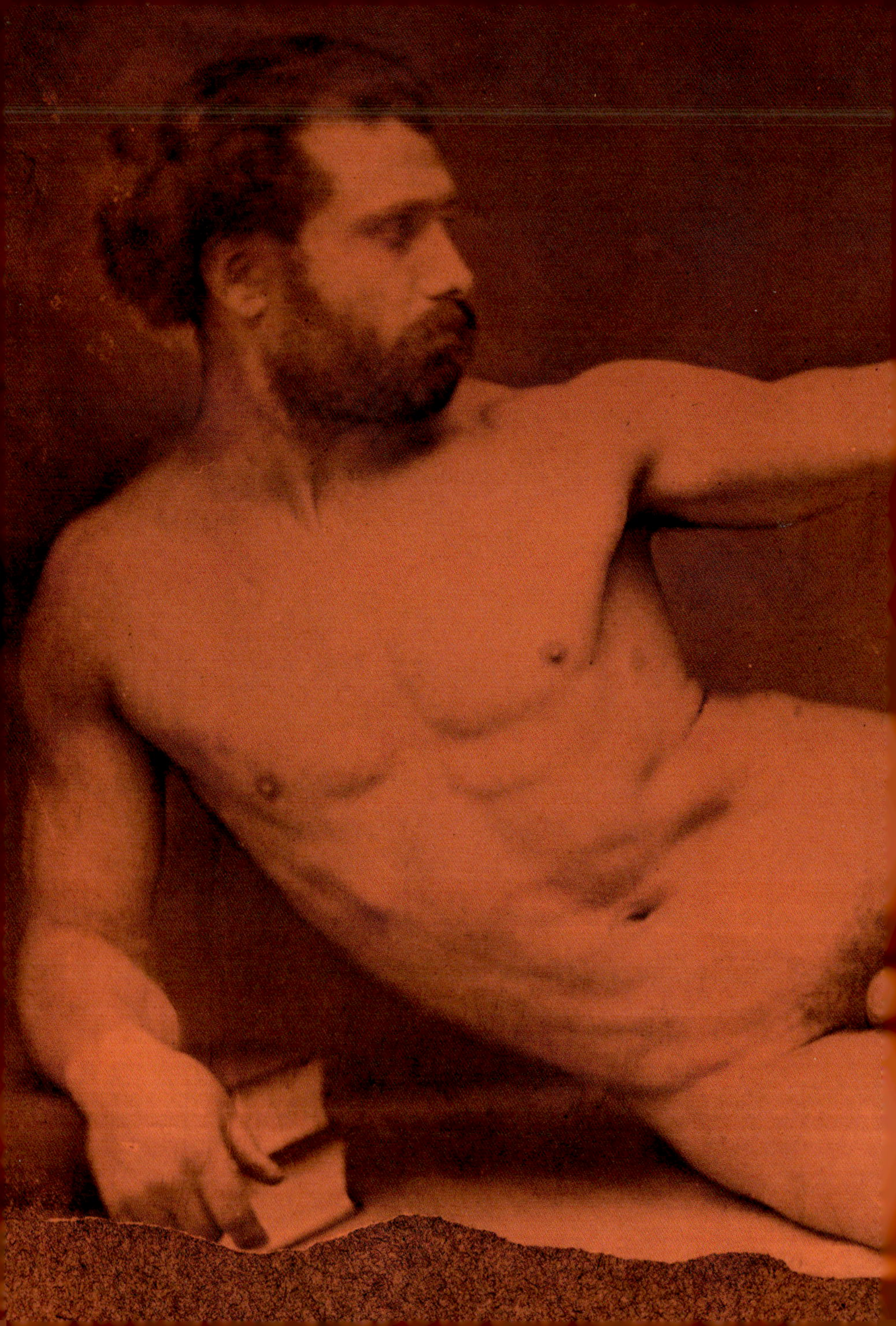

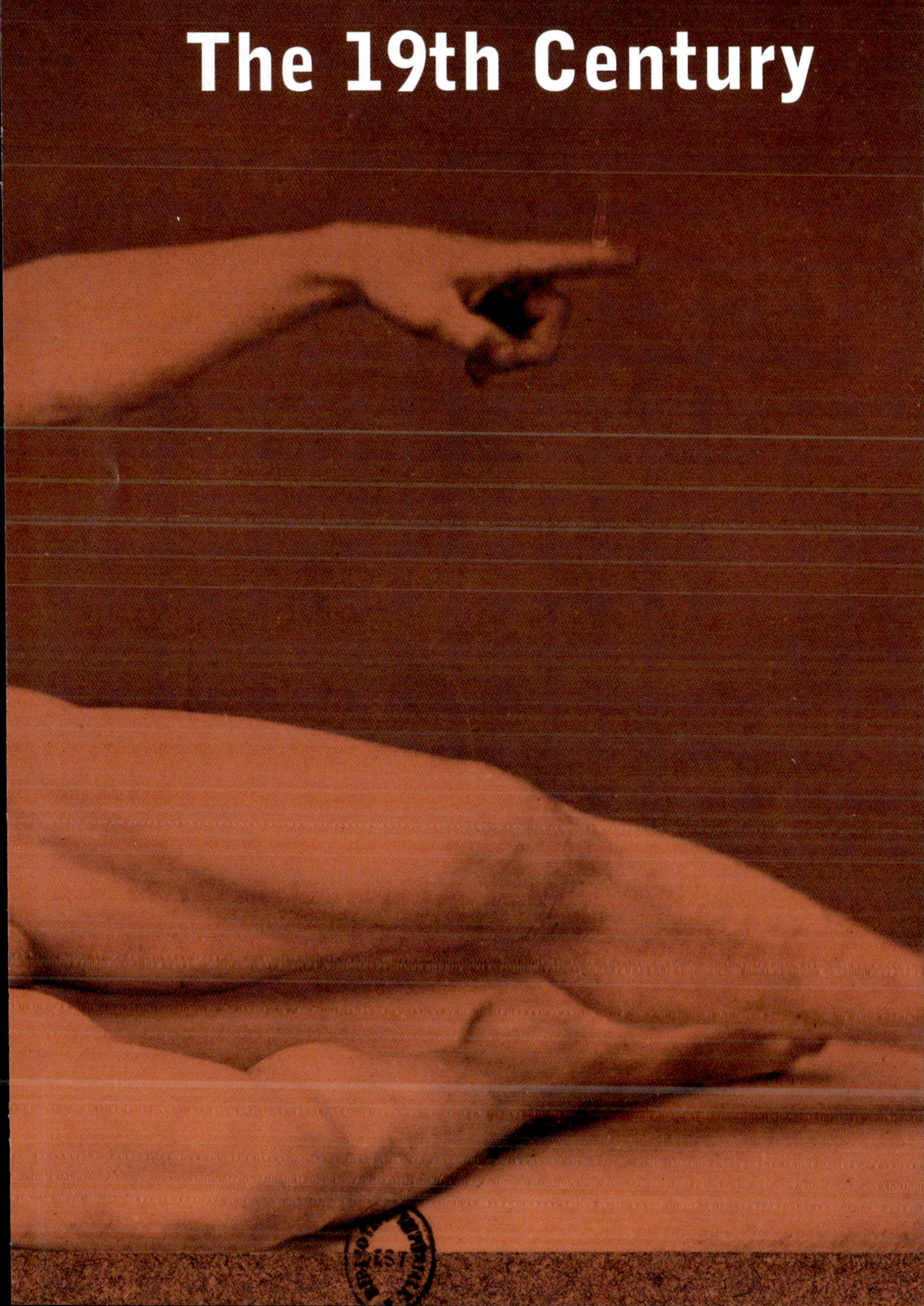
The 19th Century

The true character of the 19th century became apparent in the 1830s and 1840s. Industrialization created a new kind of man. Aristocrats still felt, as they had in previous centuries, that being "in business" was beneath them. But the kind of money being made by the barons of steel-making, shipping, railroads, oil, rubber, and the like soon began to change attitudes. Money talked and these newly rich men married their daughters into old families and quickly formed a new kind of ruling class.

This had a direct effect on art. European art exhibitions were inundated with nude females in harems, washed up on the beach, chained to rocks, and feigning to be goddesses, while their naked male counterparts were almost entirely absent. The men who ruled the world wanted to see their women naked in the guise of art, particularly in this heavily clothed period. But viewing their own sex as defenseless, and attractive other than through money and power, became a taboo.

In this same period, the 1830s and 1840s, photography began to flourish, especially for portraiture. The early daguerreotypes gave a reverse image, had no negative, and produced only one picture. These, however, were quickly replaced with glass plates that could be used to make a number of prints. Immediately artists grasped how handy this could be as a replacement for models and outdoor scenes. Businesses sprang up peddling views of fields, streets and houses, and, of course, nudes. The nudes came in all the heroic and dramatic poses that were customary in painting and, like studio models, these photographs left nothing to the imagination. Many buyers wanted the photographs of the female nudes for fun at home, not for artistic inspiration. And there must also have been men who bought and relished these artists' photographs of the nude male.

This then was the true origin of male nude photography: men posing in ways that painters found useful to copy and incorporate into their work. Other than this the male nude was strictly under wraps for the rest of the 19th century. As was everyone else. Never before in history had humans worn so much clothing. Women were more upholstered than dressed. Layer upon layer of cloth was superimposed upon the female form. Drawn up, ruffled, adorned with bows,

fringes, and lace, women were walking display cases for all the new manufac-
turers of fabrics and boots, gloves, and bonnets, cloaks and shawls.

Men wore vests, long underwear, button-up boots and top hats, and carried
canes. If you were a serious man in that century, what you wore showed just how
successful you were. And what you didn't want to wear yourself, you loaded onto
your wife. Women could hardly move once they were laced and pinned into their
hoopskirts, tight boots, tight gloves, and bonnets that left them unable to see
anywhere other than straight ahead. Never was female subjugation to men more
clearly visible. Even housemaids wore hoopskirts, knocking "objets d'art" to left
and right as they did the dusting.

Not only was the male nude invisible, but there were great taboos connected
with it. Napoleon's nephew, Napoleon III, and his wife the Empress Eugenie
encouraged commerce and the arts in the Second Empire in France, and artists
found they had plenty of work to do. The emperor liked a good female nude, and
these were omnipresent on the walls of upper class establishments. But never a
male nude. Men didn't like to see themselves nude. Being sexy was definitely not
part of their role. They were consumers of female beauty. What women might
like was never even considered. And men who liked men? Quelle horreur ! An
interest in the female formed a major part of the 19th-century male's image.
What would people have thought if he hadn't wanted to pursue it at all? Being
macho was a must.

The 18th century, when two men sleeping together would be considered a
mere peccadillo, was long since buried. Men ruled the roost from behind their
long beards. Being physically desirable was not a serious consideration for these
figures of authority.

In their new capitalistic world, money equalled power and that power had to
be displayed. A naked man was devoid of power. The 20th century had its work
cut out freeing men from this attitude.

As early as 1872 Eadweard Muybridge began his scientific studies that led
to the first male nude photographs unrelated to the work of artists. Muybridge
developed a stop-action form of photography to see exactly how humans and
other creatures move His photography revealed that a running horse has all

four hooves off the ground at one time. This was news to the painters of horses, who thought it impossible. For his stop-action work on men running, wrestling, and jumping, Muybridge insisted on his models being nude. One notices that the Muybridge models are all handsome with excellent bodies. As one suspects of Dr. Kinsey a century later, the scientist's work might have developed from his personal interests.

The Philadelphian painter Thomas Eakins also photographed male nudes for use in his painting. He was very interested in men in an undressed state and lost his teaching position when he insisted that female art students draw male models without their posing straps. There is nothing erotic about his photographs or his paintings, but his getting six male students to take off their clothes and wrestle in an orchard while he photographed them would be considered unusual in any era.

Muybridge's studies were not published until 1887, more than a decade after he completed them. But published they were. And the vague air of scandal that hung around Eakins led to interest in his photographs, too. Science lent respectability to these endeavors and so permitted a peek at male nudes towards the end of the century.

There was no such air of respectability surrounding Baron von Gloeden, a German aristocrat who settled in Sicily. The Baron took pictures of local youths in simulated scenes of ancient Greece. The models usually wore wreaths and sandals, if that. These were neither scientific studies nor guides for artists; they were the first purely artistic photographic representations of the male nude.

The pictures were sold to passing tourists. In Naples, von Gloeden's cousin Wilhelm von Plüschow, known as Guglielmo, produced similar photographs, and there were others too. It is hard to imagine many female tourists in their bustles and large hats buying this material. It was a "men only" market, aimed at men who preferred other men.

In Rome the photographers A. Calavas and Vincenzo Galdi soon began shooting male nudes for the same market but without the classical references. In Germany, Theodor Hey began similar work.

Von Gloeden and his cohorts were not operating underground. Their photography was considered art, similar to the painter Alma-Tadema's elaborate scenes of ancient Greece and Rome. But in this "Don't ask, don't tell" era there was a tacit understanding that the most enthusiastic purchasers were homosexual. Von Gloeden and the others also set up catalog businesses which flourished uninterrupted up to World War I.

Towards the end of the century the first signs of an interest in body-building emerged. Gymnasiums had begun to flourish. Empress Elizabeth of the Austro-Hungarian Empire even exercised in her bedroom in the Imperial Palace in Vienna, hanging from an overhead bar. Inevitably competitiveness arose as to whose body was the most beautiful. The German Eugene Sandow was generally conceded to be the winner. He was primarily a weightlifter, but his blond good looks and handsome body soon drew fans for his beauty alone. He went to the United States under the auspices of the theatrical manager Florenz Ziegfeld and became a star. He posed frequently wearing only sandals and a fig leaf. Supposedly the cards bearing his picture were collected by females, but men too were most certainly among his admirers.

The attention he got was an indication that the taboo against seeing men naked was collapsing. Furthermore, whereas female performers could only display their bodies encased in tights, Sandow went utterly naked. For the first time in almost one hundred years the male nude was publicly displayed and admired, and now as a frankly sexual object. The 20th century was slowly but surely to see the male nude restored to public view.

Erst in den 30er und 40er Jahren des 19. Jahrhundert bildete sich dessen
wahrer Charakter aus. Die Industrialisierung brachte einen neuen Menschentyp
hervor. Wie in den Jahrhunderten zuvor hielt es der Adel immer noch für unter
seiner Würde, sich mit kaufmännischen Dingen abzugeben. Das Geld, das die
Industriemagnaten mit Stahl, Öl, Gummi, im Schiffsbau und im Transportwesen
verdienten, brachte allerdings das festgefahrene soziale Gefüge stark ins Wanken. Geld öffnete alle Türen, die Neureichen verheirateten ihre Töchter mit den
Sprösslingen der alten Familien, und so bildete sich rasch eine neue herrschende
Gesellschaftsschicht.

Das blieb nicht ohne Folgen für die Kunst. Während in den europäischen
Kunstausstellungen nackte Frauen im Harem, an Meeresgestade gespült,
an Felsen gekettet oder als Göttinnen verkleidet die Wände zierten, war Nacktheit aus der Öffentlichkeit verbannt. Und der nackte Mann war es auch in der
Kunst. Männer wollten sich nicht nackt sehen. Das eigene Geschlecht in seiner
Kreatürlichkeit, seiner Herrschaftsinsignien beraubt, wehrlos oder gar in seiner Nacktheit anziehend zu sehen, war Tabu. Wenn man nackt war, hatte man
nichts vorzuweisen. Das 20. Jahrhundert hatte alle Hände voll zu tun, den Mann
von dieser Zwangsvorstellung zu befreien.

Das 19. Jahrhundert und das Bürgertum waren zugeknöpft. Niemals zuvor
haben sich Menschen unter derart viel Kleidung begraben. Die Männer trugen
Mäntel, Westen, lange Unterhosen, Knopfgamaschen und Zylinder. Die Kleidung
signalisierte, wie weit man es in der Gesellschaft gebracht hatte, über wieviel
Macht und Einfluss man verfügte. Herrschaft und Sinnlichkeit schlossen sich
aus, so glaubte man. Und was der einflussreiche, vermögende Mann an äußeren
Zeichen seines Status nicht selber tragen wollte, das halste er seiner Frau
auf: aufgeplustert, zugeschnürt, mit Fransen und Spitzen geschmückt stakste
die Bürgerfrau ihrem Mann hinterher, den Blick stur geradeaus. Selbst einfache
Dienstmädchen waren in Reifröcke gezwängt und fegten so neben dem Staub
auch noch kostbares Porzellan von den Schränken.

Der nackte Mann blieb nicht nur unsichtbar, er wurde tabuisiert. Napoleons
Neffe, Napoleon III., und dessen Frau, Kaiserin Eugenie, förderten nicht
nur den Handel, sondern auch die Künste. Der Kaiser fand Gefallen an guten

Frauenakten, und in den Häusern der Oberschicht waren Darstellungen des nackten weiblichen Körpers allgegenwärtig. Männerakte hingegen waren verpönt, Männer wollten sich selbst nicht nackt sehen, Geschlechtlichkeit war nicht ihre Sache. Sie ergötzten sich lieber an der Schönheit der Frau. Was den Frauen eventuell gefallen könnte, danach wurde nicht gefragt.

Und was war mit den Männern, die Gefallen an anderen Männern fanden? Wie entsetzlich! Im 18. Jahrhundert noch hatte der Geschlechtsverkehr unter Männern als Kavaliersdelikt gegolten, doch diese Zeiten waren längst vorbei.

In den 30er und 40er Jahren feierte die Fotografie die ersten Erfolge. Daguerreotypien gaben nur ein seitenverkehrtes Bild wieder. Da es kein Negativ gab, bekam man nur ein Bild. Die Metallplatten wurden jedoch bald durch Glasplatten ersetzt, von denen sich mehrere Abzüge fertigen ließen. Künstler erkannten sofort, wie gut diese neue Technik dazu taugte, einen Ersatz für echte Modelle zu finden oder wie hilfreich sie bei Landschaftsstudien war. Kleine Geschäfte, die Fotos von Feldern, Straßen, Gebäuden und natürlich auch Aktbilder anboten, schossen wie Pilze aus dem Boden. Die Aktmodelle nahmen die in der Malerei üblichen heroischen und dramatischen Posen ein. Weibliche Akte erfreuten sich großer Nachfrage und dienten oft mehr dem Vergnügen als der künstlerischen Inspiration. Doch sicherlich wird es nicht wenige Männer gegeben haben, die Gefallen an Darstellungen nackter Geschlechtsgenossen fanden.

Der Ursprung des Männeraktes lag also hier: als Hilfestellung für Maler, die diese Posen kopierten und in ihre Bilder integrierten. Doch es gab auch andere Beweggründe: 1872 hatte Eadweard Muybridge begonnen, mit einer von ihm selbst entwickelten Art von Zeitrafferfotografie die Bewegungsabläufe des Körpers zu studieren. Bei seinen Aufnahmen von laufenden, springenden und miteinander ringenden Männern sind die Modelle nackt. Dies sind die ersten männlichen Aktaufnahmen, die nicht unmittelbar zu künstlerischen Zwecken entstanden. Offensichtlich hat es seinen Modellen nichts ausgemacht, splitternackt im Freien vor seiner Kamera herumzutollen. Da seine Modelle ausnahmslos gut aussahen und gute Körper hatten, mag Muybridge neben seinem wissenschaftlichen vielleicht auch noch ein anderes Interesse getrieben haben.

Veröffentlicht wurden seine Fotografien erst über ein Jahrzehnt nach
Abschluss seiner Forschungen. Vielleicht half ihm dabei der Skandal, den der
Maler Thomas Eakins provoziert hatte. Eakins fotografierte nackte Männer,
um Vorlagen für seine Bilder zu gewinnen. Als er darauf insistierte, dass seine
Kunststudentinnen die männlichen Modelle ohne den obligatorischen Lendenschurz zeichnen sollten, war es um seinen Lehrauftrag geschehen. Weder in
seinen Fotos noch in seinen Bildern kommt eine besondere erotische Spannung
zum Ausdruck, aber sechs männliche Studenten dazu zu bewegen, sich gänzlich zu entkleiden und in einem Obstgarten miteinander zu ringen, während
sie fotografiert werden, das wäre wohl zu jeder Zeit ein ungewöhnliches Unter-
fangen.

Von ganz anderem Schlag war Baron Wilhelm von Gloeden. Der verarmte
deutsche Aristokrat hatte sich in Taormina auf Sizilien niedergelassen und fotografierte Knaben vor einer dem antiken Griechenland nachempfundenen Kulisse.
Seine Modelle waren höchstens einmal mit einem Blumenkranz oder Sandalen
bekleidet. Die Fotos waren keine wissenschaftlichen Studien oder Vorlagen für
Künstler, es waren die ersten echten Werke männlicher Aktfotografie.

Von Gloedens Vetter Wilhelm von Plüschow, der unter dem Namen Guglielmo
bekannt wurde, betrieb in Neapel ein ähnliches Unternehmen, und die beiden
sollten nicht die einzigen bleiben. Man kann sich nur schwerlich vorstellen, dass
Touristinnen mit Gesäßpolstern und wagenradgroßen Hüten diese Aufnahmen
erstanden. Nein, dieser Markt war „nur für den Herrn", und zwar für einen von
der Sorte, die ihr eigenes Geschlecht bevorzugte.

In Rom begannen wenig später die Fotografen A. Calavas und Vincenzo Galdi
den Markt mit ähnlichen Produkten zu beliefern. Sie verzichteten allerdings
auf die klassische Kulisse. In Deutschland betrieb Theodor Hey ein ähnliches
Unternehmen.

Von Gloeden und seine Nachfolger arbeiteten nicht im Verborgenen. Ihre
Fotos galten als Kunst, ähnlich der, die der Maler Alma-Tadema mit seinen
sorgfältig inszenierten Genrebildern aus dem antiken Griechenland und Rom
präsentierte. Dennoch war es auch in dieser heuchlerischen Zeit bekannt, dass
Homosexuelle besonders treue Kunden waren.

Gegen Ende des Jahrhunderts entdeckte man das Bodybuilding, und vielerorts entstanden Sportstudios. Selbst an gänzlich unerwarteten Orten knarrten die Gelenke. So heißt es von der Kaiserin Elisabeth von Österreich-Ungarn, dass sie sich in ihrem Schlafzimmer im kaiserlichen Palast in Wien begeistert an einer Reckstange ertüchtigte.

Sportlicher Ehrgeiz war überall entfacht, und bald bewunderte die Welt ihren ersten „Mr. Universum", Eugene Sandow, ein Deutscher, der in den USA zum Star wurde. Sandow war in erster Linie Gewichtheber, aber sein blondes Haar und sein hübscher Körper begeisterten weibliche wie männliche Fans. Während Frauen nur in Trikots auf die Bühne durften, präsentierte sich Sandow splitternackt und wurde als Sexobjekt bewundert. Ein erster Hoffnungsschimmer – aber erst im späten 20. Jahrhundert sollte es gelingen, den männlichen Akt der Öffentlichkeit frei zugänglich zu machen.

Ce ne fut que dans les années 1830 et 1840 que la véritable nature du XIXe siècle commença à apparaître au grand jour. L'industrialisation avait donné naissance à un nouveau type d'homme. Les aristocrates estimaient toujours, comme pendant les siècles précédents, que le «négoce» n'était pas digne d'eux. Mais les fortunes amassées par les barons de l'acier, du transport, des chemins de fer, du pétrole, du caoutchouc etc., firent rapidement évoluer les mentalités. Ces nouveaux riches épousèrent des filles de grandes familles et engendrèrent rapidement une nouvelle classe dirigeante.

Dans le domaine de l'art, cela renforça la présence du nu féminin et chassa celle du nu masculin. Dans les expositions d'art européen, on voyait des femmes nues dans des harems, échouées sur des plages, enchaînées à des rochers et se prenant pour des déesses, mais rarement leurs équivalents masculins. Les hommes qui dirigeaient le monde aimaient voir les femmes dévêtues. En revanche, voir les hommes présentés d'une manière vulnérable, et peut-être attirante, devint tabou.

Au cours des années 1830 et 1840, la photographie fit son apparition. Sa première utilisation fut le portrait. Les daguerréotypes donnaient une image inversée, n'avaient pas de négatifs et constituaient des exemplaires uniques. Ils furent bientôt remplacés par des plaques de verre à partir desquelles on pouvait réaliser un certain nombre de tirages. Les artistes comprirent aussitôt qu'ils avaient là un substitut pratique aux modèles vivants et au travail d'après nature. Des photographes diffusèrent des vues de champs, de rues, de maisons et, naturellement, des nus. Ces derniers reprenaient toutes les poses héroïques et dramatiques que l'on trouvait dans la peinture et, comme les modèles d'ateliers, ils étaient entièrement nus. Jusqu'à nos jours, les images de nus présentés sous forme de modèles d'atelier ont toujours été populaires.

Ce fut donc à partir de cette base que la photo de nu masculin se développa : des hommes prenant des poses académiques que les artistes pouvaient copier et intégrer dans leurs tableaux. En dehors de ce cadre strict, le nu masculin était soigneusement caché. Jamais dans l'histoire les êtres humains ne portèrent autant de vêtements les uns sur les autres. Les femmes étaient plus tapissées que vêtues, portant des couches de vêtements superposées. Elles étaient les vitrines ambulantes de la nouvelle industrie du tissu, des bottes, des gants, des bonnets, des manteaux et des châles.

Les hommes portaient des gilets, des caleçons longs, des guêtres, des chapeaux haut-de-forme et des cannes. La tenue vestimentaire annonçait précisément quel était le degré de réussite sociale. Quant aux femmes, une fois qu'elles étaient lacées et coincées dans leurs paniers, leurs bottines, leurs gants et leurs bonnets, qui les empêchaient de voir où elles allaient, elles pouvaient à peine marcher. Jamais la soumission de la femme à l'homme ne fut aussi manifeste. Même les femmes de chambre portaient des robes à panier, renversant au passage les objets d'art tandis qu'elles passaient le plumeau.

Sous le Second Empire, le neveu de Napoléon, Napoléon III, et son épouse, l'impératrice Eugénie, encouragèrent le commerce et l'art, et les artistes eurent beaucoup de travail. L'empereur avait un faible pour les femmes nues, et celles-ci apparaissaient partout sur les murs de la haute bourgeoisie. Mais d'homme nu, point. Les hommes n'aimaient pas se voir nus. Etre sexy ne faisait pas partie de leurs attributions. Leur rôle était de consommer la beauté des femmes. De ce que les femmes pouvaient aimer, il n'était même pas question. Quant aux hommes qui aimaient les hommes ? Horreur ! Pendant une grande partie du XIXe siècle, tout homme qui se respectait se devait de courir les jupons. Qu'auraient pensé les autres s'il n'avait pas paru s'y intéresser ? L'homme était macho ou n'était pas.

Le XVIIIe siècle, où un homme pouvait dormir avec un autre homme sans qu'on en fasse toute une histoire, était bel et bien terminé. Le fait que le frère de Louis XIV avait aimé porter des robes était complètement oublié. Derrière leur longue barbe, les hommes régnaient en maître sur le poulailler, et qu'ils puissent être aimés pour leur corps plutôt que pour leur pouvoir dépassait leur imagination.

Dans ce nouveau monde capitaliste, l'argent équivalait au pouvoir, et le pouvoir devait être montré. Nu, l'homme ne pouvait rien montrer. Il faudra attendre le XXe siècle pour que l'homme puisse se libérer de cette mentalité.

En 1872, Eadweard Muybridge entama des études scientifiques qui aboutirent à la création de photos d'hommes nus sans rapport avec les poses académiques destinées aux artistes. Au cours de ses recherches sur le mouvement humain et animal, il mit au point une technique de séquences photographiques. Grâce à ses photos, les peintres de chevaux découvrirent qu'un cheval au galop soulève ses quatre sabots de terre en même temps. Pour ses séquences d'hommes courant, luttant et sautant, Muybridge tenait à ce que ses sujets soient nus. Ce qui ne semblait d'ailleurs pas les gêner. On remarquera également que les modèles étaient tous de beaux spécimens humains aux corps avantageux. Comme on a pu le soupçonner plus tard, les recherches scientifiques du docteur Kinsley étaient peut-être motivées par d'autres intérêts, moins avouables.

Thomas Eakins, le peintre de Philadelphie, photographiait lui aussi des hommes nus pour s'en inspirer dans ses tableaux. Dénuder les hommes semble avoir été une fixation chez lui et il se fit remercier par l'école où il enseignait après avoir insisté pour que ses étudiantes d'art dessinent des modèles masculins vivants sans leur cache-sexe. Ni ses photographies ni ses tableaux n'ont un caractère érotique, mais parvenir à convaincre six étudiants de se déshabiller dans un verger pour les photographier en train de lutter ensemble peut être considéré comme un tour de force, quelle que soit l'époque.

Le vague parfum de scandale qui entourait Eakins fit qu'on s'intéressa à ses photographies. Les études de Muybridge ne furent publiées qu'en 1887, plus de dix ans après qu'il les ait réalisées. Mais elles furent néanmoins publiées, la science conférant une certaine respectabilité à ces expériences.

Cette respectabilité ne s'étendait pas au baron von Gloeden, un aristocrate allemand habitant en Sicile. Celui-ci prenait des photos de jeunes garçons dans des scènes qui se voulaient une reconstitution de la Grèce antique. Ses modèles ne portaient que des sandales et des couronnes de fleurs, quand ils portaient quelque chose. Ces images, vendues à des touristes, n'étaient ni des études scientifiques ni des épreuves académiques pour artistes, elles étaient purement et simplement des représentations artistiques de nu masculin. A Naples, le cousin de von Gloeden, Wilhelm von Plüschow, connu sous le nom de Guglielmo, travaillait dans la même veine. On imagine mal des dames en villégiature, en faux cul et en grandes capelines de paille, achetant ce genre de photos. Elles étaient destinées à un marché exclusivement masculin.

A Rome, les photographes A.Calavas et Vincenzo Galdi se mirent bientôt à photographier des nus pour le même marché, mais sans les références classiques, de même que Theodor Hey en Allemagne.

Von Gloeden et ses disciples ne travaillaient pas en cachette. Leurs images étaient considérées comme de l'art, semblables aux tableaux que réalisait le peintre Alma-Tameda, avec ses grandes scènes de la Grèce et de la Rome antiques. Mais dans cette époque de «discrétion», il était implicitement entendu que les acheteurs les plus intéressés étaient homosexuels. Von Gloeden et les autres firent même circuler des catalogues de vente par correspondance et travaillèrent sans interruption jusqu'à la Grande Guerre.

Vers la fin du siècle, on commença également à s'intéresser à la culture physique et les gymnases fleurirent. L'impératrice Sissi, par exemple, faisait de la gymnastique dans sa chambre à coucher du palais impérial de Vienne. Inévitablement, il s'installa une rivalité entre ceux qui voulaient avoir le plus beau corps. L'Allemand Eugene Sandow était généralement considéré comme le champion incontesté. Il était avant tout culturiste mais sa chevelure blonde et son corps sculptural lui attirèrent bientôt des admirateurs pour sa seule beauté. Il se rendit aux Etats-Unis sous les auspices du directeur de théâtre Florenz Ziegfeld et devint une star. Les cartes postales avec sa photo étaient censées être achetées par des femmes, mais il devait sûrement compter des hommes parmi ses admirateurs.

Son succès montre que le tabou envers les hommes nus commençait à se fissurer. Détail intéressant, alors que les artistes femmes ne pouvaient se montrer qu'en collants, Sandow, lui, était entièrement nu. Pour la première fois depuis près d'un siècle, le corps de l'homme était exposé et admiré en public, avec cette différence toute moderne qu'il était cette fois ouvertement présenté comme un objet sexuel. Ce devait être le point de départ d'une restauration du nu masculin dont le XX⁰ siècle allait lentement se charger.

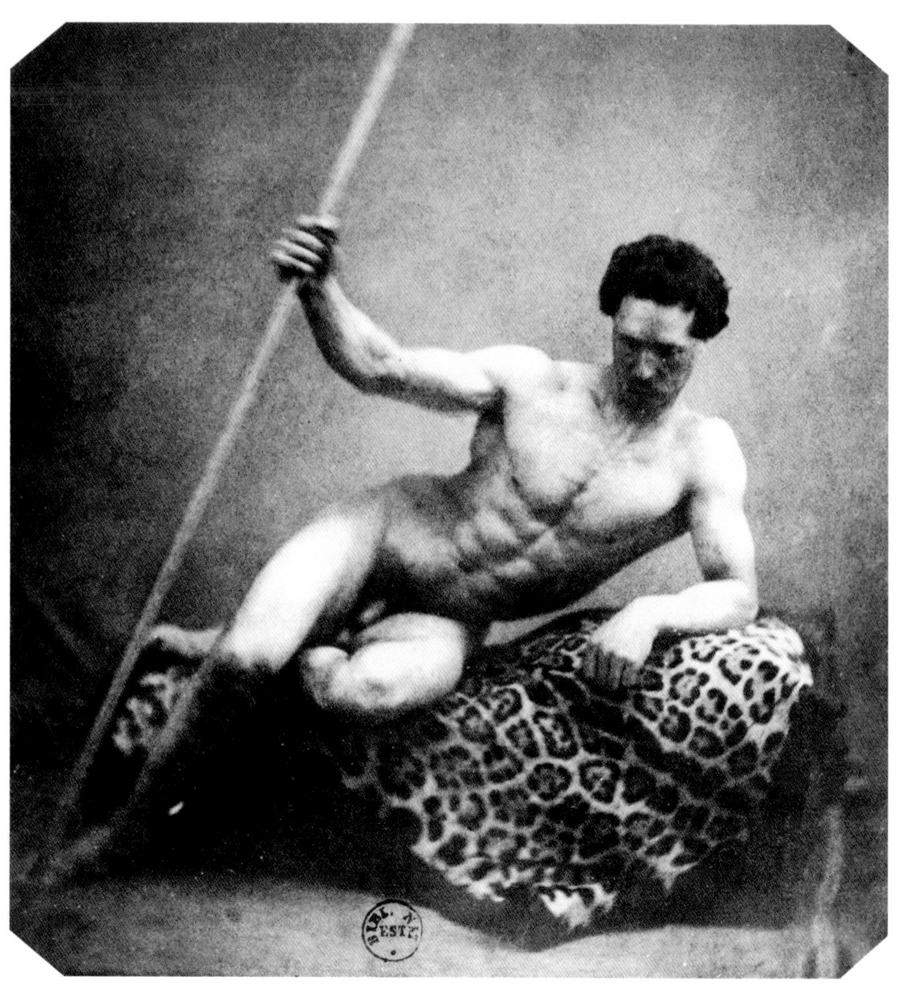

Eugène Durieu, Nu masculin assis, 1854

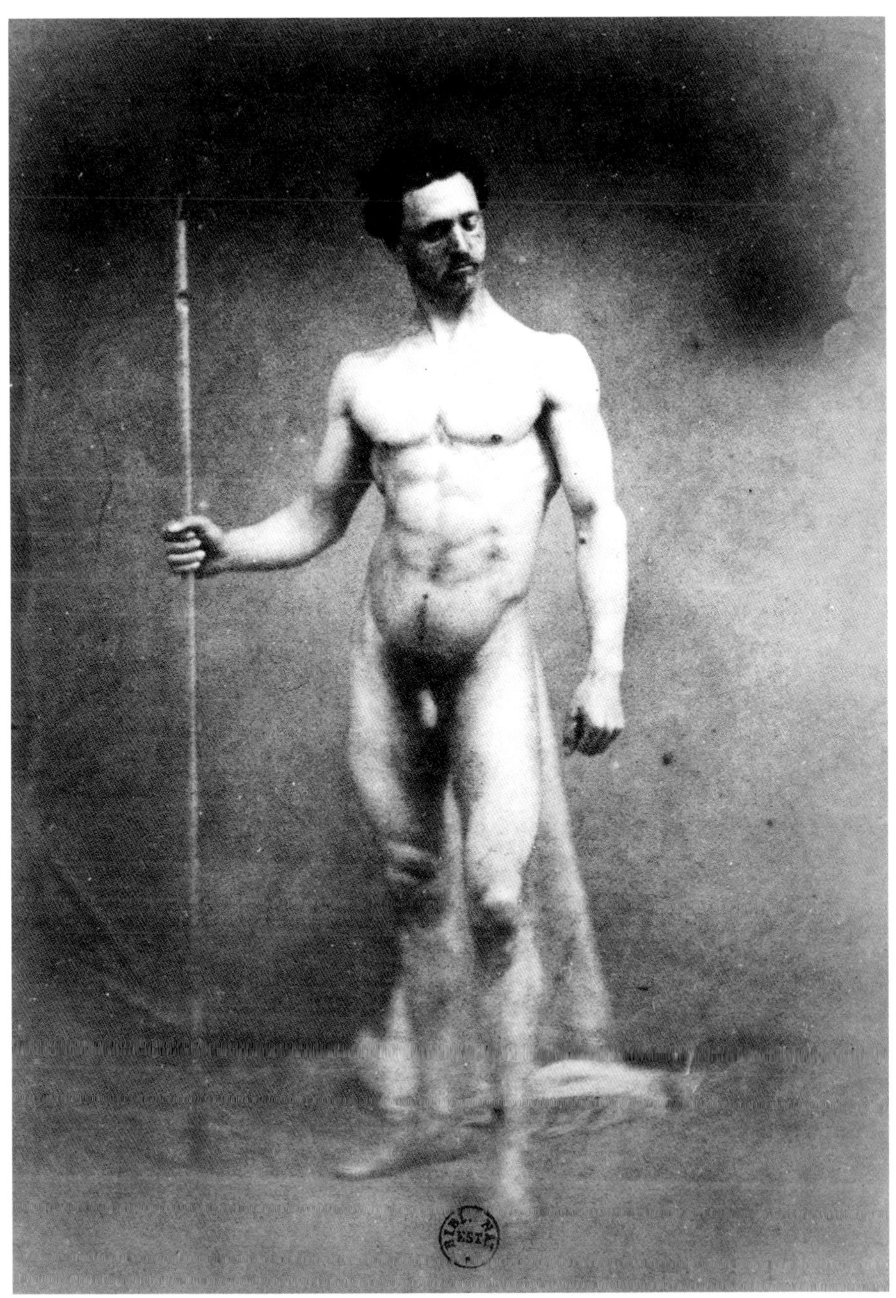

Eugène Durieu, Nu masculin debout, 1854

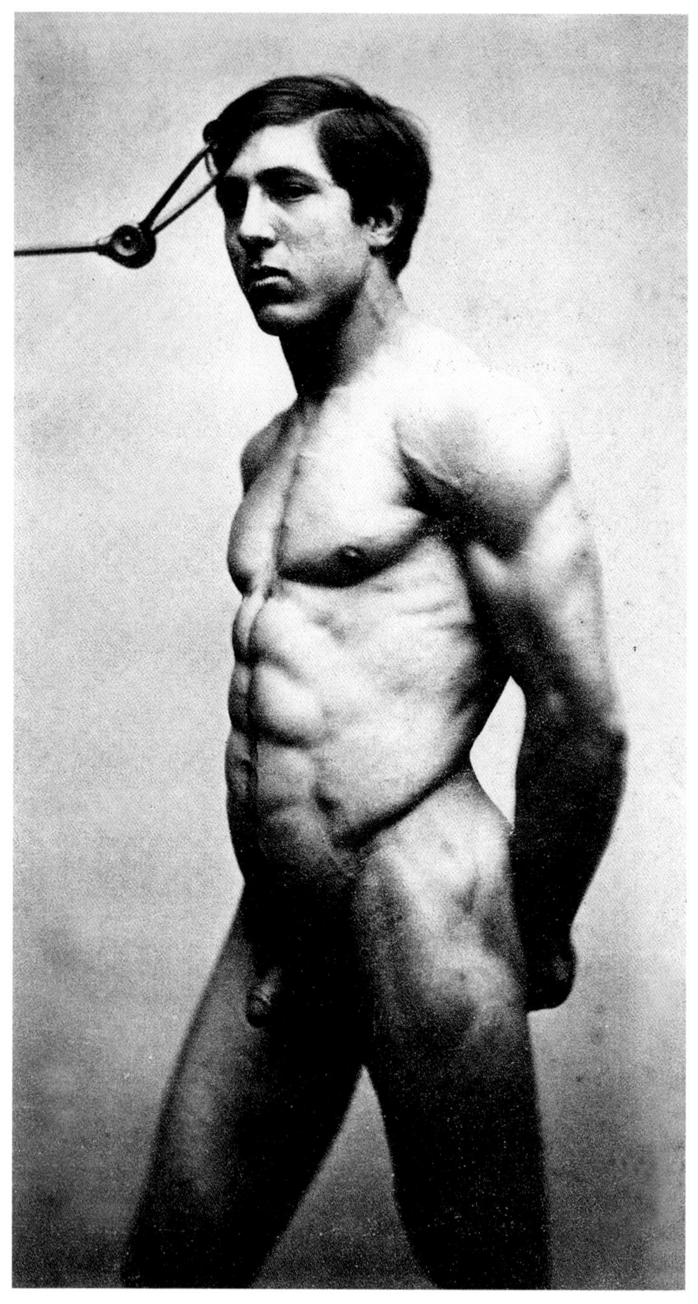

46

Anonymous, c. 1855

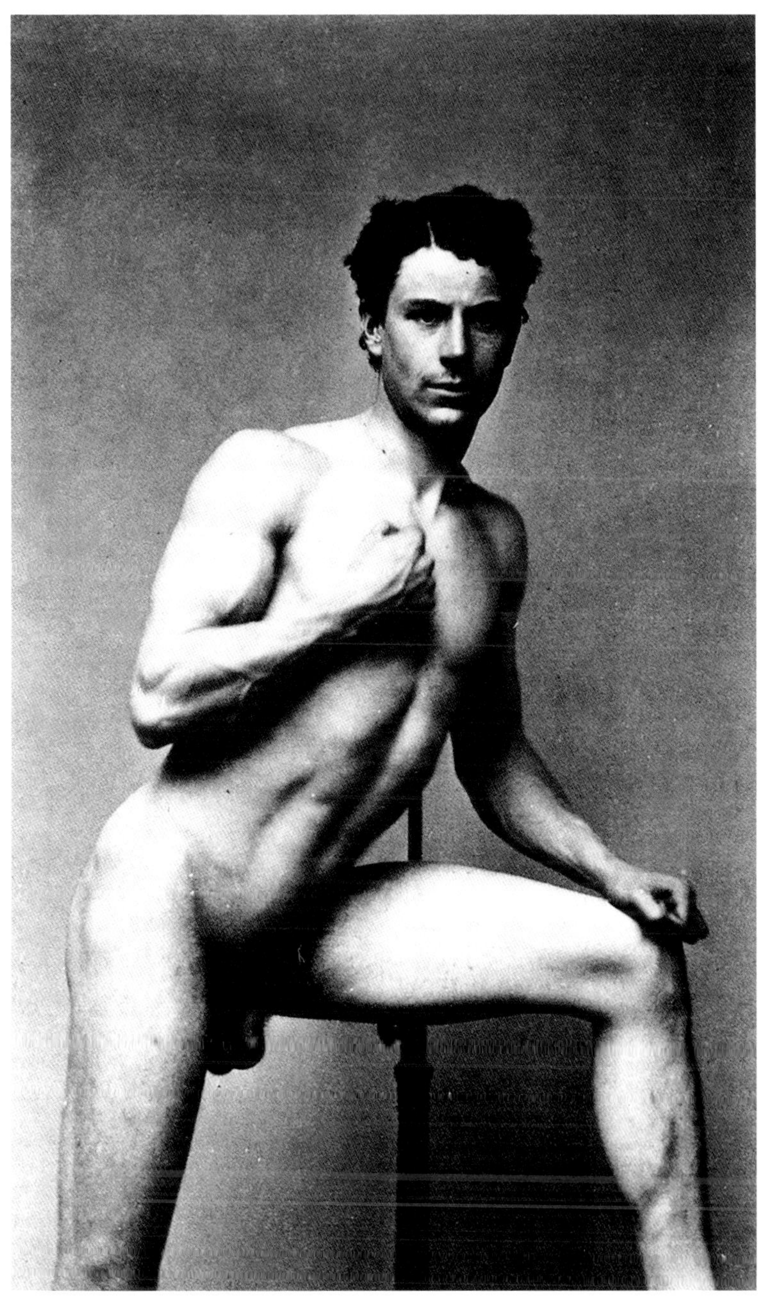

Anonymous, c. 1855

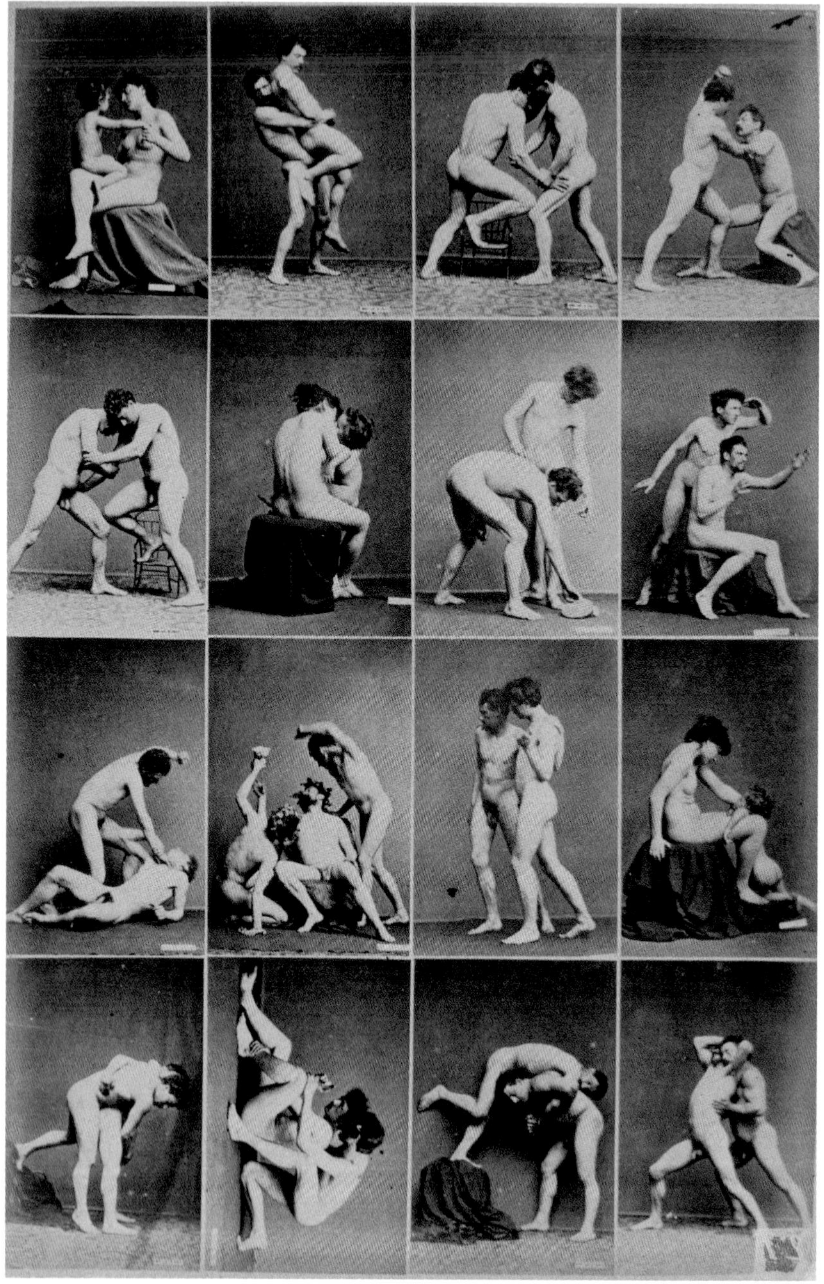

A. Calavas, c. 1895

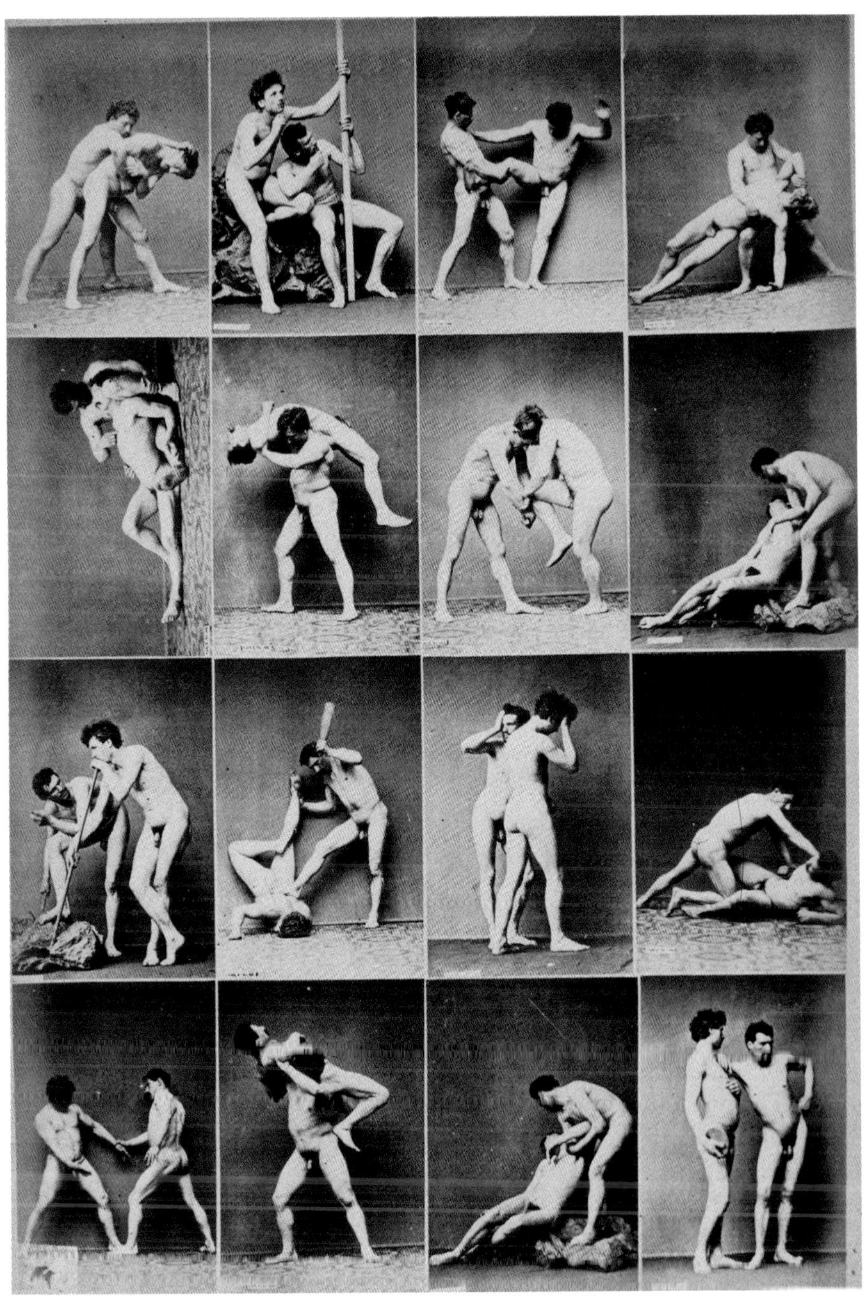

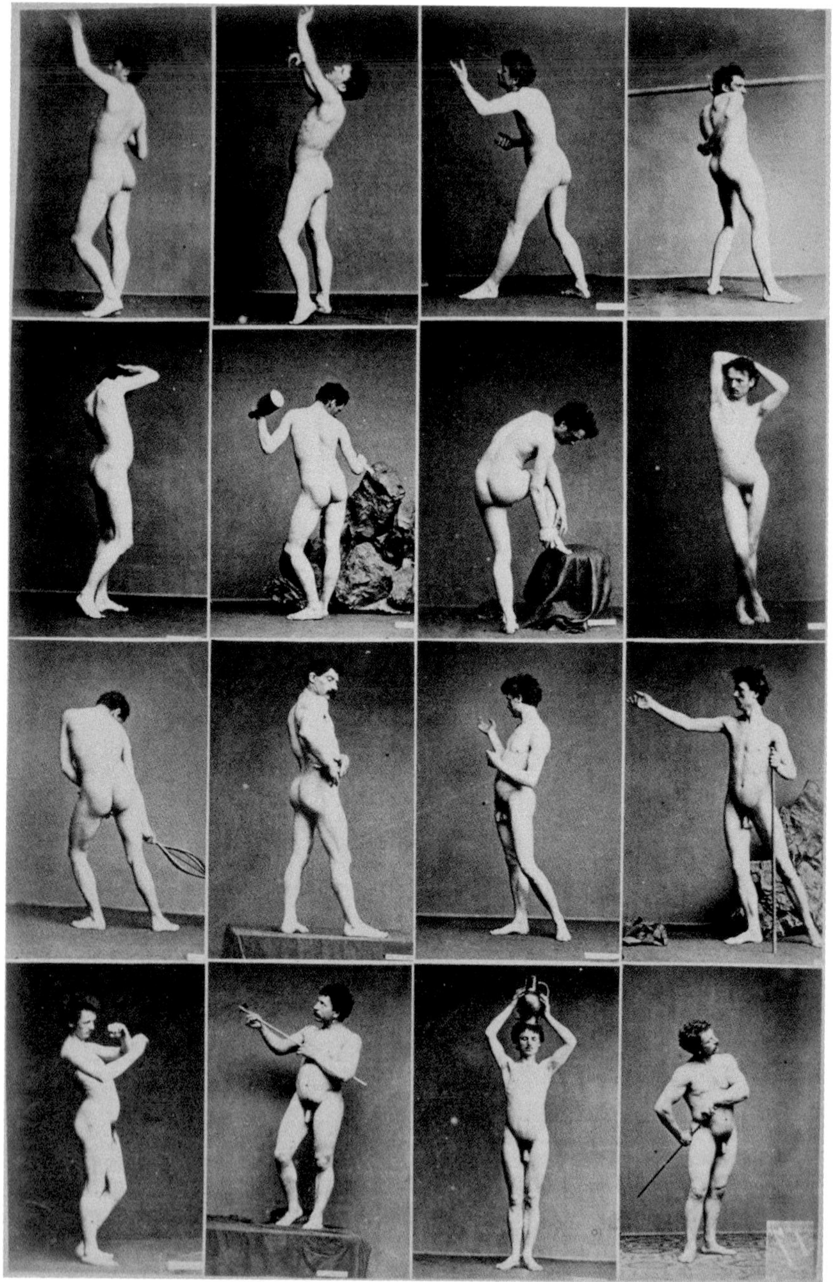

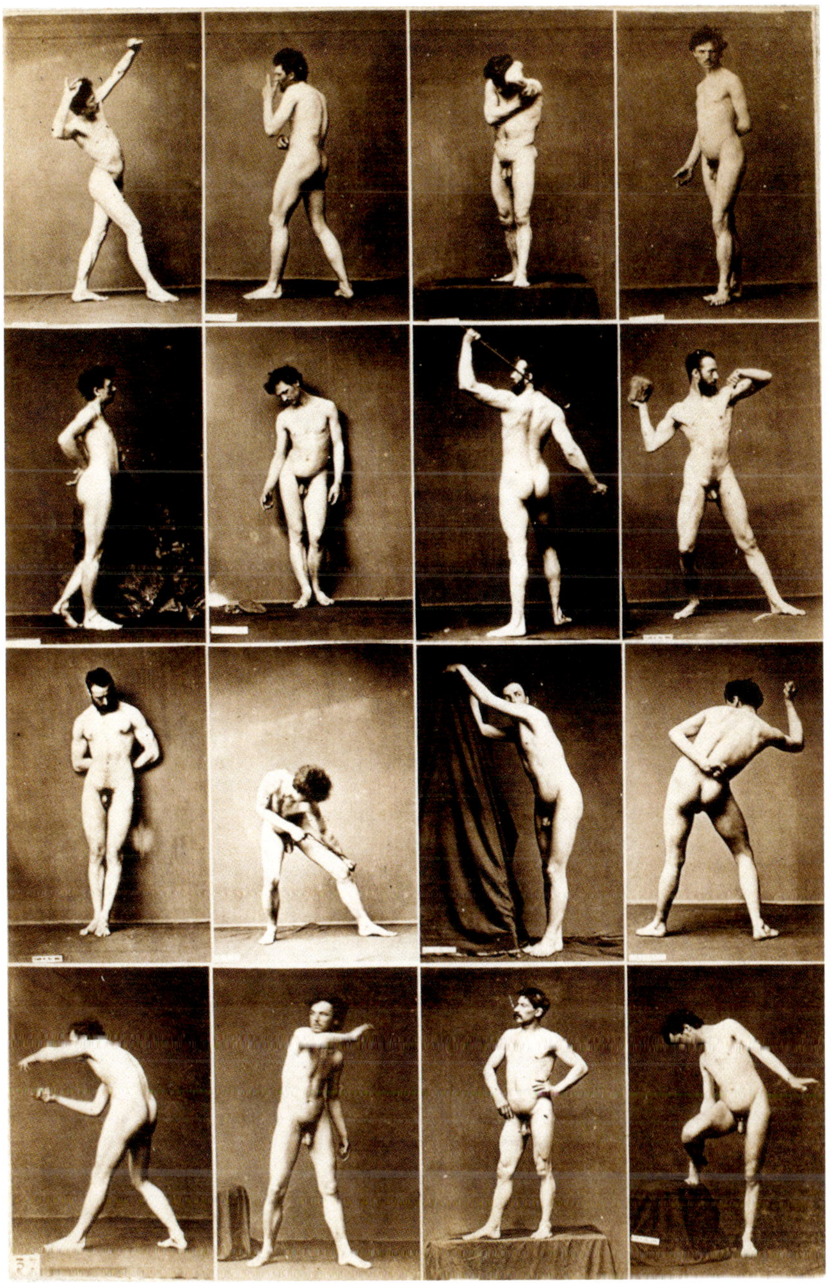

A. **Calavas,** c. 1895

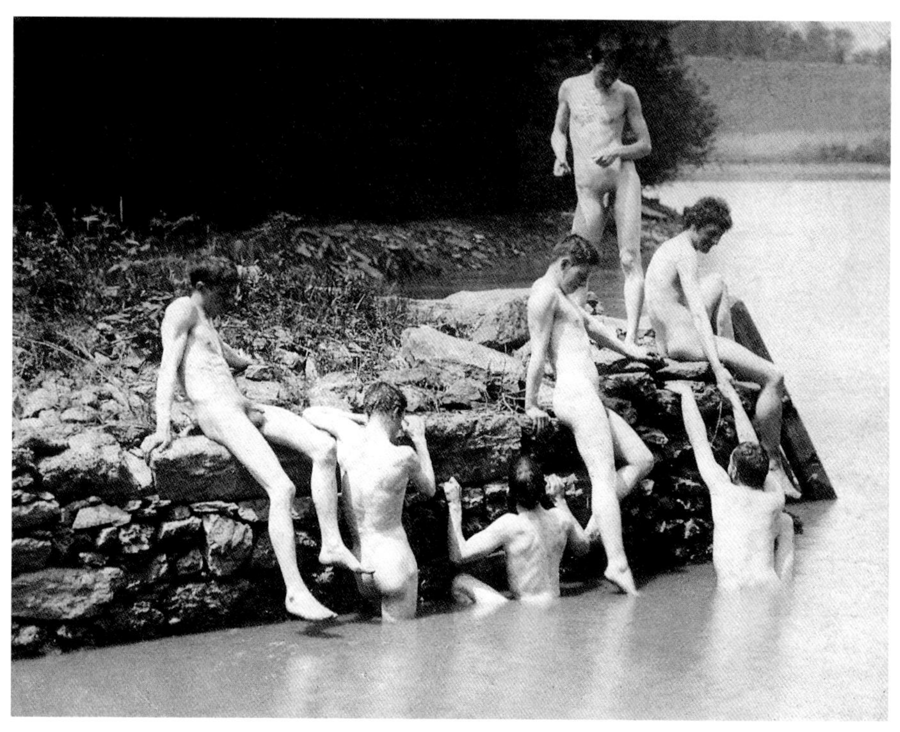

Thomas Eakins, 1883

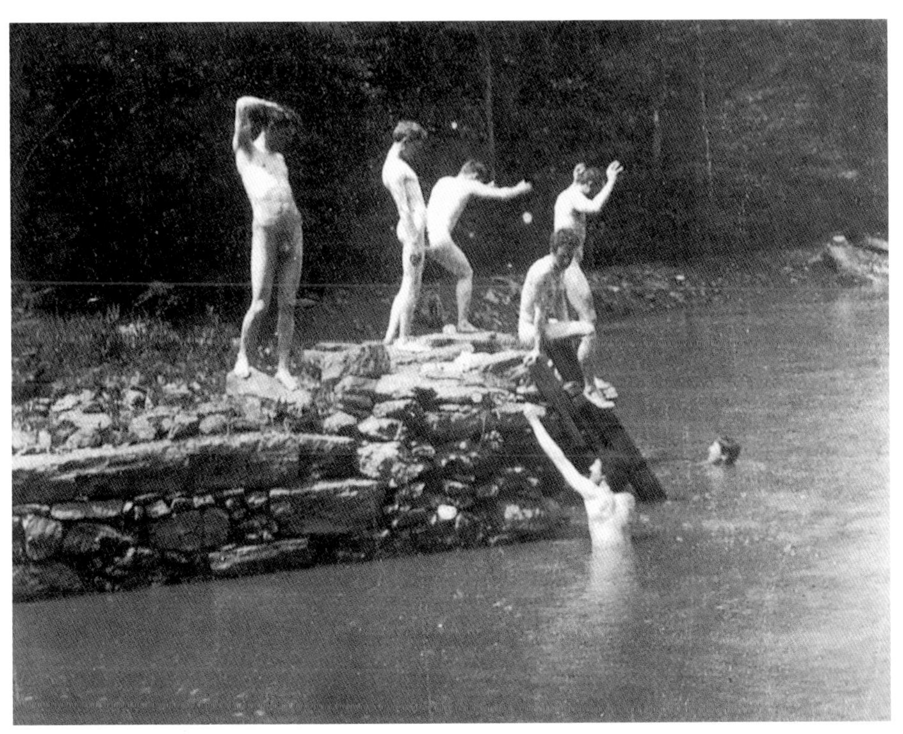

Thomas Eakins, 1883

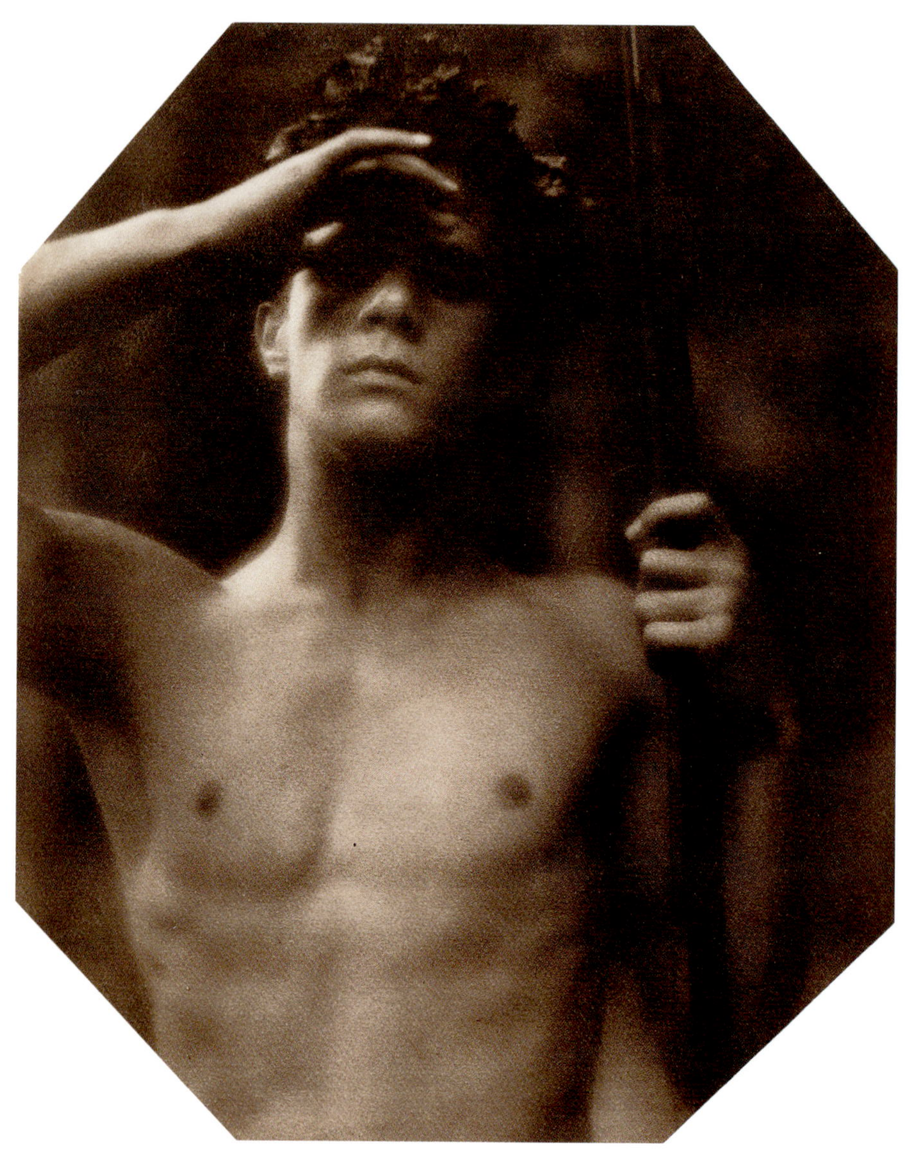

Fred Holland Day, Torso, 1908

Fred Holland Day, Hypnos, c. 1896

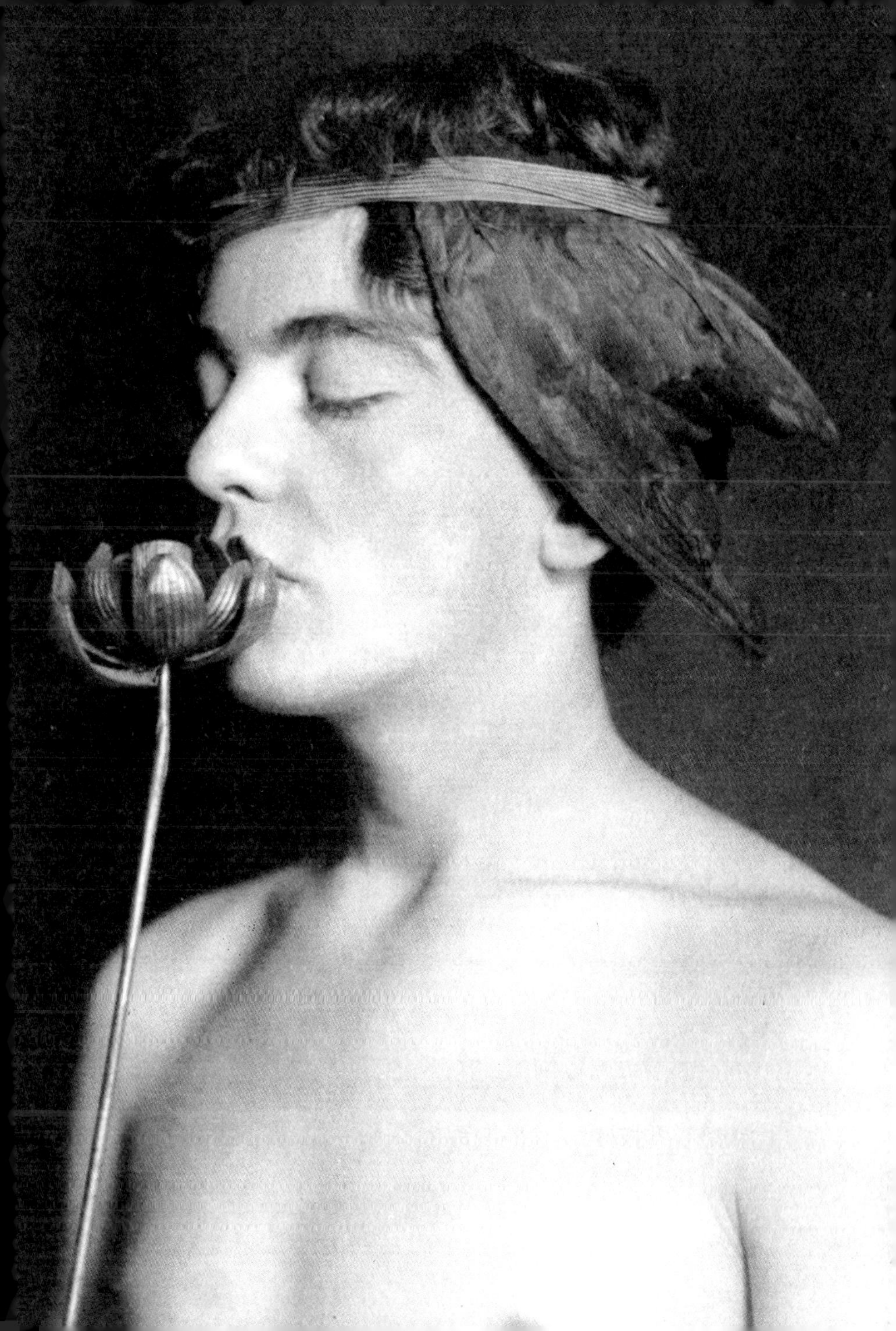

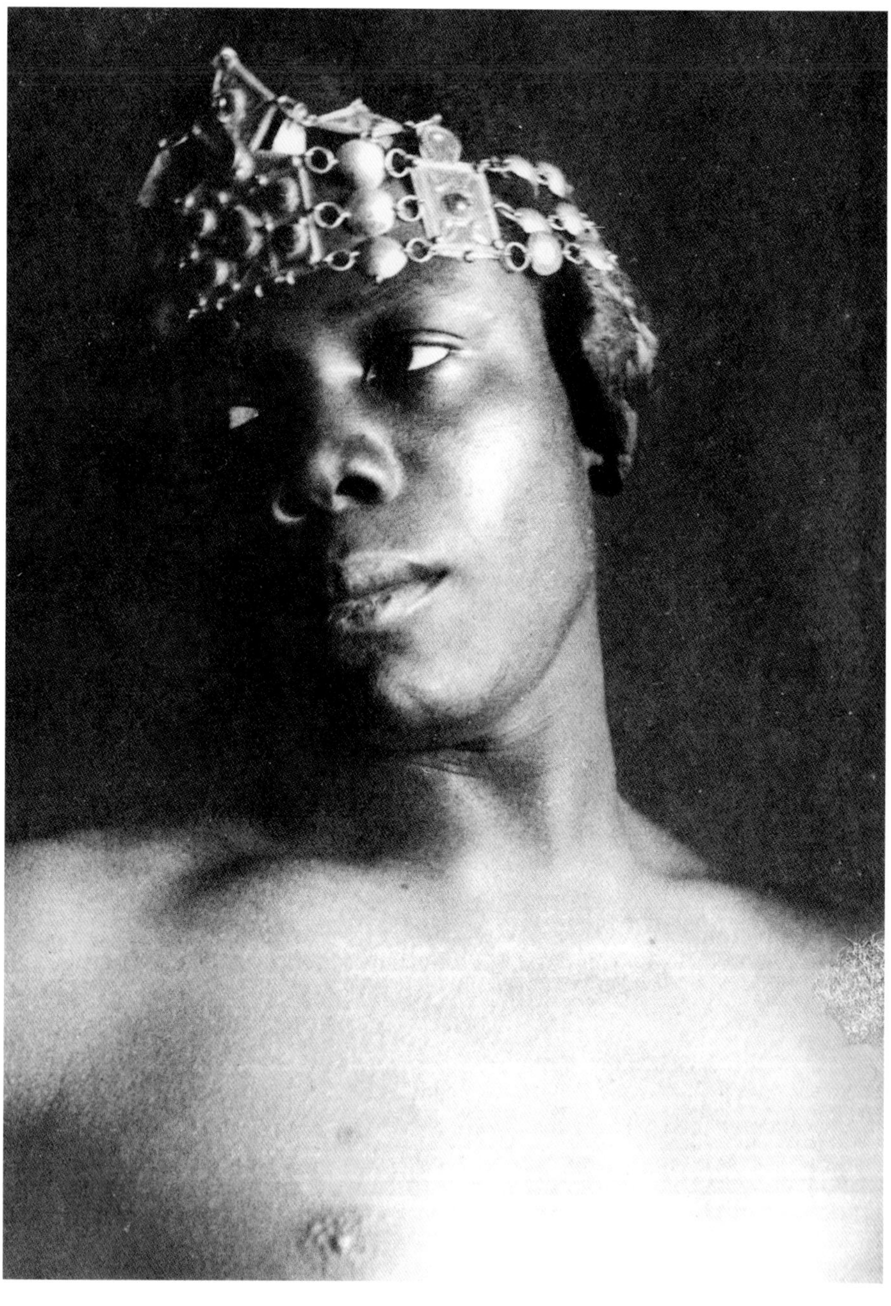

Fred Holland Day, Ethiopian Head Crowned, 1897

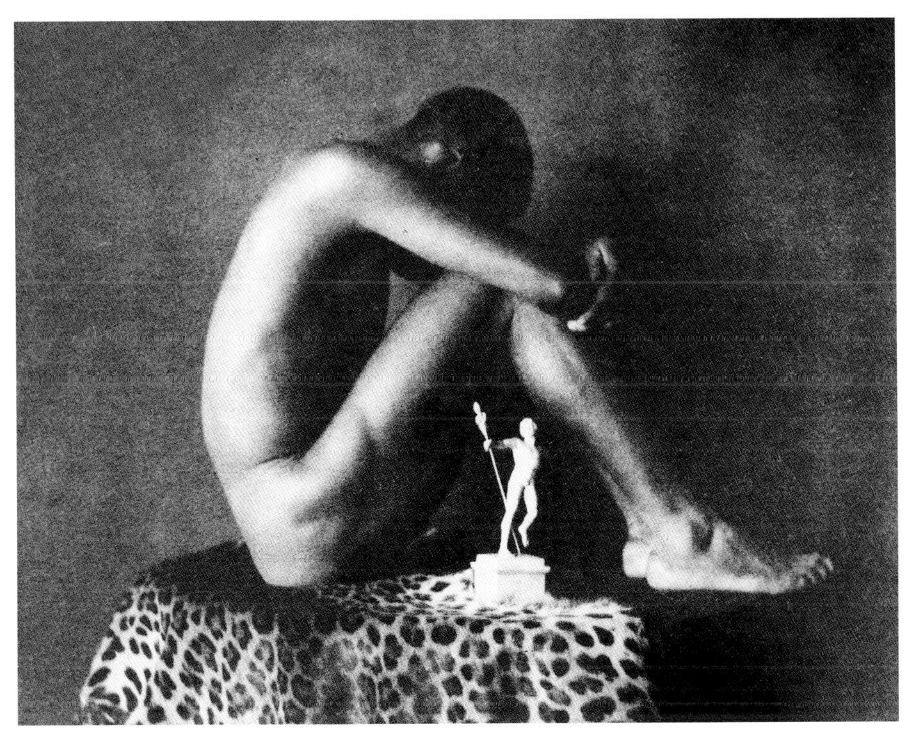

Fred Holland Day, Ebony and Ivory, 1897

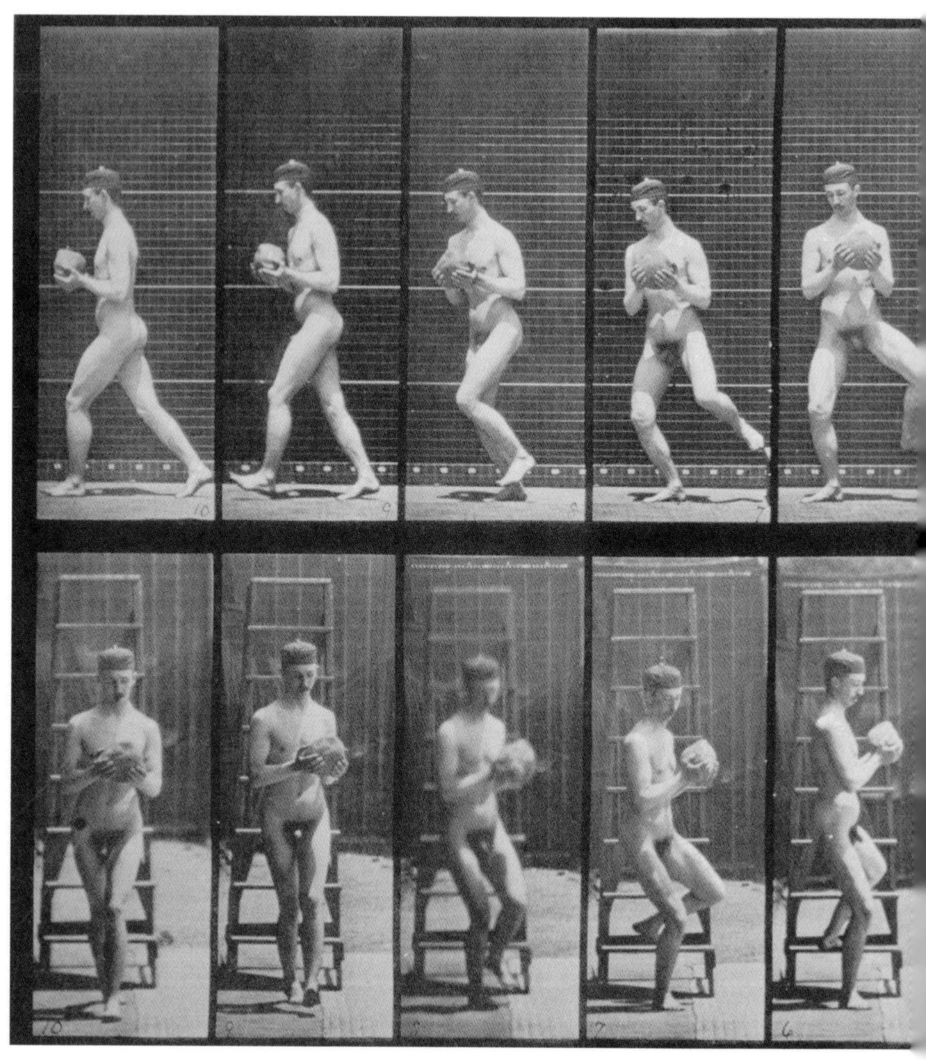

Eadweard Muybridge, Animal Locomotion, Plate 151, 1887

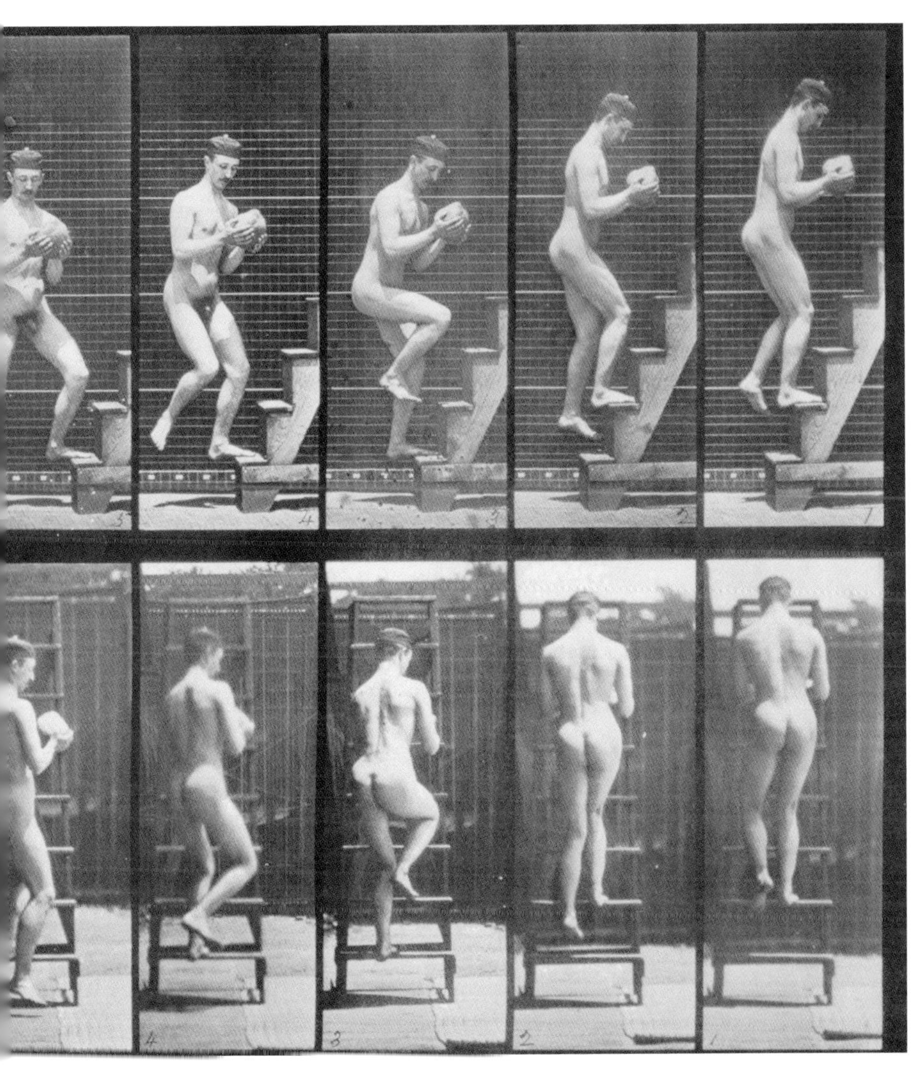

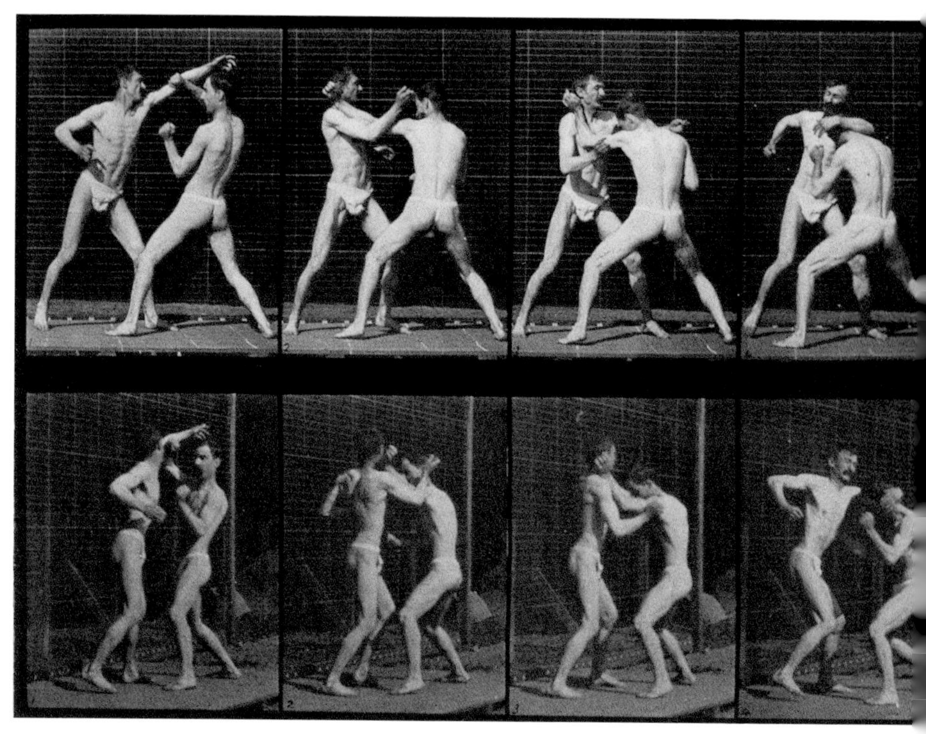

Eadweard Muybridge, Animal Locomotion, Plate 342, 1887

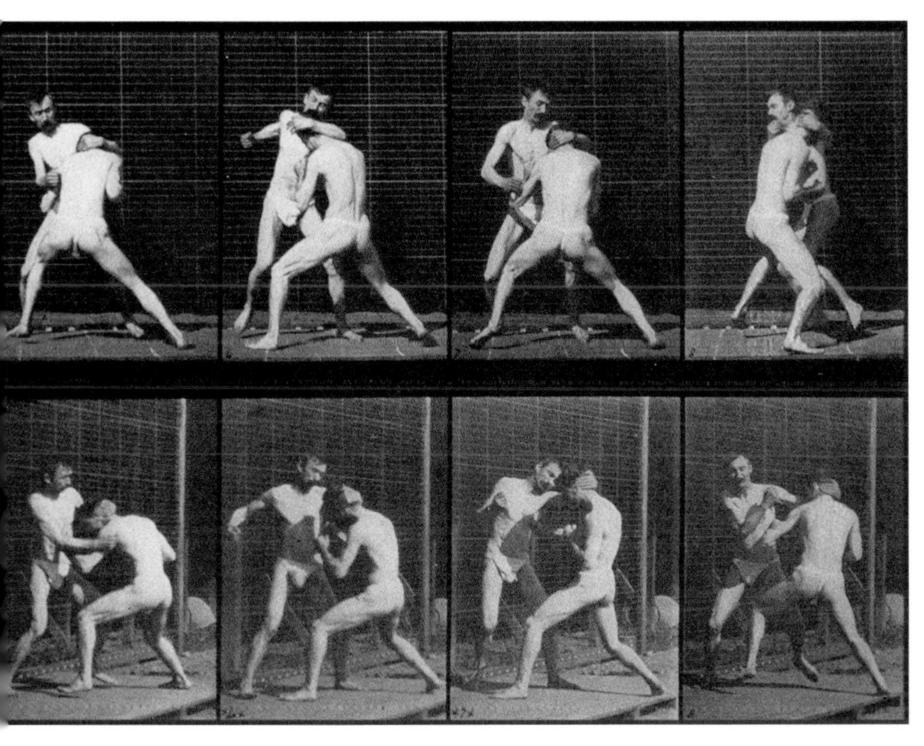

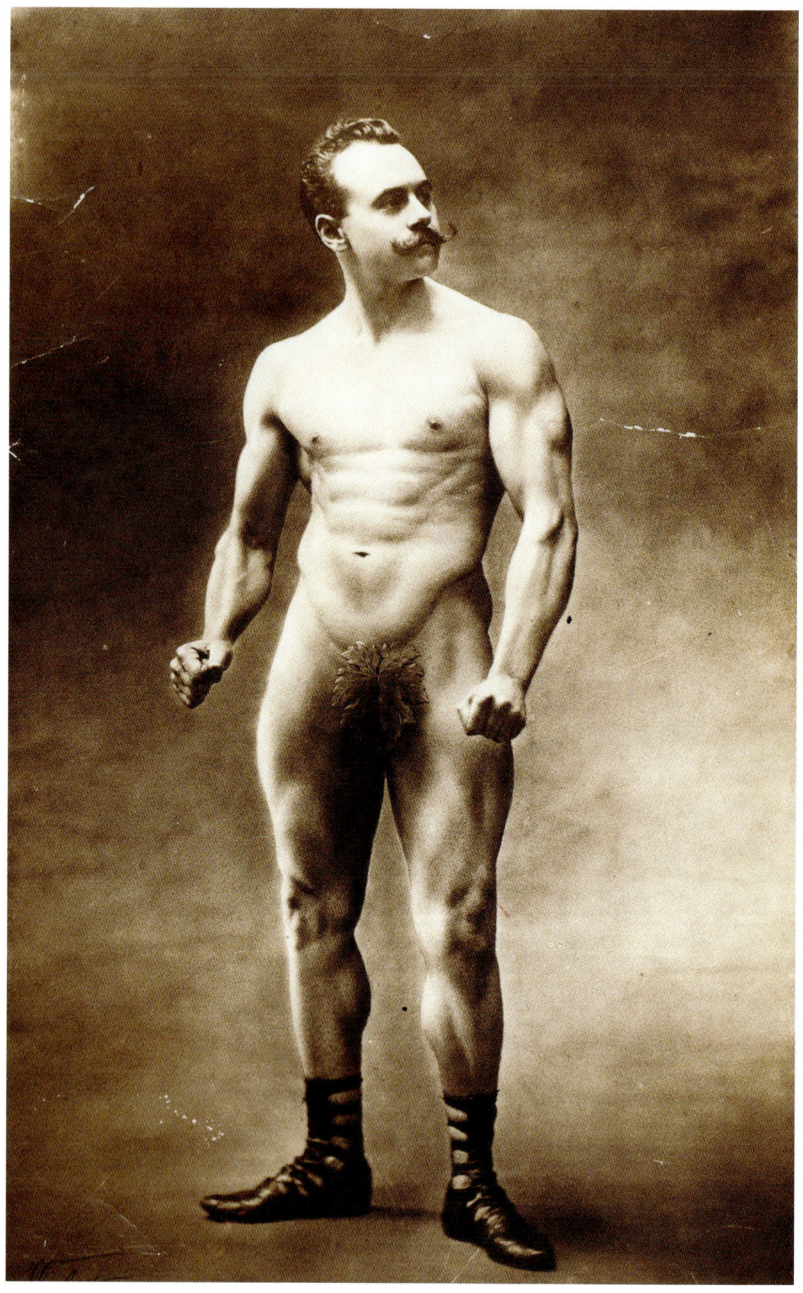

Anonymous, Collection Athlétique, c. 1890

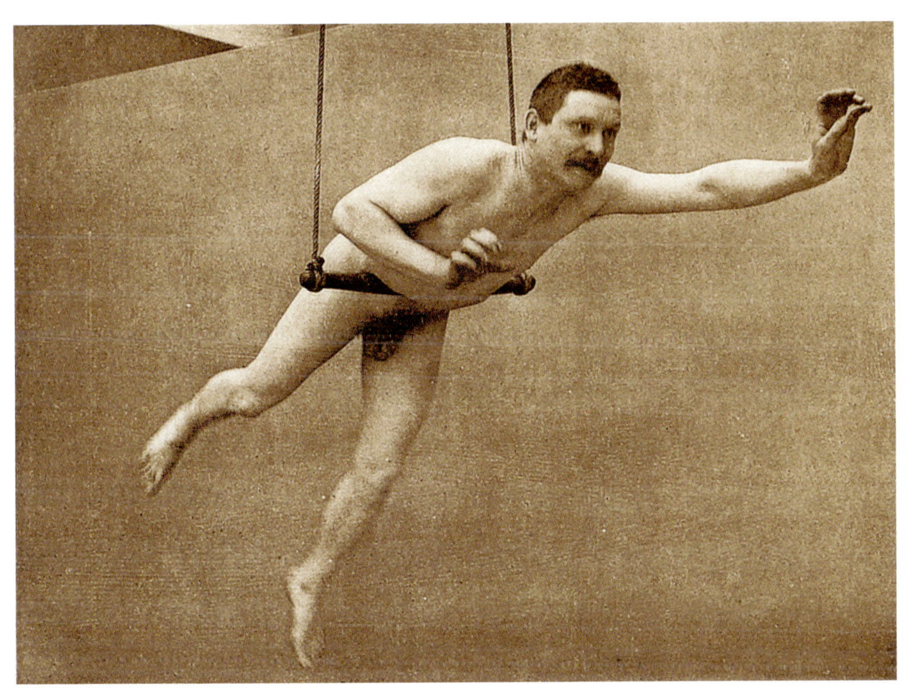

Max Koch/Otto Rieth, Der Act, 1894

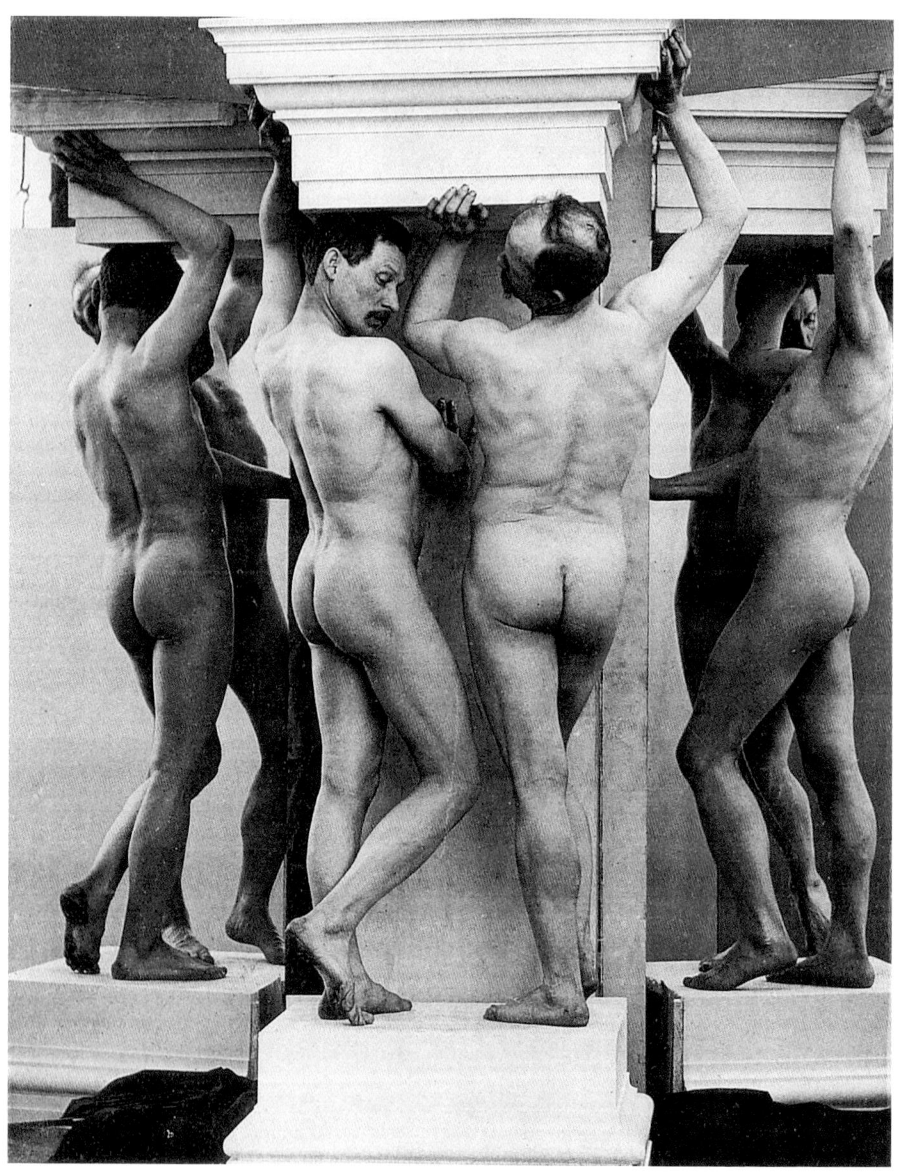

Max Koch/Otto Rieth, Der Act, 1895

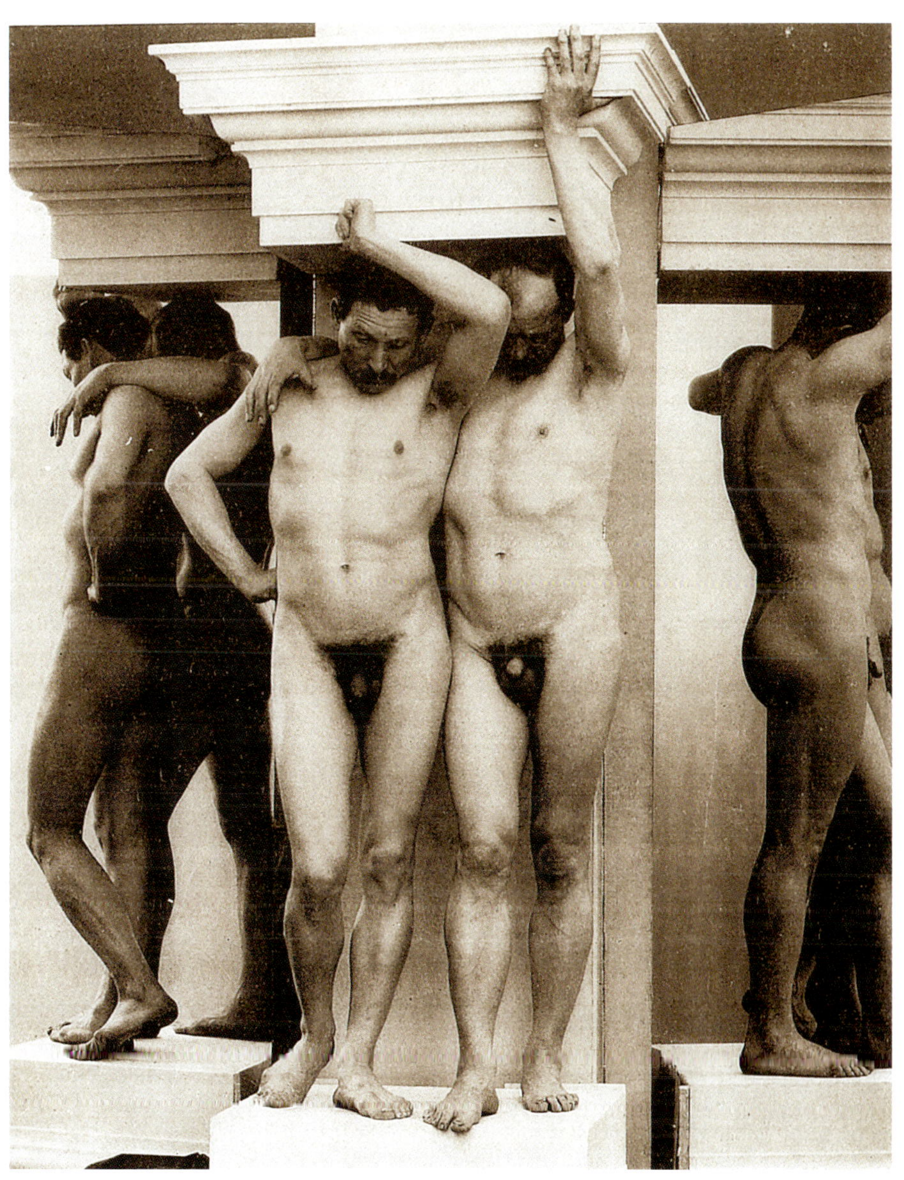

Max Koch/Otto Rieth, Der Act, 1895

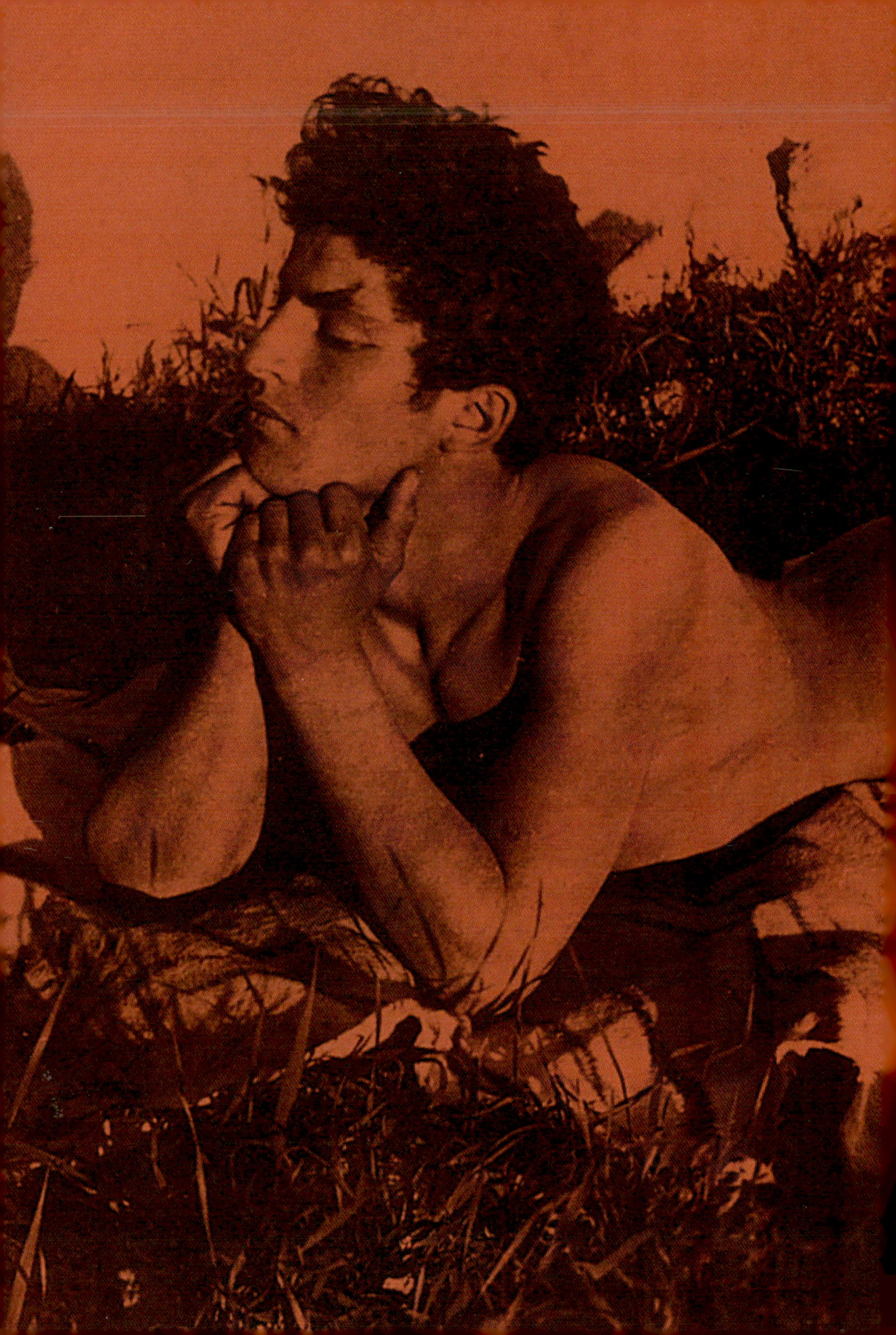

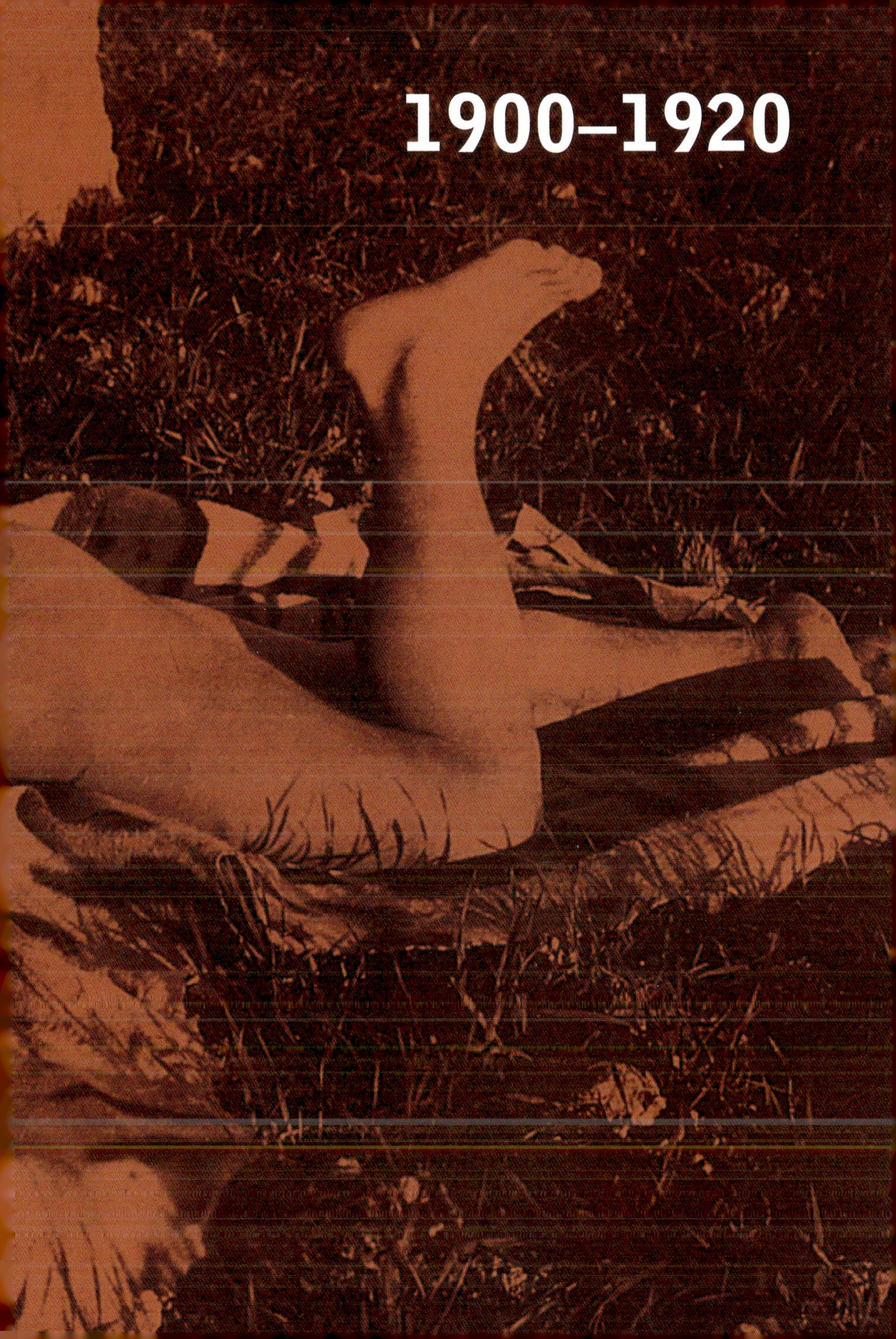

1900–1920

The first two decades of the 20th century differed greatly in character. The years up to 1910 drifted along very much in the manner of the previous century. Although automobiles, electricity, and the telephone were becoming increasingly commonplace, morals and mores continued as they had for many decades before. Men and women both remained tightly buttoned-up, laced-in, and booted.

Photographs of New York City at the turn of the century show the populace dressed mostly in black. The men are wearing buttoned-up coats, and bowler hats, while the women are burdened by long, dragging skirts, long sleeves, and very large hats – even under a blazing summer sun. Black shadows match their black clothes as they struggle in the heat and humidity. How shocking, yet appealing nude photographs must have been. Someone somewhere was comfortable at least!

As high society drifted along giving garden parties and ignoring the tensions that were building up everywhere, the only possibility of photographing male nudes was to place them in a faraway never-never land. This Baron Wilhelm von Gloeden was doing very well and exhaustively on the island of Sicily.

Von Gloeden was born in 1856 and lived until 1931. In his mid-20s he came to the town of Taormina on Sicily. He hoped the warmer climate would help his tuberculosis and he did regain his health there. But he lost his family fortune and was forced to look for some kind of work. He had a cousin Wilhelm von Plüschow in Naples who was working as a commercial photographer, and von Gloeden decided to try his hand at this in Taormina. Biographies fail to mention that von Gloeden had a German cousin working in Naples. Commercial photography hardly having developed at the time, one wonders what his real motives were.

The Baron soon combined his interest in his large-view camera and attractive young men very profitably. He produced some postcard views of Sicily and its monuments, but he also recreated his idea of life in early Greece. He peopled this fantasy world with naked boys.

In this highly repressed period, an interest in the classical period was entirely acceptable. As we will come to see, depicting male nudity always had to be cloaked in an ulterior motive; and so von Gloeden placed his youths in an imaginary past where the majority of young men ran around nude. The Greek concept of an older man nurturing and helping a younger man to reach maturity was a very appealing one to closeted gay men.

Many relationships between men of approximately the same age and class must have existed, such as that of Sherlock Holmes and his assistant Dr. Watson. But most men who preferred their own sex seemed to focus on boys as their romantic ideal. Von Gloeden's photographs of wistful and not terribly attractive Sicilian boys seemed to fit the bill for many of them. The photographer sold his prints by mail order and was very successful. That his clients' interests weren't purely philanthrophic is evidenced in all the full-frontal penises featured. Many of the models were obviously selected primarily for penis size. It would be very interesting to know how von Gloeden presented his work to his clients. We know that many customers were tourists passing through Italy and Sicily. He had several levels of available material, some of it verging on hard core.

His cousin Wilhelm von Plüschow, known as Guglielmo, worked on similar themes, and there has been much difficulty in attributing the photographs, which were often left unsigned.

Italian photographers like Gaetano d'Agata, Vincenzo Galdi, and A. Calavas followed the German cousins into the business. Their work was the precursor of latter-day "beefcake," and open legs and a large penis as the centerpiece of the photograph was often the format.

Another German photographer, Arthur Schulz, seems to have been influenced by von Gloeden but avoided placing his nudes in a classical context. He also chose adult, well-built males as models, rather than boys. Working at the turn of the century, Schulz was the first to use an interest in sports as a pretext for nude male activities. His men wrestled and sparred and appeared to be enjoying themselves.

Schulz's countryman Hugo Erfurth was producing male nudes of a more artistic sort, as was Theodor Hey. Paul Pichier followed suit in France, and Frank Eugene Smith in England.

These kinds of "arty" photographs found publishers under the traditional guise of offering material for artists or the medical profession. In Germany several volumes were published in 1906, edited by a professor of anatomy at the University of Berlin. They were largely heavy-bottomed young men striking the same poses as in antique statuary. Any possibility of a frontal view was obscured with bits of drapery or an unusually low-slung kind of tie-belt, the purpose of which was merely to conceal the genitalia. None of the models seem to be very happy about being outdoors without any clothing, unlike their Italian counterparts, who always seemed quite cheerful and content.

In the United States, Fred Holland Day was using both religious settings and the "pagan past" to display the male nude. Frontal male nudity was lost in shadows and distance, and all his photographs had the soft fuzziness that was considered most desirable in contemporary art photography.

His romantic male nudes were accepted as artistic by the public, but his photographs of himself as the dead, naked Christ, for which he dieted himself down to a skeletal appearance, caused a furor. A dead Christ was one thing, but a naked one was quite another. No matter that for centuries artists had depicted the Saviour's figure naked but for a wisp of drapery; this photograph of Christ had a real human body and no one was quite prepared for it.

The 1910s, when World War I brought the Victorian era and golden Edwardian times to an abrupt end, ushered in much more freedom in styles of dress as men went into uniform and women began war work and needed more functional clothing. This also affected the kind of nude photographs that people wanted to see. The war moved men on both sides of the trenches out of their small town worlds and into new environments. Often they came into contact with kinds of people they had never known before. Sex was more easily available and if a man was interested in other men, that wasn't out of the question either. Unformed dreams became reality and the repressiveness of Victorian society was shattered.

Although they still took pictures with a soft, "painterly" quality, a new breed of photographers was emerging in the United States as the war began in Europe. Imogen Cunningham, who in 1915 was 32, took photographs of her new husband Roi Partridge on Mount Rainier. She did not feel it necessary to name her photographs "Narcissus" or the like, or to place them in a classical context. Although soft-edged, they were simply admiring glances at a beautiful male body. Being a woman's photographs of her husband, they were free of the taint of homosexuality, although many gay men must have enjoyed looking at Roi's body. The pictures caused a scandal when they were printed in Imogen's hometown newspaper.

Edward Weston, another West Coast photographer, also began shooting nudes that were just that and nothing else. They had no relationship to the romantic "genre" photography of von Gloeden and Holland Day, which always required some kind of artistic pretext for presenting the naked male body. Weston produced many more female than male nudes, and his work of this period incorporated the soft haze thought necessary for art photography, but he was one of the harbingers of a new kind of reality in photographing the male nude. The work of Cunningham and Weston was to develop a great deal in the decades ahead, bringing the male body into ever sharper focus. Others were set to follow. Slowly the mists enshrouding the naked male were being blown aside. The pretexts of health and sport would still be thought necessary for quite a few years to come, though; the idea that men might actually be enjoying the view of another naked male body was still a frightening one, and the idea that women might enjoy this same view was inconceivable.

Die ersten beiden Dekaden des 20. Jahrhunderts unterschieden sich gründlich
in ihrem Charakter. Obwohl unzählige technische Errungenschaften wie das
Automobil, die Elektrizität und das Telefon sich anschickten, Allgemeingut zu
werden, blieben Sitten und Gebräuche im 19. Jahrhundert verhaftet. Das Bürgertum ignorierte die sich im Zuge fortschreitender Industrialisierung anbahnenden
gesellschaftlichen und sozialen Spannungen, es gab sich auf diversen Festlich-
keiten dem Vergnügen hin. Die entscheidende Wende sollte erst nach dem Ersten
Weltkrieg eintreten.

Fotografien aus einem New Yorker Hochsommer zu Beginn des Jahrhunderts
zeigen die Menschen ganz in Schwarz gekleidet; Mäntel und Zylinder für die
Männer, die Frauen in knöchellangen Kleidern, langärmligen Oberteilen und
unter breitkrempigen Hüten. Alle sozialen Spannungen und alle Zeichen ignorie-
rend, die auf einen nötigen Wandel hinwiesen, stakste das Bürgertum mit stei-
fem Kragen und strenger Moral auf alten Pfaden. Wie schockierend, aber auch
wie anziehend müssen Aktaufnahmen den schwitzenden Gestalten erschienen
sein. Irgendwo hatte irgend jemand tatsächlich Spaß!

Nach wie vor ließen sich Aktaufnahmen von Männern nur veröffentlichen,
wenn man sie in einer arkadischen Phantasiewelt ansiedelte, und der Fach-
mann hierfür war weiterhin der uns schon bekannte Baron Wilhelm von Gloeden
(1856–1931). Mit Mitte Zwanzig war von Gloeden nach Sizilien gereist, weil
er sich von dem warmen Klima die Heilung seiner Tuberkulose versprach. Als er
sein Familienvermögen verlor, entschloss er sich, dem Vorbild seines in Neapel
tätigen Vetters Wilhelm von Plüschow folgend, seinen Lebensunterhalt als Fotograf zu verdienen. Beide verstanden es, ihre Vorliebe für die Fotografie und ihr
Interesse an jungen Männern auf einträgliche Weise miteinander zu verknüpfen.
Von Gloeden fotografierte einige Postkartenansichten von Sizilien und seinen
Baudenkmälern, aber vornehmlich inszenierte er Szenen einer antiken griechi-
schen Phantasiewelt, bevölkert mit nackten Knaben.

Der Bezug zur Antike legitimierte seine Arbeiten, auch wenn die meisten
seiner Kunden die Antike in erster Linie als Paradies der Knabenliebe verstanden. Sicherlich gab es zu von Gloedens Zeit viele Beziehungen zwischen
Männern, die ungefähr gleichaltrig waren oder derselben sozialen Schicht

angehörten, Sherlock Holmes und Dr. Watson sind nur ein bekanntes Beispiel hierfür. Aber die meisten Männer, die Männer liebten, hingen ihrer Liebe zu Knaben zumeist als einem romantischen Ideal nach. Von Gloedens Fotos von verträumten und nicht gerade außergewöhnlich hübschen sizilianischen Jungen schienen diese Phantasien genau zu treffen. Dass das Interesse seiner Kunden nicht nur vom Kunstsinn gespeist wurde, belegt der auffällige Umstand, dass der Penis der Jungen auf den Bildern deutlich ins Blickfeld gerückt ist. Viele Modelle scheinen allein der Größe ihrer Geschlechtsorgane wegen ausgewählt worden zu sein. Manche seiner Arbeiten grenzen an Hardcore. Es wäre interessant herauszufinden, wie von Gloeden den Kunden seine Arbeiten präsentierte. Man weiß, dass viele seiner Kunden Touristen waren. Von Gloeden hatte immer Material unterschiedlicher Qualität auf Lager.

Sein Vetter Wilhelm von Plüschow, auch als Guglielmo bekannt, griff in seiner Arbeit ähnliche Themen auf. Da sowohl er als auch von Gloeden ihre Abzüge häufig nicht signierten, fällt die Zuordnung nicht immer leicht.

Die italienischen Fotografen Vincenzo Galdi und A. Calavas traten in die Fußstapfen der beiden Deutschen. In ihrer Arbeit nehmen sie die nackten Muskelprotze späterer Jahre vorweg, so auch gespreizte Beine und ein in den Bildmittelpunkt gerücktes Geschlecht.

Auch der deutsche Fotograf Arthur Schulz ließ sich von den Arbeiten von Gloedens inspirieren, allerdings platzierte er seine Männerakte nicht in antikisierenden Szenarien. Zudem suchte er sich gut gebaute erwachsene Männer als Modelle. Das Thema Sport, das später zum häufigsten Vorwand wurde, Nacktheit zu präsentieren, hatte Schulz bereits um die Jahrhundertwende für sich entdeckt und als erster in die Fotografie aufgenommen. Seine Modelle sieht man beim Boxen oder Ringen, und anscheinend hatten sie einigen Spaß daran.

Stärkeren Wert auf die künstlerische Note ihrer Arbeiten legten die deutschen Fotografen Hugo Erfurth und Theodor Hey. In Frankreich folgte Paul Pichier, in England Frank Eugene Smith. Männerakte in einem historischen oder sportlichen Kontext zu zeigen, verlor zunehmend an Attraktivität.

Veröffentlicht wurden diese „künstlerischen" Fotos weiterhin unter dem Vorwand, Künstlern, aber auch Medizinern als Studienmaterial zu dienen. 1906

erschienen mehrere Bildbände, herausgegeben von einem Anatomieprofessor
der Universität Berlin. Die meisten Bilder zeigen junge Männer mit breitem
Becken, die die altbekannten, von antiken Statuen abgeschauten Posen ein-
nehmen. Frontalansichten wurden tunlichst vermieden und jeder Blick auf
die Genitalien durch kunstvoll drapierten Stoff verwehrt. Anders als bei ihren
italienischen Kollegen, scheinen die Modelle keinen besonderen Spaß an der
Arbeit empfunden zu haben.

In den Vereinigten Staaten bediente sich Fred Holland Day der heidnischen
Vergangenheit und der Religionsgeschichte als Kulisse für seine Männerakte.
Frontalansichten verlieren sich in fernen, dunklen Schatten, wie überhaupt alle
seine Fotos durch eine weichgezeichnete Unschärfe charakterisiert sind, die
zur damaligen Zeit als Markenzeichen guter Kunstfotografie galt.

Seine verträumten Aktfotos akzeptierte die Öffentlichkeit als Kunst, doch
als er sich selbst als nackten, gekreuzigten Jesus porträtierte, löste er einen
Skandal aus. Obwohl seit Jahrhunderten in der Kunst kaum verhüllt dargestellt,
war dieser gänzlich nackte Christus ein wirklicher Mensch, und darauf war
niemand gefasst.

Der Erste Weltkrieg brachte auch die überkommenen Moralvorstellungen
ins Wanken. In einer Welt, in der Chaos regiert, verlieren alte Werte und Konventionen schnell an Bedeutung. Mit Ausbruch des ersten Weltkriegs trugen
die Männer Uniformen und die Frauen in der kriegsbedingten Produktion
Arbeitskleidung – das Ende der viktorianischen Kleiderordnung, was auch seine
Wirkung auf die Aktfotos nicht verfehlte. Der Krieg riss die Männer auf beiden
Seiten der Schützengräben aus ihrer kleinstädtischen Welt heraus, stellte sie
in eine neue Umgebung und brachte sie in Kontakt mit Menschen, die ihnen
bislang fremd gewesen waren. Sex war leicht zu haben, und auch wenn ein Mann
Interesse an anderen Männern hatte, war das kein Problem. Träume wurden
Wirklichkeit, und die repressive Atmosphäre der viktorianischen Gesellschaft
war erschüttert.

In den USA fotografierte Imogen Cunningham, die 1915 gerade 32 Jahre
alt war, ihren neuen Ehemann Roi Partridge auf dem Mount Rainier und hielt es
nicht mehr für nötig, die Bilder mit Titeln wie „Narzissus" zu verbrämen. Die

Aufnahmen werfen, wenn auch weich gezeichnet, bewundernde Blicke auf den nackten Körper eines schönen Mannes, und da sie von einer Frau stammten, waren sie auch frei vom Ruch der Homosexualität. Aber der nackte Roi wird auch manchem Mann gefallen haben. Natürlich gab es einen Skandal, als sie tatsächlich in Cunninghams Lokalzeitung erschienen.

Auch Edward Weston, ein weiterer Fotograf von der Westküste, begann Akte zu fotografieren, die nichts anderes als eben das sein wollten: Fotos von nackten Menschen. Sie hatten keinen Bezug mehr zur romantischen Genrefotografie eines von Gloeden oder Holland Days. Weston nahm mehr Akte von Frauen als von Männern auf, und seine Bilder aus dieser Zeit sind immer noch von dem für die Aktfotografie unabdingbaren Dunstschleier überzogen, dennoch war er einer der Vorreiter einer neuen Art von Wirklichkeit in der männlichen Aktfotografie. Weston und Cunningham trugen wesentlich zur Entwicklung der Fotografie in den kommenden Jahrzehnten bei. Der nackte männliche Körper rückte zunehmend schärfer konturiert ins Blickfeld, und die schamhaften Schleier begannen sich zu lüften.

Les photographies de New York à cette époque montrent des hommes et des femmes habillés de noir. Les hommes portent des manteaux boutonnés jusqu'au cou et des chapeaux melon, et les femmes, de longues jupes, de longues manches et de très grands chapeaux, le tout sous un soleil torride. Leurs silhouettes noires projettent des ombres noires tandis qu'ils souffrent en silence dans la chaleur et l'humidité.

Tandis que le beau monde coulait des jours tranquilles, donnant des garden-parties et faisant la sourde oreille aux rumeurs de guerre qui grondaient un peu partout, la seule possibilité de faire des photographies de nus était de les placer dans un contexte complètement irréel. C'était le cas de Wilhelm von Gloeden, qui le faisait très bien et souvent en Sicile.

Von Gloeden, né en 1856, en pleine ère victorienne, vécut jusqu'en 1931. Alors qu'il avait une vingtaine d'années, il se rendit dans la ville de Taormina pour soigner sa tuberculose au soleil de la Sicile. Il guérit mais, entre-temps, il perdit sa fortune familiale et se vit contraint de chercher une source de revenus.

Le baron parvint rapidement à associer sa passion pour son grand angle et les adolescents nubiles d'une manière très lucrative. Il réalisait quelques cartes postales de paysages et de monuments siciliens, mais recréait surtout des scènes de ce qu'il imaginait être la Grèce antique, à savoir, peuplée de jeunes éphèbes dans le plus simple appareil.

Dans cette époque très étriquée, l'intérêt pour l'Antiquité était considéré comme parfaitement acceptable. Comme nous le verrons plus loin, il fallait toujours une bonne raison pour montrer la nudité et, dans ce cas précis, von Gloeden cherchait à évoquer un passé imaginaire où, par le plus grand des hasards, la plupart des jeunes hommes étaient nus. Il y avait sûrement de nombreuses relations entre des hommes du même âge, comme Sherlock Holmes et son inséparable docteur Watson, mais la plupart des hommes qui aimaient les hommes semblent avoir reporté tout leur érotisme sur les jeunes garçons. Aussi, les photographies de von Gloeden montrant des adolescents siciliens songeurs, mais pas très beaux, trouvèrent rapidement leur public. Le photographe vendait également ses tirages par correspondance. L'intérêt de ses clients n'était pas purement philanthropique : en témoignent les nombreux clichés de pénis vus de face, un bon nombre des modèles ayant manifestement été choisis pour la taille généreuse de leur organe. Il serait très intéressant de savoir comment von Gloeden présentait son travail à ses clients. Nous savons que bon nombre d'entre eux étaient des touristes de passage. Von Gloeden avait différentes catégories d'images à leur montrer, certaines frôlant la pornographie pure et dure.

Wilhelm von Plüschow, le cousin de von Gloeden, également connu sous le prénom de Guglielmo, travaillait dans la même veine, ce qui entraîna une grande confusion quand on voulut répertorier les images des deux cousins. Leurs photos étaient en effet rarement signées.

Des photographes italiens tels que Vincenzo Galdi et A. Calavas emboîtèrent le pas aux deux Allemands. Leurs travaux préfiguraient le culturiste des années 50, et les cuisses écartées et les gros pénis étaient souvent bien mis en évidence au centre de l'image.

Un autre photographe allemand, Arthur Schulz, semble avoir été influencé par von Gloeden, mais il évitait de placer ses modèles dans un contexte classique. En outre, il photographiait des sujets adultes et bien bâtis. Le sport comme prétexte pour montrer des hommes nus allait venir plus tard, mais Schulz fut un des premiers à s'en servir. Ses hommes luttaient, boxaient et avaient l'air de bien s'amuser. Son compatriote Hugo Erfurth réalisait aussi des nus masculins dans un genre plus artistique, tout comme Theodor Hey. Paul Pichier faisait de même en France, et Frank Eugene Smith en Angleterre. Le besoin de placer les nus masculins dans un cadre historique ou académique commençait à disparaître.

Ce genre de photographies «artistiques» ne trouvait des éditeurs que sous le prétexte traditionnel d'être destiné à un public d'artistes ou de médecins. En Allemagne, plusieurs volumes furent publiés en 1906 par un anatomiste de l'université de Berlin. Ils montraient principalement de jeunes hommes au derrière imposant, prenant les mêmes poses inspirées de l'art antique. Leur sexe était caché par des morceaux de draperie ou des boucles de ceinture qui ne retenaient rien, mais avaient l'avantage de retomber devant l'entrejambe.

Aux Etats-Unis, Fred Holland Day montrait ses nus dans un passé païen imaginaire, ou dans l'histoire religieuse. La nudité frontale se perdait dans les ombres ou la distance, et toutes ses images étaient noyées dans le flou savant très prisé à l'époque pour les photographies d'art.

Les photos de ses hommes songeurs et mélancoliques étaient acceptées par le public comme artistiques, mais son autoportrait en Christ, pour lequel il suivit un régime jusqu'à paraître squelettique, provoqua un scandale. Un Christ mort était une chose, mais un Christ nu en était une autre. Du moins sur une photographie. Bien qu'il ait été peint ne portant qu'un soupçon de linge autour des hanches depuis des siècles, ce Christ-là avait un corps bien humain, et personne n'était encore prêt à le voir.

La seconde décennie, au cours de laquelle la guerre fit éclater la bulle victorienne, entraîna une révolution vestimentaire, libérant les corps. Elle eut également un effet majeur sur le genre de photos de nu que les gens voulaient voir. Des deux côtés des tranchées, la guerre fit sortir les hommes de leur petit monde étriqué et les plongea dans de nouveaux environnements. Ils rencontrèrent des gens comme ils n'en avaient jamais vu auparavant. Les rapports sexuels étaient beaucoup plus faciles, et si un homme s'intéressait à un autre homme, ce n'était pas forcément hors de question. Les rêves les plus profondément enfouis devenaient réalité, et la répression de l'ère victorienne s'effondrait en miettes.

Une nouvelle génération de photographes apparut aux Etats-Unis alors que la guerre éclatait en Europe. Imogen Cunningham, qui avait 32 ans en 1915, réalisa des photographies de son nouveau mari, Roi Partridge, escaladant le Mount Rainier entièrement nu. Elle ne ressentit pas le besoin de baptiser ses images « Narcisse », ou autre chose du même genre, ni de les placer dans un contexte classique. Bien qu'artistiquement floues, elles étaient simplement des images admiratives d'un beau corps d'homme. Comme elles avaient été prises par sa femme, on ne pouvait pas accuser le photographe d'être homosexuel, même si de nombreux gays ont sans doute contemplé avec plaisir les formes avantageuses de Roi. Ces images firent couler beaucoup d'encre lorsqu'elles parurent dans le journal local de la ville d'Imogen.

Edward Weston, un autre photographe de la côte ouest, se mit à photographier des nus qui n'avaient plus rien à voir avec la photographie du « genre » de von Gloeden et de Holland Day. Weston réalisa beaucoup plus de nus féminins que masculins, et ses œuvres de cette période ont ce flou que l'on considérait alors indispensable à la photographie d'art, mais il fut l'un des précurseurs d'un nouveau réalisme dans le nu masculin. Cunningham et lui devaient aller beaucoup plus loin dans les décennies suivantes, mettant de plus en plus le corps masculin en valeur. Comme beaucoup d'autres. L'homme nu n'avait plus besoin d'être nimbé dans les brumes d'un passé romantique.

Toutefois, les prétextes de la communion avec la nature et du sport n'étaient pas encore prêts de disparaître. L'idée que des hommes puissent apprécier la vue d'un corps d'homme nu faisait encore peur, et que des femmes puissent avoir le même plaisir était carrément inconcevable.

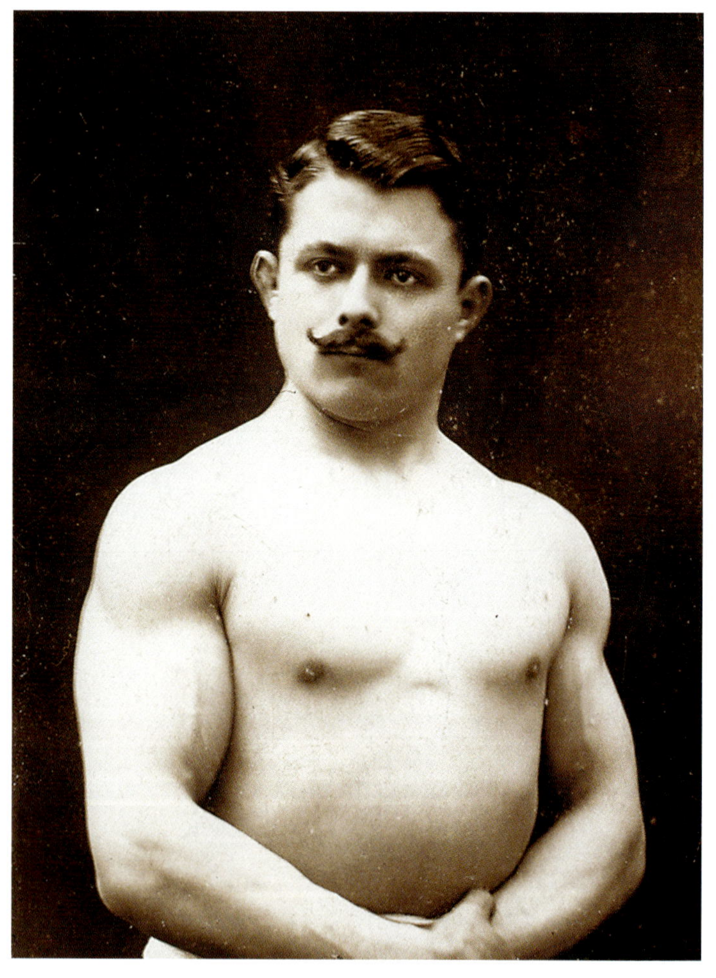

Anonymous, c. 1900

Anonymous, c. 1910

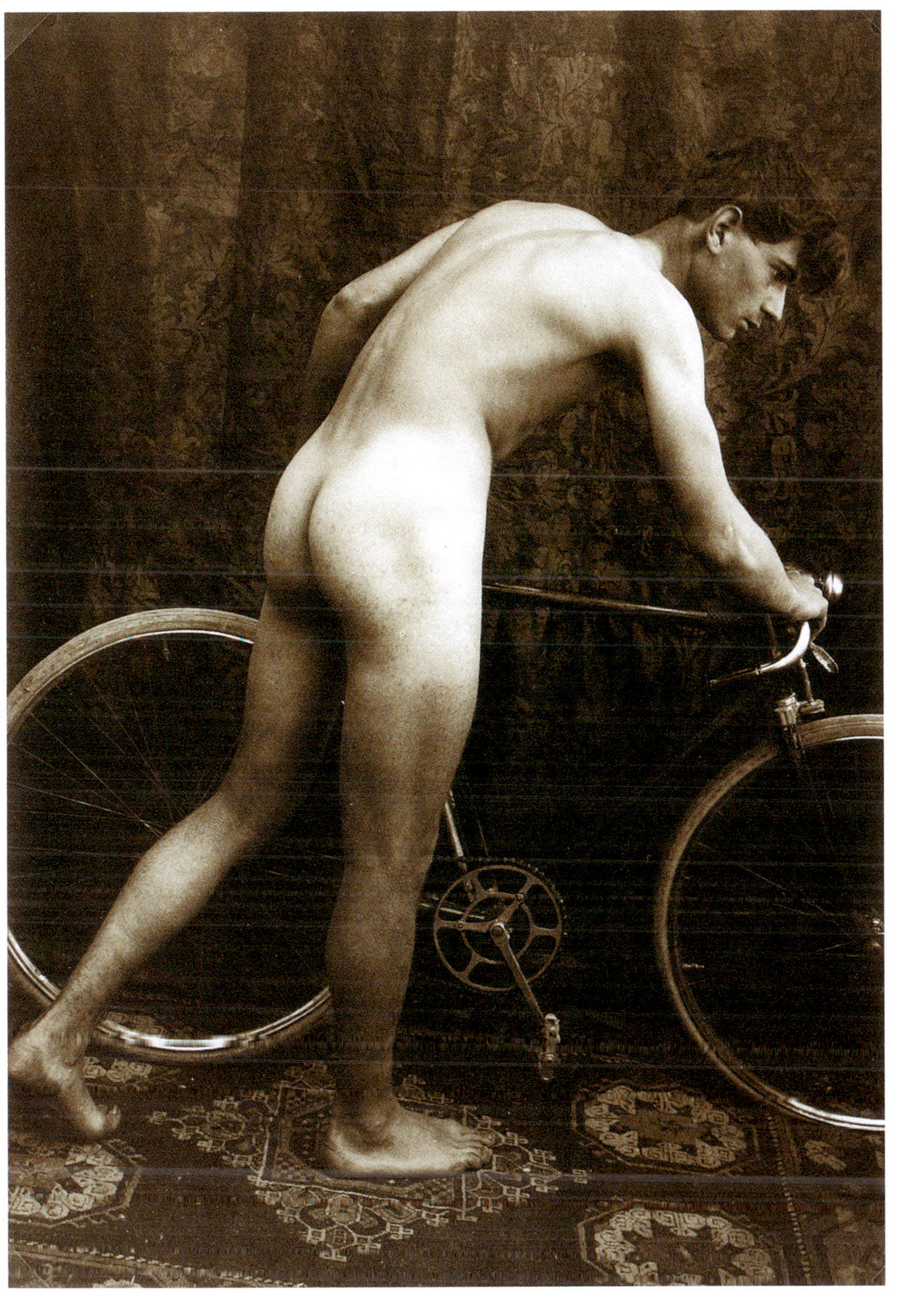

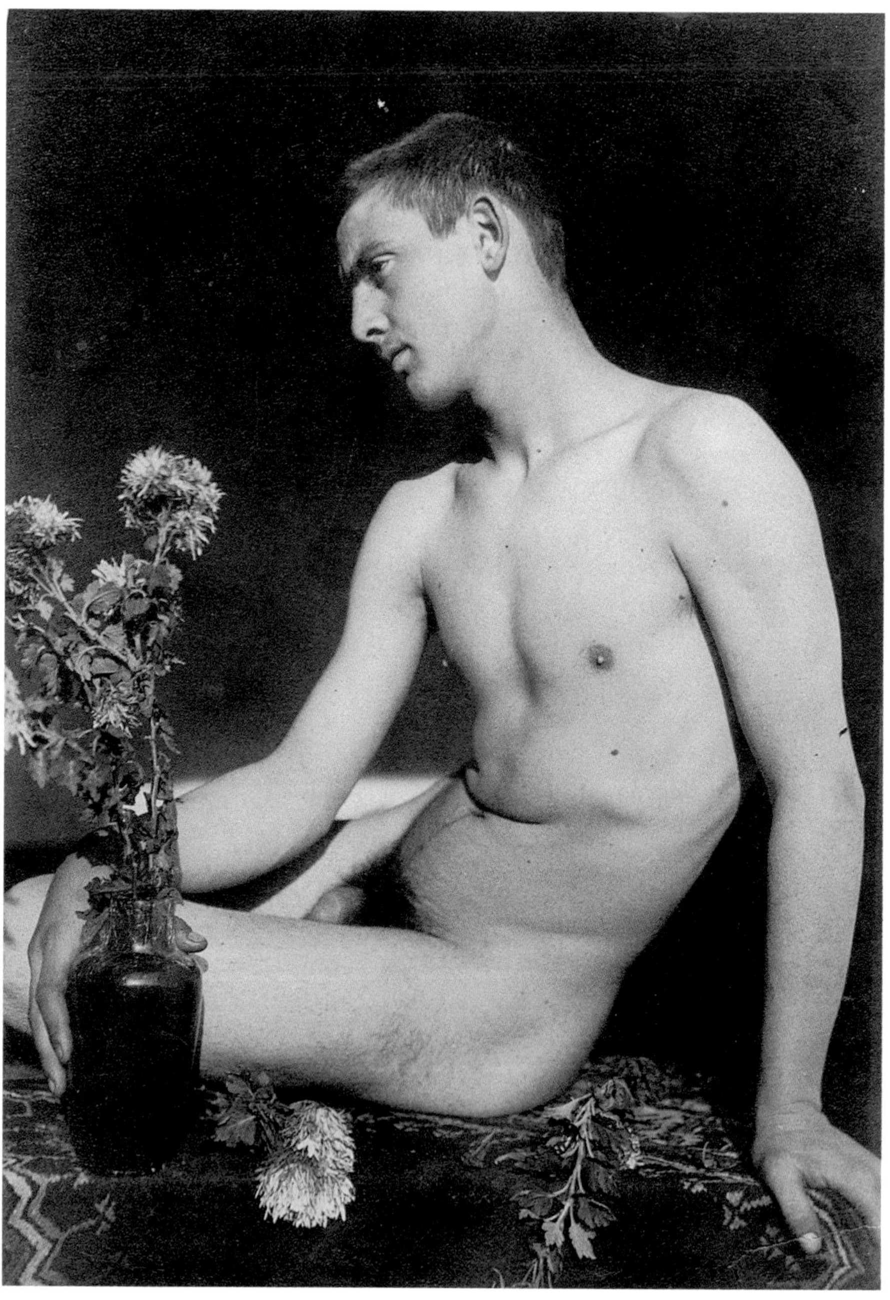

Guglielmo Plüschow, c. 1900

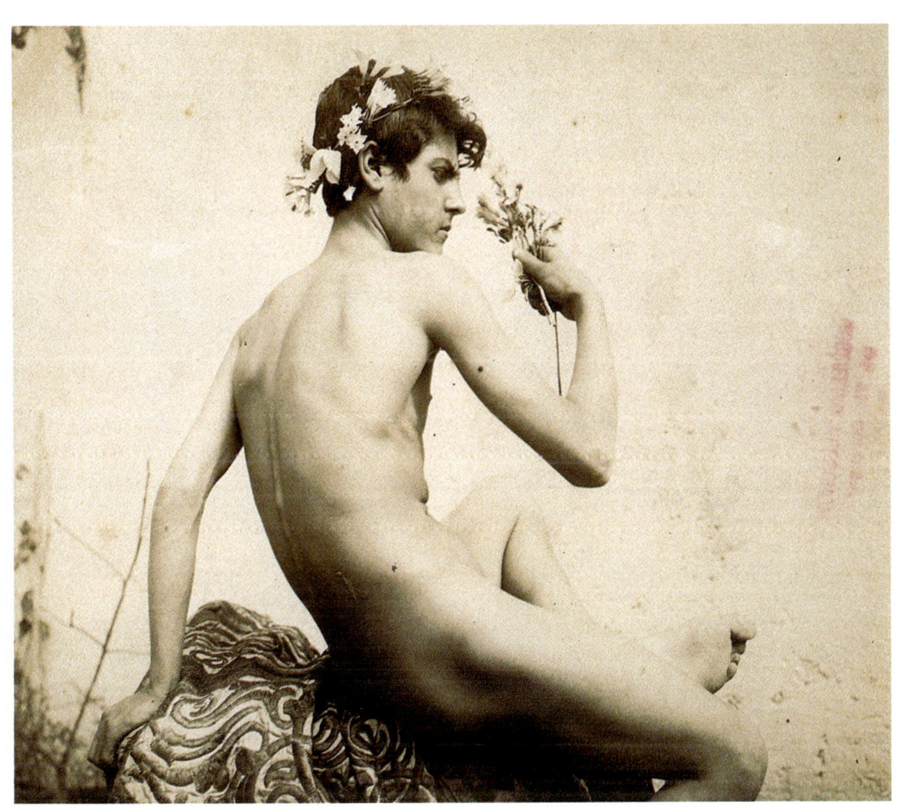

Guglielmo Plüschow, c. 1900

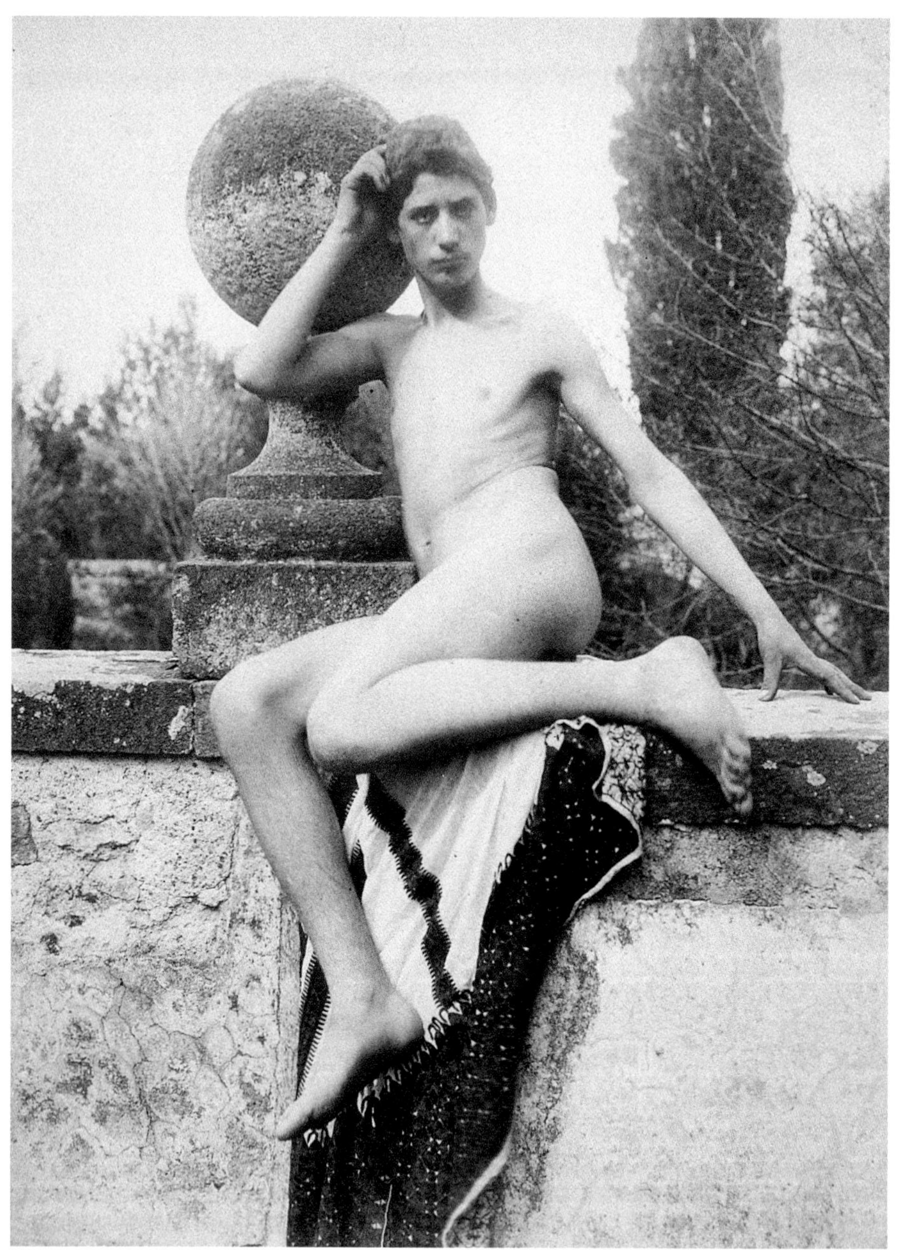

Guglielmo Plüschow, c. 1900

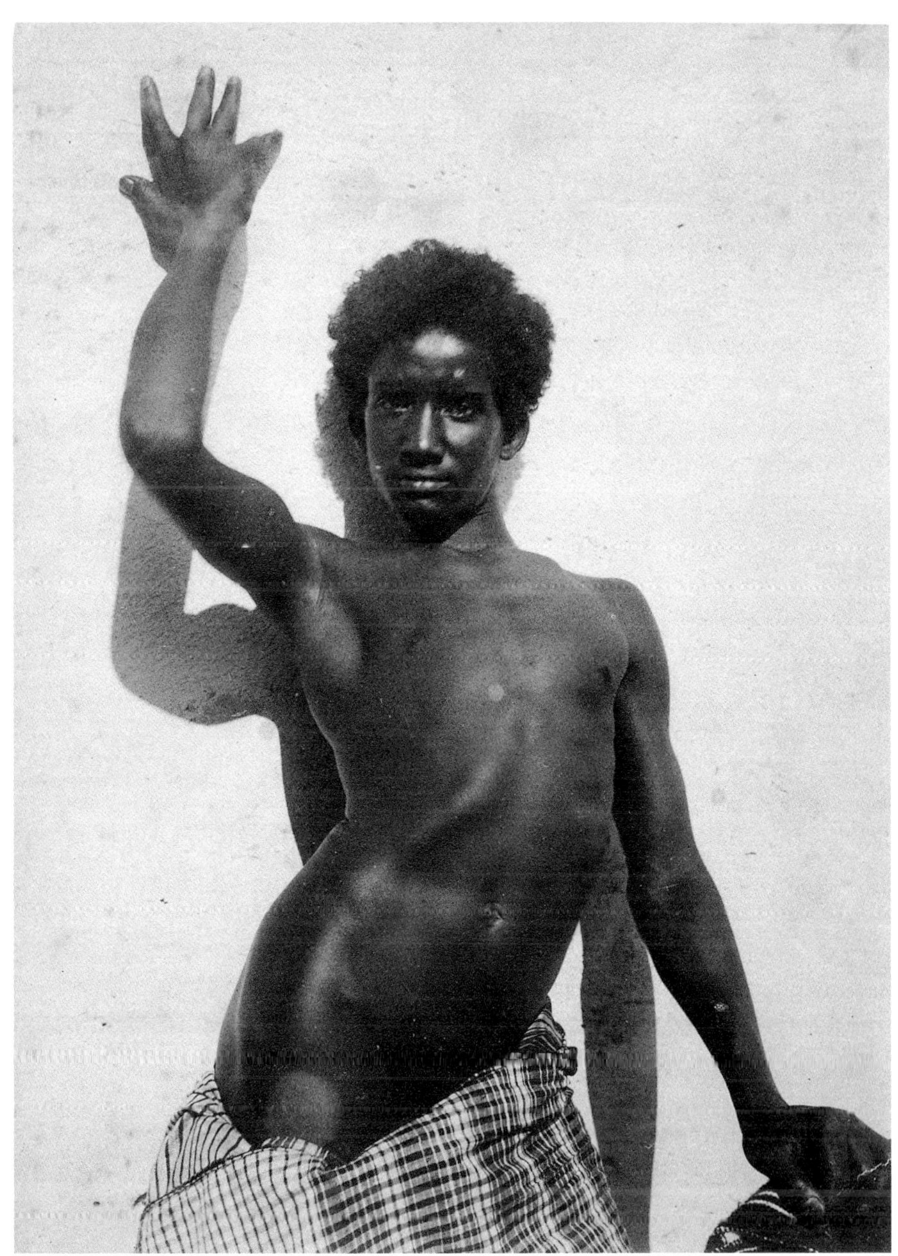

Guglielmo Plüschow, c. 1900

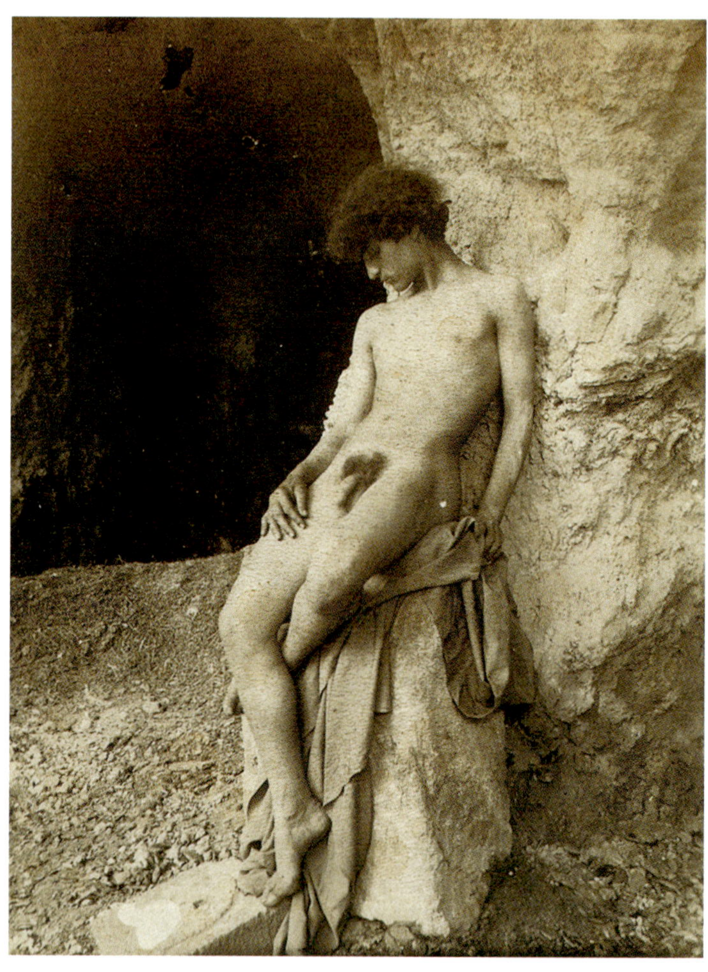

Guglielmo Plüschow, c. 1900

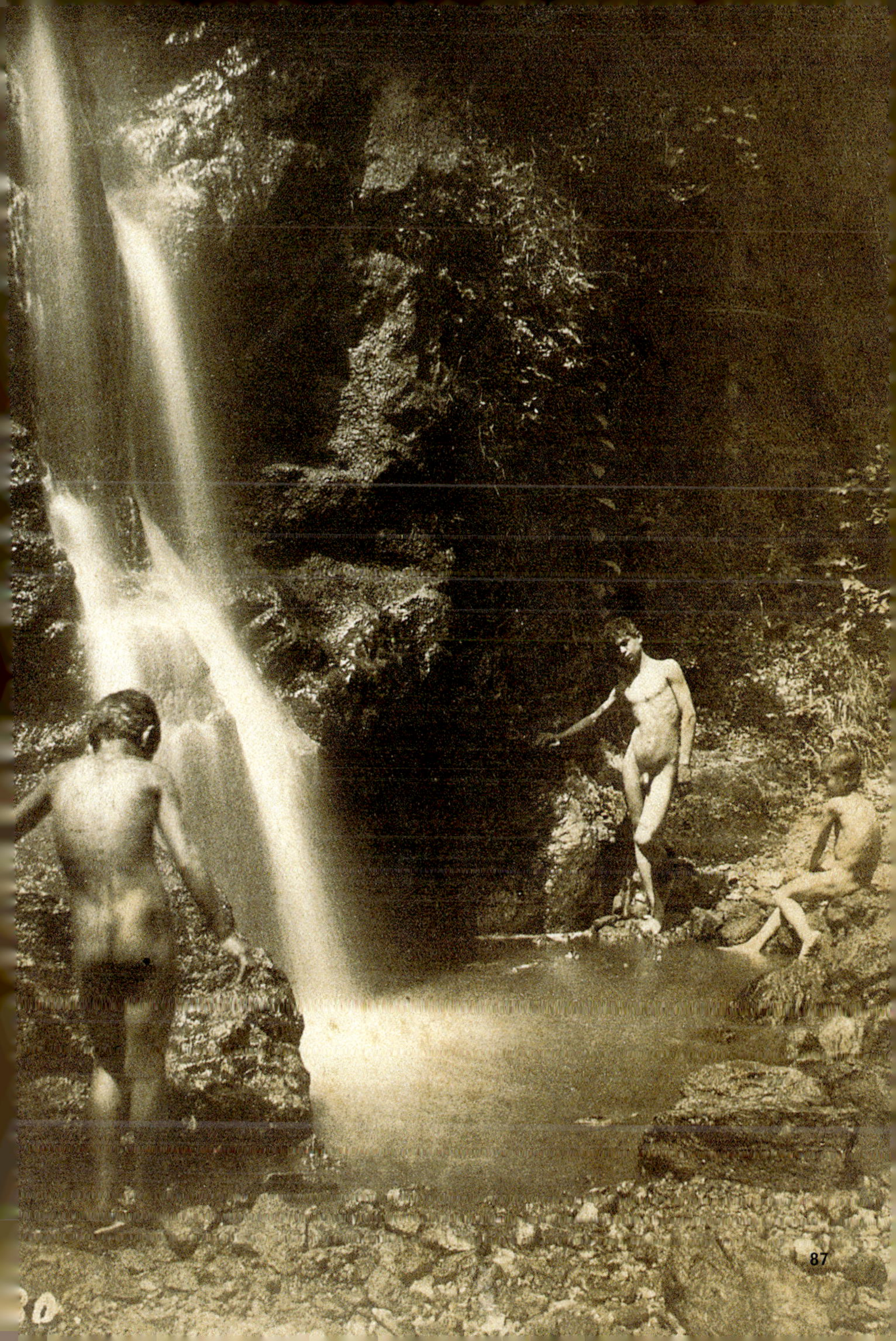

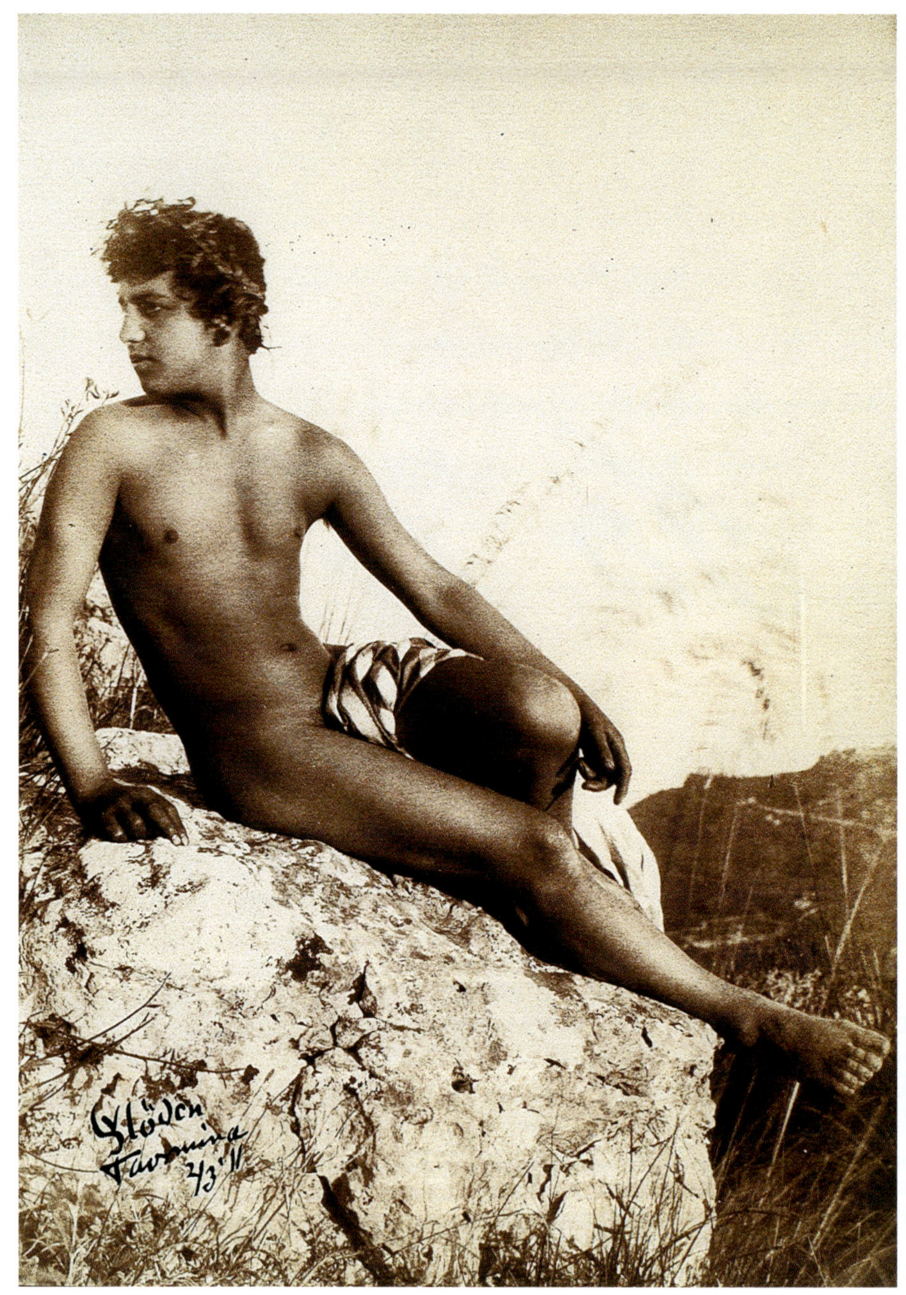

Wilhelm von Gloeden, c. 1911

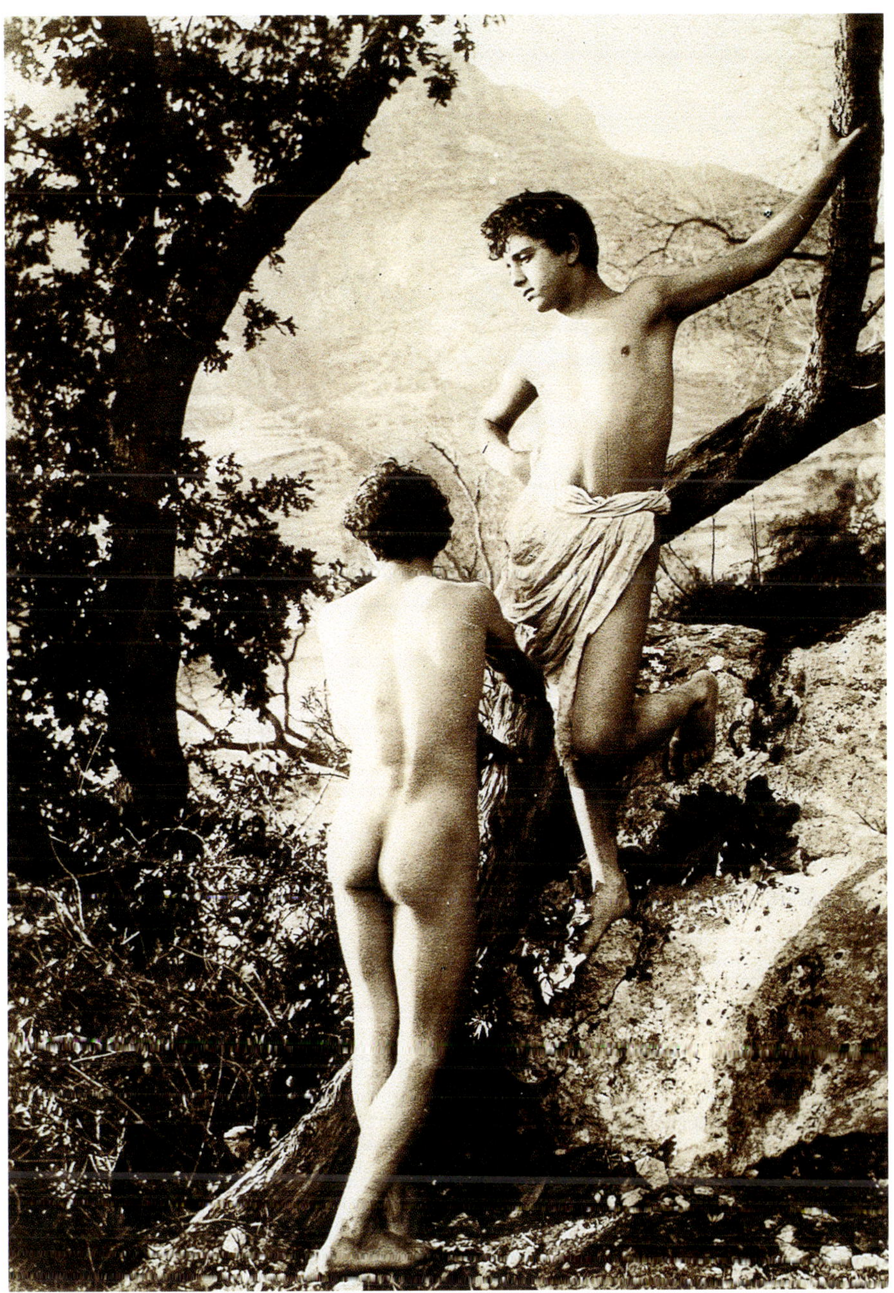

Wilhelm von Gloeden, c. 1905

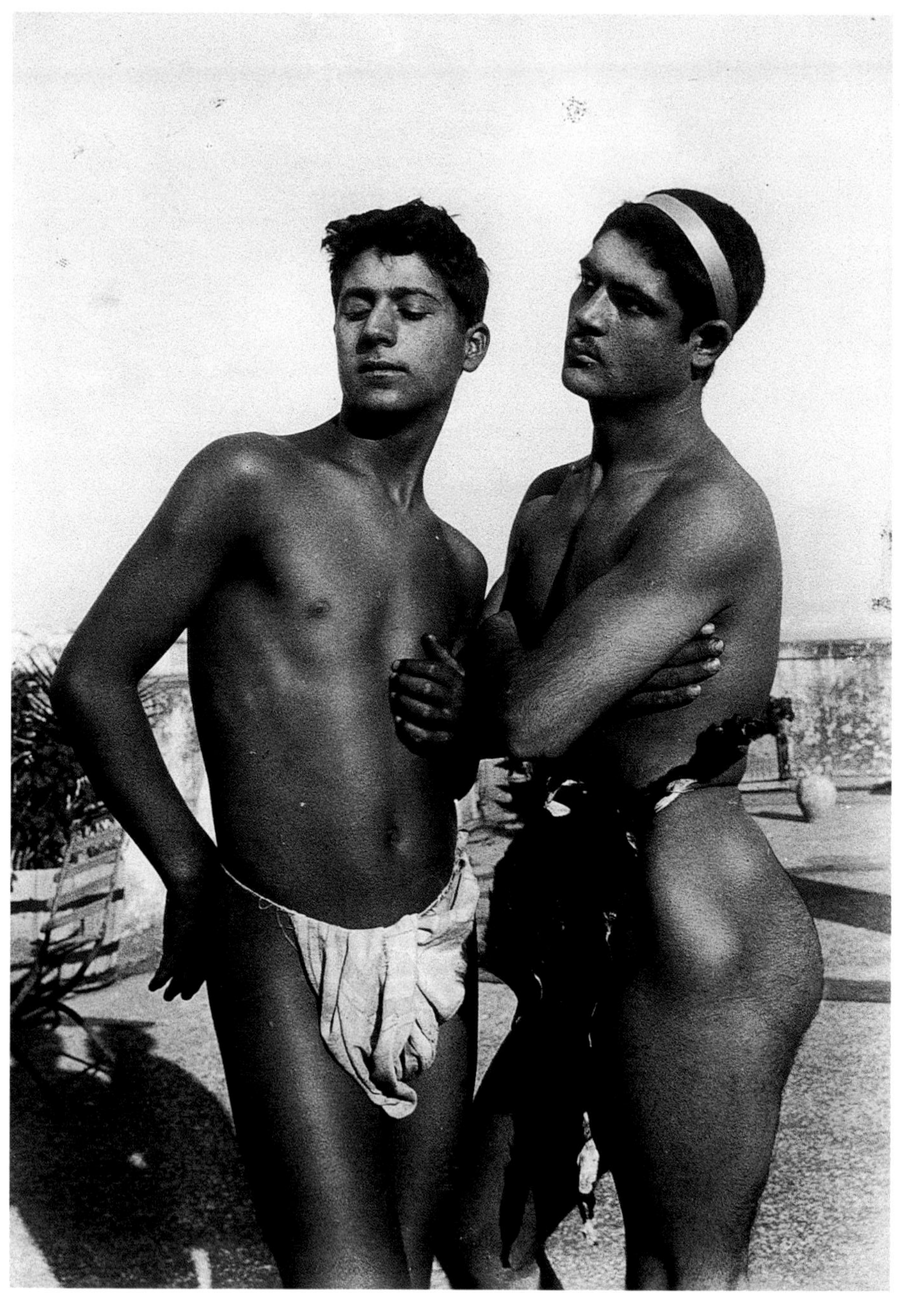

Wilhelm von Gloeden, c. 1900

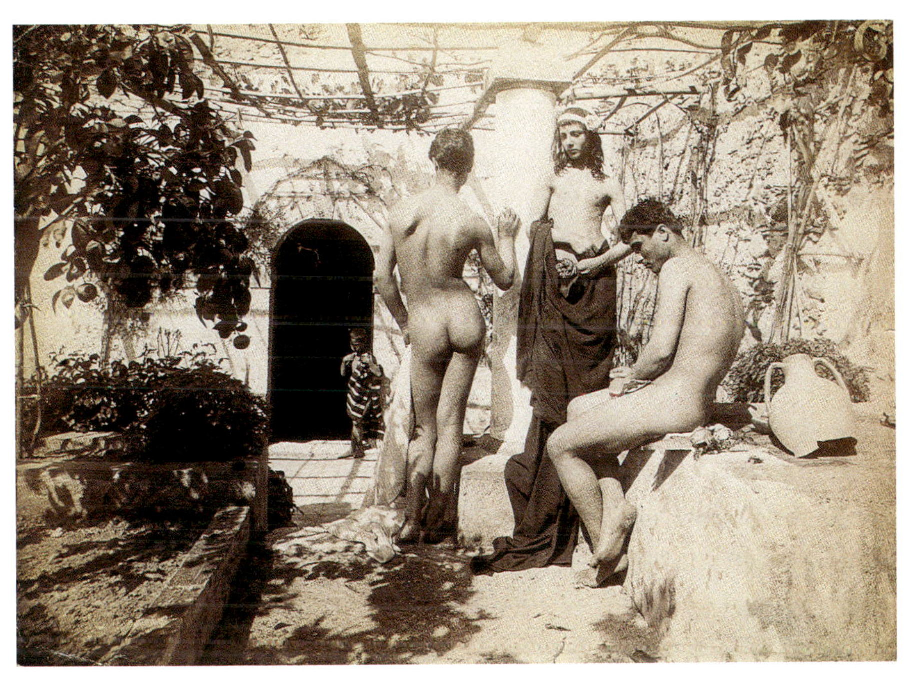

Wilhelm von Gloeden, c. 1905

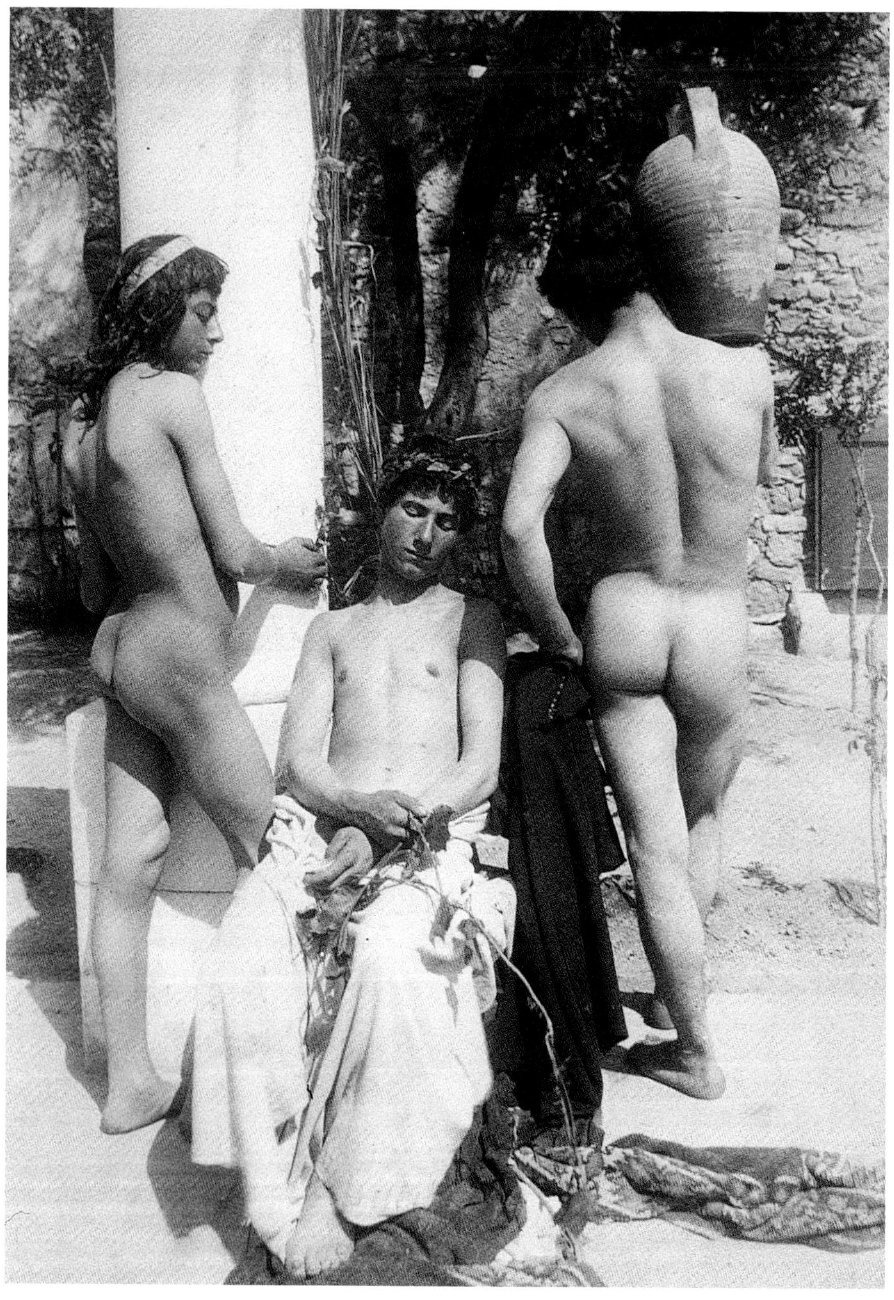

Wilhelm von Gloeden, c. 1905

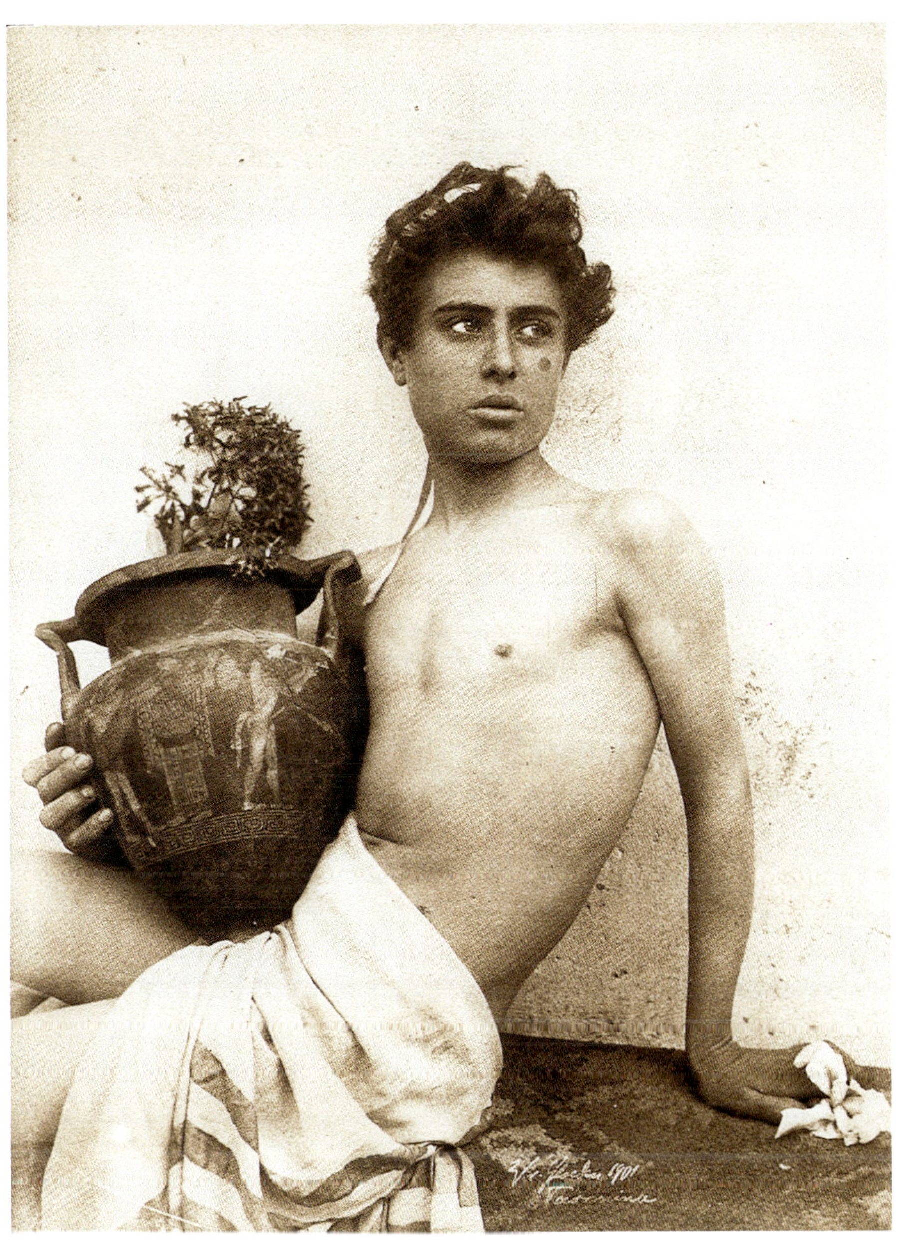

Wilhelm von Gloeden, c. 1901

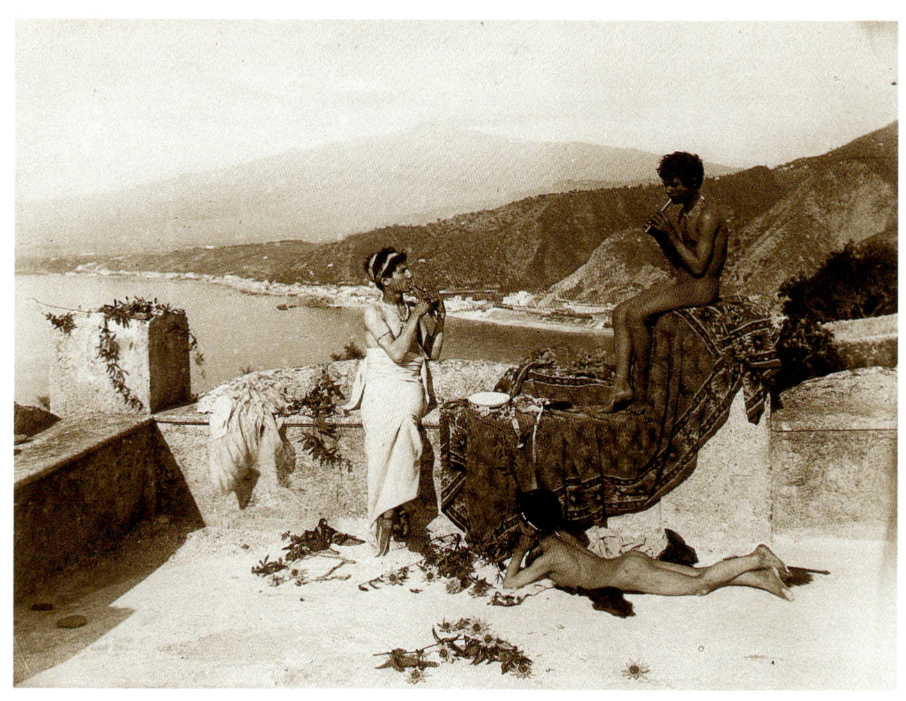

Wilhelm von Gloeden, c. 1900

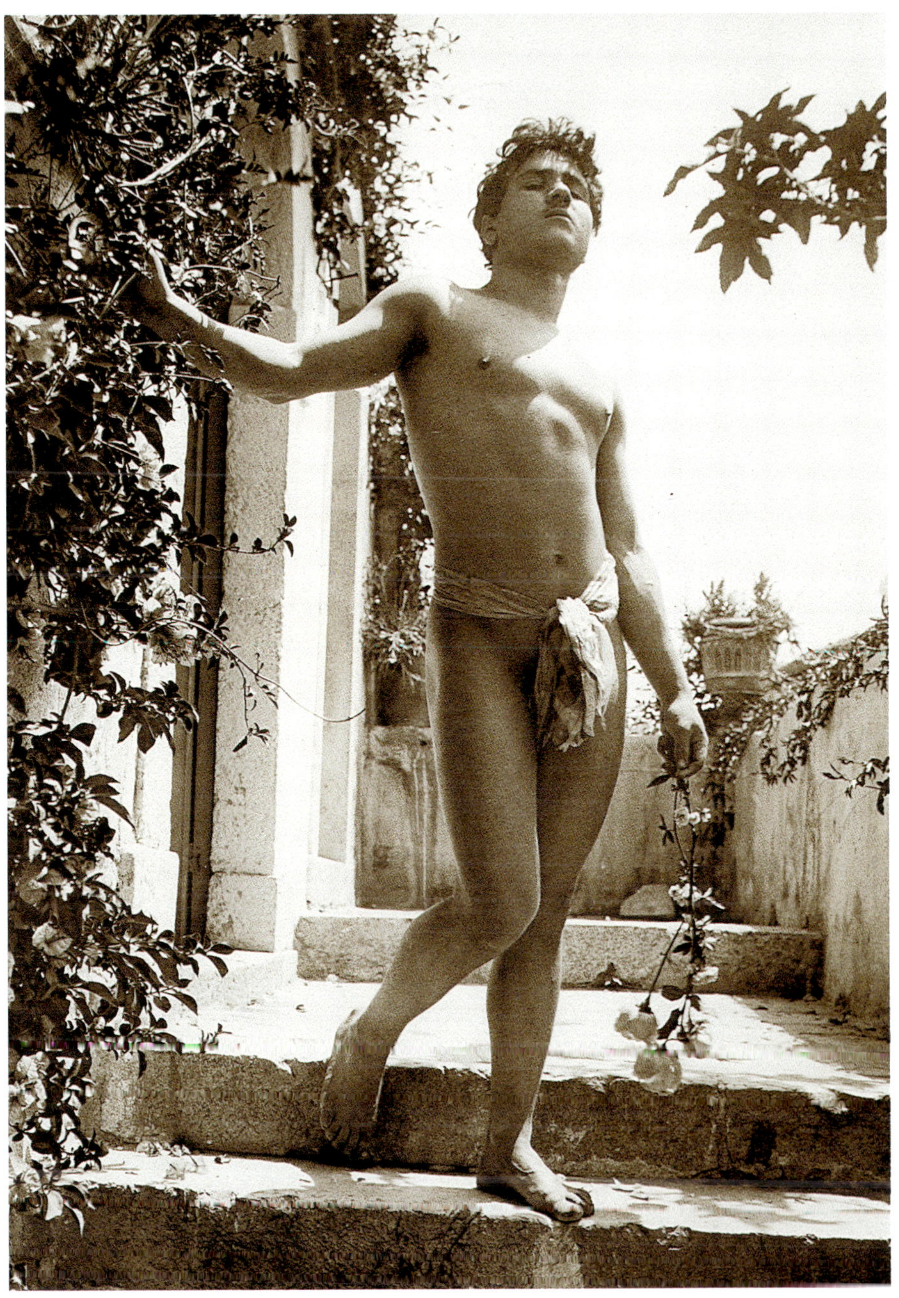

Wilhelm von Gloeden, c. 1900

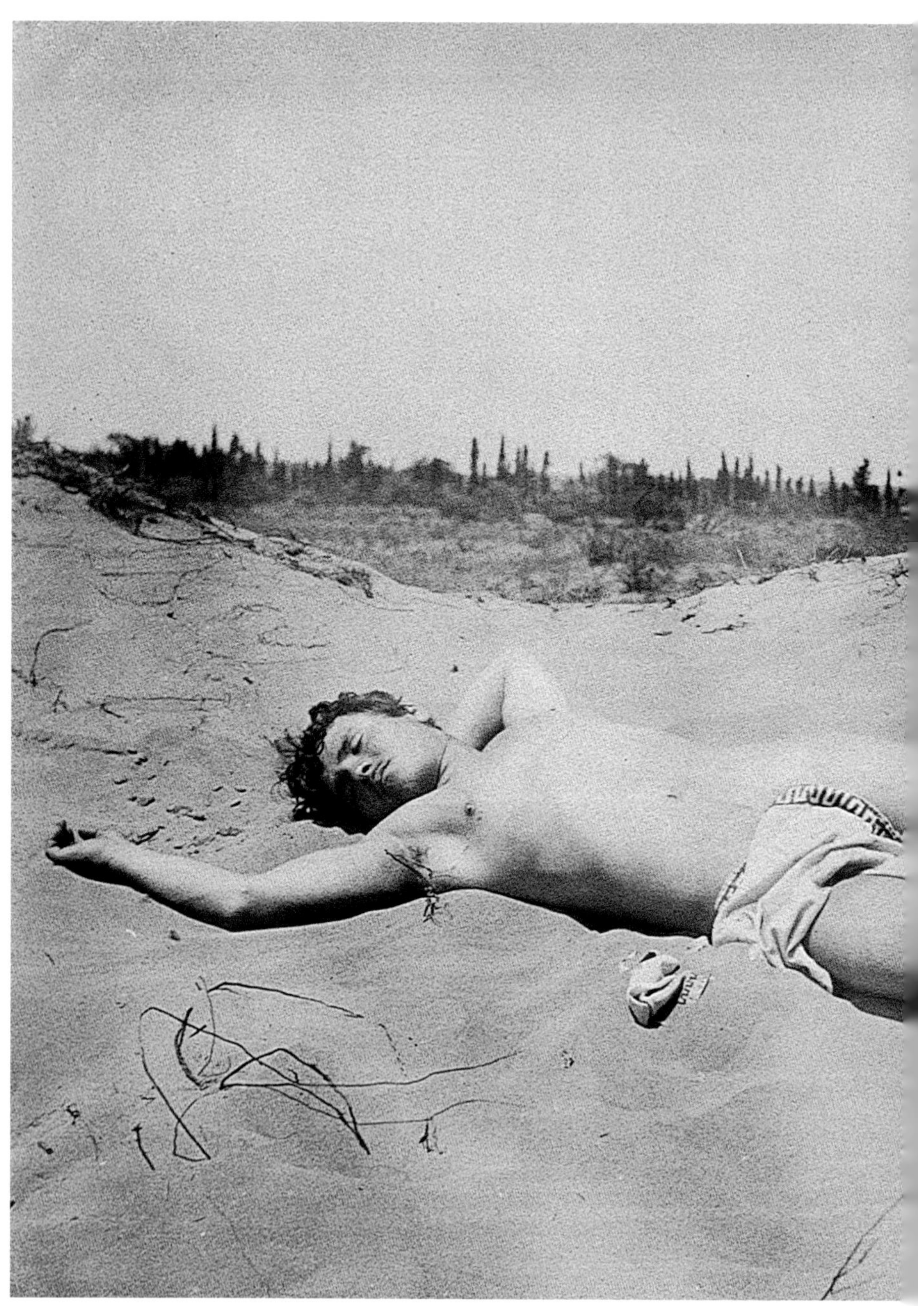

Wilhelm von Gloeden, c. 1905

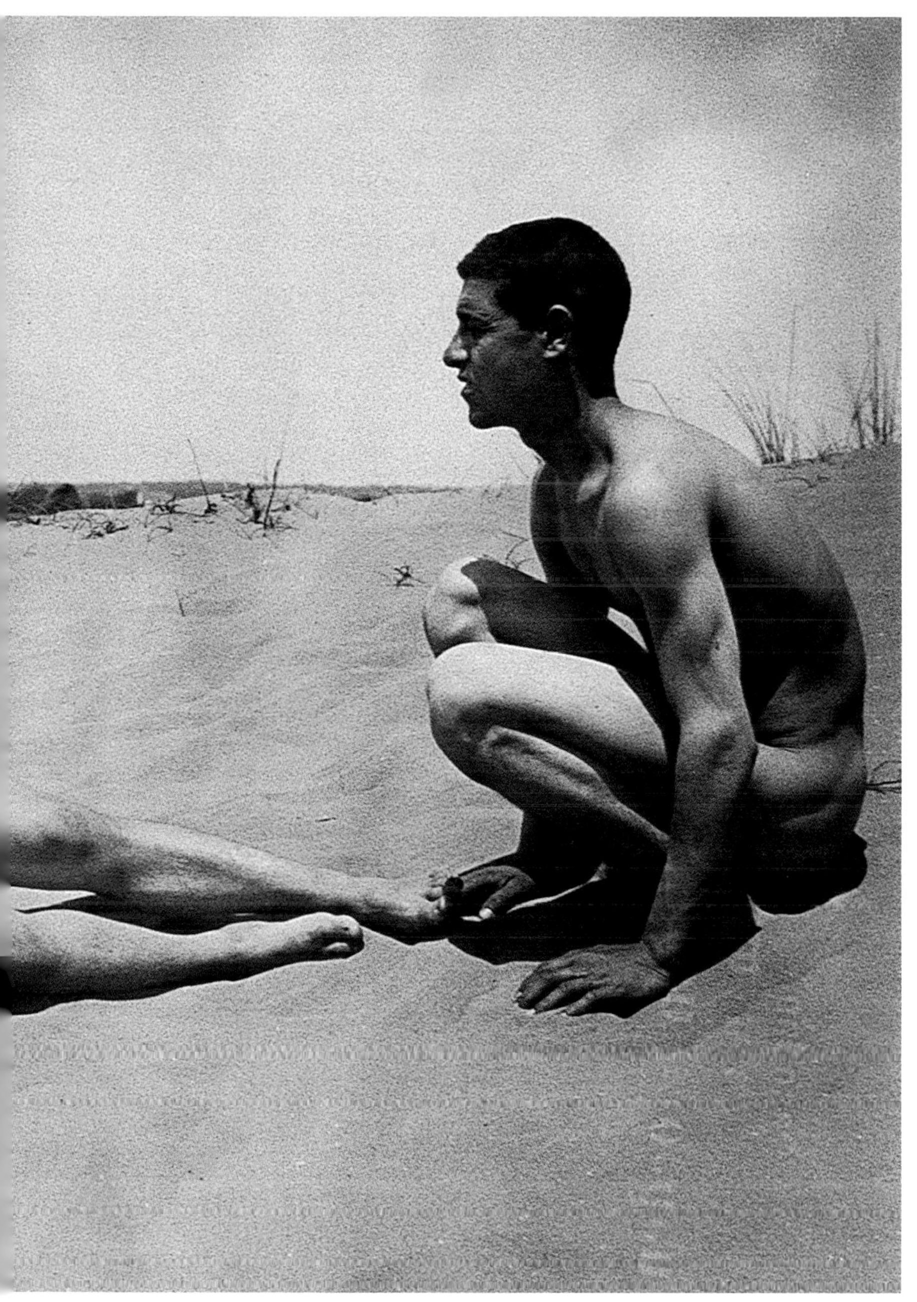

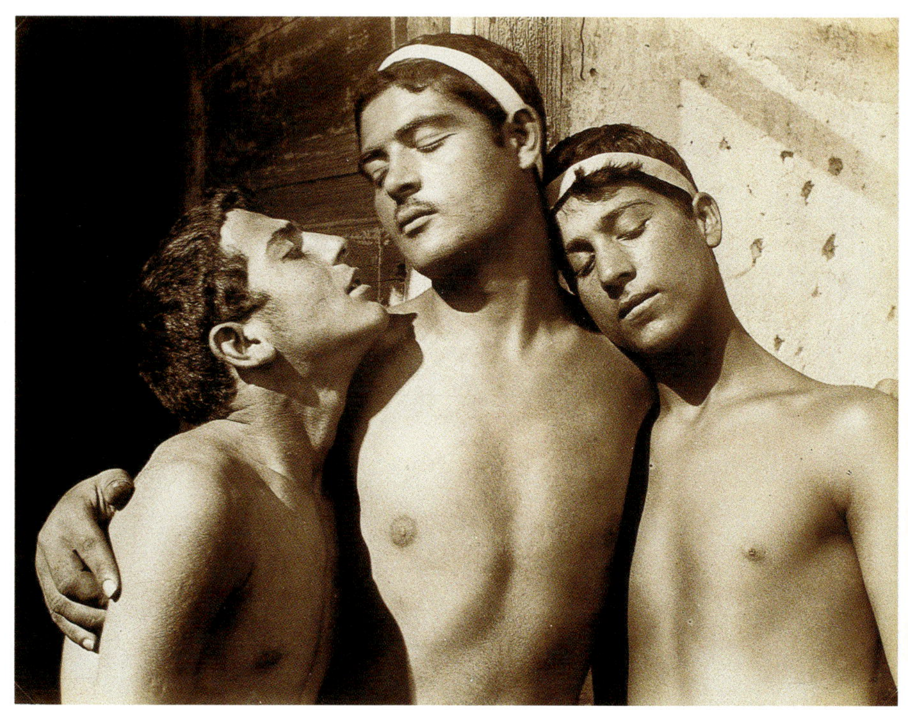

Wilhelm von Gloeden, c. 1900

Wilhelm von Gloeden, c. 1900

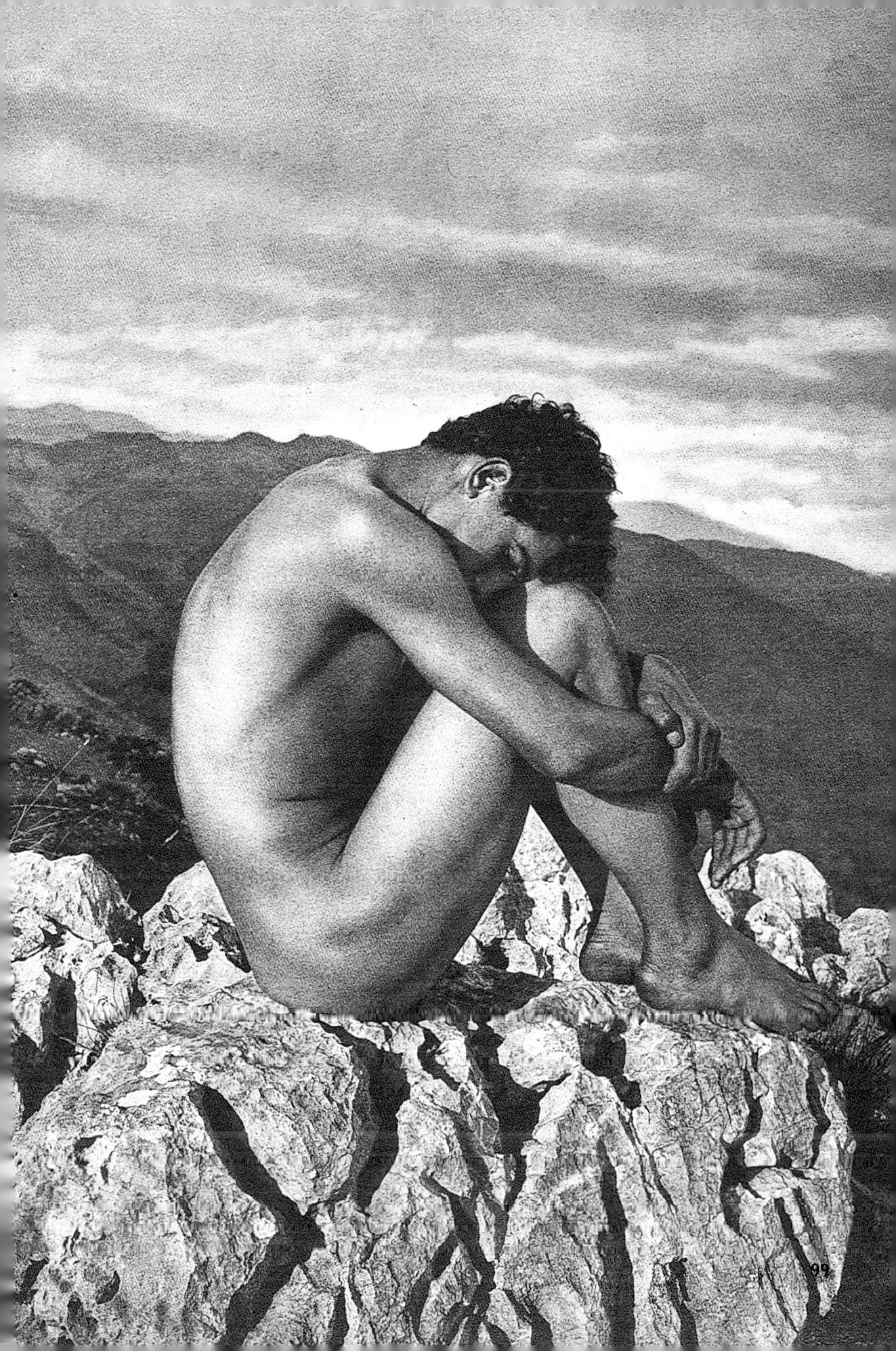

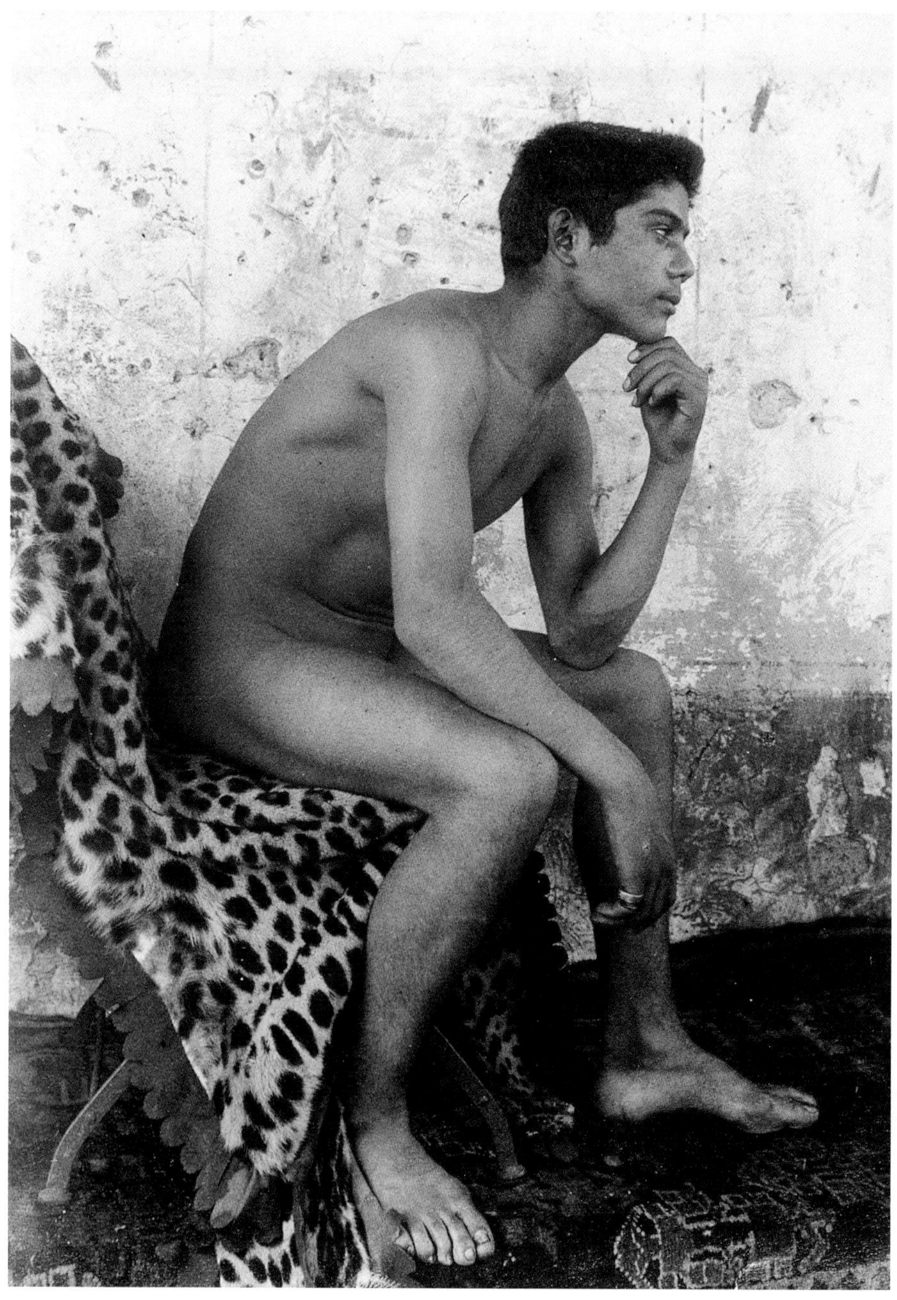

Wilhelm von Gloeden, 1901

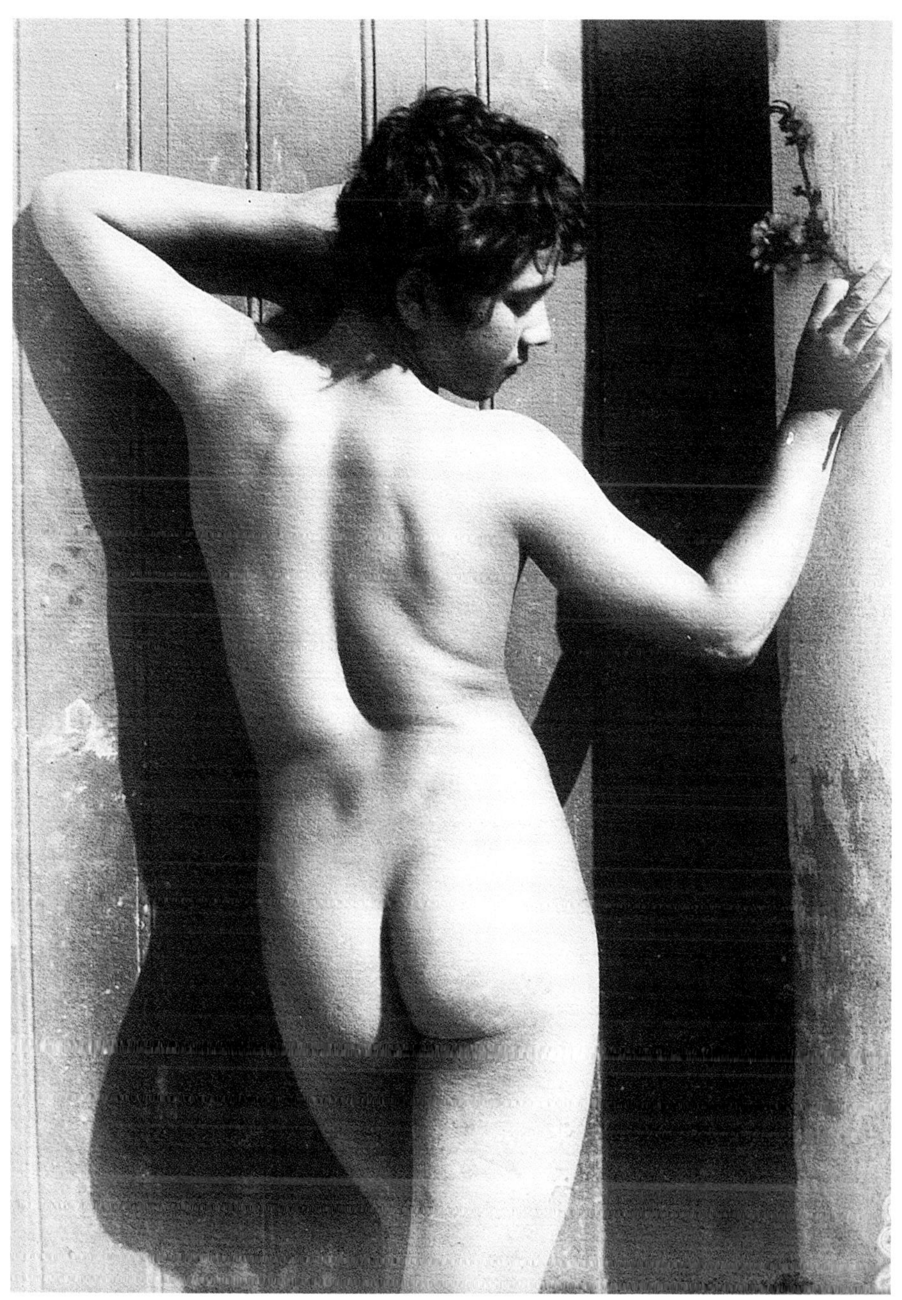

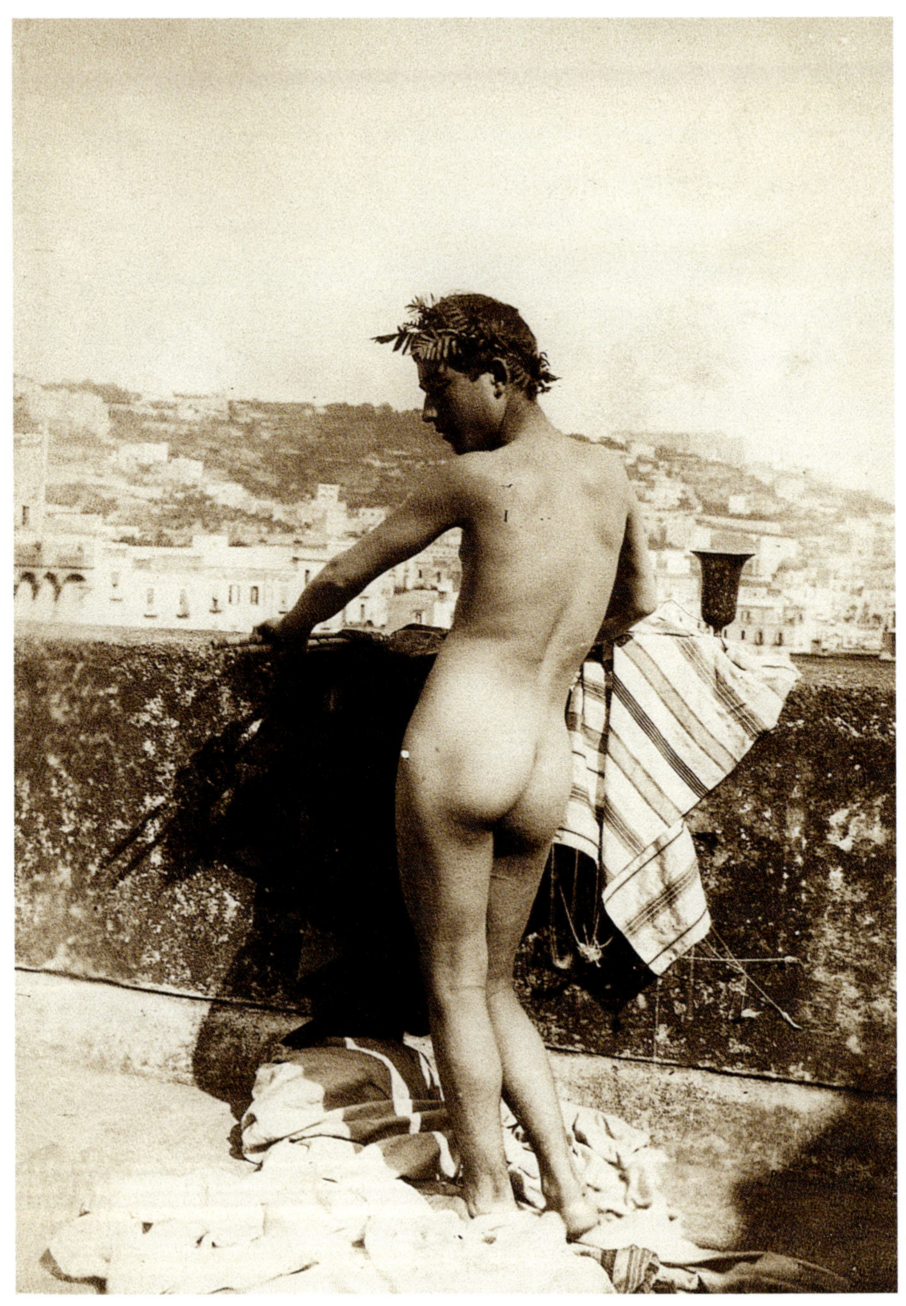

Wilhelm von Gloeden, c. 1900

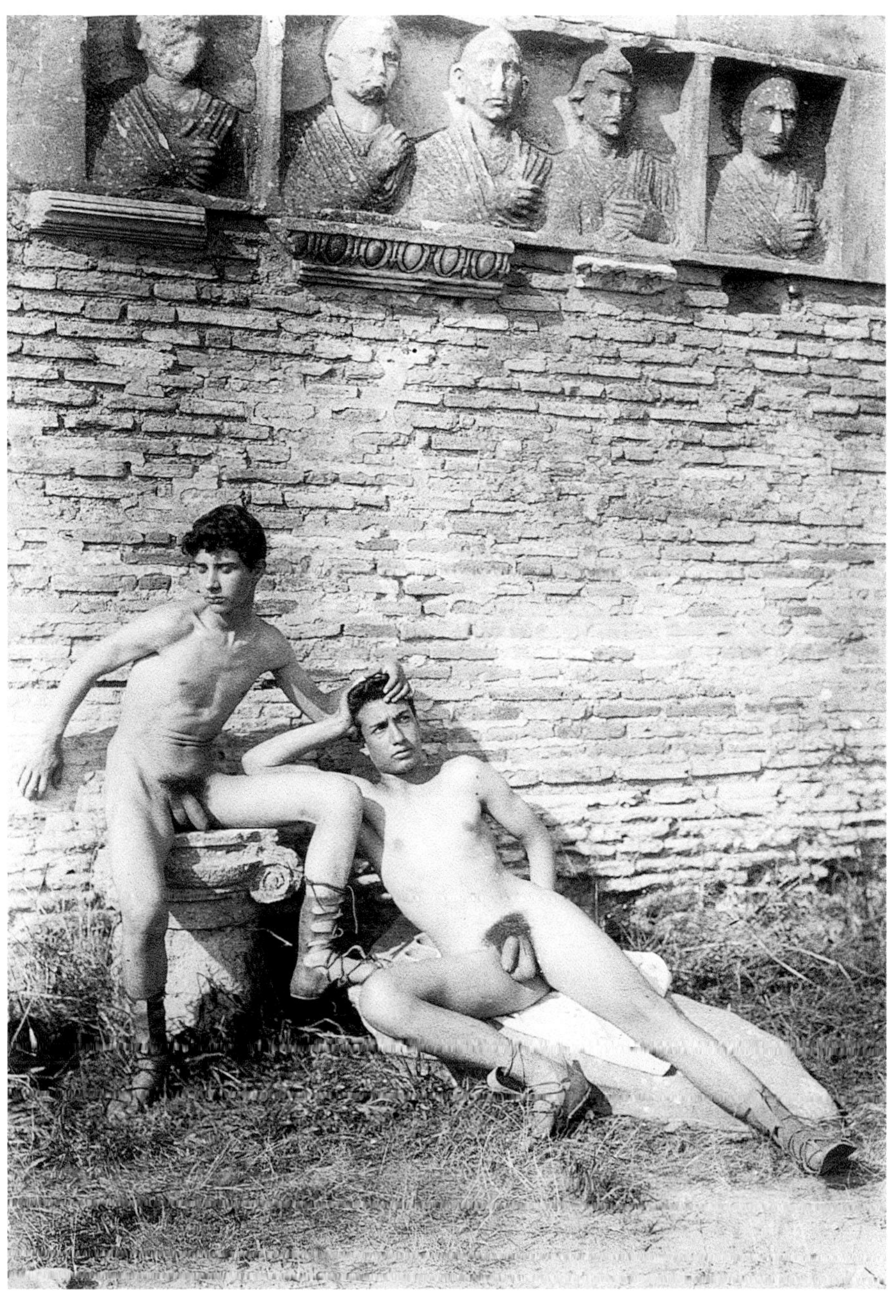

Vincenzo Galdi, c. 1900

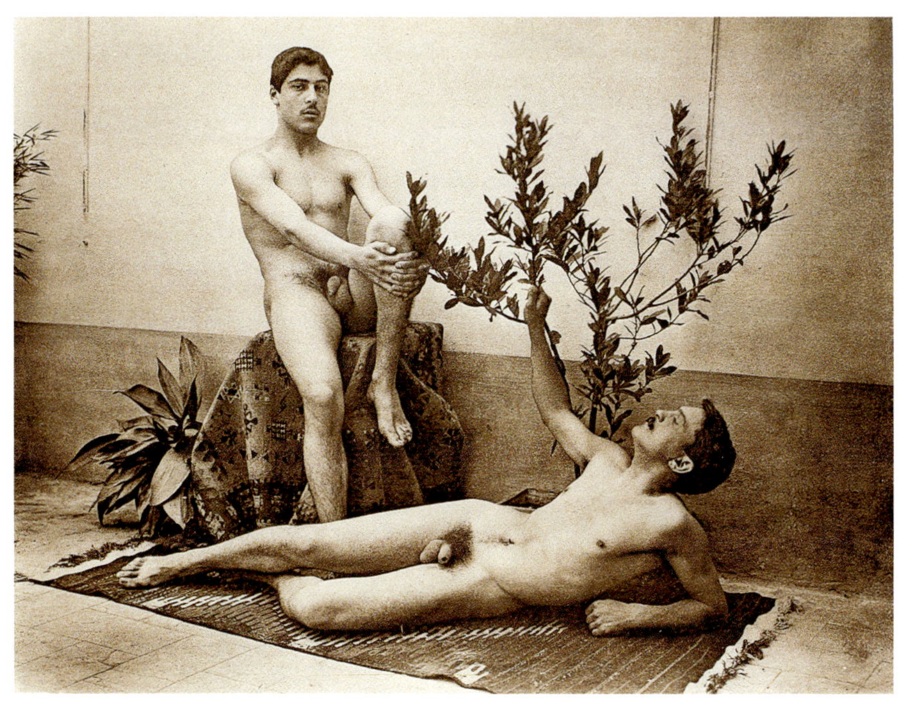

Arthur Schulz, c. 1900

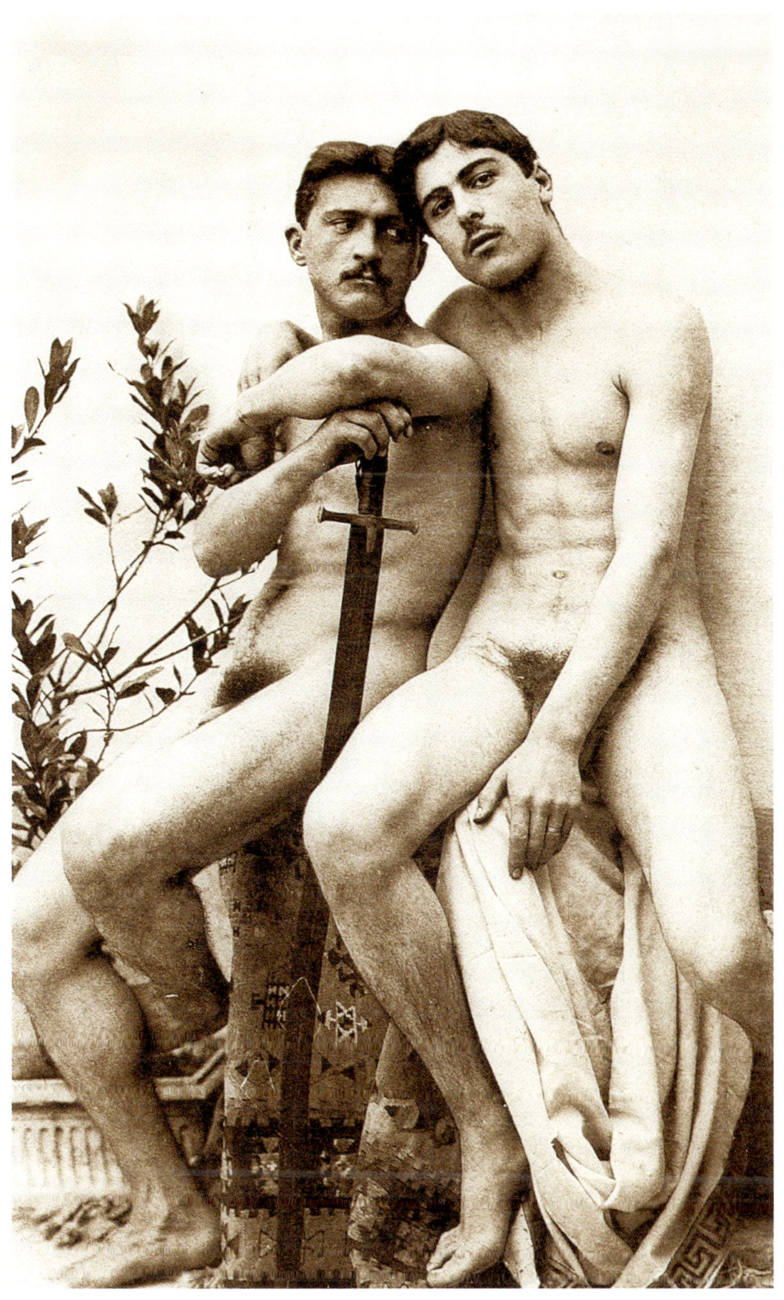

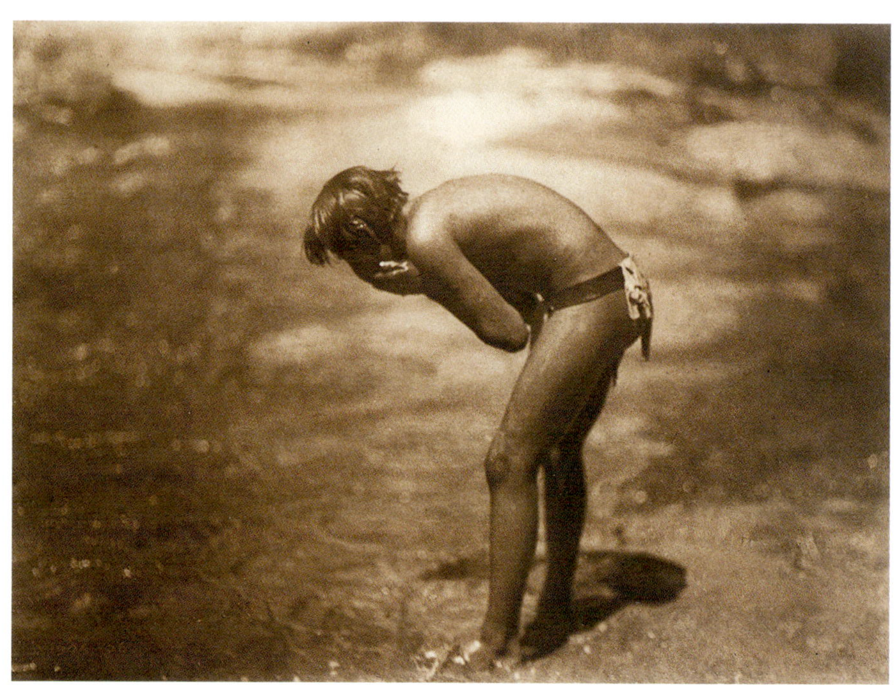

Edward S. Curtis, The Morning Bath – Apache, 1907

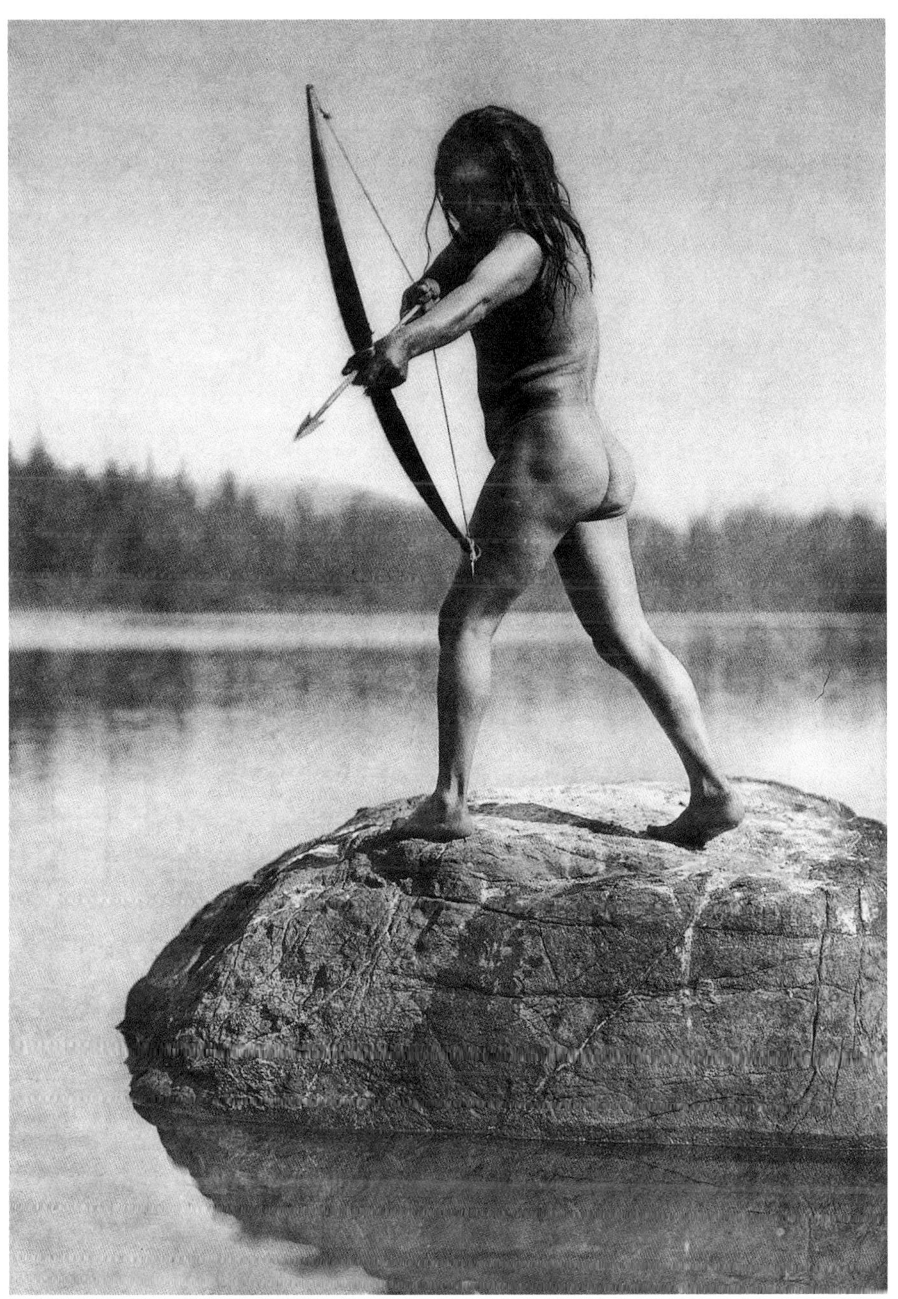

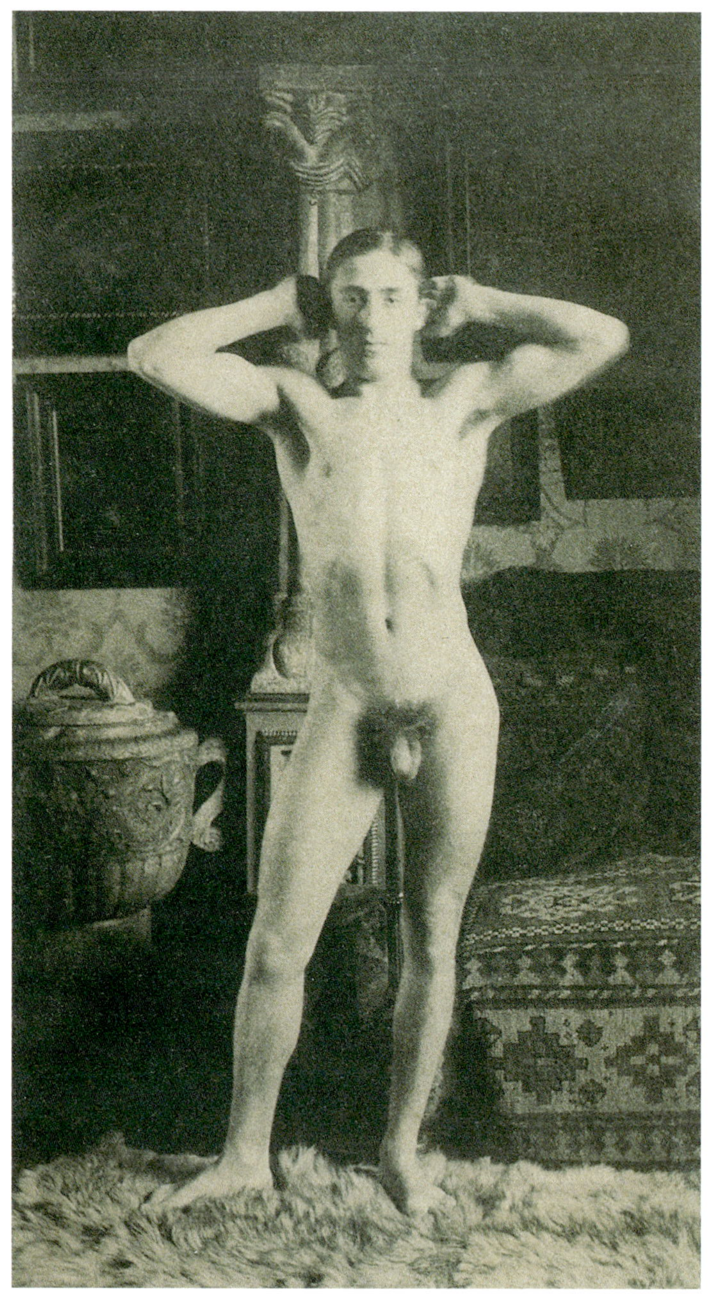

Theodor Hey, c. 1900

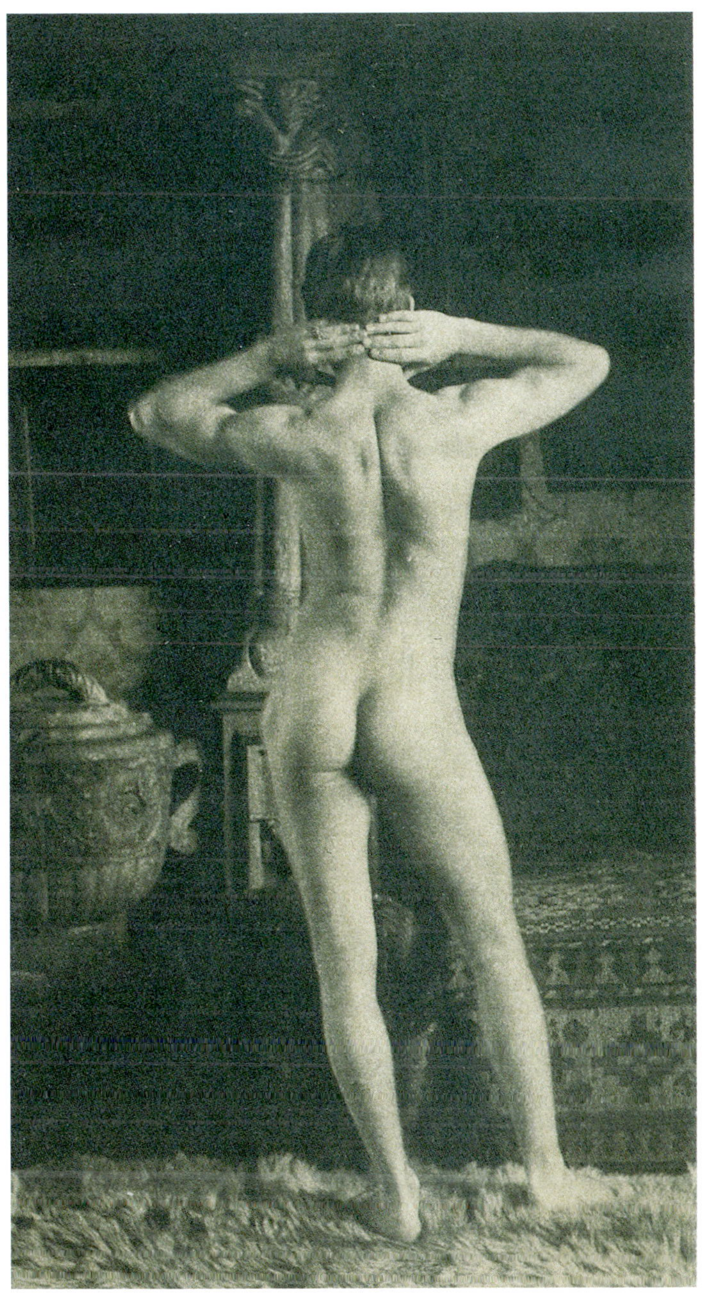

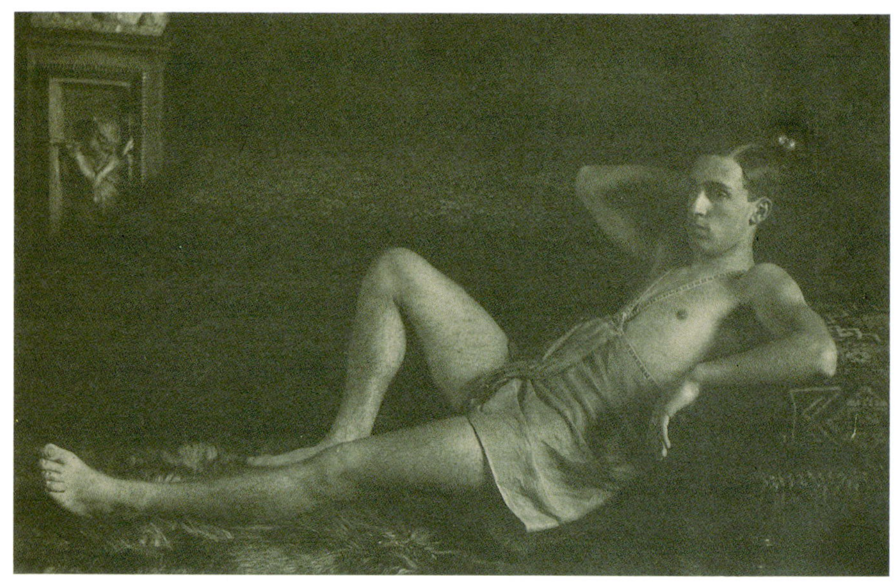

Theodor Hey, c. 1900

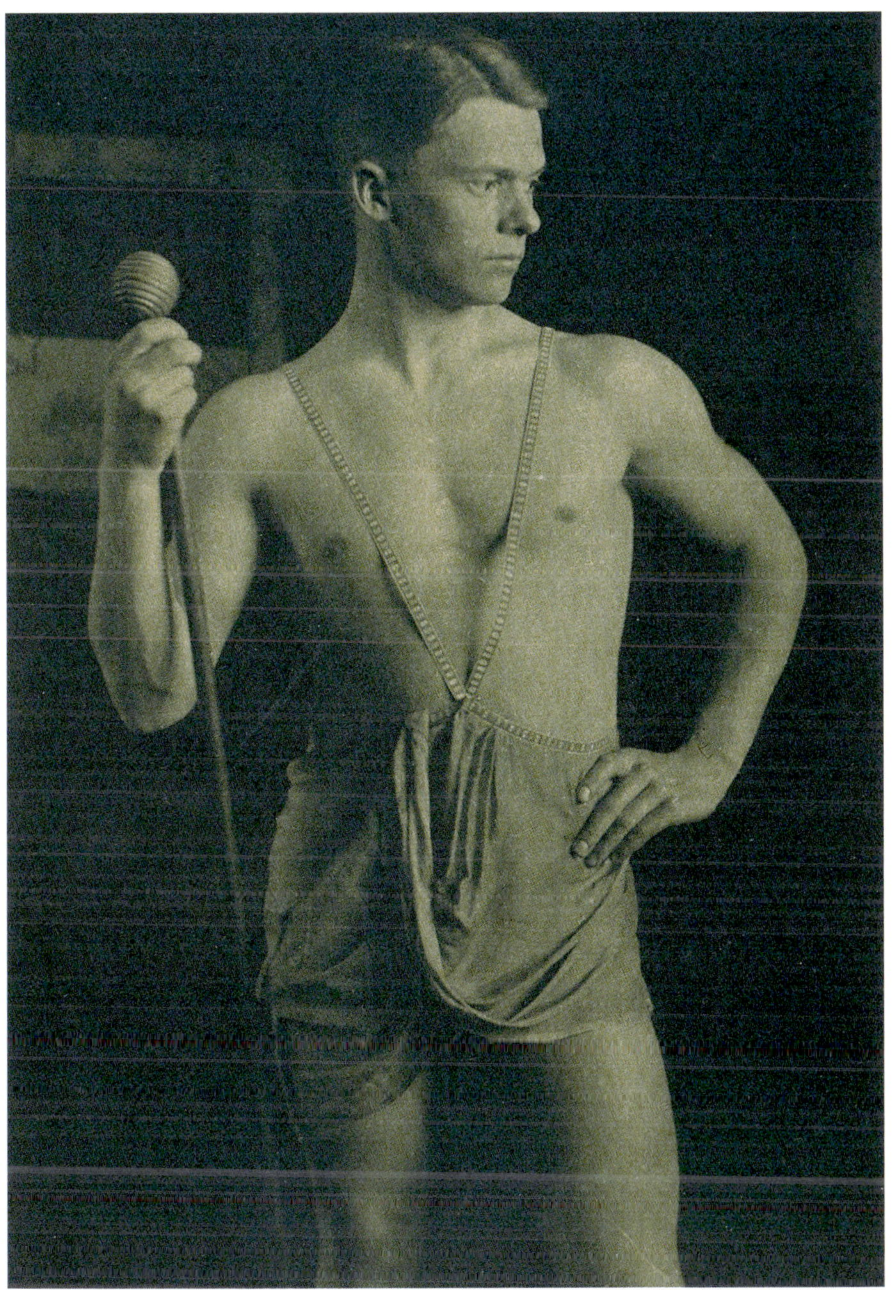

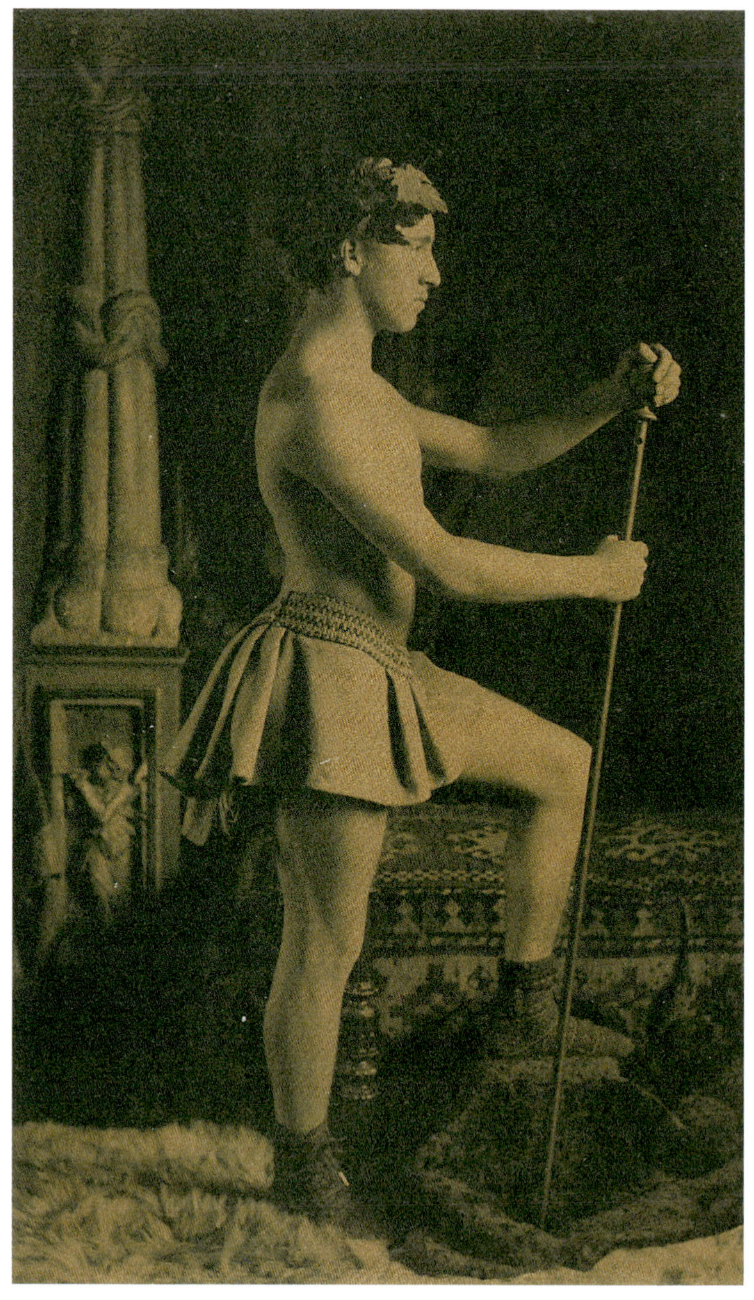

Theodor Hey, c. 1900

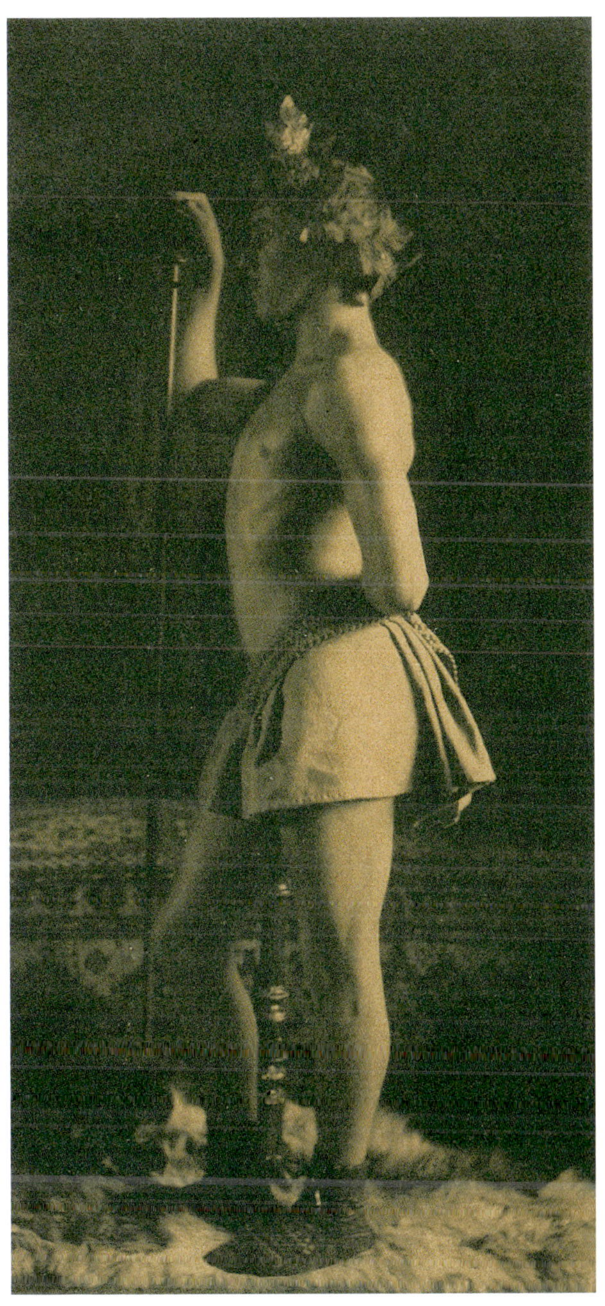

Theodor Hey, c. 1900

113

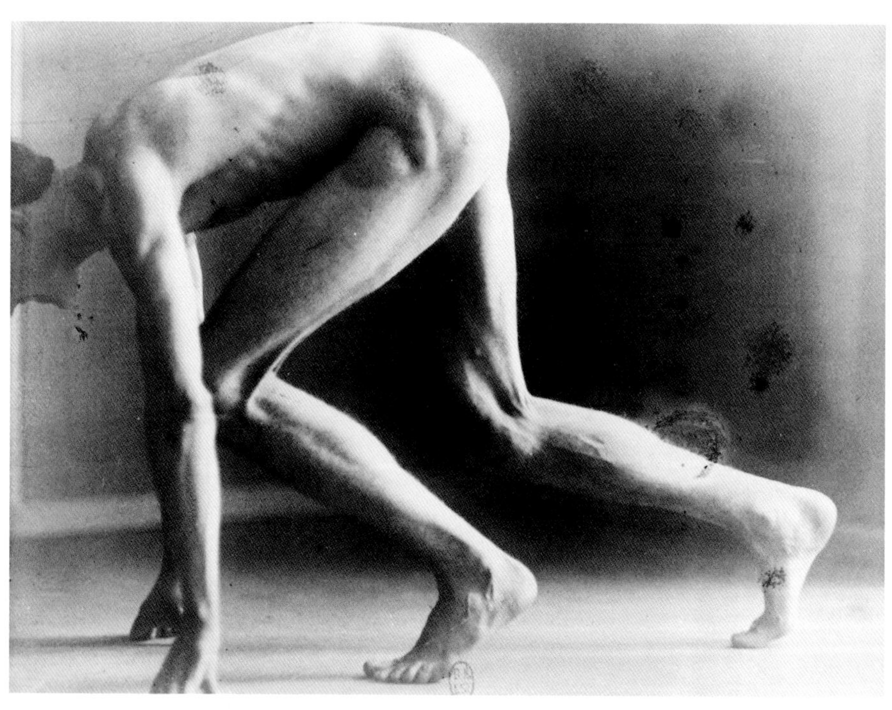

Jean-Léo Reutlinger, Hans Braun, coureur à pied, 1912

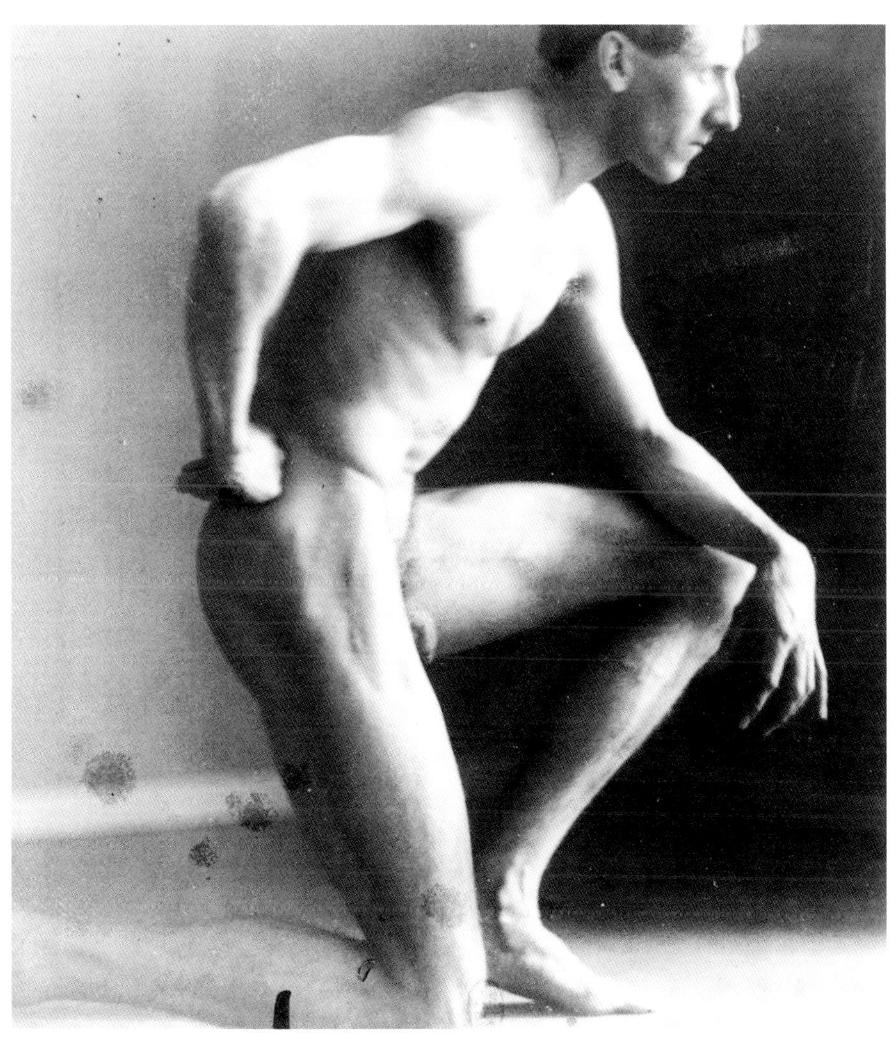

Jean-Léo Reutlinger, Hans Braun, 1912

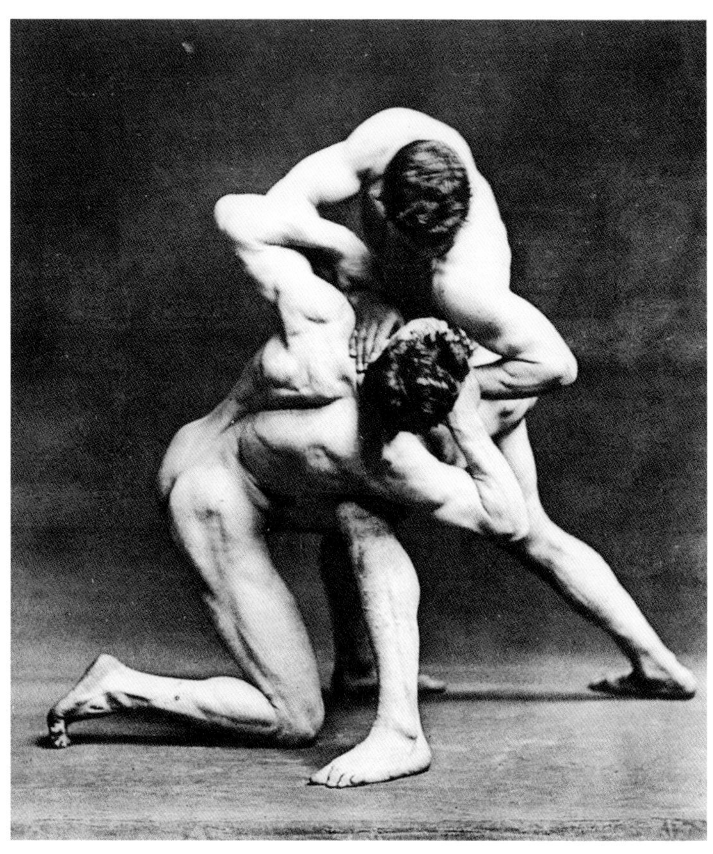

W. G. Hill, The Combat, c. 1918

          Paul Martin, Hackenschmidt, Russian Wrestler, c. 1910

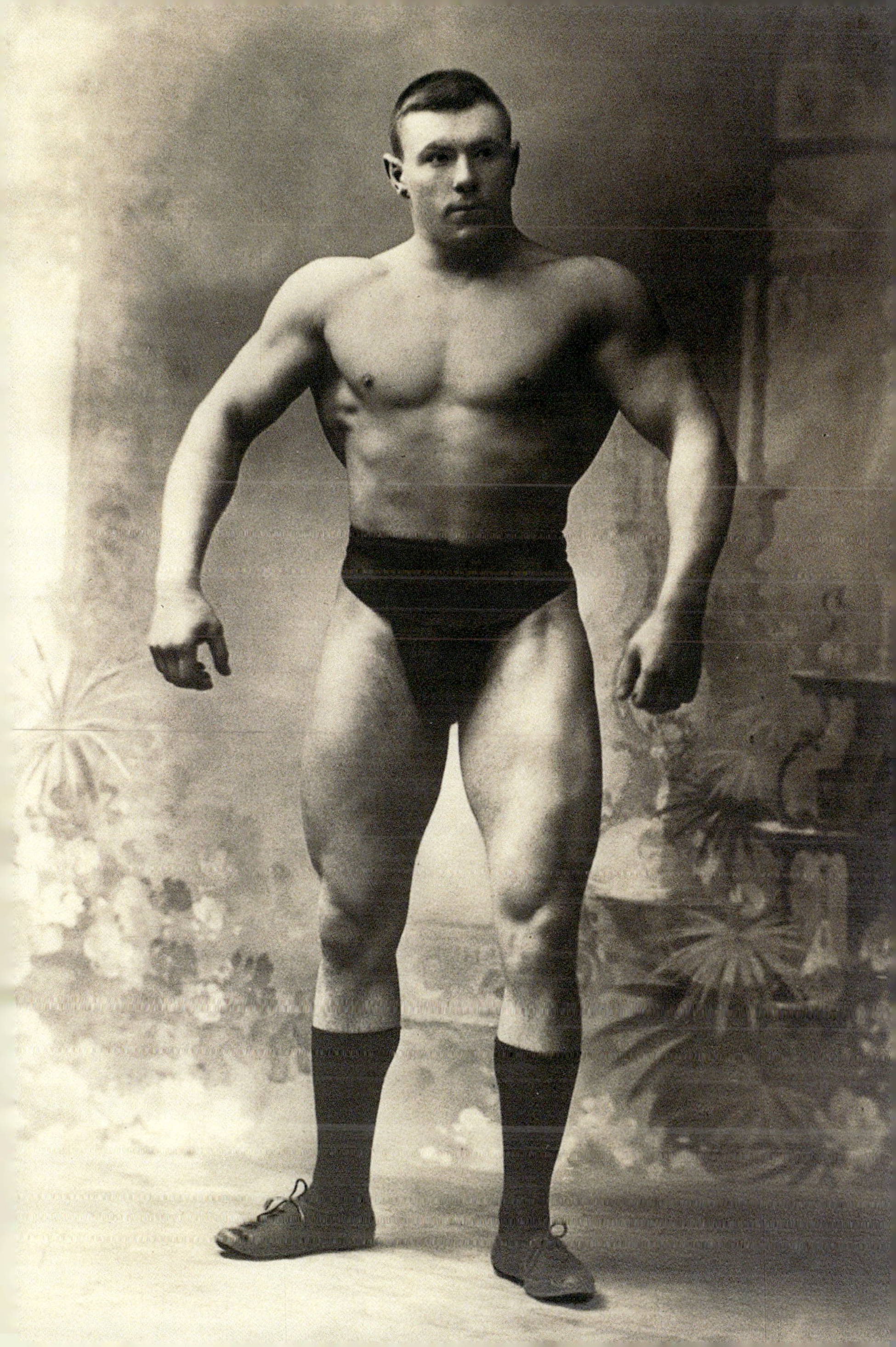

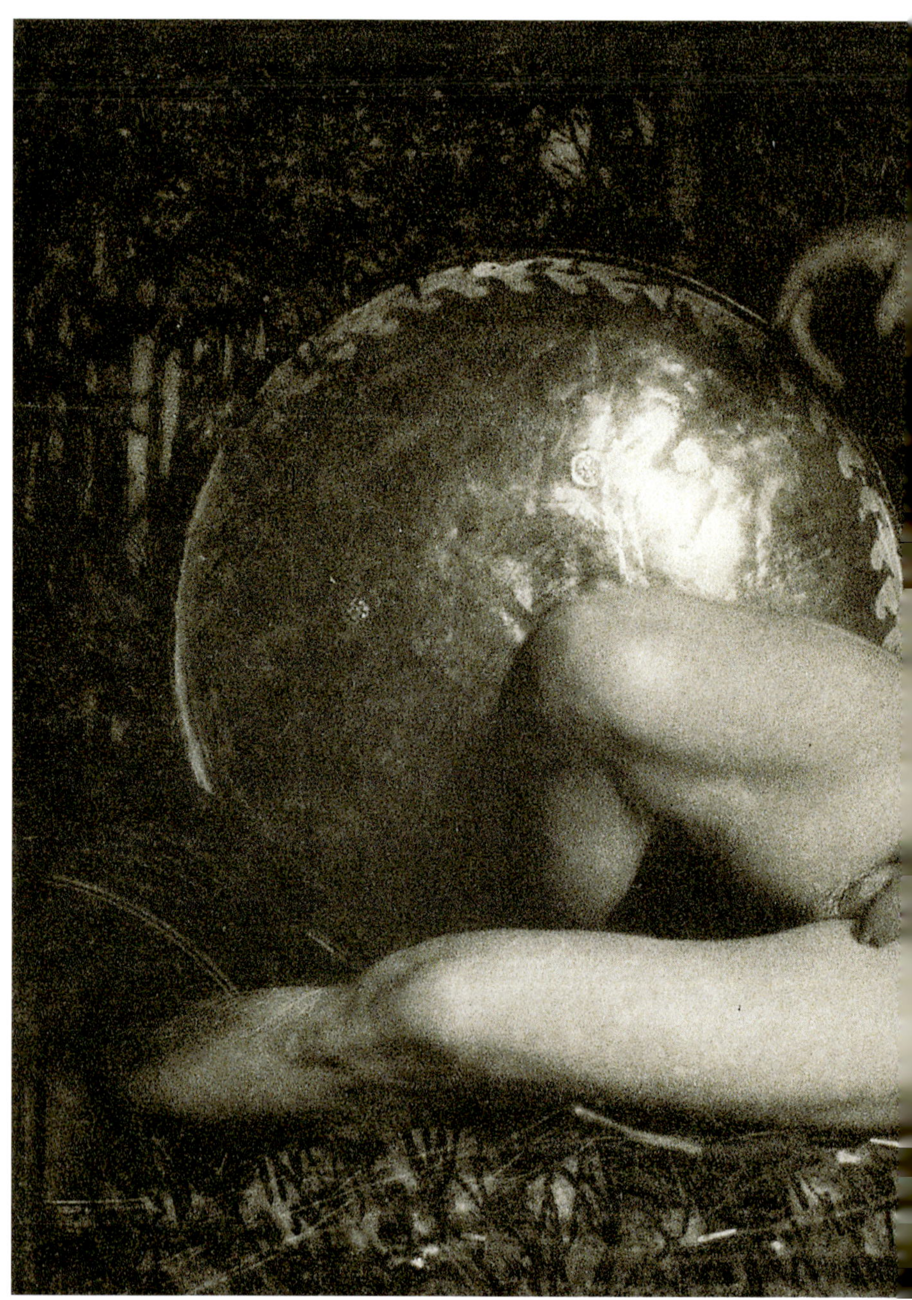

Frank Eugene Smith, c. 1914

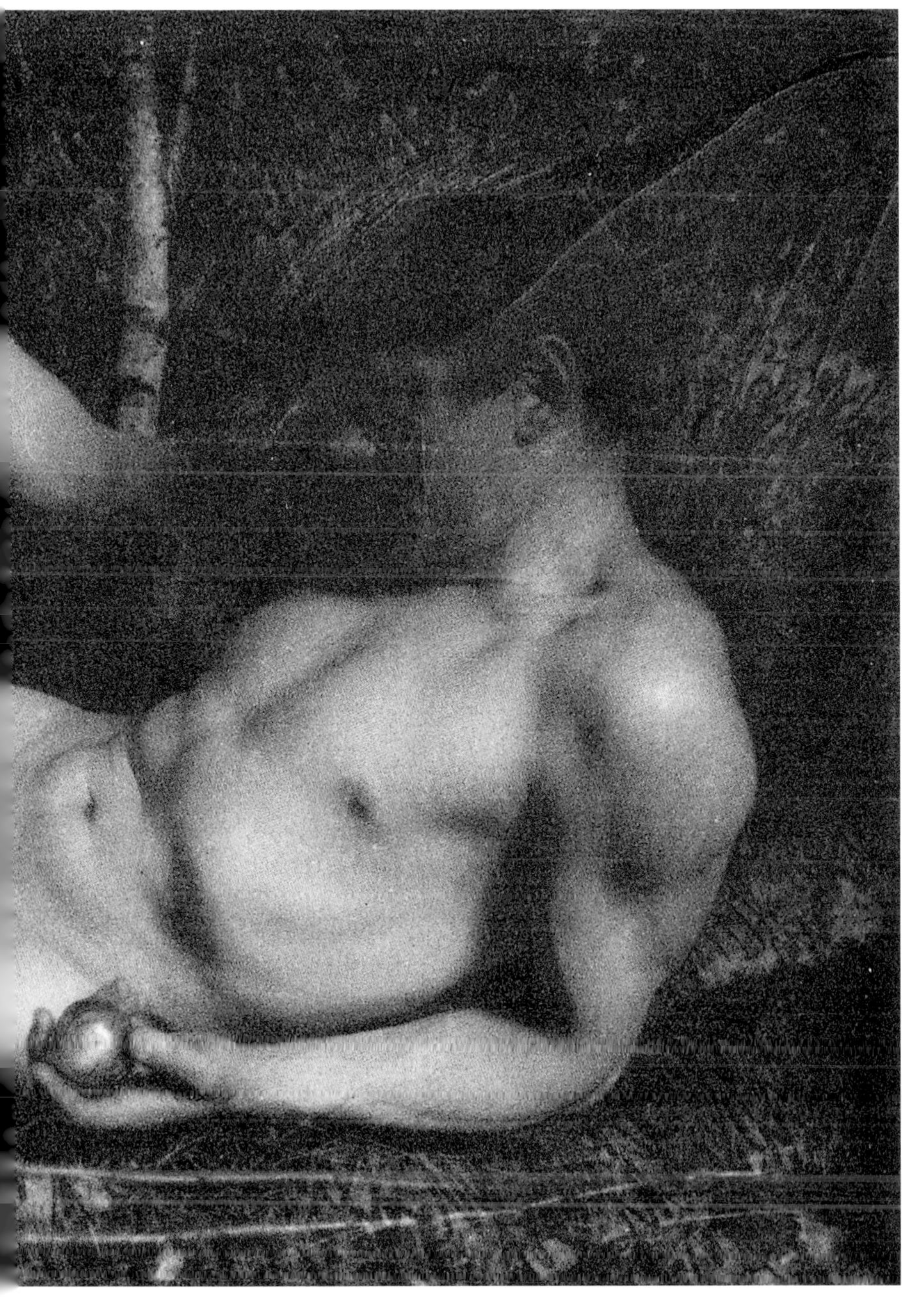

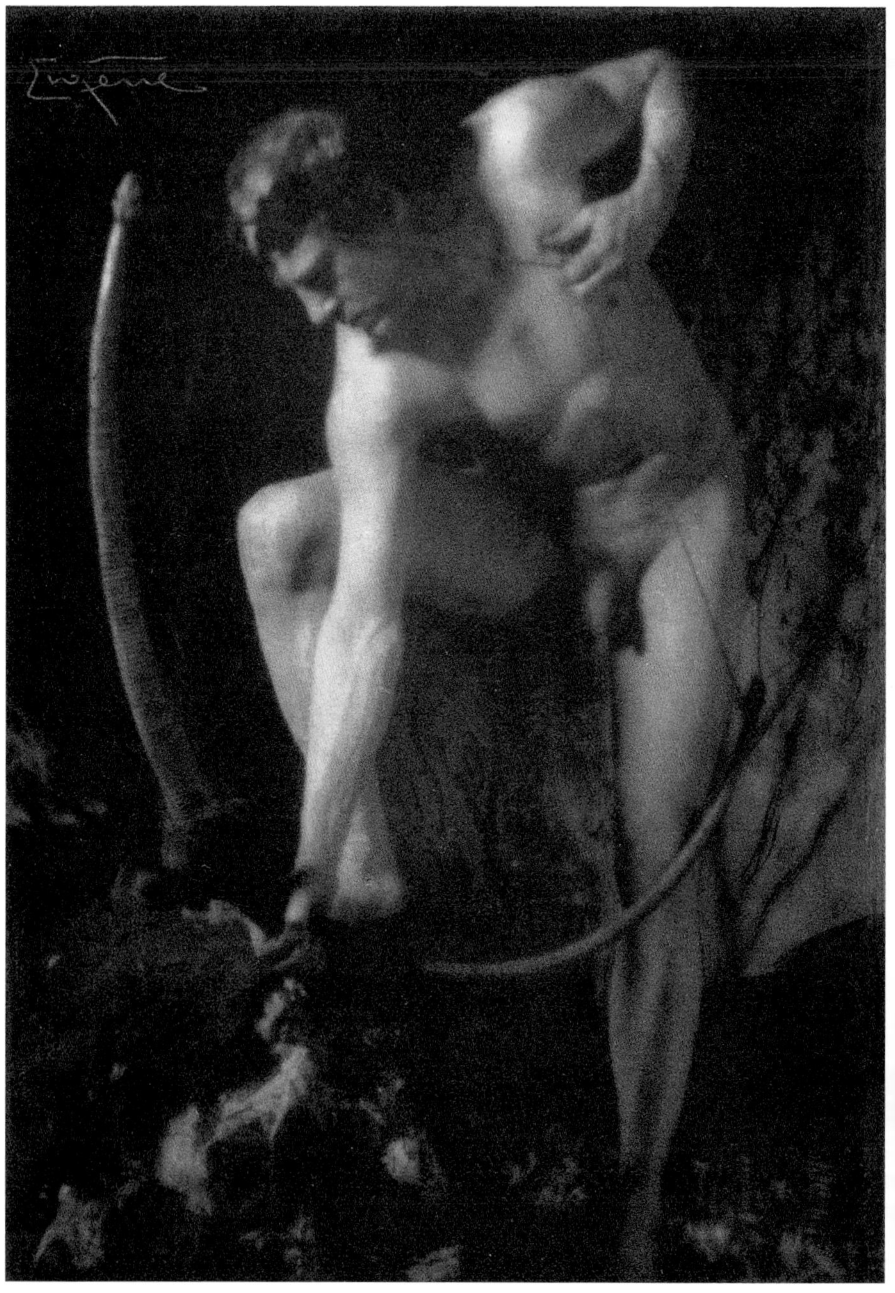

Frank Eugene Smith, c. 1914

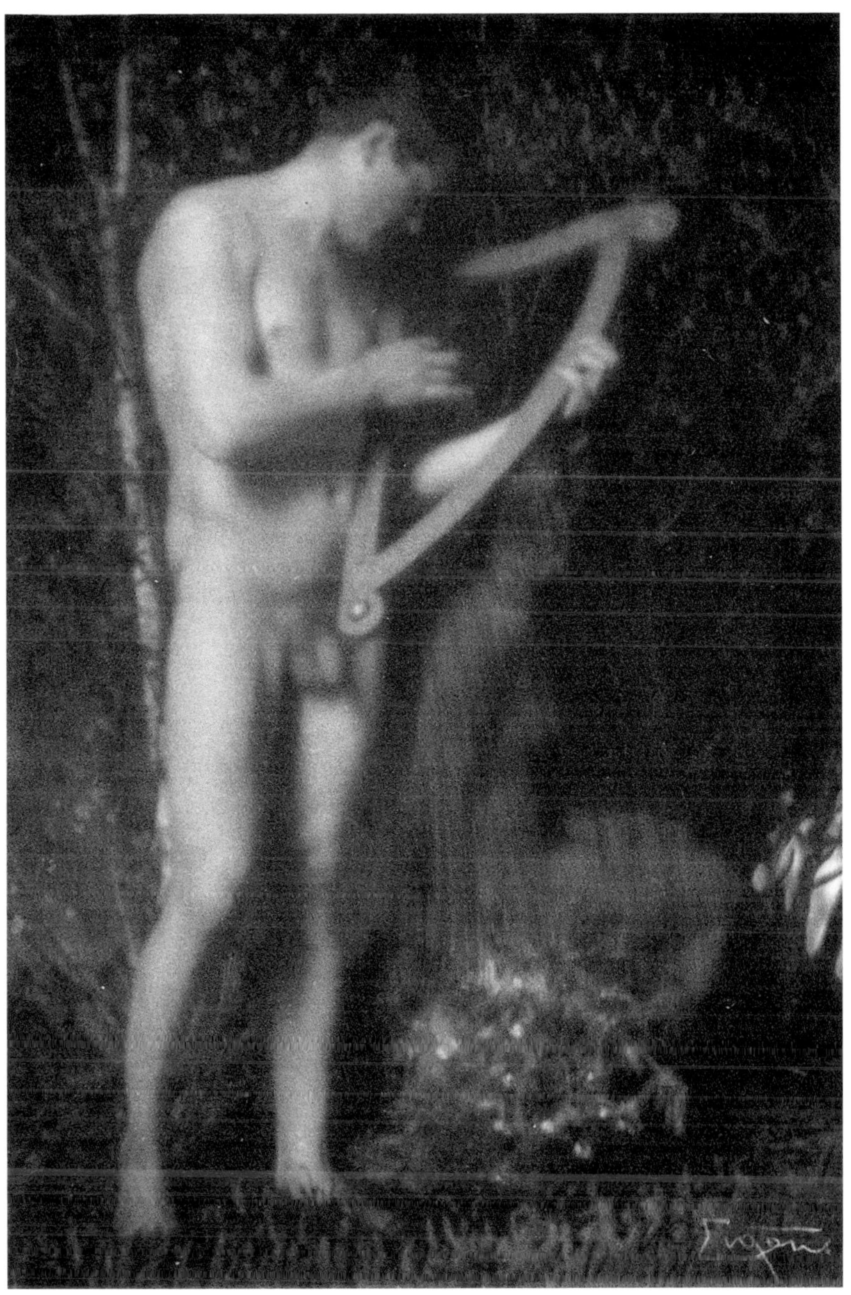

Frank Eugene Smith, c. 1914

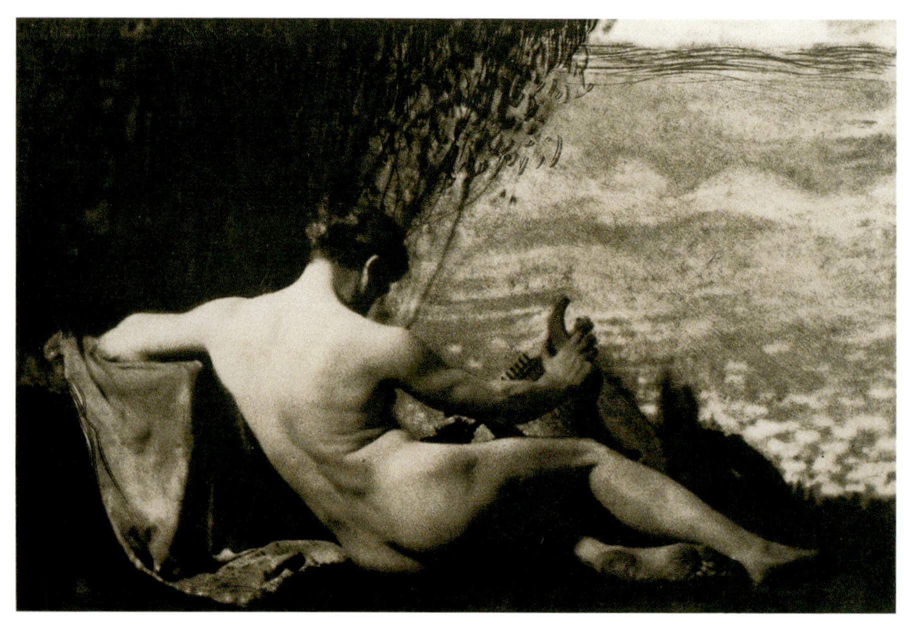

Frank Eugene Smith, c. 1914

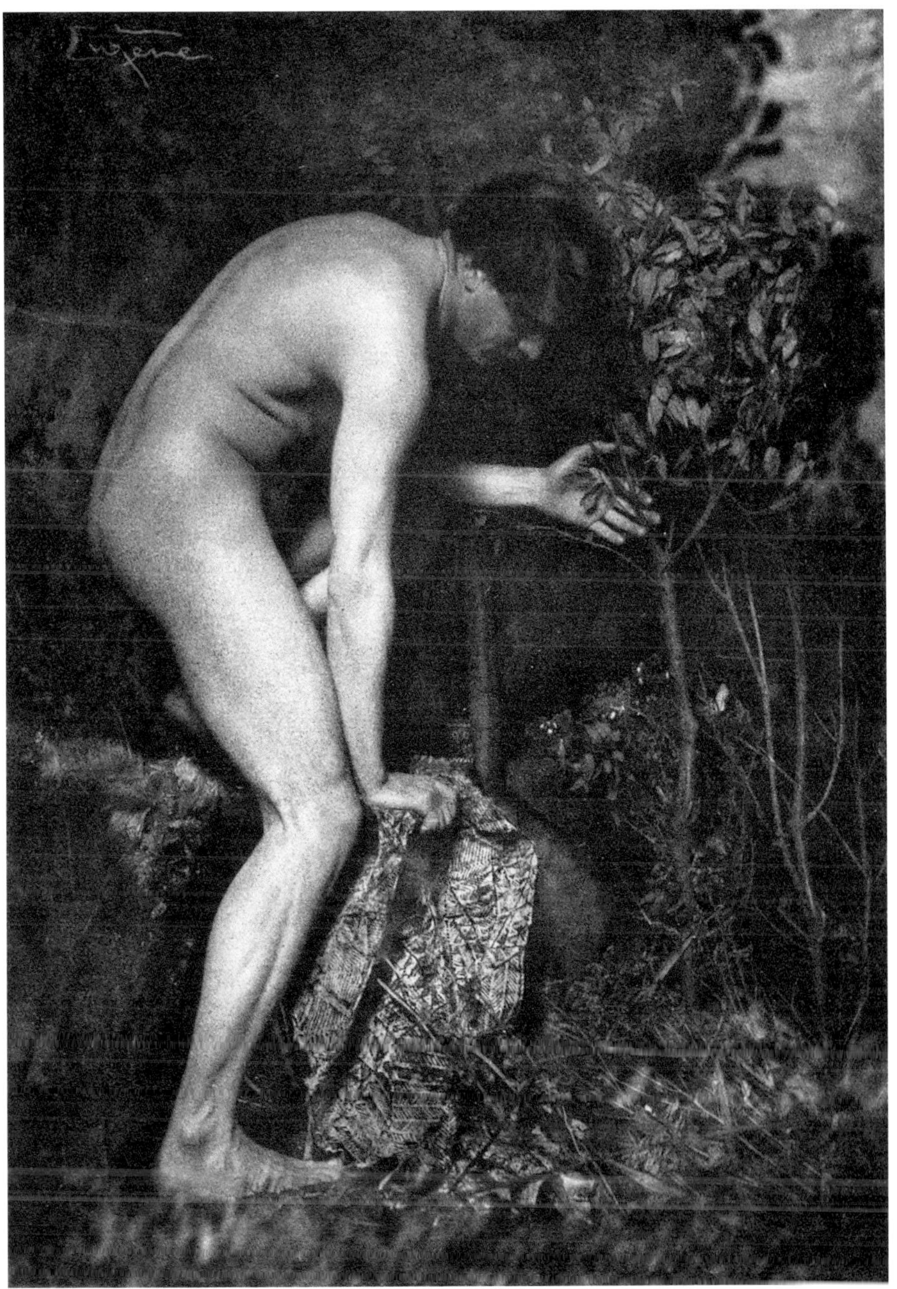

Frank Eugene Smith, c. 1914

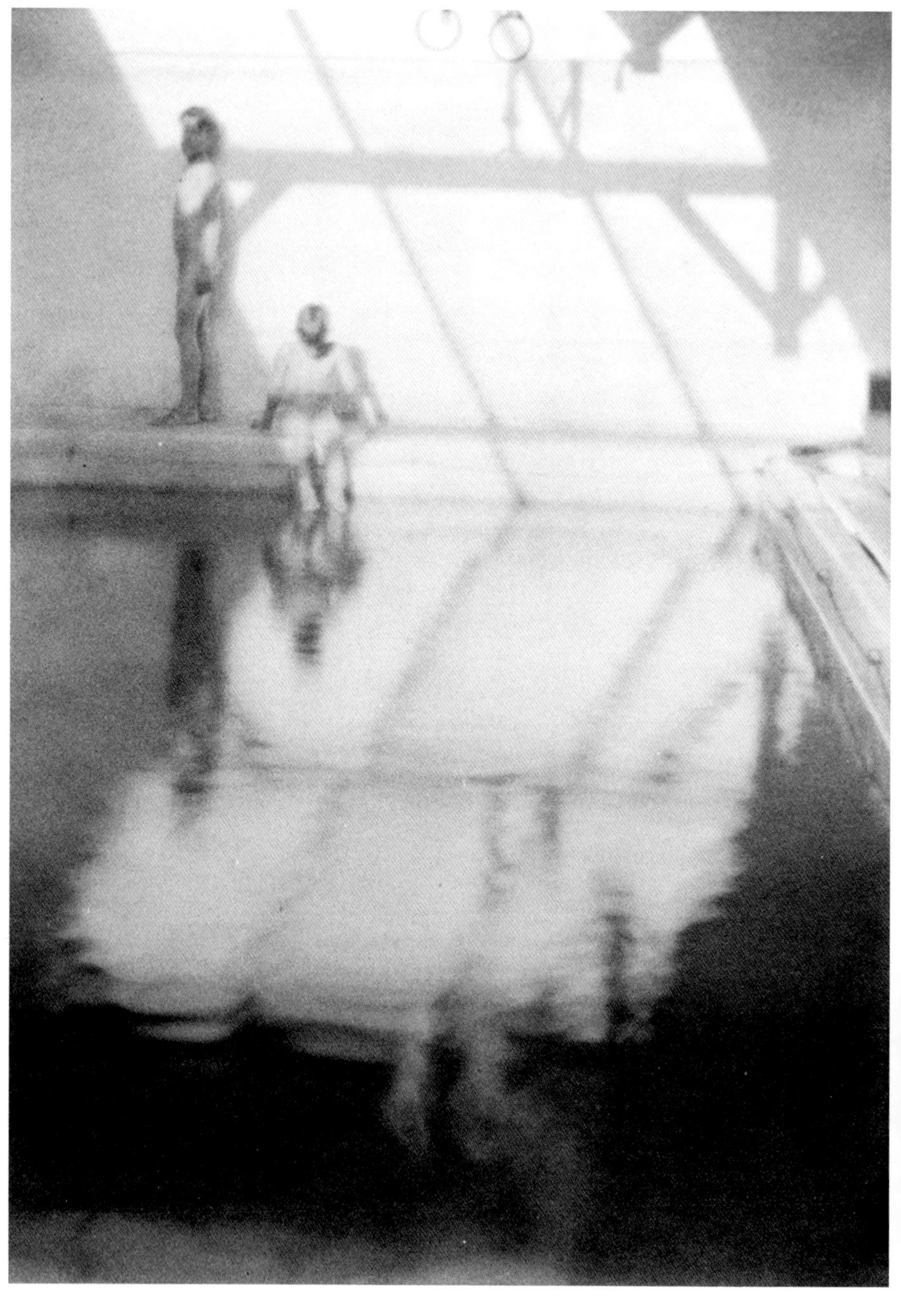

Edward Weston, The Bathing Pool, 1919

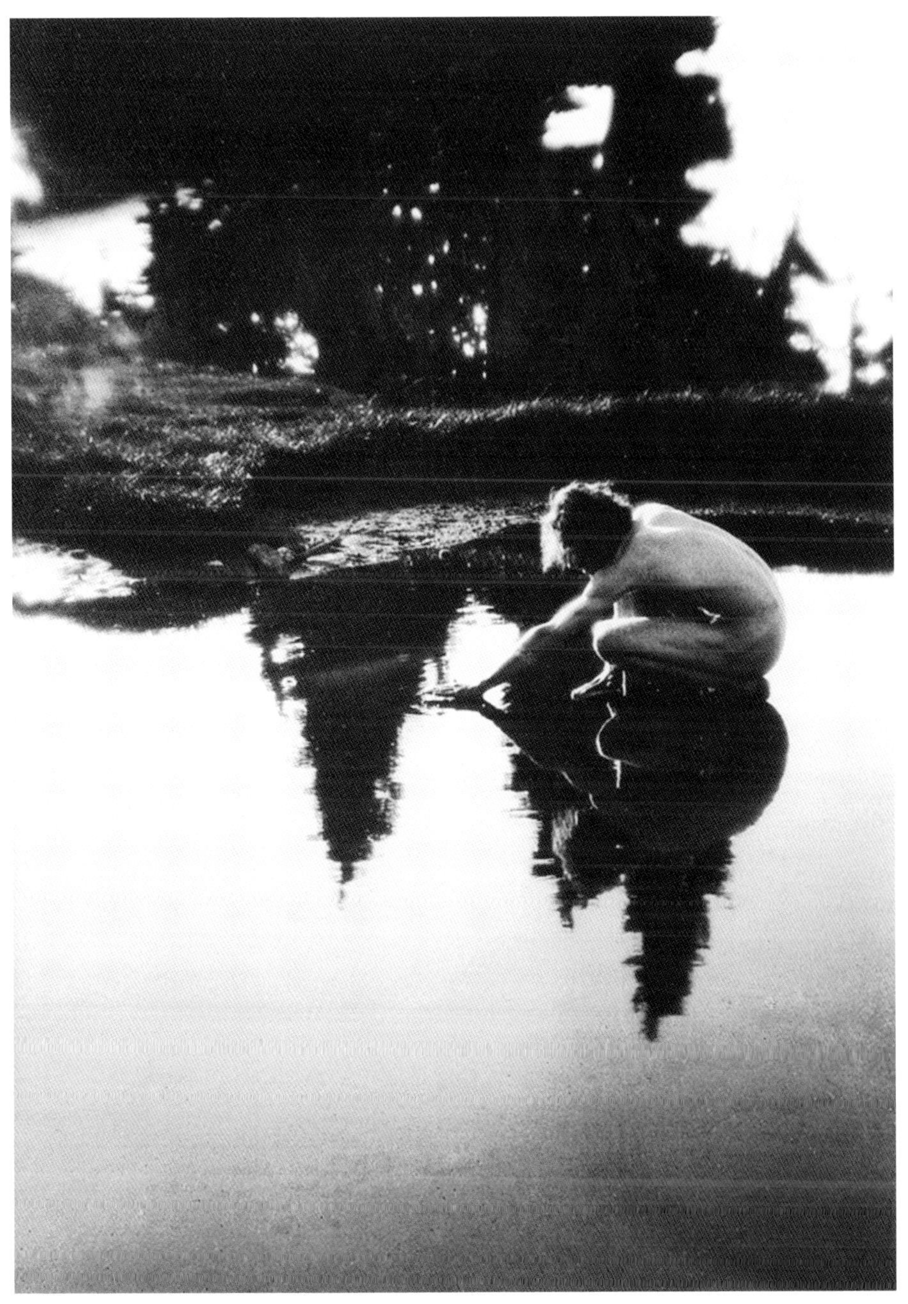

Imogen Cunningham, Roi on the Dipsea Trail, 1918

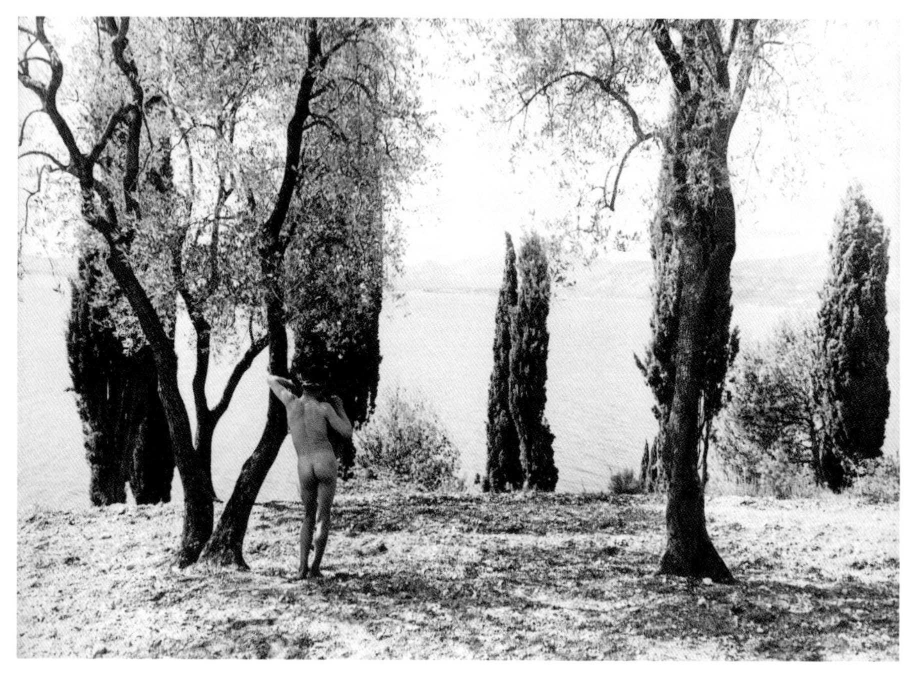

Paul Pichier, Nackter Jüngling in arkadischer Landschaft, c. 1905

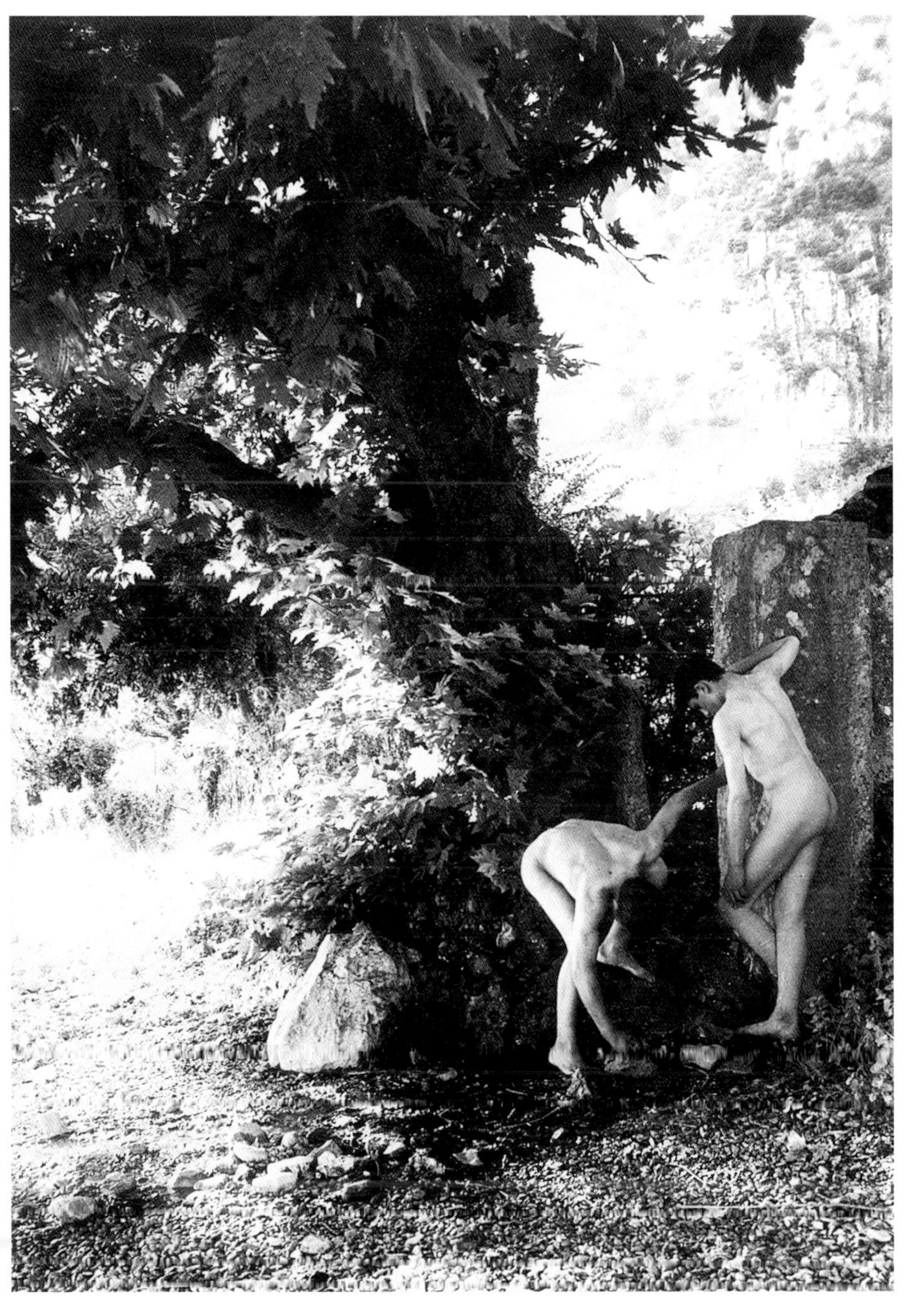

Paul Pichier, Aktstudie zweier Jünglinge in romantischer Landschaft, 1890-1910

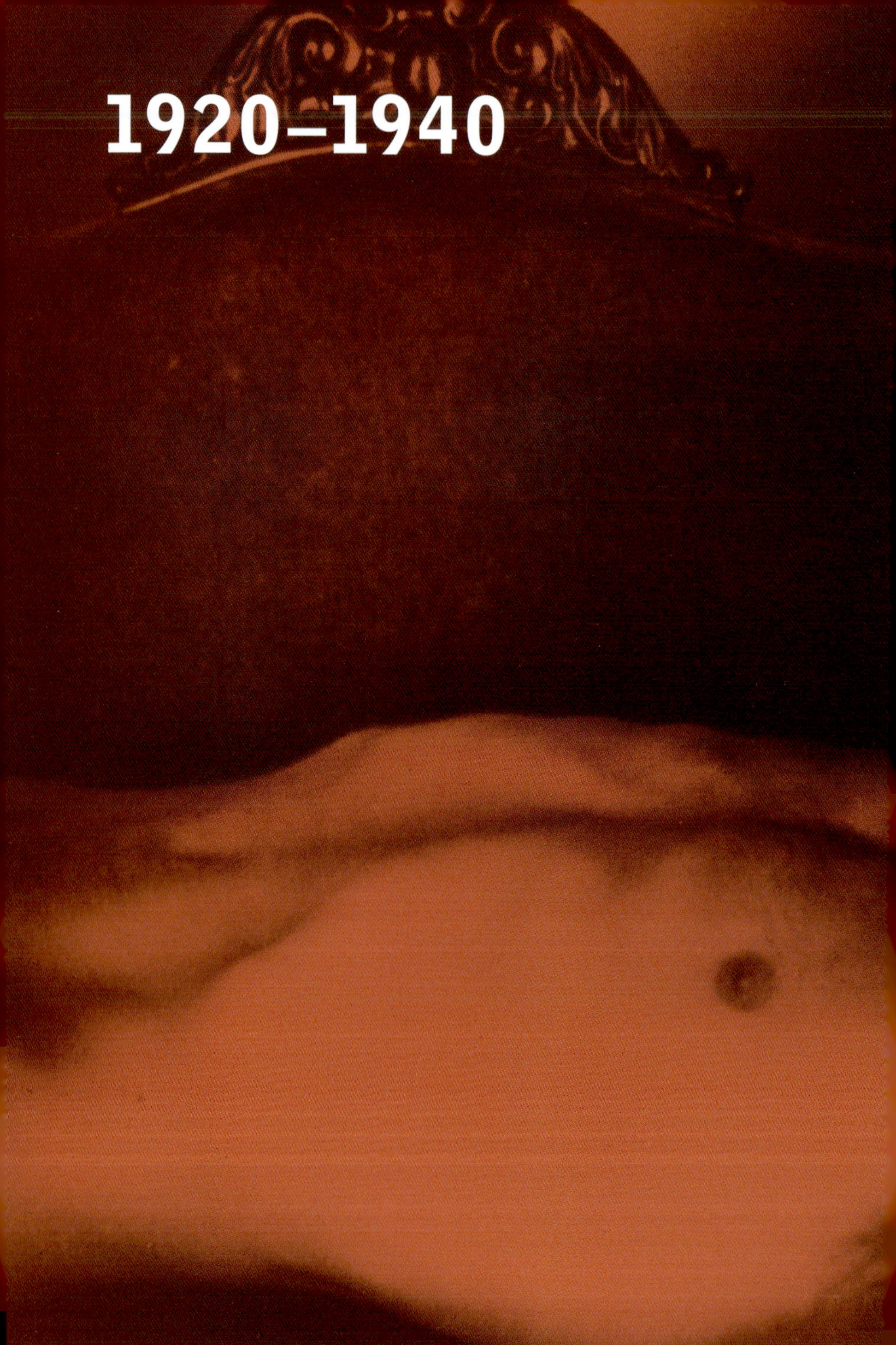
1920–1940

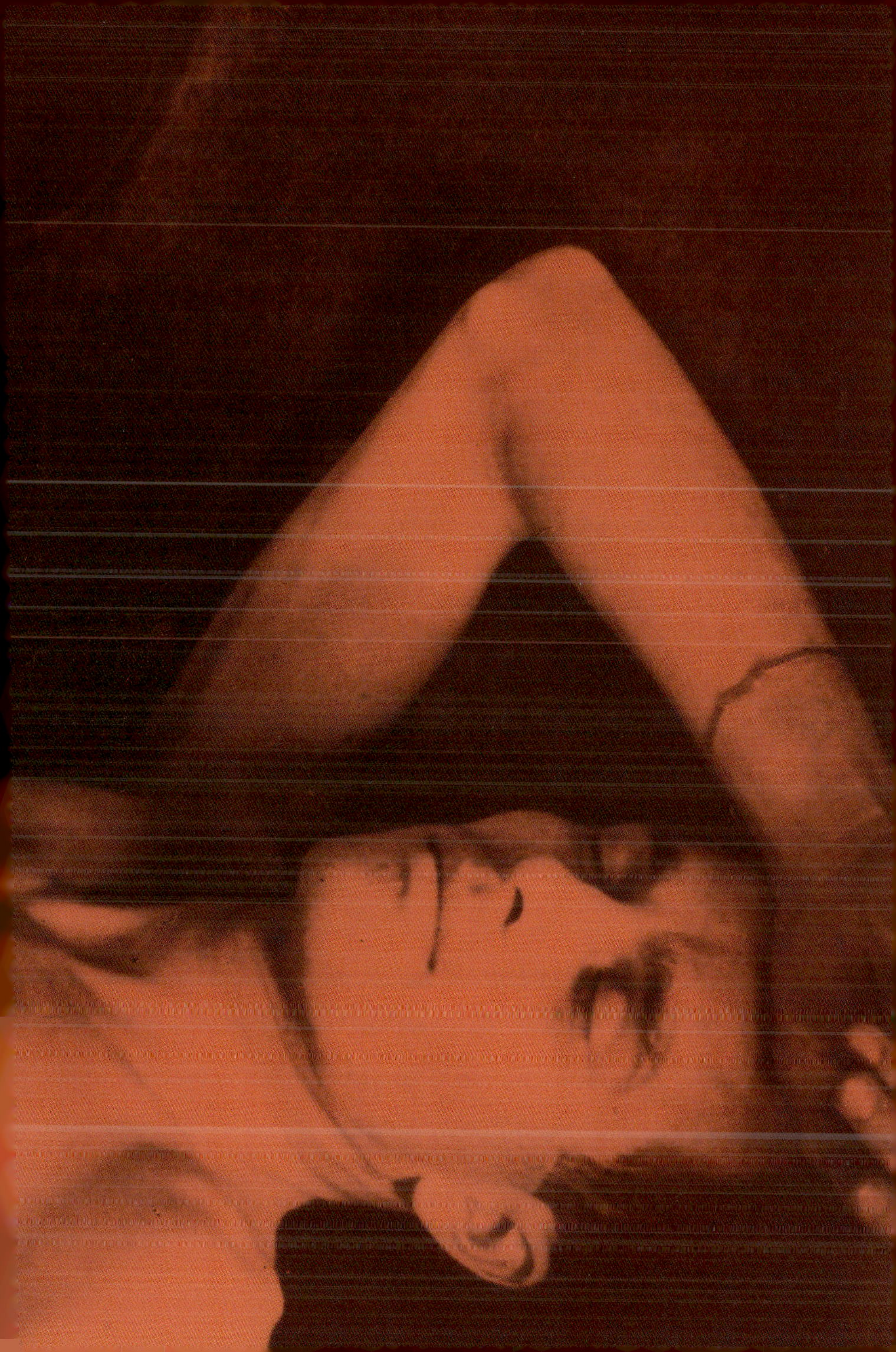

The greater freedom in dress and morals introduced by World War I brought a new interest in healthier, or at least more attractive, bodies with it. Fashion for women now demanded a slight, hipless, boyish body. It took a lot of dieting and exercise to get the ample hips and bosoms favored by the Victorians into this kind of shape, and men were the natural instructors. Military training during the war had also stressed fitness, and the homecoming men were accustomed to exercise and keeping in shape. Thus the idea was born that men and women should look dashing and elegant, both in and out of their clothes.

There were exponents, like Bernarr McFadden in the United States, of the concept that true health lay in being out of your clothes as much as possible. Thus nudism was born. McFadden himself graced the cover of his magazine "Physical Culture". Magazines like "Vim" in England, which became "Health and Efficiency", and then "Health and Strength", carried many jolly pictures of nudists. These were certainly bought by a number of people who were interested in neither health nor in being efficient or stronger. Rather, they wanted to see naked bodies. These magazines were to lead later to girly magazines for hetero-sexual men as well as the physique magazines, which still fascinate people of all sexual leanings.

People who believed in exposing their bodies to sunlight and air as much as possible had been grouping together since the turn of the century and called themselves naturists; they included George Bernard Shaw, the playwright. But photographs taken in the nudist colonies that began to spring up in Germany, France, and Scandinavia were something new. The law was always equivocal as to whether the magazines that carried these photos were concerned with health or sex. That it might be both was inconceivable. Sex was definitely not healthy in the mind of the law.

The German military of the 1920s, however, thought nudity was healthy and strengthening. Major Hans Suren had written "Der Mensch und die Sonne" (mankind and the sun) expounding his views about the importance of exercise and sunlight in the building of strong bodies. Some German commandants liked his ideas and trained their men outdoors in the nude and even had the cavalry ride bareback into nearby lakes.

The trend of photographing male nudes in a health context continued with the work of Josef Bayer, Karlwilli Damm, Gerhard Riebicke, Kurt Reichert, and Herbert Lehmitz. Two women joined them, Ingeborg Boysen and Lotte Herrlich.

In addition to this photography, which was never designed to beautify or eroticize the male body, there were photographers doing studio stills of men without clothes. Modern dance had freed dancers of their toe shoes and tutus, and the growth of the vaudeville theater in the United States had brought more men into this field. Ted Shawn and Ruth St. Denis took a company of dancers on the road, among them the young Martha Graham, and later Shawn was to have a company of all male dancers.

Their production numbers were exotic, suggestive of the Far East or the American Indian. Shawn took every opportunity to work with his clothes off and he and his dancers posed regularly for theater photographers nude, or nearly nude. There was a great vogue for pictures of nude men posed as if performing in some kind of exotic theater piece. In fact these photographs were just an opportunity to get naked in front of the camera. Again there had to be an excuse for it. Otherwise those who purchased the pictures might feel they were just letting their baser instincts run amok. Or more likely, they just wanted an excuse to offer the salesperson. "These are for my theater collection, you know."

The movies and their stars also provided a few glimpses of male nudity. Ramón Navarro had stripped for "Ben Hur" in the 1920s. And the Tarzan films were always good for a display of masculine flesh. Cecil Beaton's photograph of Johnny Weissmüller in 1932 is very sensual, even if Hollywood was trying to clean up its act by creating the self-censoring Hays Office at the time.

In the 1930s there were two developments on the nude male photographic front. The first was a modern rebirth of photographs for the use of artists. However, while in the 19th century there was obviously a sincere interest in photographing nudes to provide accurate guidelines for artists and to lower the cost of models, the photographs of the 1930s seem more clearly aimed at men who wanted to look at other men naked.

The Ritter Brothers advertised as models in the newly emerging physique magazines. They also offered sheets of miniature photos, obtainable by mail order. They were sleek-haired young men with gym-built, stream-lined physiques, and in their photographs they are always hairless (except for their brilliantined heads) and lightly oiled. They usually wore the ubiquitous posing strap in their pictures, although there are some in which they are full-frontally nude.

Fred and William Ritter, as they were known, worked out at the YMCA in New York and developed a business taking pictures of themselves, which they printed in their own darkroom, and sold by mail order. Prints in an 8 x 10-inch format sold for one dollar. This, in addition to their modeling work, must have provided them with an excellent living in the tough times of the Depression.

In Columbus, Ohio, another professional bodybuilder named Dick Falcon developed a mail-order business selling photographs of students he had trained in his own gymnasium. He also did photography and printing.

In New York at this time, Edwin F. Townsend was photographing male actors and athletes in the nude. He was best known for his photographs of Tony Sansone, a dancer and athlete of the period with outstanding good looks and a beautiful body. He too owned a well-known gymnasium in New York where many of the most beautiful male bodies of later years were developed.

The second major development in the period stemmed from the photographer George Platt Lynes, although his male nude photographs were mainly undercover or circulated among his friends and acquaintances.

Platt Lynes, from Paris, had the benefit of well-connected lovers and friends, and became a successful fashion photographer quite soon after his arrival in New York. As a very young acquaintance of Gertrude Stein he had met many artists in Paris when trying to make his way as a writer. His photography was strongly influenced by the Surrealists, the art movement that placed real objects in dreamlike settings. Many of his highly talented male nudes are photographed in the same kind of settings of unusual shapes and objects that he used for his fashion work. In fact, after a fashion shoot, he would often enroll friends and other handsome young men to disrobe in the same settings used for frocks.

He employed the Ritter Brothers for some of his very early experimental work. His assistant of the late 1930s, James Ogle, remembers him saying to the

Ritters as they appeared on the set in their posing straps, "We don't use those, we use shadows." With the brothers he did some very intimate work.

Throughout his career, which continued into the '40s and '50s, Platt Lynes photographed many hundreds of male nudes; his work was beautifully lit and endlessly inventive. The only time his nudes were seen publicly was in an occasional photographic exhibition, where a single male nude would be carefully balanced by a female nude and a flood of celebrity portraits. His great influence would come later in the century when his originality sparked many other photographers' work.

He produced a series of nude photographs based on mythology, reverting to the subterfuges of the turn of the century when nudes were only acceptable in a classical context. These photographs met with little enthusiasm and only a handful have appeared in the occasional anthology.

Through his long-time friend Lincoln Kirstein, founder of the School of American Ballet and of several dance groups that were to become the New York City Ballet, he also took many outstanding photographs of dancers. For the ballet "Orpheus", designed by his friend, the Russian artist Pavel Tchelitchew, he did manage to involve some nudity, largely because the costumes for the ballet were skimpy.

Successful fashion and theater photographers were also doing male nude work: George Hoyningen-Huene in the United States and Europe, Cecil Beaton and Angus McBean in England, Raymond Voinquel in France, and the American Man Ray in Paris. The German photographer Herbert List was also doing beautiful outdoor studies in Greece.

The strides made in the 1920s towards photographing the male nude with no excuses receded a little in the '30s. Magazines of the period like "Strength and Health", "Tomorrow's Man" and "Body Beautiful" may have had some sincere readers, but they were largely pretexts for displaying homoerotic photography. However, something was brewing, besides World War II, and an interest in seeing nude men without pretexts was clearly emerging, though such images had yet to make their appearance in a format readily available to the public.

Mit der Lockerung in Bekleidungsfragen und moralischen Dingen nach dem Weltkrieg nahm auch das Interesse an einem gesünderen oder doch zumindest attraktiveren Körper zu. Die Freikörperkultur erlebte einen neuen Auftrieb.

In den USA vertrat beispielsweise Bernarr McFadden die Vorstellung, dass wahre Gesundheit nur zu erreichen sei, wenn man so häufig wie möglich die Kleidung ablegte. Das war die Geburt der Freikörperkultur. McFadden persönlich zierte das Titelblatt seiner Zeitschrift „Physical Culture". In England zeigte die Zeitschrift „Vim", aus der dann „Health and Efficiency" und „Health and Strength" wurden, Bilder fröhlicher Nudisten. Zweifellos wurden diese Hefte auch von Menschen gekauft, deren Interesse nicht unbedingt der körperlichen Ertüchtigung galt. In direkter Nachfolge dieser Zeitschriften entstanden die „Physique Magazines", die Körperkult- und Bodybuildingzeitschriften, die auch heute noch ein nicht nur heterosexuelles Publikum finden.

Freikörperkultur hatte es eigentlich schon seit der Jahrhundertwende gegeben. In England nannten sie sich Naturists, und einer ihrer prominentesten Vertreter war der Dramatiker George Bernard Shaw. Doch Fotos aus den Nudistenkolonien, die in Deutschland, Frankreich oder Skandinavien entstanden waren, waren etwas Neues. Von gesetzlicher Seite wurde immer wieder diskutiert, ob es in diesen Magazinen um den gesundheitlichen Aspekt oder um Sex ging, denn Sex hatte im Sinne des Gesetzes nun wirklich nichts mit Gesundheit zu tun.

Der allgemeine Trend, Männerakte im Kontext körperlicher Gesundheit und Ertüchtigung zu fotografieren, setzte sich in der Arbeit von Josef Bayer, Karl-Willi Damm, Gerhard Riebicke und Kurt Reichert fort. Einige Frauen, etwa Ingeborg Boysen und Lotte Herrlich, folgten ihrem Beispiel.

Neben dieser Fotografie, die nicht angetreten war, den männlichen Körper als schönes und erotisches Objekt darzustellen, gab es auch Fotografen, die Studioaufnahmen unbekleideter Männer machten. Zu ihren Modellen zählten vielfach Tänzer und Bühnenstars. Der Modern Dance hatte die Tänzer von ihren Spitzenschuhen und Trikots befreit, und der Boom des Vaudeville in den Vereinigten Staaten hatte zahlreiche Männer in dieses Metier gelockt. Ted Shawn und Ruth St. Denis zogen mit einer Tanztruppe durchs Land, zu der auch die junge Martha Graham gehörte, und Shawn gründete schließlich eine Company, die nur aus männlichen Tänzern bestand.

Ihre Auftritte hatten immer etwas Exotisches, suggerierten fernöstliche und indianische Szenen, und Shawn nutzte jede Gelegenheit, unbekleidet zu arbeiten. Er und seine Tänzer standen nackt oder halbnackt Modell für die Theaterfotografen. Zusätzlich ließen sich zahlreiche Männer in Posen und Kulissen ablichten, die sie wie Akteure in einer exotischen Theaterproduktion erscheinen ließen. So war eine neue Entschuldigung gefunden, sich nackt ablichten zu lassen, und der Käufer der Aufnahmen durfte sich darauf berufen, ja nur Bilder für seine Theatersammlung erstehen zu wollen.

Auch der Film gewährte schon einmal erste kurze Blicke auf nackte Männer. Ramón Navarro hatte in den 20er Jahren in „Ben Hur" die Hüllen fallen lassen, und auch die Tarzanfilme eigneten sich immer gut für ein bisschen nacktes Männerfleisch. Cecil Beatons Aufnahme von Johnny Weissmüller aus dem Jahre 1923 ist sehr sinnlich, auch wenn Hollywood damals mit der Einrichtung des Hays Office Selbstzensur zu üben begann.

In den 30er Jahren gab es zwei wichtige Strömungen in der männlichen Aktfotografie. Die erste war so etwas wie eine moderne Wiedergeburt der Aktfotografie für den künstlerischen Gebrauch. Doch während es im 19. Jahrhundert dafür sicherlich diesbezüglich ein ernsthaftes Interesse gegeben hatte, zielten diese Aufnahmen nun eindeutig auf ein homosexuelles Publikum.

Die Ritter Brothers boten sich in den Körperkult-Magazinen als Modelle an und verschickten Blätter mit Kontaktabzügen für ihren Mailorder. Die beiden waren junge, athletisch gebaute Männer, die sich auf den Aufnahmen immer eingeölt und unbehaart (abgesehen vom pomadetriefenden Haupthaar) präsentierten. Gewöhnlich trugen sie den unvermeidlichen Lendenschurz, doch es gibt auch einige Fotos, die sie gänzlich unverhüllt zeigen.

Frad und William Ritter trainierten im YMCA von New York, fotografierten sich selbst, entwickelten die Aufnahmen in der eigenen Dunkelkammer und verschickten die Aufnahmen auf Bestellung. Ein Bild im Postkartenformat kostete einen Dollar. Dieser Zusatzverdienst zu ihrem Salär als Models muss ihnen in den Zeiten der Depression einen einträglichen Lebensunterhalt gesichert haben.

In Columbus, Ohio, baute ein professioneller Bodybuilder, Dick Falcon, ebenfalls ein Versandgeschäft mit Fotos von Schülern auf, die er in seinem eigenem Sportstudio trainierte. Auch er stellte die Aufnahmen und Abzüge in Eigenregie her. In New York war es Edwin F. Townsend, der Aktaufnahmen von Schauspielern und Sportlern machte. Am bekanntesten sind seine Fotos von Tony Sansone, einem Tänzer und Athleten, der blendend aussah und einen makellosen Körper besaß. Sansone betrieb später in New York ein eigenes Sportstudio, in dem viele zukünftige Stars der Aktfotografie geschmiedet wurden.

Die andere wichtige Entwicklung dieser Zeit leitete der Fotograf George Platt Lynes ein, dessen Männerakte allerdings nicht für die Öffentlichkeit gedacht waren, sondern nur im Freundes- und Kennerkreis kursierten. Platt Lynes konnte auf die guten Beziehungen seiner Freunde und Lover bauen und stieg schon bald nach seinem Wechsel von Paris nach New York zu einem erfolgreichen Modefotografen auf. Als junger Vertrauter von Gertrude Stein hatte er bei dem Versuch, sich in Paris als Schriftsteller einen Namen zu machen, Bekanntschaft mit vielen Künstlern geschlossen. Seine Fotografie ist stark von den Surrealisten geprägt, und viele seiner Männerakte entstanden in derselben Kulisse aus seltsamen Objekten und Formen, die er auch für seine Modefotos verwandte.

Für seine ganz frühen Fotoexperimente heuerte er auch die Ritter-Brüder an. James Ogle, Ende der 30er Jahre sein Assistent, erinnert sich noch gut daran, wie Platt Lynes die Brüder begrüßte, als sie mit ihren Lendenschurzen zum Fototermin erschienen: „Das brauchen wir hier nicht. Wir arbeiten mit Schatten." Mit den Ritter Brothers sind Platt Lynes einige sehr intime Aufnahmen gelungen. Während seiner aktiven Zeit als Fotograf, die bis in die 40er und 50er Jahre reichte, entstanden Hunderte von Aktaufnahmen, alle sehr gut ausgeleuchtet und verblüffend originell. In Fotoausstellungen taucht zur damaligen Zeit nur ganz vereinzelt einmal ein Männerakt von Platt Lynes auf, und dann ist er stets neutralisiert durch einen weiblichen Akt und zahllose harmlose Bilder von Stars und Berühmtheiten. Platt Lynes gewann erst viel später Einfluss, als sich eine neue Generation von Fotografen durch seine einzigartigen Werke inspirieren ließ.

Platt Lynes machte auch eine Serie von Aktfotos mit mythologischer
Thematik und kehrte damit zu der Verschleierungstaktik der Jahrhundertwende
zurück. Sie fanden trotz ihrer unbestrittenen Qualität wenig Anklang. Dank sei-
nes langjährigen Freundes Lincoln Kirstein, dem Gründer der School of American
Ballet und verschiedener Tanzgruppen, aus denen das New York City Ballet
entstehen sollte, konnte er auch einige hervorragende Ballettfotos aufnehmen.
Er schaffte es sogar, in dem Ballett „Orpheus", das sein Freund, der russische
Künstler Pavel Techelitschev, entworfen hatte, etwas Nacktheit unterzubringen.

Erfolgreiche Mode- und Theaterfotografen nahmen ebenfalls männliche
Akte auf. George Hoyningen-Huene und Cecil Beaton arbeiteten sowohl in den
USA wie auch in Europa, zur gleichen Zeit schoss in England Angus McBean
Aktfotos. Raymond Voinquel und Man Ray fotografierten Akte in Paris, und
der Deutsche Herbert List machte phantastische Außenaufnahmen von unbeklei-
deten Männern in Griechenland.

Der stärkere Realitätsbezug in der Fotografie des Männeraktes, wie er in
den 20ern zu entdecken war, wurde in den 30er Jahren wieder etwas zurück-
genommen, doch die Richtung war vorgegeben und das Interesse erwacht, den
nackten Mann ohne verbrämendes Beiwerk betrachten zu können.

Avec la nouvelle liberté vestimentaire et morale apportée par la Première Guerre mondiale, on commença à s'intéresser à des corps plus sains ou, du moins, plus beaux. La mode féminine nécessitait un corps svelte et longiligne.

L'entraînement militaire durant la guerre avait également mis l'accent sur la forme physique. Les hommes qui rentrèrent du front étaient habitués aux exercices et à l'entretien de leur musculature. C'est ainsi que naquit l'idée selon laquelle les hommes et les femmes devaient avoir l'air fringant et élégant, tant habillés que nus.

Certains, comme Bernarr McFadden aux Etats-Unis, annoncèrent que, pour être en bonne santé, il fallait être nu le plus souvent possible. Le nudisme était né. McFarren en personne ornait la couverture de son magazine « Physical Culture ». Des revues telles que « Vim » en Angleterre, qui devint « Health and Efficiency », puis « Health and Strength », présentaient des photos de nudistes épanouis. Ces revues devaient déboucher plus tard sur les magazines de charme pour les hommes hétérosexuels et sur les revues de culture physique, qui continuent encore aujourd'hui de fasciner certains hétérosexuels, de nombreux homosexuels et des bisexuels.

Les naturistes existaient depuis le début du XXe siècle et comptaient le dramaturge George Bernard Shaw parmi leurs membres. Toutefois, les photographies de camps de nudistes qui commençaient à apparaître en Allemagne, en France et en Scandinavie étaient d'un autre genre. Les législateurs avaient beaucoup de mal à décider si les revues qui les publiaient relevaient du domaine de « la santé » ou de « la sexualité ». L'idée qu'elles puissent appartenir un peu aux deux était trop déroutante pour qu'on y songe. Dans l'esprit de la loi, la sexualité n'avait rien de sain.

Dans les années 20, l'armée allemande pensait que la nudité était saine et revigorante. Le major Hans Surren publia « Der Mensch und die Sonne », exprimant ses idées sur l'importance de l'exercice et du soleil pour renforcer le corps.

La tendance à photographier les nus masculins dans un contexte de santé se poursuivit avec les œuvres de Josef Bayer, Karlwilli Damm, Gerhard Riebicke et Kurt Reichert et Herbert Lehmitz. Certaines femmes les rejoignirent, telles Ingeborg Boysen et Lotte Herrlich.

Outre ces photographies, qui n'étaient pas destinées à rendre le corps de l'homme beau ou érotique, il y avait des photographes de studio qui prenaient des photos d'hommes sans vêtement. La danse moderne avait libéré les danseuses de leurs tutus et de leurs pointes, et l'essor du théâtre de vaudeville aux Etats-Unis attira de nombreux hommes dans ce domaine.

Ted Shawn et Ruth St. Denis emmenèrent une compagnie de danseurs en tournée, parmi lesquels la jeune Martha Graham. Plus tard, Shawn devait monter une compagnie de danse exclusivement masculine.

Leurs chorégraphies étaient originales, suggérant l'Extrême-Orient ou les Indiens d'Amérique. Shawn saisissait la moindre occasion d'enlever ses vêtements. Ses danseurs et lui-même posaient, nus ou presque, pour des photographes de théâtre. Il y avait également une mode de photos de modèles nus, posant comme s'ils étaient des artistes pratiquant un genre théâtral exotique. A vrai dire, ces photographies étaient surtout une chance de s'exhiber devant un objectif. Là encore, il fallait un bon prétexte. Dans le cas contraire, les acheteurs potentiels risquaient d'avoir le sentiment de se laisser aller à leur instinct le plus vil. Ou encore, il leur fallait une excuse à avancer au marchand de journaux. « C'est pour ma collection de photos de théâtre, vous savez. »

Les films et leurs vedettes permirent d'entrevoir quelques hommes dévêtus. Dans les années 20, Ramón Navarro, lui, avait tout enlevé dans « Ben Hur ». Quant aux films de Tarzan, ils étaient l'occasion rêvée de montrer un peu de chair masculine. Le portrait de Johnny Weissmüller par Cecil Beaton, réalisé en 1932, est très sensuel, malgré les tentatives de Hollywood pour s'autocensurer au travers de son « Hays Office ».

Les années 30 virent deux nouveautés dans le domaine du nu masculin. La première était une variante de la photographie destinée aux artistes. Mais si, au XIXe siècle, les photos de nu correspondaient à une démarche sincère pour aider à la précision anatomique et fournir des modèles à moindre prix, leurs équivalents du XXe siècle s'adressaient clairement aux hommes qui aimaient regarder des hommes nus.

Dans les magazines de culture physique qui commençaient juste à paraître, les frères Ritter passaient des annonces pour se proposer comme modèles.

Ils étaient tous deux élancés avec un corps musclé. Sur leurs photographies, ils avaient le corps rasé et légèrement huilé. Ils portaient généralement l'inévitable cache-sexe, quoique sur certaines photos, ils soient entièrement nus et montrés de face.

Fred et William Ritter s'entraînaient à la YMCA de New York et mirent au point une petite activité commerciale : ils se prenaient mutuellement en photo, les tiraient dans leur chambre noire, puis les vendaient par correspondance. Des tirages de 8x10 se vendaient 1$ pièce.

A Colombus, dans l'Ohio, un autre culturiste professionnel nommé Dick Falcon développa une affaire de vente par correspondance avec des photos d'étudiants qu'il entraînait lui-même au gymnase. Il s'occupait lui aussi de faire les photos et de les tirer. A la même époque, à New York, Edwin F. Townsend faisait des nus d'acteurs et d'athlètes. Il était surtout connu pour ses photos de Tony Sansone, un danseur et athlète qui avait un visage superbe et un corps magnifique. Sansone monta plus tard son propre gymnase où furent formés les plus beaux corps de son temps.

Le second événement majeur de l'époque fut l'arrivée de George Platt Lynes, bien que ses nus masculins aient seulement été diffusés sous le manteau à des prix réduits, ou comme cadeaux, à des amis et des relations. Platt Lynes bénéficia d'un réseau d'amants et d'amis bien placés et, peu après son arrivée à New York, il devint un photographe de mode renommé. Très jeune, il avait fait la connaissance de Gertrude Stein à Paris, chez qui il avait rencontré de nombreux artistes alors qu'il essayait de devenir écrivain. Ses photographies étaient très influencées par les surréalistes. Un grand nombre de ses nus masculins étaient pris dans les mêmes décors étranges que ses photos de mode.

Pour ses premiers travaux expérimentaux, il engagea les frères Ritter comme modèles. Son assistant à la fin des années 30, James Ogle, se souvient de l'avoir entendu dire, alors que les Ritter se présentaient sur le plateau avec leur cache-sexe : « Ici, on n'utilise pas de ça, on se sert des ombres. » Il réalisa avec eux des travaux très intimes.

Tout au long de sa carrière, qui se poursuivit dans les années 40 et 50, Platt Lynes photographia des centaines de nus masculins, tous superbement éclairés et plus inventifs les uns que les autres. Durant la période dont il est question ici, ses nus n'apparurent que rarement dans quelques expositions photographiques, où un nu masculin était toujours soigneusement contrebalancé par un nu féminin et une avalanche de portraits de célébrités. Plus tard, ses œuvres originales allaient avoir une influence considérable sur les nouvelles générations de photographes.

Il réalisa également une série de nus dans un contexte mythologique, retombant sur les subterfuges du début du siècle quand les nus n'étaient acceptables que dans un cadre classique. Bien que très belles et originales, ces photographies éveillèrent peu d'enthousiasme, et seule une poignée furent publiées dans quelques anthologies.

Grâce à son ami de toujours, Lincoln Kirstein, fondateur de la School of American Ballet, et à plusieurs groupes de danse qui allaient plus tard devenir le New York City Ballet, il réalisa également d'admirables photos de ballet. Pour « Orpheus », de son ami l'artiste russe Pavel Techelitchev, il parvint à montrer un peu de nudité, notamment parce que les costumes des danseurs étaient plus que sommaires.

D'autres grands photographes de mode et de théâtre réalisaient également des nus masculins. George Hoyningen-Huene et Cecil Beaton travaillèrent aux Etats-Unis aussi bien qu'en Europe. A la même époque, Angus McBean faisait des nus en Angleterre, tout comme Raymond Voinquel et Man Ray en France. L'Allemand Herbert List réalisait de superbes études en extérieur, le plus souvent en Grèce.

La percée du réalisme dans la photo de nu masculin, apparue dans les années 20, perdit un peu de terrain dans les années 30. Platt Lynes lui-même avait dû se retrancher derrière des illustrations de mythes, sans grand succès. Mais quelque chose couvait, outre la Seconde Guerre mondiale, et un intérêt pour les hommes nus vus de face commençait à poindre, même si ces derniers étaient encore loin d'apparaître dans un format accessible à un large public.

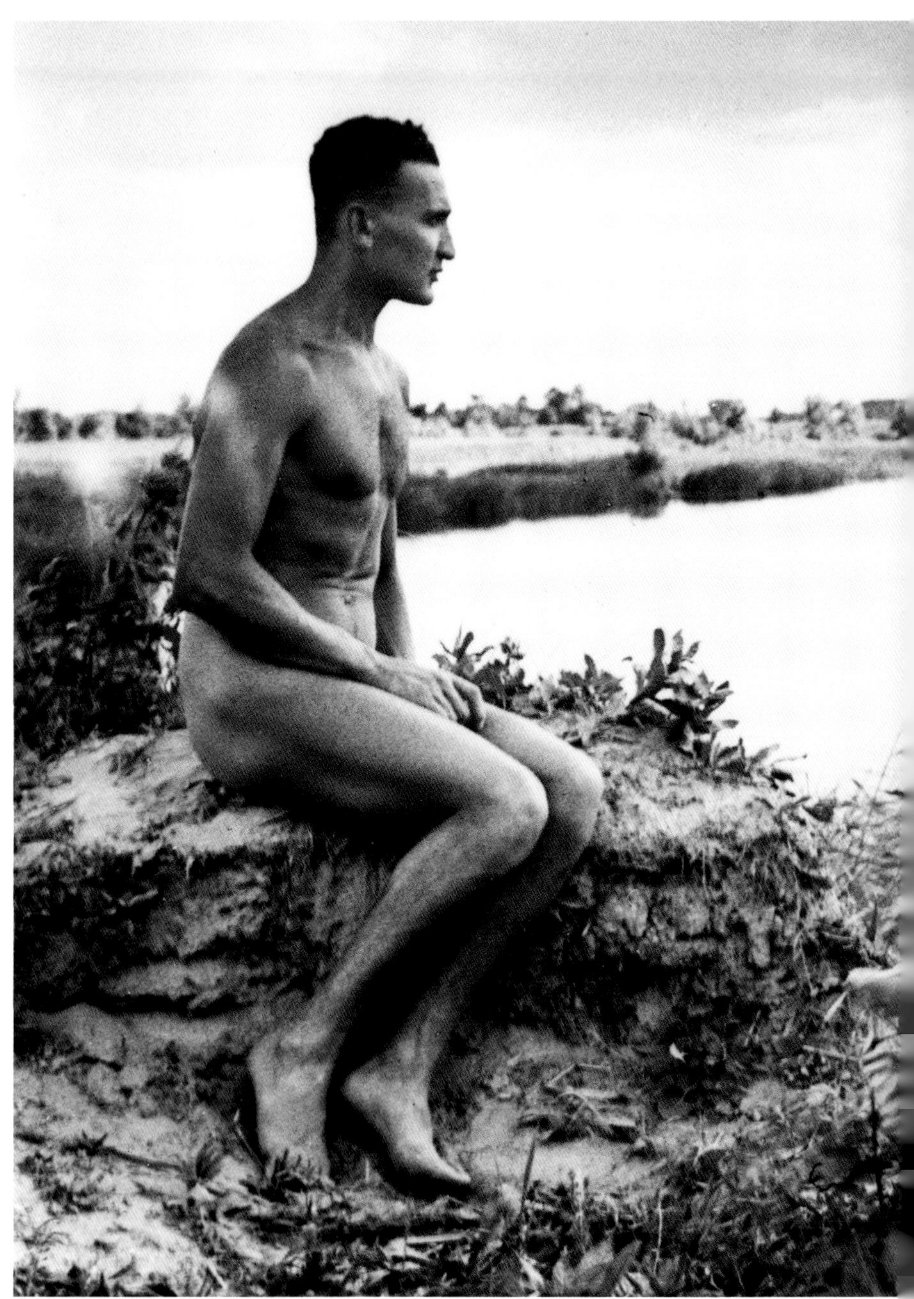

André Kertész, Duna Haraszti, May 30, 1920

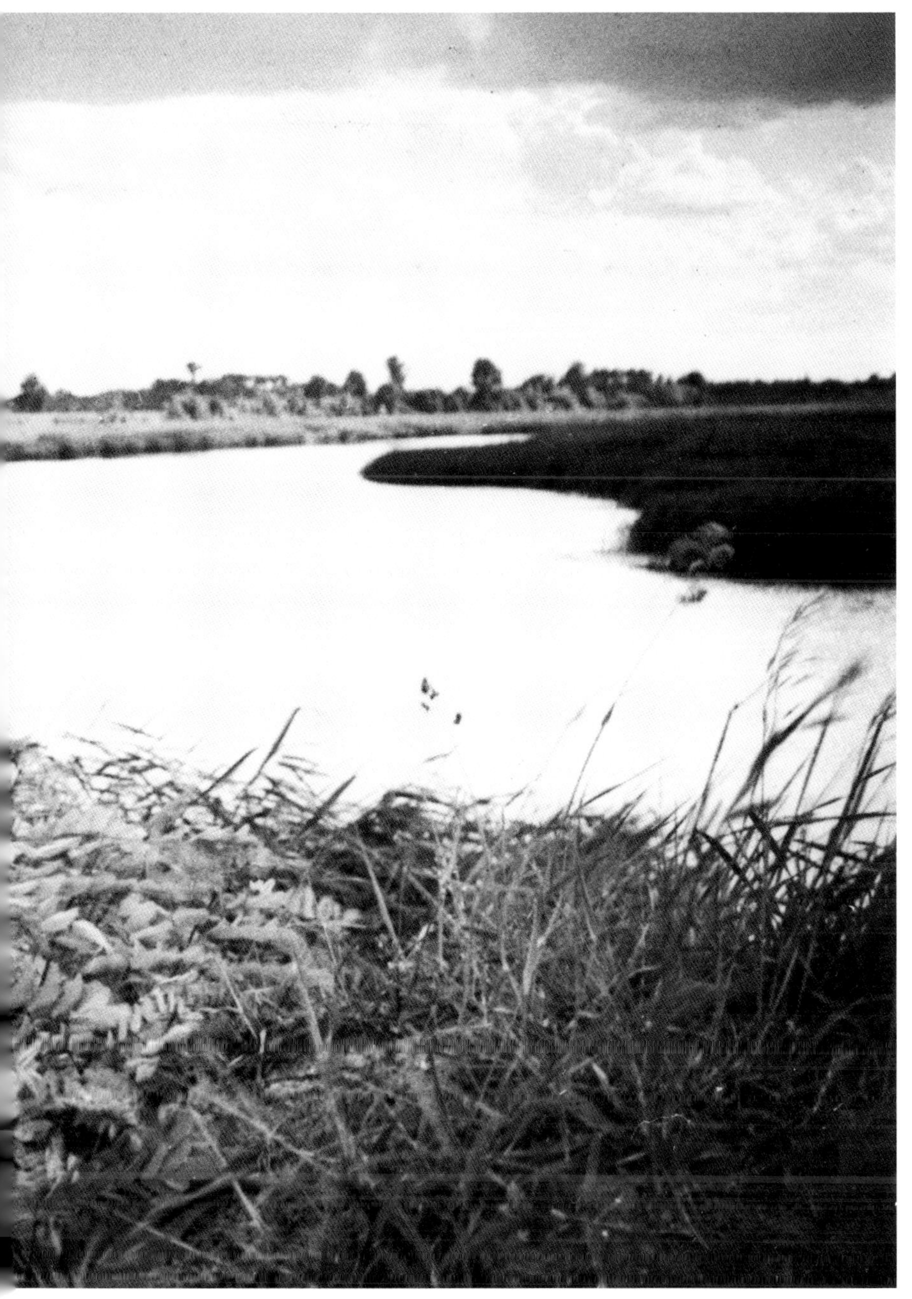

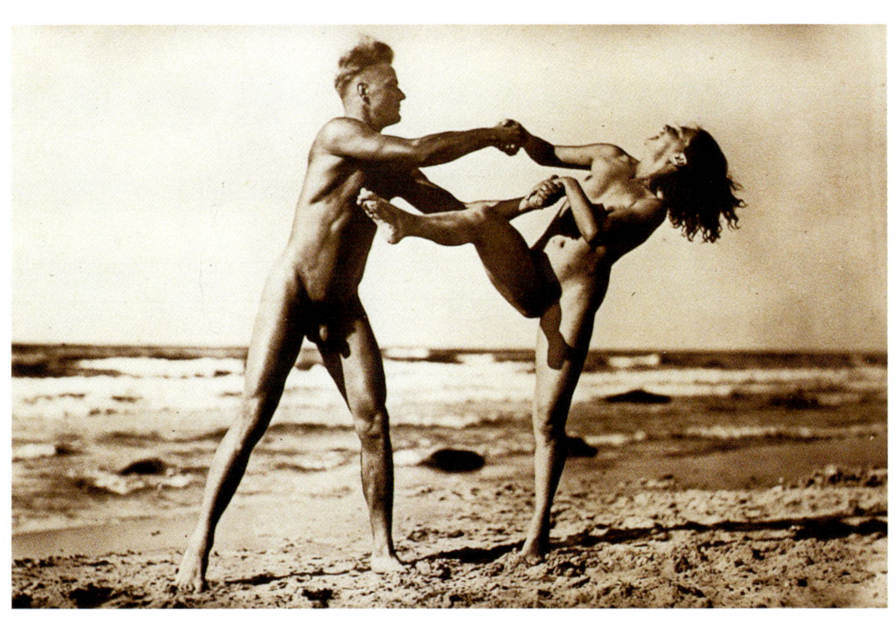

Anonymous, c. 1935

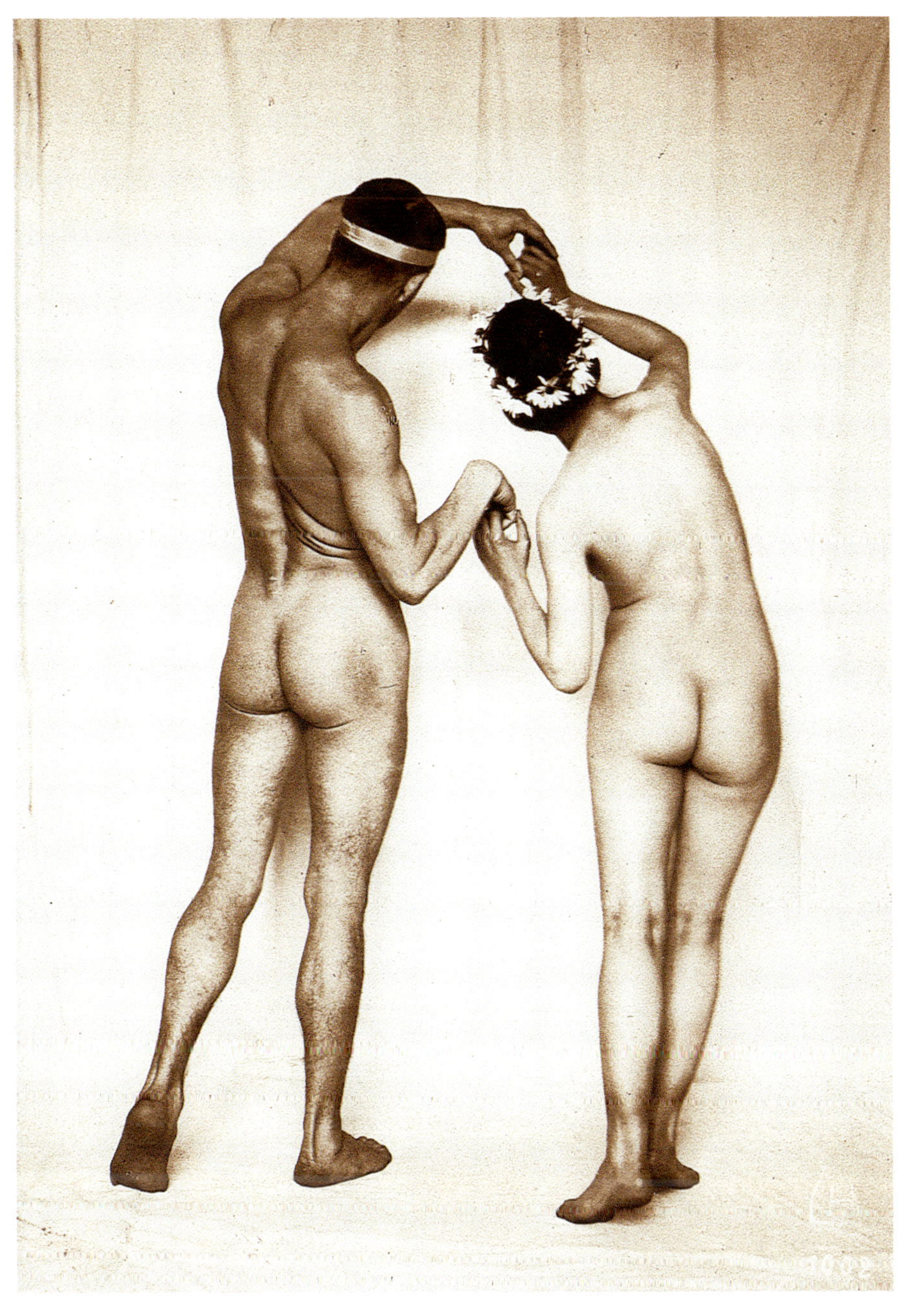

Lotte Herrlich, c. 1920

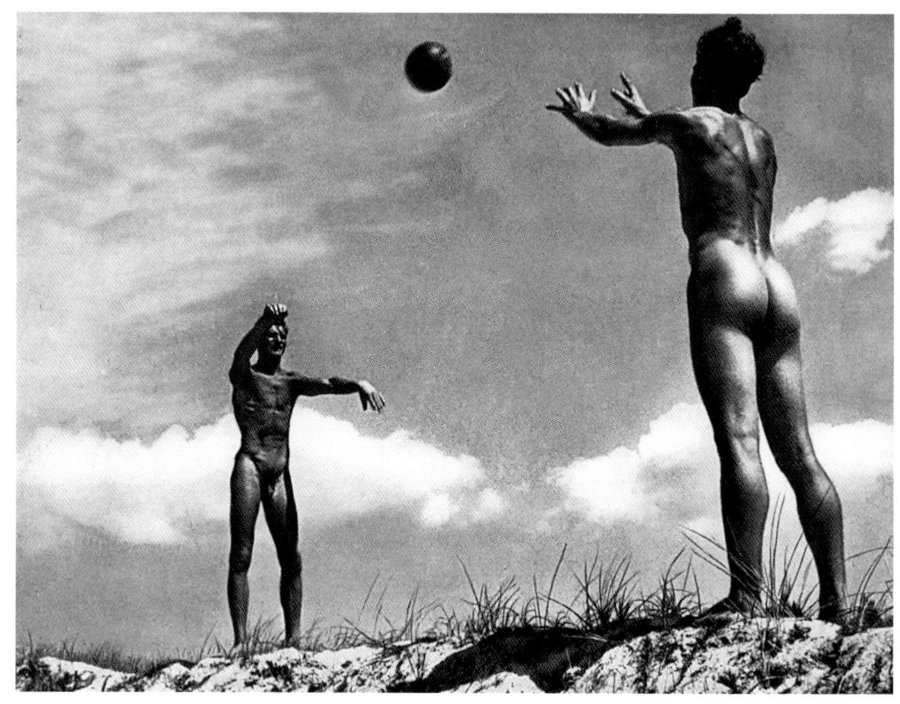

Anonymous, c. 1930

Anonymous, c. 1920

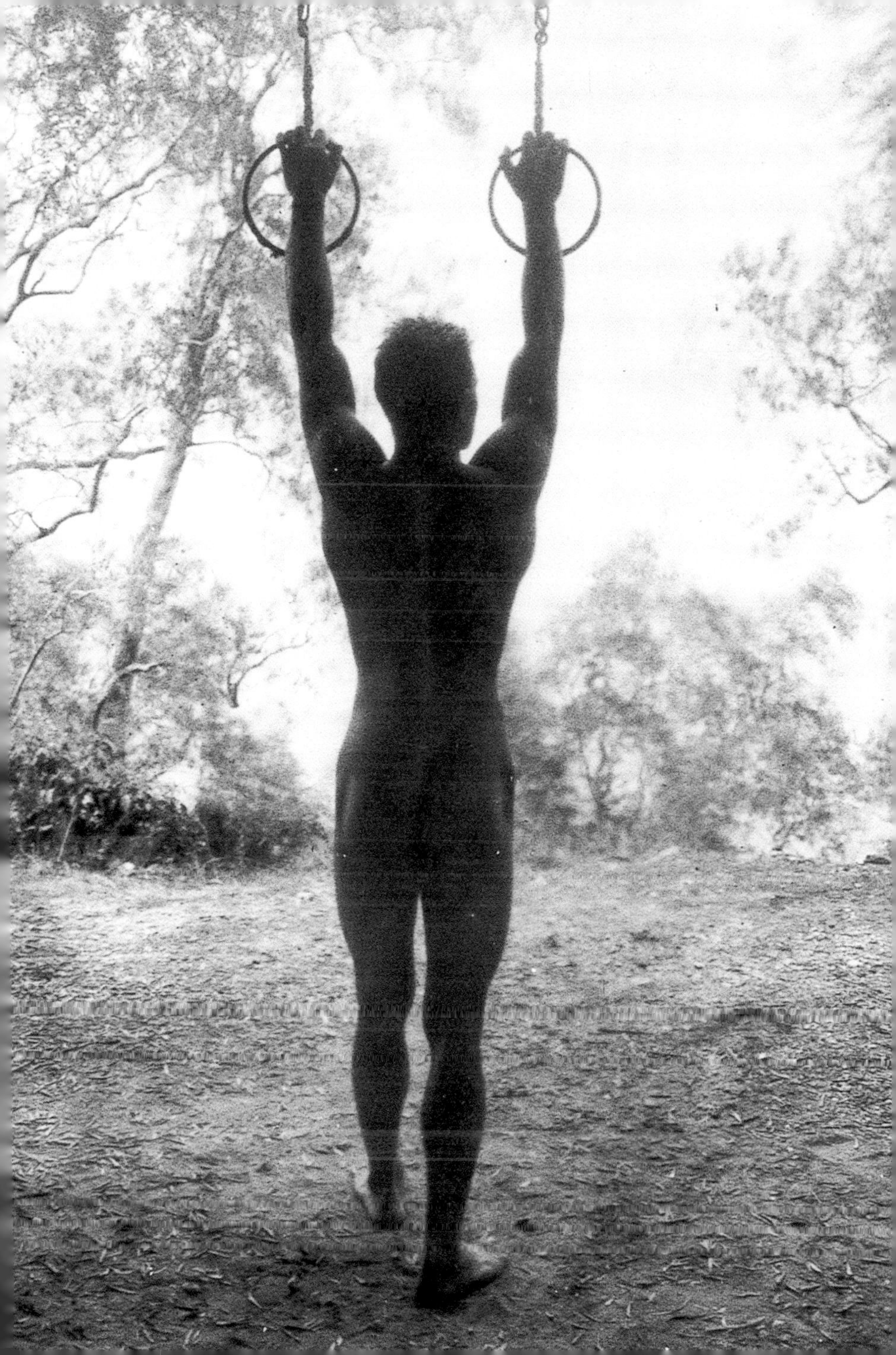

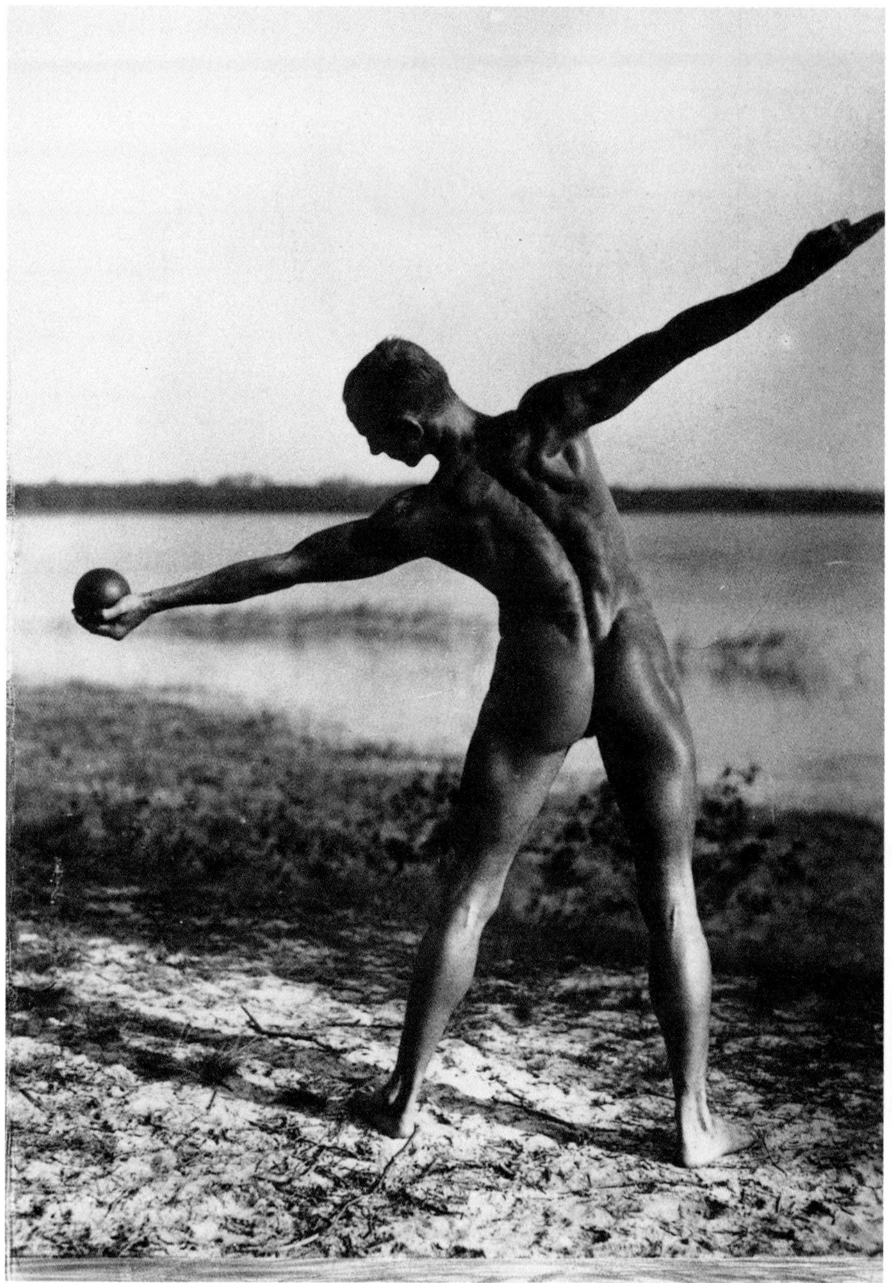

Anonymous, c. 1925

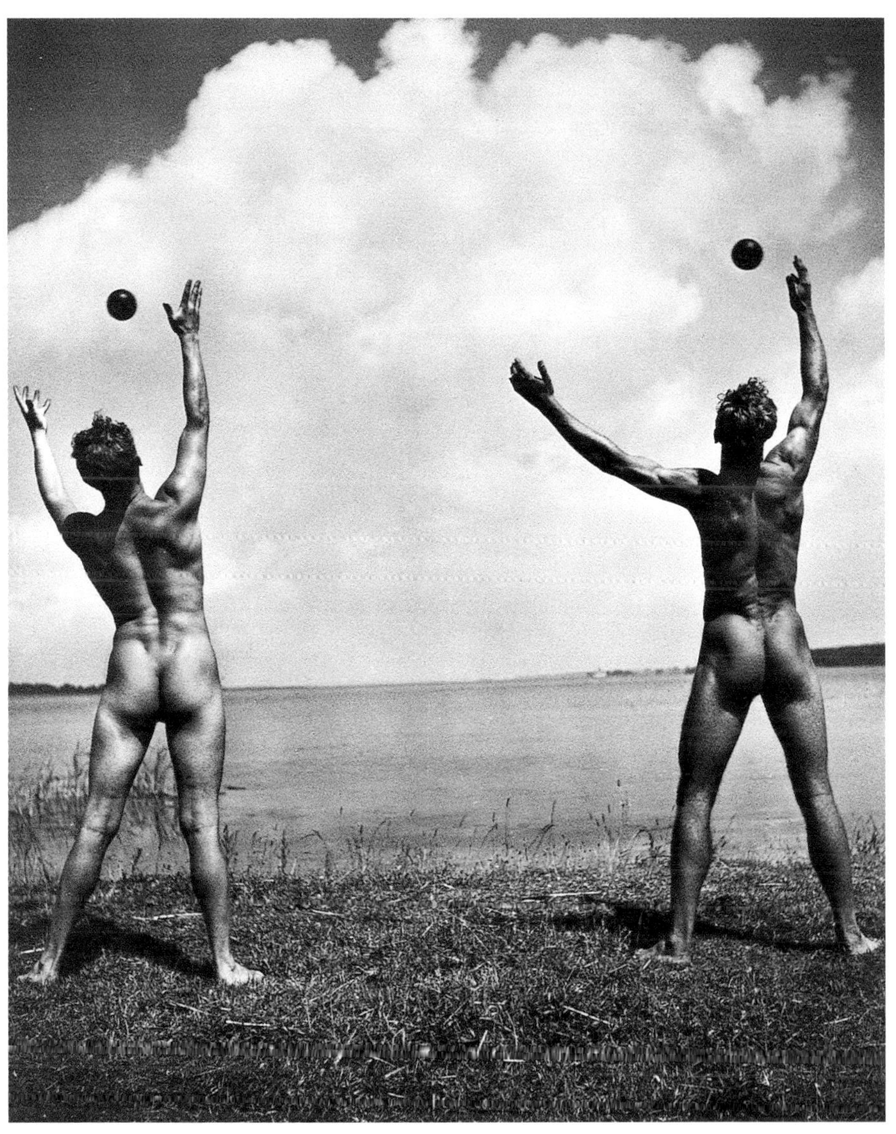

Kurt Reichert, c. 1935

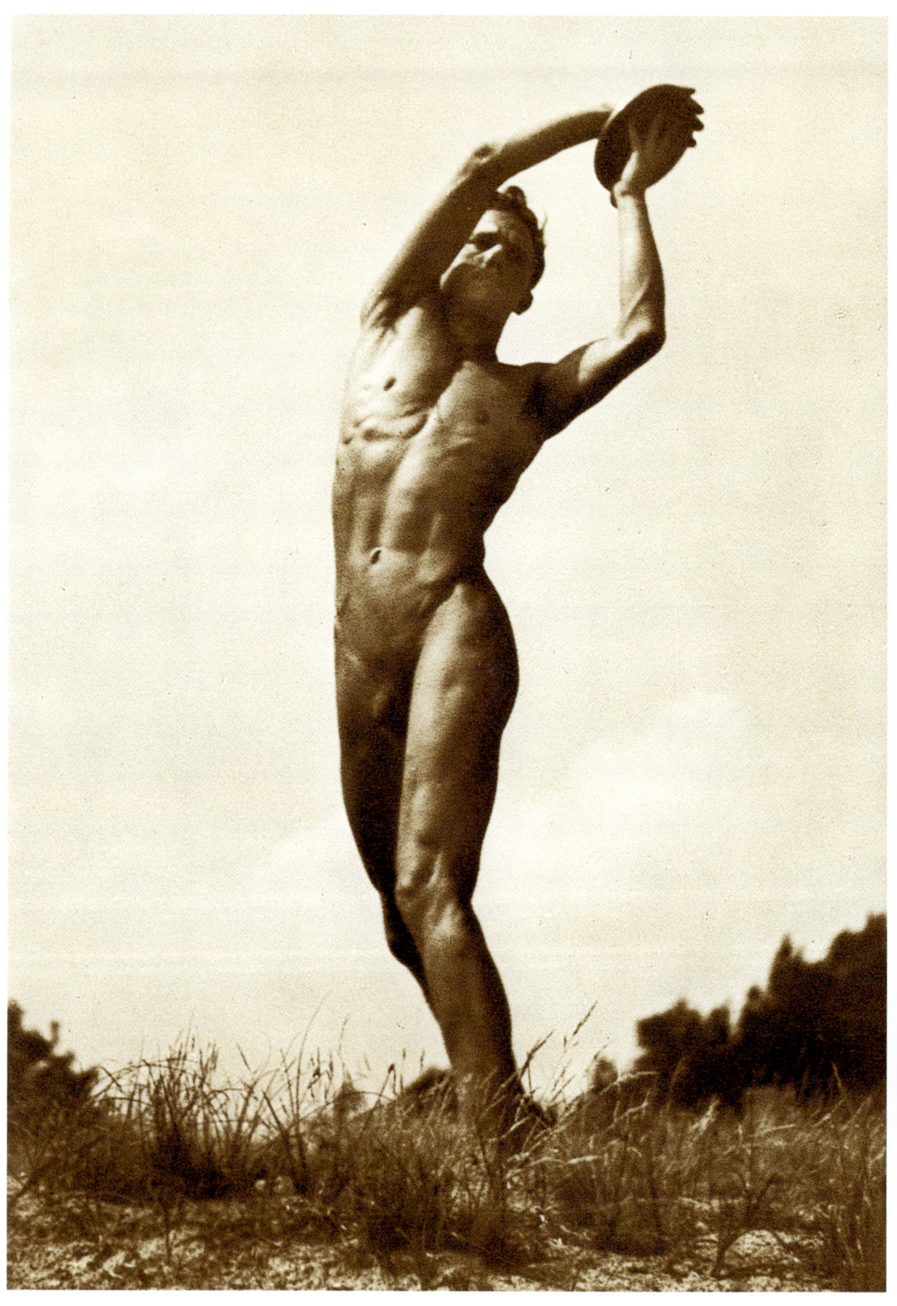

Kurt Reichert, c. 1935

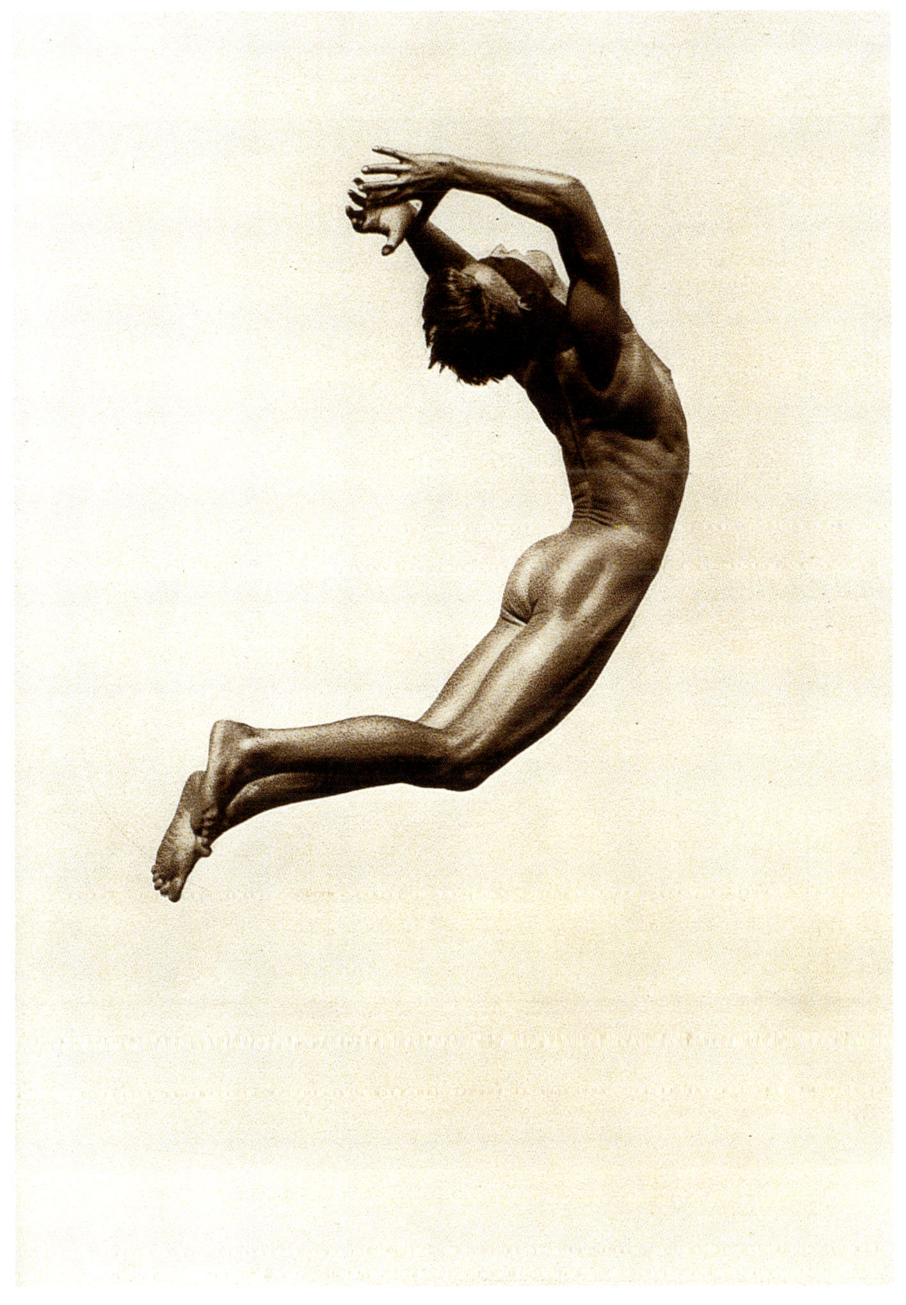

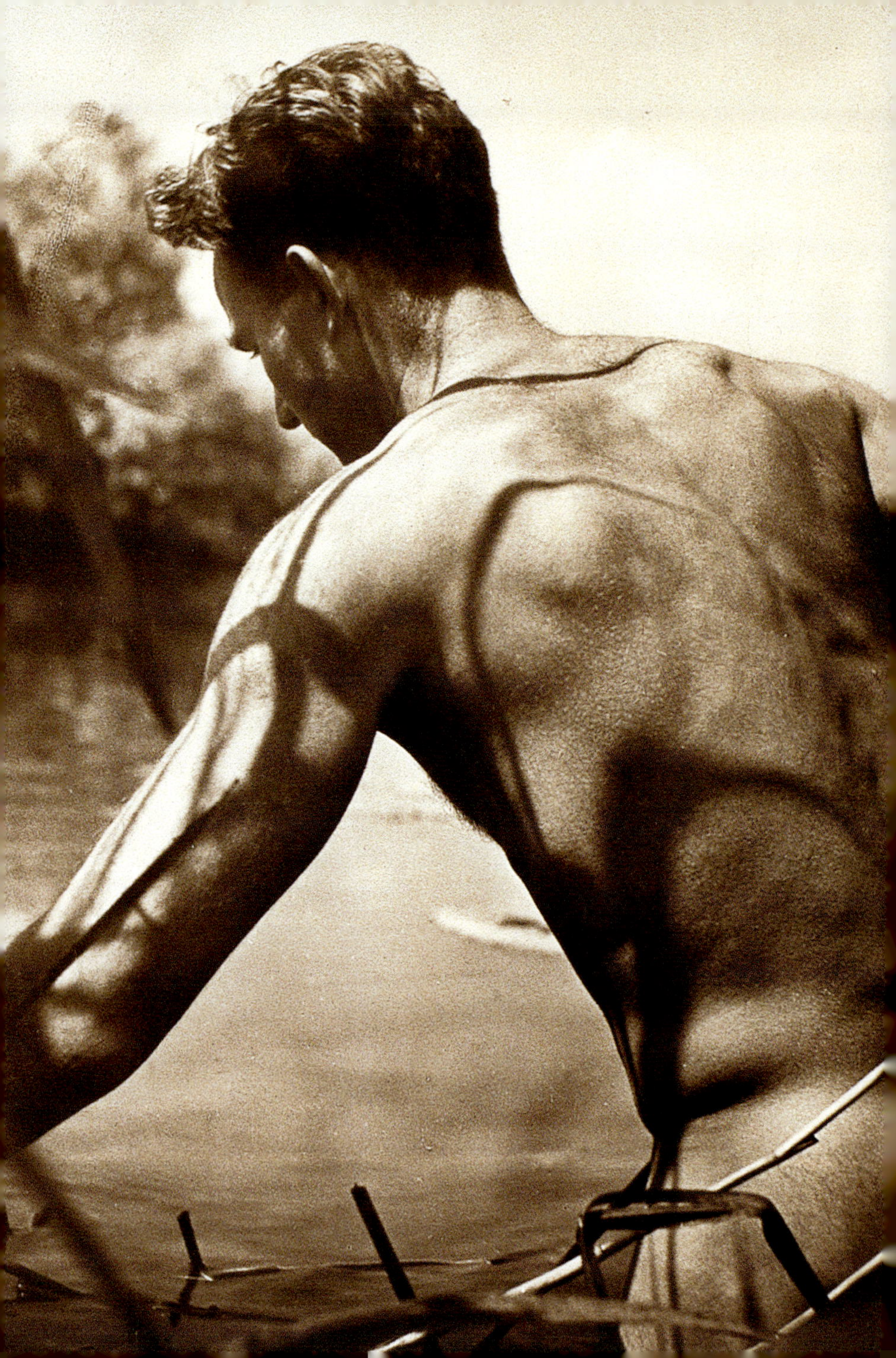

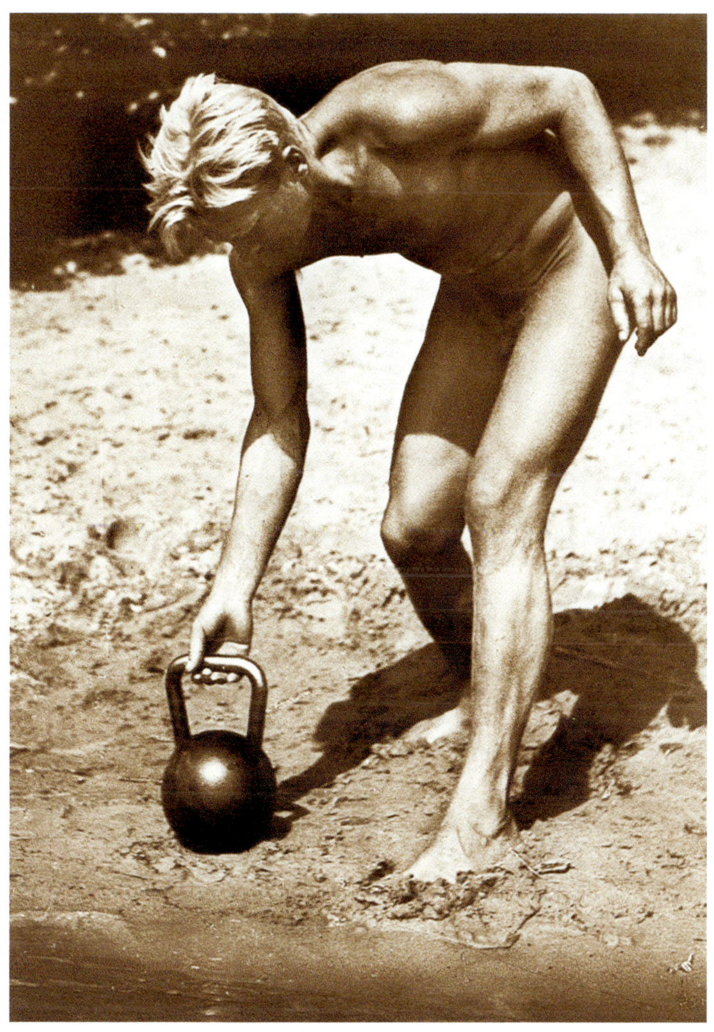

Kurt Reichert, c. 1935

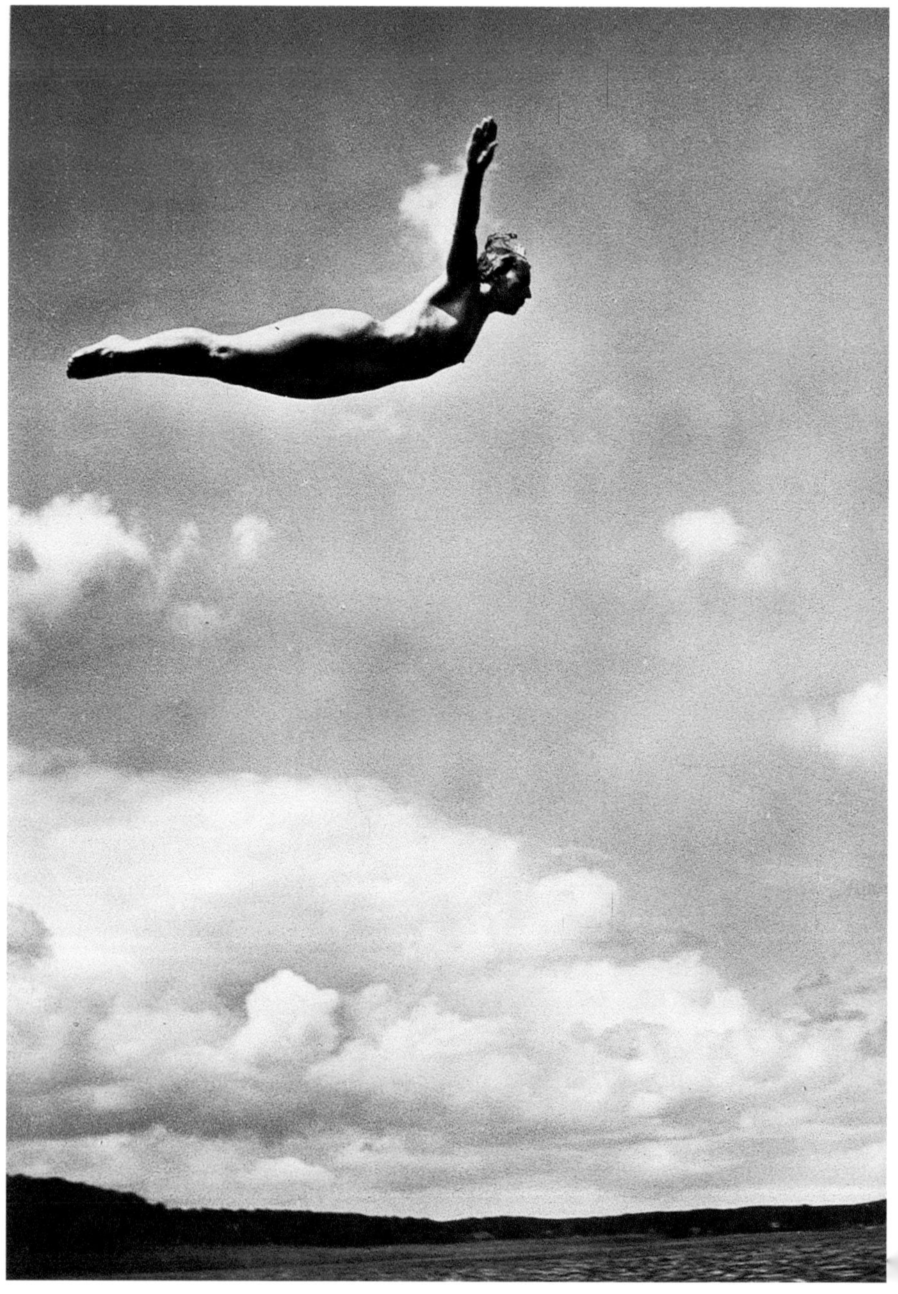

Kurt Reichert, c. 1935

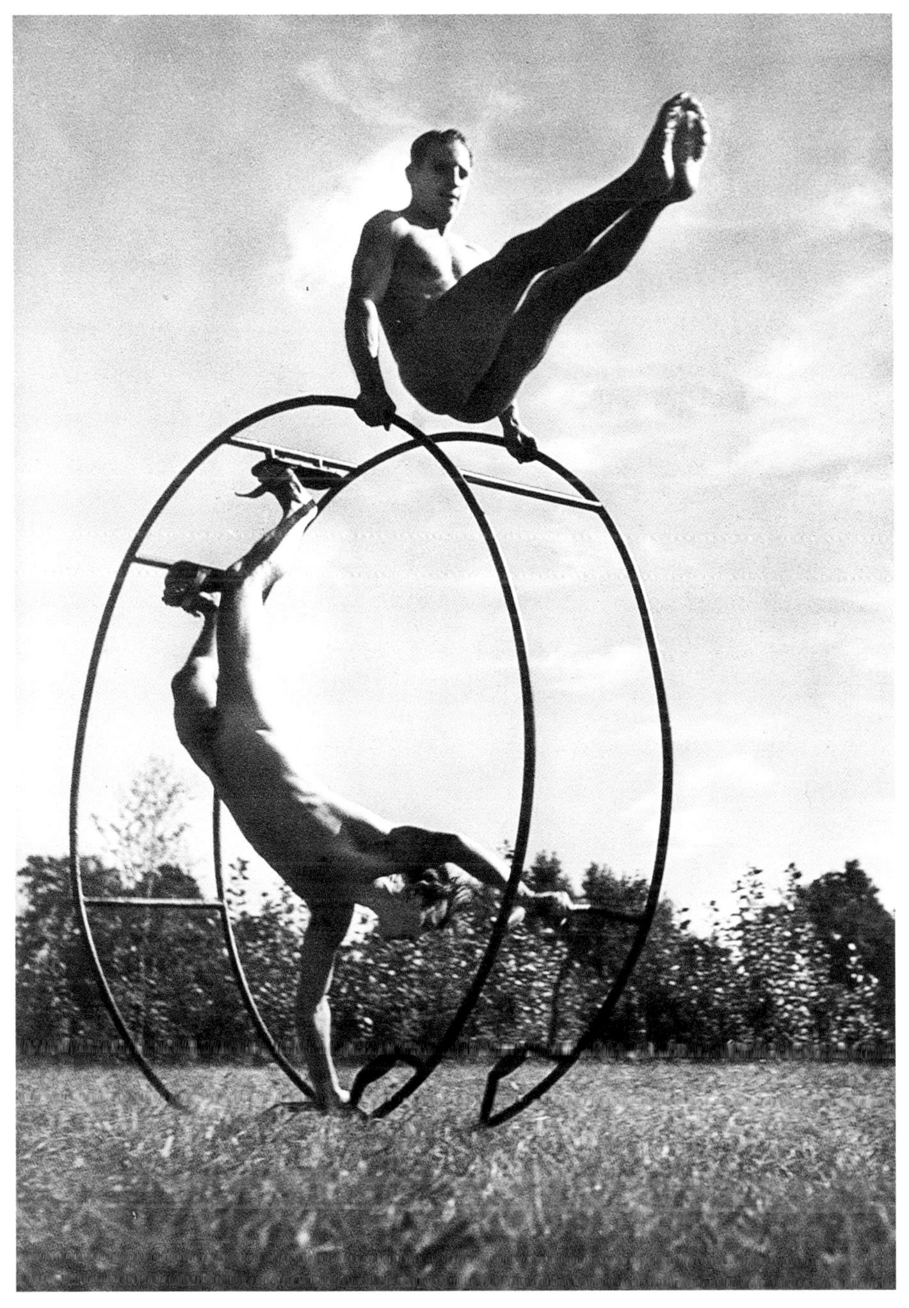

Kurt Reichert, c. 1935

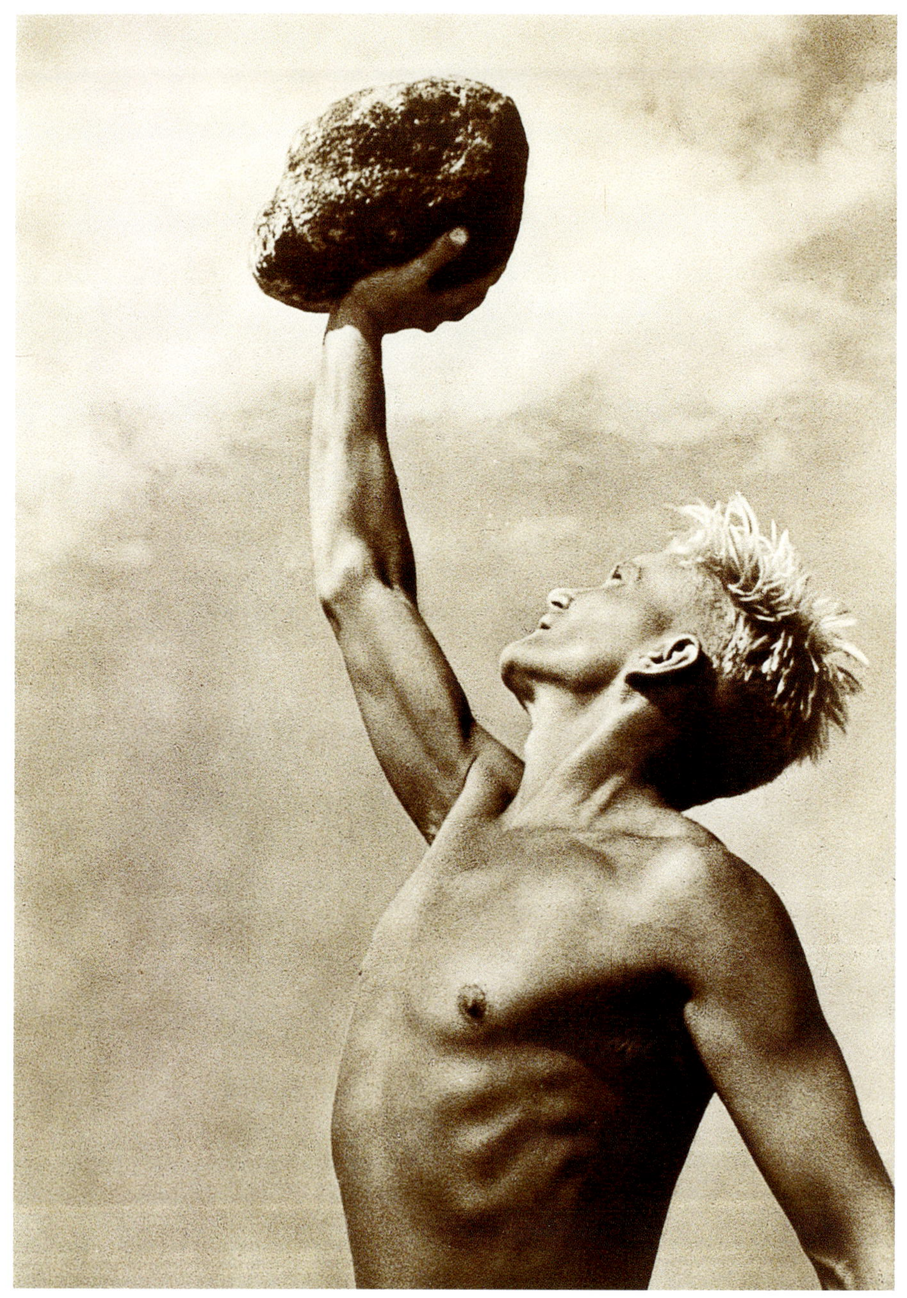

Kurt Reichert, c. 1935

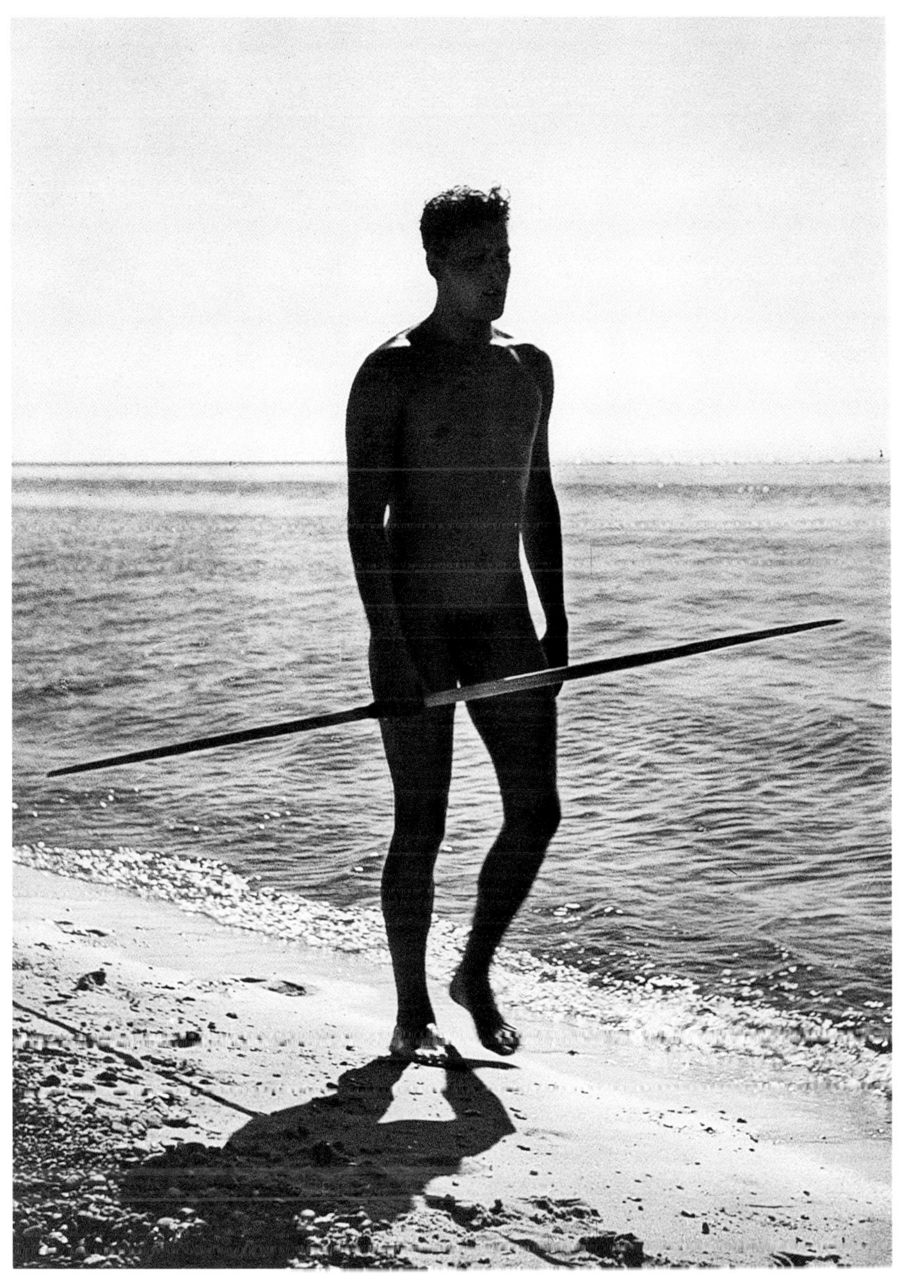

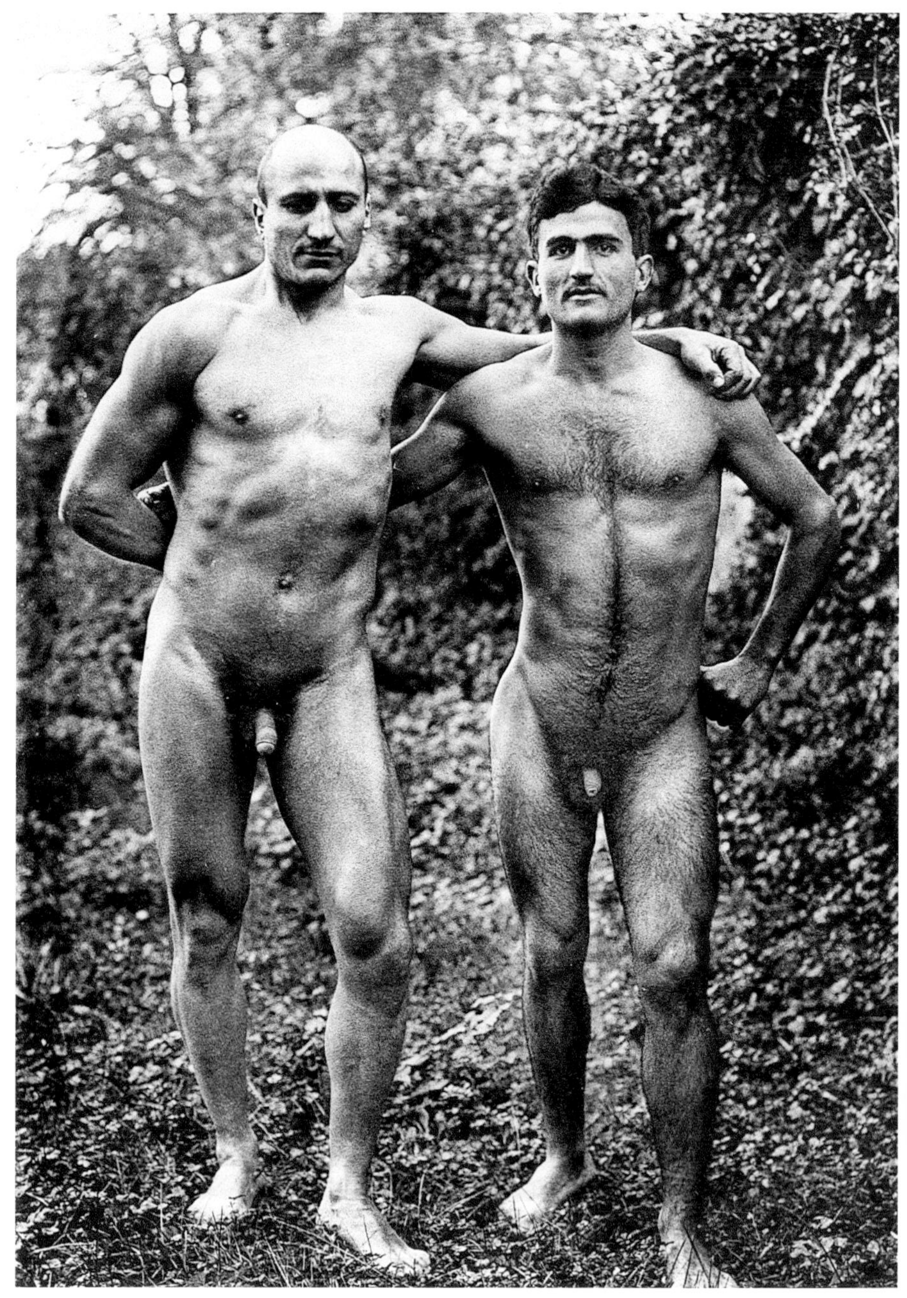

Arthur Schulz, c. 1920

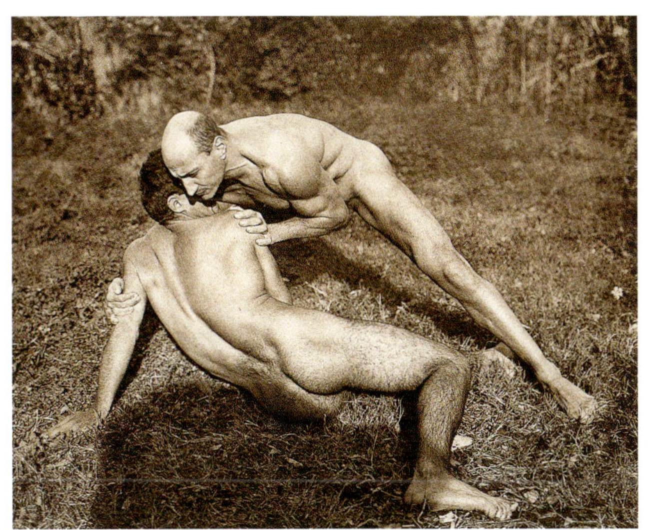

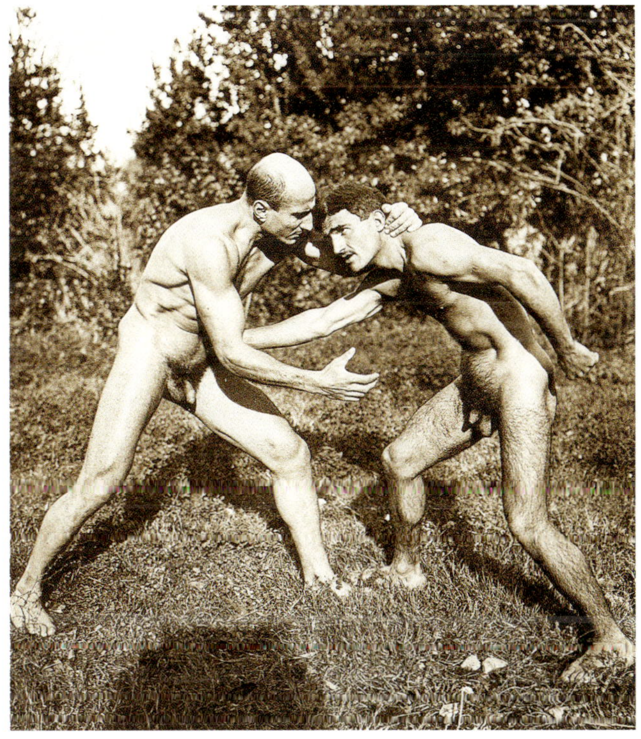

Arthur Schulz, c. 1920

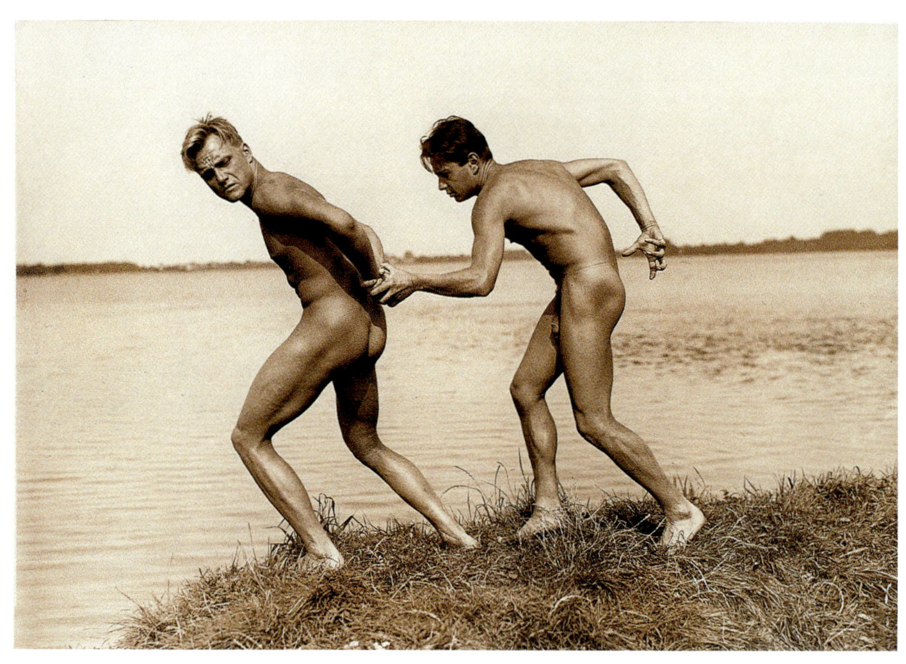

Gerhard Riebicke, c. 1935

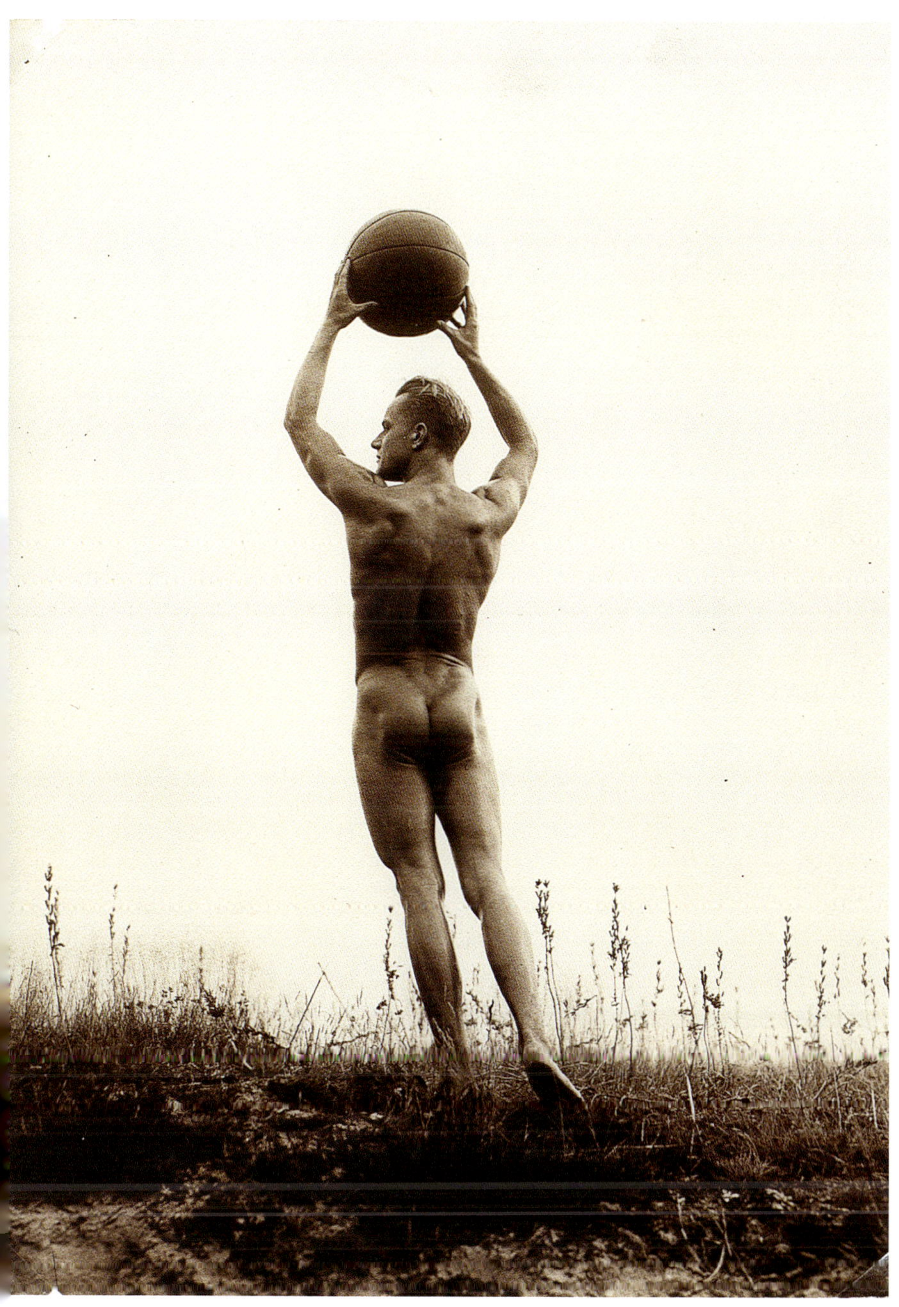

Gerhard Riebicke, c. 1930

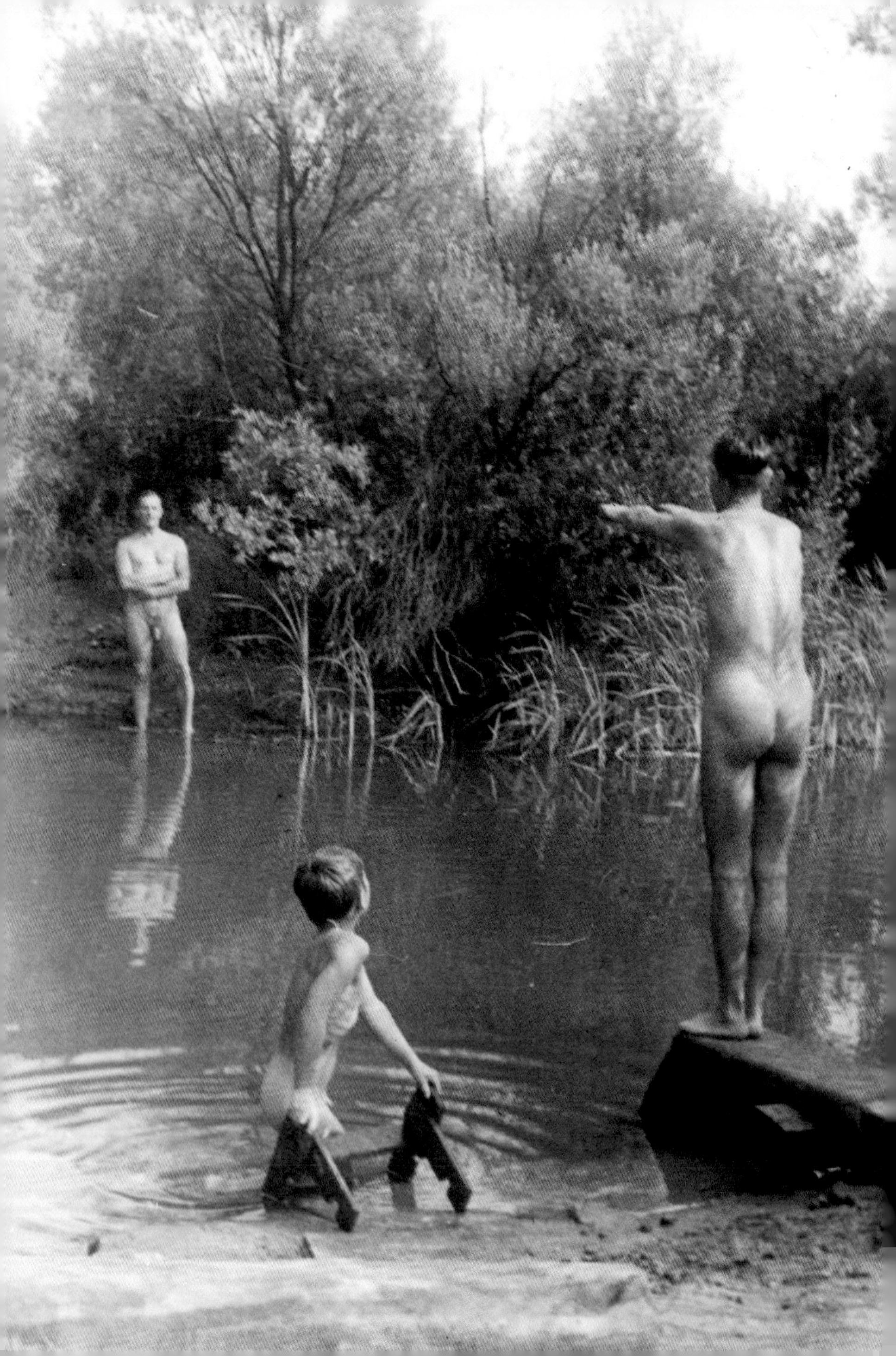

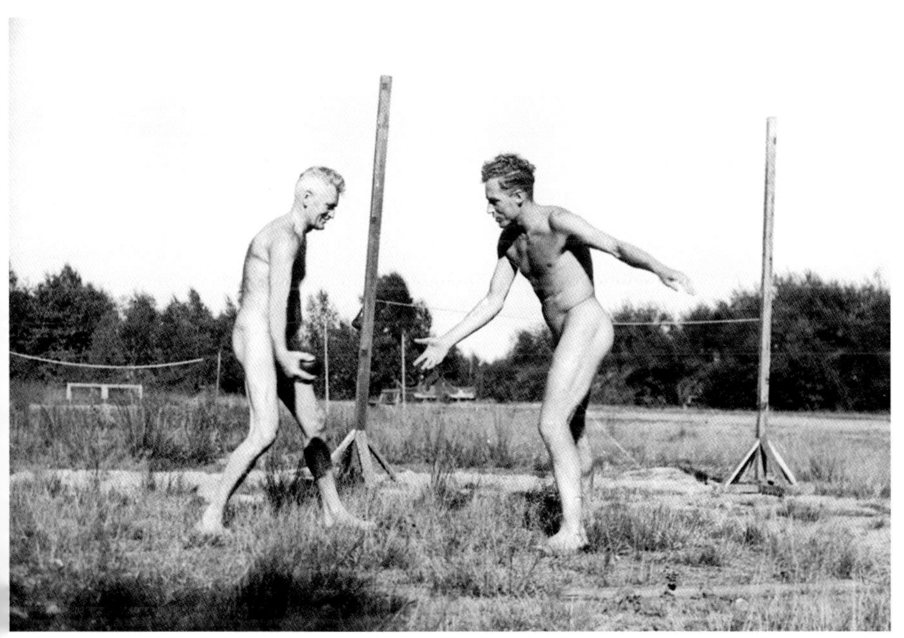

Ingeborg Boysen, c. 1925

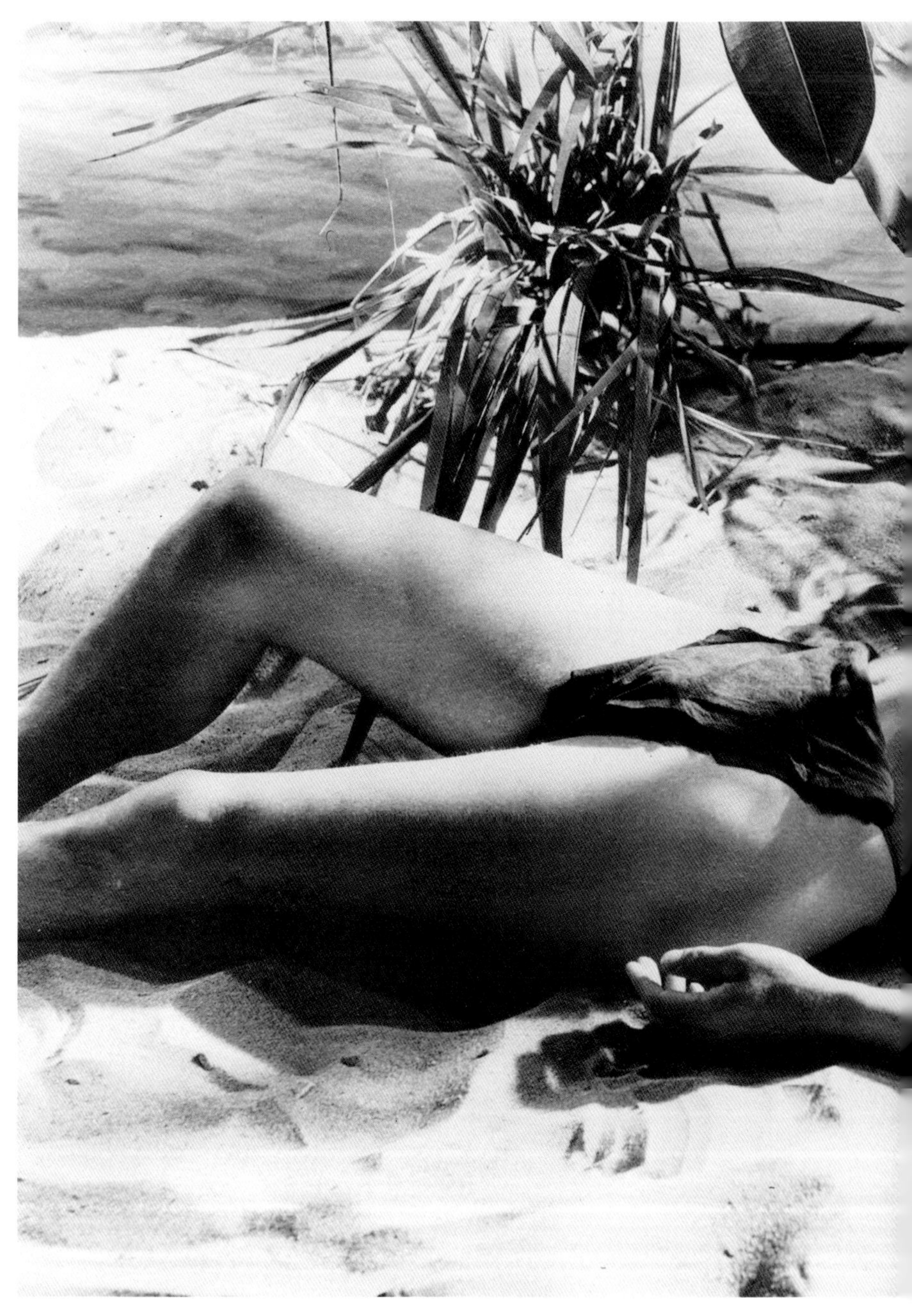

Cecil Beaton, Johnny Weissmüller, 1932

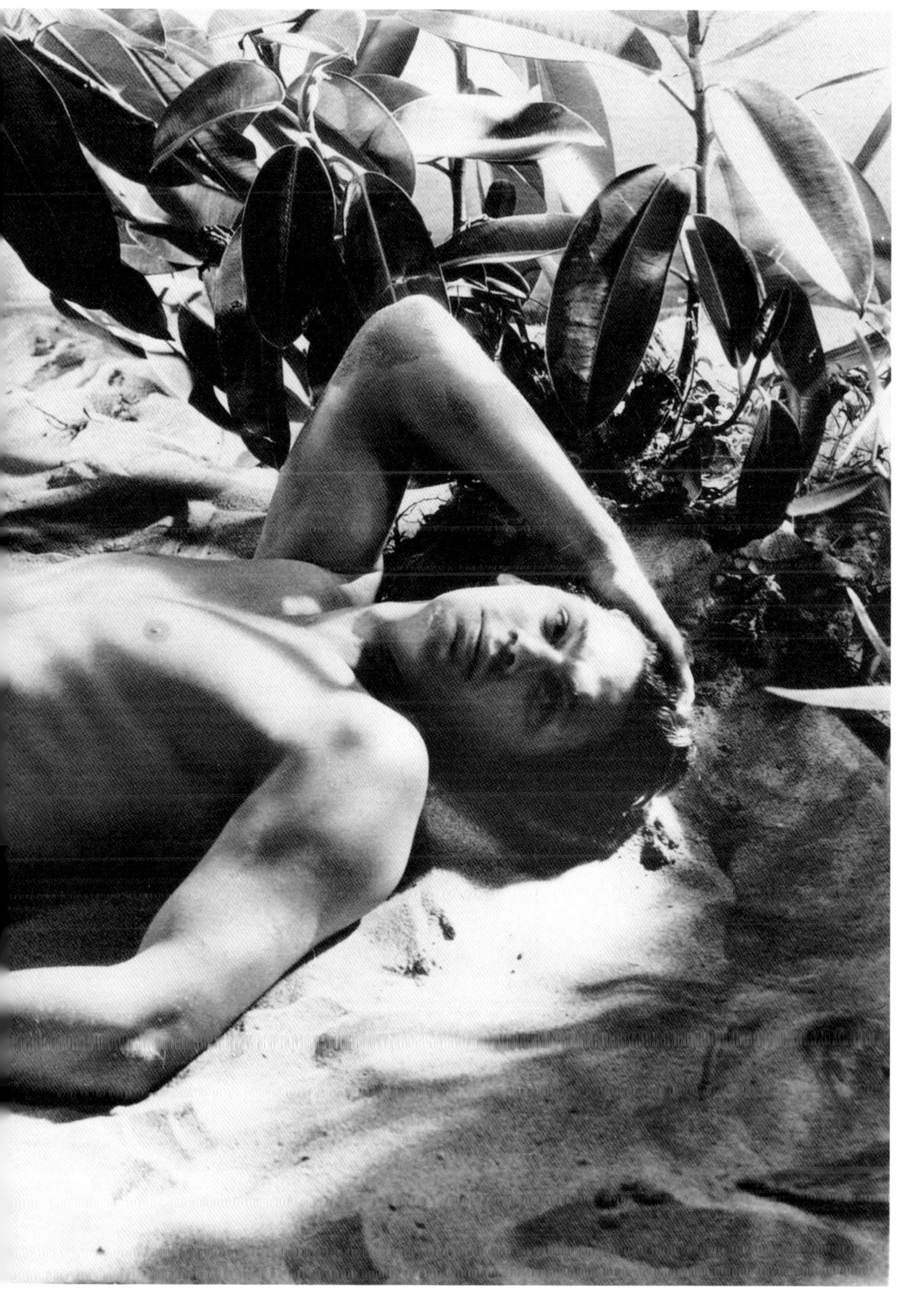

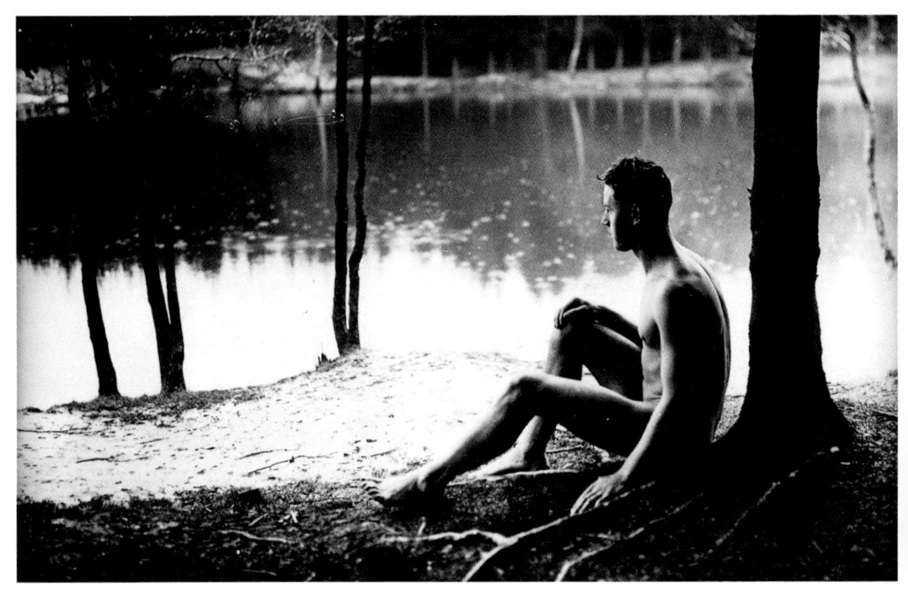

Anonymous, 1925

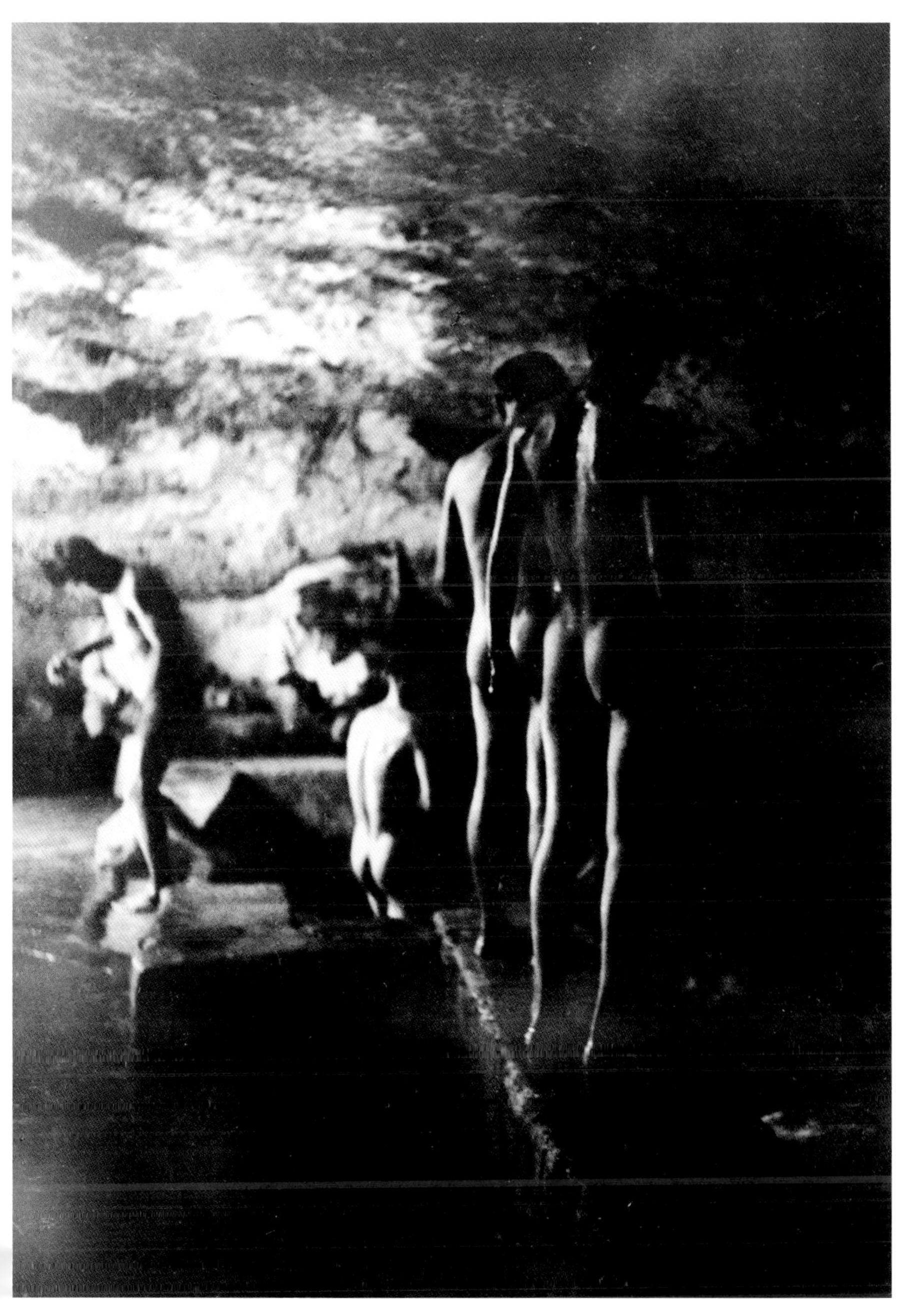

Cecil Beaton, Photograph in the Manner of El Greco, 1935

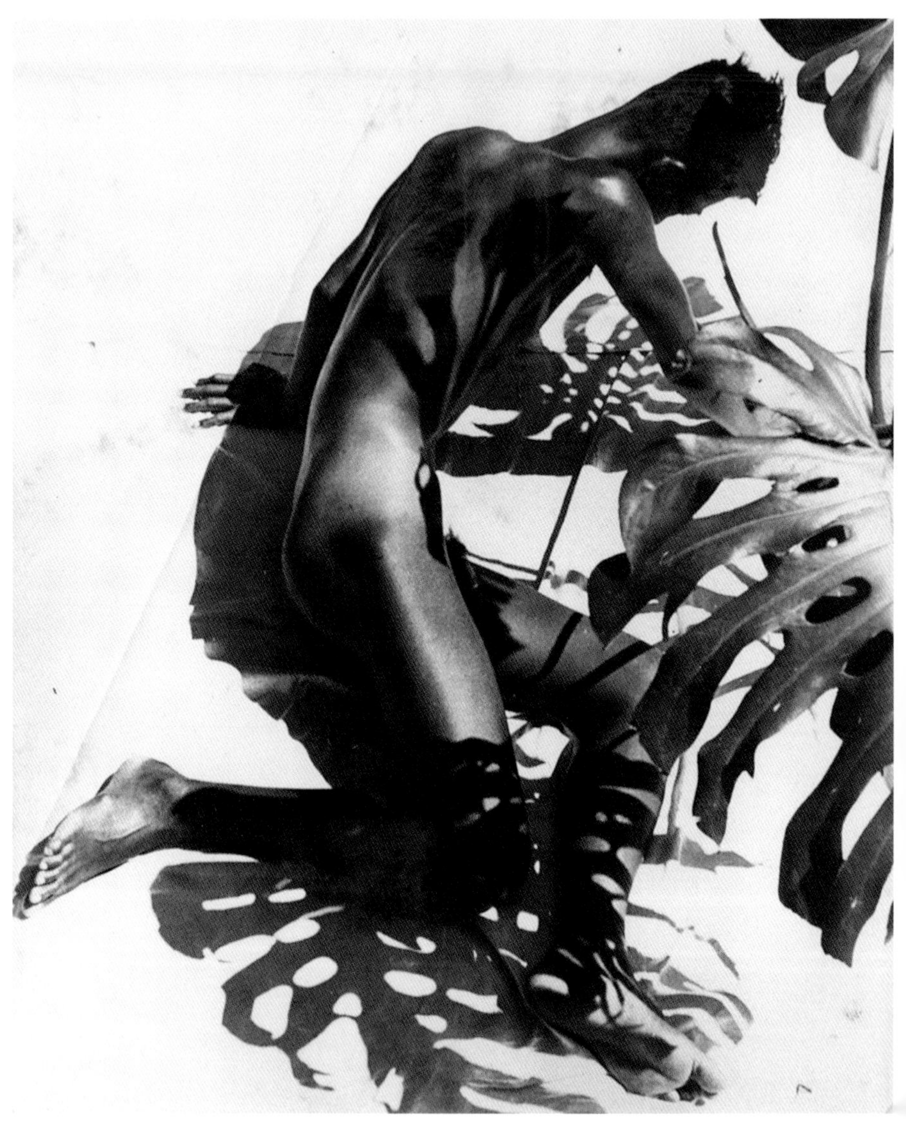

George Hoyningen-Huene, c. 1930

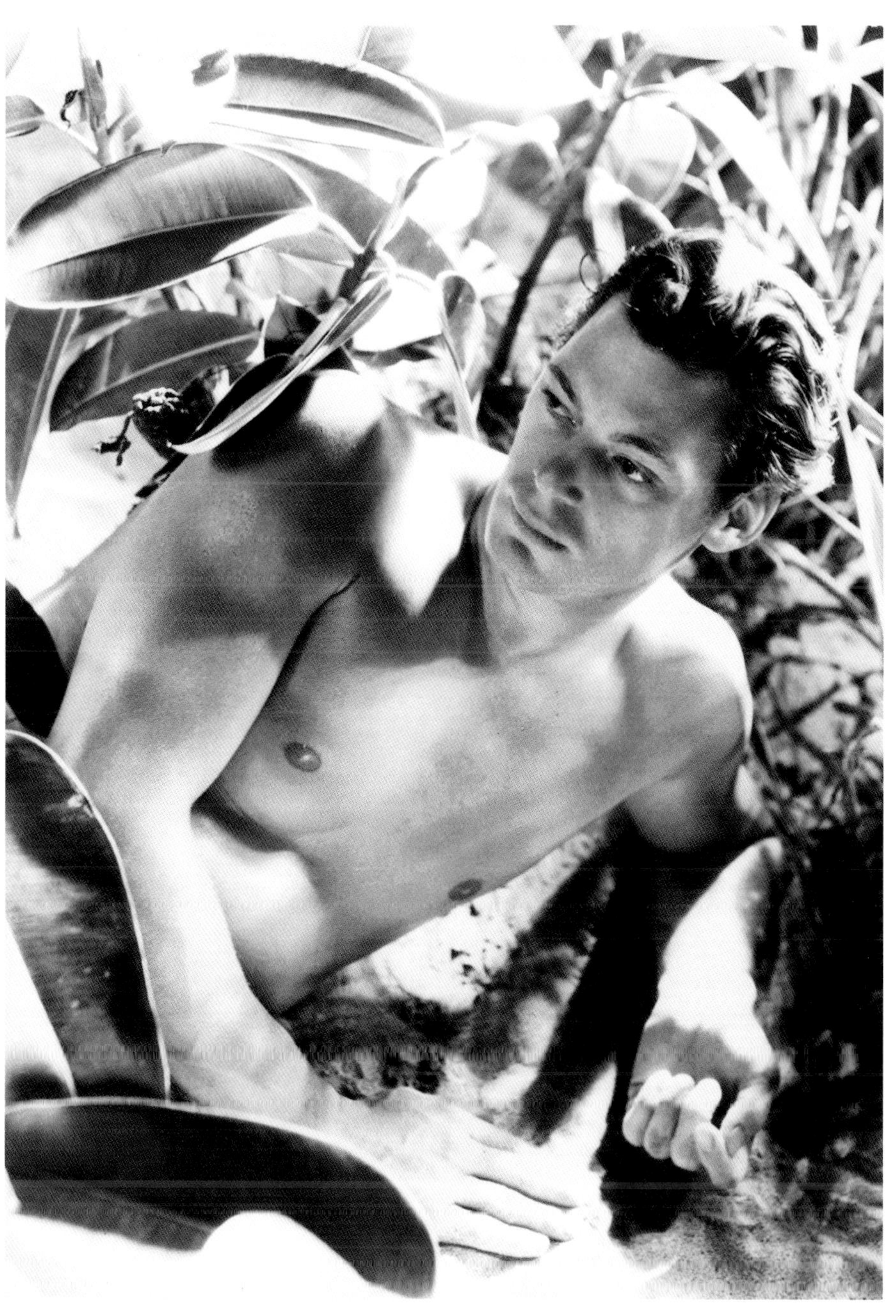

Cecil Beaton, Johnny Weissmüller, 1932

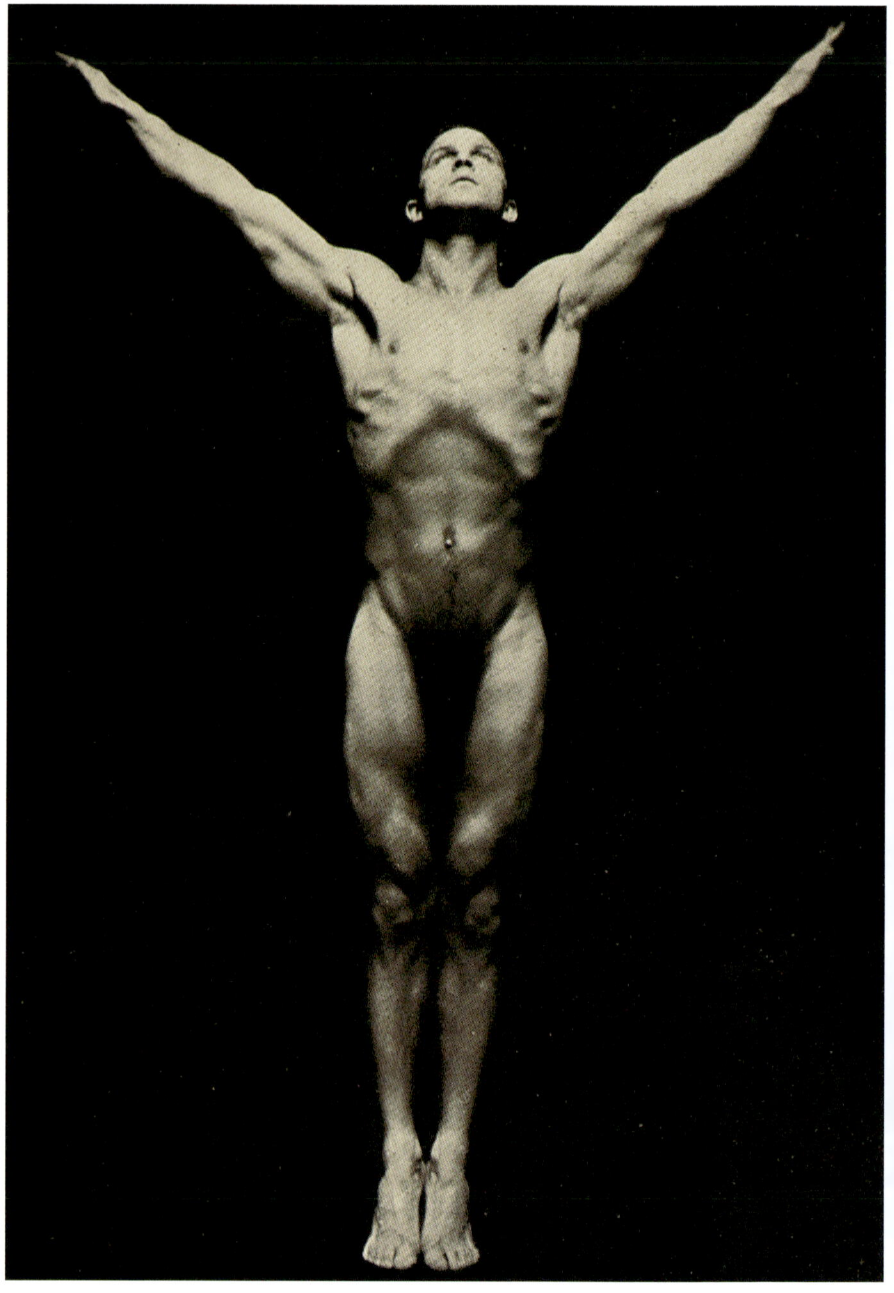

Edwin F. Townsend, Tony Sansone, c. 1930

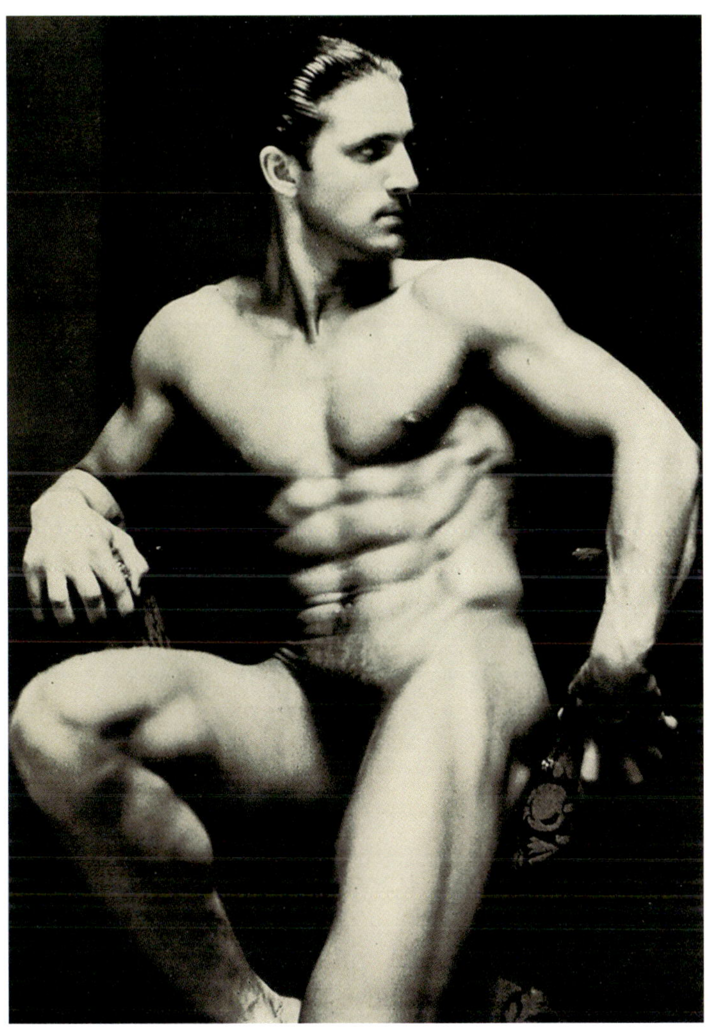

Edwin F. Townsend, Tony Sansone, c. 1930

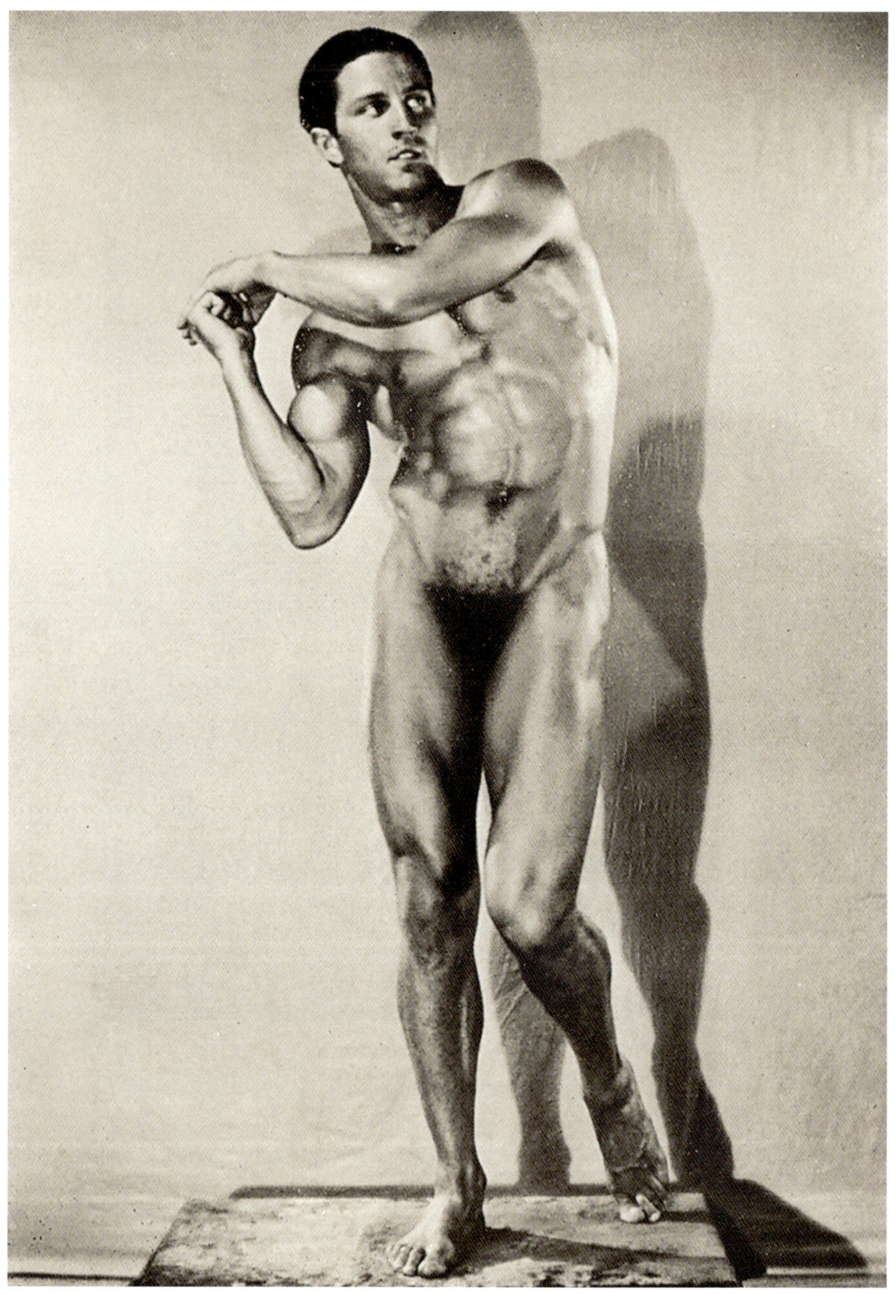

Edwin F. Townsend, Tony Sansone, c. 1930

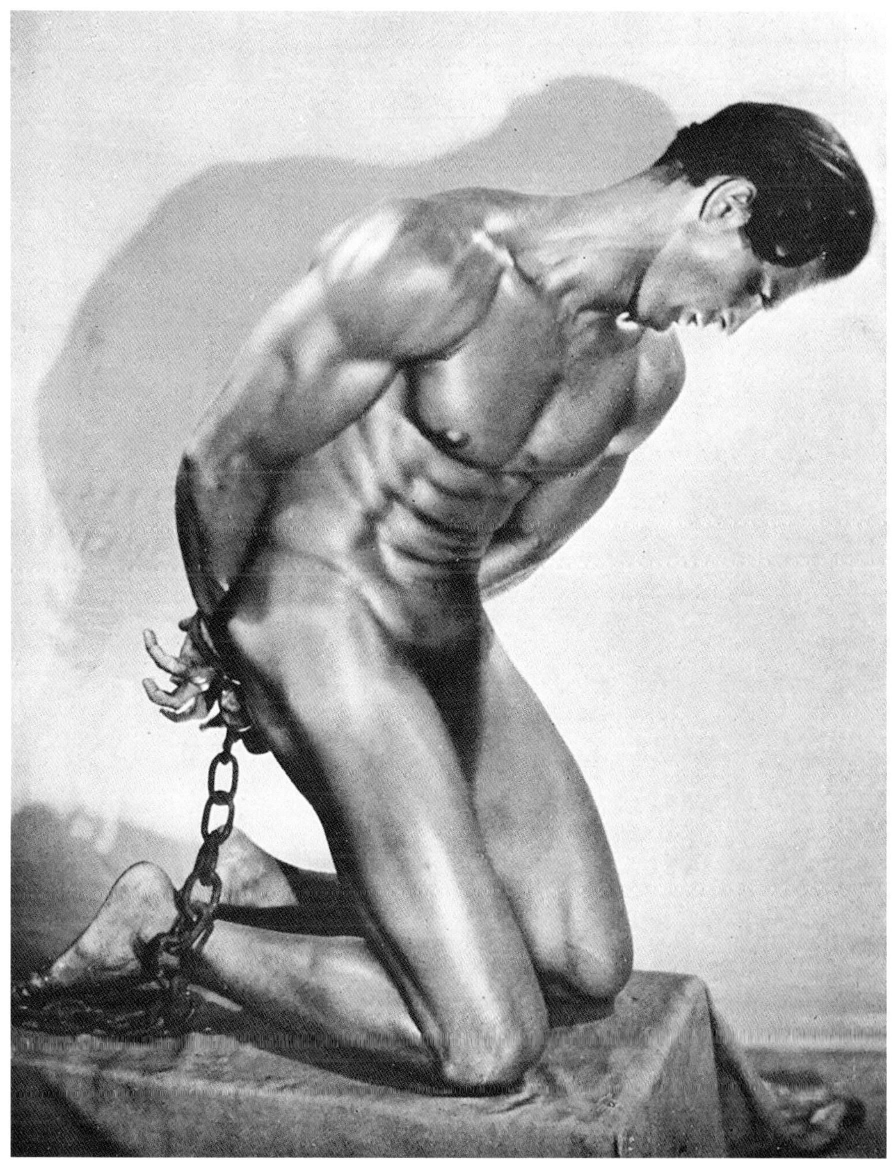

Edwin F. Townsend, Tony Sansone, c. 1930

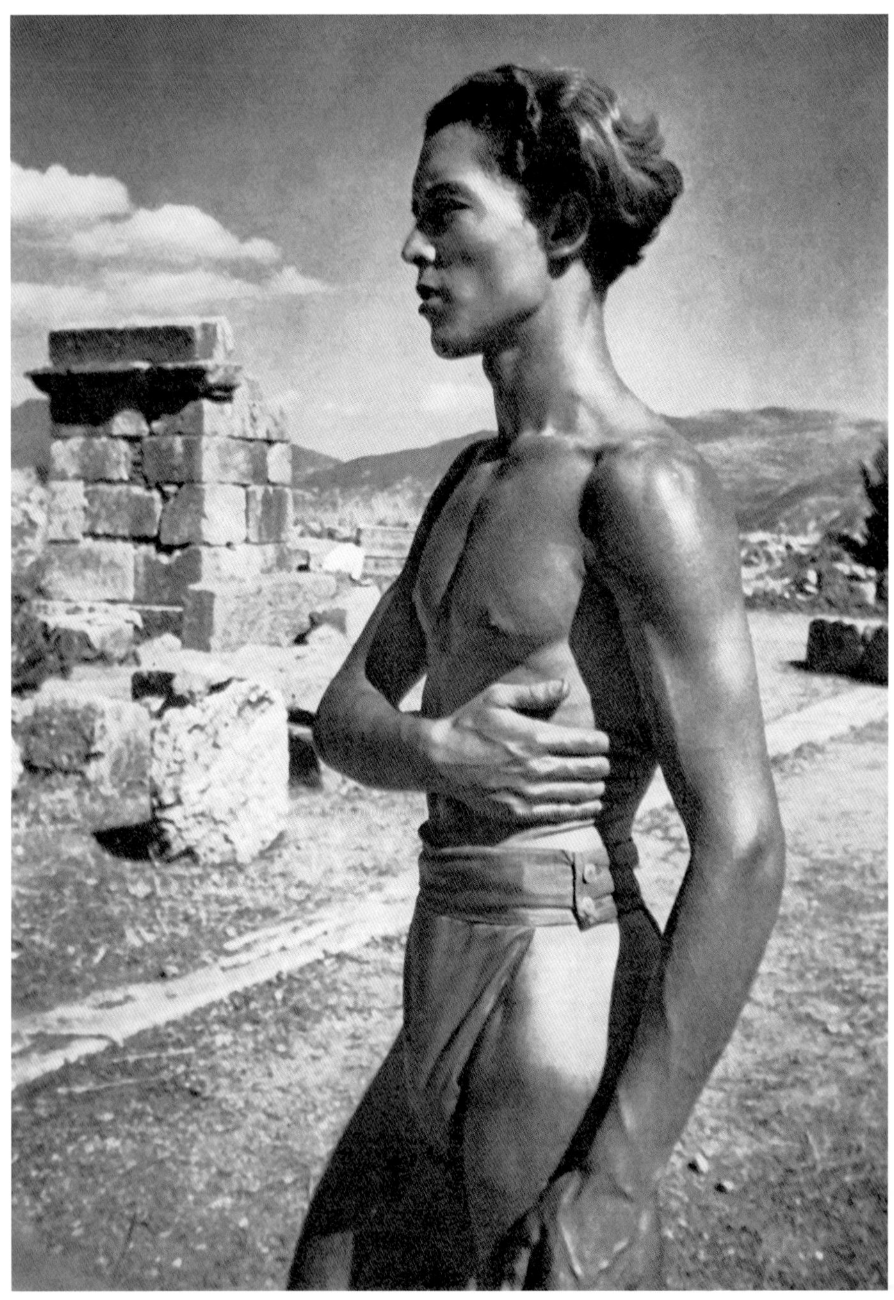

  Leni Riefenstahl, Junger Grieche aus Pyrgos, 1936

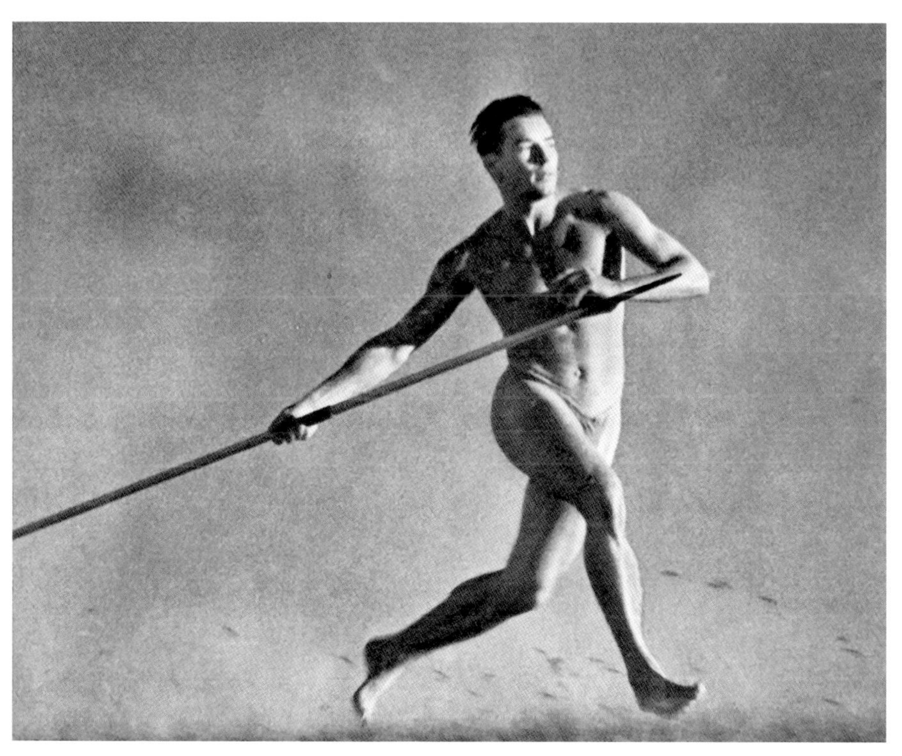

Leni Riefenstahl, Der Speerwerfer, 1936

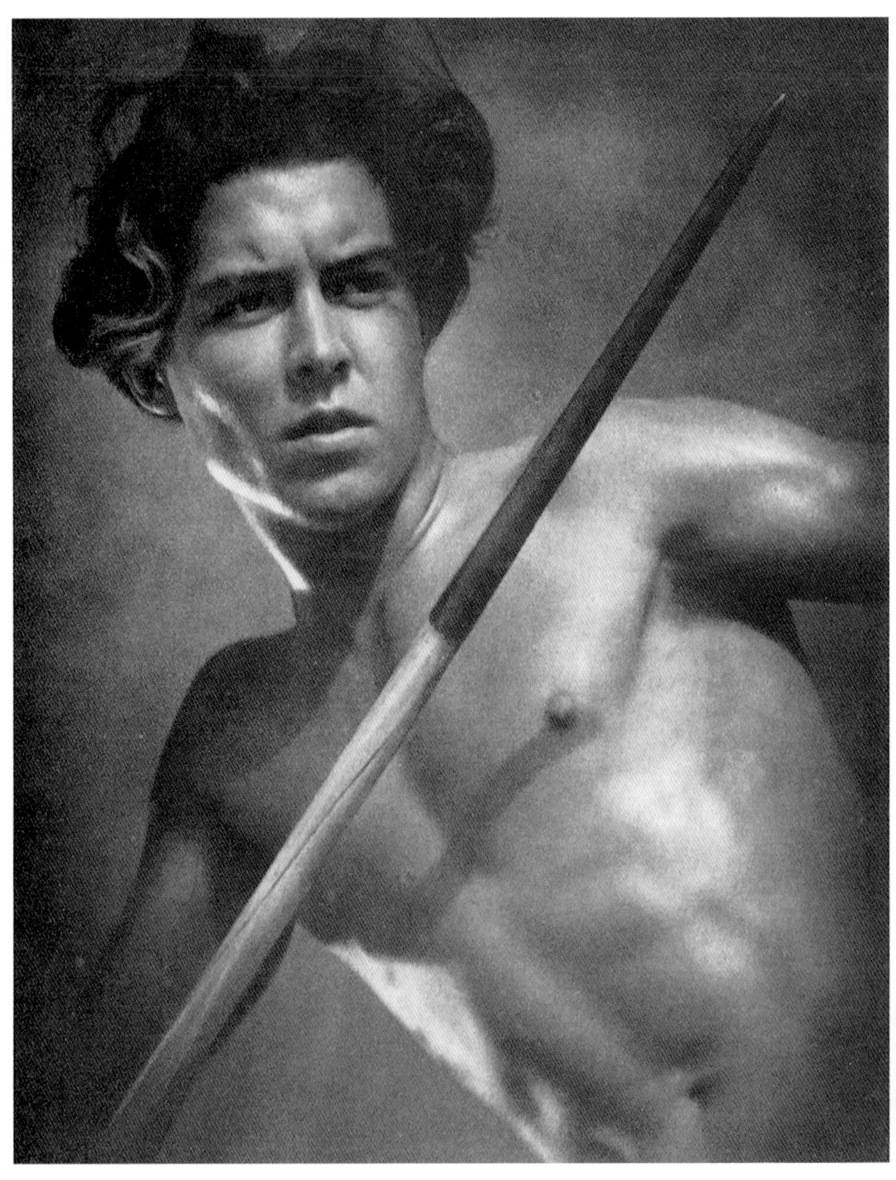

Leni Riefenstahl, Junger Athlet, 1936

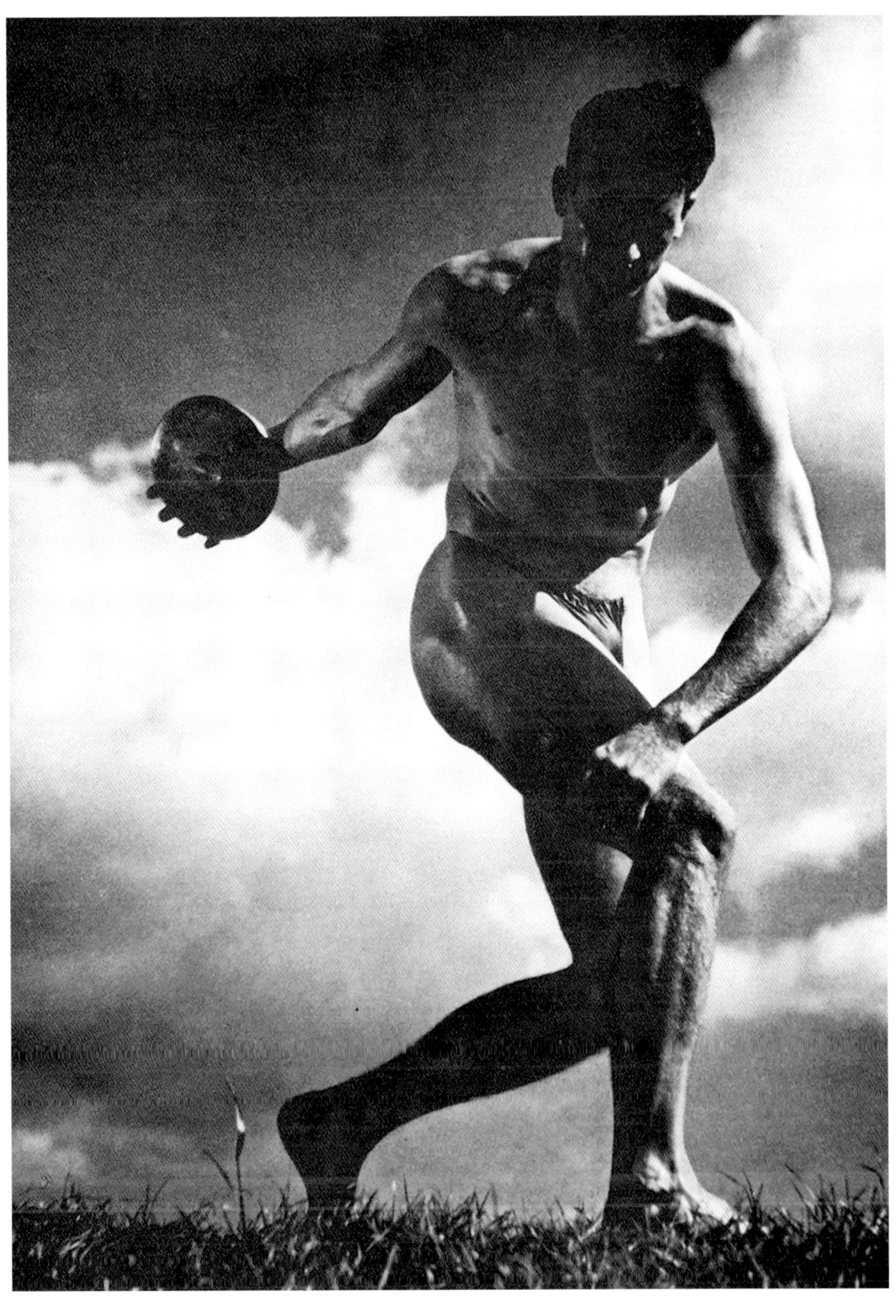

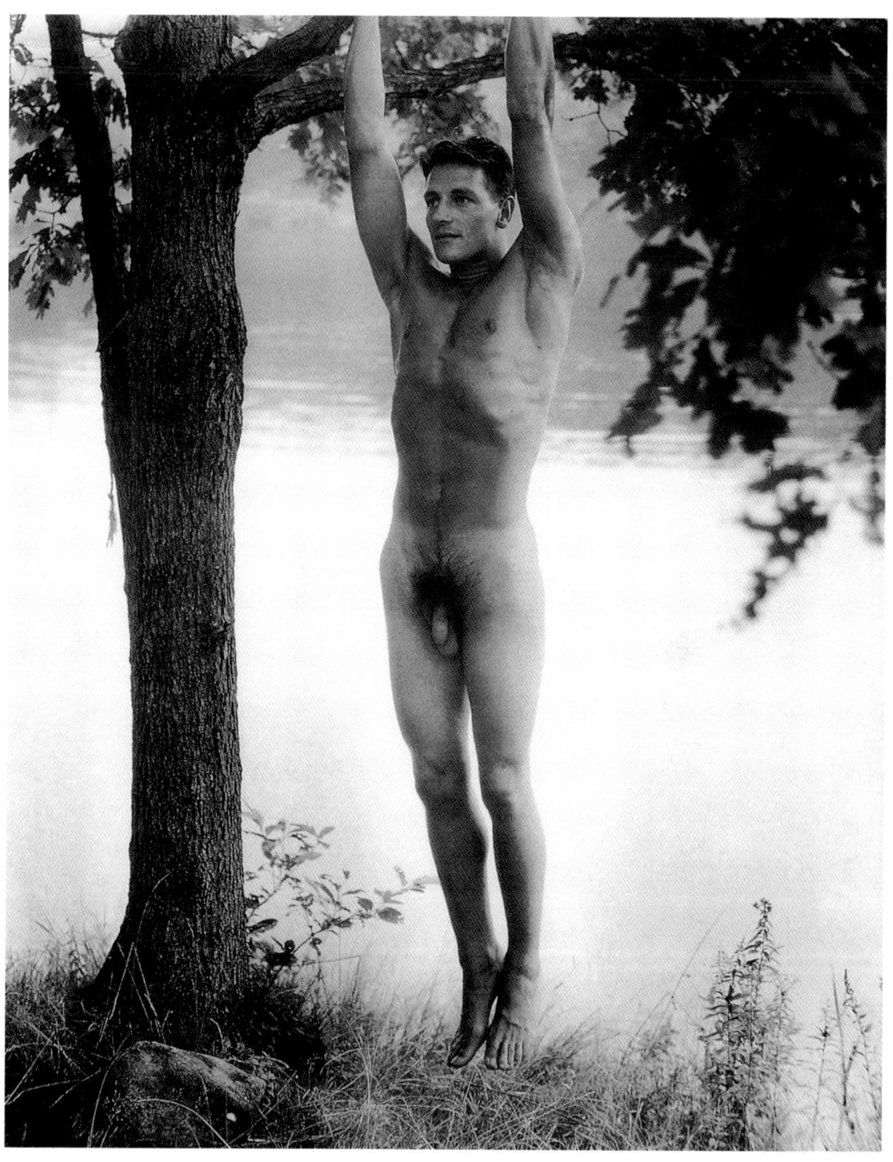

The Ritter Brothers, 1932–35

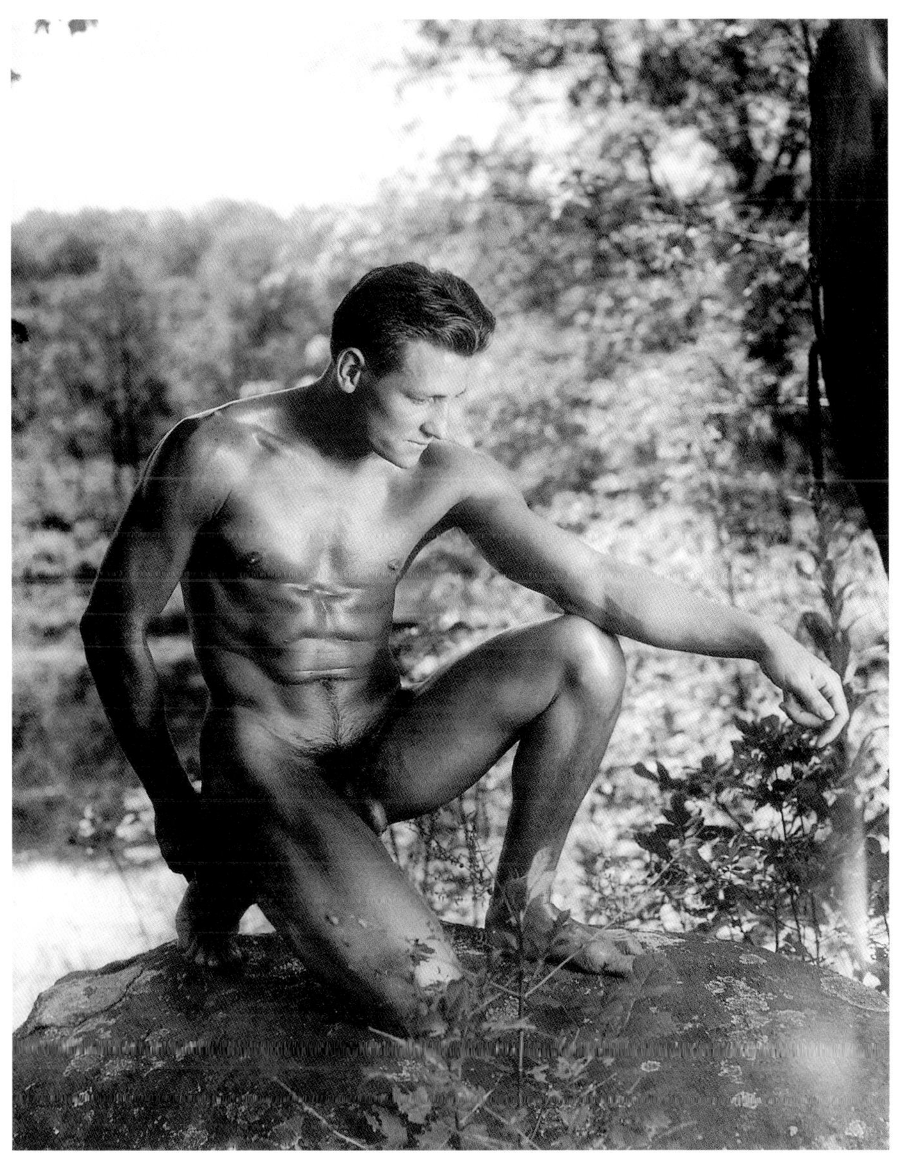

The Ritter Brothers, 1932–35

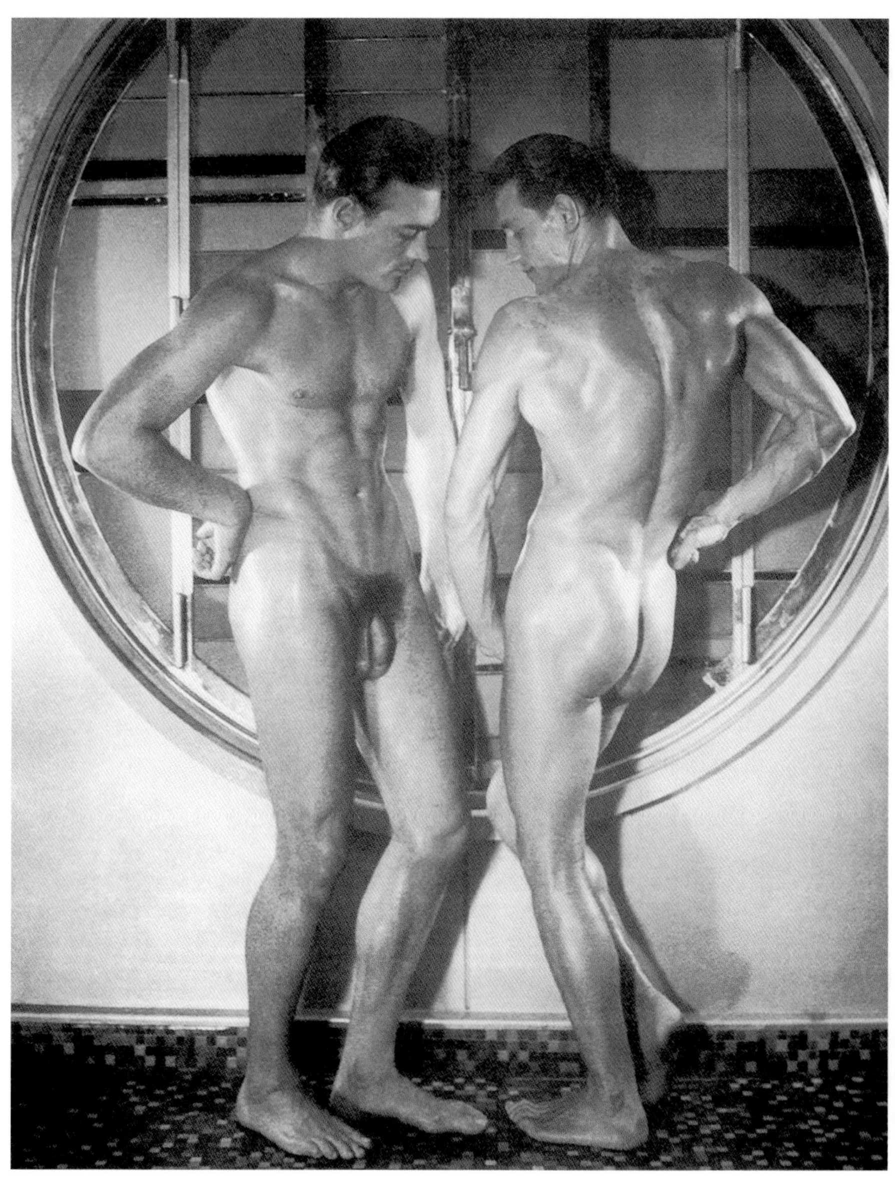

The Ritter Brothers, 1932–35

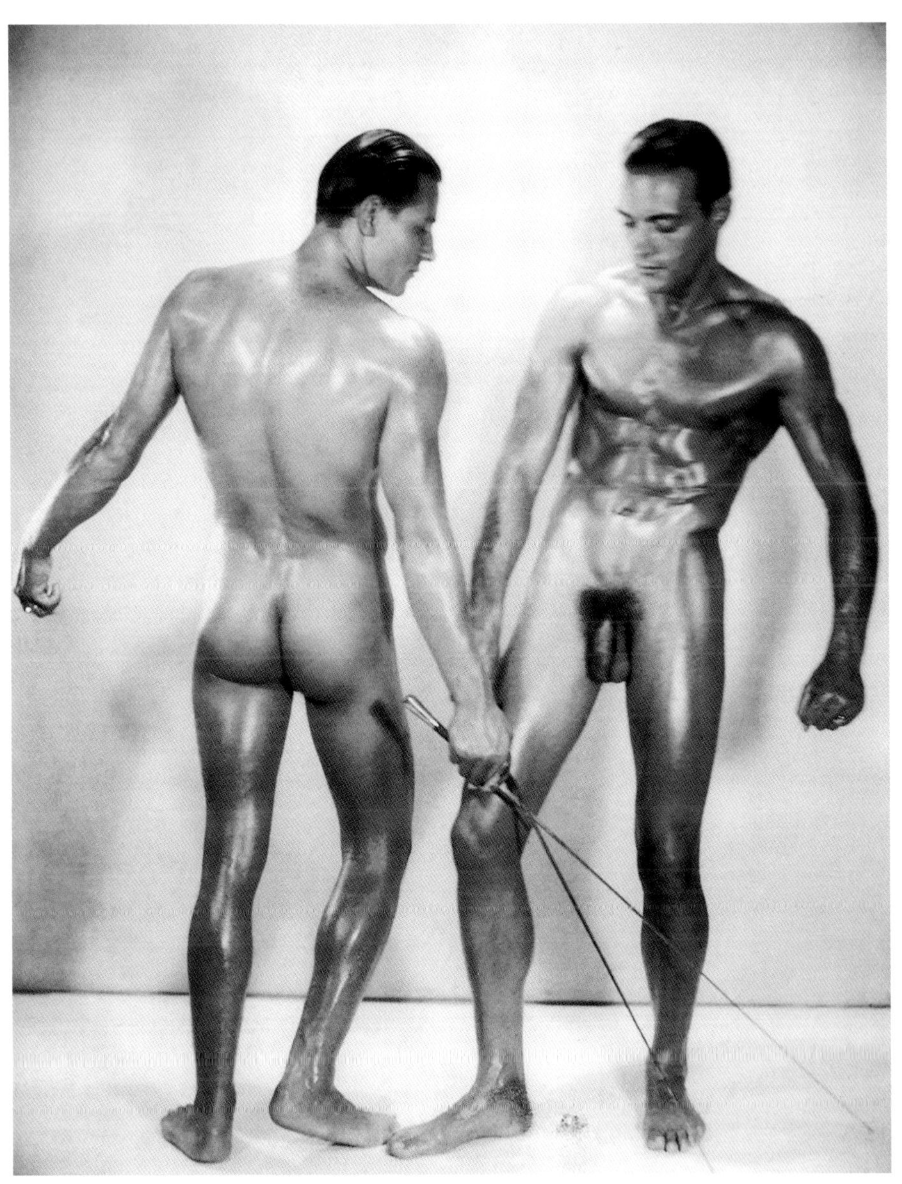

The Ritter Brothers, 1932–35

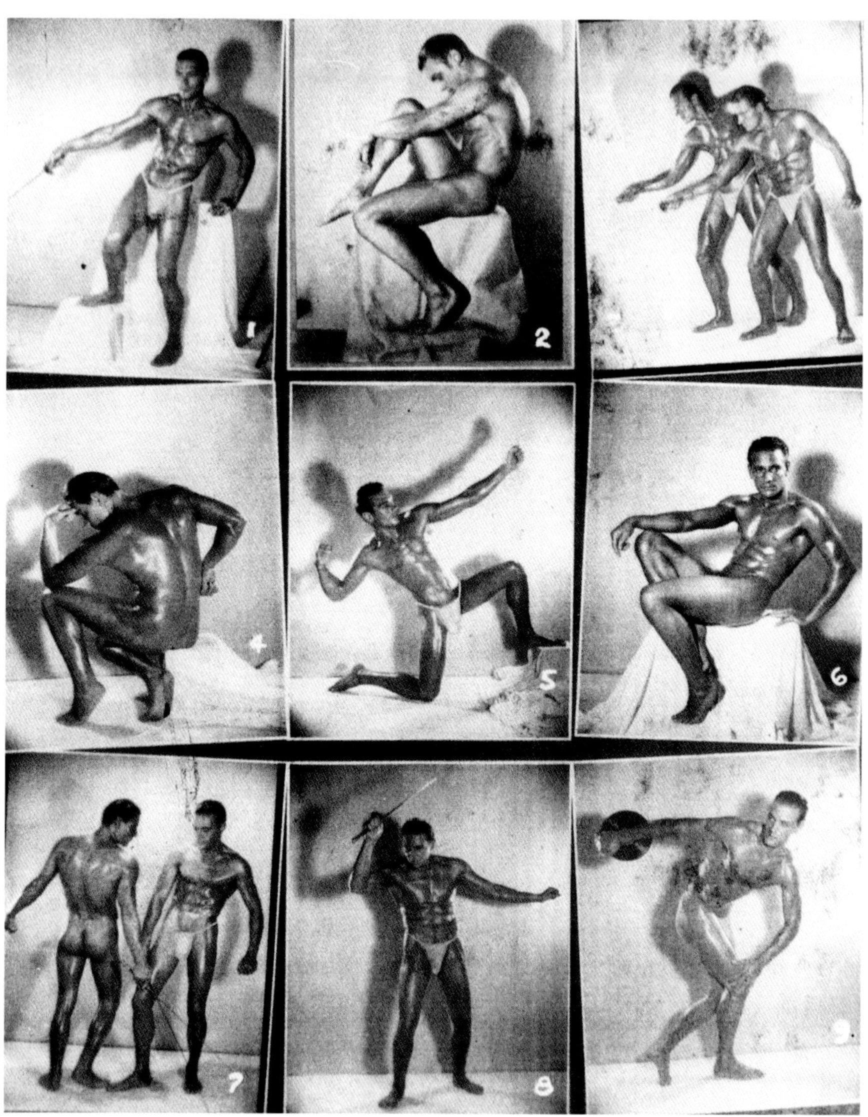

The Ritter Brothers, c. 1934

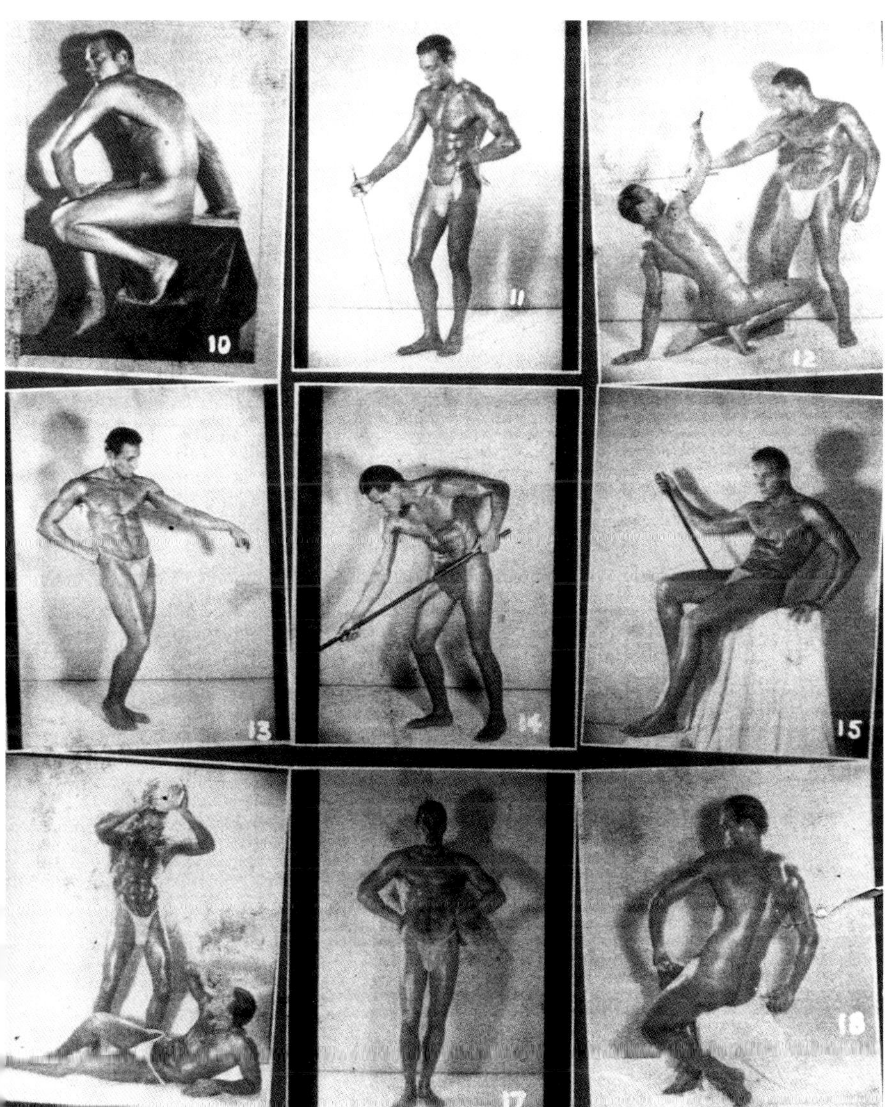

The Ritter Brothers, c. 1934

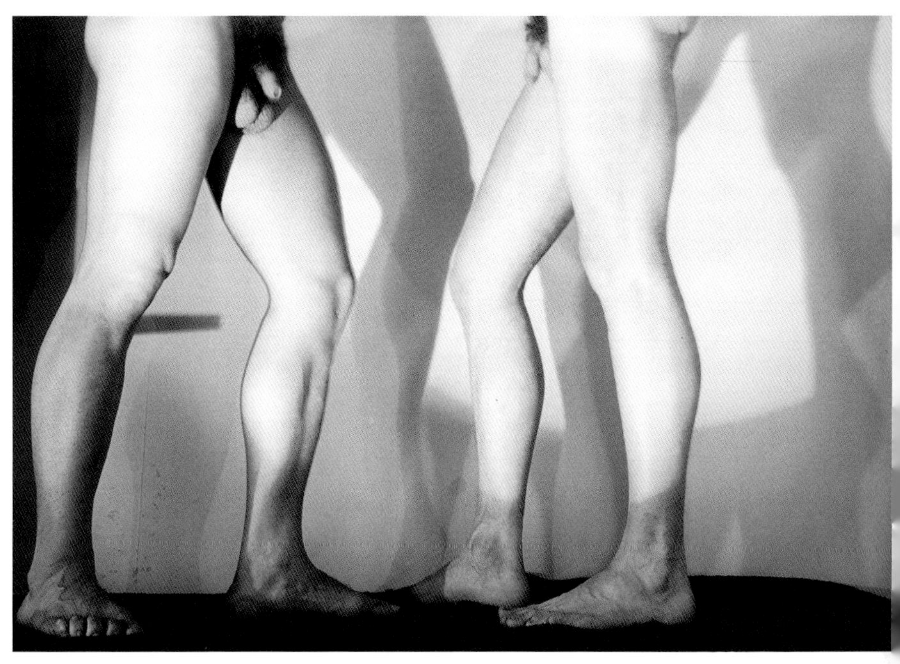

George Platt Lynes, Fred Ritter and his Brother, c. 1934

George Platt Lynes, Fred Ritter and his Brother, c. 1934

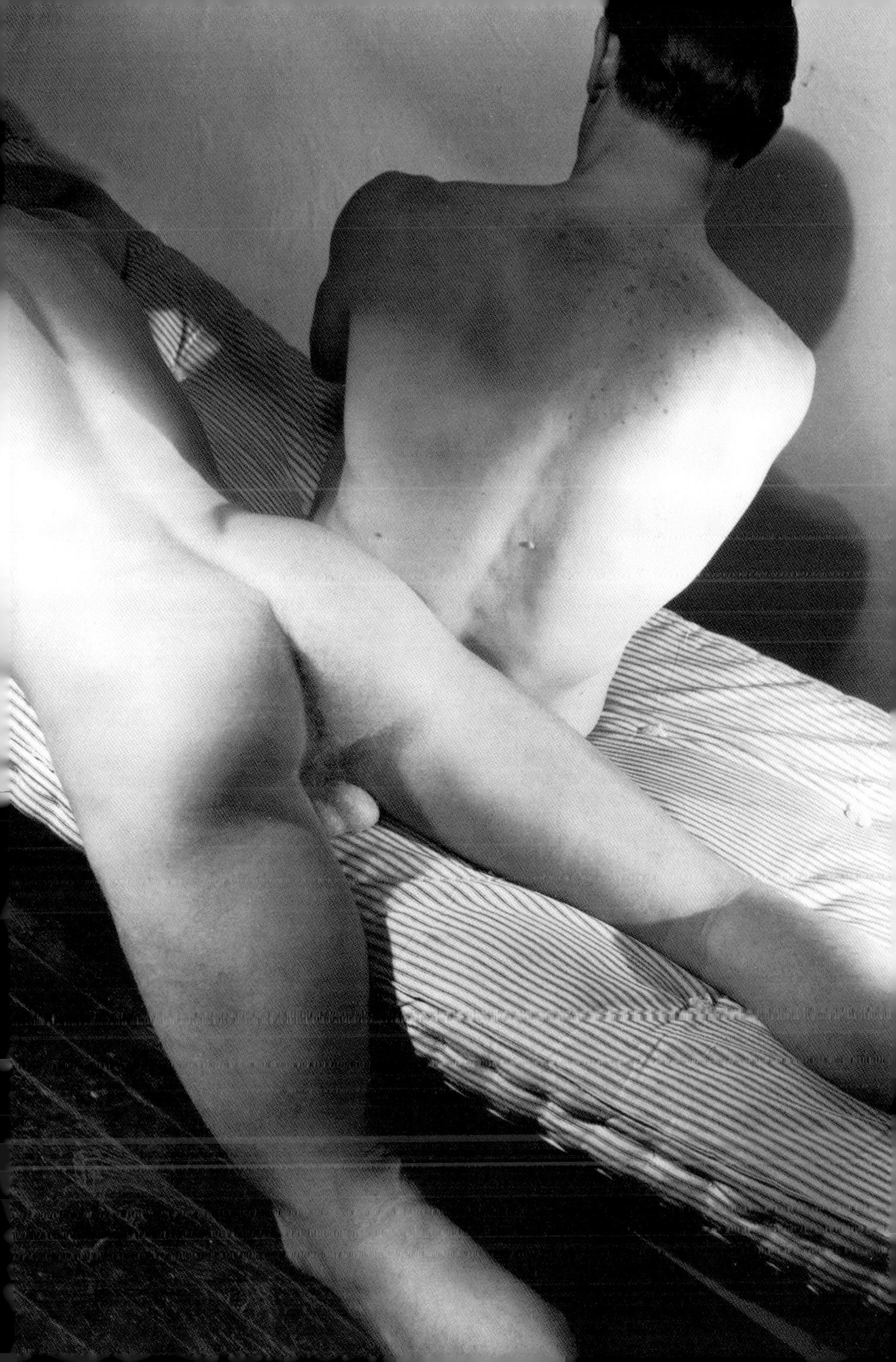

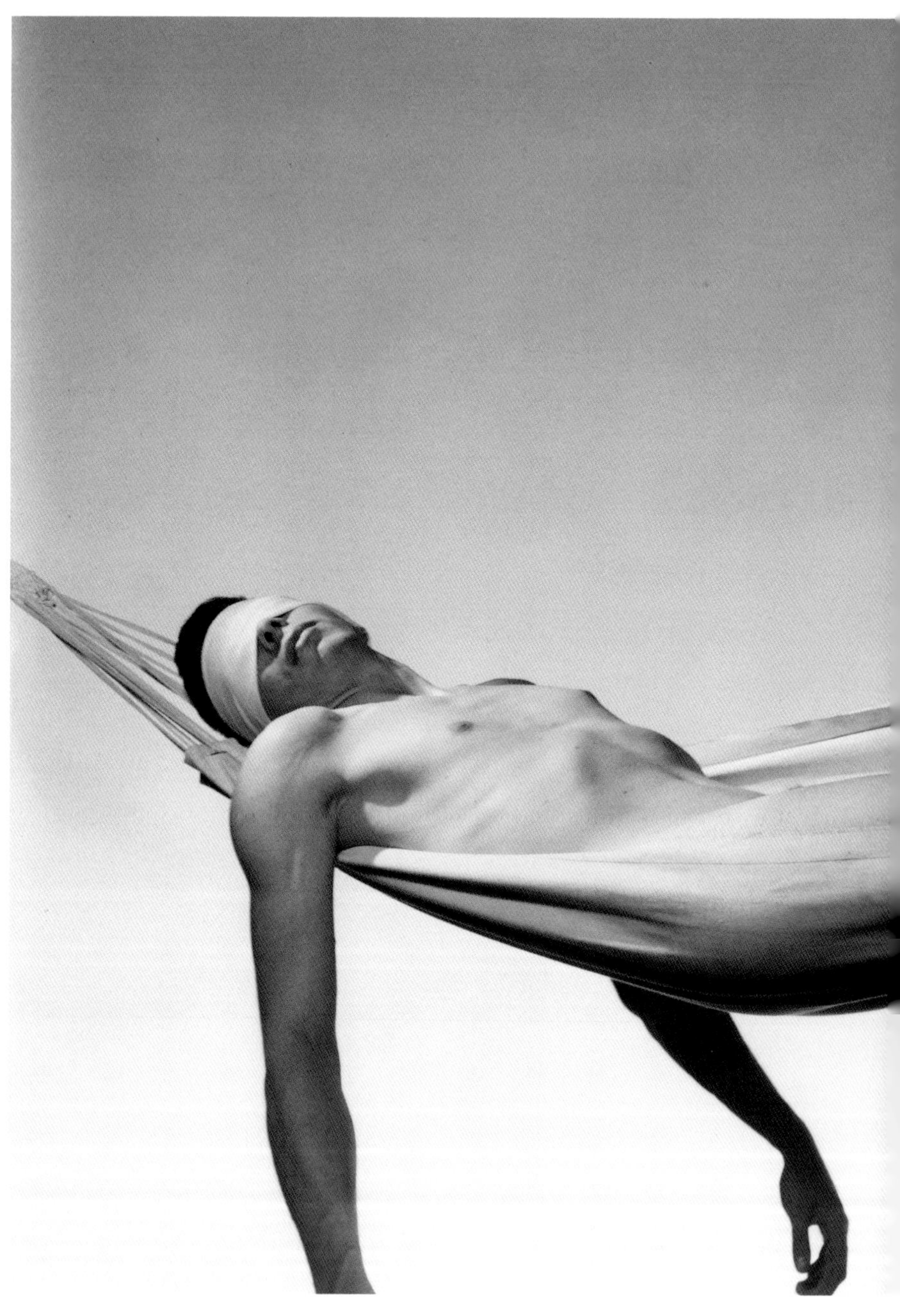

George Platt Lynes, George Tichenor, c. 1940

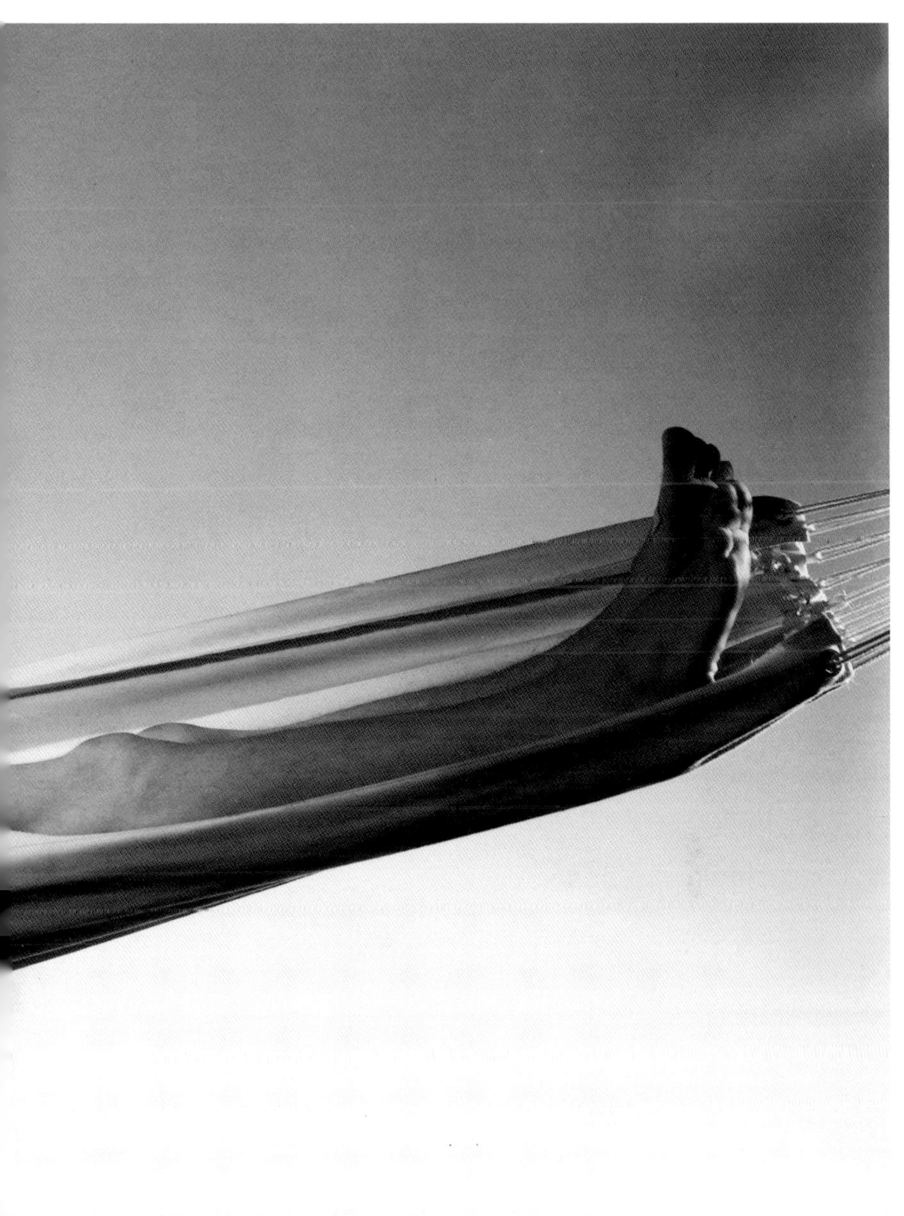

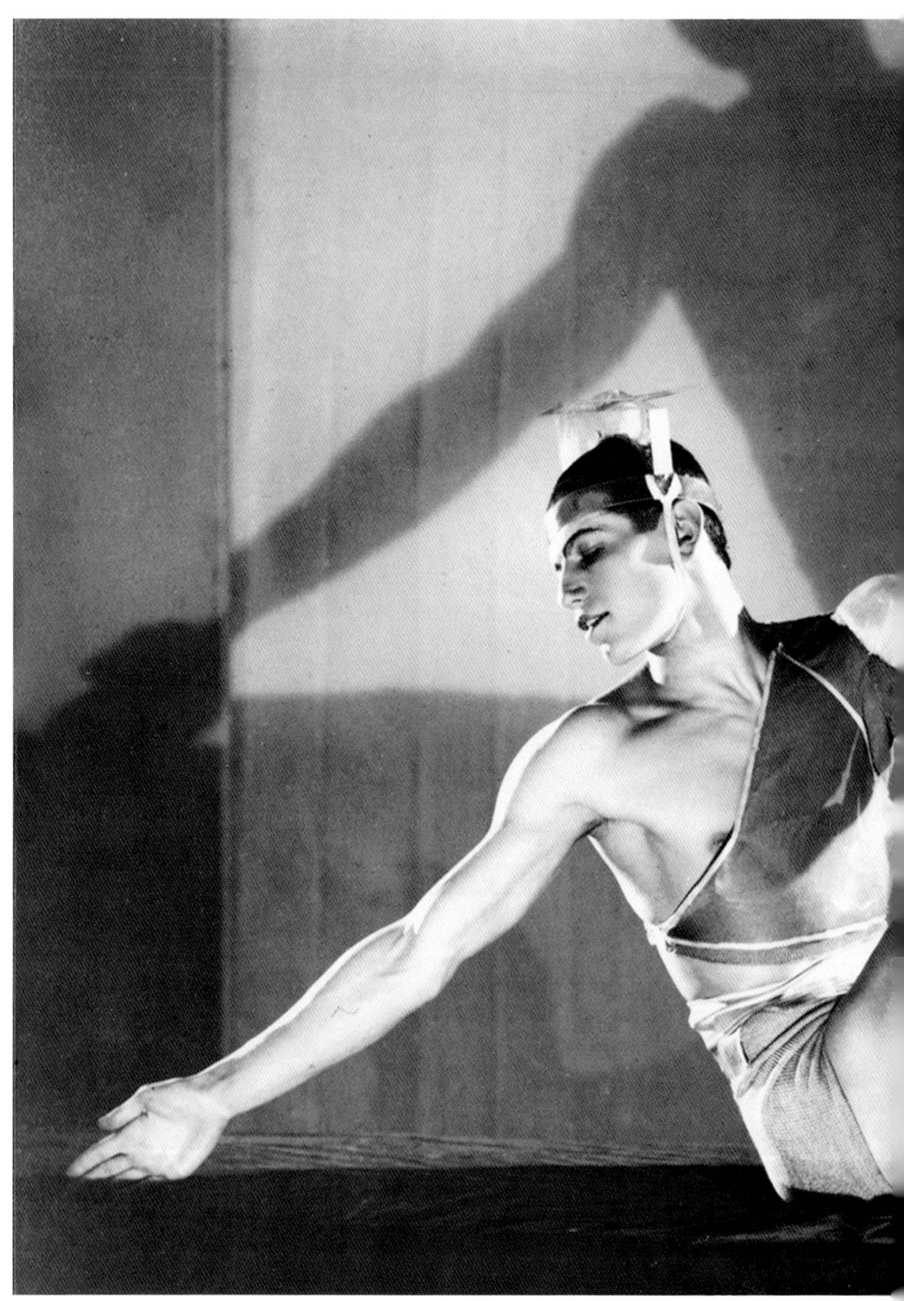

George Hoyningen-Huene, Serge Lifar in "La Chatte", 1927

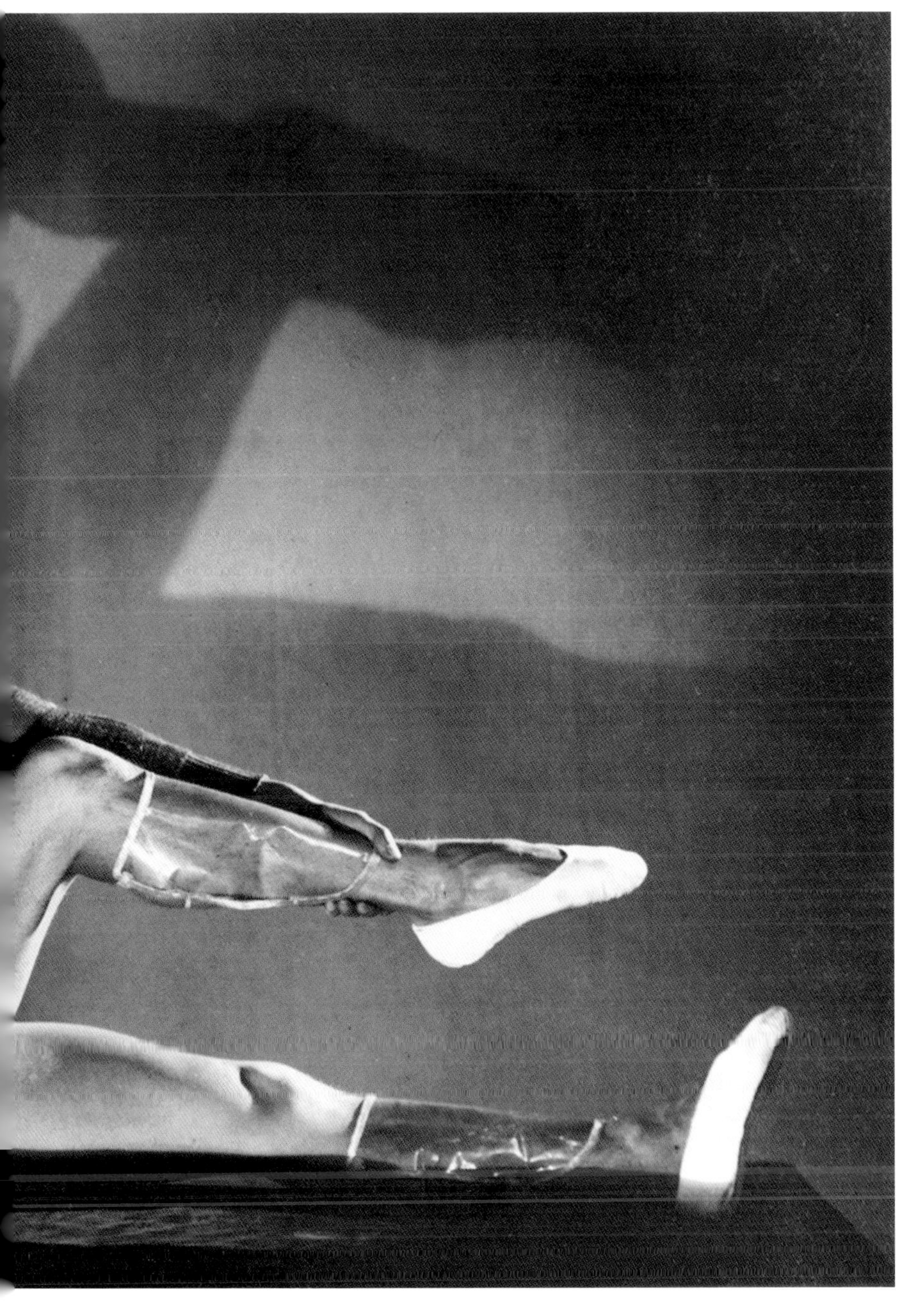

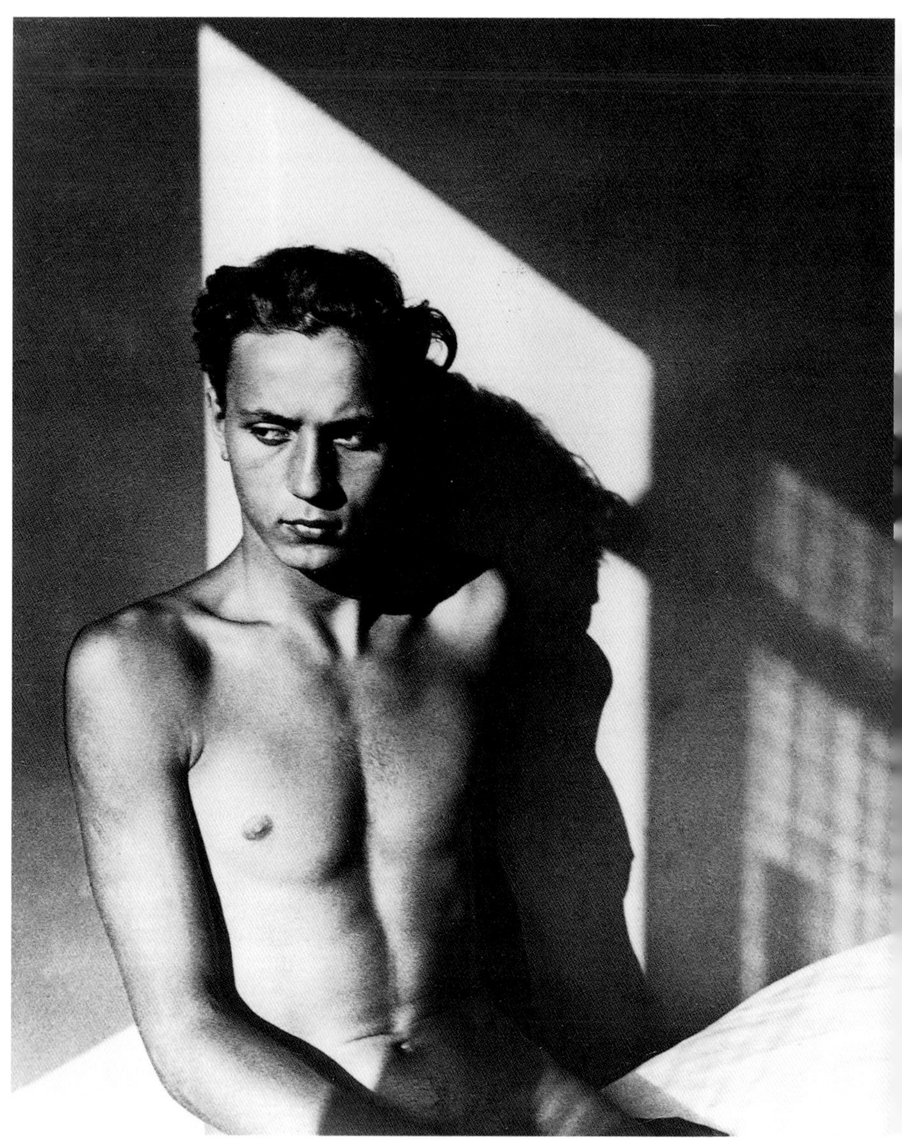

Herbert List, Junger Mann im Morgenlicht, 1932

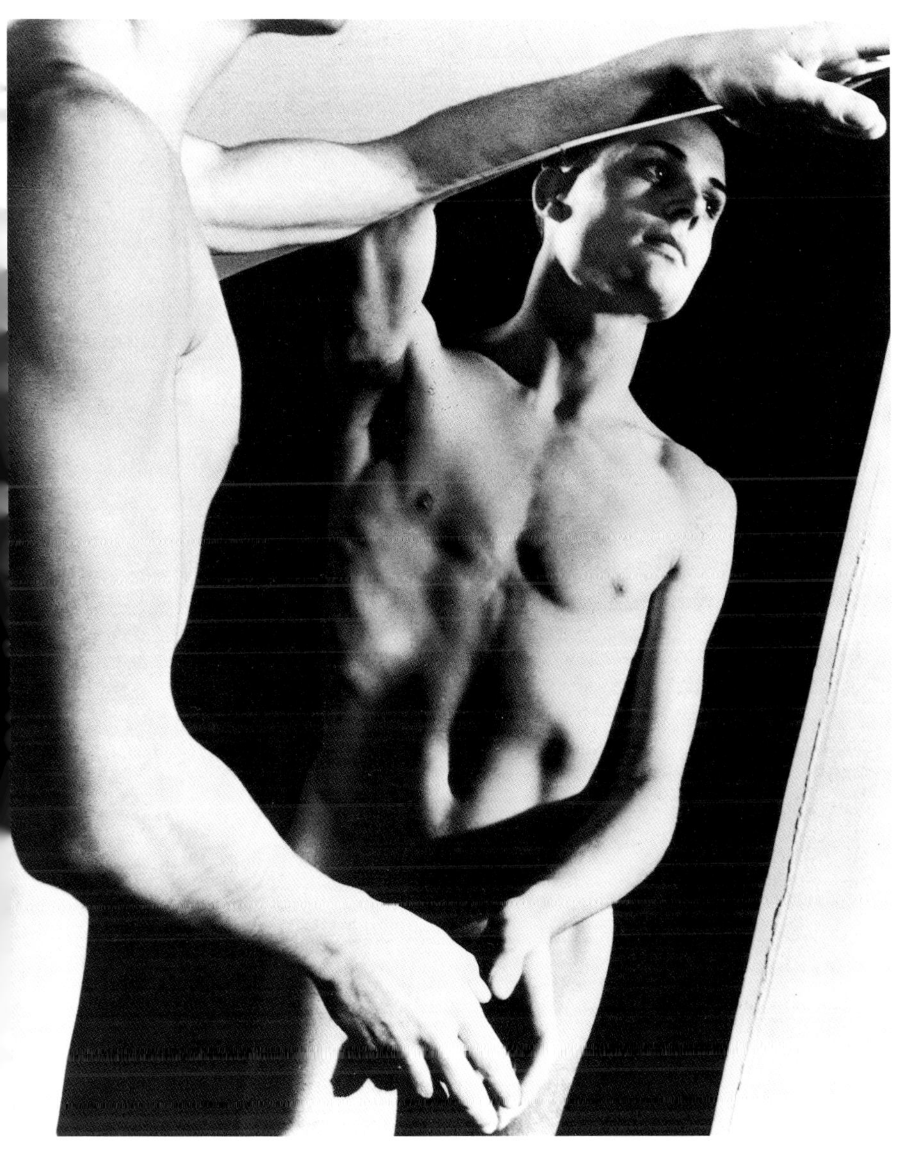

Herbert List, Junger Mann im Spiegel, 1931

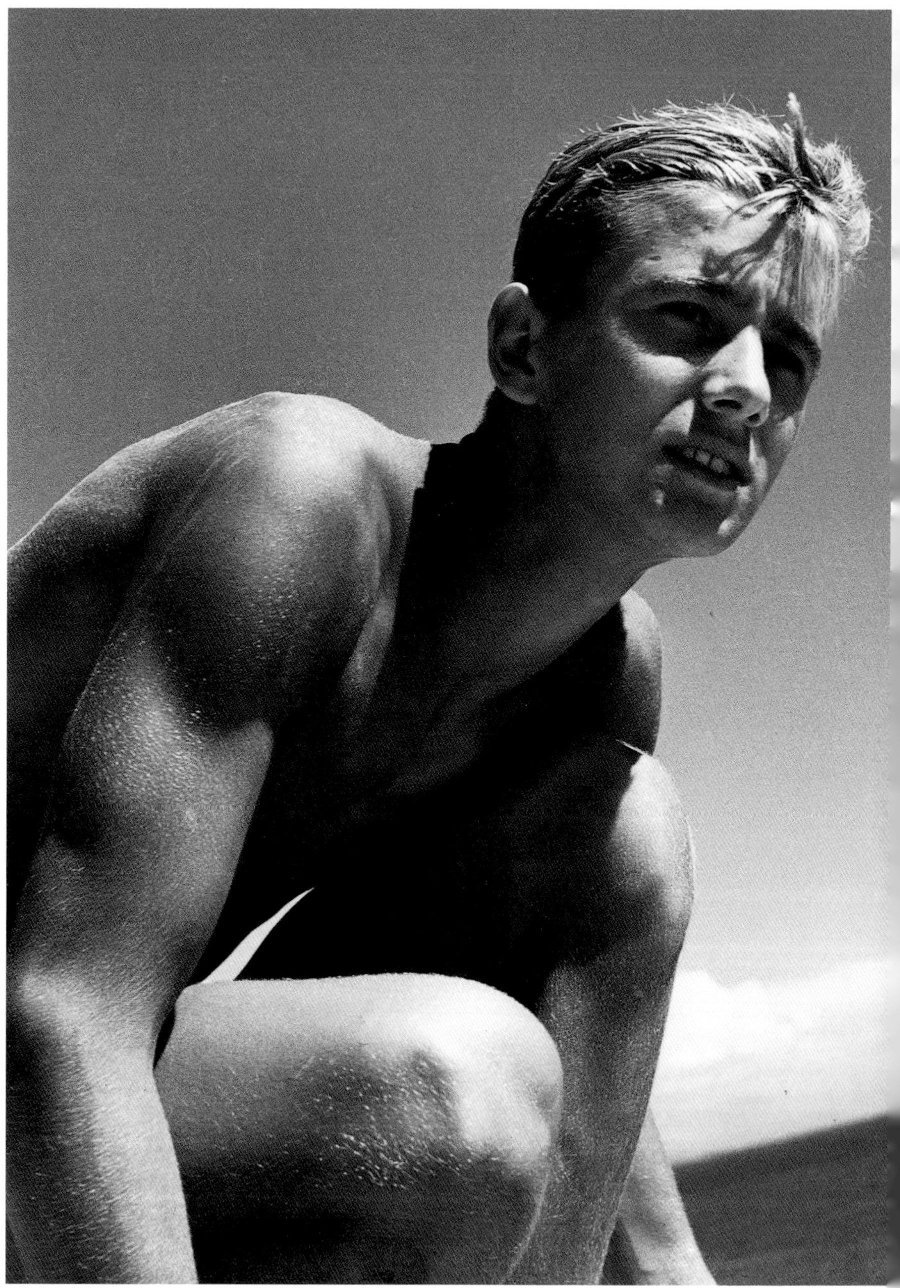

Herbert List, Knieender junger Mann, 1933

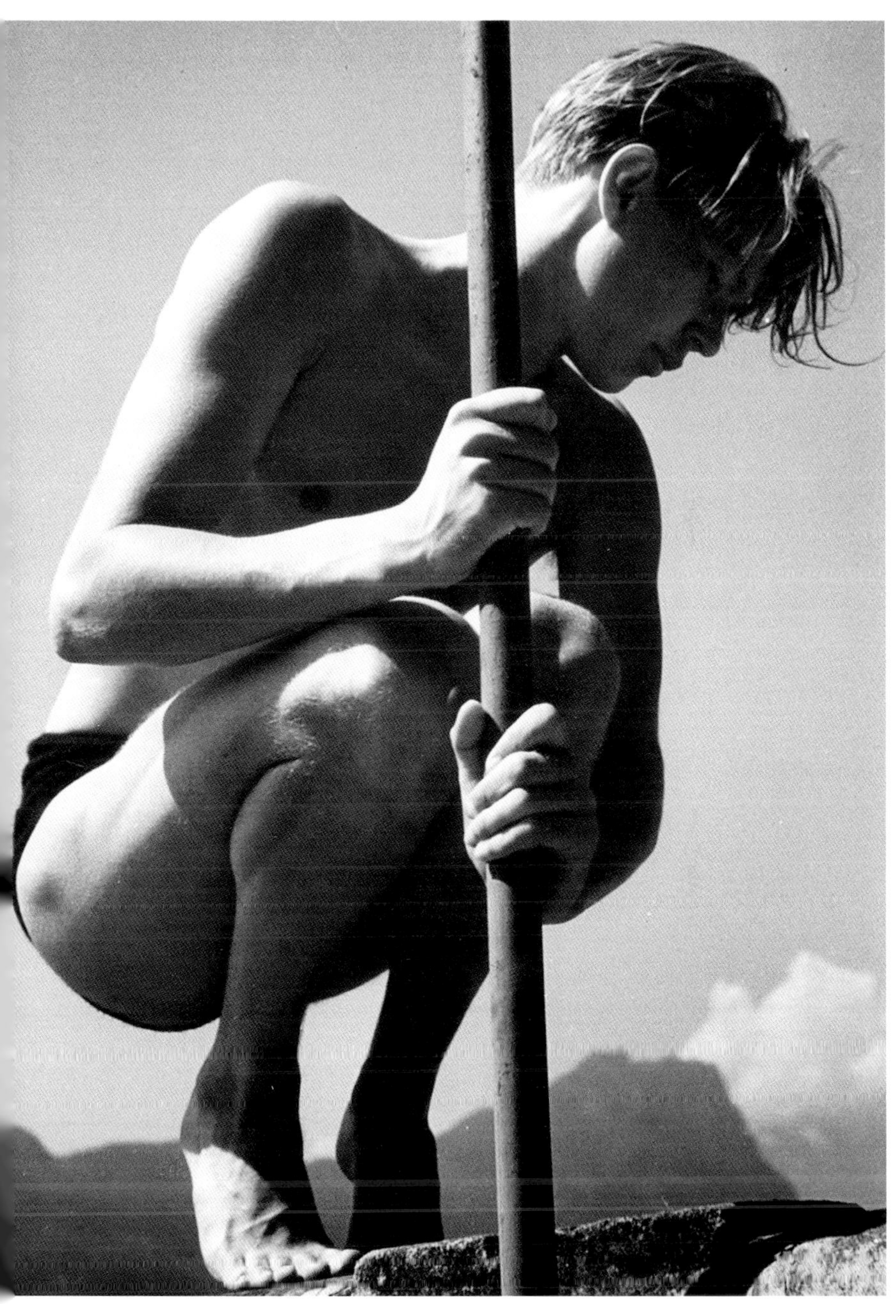

erbert List, Ritti mit Angel, 1936

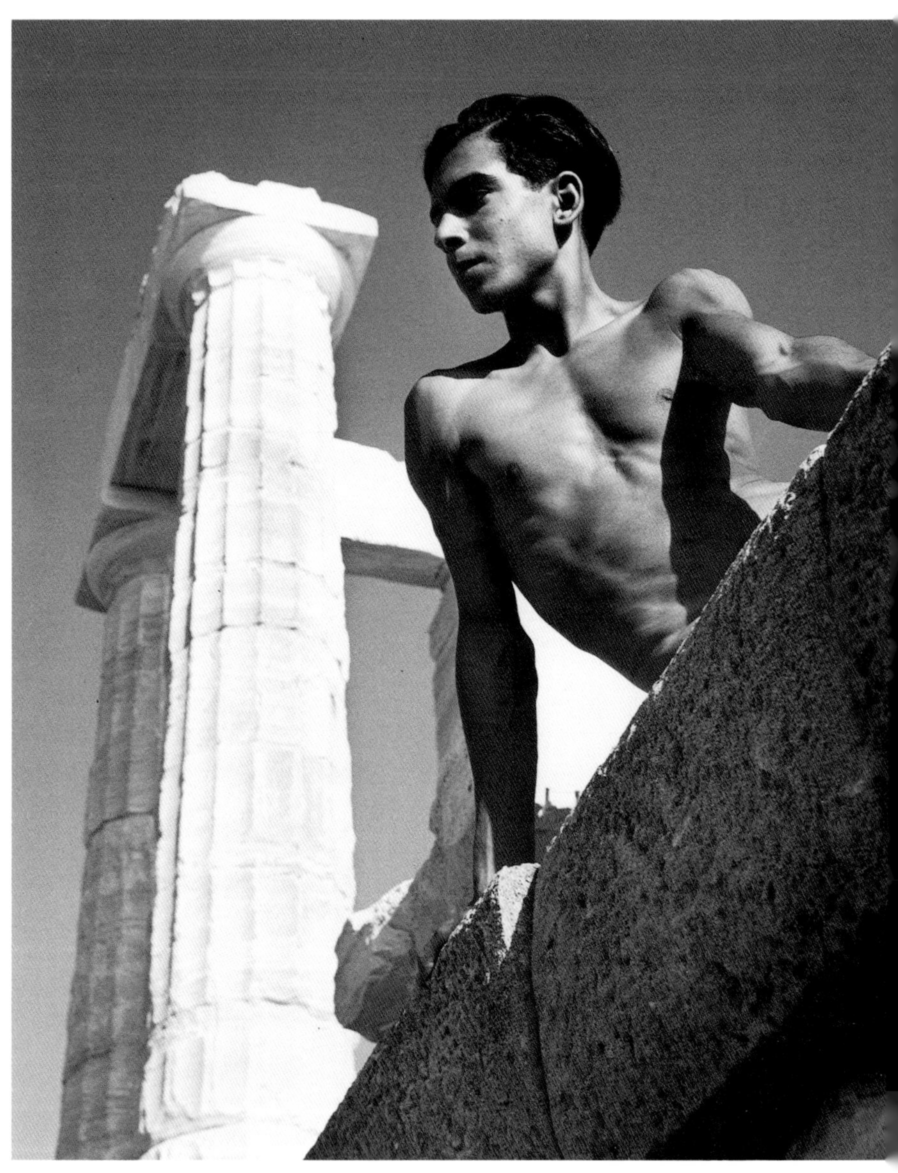

Herbert List, Junge unter dem Poseidon-Tempel, 1937

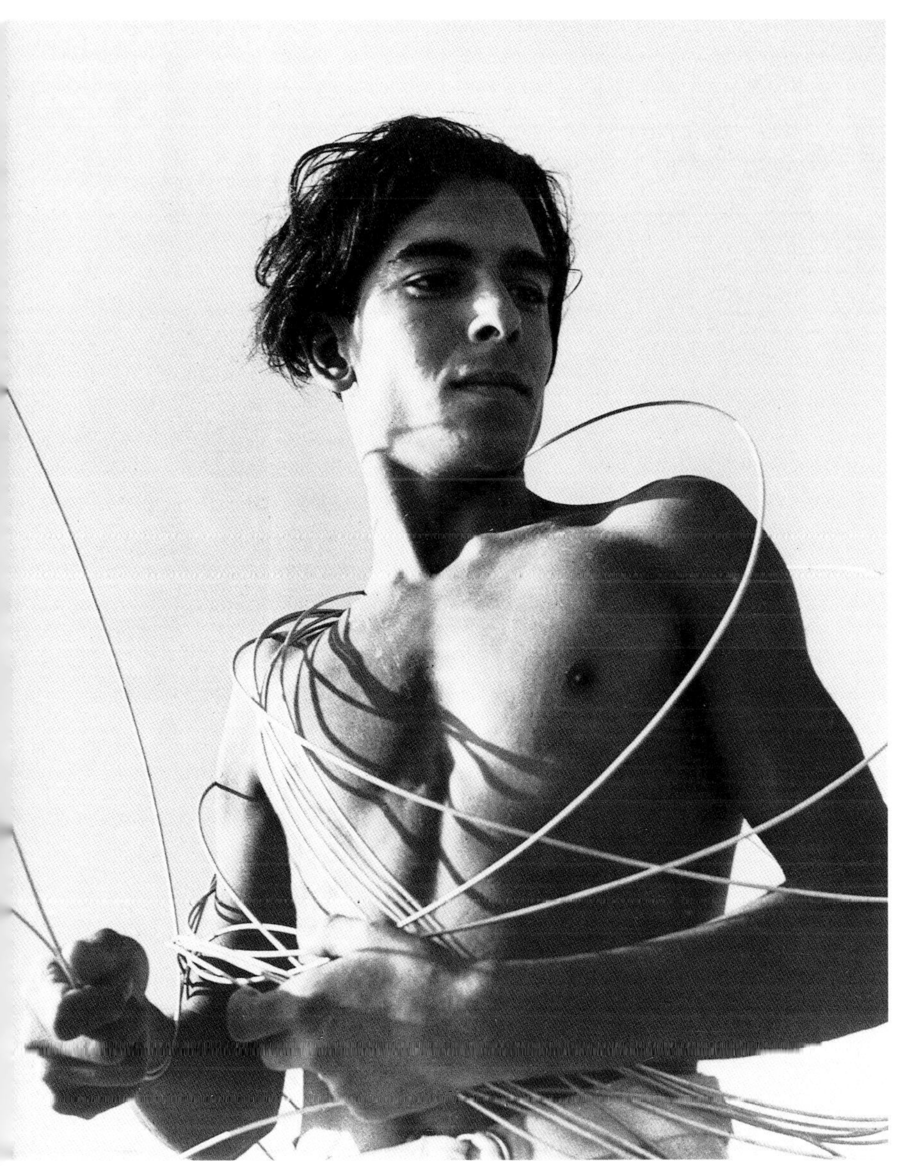

Herbert List, Junge mit Draht, 1934

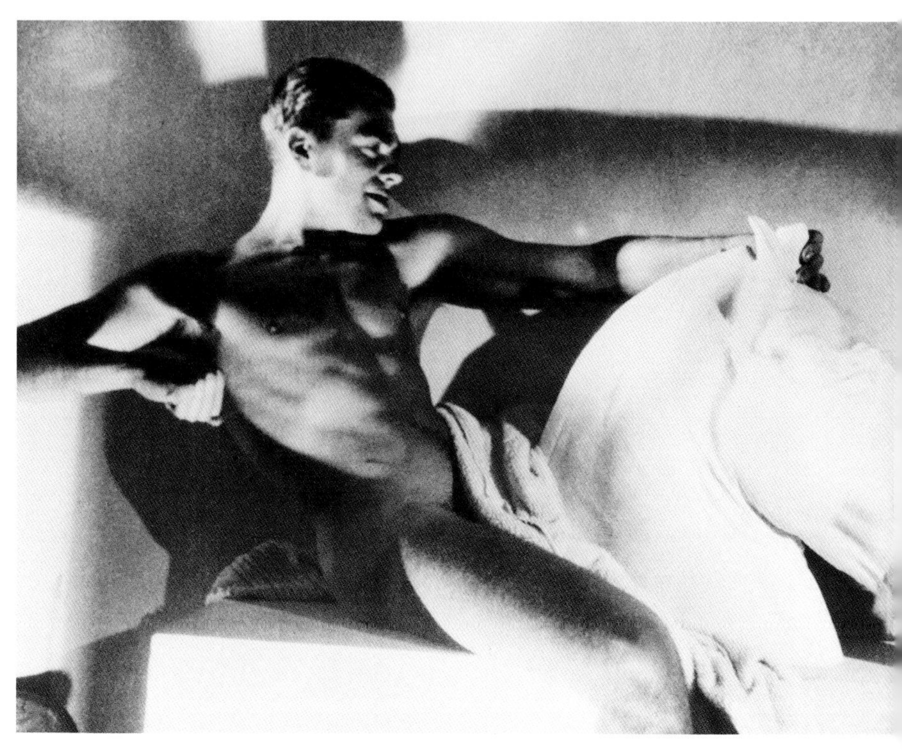

George Hoyningen-Huene, Horst P. Horst, 1932

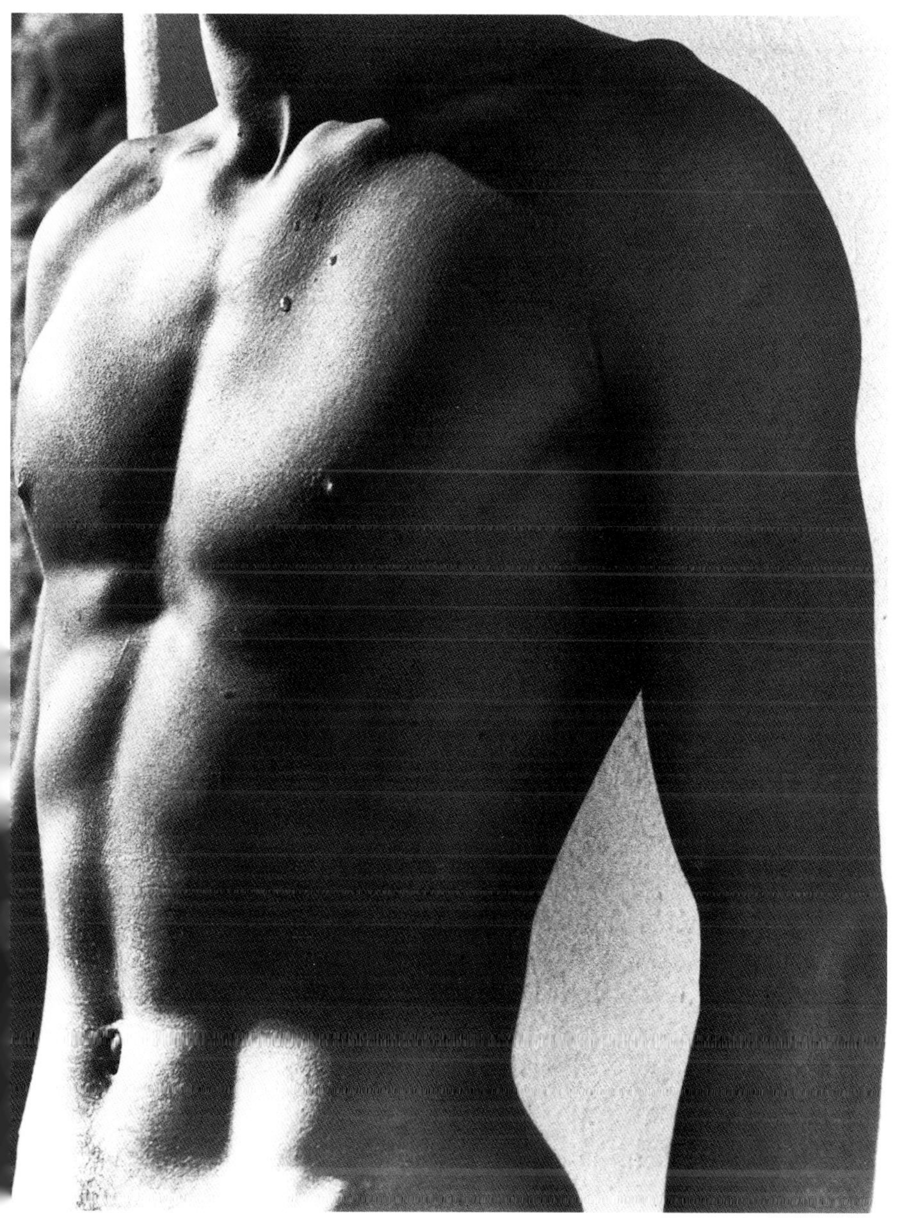

Herbert List, *Tursu, 1936*

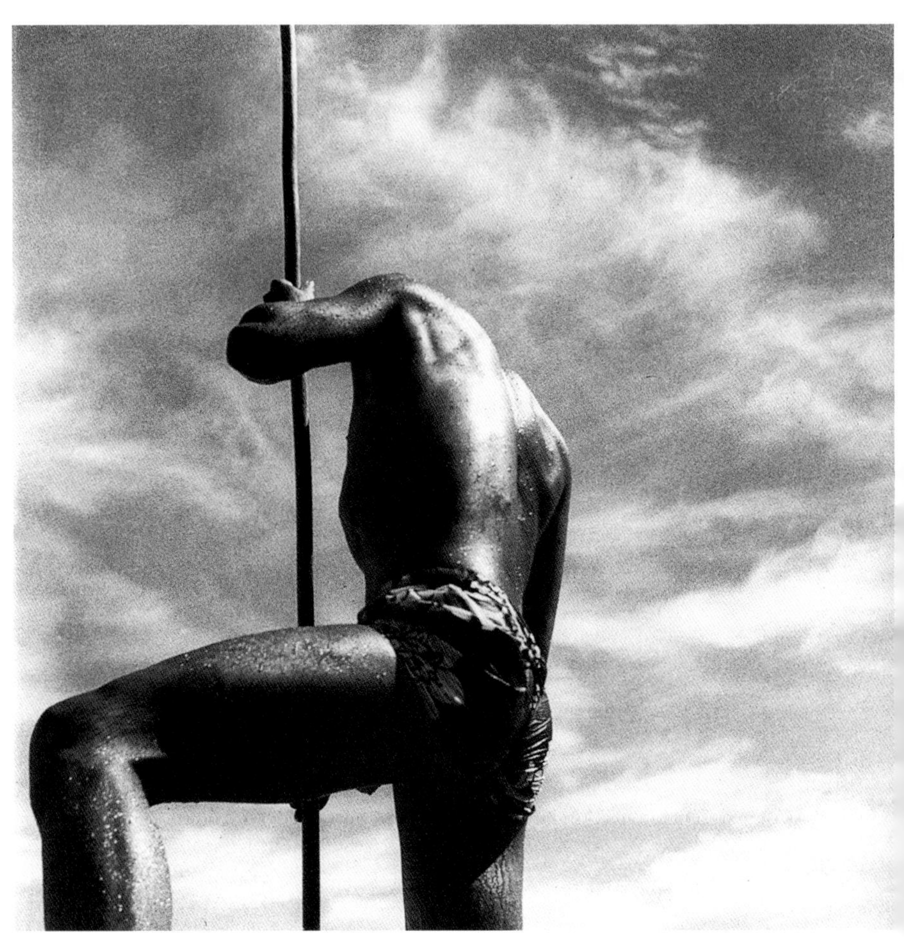

Pierre Verger, Moorea, 1933

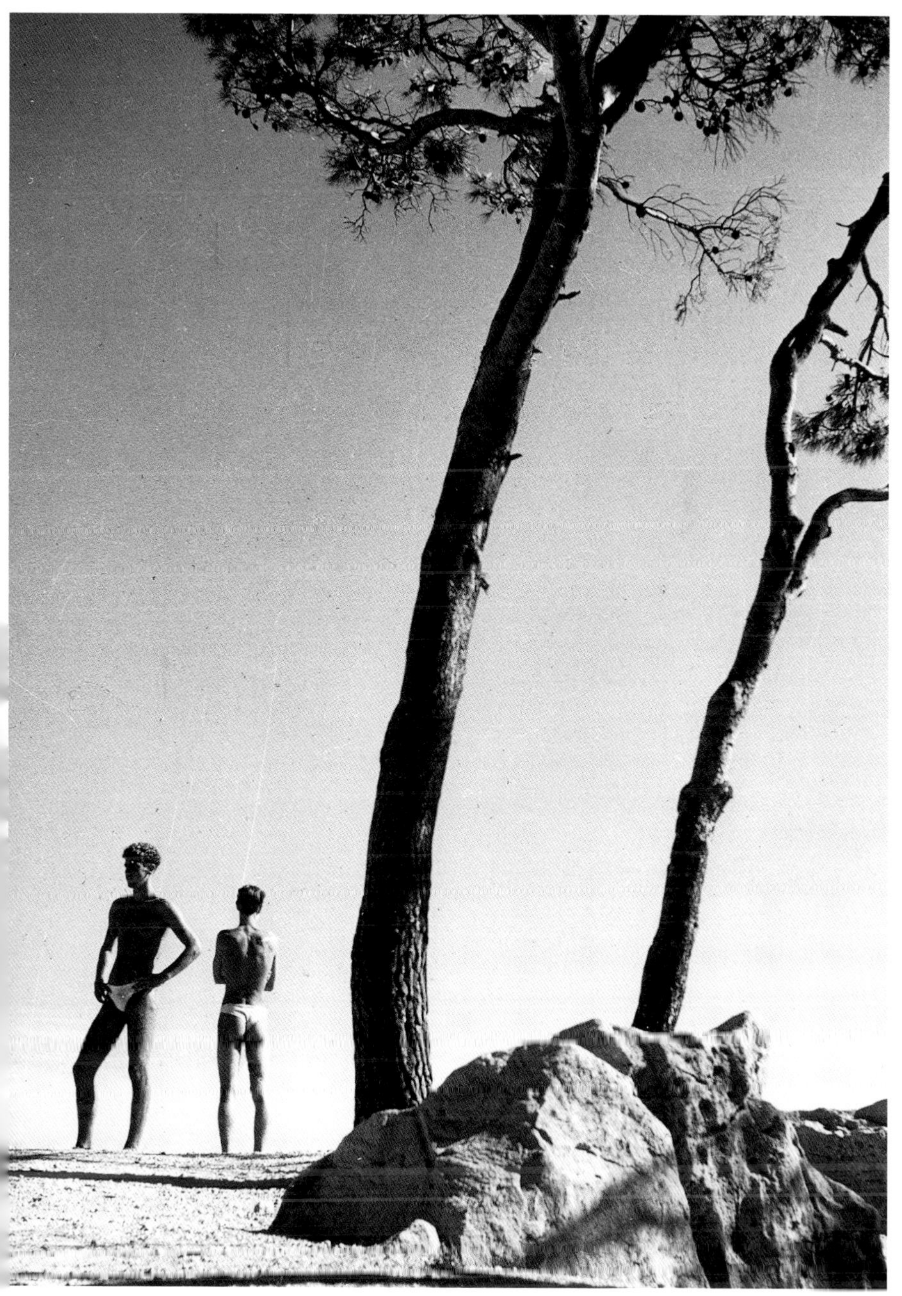

Herbert List, Freunde, 1937

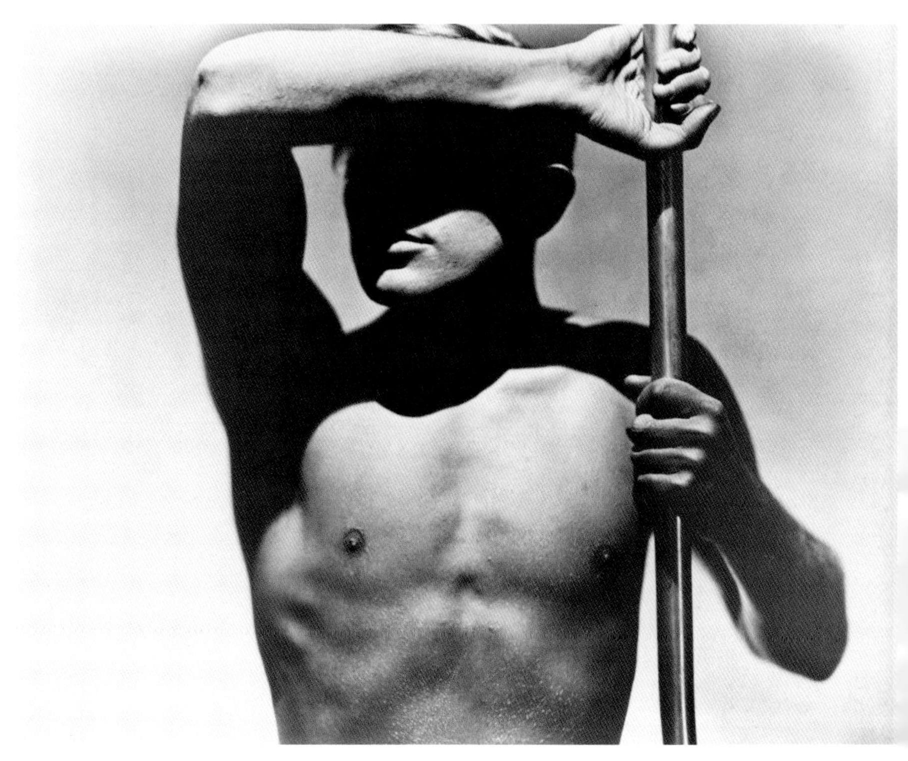

George Hoyningen-Huene, Horst P. Horst, 1931

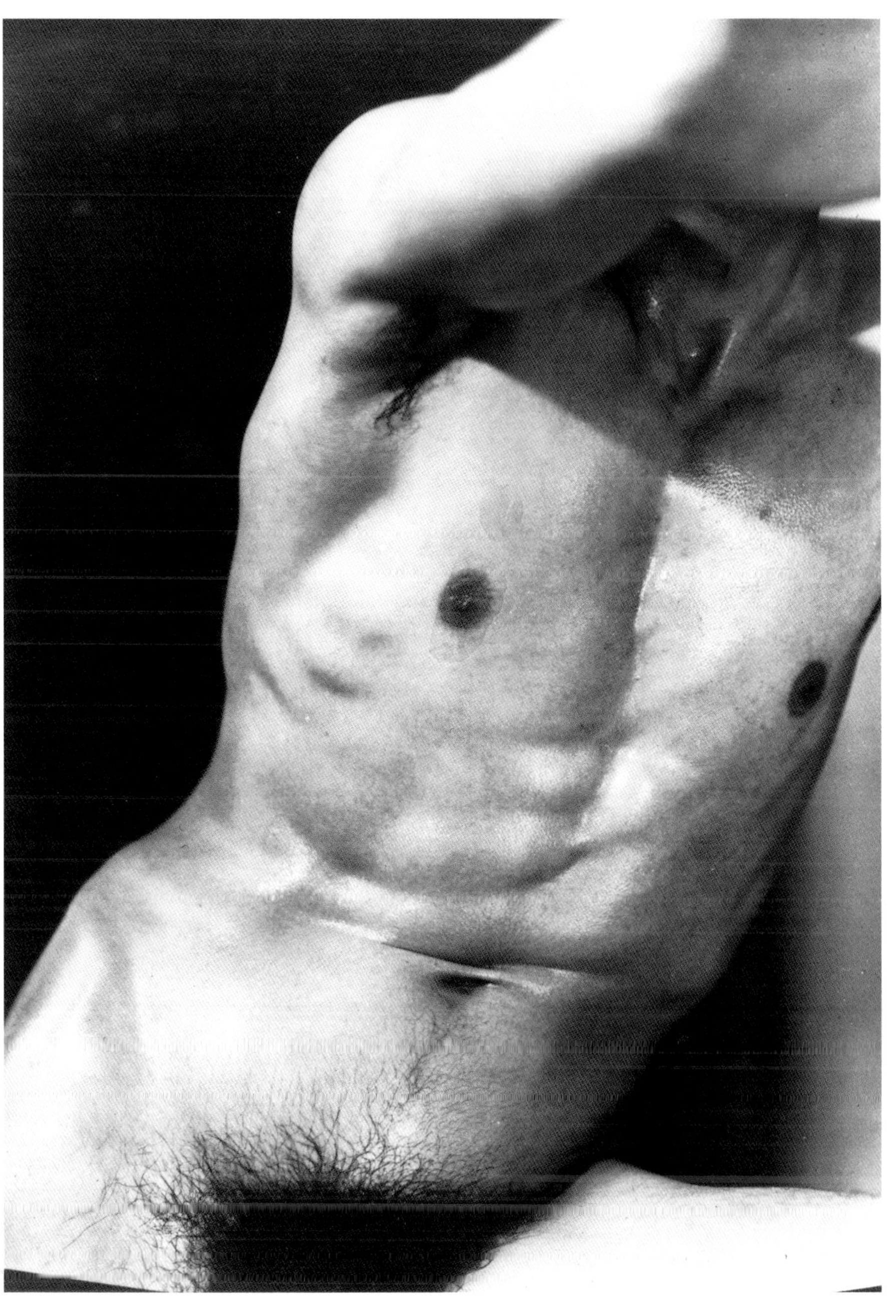

George Hoyningen-Huene, Ohne Titel, c. 1940

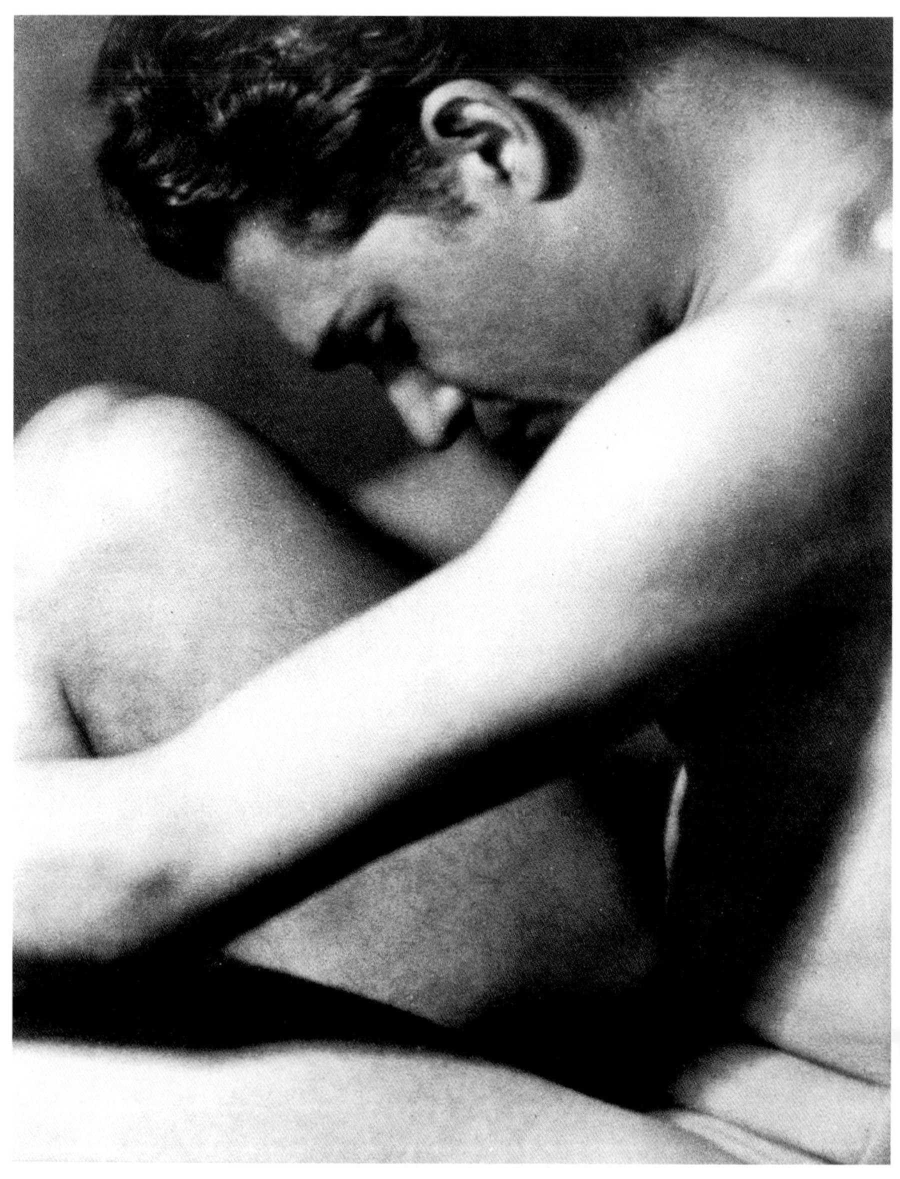

Laure Albin-Guillot, Untitled, c. 1930

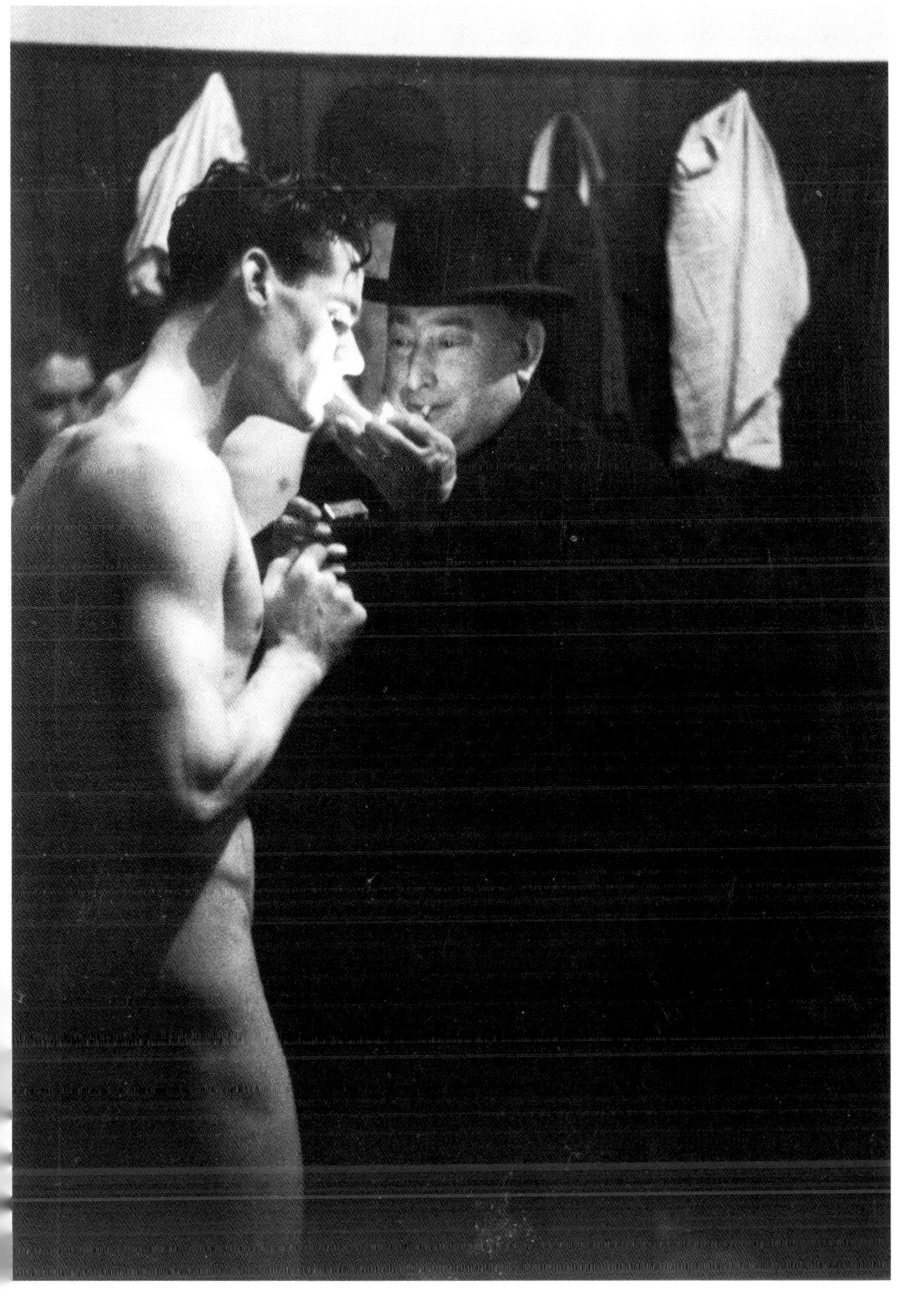

Humphrey Spencer, Newcastle United Football Club Changing Room, 1938

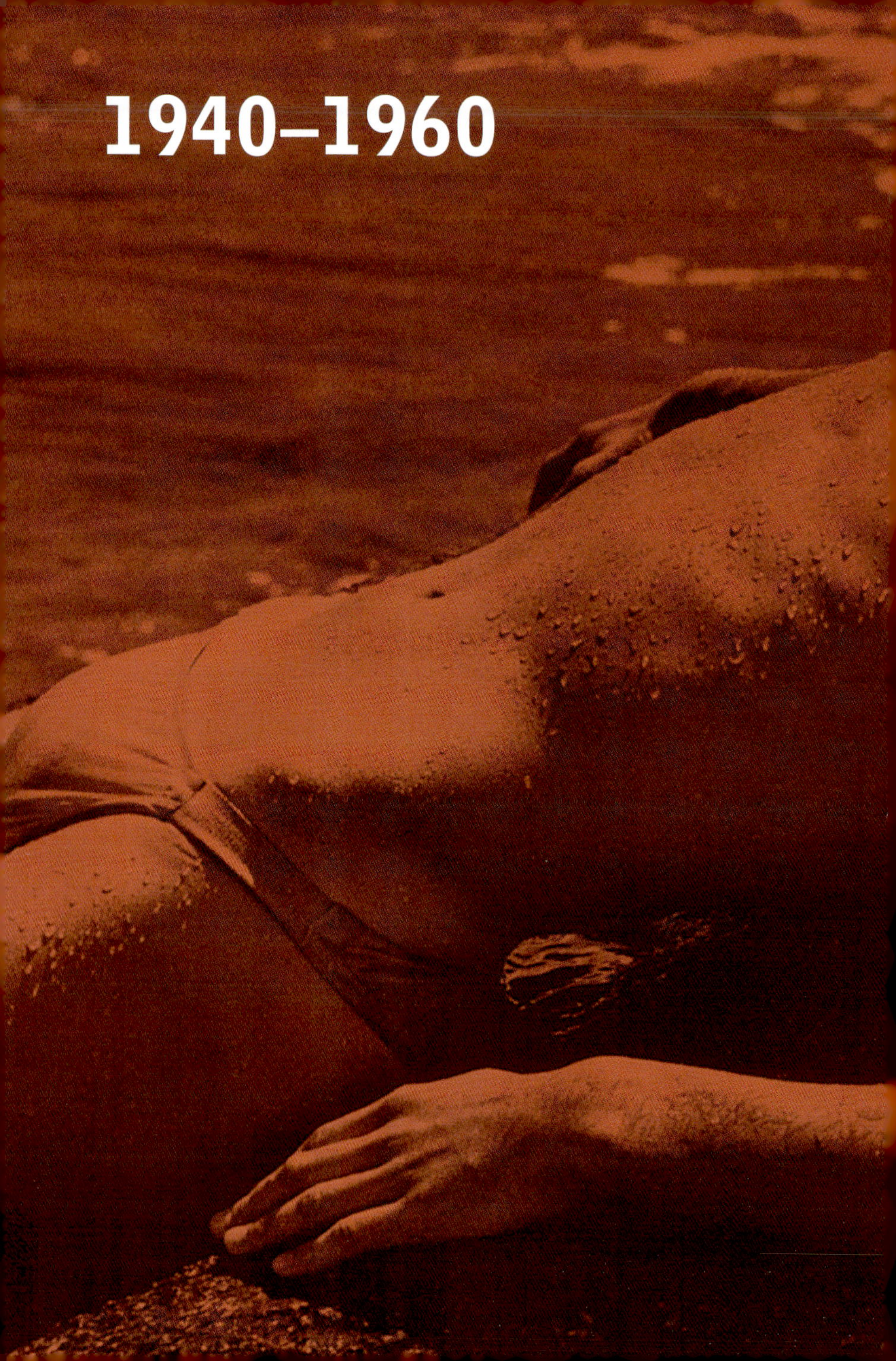
1940–1960

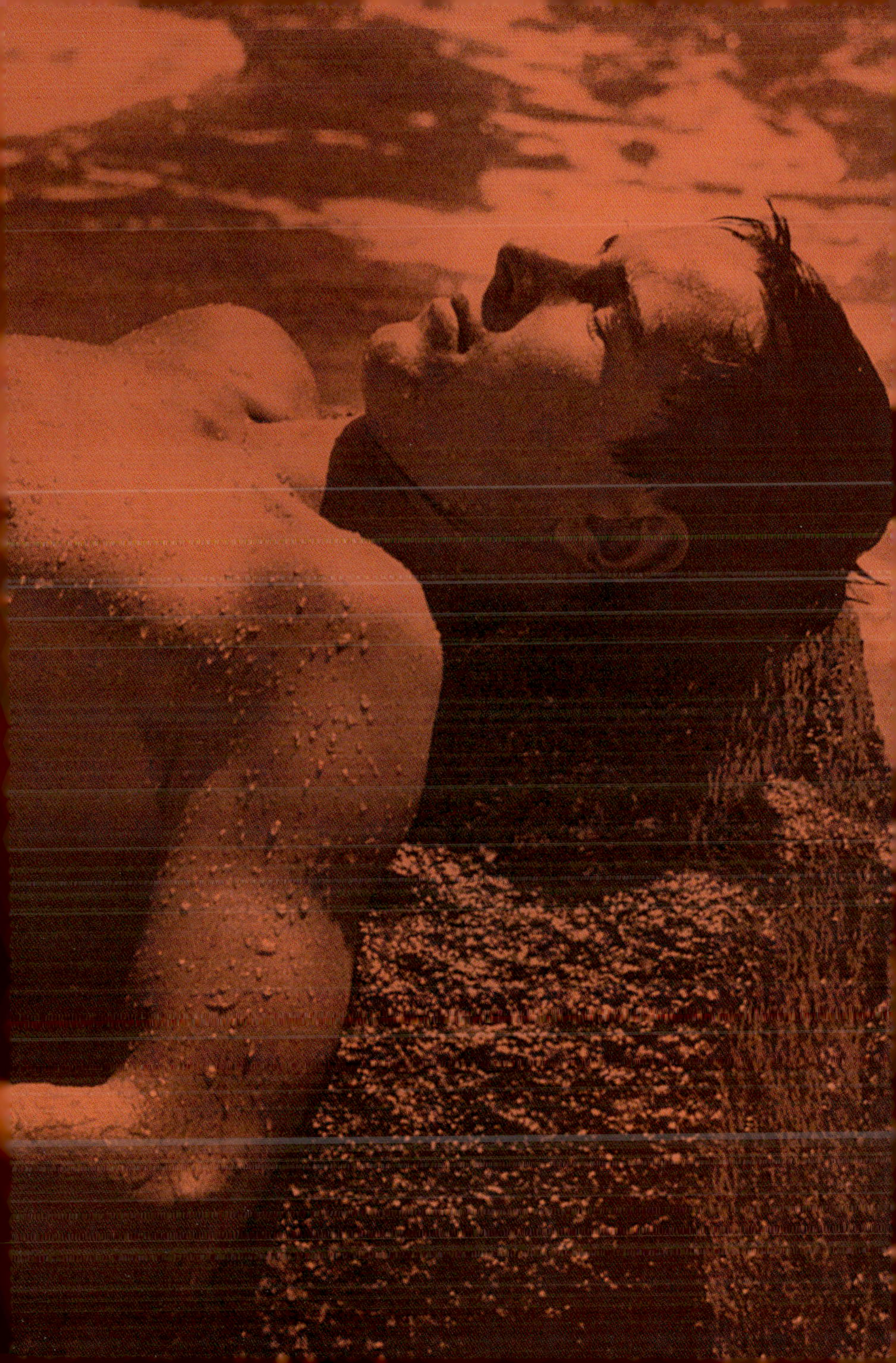

Just as World War I had ended Victorian prudery and introduced a new reality into the photographing of male nudes, World War II was to free the image that bit more. As in the previous war, men were torn from their provincial homes and thrust into exotic new situations and countries. They were surrounded by many different kinds of friends and companions from a variety of backgrounds. And in a wartime world, the constant presence of death made repression and conformity seem pointless.

In this atmosphere, photographers already doing male nude work thrived. After the war, an entirely new group of photographers, usually identified by the city in which they worked, came on the scene, using sports and outdoor themes to create overtly erotic pictures.

Among the established photographers, George Platt Lynes continued his unpublished but groundbreaking work. He was no longer interested in surreal or mythological settings but frequently used young athletes he had discovered at the YMCA gymnastic poses. Frontal nudity was no longer concealed but there was no special emphasis on genitalia either. He tended to show either the face or the genitalia.

After the war, many things changed. Platt Lynes' fashion photography career declined, and a new mode of spontaneous outdoor pictures introduced by Richard Avedon swept the magazine world. Lynes' interest in fashion work waned as his fascination with photographing the naked male body grew. By the time of his early death in 1955, his files held hundreds of photographs of young men, most of them with natural, un-pumped up bodies who looked beautiful and accessible. These were handsome young men, whom the viewer could imagine meeting and perhaps even sleeping with. This was a major departure from the earlier work of Platt Lynes and others, which had presented a kind of male beauty one could only hope to encounter in one's dreams.

Painter friends of Platt Lynes – Paul Cadmus, Jared French, and his wife Margaret French – formed the PAJAMA group. They took photographs to inspire their largely Magic Realist painting, which depicted recognizable human beings and places in a magical and idealized way. Their photographs often included nude males, among them the beautiful George Platt Lynes himself.

They belonged to a New York art world where many artists and photographers took turns posing for one another. Platt Lynes frequently photographed Cadmus and the Frenches, the men from time to time nude. They were all handsome people with fine bodies. In the early '40s Platt Lynes had photographed groups of naked young men garnered from the YMCA for the painter Jared French, who had posed them for the camera. What use French made of these pictures is not known.

Whereas Platt Lynes' photographs were almost all taken in the studio, the PAJAMA pictures (PAJAMA being an acronym of the first letters of the names Paul, Jared, and Margaret, used because they were never sure who had taken which photographs) were shot almost entirely out of doors. This usually happened during seashore vacations on Fire Island and other beach resorts. They made no special effort to glamorize the men they photographed, but their subjects were always handsome and well built. They did create a magical atmosphere in their photographs – the same that suffused their paintings.

These photographs had to wait until the 1990s to be seen by the world, but Platt Lynes did find an outlet for some of his male nude work in a small magazine "Der Kreis" (The Circle) printed in Switzerland. He used the name Roberto Rolfe for this work in order not to jeopardize his standing as a fashion photographer.

Horst P. Horst, the protégé of Hoyningen-Huene, did powerful graphic work with male nudes in the early '50s, while another fashion photographer, Clifford Coffin, was taking shots of male nudes that were clearly erotic. Most of his work was lost in a fire.

Completely aside from this artistic photography of the male nude, another kind of photography was emerging: the physique photograph. This had been slowly making its appearance before the war with the Ritter Brothers and Tony Sansone posing for photographs that were sold to a private clientele. In 1945 Bob Mizer had founded the Athletic Model Guild in Los Angeles as a model agency for bodybuilders. Many young men had not returned to their home towns after the war and were hanging around the movie capital hoping their good looks might lead to a career in motion pictures. Mizer soon developed a thriving mail-order business with these photographs, and in 1951 launched the magazine

"Physique Pictorial". This was a magazine devoted to physical culture, in which the publishers presented human bodies reminiscent of classical sculpture shaped by special exercises and the lifting of weights. Their product was clearly meant for the homosexual market and no other. It was aimed neither at health enthusiasts nor at those in the actual business of building their bodies. It was solely intended for those who enjoyed the sight of nude males. Each model was identified, and a short biography and interests were included. The nude image was becoming more and more realistic.

Mizer published the work of other photographers as well as his own, and a rich culture began to grow. Lon of New York (Lon Hanagan) had done some photographic work before the war and the market developed by "Physique Pictorial" did much to boost his postwar business. Bruce of Los Angeles (Bruce Bellas) soon followed suit. His speciality was photographing contestants in bodybuilding competitions. The stage props of swords, spears, and bows and arrows often used in the "Physique Pictorial" studies to link the subject to classic antiquity were largely abandoned by Bruce. His young men occasi+onally wrestled or lifted one another in the air, but for the most part they just stood about in their sunny, healthy American bulk and let themselves be examined by the camera. The enormous volume of his work is now administered in California by John Sonsini, a talented young photographer in his own right.

In other parts of the U.S., trade was equally brisk. Douglas of Detroit (Douglas Juleff) was recruiting young local bodybuilders for photographs to be sold by mail, as was Al Urban Jr. in Chicago. A number of other photographers were working in the Los Angeles and San Francisco area, and in New York.

One of the most successful new enterprises was Don Whitman's Western Photography Guild in Denver, Colorado. His specialty was posing brawny young men in the sunlit Rocky Mountains wearing only cowboy hats and boots, and frequently not even that. With this fresh attitude to the photographing of nude males, no pretext was needed to look at such pictures.

There was a lot of harassment of these photographers by the law; Bob Mizer and his "Physique Pictorial" were forced to close in the 1960s, following a lawsuit that went all the way to the United States Supreme Court.

"Grecian Guild Pictorial" won a similar case in 1968. Now nudity was no longer judged obscene.

But even in the repressive atmosphere of the McCarthy era of the 1950s, with its Communist witch hunts, there had been a big shift in attitude in favor of the male nude image. Many men had come home from the war convinced that they should not marry the girl next door but should seek their sexual identities elsewhere. That elsewhere often involved a subscription to "Physique Pictorial" and the purchase of similar material.

Art photographers working at this time included Minor White who took very personal photographs of men he obviously cared for very much. Herbert Tobias in Germany was producing dark and disturbing work which was to be imitated by many other photographers in later decades.

In England the photographer John Barrington was doing something similar; he started his magazine "Male Model Monthly" in 1954. Barrington also published books on anatomy and related subjects. He was influenced by the big British names of the day, Cecil Beaton and Angus McBean, and although he was prolific, his photographs were of consistently high quality.

Beaton and McBean also produced some male nude studies. Beaton's were rather impromptu but McBean shot a good number of very fine studio nudes.

Raymond Voinquel's work appeared in France around the same time; it was imbued with the magic and romance that were his hallmark.

Herbert List in postwar Germany added more male nudes to his opus, but these were much more realistic in manner than his prewar studies, while Konrad Helbig and Jo von Kalckreuth, two contemporary German photographers, were also exploring new possibilities in this field.

Der Zweite Weltkrieg sollte – den Veränderungen nach dem Ersten Weltkrieg vergleichbar – das Bild des nackten Mannes noch stärker von seinen Fesseln befreien.

Wie schon im Ersten Weltkrieg wurden die Männer ihrer alltäglichen provinziellen Umgebung entrissen und in fremde Länder verschlagen, wo sie Menschen aus den unterschiedlichsten sozialen Schichten begegneten. Im Krieg lässt die ständige Gegenwart des Todes vor allem vorgeblich moralische Werte wie Konformität oder Verdrängung als bedeutungslos erscheinen.

Die Geschäfte der Fotografen, die sich bereits der Aktfotografie verschrieben hatten, blühten. Nach dem Krieg betrat eine neue Generation von Fotografen die Szene und bediente sich der Themen Sport und Natur, um offen erotische Bilder zu schaffen.

Unter den etablierten Fotografen setzte George Platt Lynes seine bahnbrechende Arbeit fort – auch wenn sie weitgehend unveröffentlicht blieb. Surreale und mythologische Kulissen als Deckmäntelchen für ein Interesse am männlichen Akt interessierten ihn nicht länger. Platt Lynes fand seine Modelle, junge Sportler, im YMCA und lichtete sie in sportlichen Posen ab. Der Fokus war entweder auf das Gesicht oder die Genitalien gerichtet. Platt Lynes Karriere als Modefotograf ging in der Nachkriegszeit zu Ende, als eine neue, von Richard Avedon initiierte Richtung mit „spontanen" Freiluftaufnahmen die Magazine eroberte. Platt Lynes Interesse an der Modefotografie erlosch, seine Begeisterung für den männlichen Akt rückte vollends in den Vordergrund. Als er 1955 verstarb, fanden sich in seinem Nachlass Hunderte Fotos junger Männer, die sich deutlich von seinen früheren Arbeiten unterschieden. Waren die sportlich gestählten Modelle der älteren Aufnahmen wie ferne Traumgestalten erschienen, so suggerierten die hübschen, aber durchschnittlich gebauten Modelle der Spätphase Erreichbarkeit.

Der Freundeskreis von Platt Lynes schloss sich zur PAJAMA-Gruppe zusammen, zu der die Maler Paul Cadmus, Jared French und dessen Frau Margret gehörten (der Name setzt sich aus den Initialen ihrer Vornamen zusammen und diente ihnen als Signatur). Als Inspirationsquelle für weitgehend im Stil des magischen Realismus gehaltene Gemälde dienten ihnen zumeist Fotos, unter ihnen oft solche

nackter Männer, darunter auch der gutaussehende George Platt Lynes persönlich.
In der New Yorker Kunstszene, zu der sie alle gehörten, war es üblich, dass man
sich häufig gegenseitig Modell stand. Platt Lynes hat Cadmus und das Ehepaar
French vielfach porträtiert, die beiden Männer gelegentlich auch nackt.

Während die Fotos von Platt Lynes fast ausschließlich im Studio entstan-
den, fotografierte die PAJAMA-Gruppe draußen im Freien, zumeist während der
Urlaubssaison auf Fire Island oder in anderen Badeorten. Sie unternahmen keine
besonderen Anstrengungen, die Männer, die sie fotografierten, in irgendeiner
Weise zu idealisieren, doch haftet ihren Aufnahmen wie ihren Gemälden etwas
Magisches an.

All diese Aufnahmen wurden der Öffentlichkeit erst in den 90er Jahren zugänglich gemacht, nur Platt Lynes veröffentlichte einige seiner Männerakte
in der Zeitschrift „Der Kreis", die in kleiner Auflage in der Schweiz erschien.
Um seinen Ruf als Modefotograf nicht zu gefährden, hatte er diese Arbeiten mit
dem Namen Roberto Rolfo signiert.

Anfang der 50er Jahre schuf Horst P. Horst seine stark plastisch wirkenden
Aktfotos, und auch Clifford Coffin, ein weiterer Modefotograf, nahm in dieser
Zeit Männerakte auf, von denen die meisten unverhüllt erotisch waren.

Neben diesen künstlerischen Aktaufnahmen gab es noch die gänzlich andere
Richtung der „Physique-Fotografie", die sich bereits vor dem Krieg mit den
Ritter Brüdern und Tony Sansone etabliert hatte. Abnehmer für diese Bilder
waren vornehmlich Privatkunden. 1945 gründete Bob Mizer in Los Angeles
die Athletic Model Guild, eine Modellagentur für Bodybuilder. Nach dem Krieg
hatten viele junge Männer ihrer Heimatstadt den Rücken gekehrt und waren
mit der Hoffnung auf eine Schauspielerkarriere in Hollywood gestrandet. Mizer
stellte ein schnell florierendes Versandgeschäft mit Fotos seiner Modelle auf die
Beine und rief 1951 „Physique Pictorial" ins Leben. Das Magazin hatte sich dem
Körperkult verschrieben, worunter die Herausgeber die Formung des Körpers
nach dem Vorbild der antiken Statuen verstanden. „Physique Pictorial" richtete
sich eindeutig an einen homosexuellen Leser. Jedes Modell wurde namentlich
genannt, und ein kurzer Lebenslauf nannte Hobbys und Interessen. Das Bild des
nackten Mannes bekam zunehmend Realitätsnähe.

Mizer veröffentlichte neben seinen eigenen Arbeiten auch die anderer Akt-
fotografen, sodass eine breite Plattform für das Genre entstand. Lon of New
York (Lon Hanagan) hatte bereits vor dem Krieg Aktfotos gemacht und erlebte
durch den Erfolg von „Physique Pictorial" neue Popularität. Bruce of Los
Angeles (Bruce Bellas) machte es ihm nach. Er hatte sich auf Fotos von Teil-
nehmern an Bodybuilding-Wettbewerben spezialisiert. Bruce verwarf die bei
„Physique Pictorial" häufig verwendeten Bühnenrequisiten wie Schwerter,
Speere, Pfeil und Bogen und ließ seine Modelle meist im Freien unter der Sonne
Kaliforniens posieren. Seinen umfangreichen Nachlass verwaltet heute John
Sonsini, der selbst ein begabter Fotograf ist.

Das Geschäft boomte. Douglas of Detroit (Douglas Juleff) rekrutierte für
seine auf dem Versandweg vertriebenen Fotos ebenfalls junge Bodybuilder, Al
Urban junior betrieb seinen Versand von Chicago aus. Andere wirkten wiederum
in den Großräumen San Francisco und Los Angeles, und auch in New York tat
sich neue Konkurrenz auf.

Eines der erfolgreichsten Unternehmen dieser Art war Don Whitmans
„Western Photography Guild" in Denver, Colorado. Er hatte sich auf Bilder kräf-
tiger junger Männer vor der Kulisse der Rocky Mountains spezialisiert. An ihre
Körper ließen sie höchstens Cowboyhut und Stiefel.

Die Fotografen und Verleger dieser Art von Aktfotografie sahen sich beharr-
lichen Angriffen der Gesetzeshüter ausgesetzt. Bob Mizer musste sein Magazin,
nach einem Verfahren, das bis zum Obersten Gerichtshof ging, in den 60ern
einstellen. 1968 sollte „Grecian Guild Pictorial" einen ähnlich Prozess gewinnen.

Trotz der repressiven Atmosphäre der McCarthy-Ära in den 50ern wurde die
männliche Aktfotografie in der Öffentlichkeit zunehmend toleriert. Viele Kriegs-
teilnehmer hatten neue Erfahrungen gesammelt, sie wollten nicht mehr gleich
das nächstbeste Mädchen heiraten, sondern sich erst ihrer sexuellen Identität
bewusst werden. Ein Abonnement des „Physique Pictorial" oder einer vergleich-
baren Publikation konnte da ein erster Schritt sein.

Zu den Kunstfotografen dieser Epoche zählten Minor White, der außerordentlich intime Fotos von Männern machte, und Herbert Tobias, der sich
düsteren, verstörenden Themen widmete und damit zahlreiche Fotografen der

kommenden Jahrzehnte beeinflusste. In England gründete John Barrington 1954 die Zeitschrift „Male Model Monthly". Zu den Vorbildern des überaus talentierten Barrington, der u.a. auch zur Anatomie veröffentlichte, gehörten Cecil Beaton und Angus McBean. Ungeachtet seiner immensen Produktivität zeugen alle seine Arbeiten von hoher Qualität.

Auch Beaton und McBean nahmen einige männliche Akte auf. Während es bei Beaton schnell improvisierte Aufnahmen waren, produzierte McBean eine beachtliche Anzahl sehr beeindruckender Studioaufnahmen.

Raymond Voinquel schuf in dieser Ära ein Großteil seines Werkes, durchdrungen von Magie und Romantik, und in Deutschland fotografierte Herbert List weiterhin männliche Akte, die jetzt realistischer wirkten als seine Arbeiten vor dem Krieg. Auch die Deutschen Konrad Helbig und Jo von Kalckreuth gingen in dieser Zeit neue Wege in der Fotokunst.

La Grande Guerre avait mit un terme à la pudibonderie victorienne et introduit un nouveau réalisme dans le nu masculin, mais la Seconde Guerre mondiale
devait libérer encore plus l'image.

Comme lors de la guerre précédente, les hommes furent arrachés à leurs
petites villes de province et jetés dans des situations et des contrées déconcer-
tantes. Ils se retrouvèrent au milieu de nouveaux compagnons venus d'horizons
très différents. Dans un monde en guerre, l'omniprésence de la mort rendait
les inhibitions et le conformisme désuets.

Dans cette atmosphère, ceux qui faisaient déjà des nus prospérèrent. Après
la guerre, de nouveaux photographes apparurent, utilisant les thèmes du sport
ou de la nature pour créer des images ouvertement érotiques.

Parmi les photographes établis, George Platt Lynes poursuivit son œuvre
non publiée mais avant-gardiste. Les décors surréalistes et mythologiques ne
l'intéressaient plus, et il faisait souvent poser dans des attitudes gymniques
de jeunes athlètes qu'il découvrait à la YMCA. Il ne cherchait plus à masquer les
organes génitaux sans pour autant les mettre en valeur. Il avait pour principe de
photographier soit le sexe soit le visage, un principe qu'il transgressait souvent.

Après la guerre, beaucoup de choses changèrent. La carrière de photographe de mode de Platt Lynes déclina, un nouveau genre de clichés spontanés
en extérieur, introduit par Richard Avedon, ayant envahi le monde de la mode.
Lorsqu'il mourut prématurément en 1955, les archives de Platt Lynes con-
tenaient des centaines de photos de jeunes hommes, la plupart avec des corps
naturels non travaillés, qui étaient beaux tout en étant accessibles. Ils étaient
simplement beaux, des hommes comme celui qui regardait la photo pouvait
imaginer en rencontrer, voire même passer la nuit avec eux. Ces images se
démarquaient radicalement des travaux antérieurs de Platt Lynes et d'autres
photographes, qui suggéraient que l'on ne pouvait rencontrer ce genre de
beauté que dans les rêves.

Platt Lynes était un ami du groupe PAJAMA, à savoir Paul Cadmus, Jared
French et sa femme Margaret French, trois peintres appartenant au courant du Réalisme magique. Ils prenaient des photos pour s'en inspirer dans
leurs peintures, qui représentaient des êtres humains et des lieux baignant

dans une atmosphère irréelle et idéalisée. Leurs photographies incluaient souvent des hommes nus, parmi lesquels le très séduisant George Platt Lynes lui-même.

Tous faisaient partie du monde artistique new-yorkais, où de nombreux artistes et photographes posaient souvent les uns pour les autres. Platt Lynes photographia souvent Paul Cadmus et les French, les deux hommes parfois nus. Au début des années 40, Platt Lynes avait également photographié des groupes de jeunes hommes nus recrutés à la YMCA pour Jared, qui les avait lui-même disposés devant l'objectif. On ignore quel usage il fit de ces photos.

Si les photos de Platt Lynes étaient presque toutes réalisées en studio, celles du PAJAMA (Paul Cadmus, Jared et Margaret French utilisaient cet acronyme formé avec les premières lettres de « Paul, Jared et Margaret », car ils ne se souvenaient pas qui était l'auteur des photos) étaient presque toutes en extérieur, généralement prises pendant des vacances au bord de la mer sur Fire Island ou d'autres stations balnéaires. Ils ne faisaient pas d'efforts conscients pour rendre particulièrement séduisants les hommes qu'ils photo- graphiaient et recréaient dans leurs photos la même atmosphère magique que dans leurs peintures.

Ces images devraient attendre les années 90 pour être montrées. Pendant ce temps, Platt Lynes avait trouvé un débouché pour certains de ses nus : une petite revue imprimée en Suisse, « Der Kreis » (Le Cercle). Il utilisa le pseudo- nyme Roberto Rolfe afin de ne pas mettre en danger sa carrière de photographe de mode.

Horst P. Horst, le protégé de Hoyningen-Huene, réalisa des nus impression- nants au début des années 50. Un autre photographe de mode, Clifford Coffin, faisait des nus masculins à la même époque, souvent ouvertement érotiques.

Aux antipodes de ces nus artistiques se trouvait un autre genre de photo- graphie : les clichés d'athlètes. Ces derniers étaient progressivement appa- rus depuis la guerre avec les frères Ritter et Tony Sansone, posant pour des photographies qui étaient ensuite vendues à une clientèle privée. En 1945, Bob Mizer avait fondé l'Athletic Model Guild à Los Angeles, une agence de modèles culturistes. De nombreux jeunes hommes, qui n'étaient pas rentrés chez eux après la guerre, s'étaient rendus dans la capitale du cinéma où ils espéraient faire carrière. Mizer développa bientôt un service de vente par correspondance florissant en vendant leurs photos et, en 1951, il lança la revue « Physique Pictorial ».

Il s'agissait d'un magazine consacré à la culture physique, ce qui, pour ses éditeurs, signifiait reproduire la sculpture classique en sculptant le corps humain à travers des exercices spéciaux et de la musculation. Il s'adressait clairement à une clientèle homosexuelle. Chaque modèle était accompagné de sa fiche signalétique, comprenant une brève biographie et ses activités favorites. Manifestement, le nu masculin devenait de plus en plus pragmatique.

Outre le sien, Mizer publiait le travail d'autres photographes. Une riche culture commença alors à apparaître. Lon of New York (Lon Hanagan) avait commencé à travailler avant la guerre, et le marché développé par « Physique Pictorial » aida beaucoup à relancer sa carrière dans les années 50. Bruce of Los Angeles (Bruce Bellas) marcha bientôt dans ses pas. Sa spécialité était les portraits de concurrents dans les concours de culturisme. Il n'avait que faire des accessoires tels que des épées, des lances, des arcs et des flèches, couramment utilisés dans « Physique Pictorial » pour associer ses sujets à l'Antiquité. L'énorme volume de son travail est aujourd'hui géré en Californie par John Sonsini, lui-même un talentueux jeune photographe.

Dans d'autres régions des Etats-Unis, Douglas of Detroit (Douglas Jeff) recrutait de jeunes culturistes locaux pour vendre leurs photos par correspondance, tout comme Al Urban Jr. à Chicago. Un bon nombre d'autres photographes travaillaient dans la région de Los Angeles et de San Francisco.

L'une des nouvelles entreprises les plus florissantes était la Western Photography Guild de Don Whitman à Denver, dans le Colorado. Ce dernier était spécialisé dans les jeunes hommes musclés posant au soleil dans les montagnes rocheuses, ne portant qu'un chapeau de cow-boy et des bottes, et souvent moins que ça. Là encore, il n'y avait pas besoin de prétextes pour prendre son plaisir à regarder ces images: ni art, ni santé, ni un intérêt pour le culturisme.

Ces photographes étaient souvent harcelés par les autorités, notamment Bob Mizer et son « Physique Pictorial ». Cela devait durer jusque dans les années 60,

quand un procès remonta jusqu'à la Cour Suprême. «Grecian Guild Pictorial»
l'emporta en 1968. La nudité n'était plus obscène.

Malgré l'atmosphère répressive du maccarthysme des années 50, avec sa
chasse aux sorcières communistes, les mentalités avaient changé à l'égard du
nu masculin. De toute évidence, de nombreux jeunes étaient rentrés de la guerre
convaincus qu'au lieu de rentrer chez eux pour épouser leur copine de lycée,
ils feraient mieux d'aller chercher leur identité sexuelle ailleurs. Cet ailleurs se
traduisait souvent par un abonnement à «Physique Pictorial» et l'achat de nombreuses photographies du même genre.

Parmi les photographes d'art qui travaillaient à cette époque se trouvait
Minor White, qui faisait des photos très personnelles d'hommes auxquels il
tenait manifestement beaucoup. De son côté, Herbert Tobias en Allemagne
réalisait des images troublantes et sombres qui allaient influencer de nombreux
autres photographes les décennies suivantes.

En Angleterre, John Barrington fit quelque chose de semblable avec la
création de sa revue «Male Model Monthly» en 1954. Il était influencé par les
grands noms anglais de l'époque, comme Cecil Beaton et Angus McBean et, bien
que prolifique, ses photographies étaient toujours très soignées et recherchées.

Beaton et McBean faisaient aussi des nus masculins. Ceux de Beaton étaient
très impromptus, mais McBean réalisa beaucoup de superbes nus de studio. A la
même époque, Raymond Voinquel accumulait en France une œuvre importante
et volumineuse, imprégnée de la magie et du romantisme qui faisaient son image
de marque.

Dans l'Allemagne de l'après-guerre, Herbert List ajouta d'autres nus masculins à sa collection, mais plus réalistes que ceux des années 30. Konrad Helbig
et Jo von Kalckreuth, eux, exploraient de nouvelles voies.

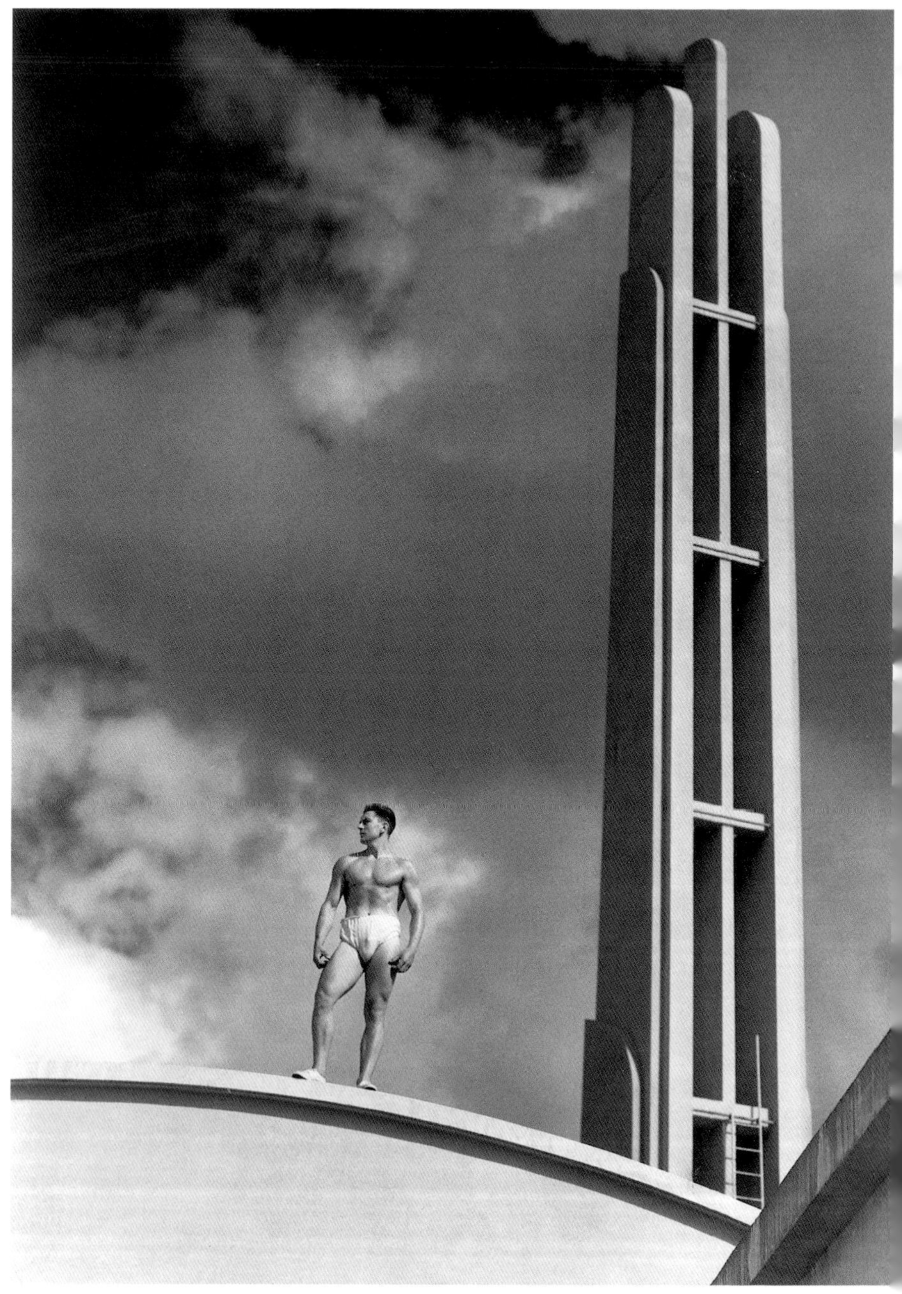

Raymond Voinquel, Le Garde du Stade, 1941

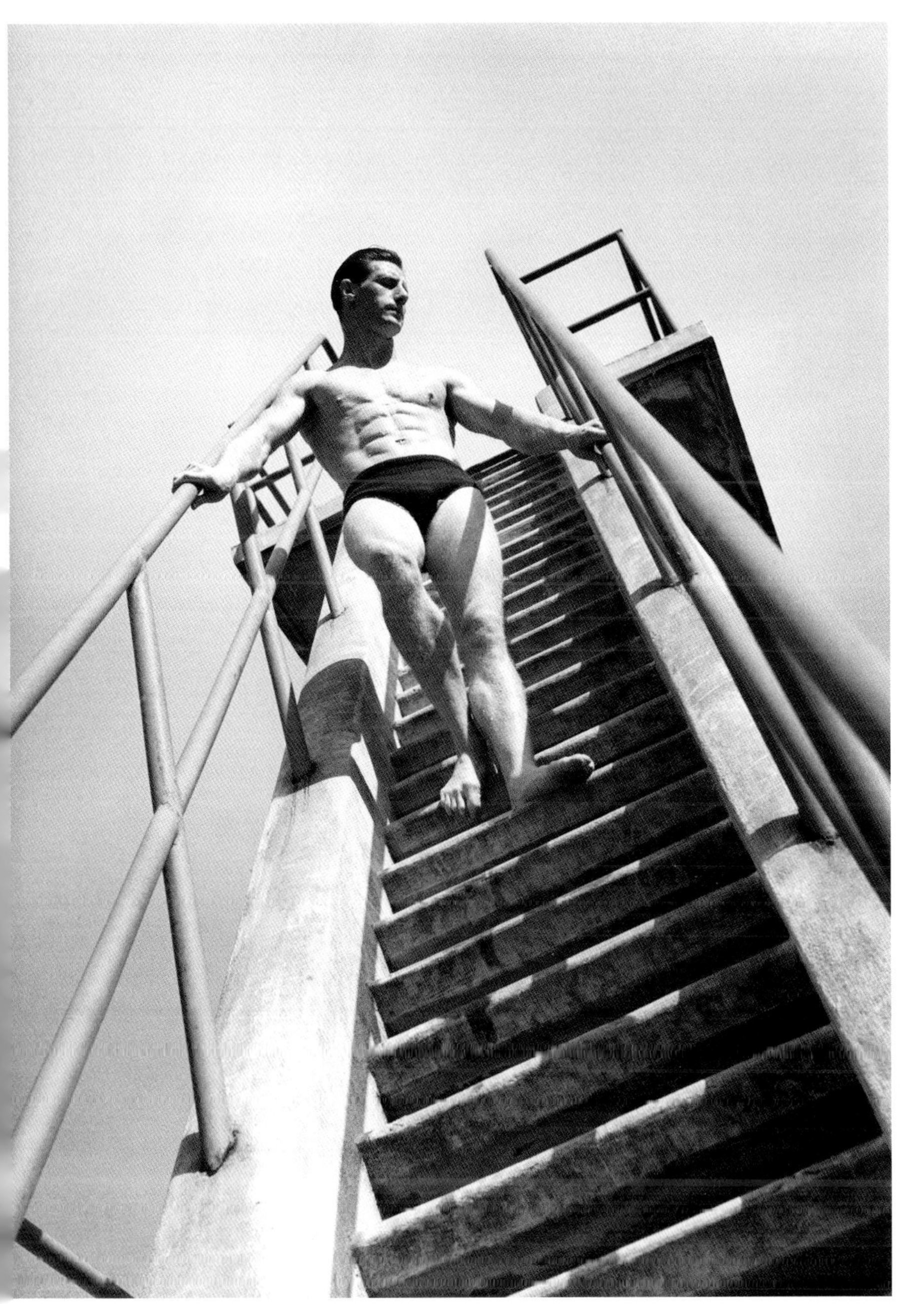

Raymond Voinquel, Au Stade de Bordeaux, 1941

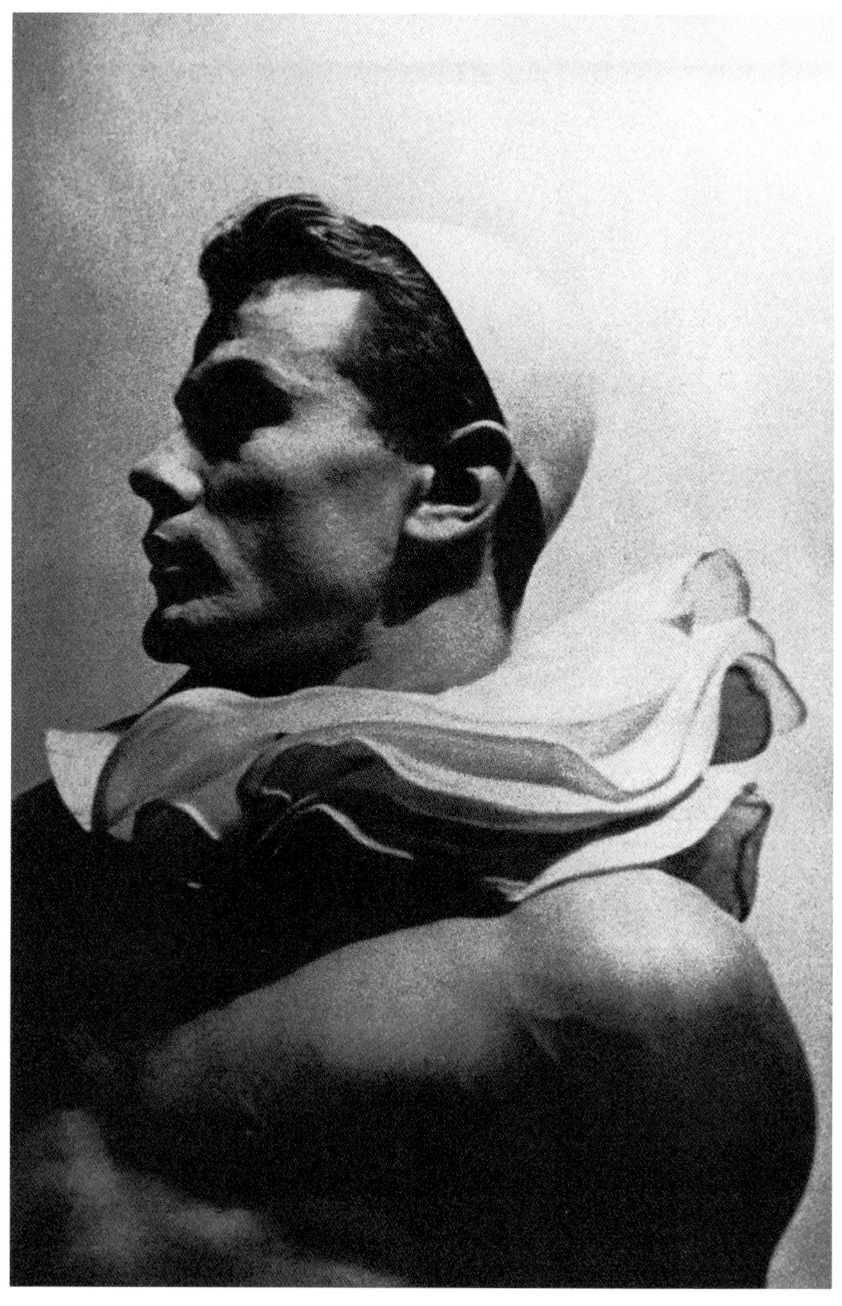

220   **Cecil Beaton,** Dick Beard, from the Ballet "Illuminations" by Sir Frederick Ashton, c. 1950

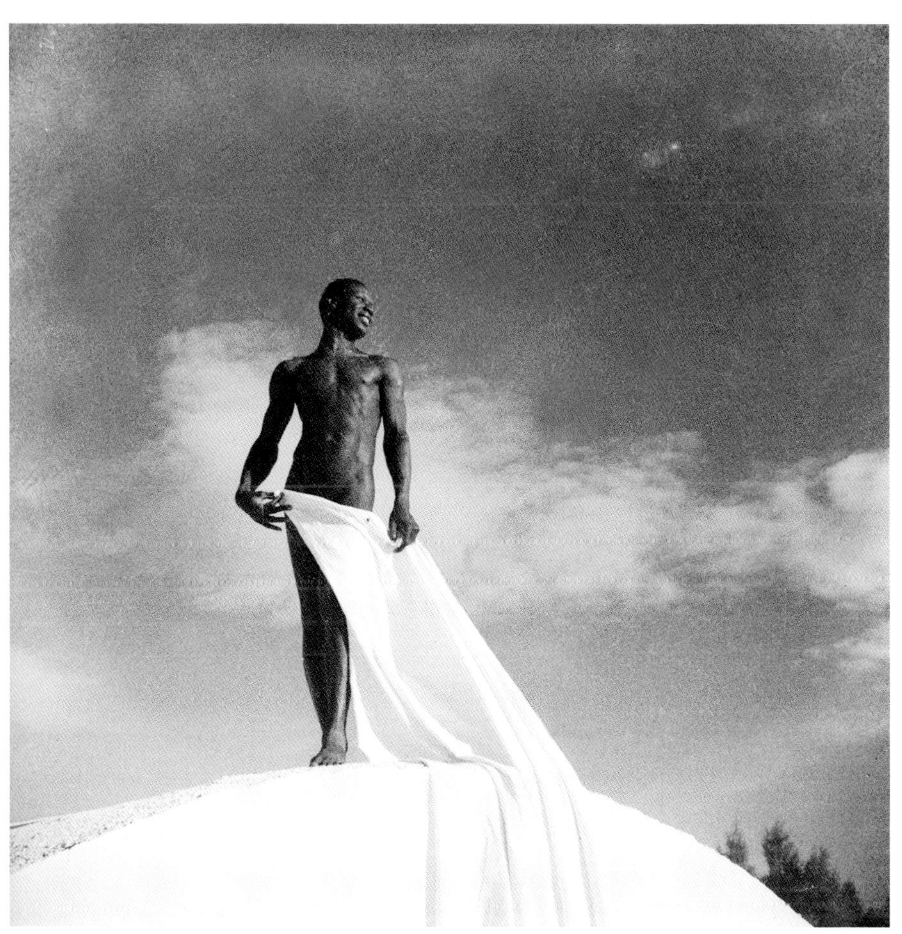

Cecil Beaton, Morocco, 1958

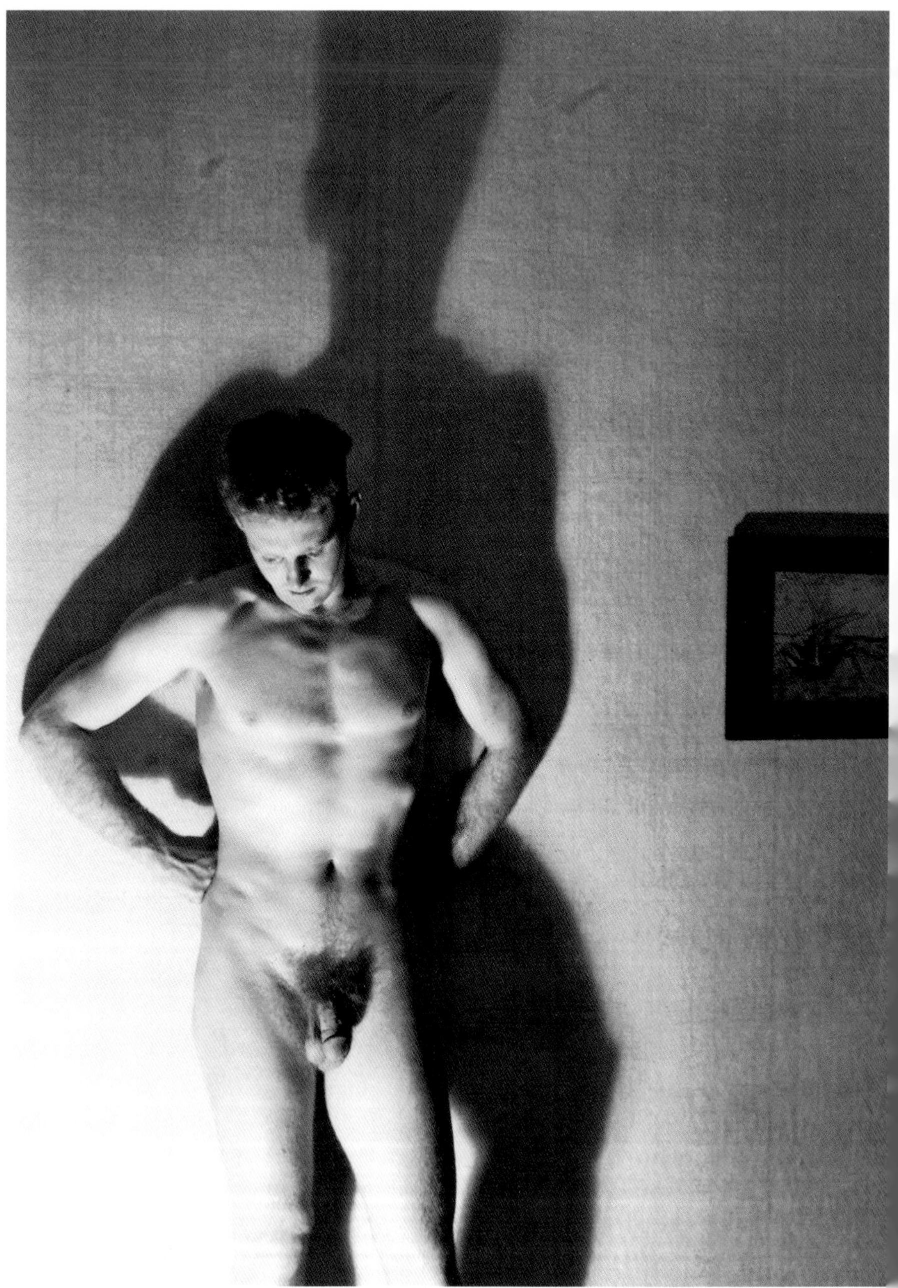

Minor White, Portland, 1940

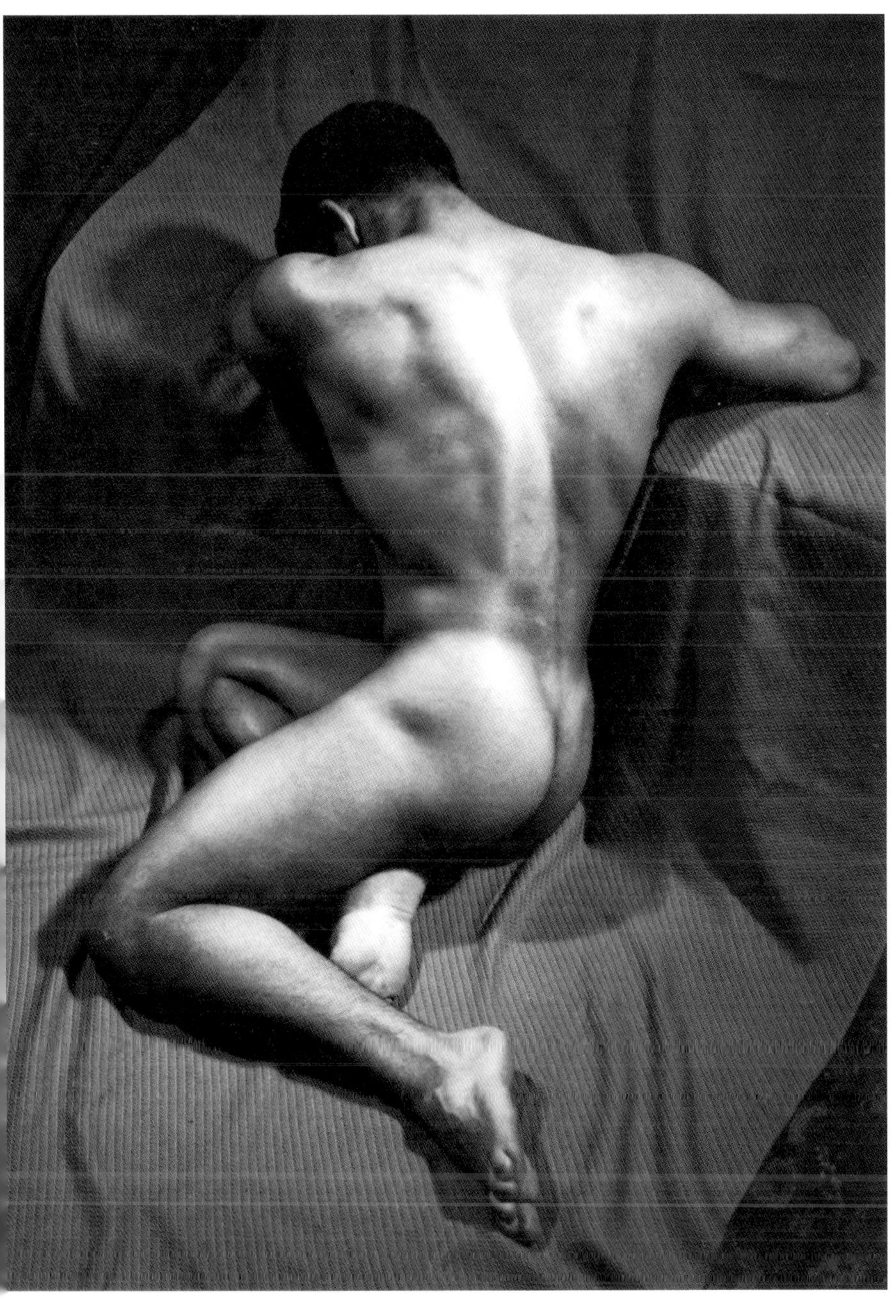

Minor White, Gino Cipolla, 1940

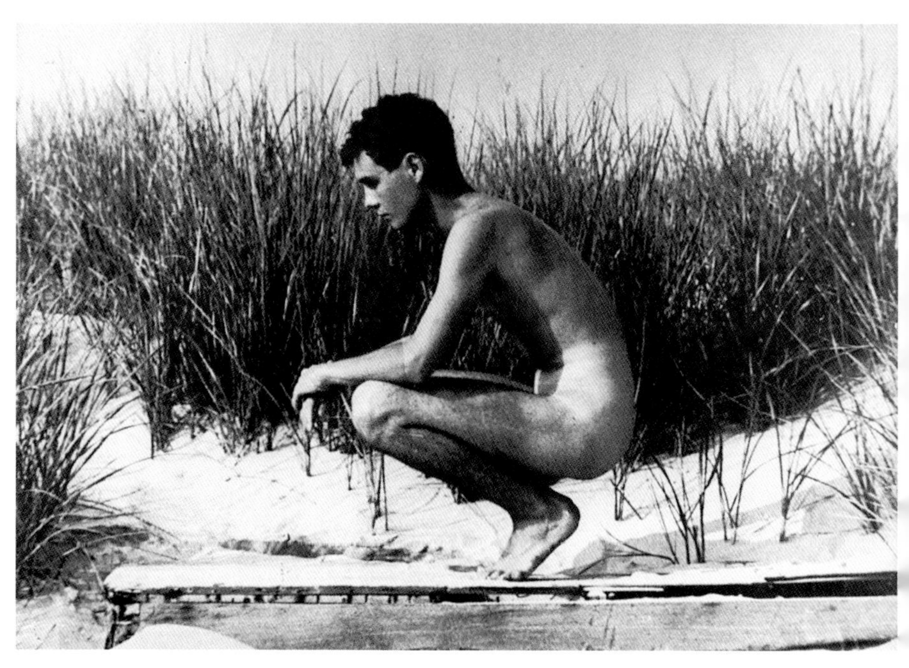

PAJAMA, Donald Windham, 1942

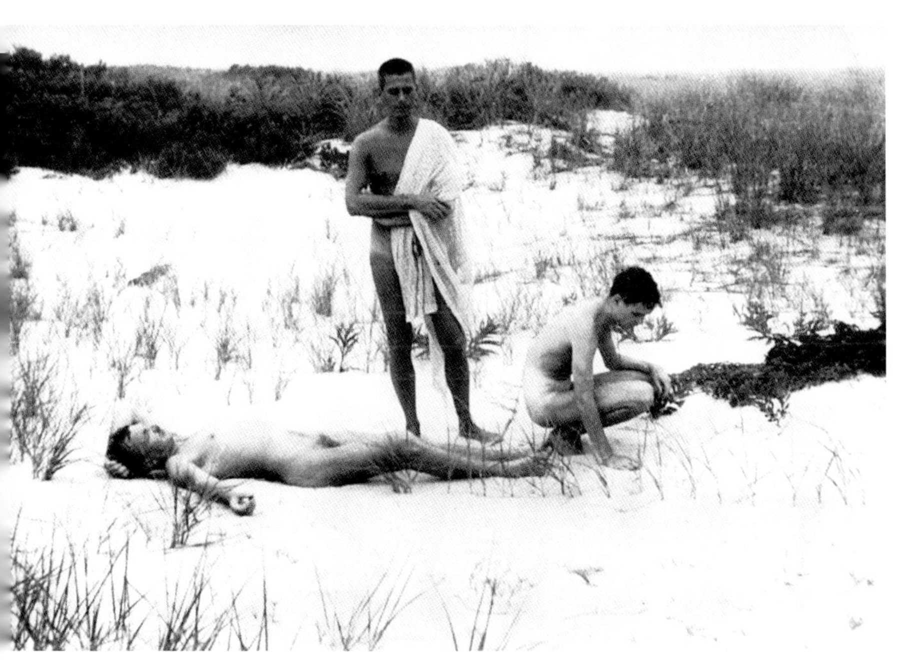

PAJAMA, Jared French, Paul Cadmus, Donald Windham, 1942

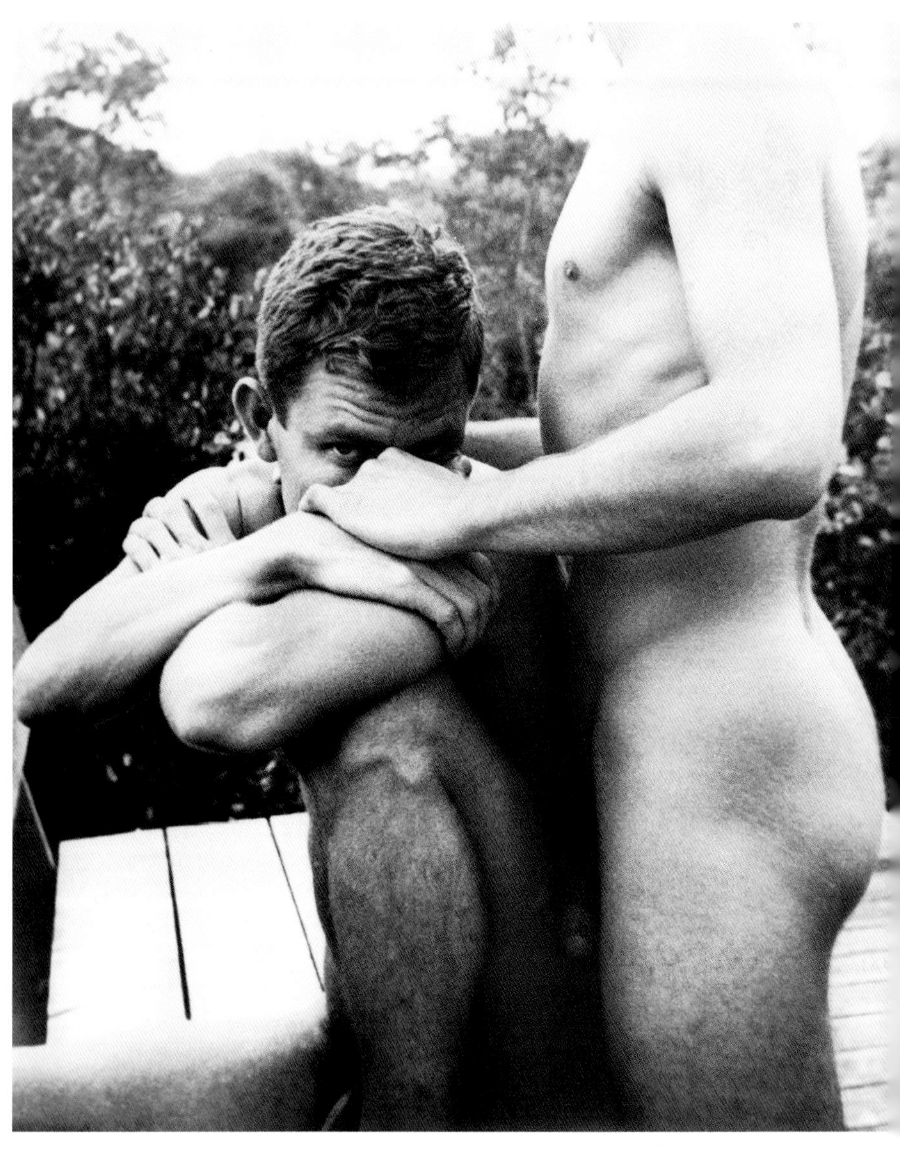

PAJAMA, Chuck and Ted, 1953

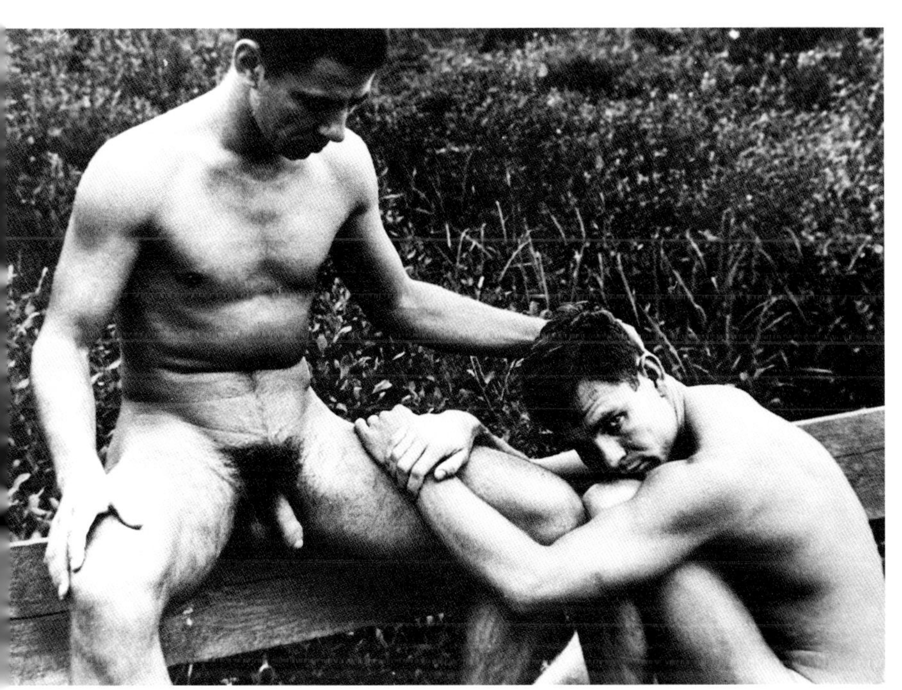

PAJAMA, Ted and Chuck, 1953

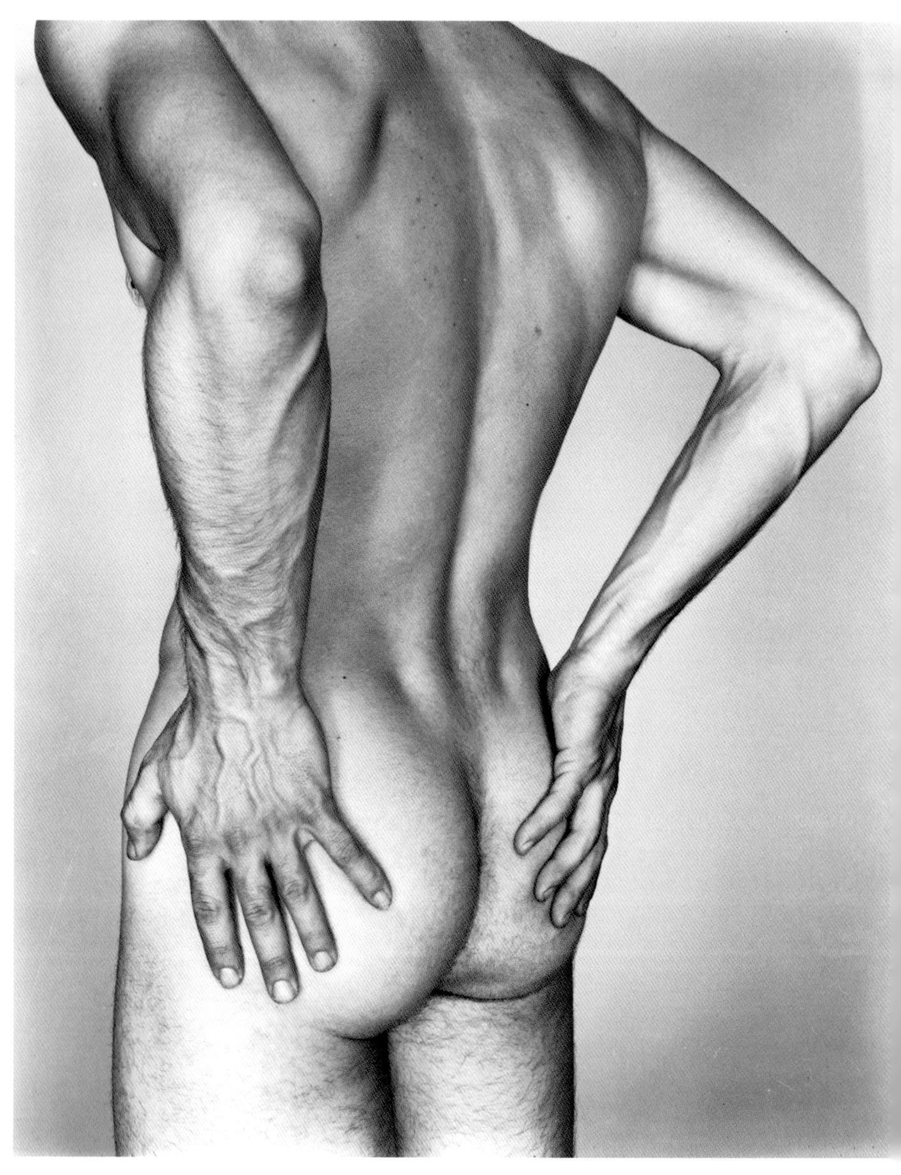

George Platt Lynes, Ted Starkowski, May 19, 1955

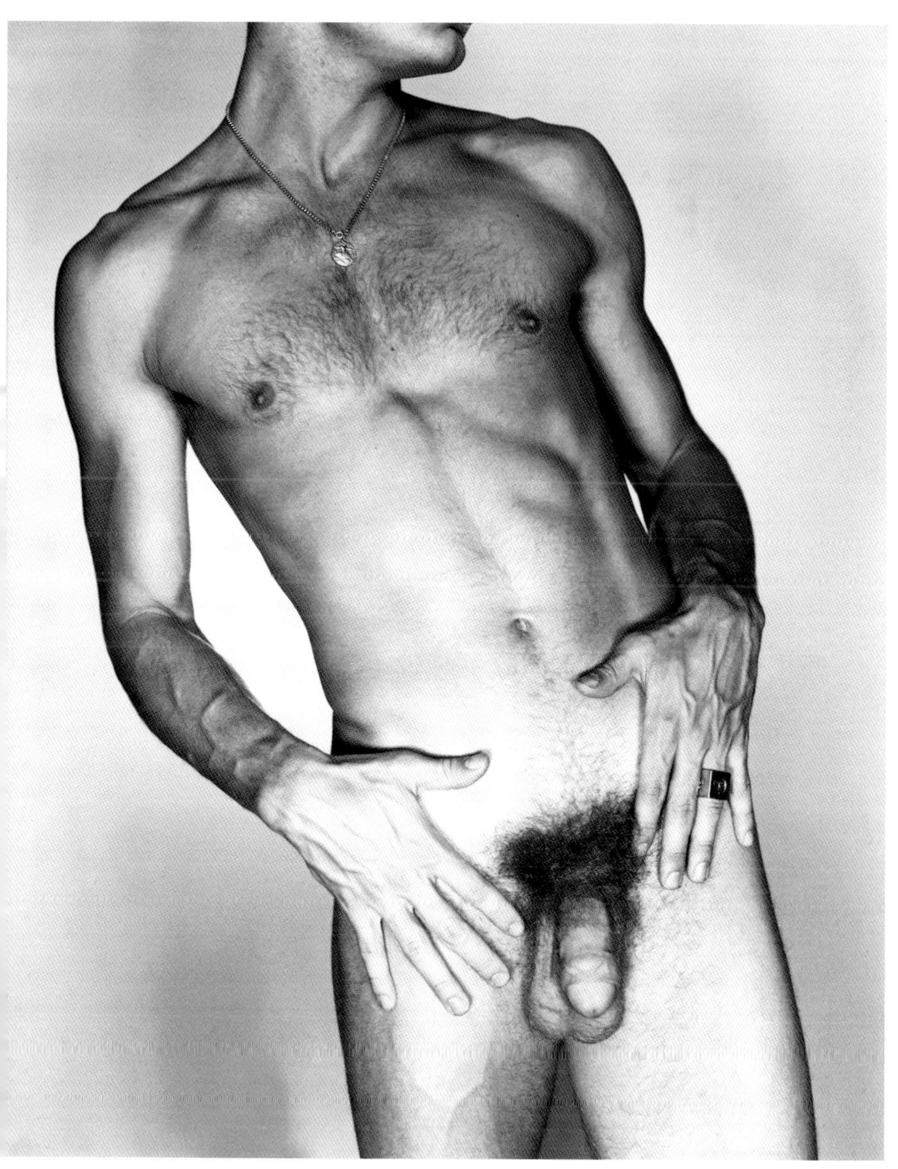

George Platt Lynes, Chuck Howard, c. 1950

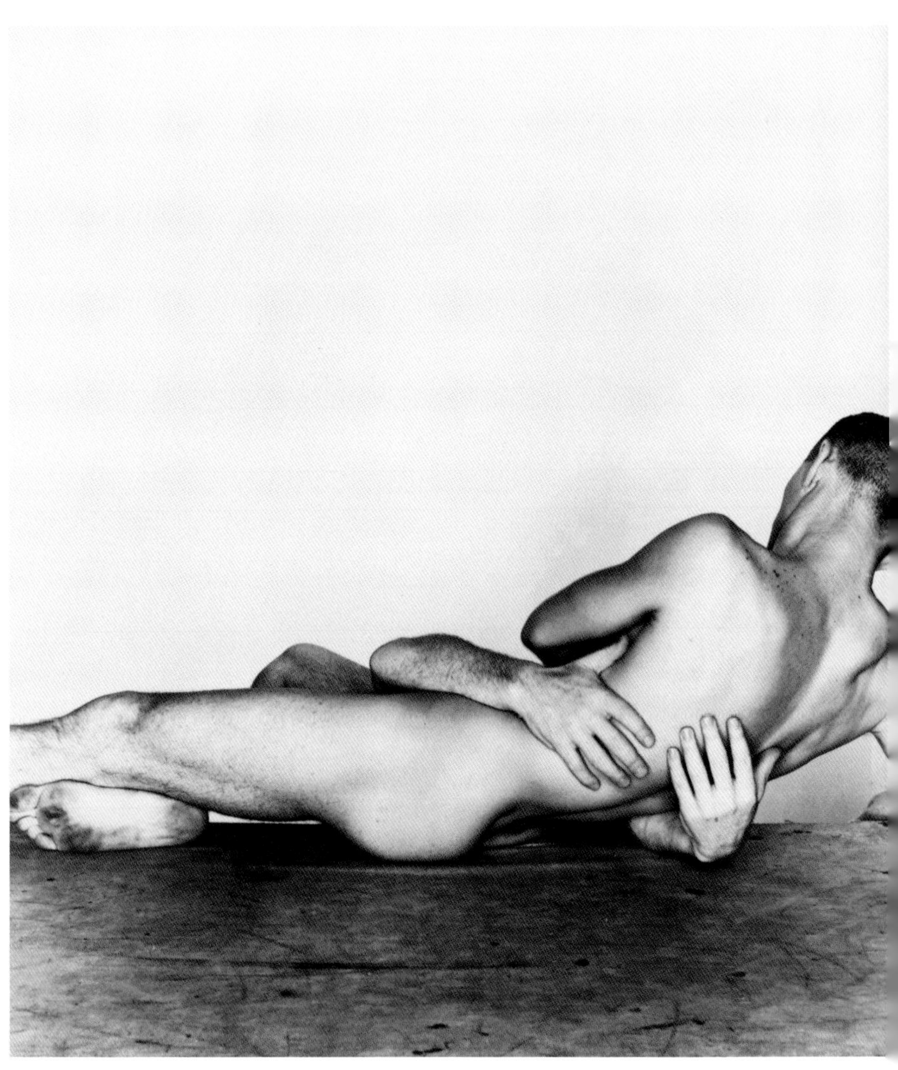

George Platt Lynes, Ernest Henry in the Arms of Neel Bate, c. 1953

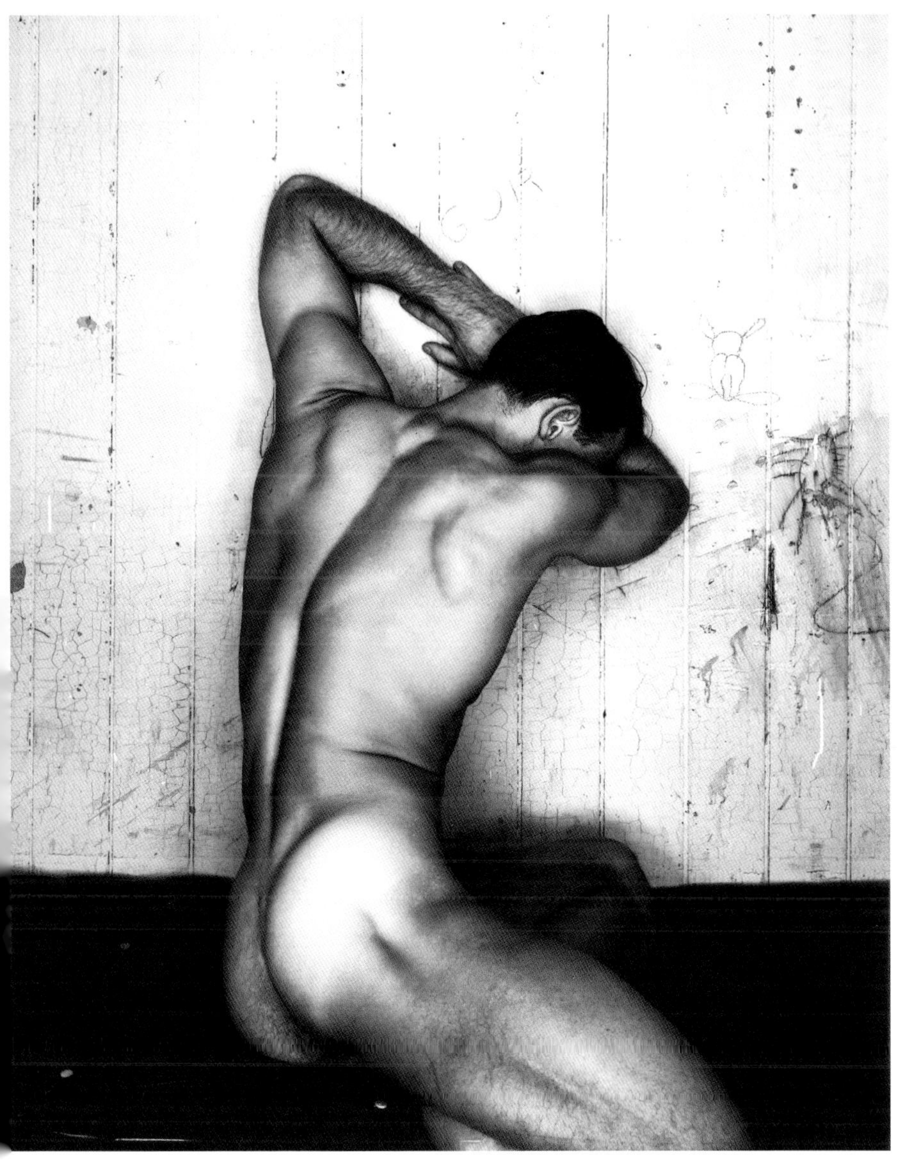

George Platt Lynes, Gordon Hanson, November 11, 1954

231

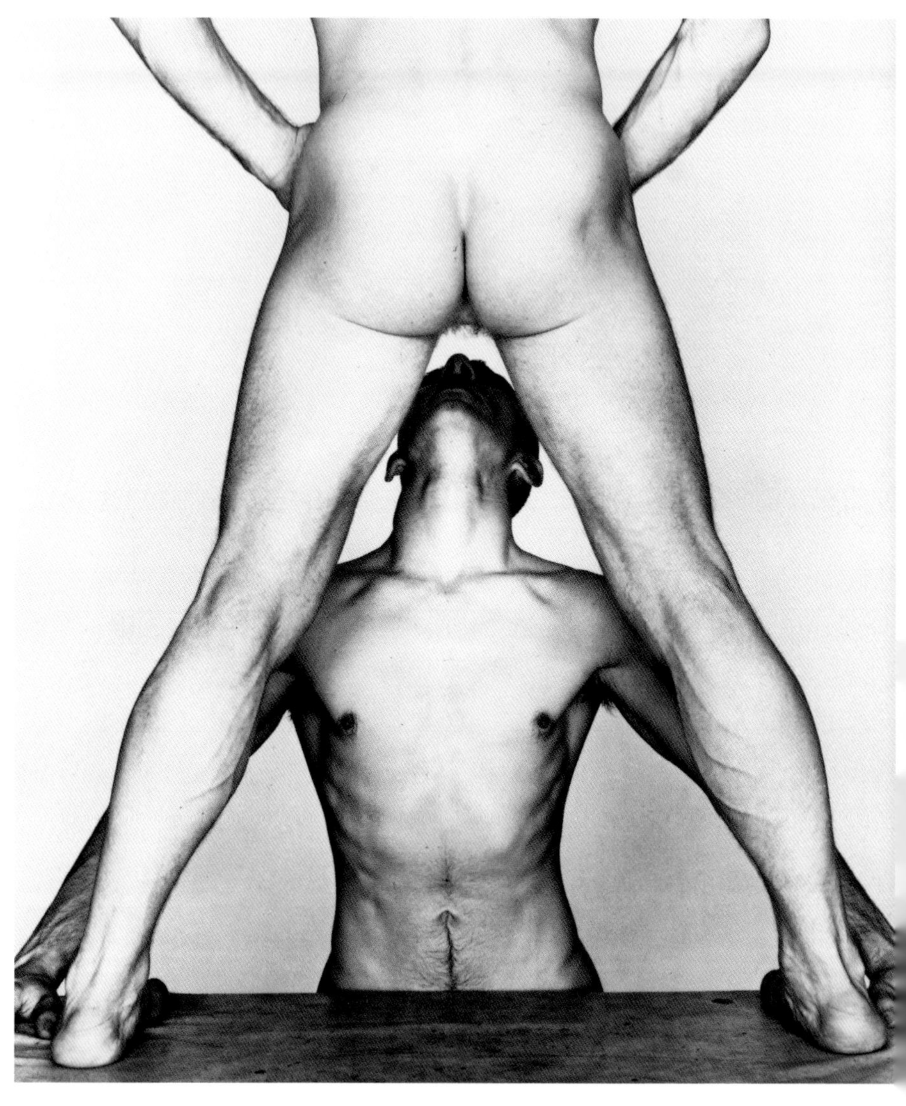

George Platt Lynes, Mel Fillini and Ted Starkowski in Background, 1954

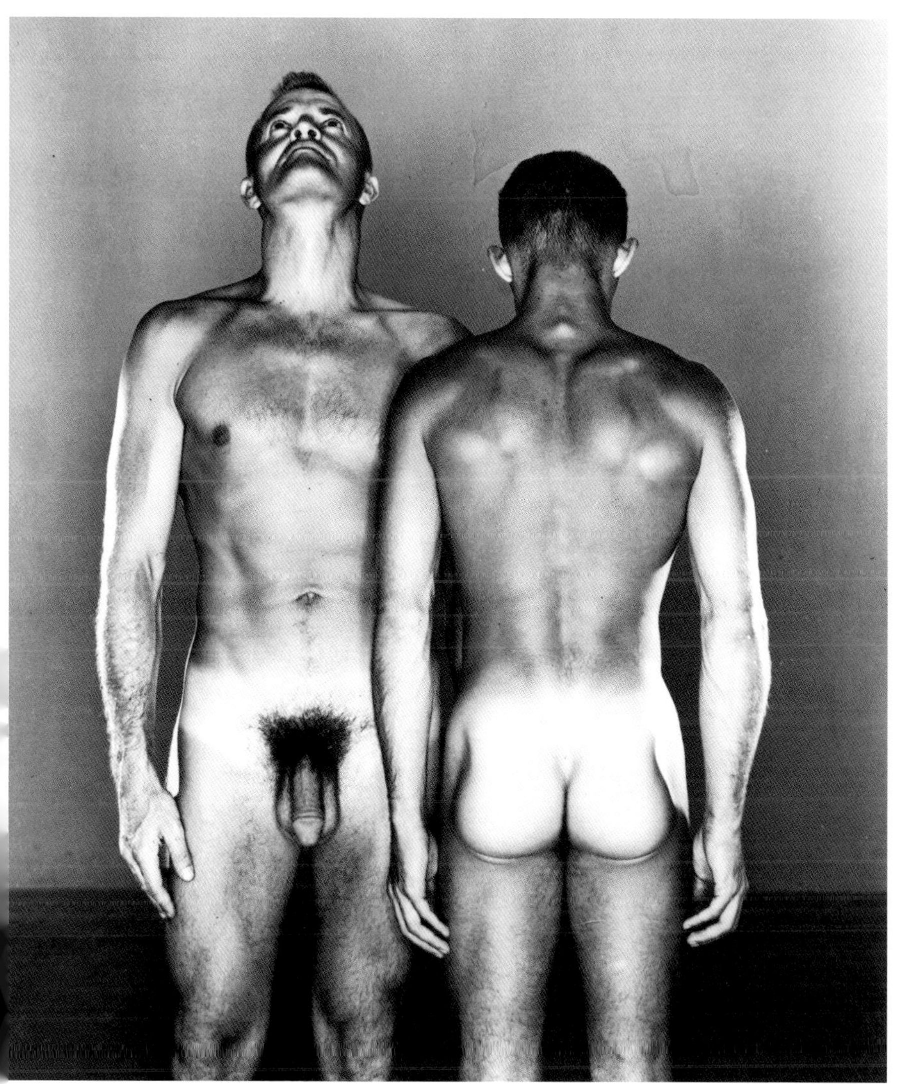

George Platt Lynes, Neel Bate and Ernest Henry, 1954

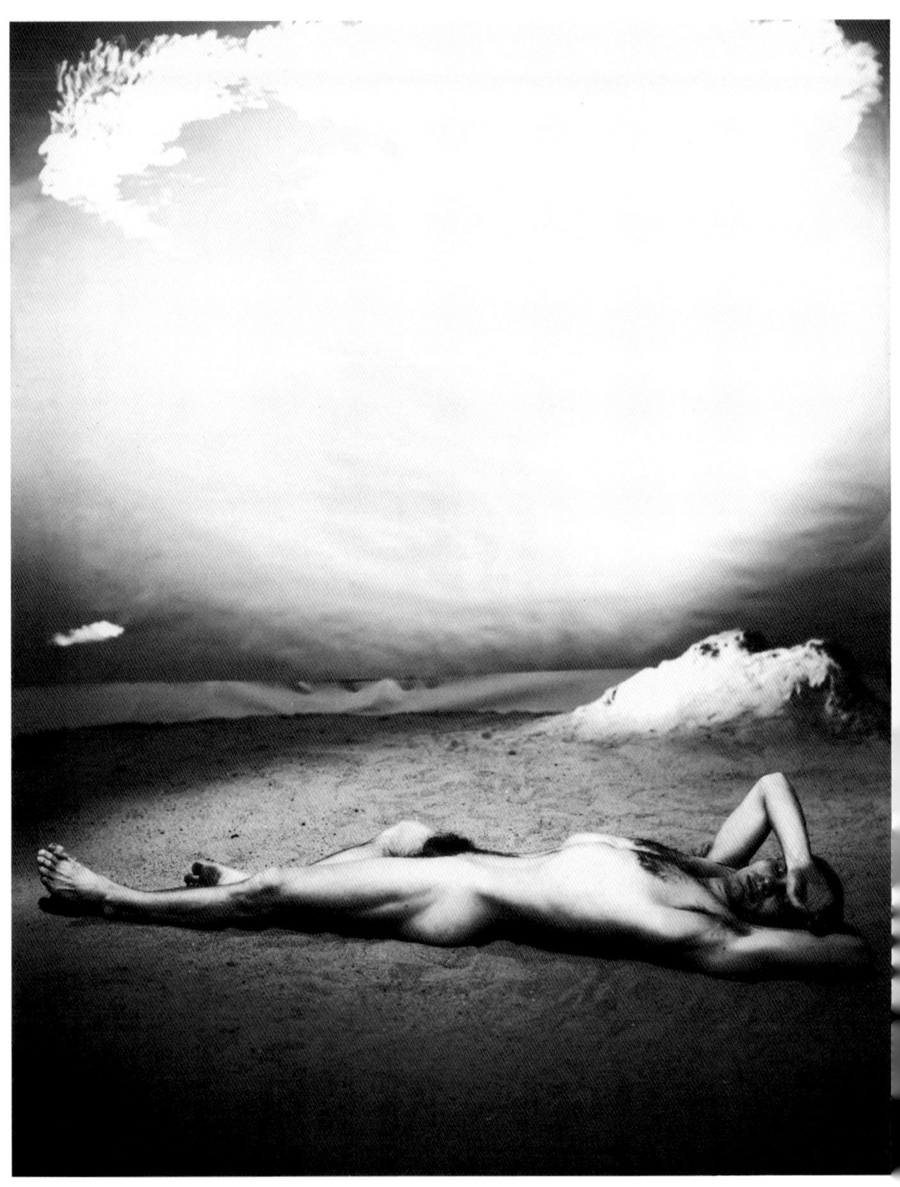

George Platt Lynes, Chuck Howard, March 11, 1950

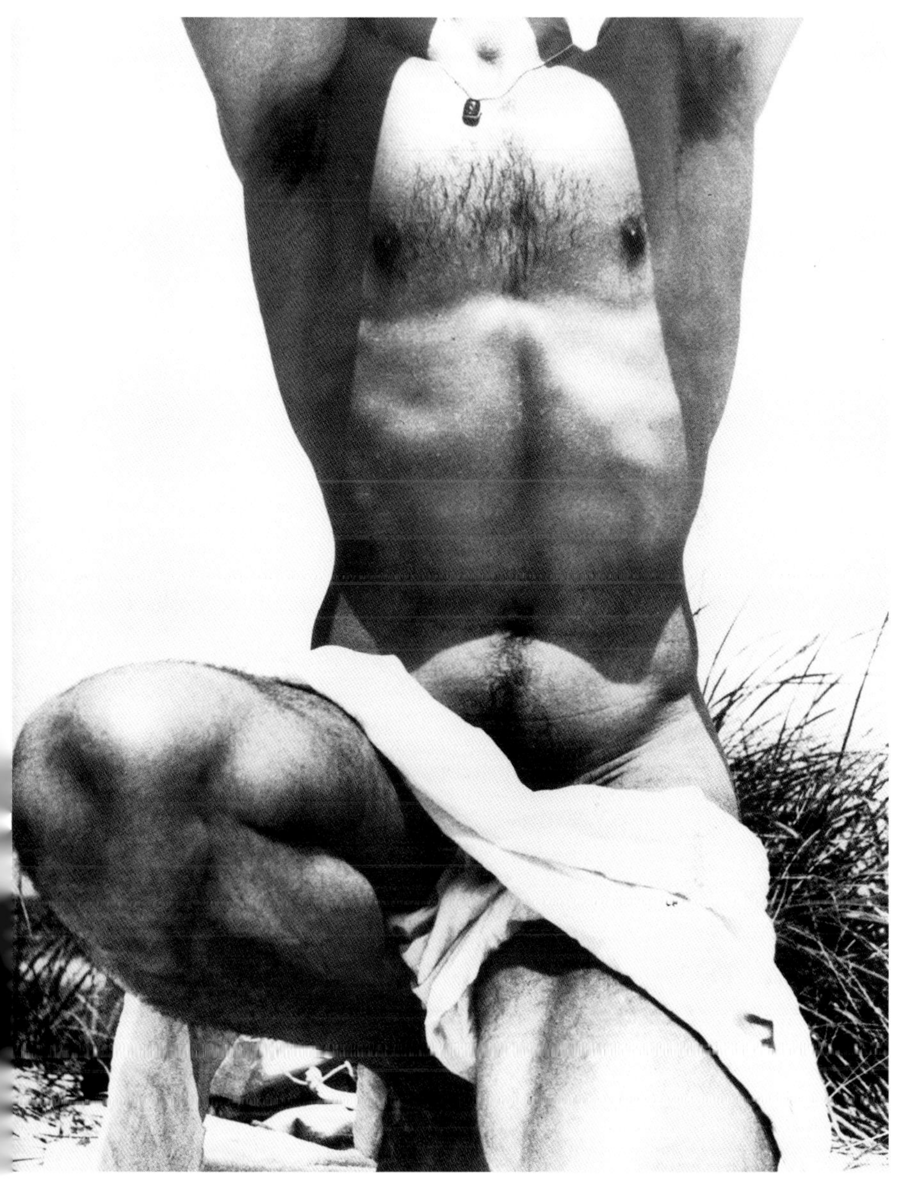

George Platt Lynes, Francisco Moncion, c. 1948

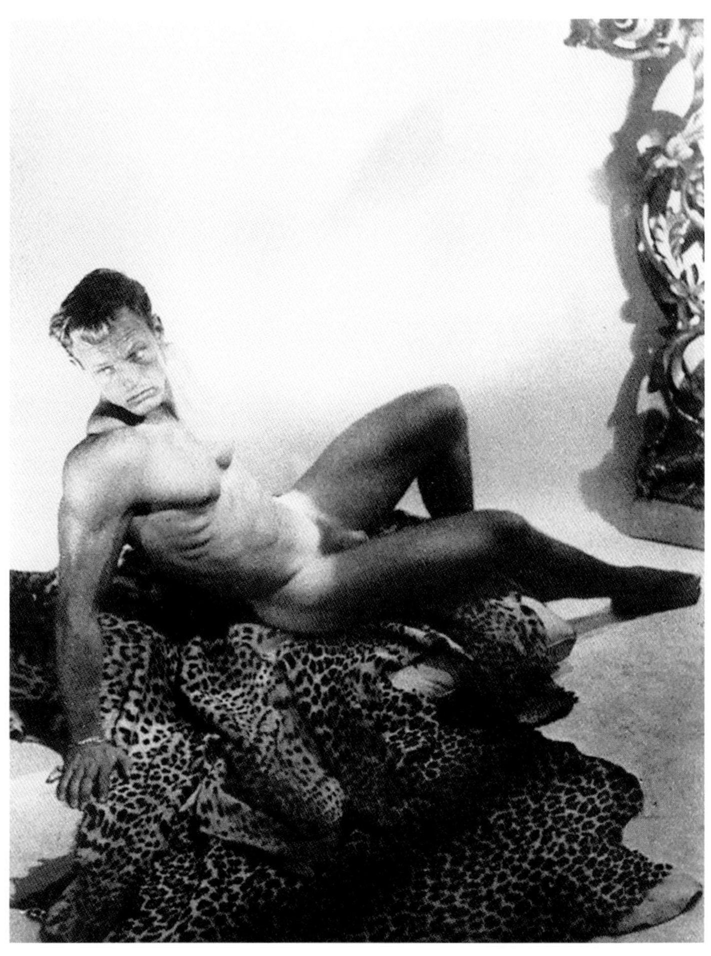

James Pendelton, Gordon Hanson, c. 1955

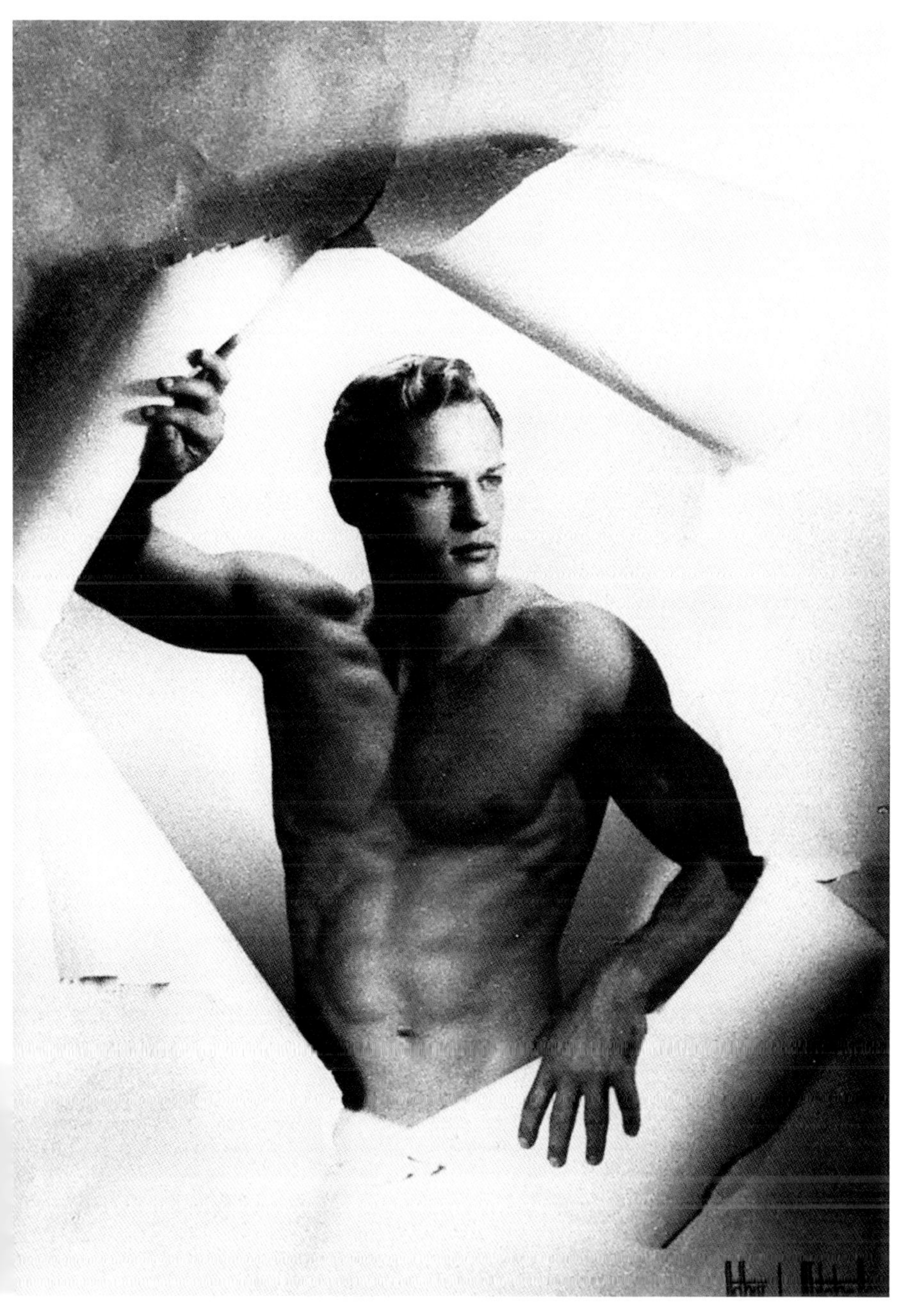

James Pendelton, Gordon Hanson, c. 1955

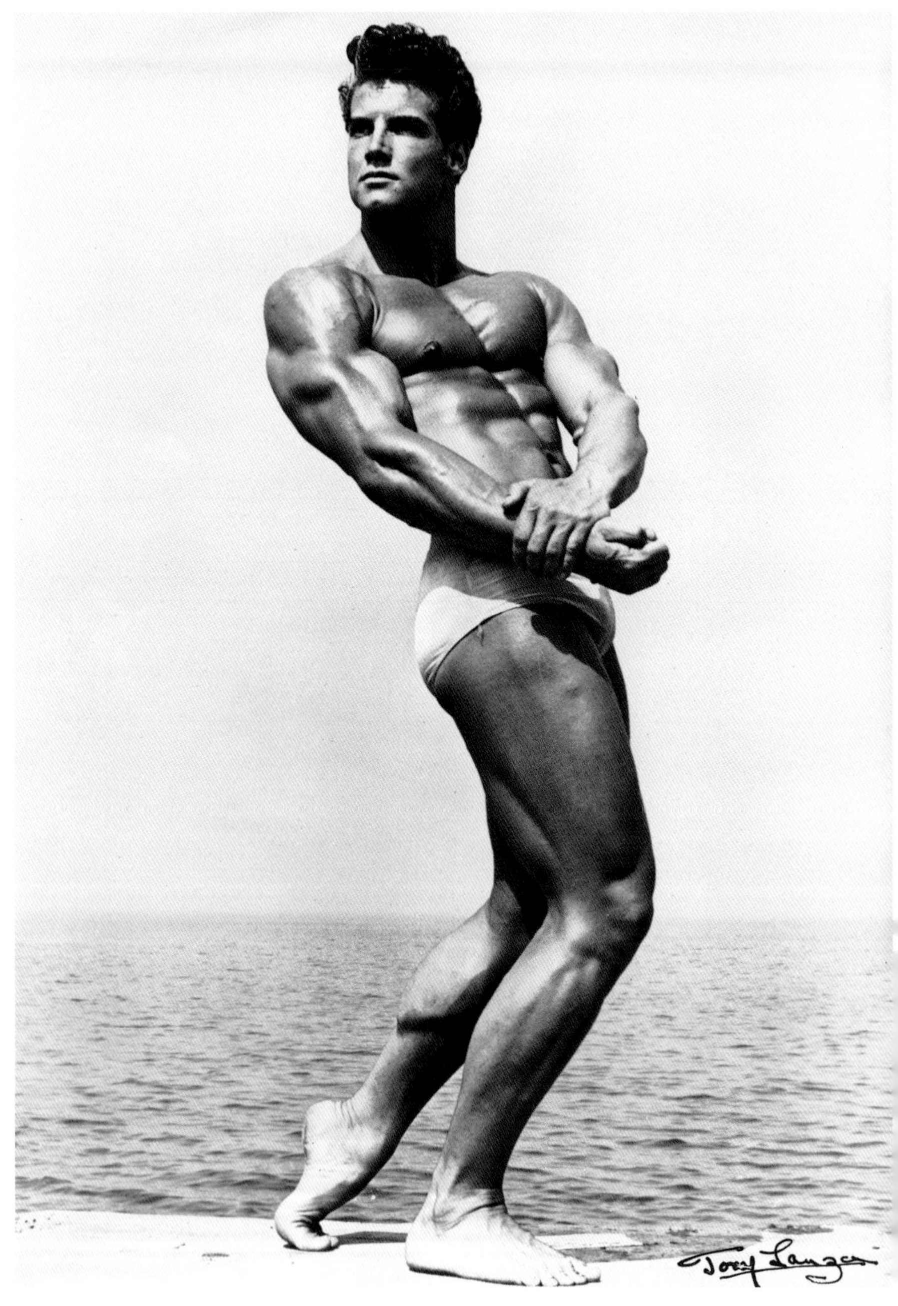

Tony Lanza, Steve Reeves, 1947

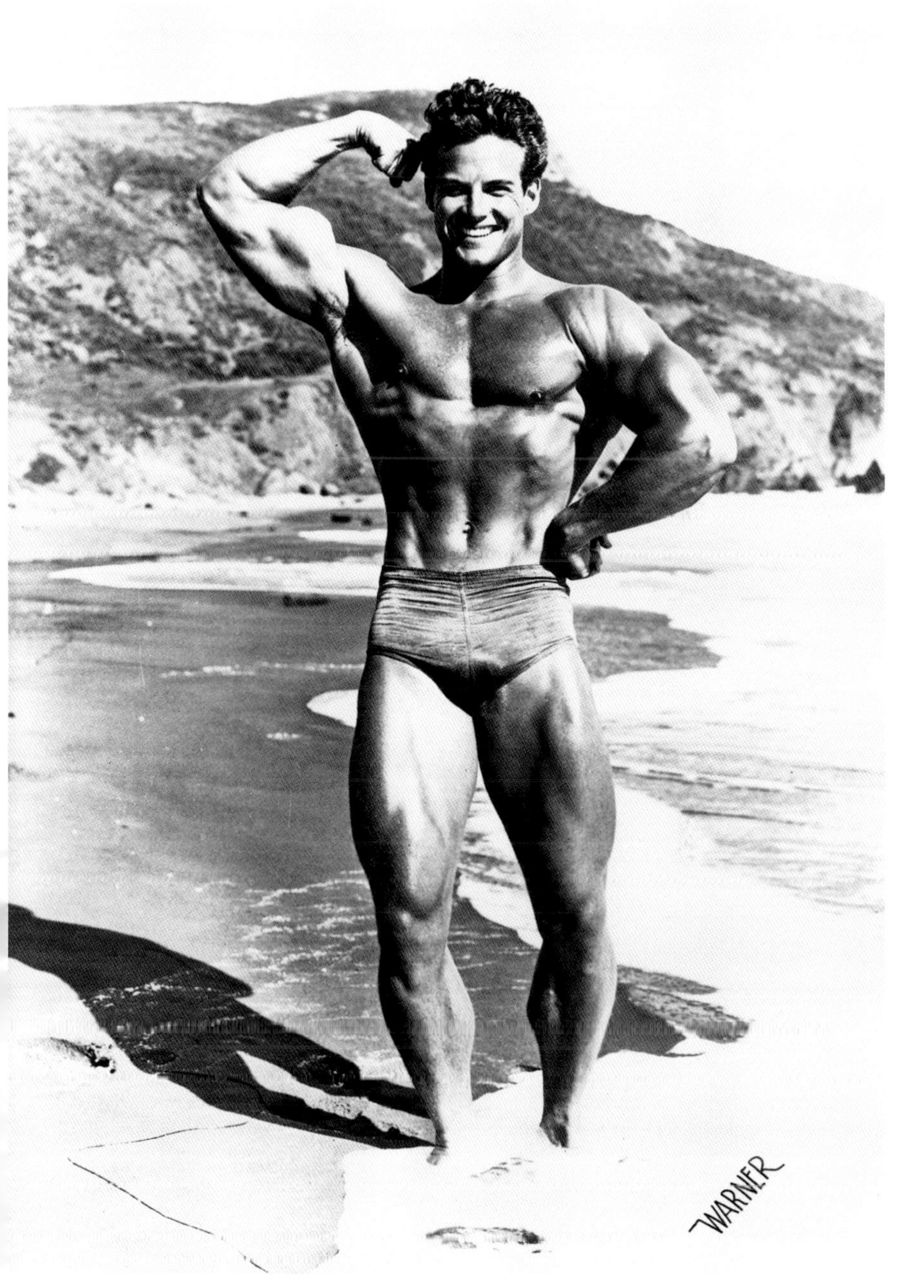

Russ Warner, Steve Reeves, 1947

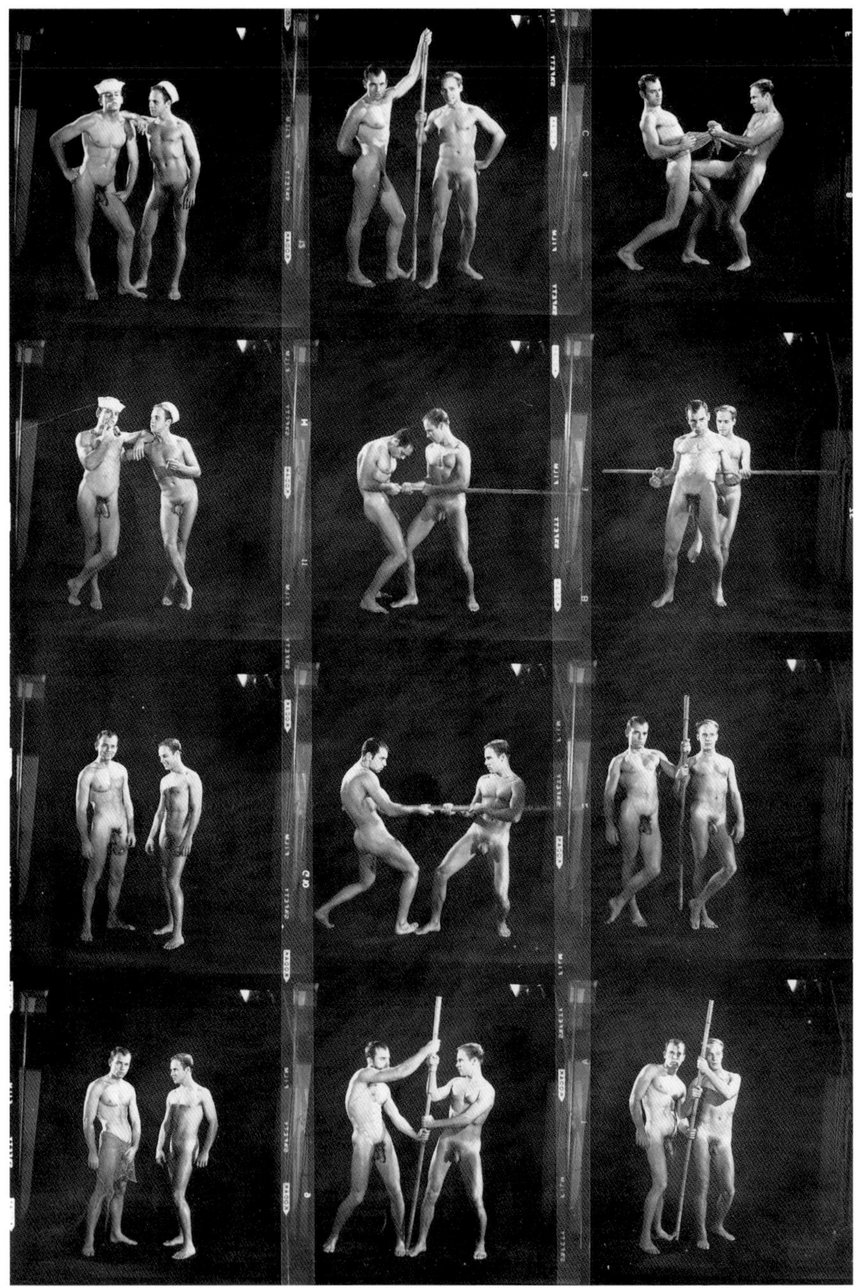

Anonymous, 1950s

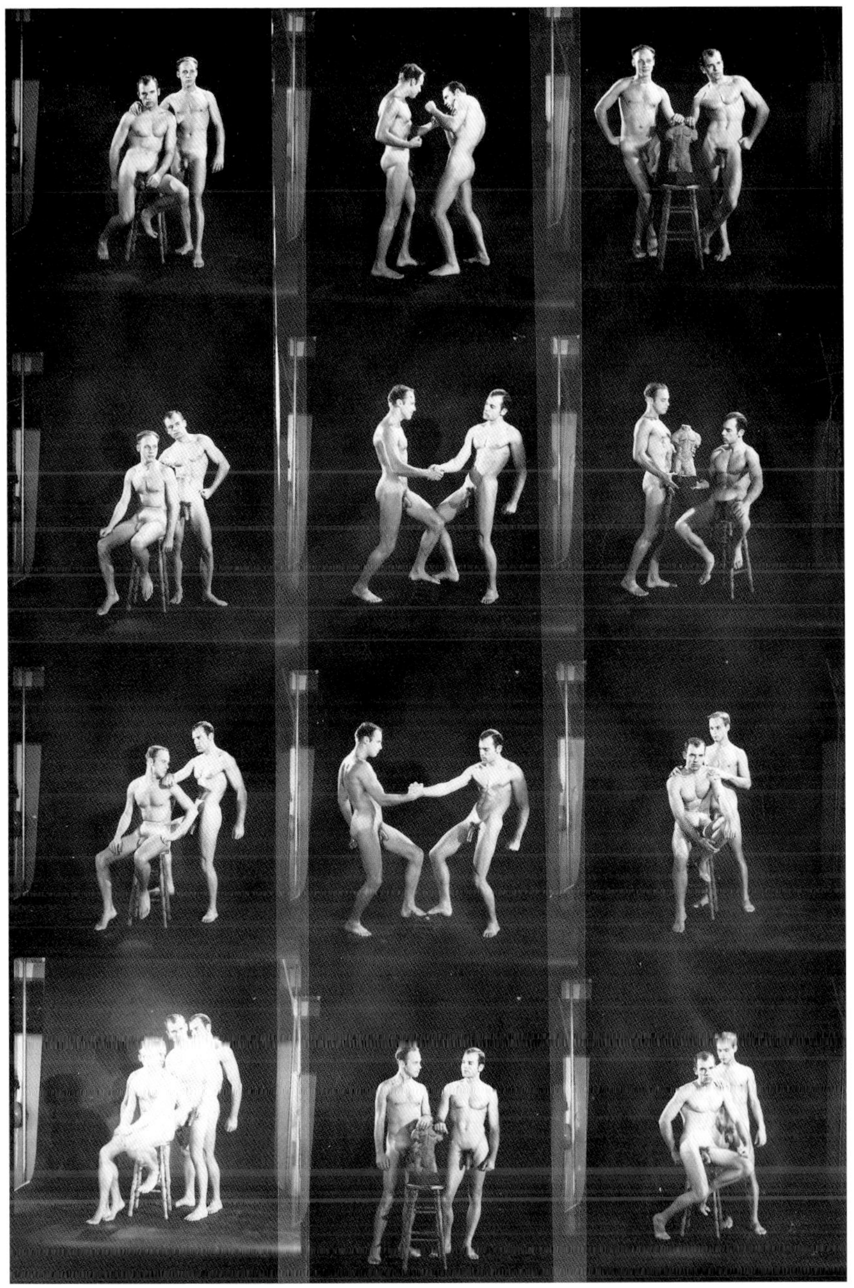

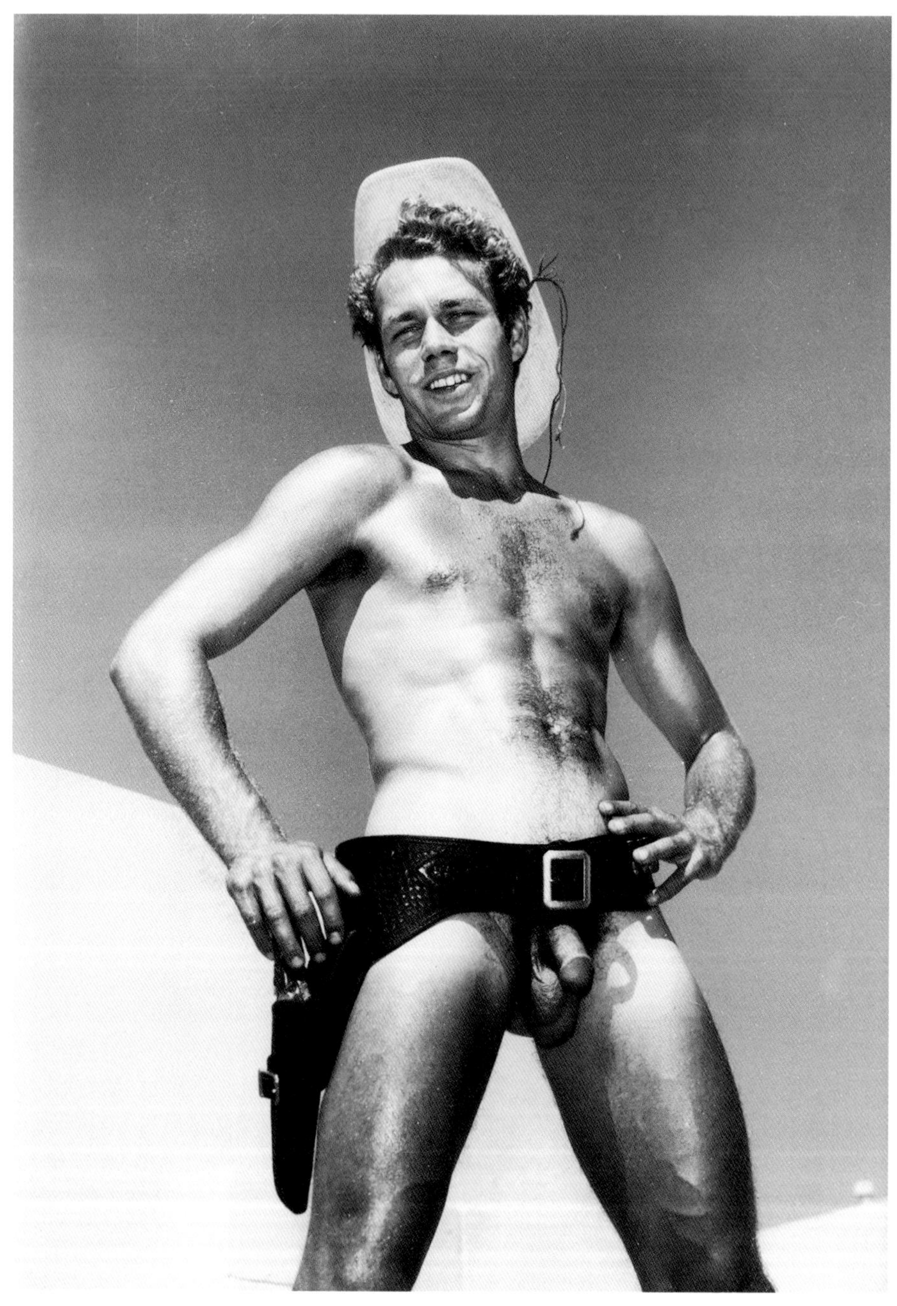

Bob Mizer, c. 1955

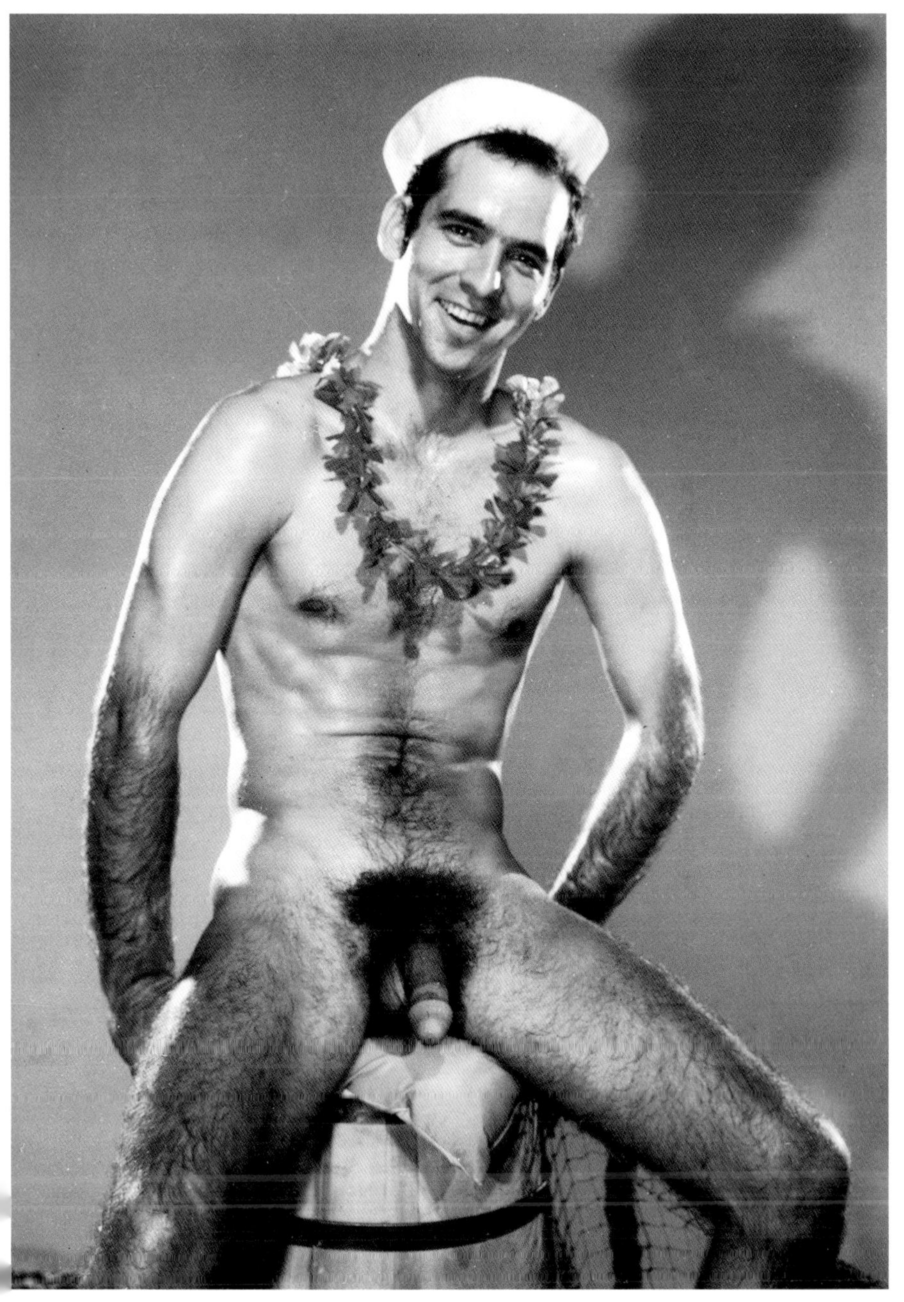

Bob Mizer, c. 1955

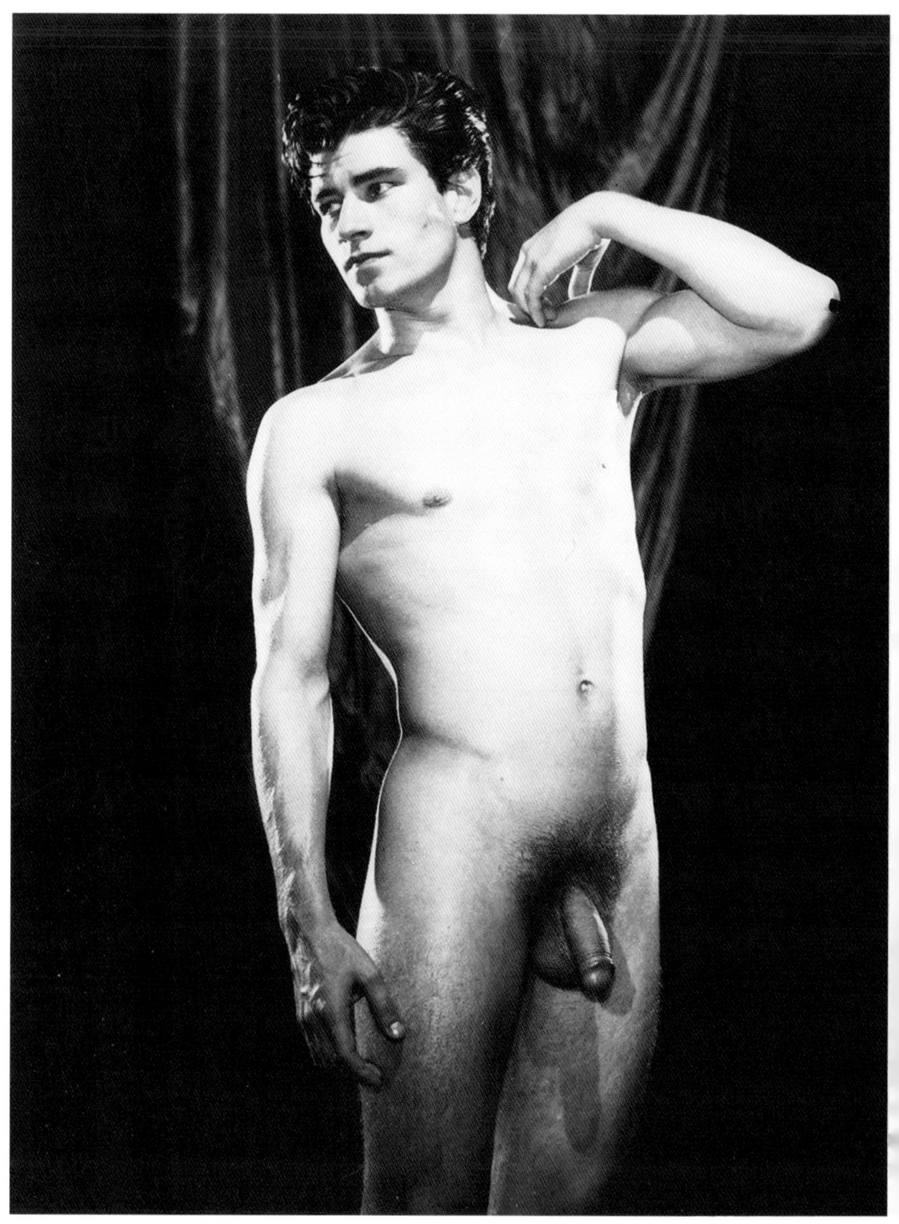

244

Bob Mizer, c. 1955

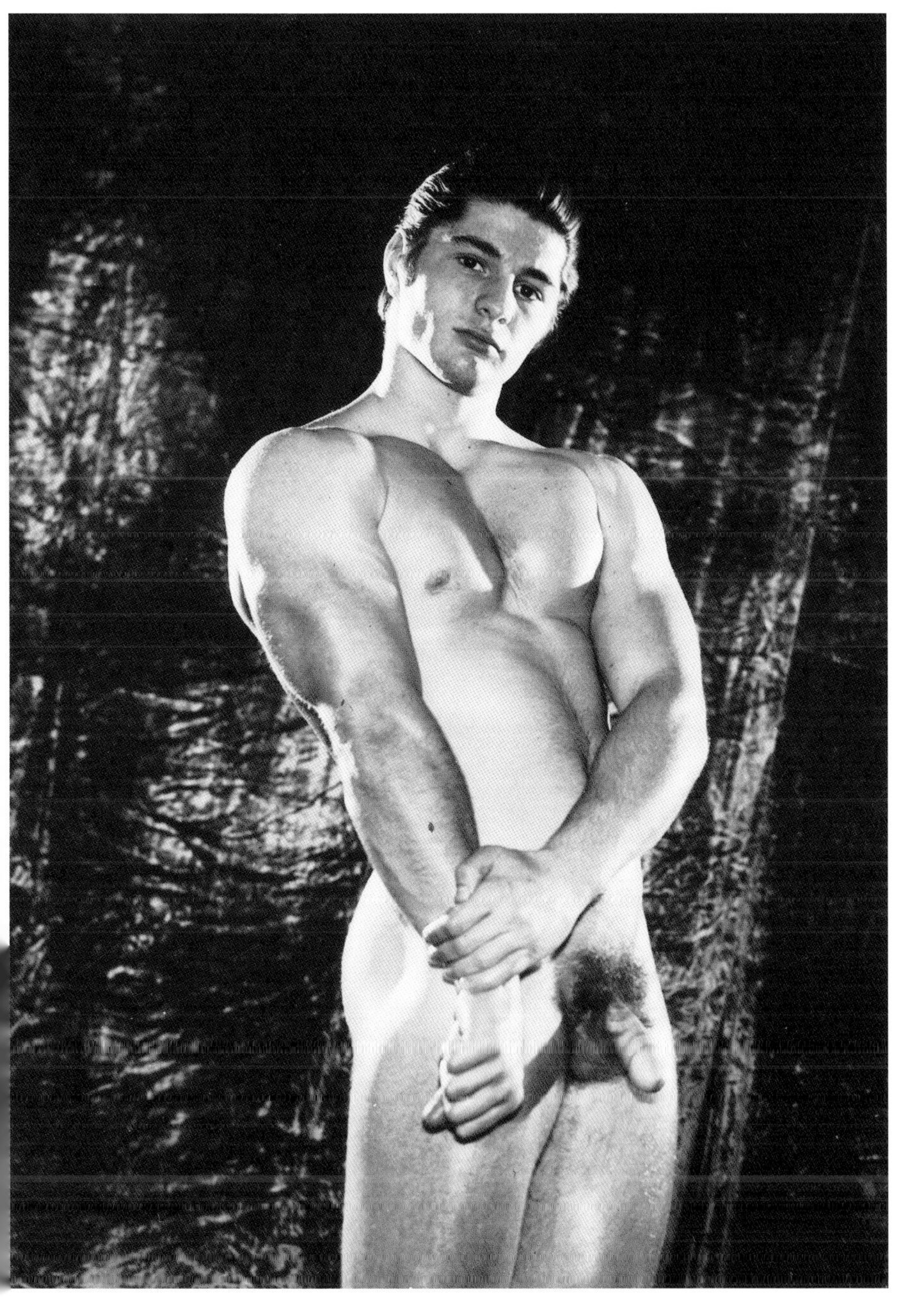

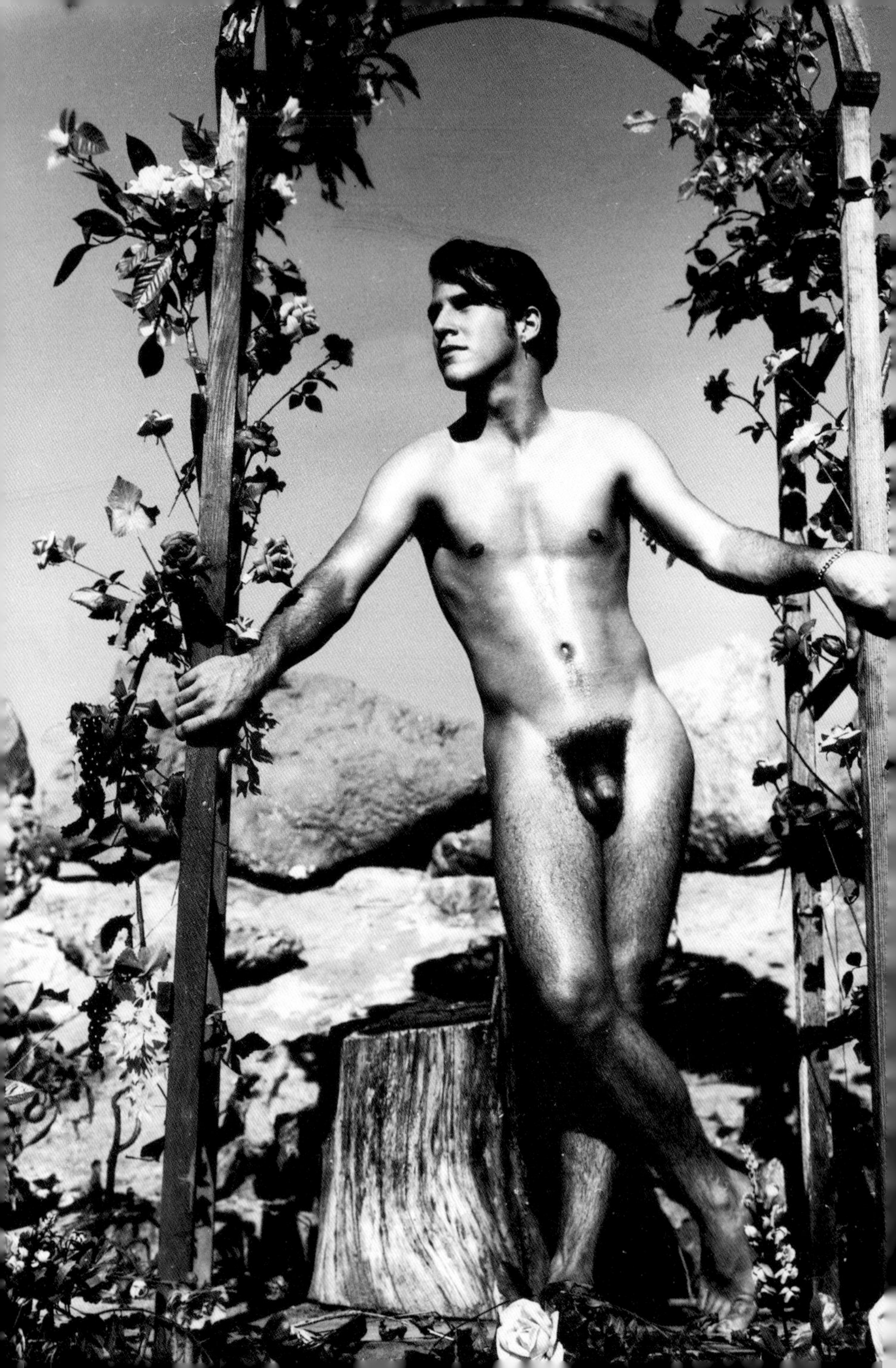

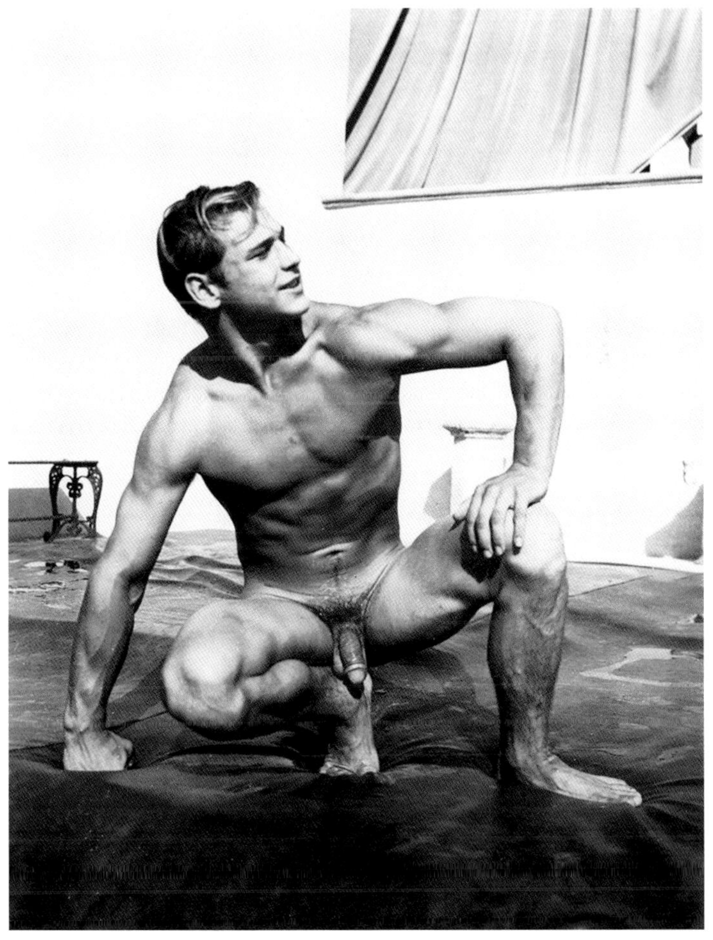

Bob Mizer, c. 1955

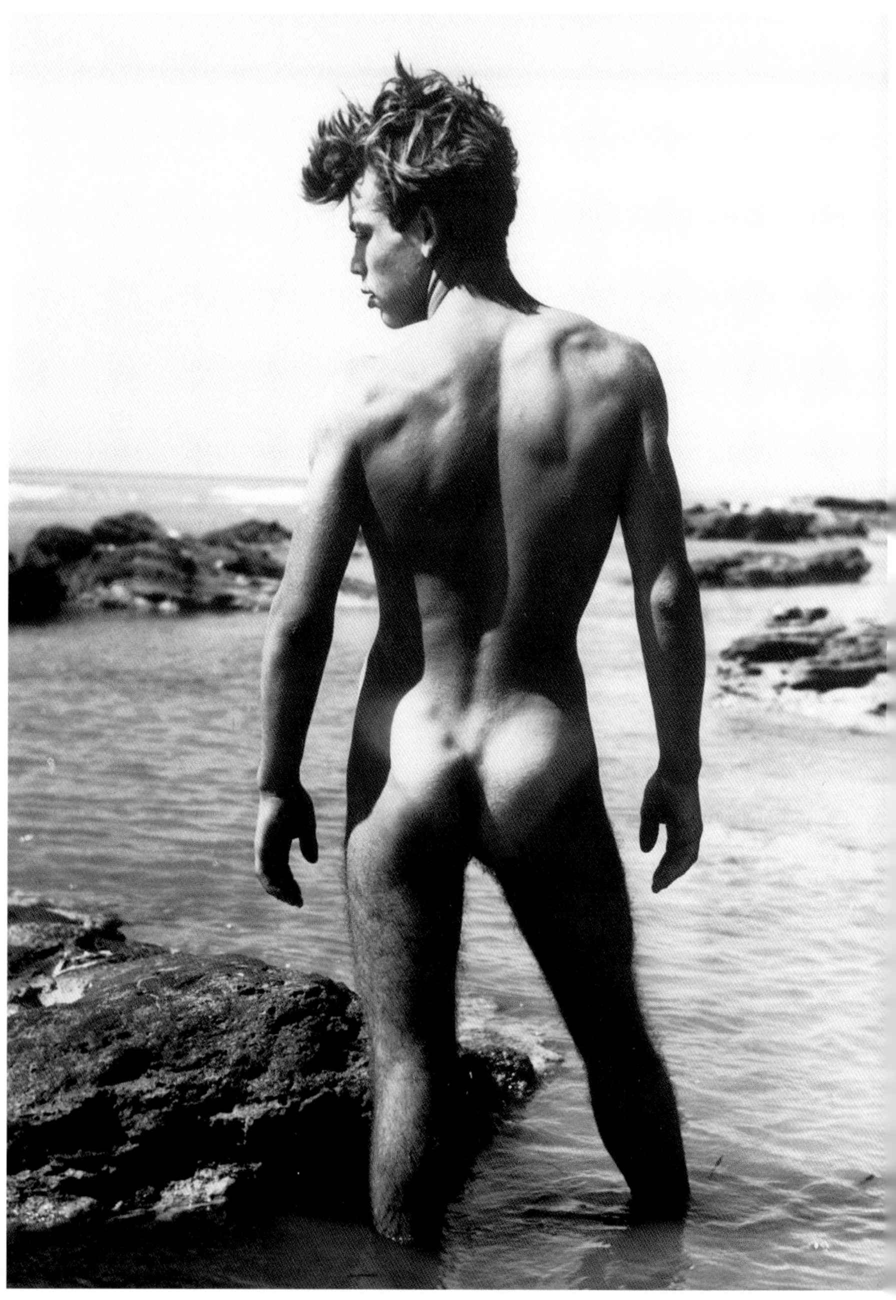

Konrad Helbig, Sicily, c. 1950–55

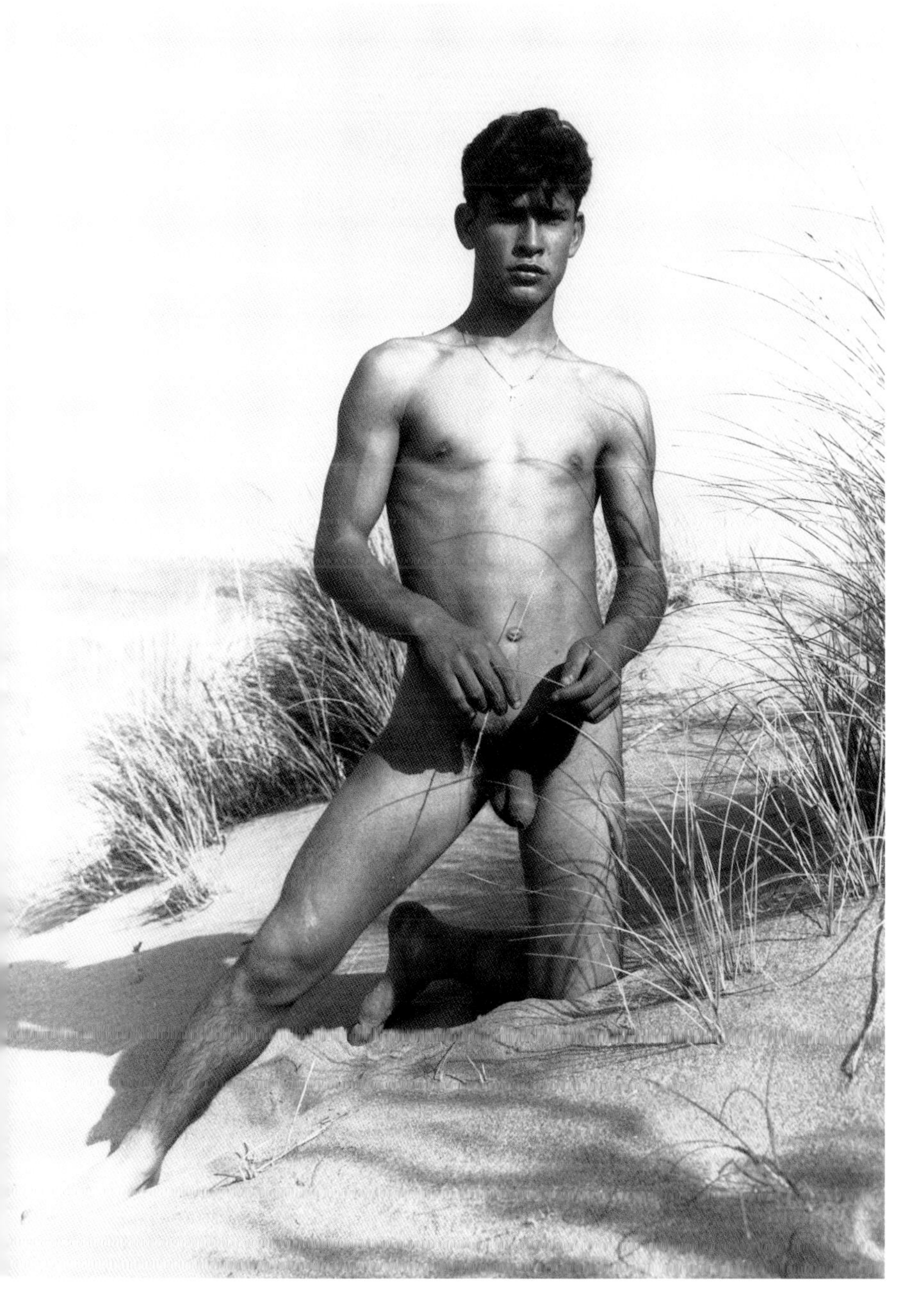

Konrad Helbig, Sicily, c. 1950–55

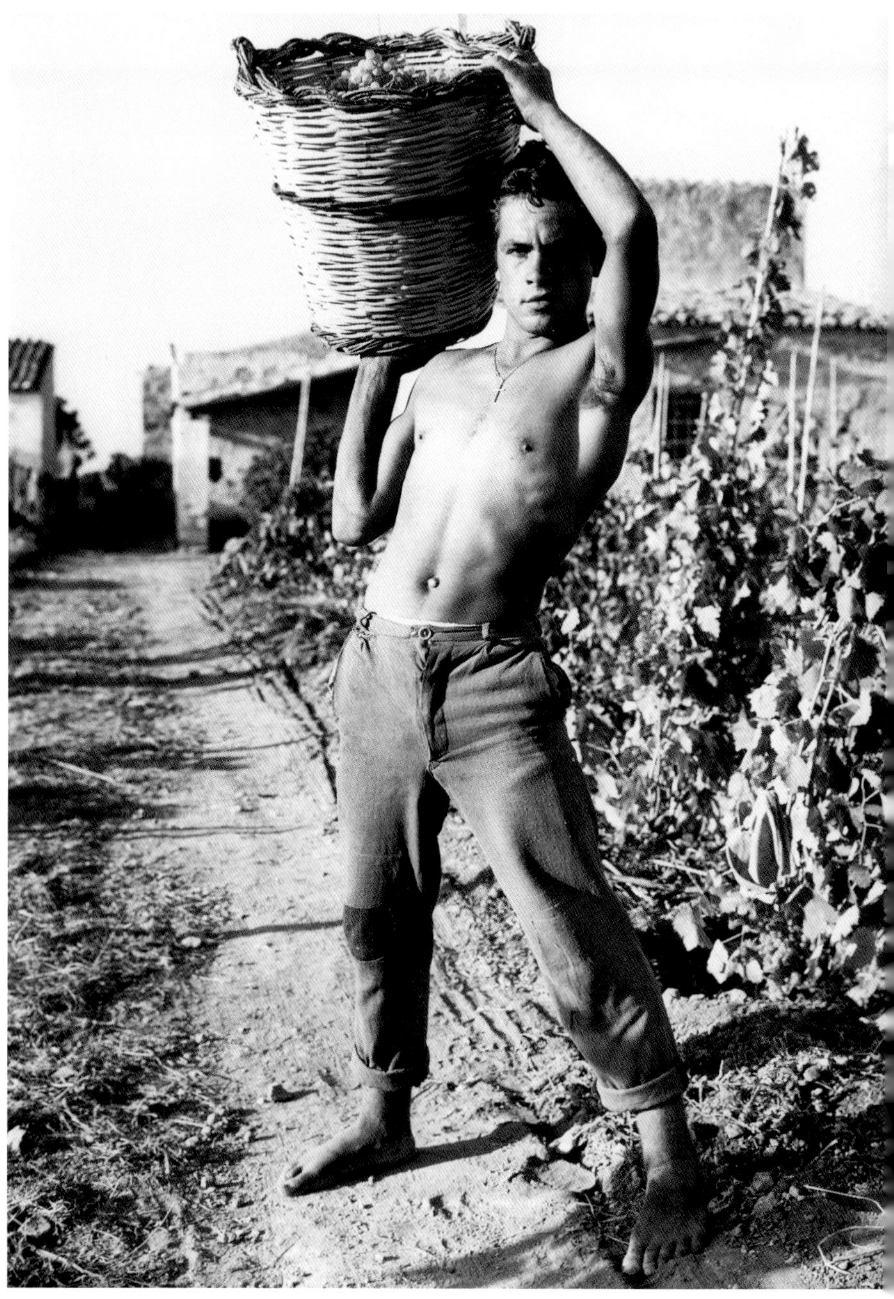

Konrad Helbig, Sicily, c. 1950–55

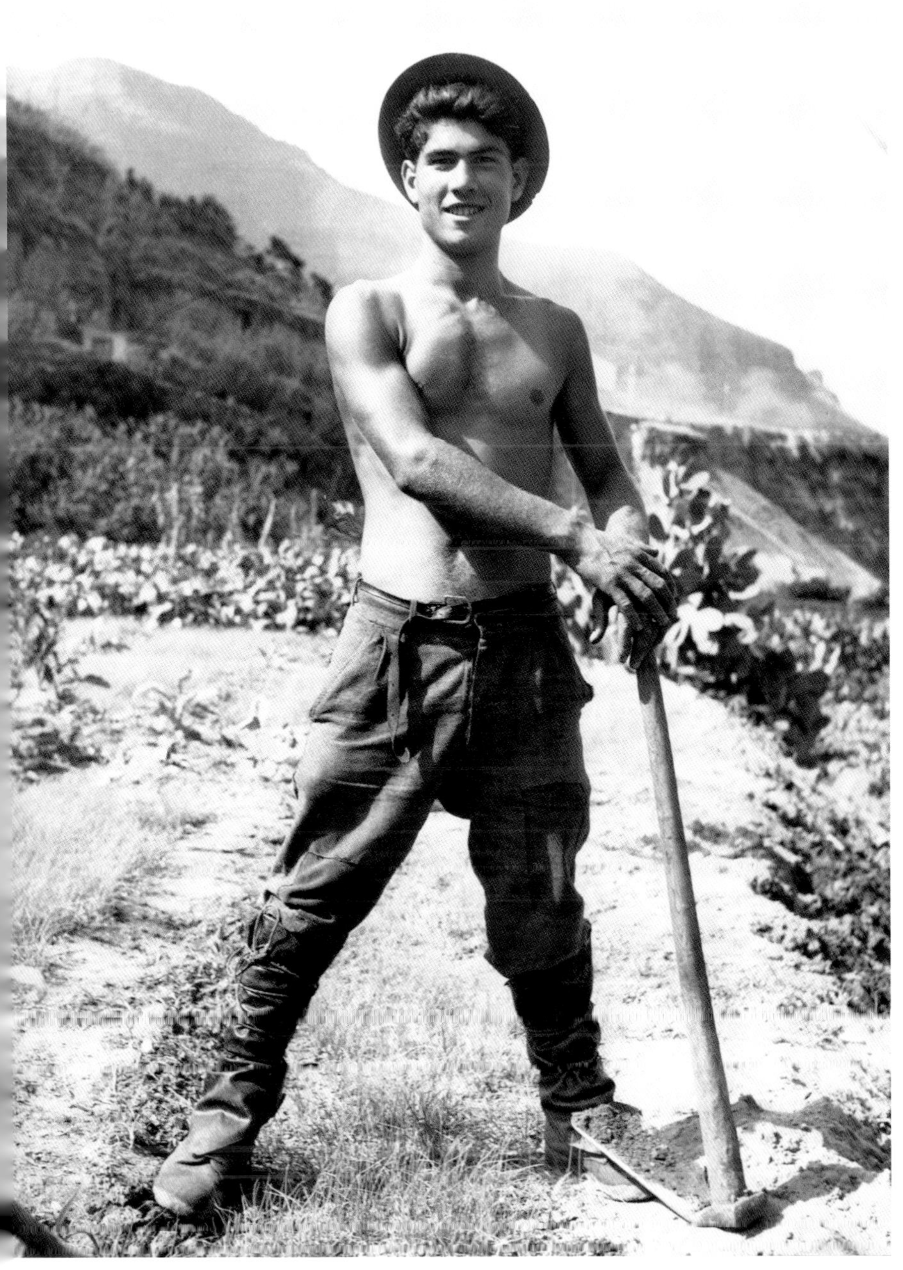

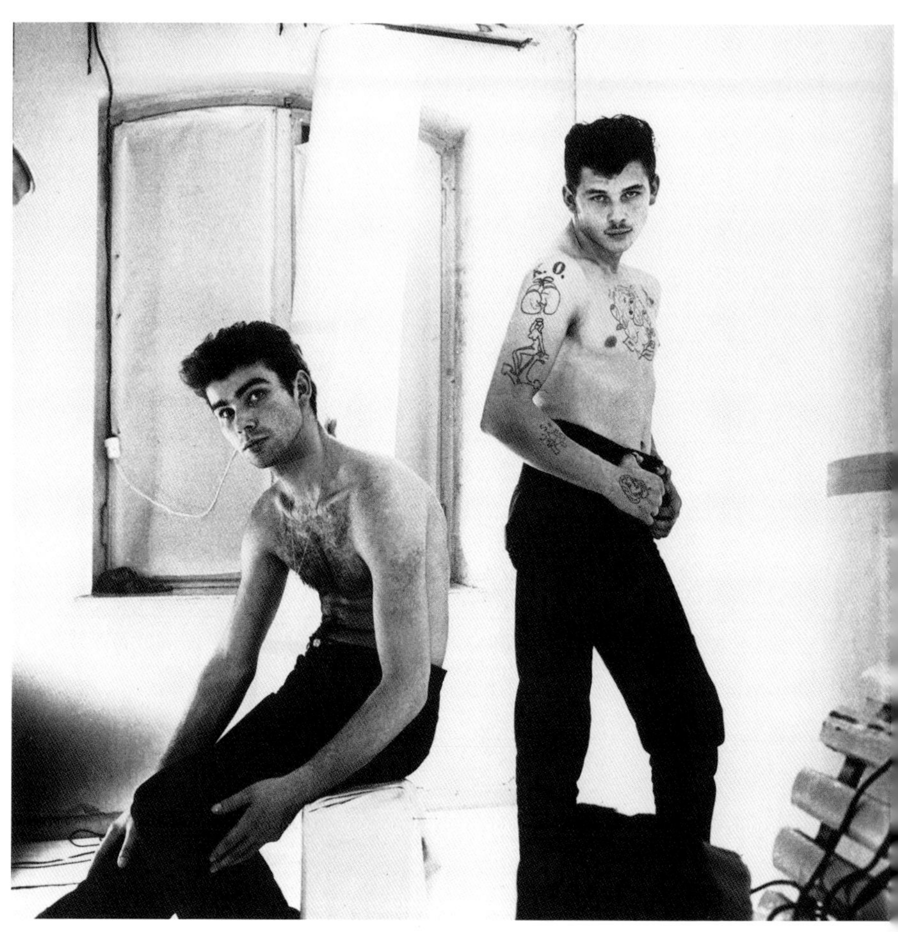

Herbert Tobias, Alle lieben Elvis, 1958

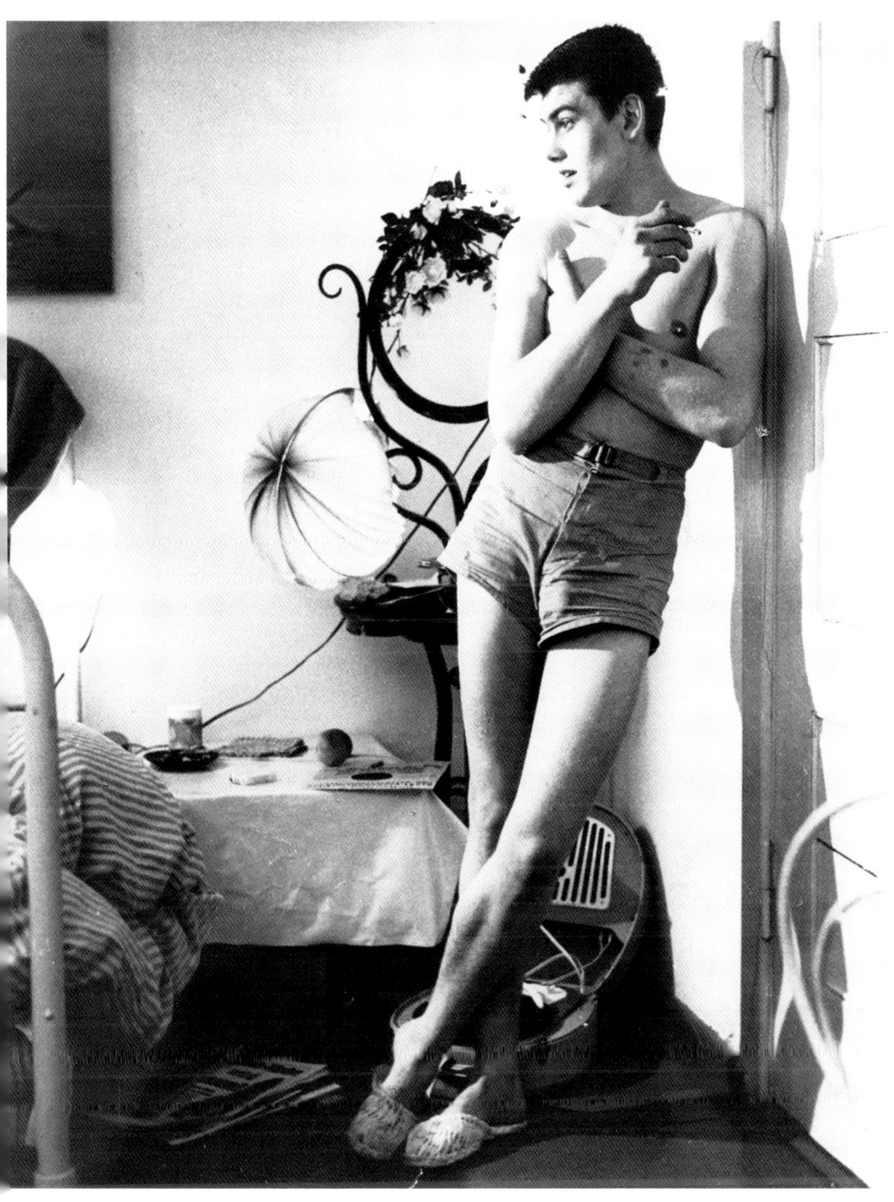

Herbert Tobias, 1957

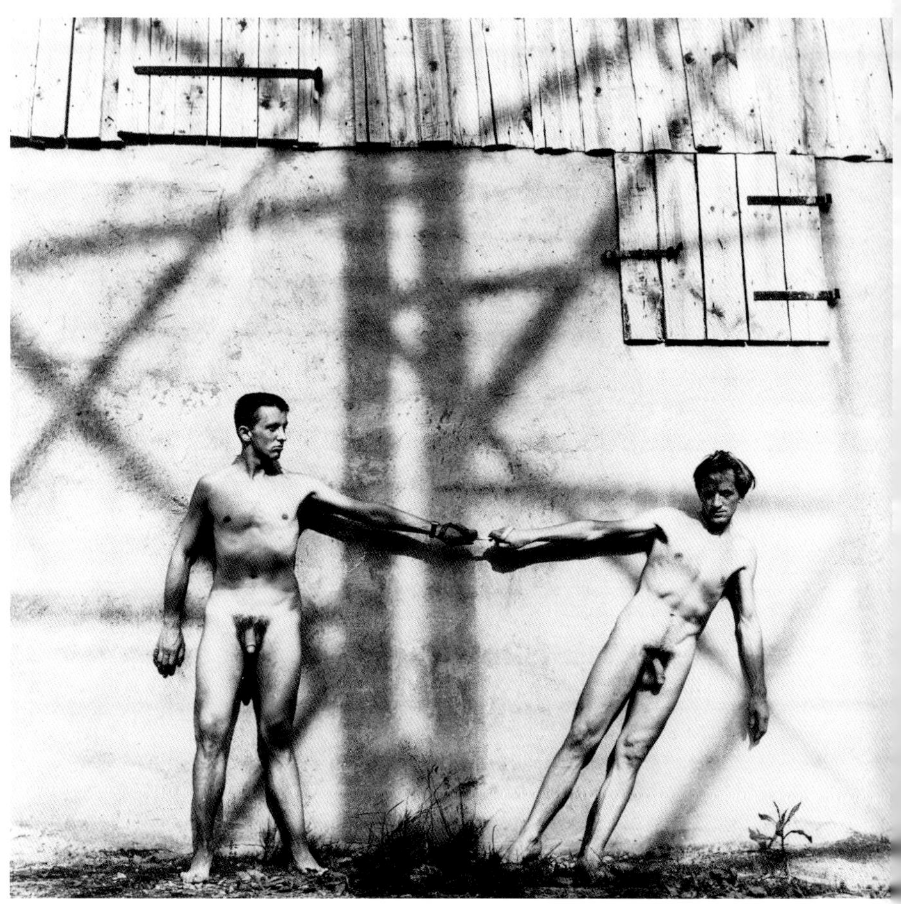

Herbert Tobias, Das Lied von der sexuellen Hörigkeit, 1954

     Herbert Tobias, Muskel-Träume, 1960

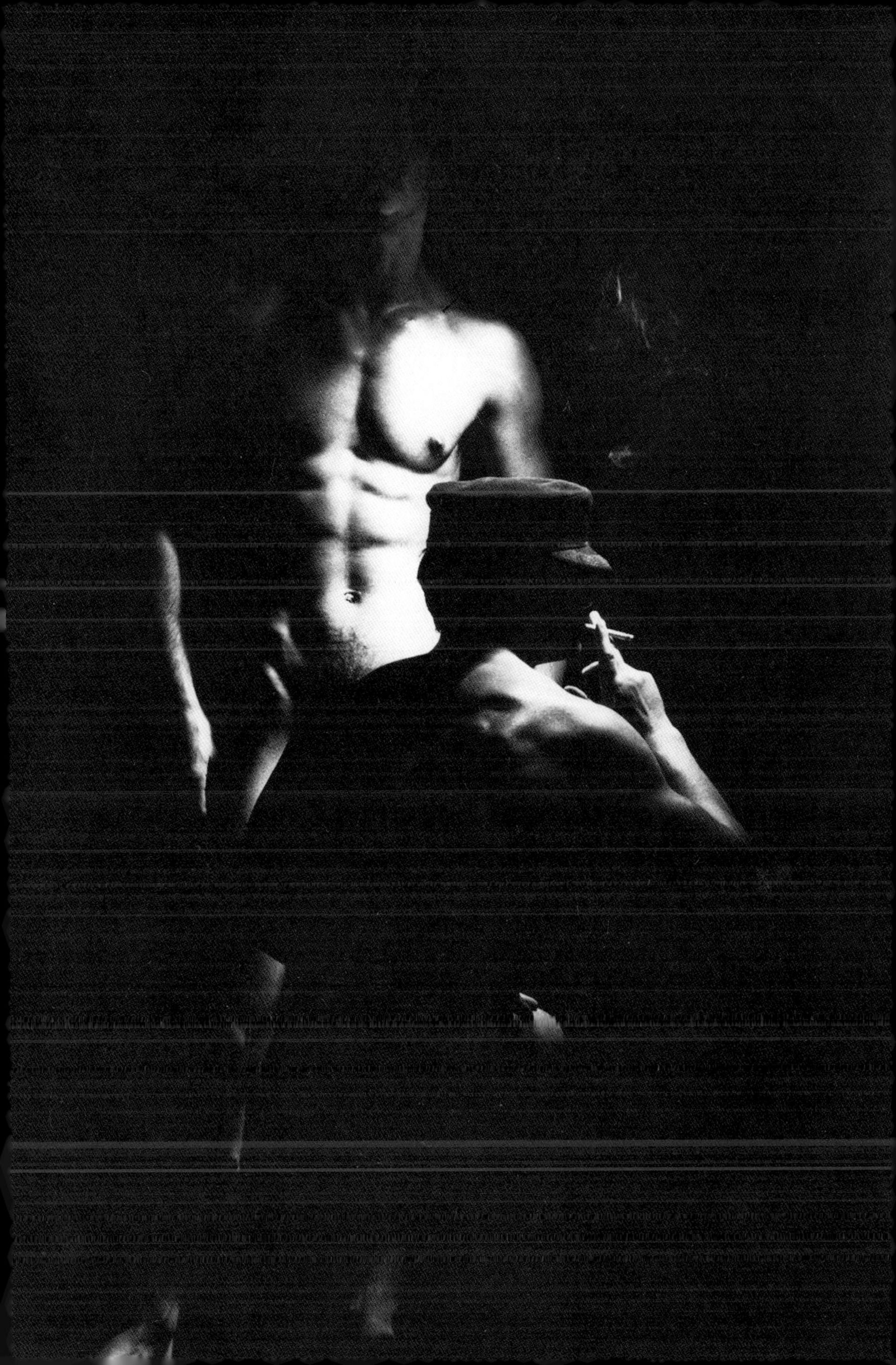

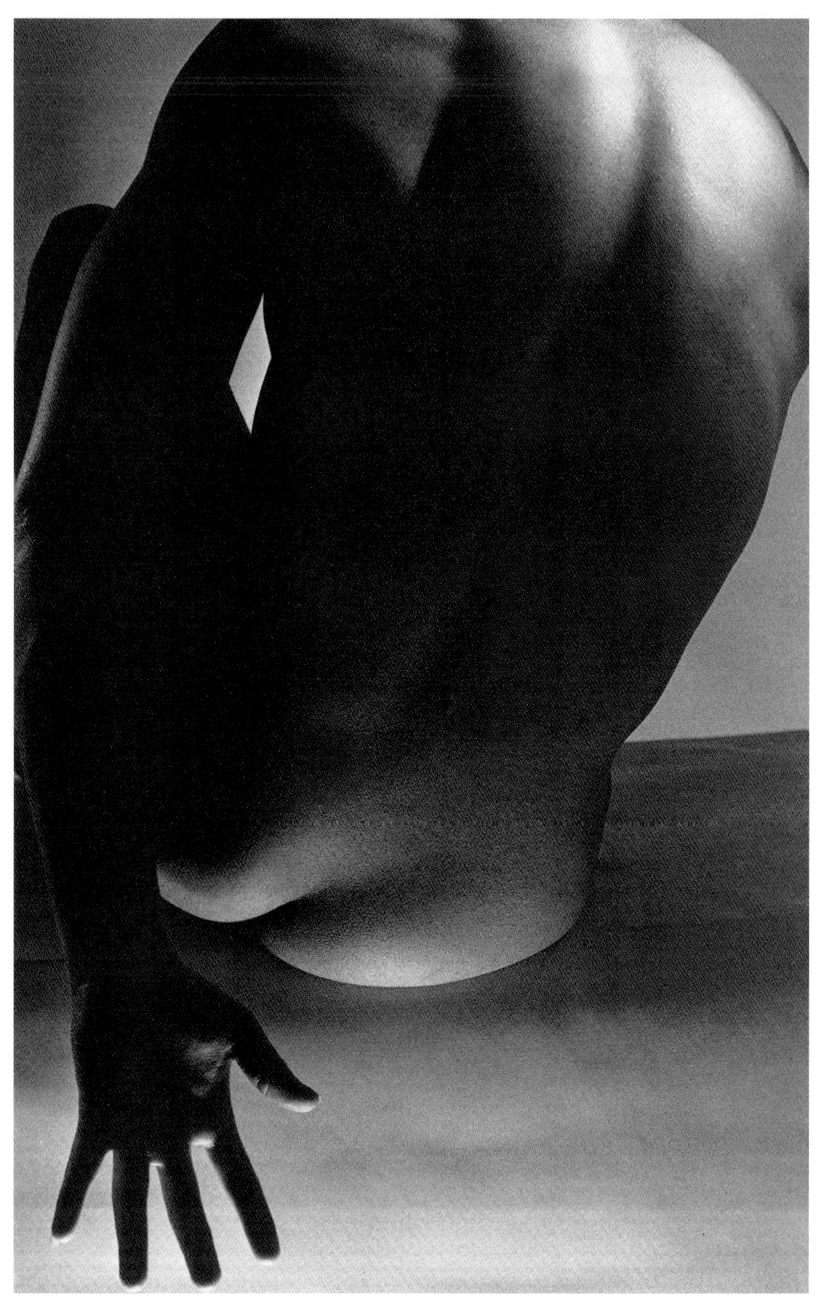

 Horst P. Horst, One-Armed Nude (backside), 1953

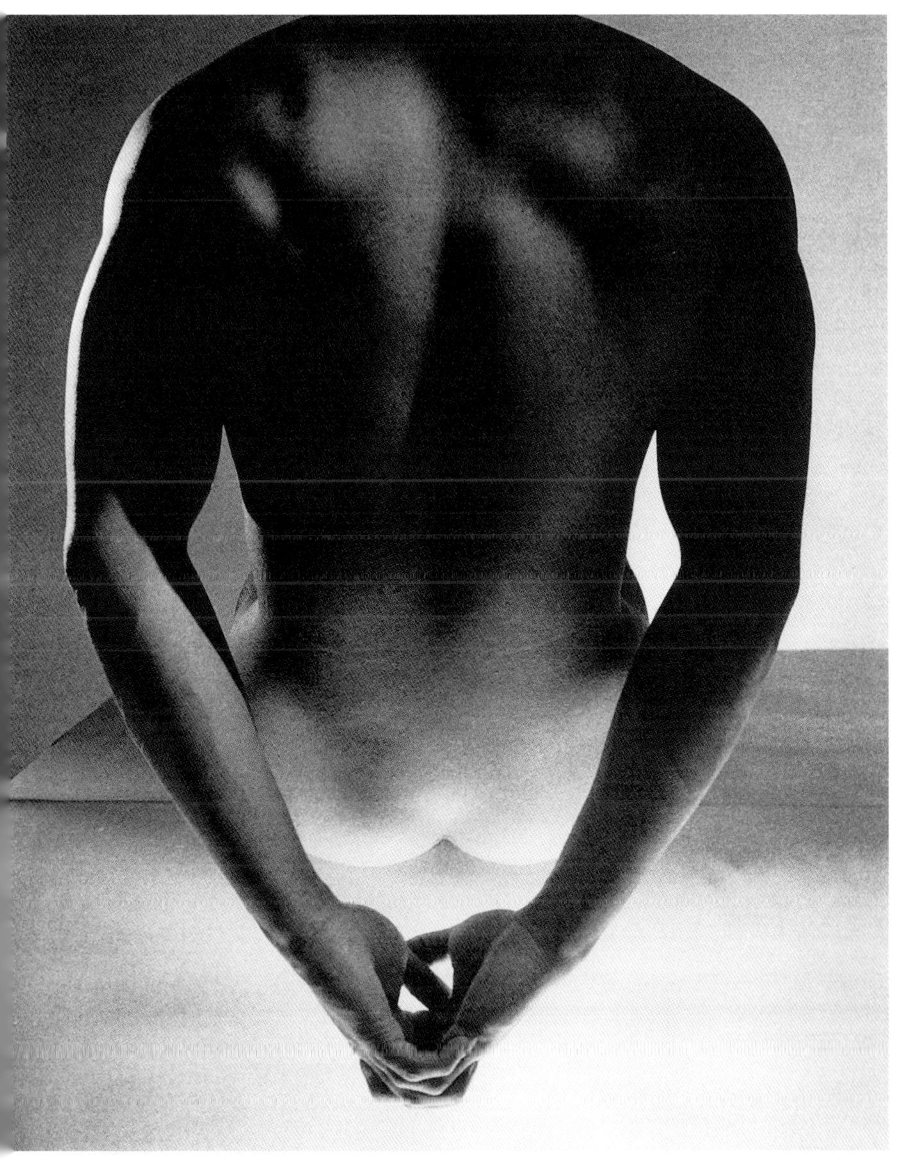

Horst P. Horst, Male Nude – "Hands behind Buttocks", 1952

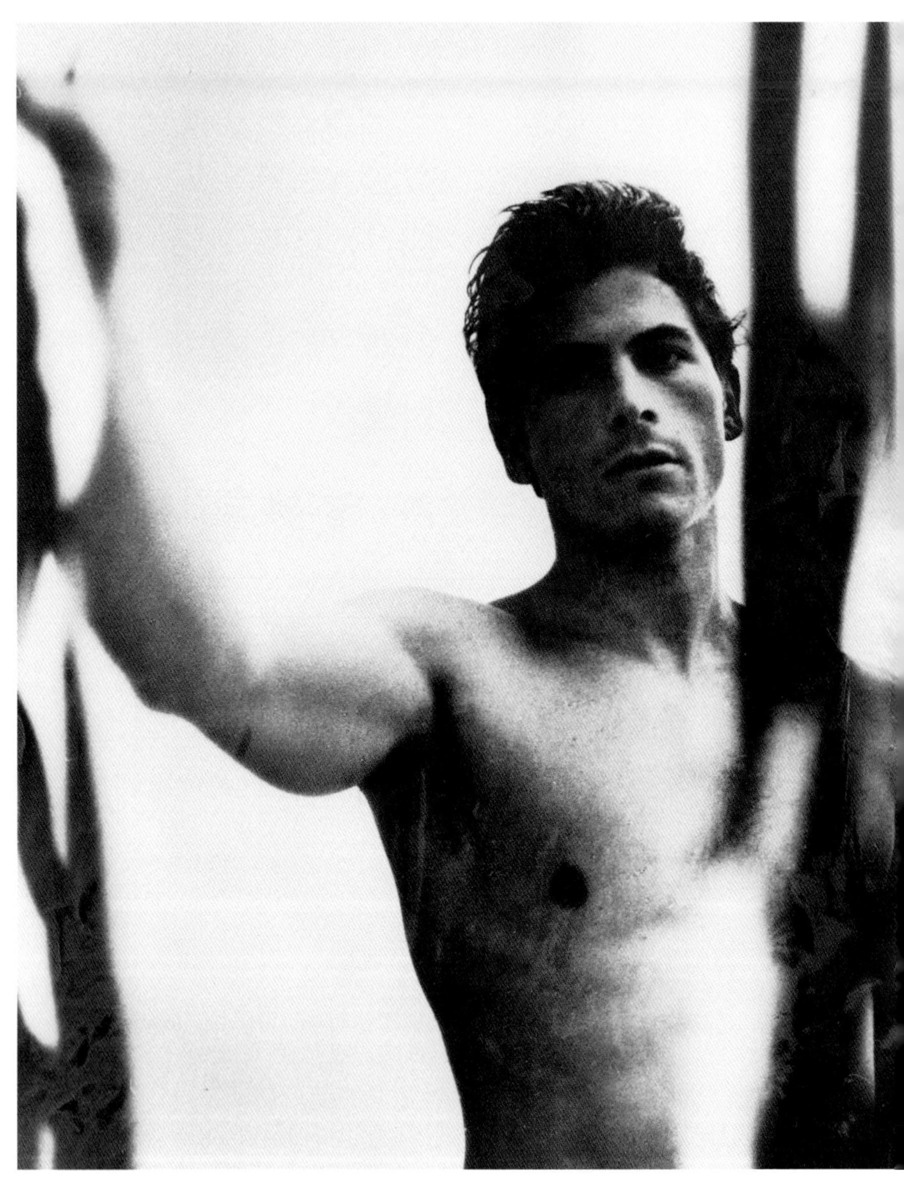

Clifford Coffin, Robert Bishop, 1954

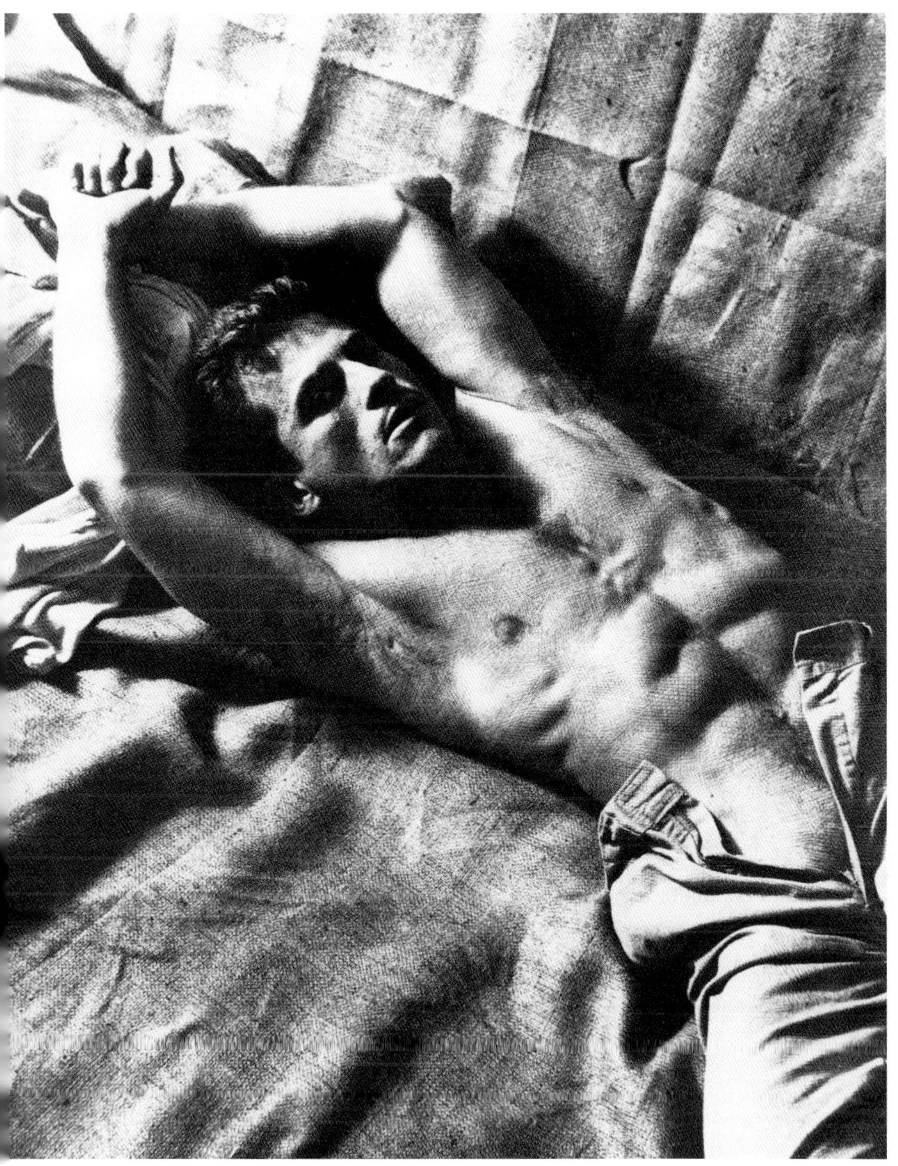

Clifford Coffin, Robert Bishop, 1954

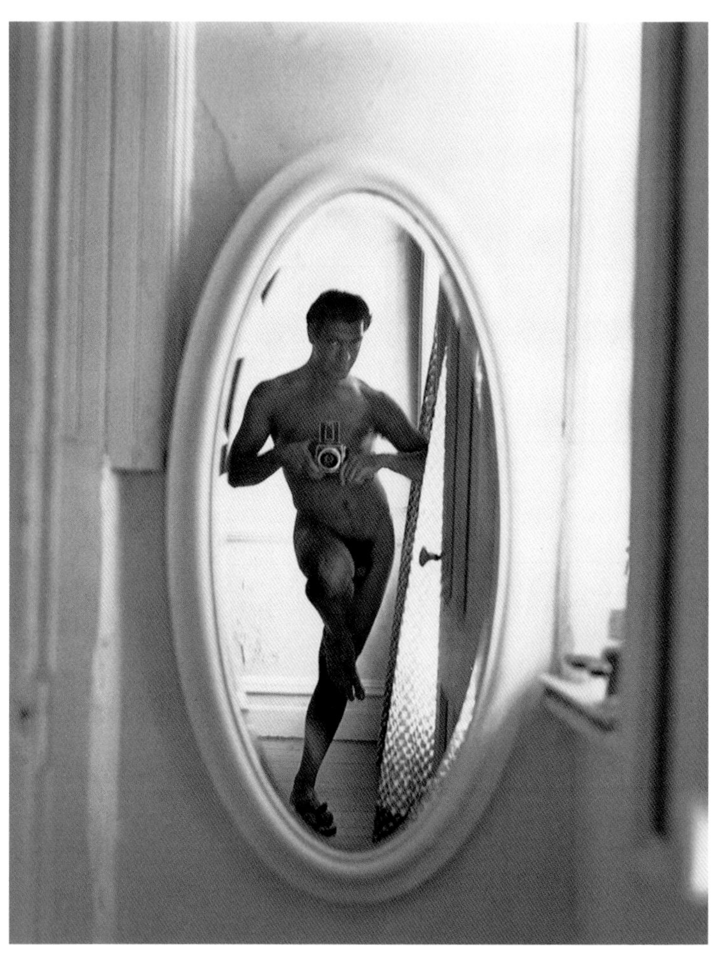

Emerick Bronson, Self-Portrait, 1956

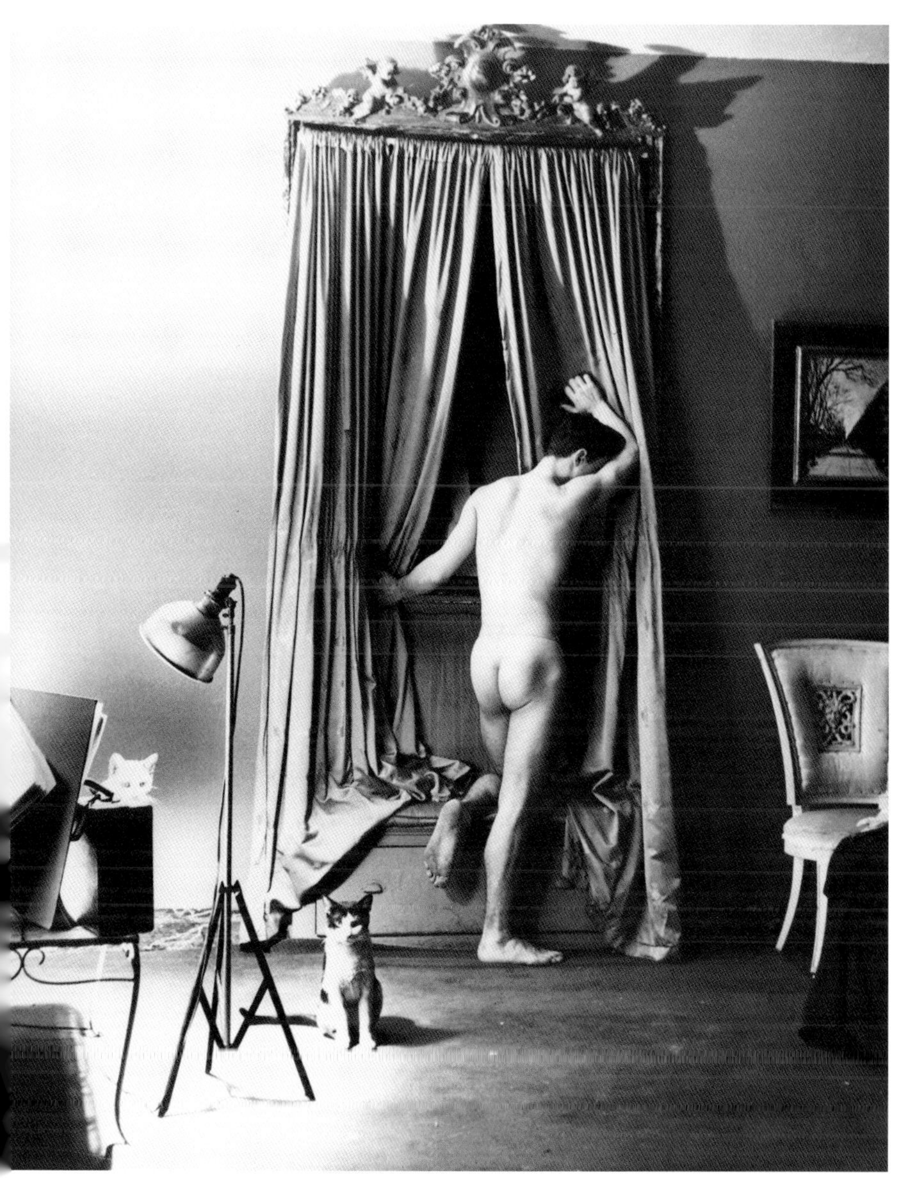

Emerick Bronson, Self-Portrait, 1954

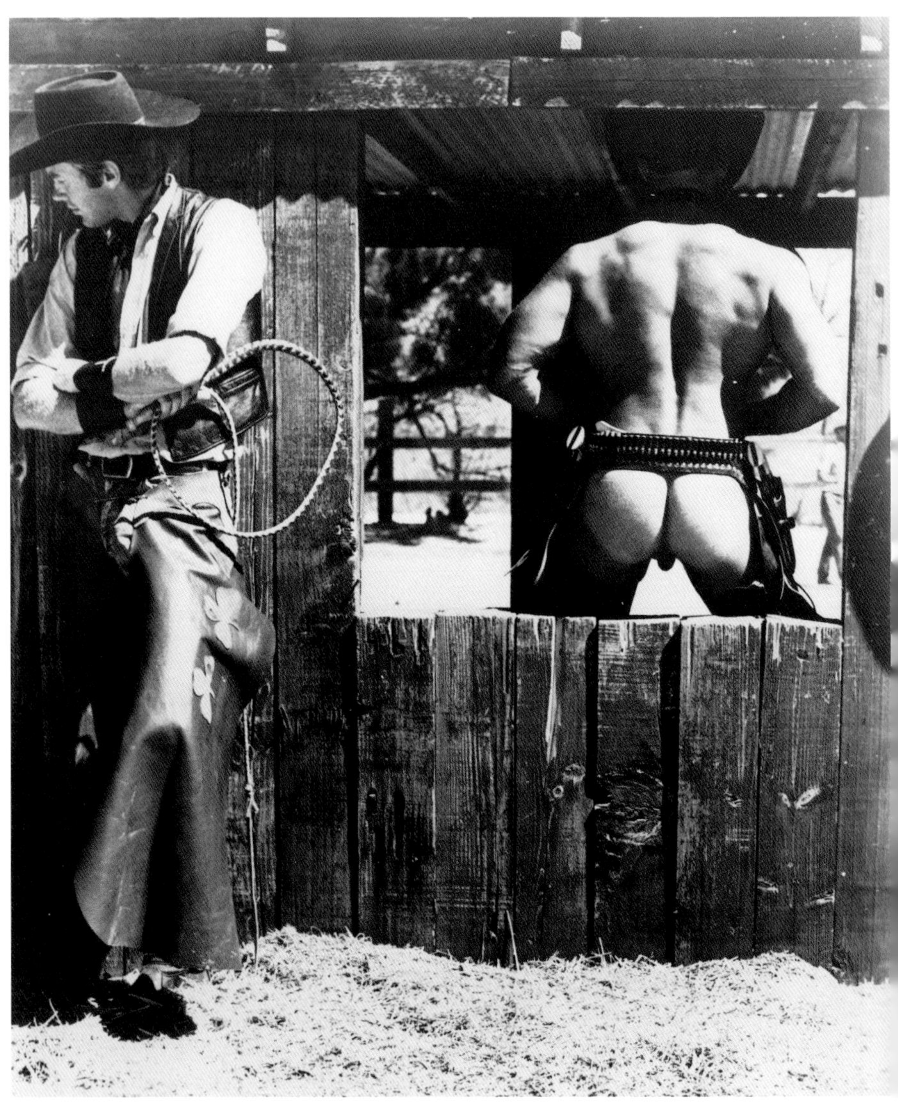

Jim French, c. 1955

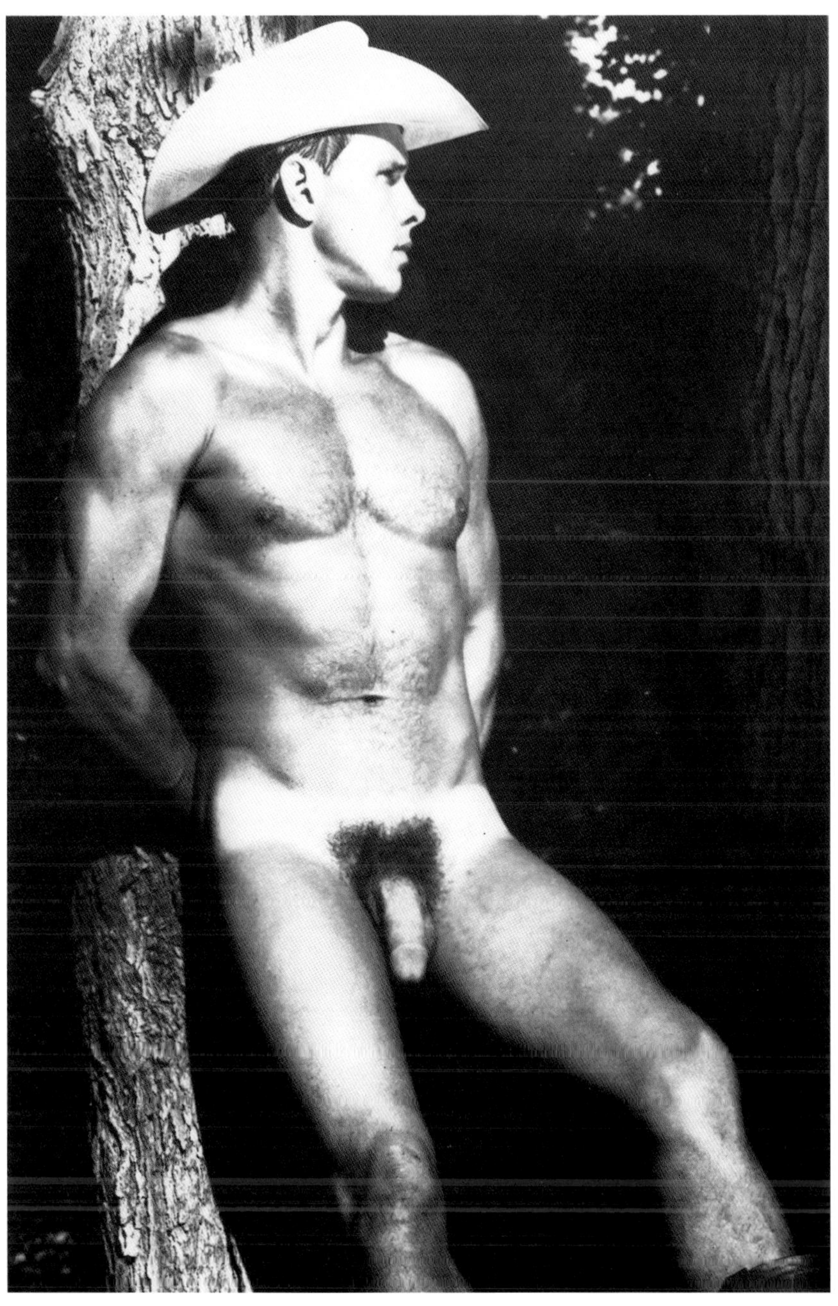

Anonymous, c. 1955

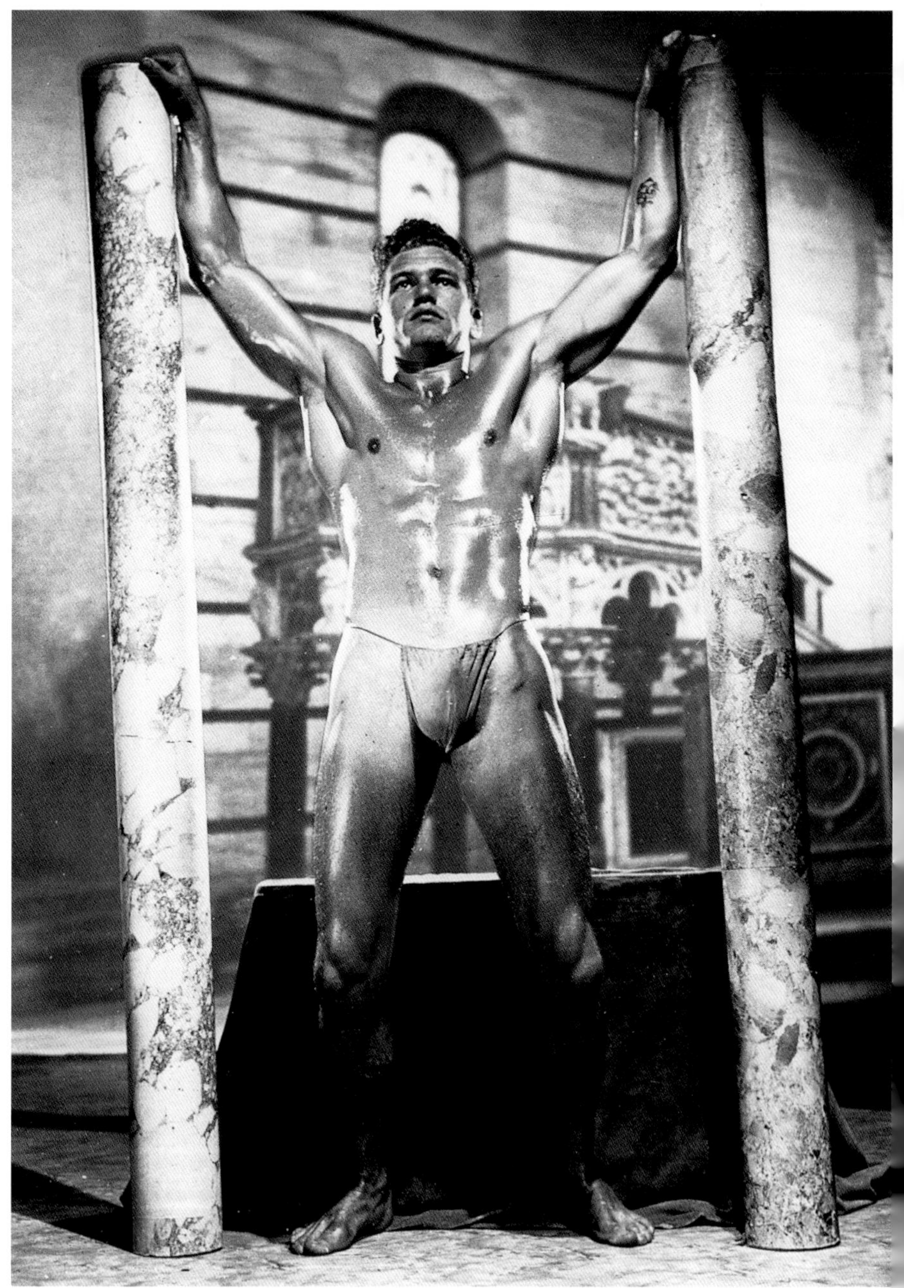

Wally Shilacut, c. 1950

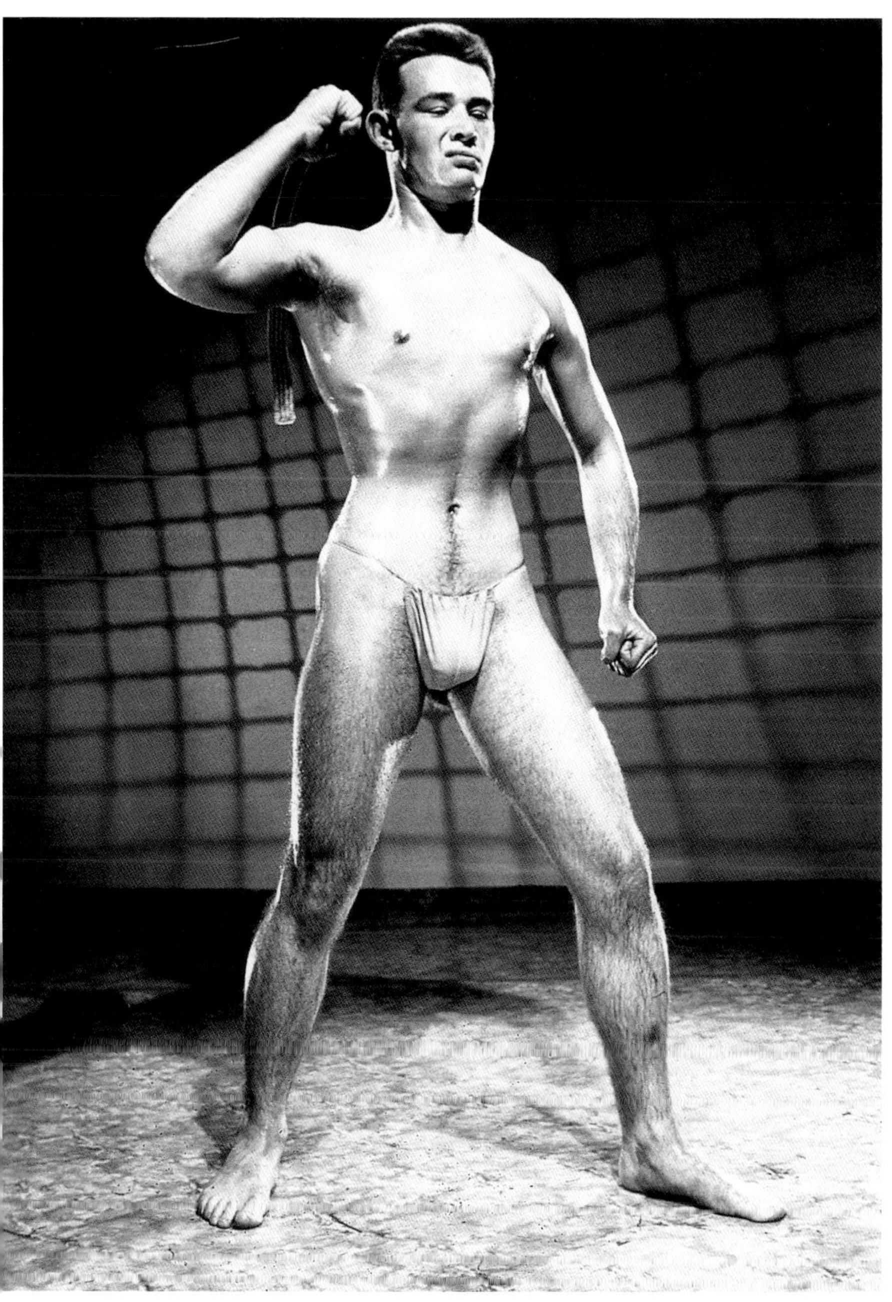

Josef Wilhelm, c. 1950   265

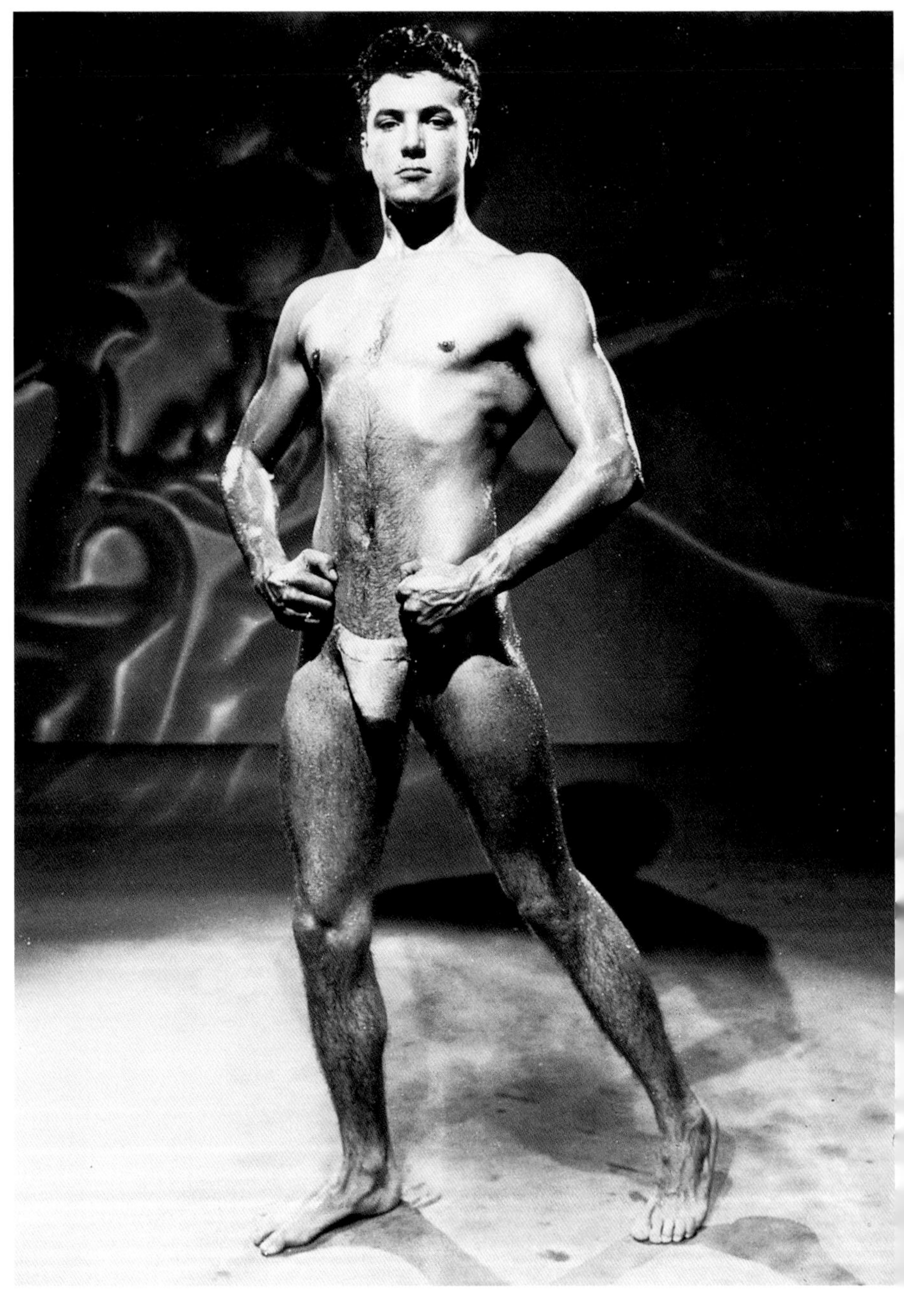

Steve Revere, c. 1950

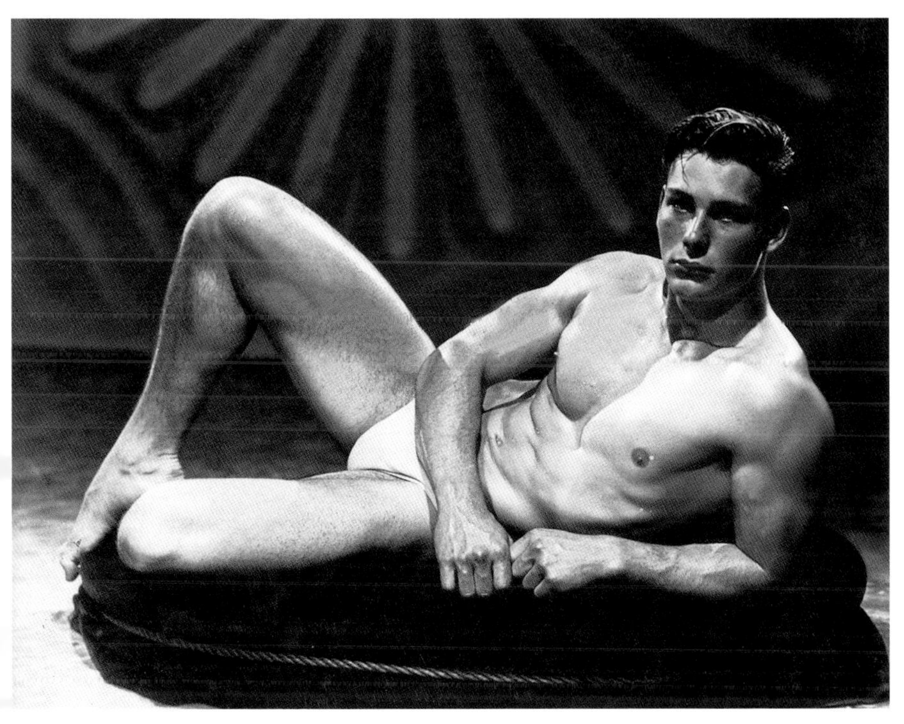

Joe Schuler, c. 1950

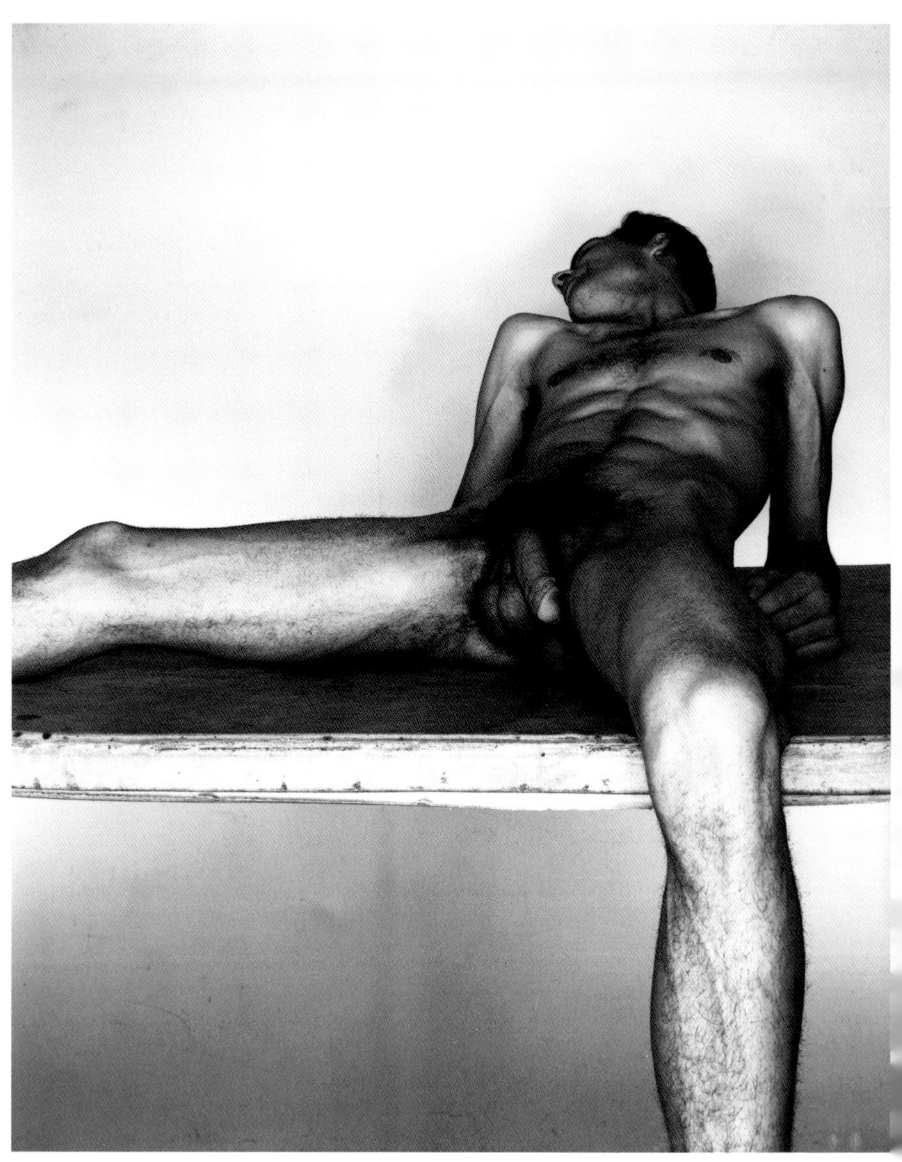

George Platt Lynes, Robert Harris, March 28, 1955

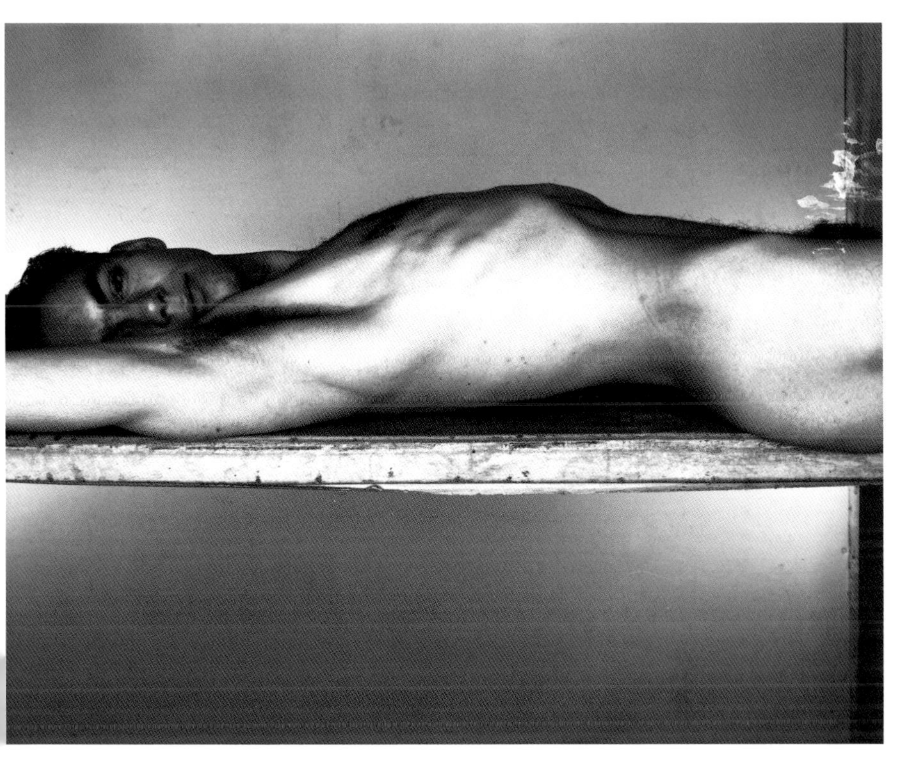

George Platt Lynes, Robert Harris, March 22, 1955

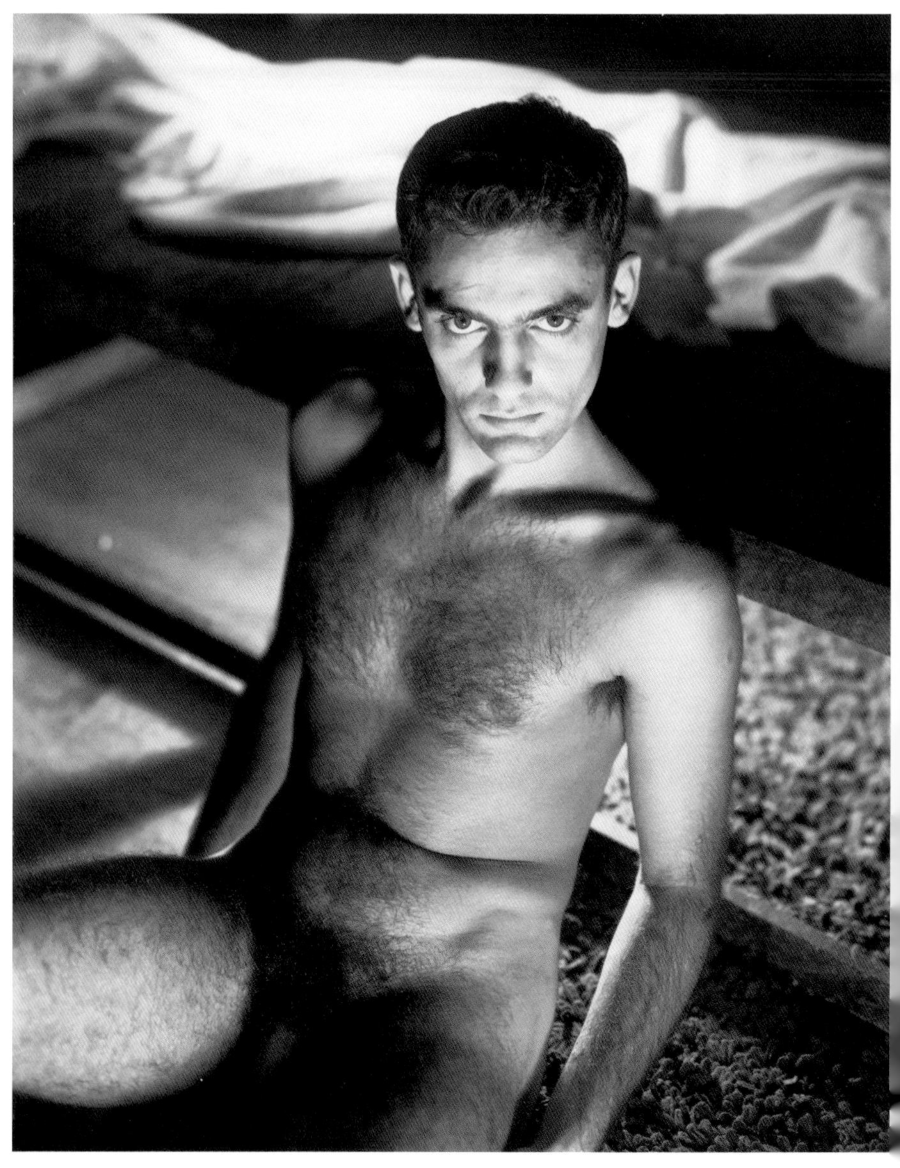

George Platt Lynes, Joseph Santoro, November 12, 1949

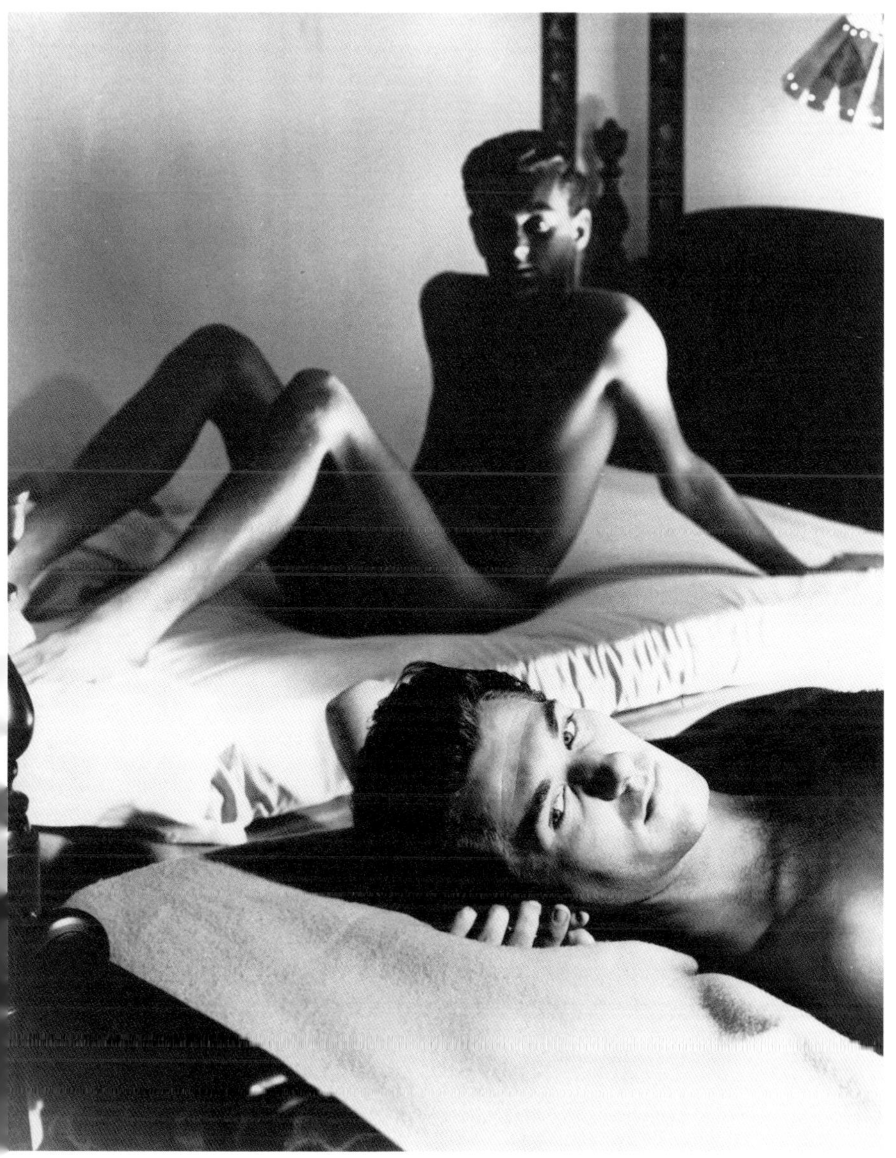

George Platt Lynes, Peter Hanson in Background and Richard Sisson, 1948

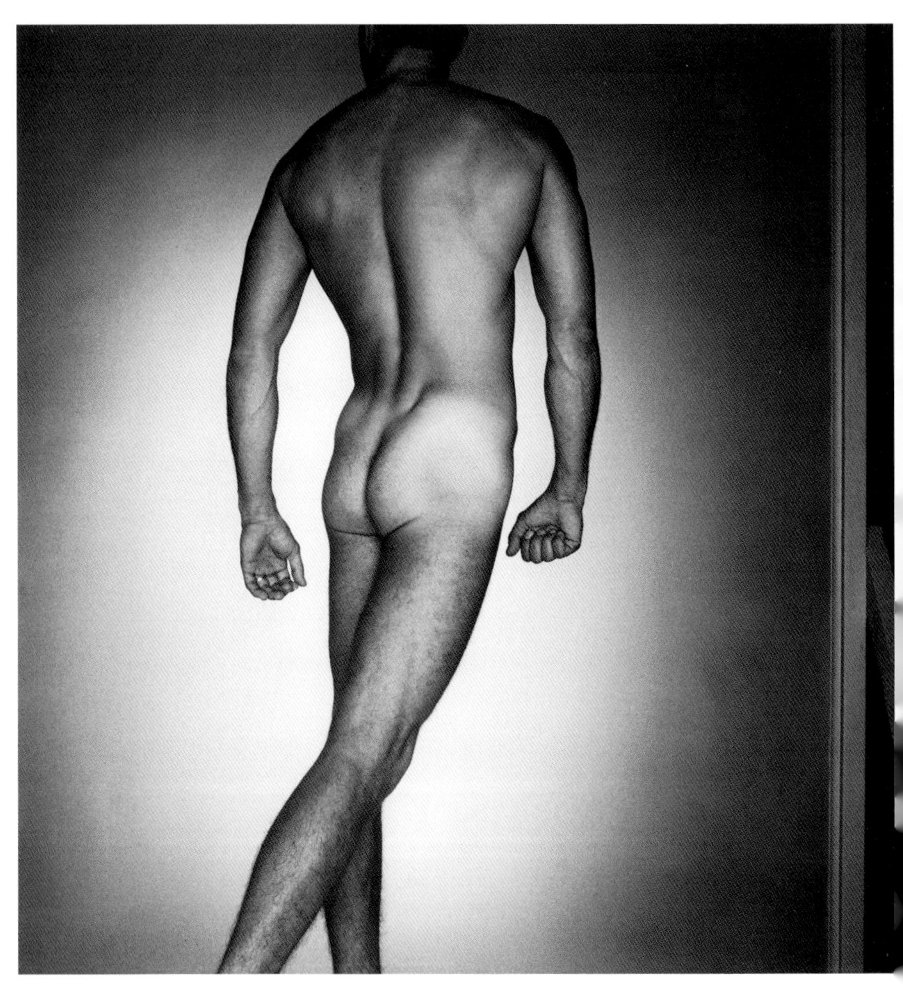

George Platt Lynes, Robert Hassa, October 19, 1954

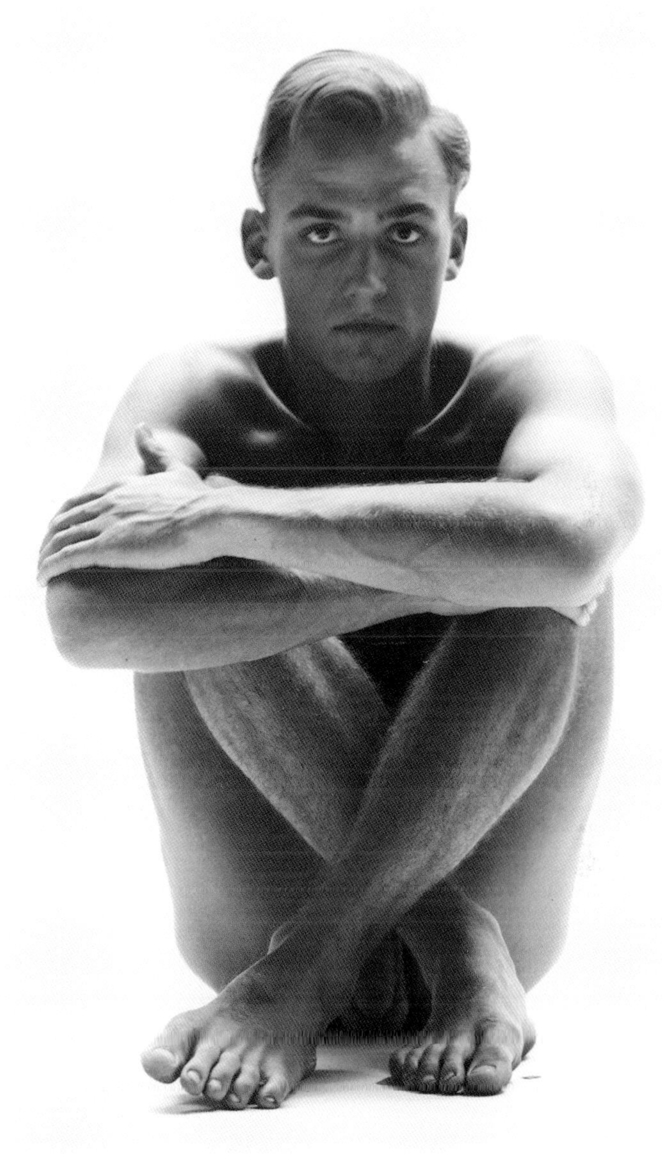

George Platt Lynes, Bill Harris, October 14, 1945

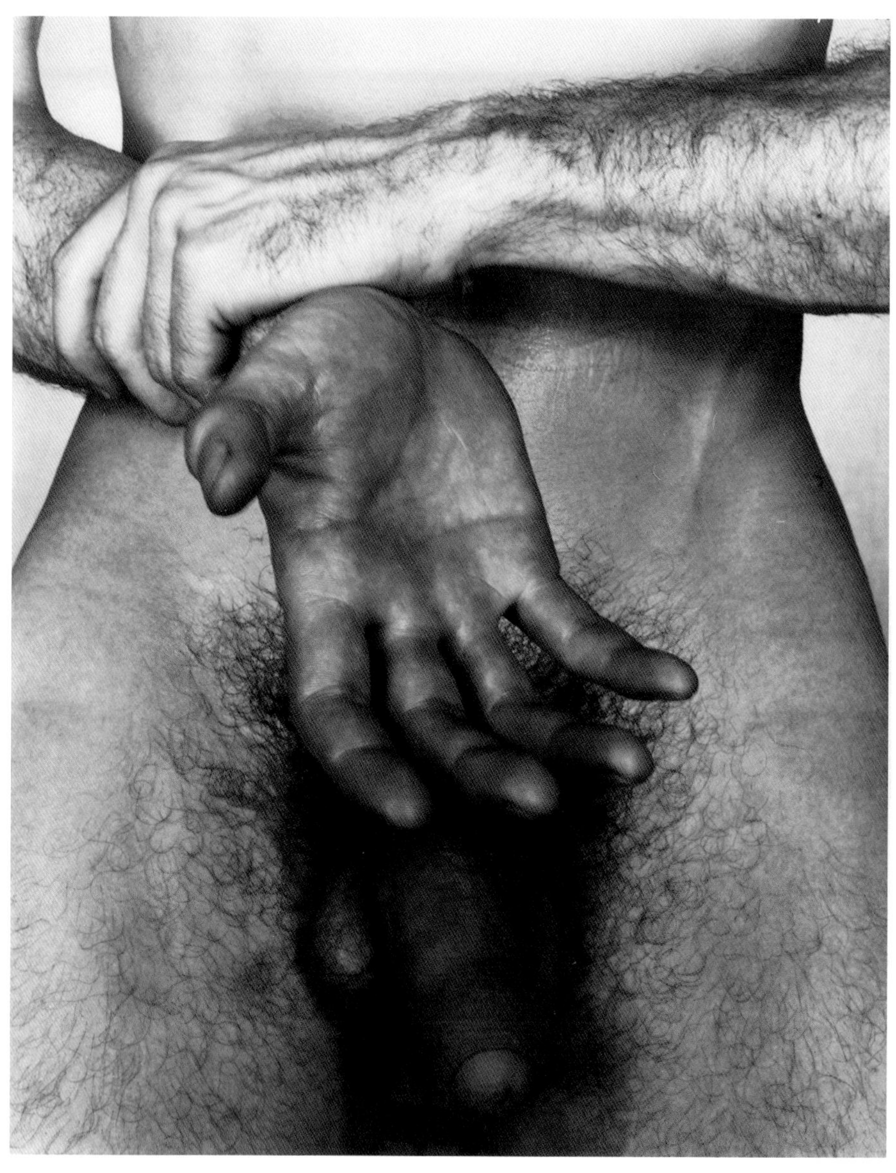

George Platt Lynes, Ralph McWilliams, March 19, 1953

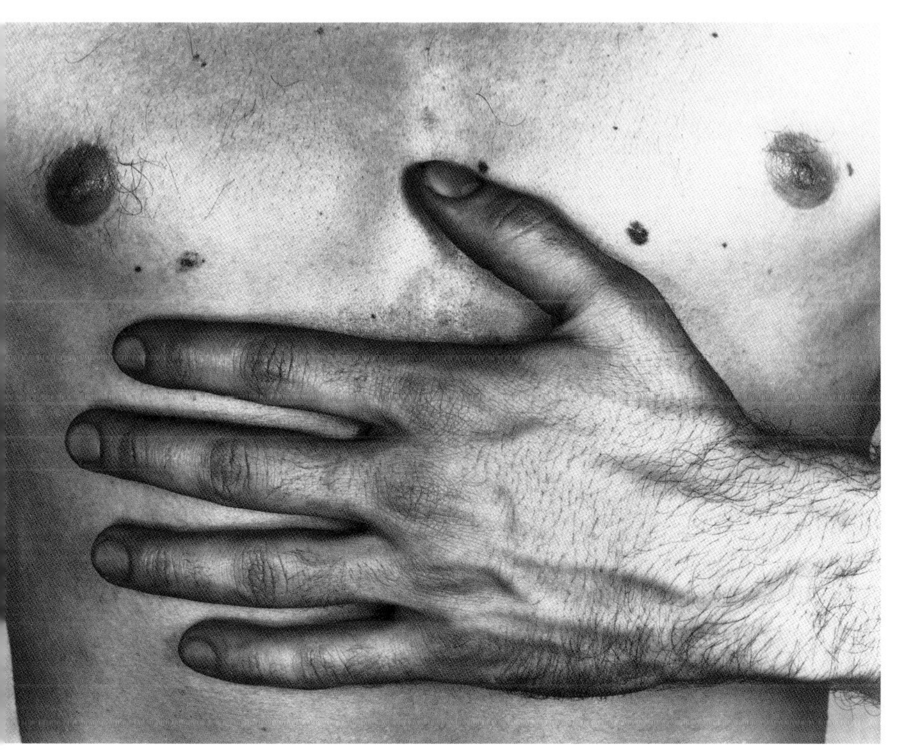

George Platt Lynes, Ralph McWilliams, March 19, 1953

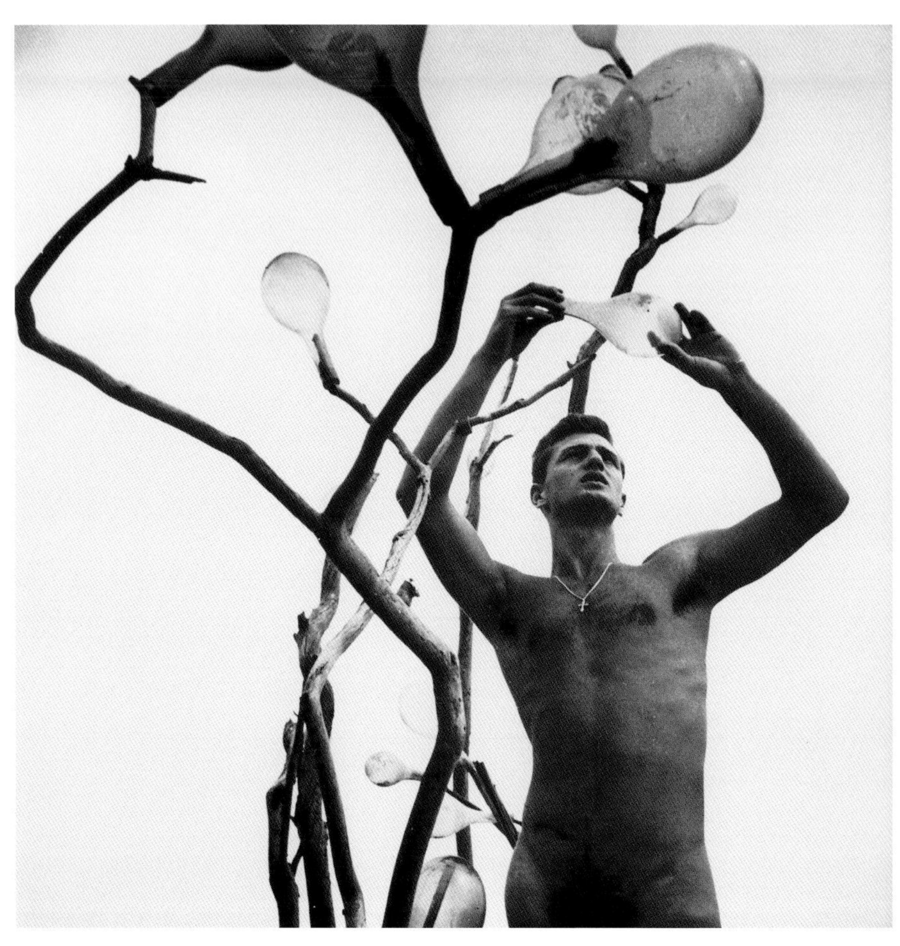

George Daniell, The Chianti Tree, 1950

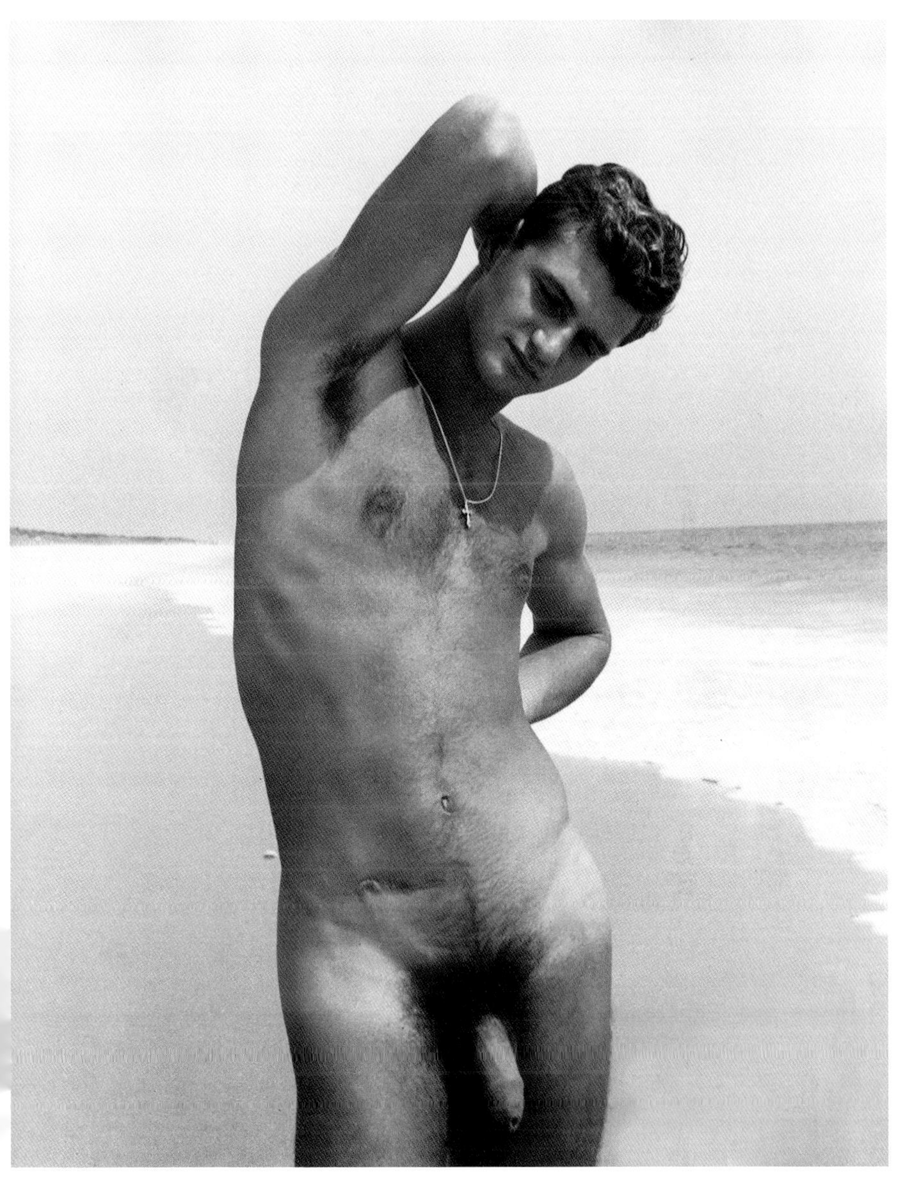

George Daniell, Fire Island, 1955

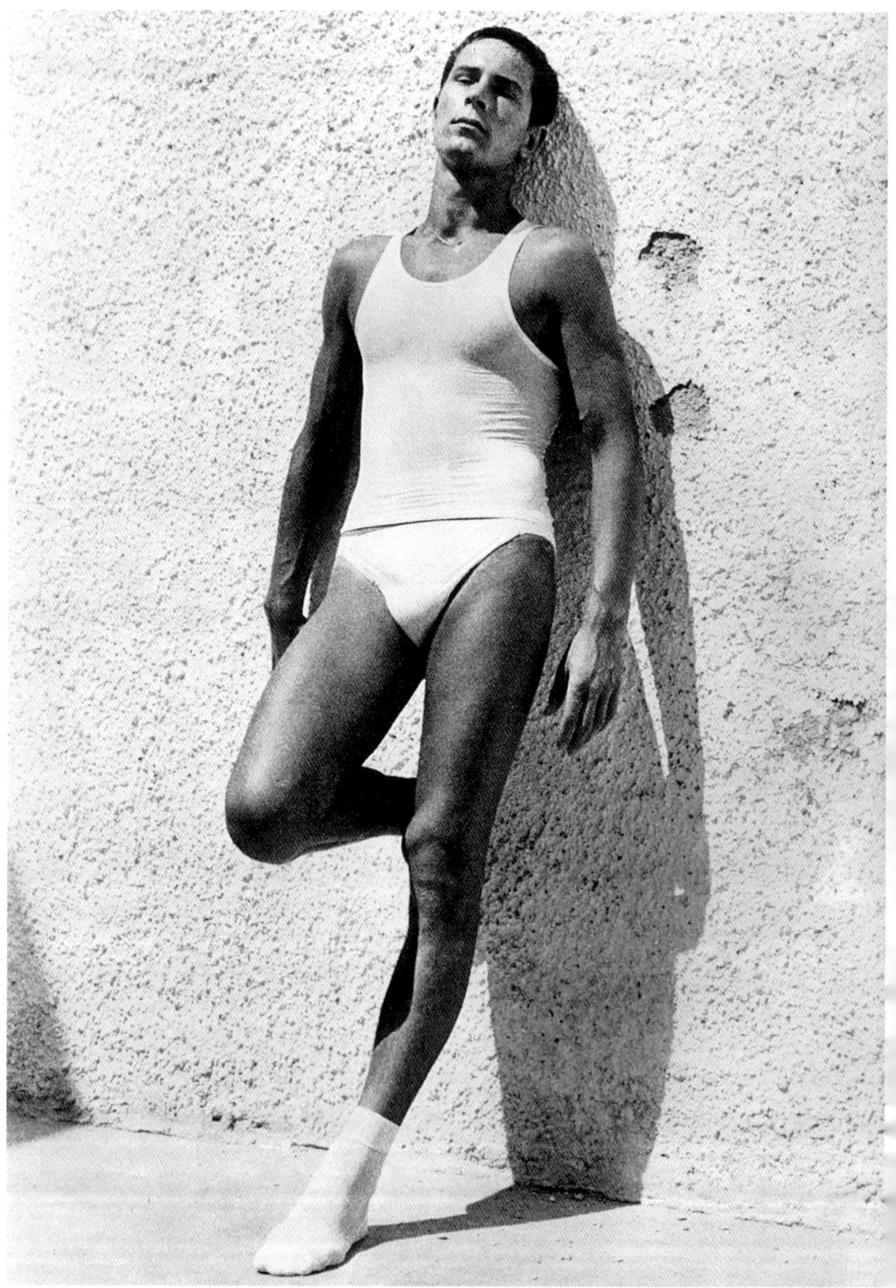

Herbert List, Sonnenbad (1), 1955

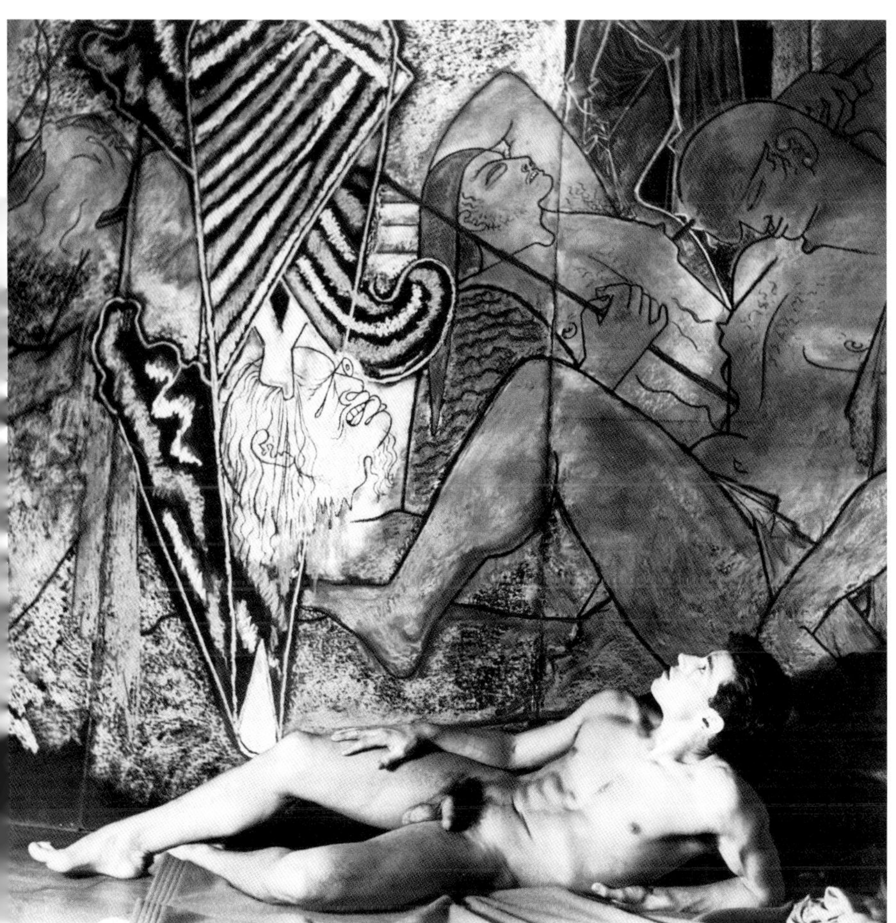

Herbert List, Edouard Dermit, 1948

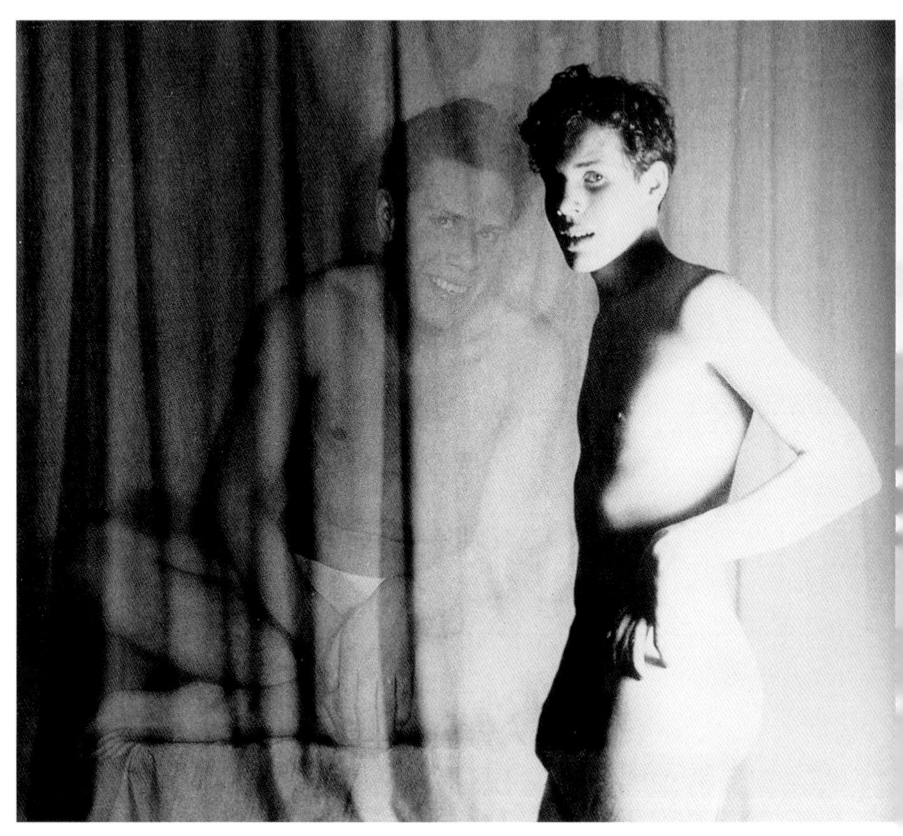

Jo von Kalckreuth, c. 1955–60

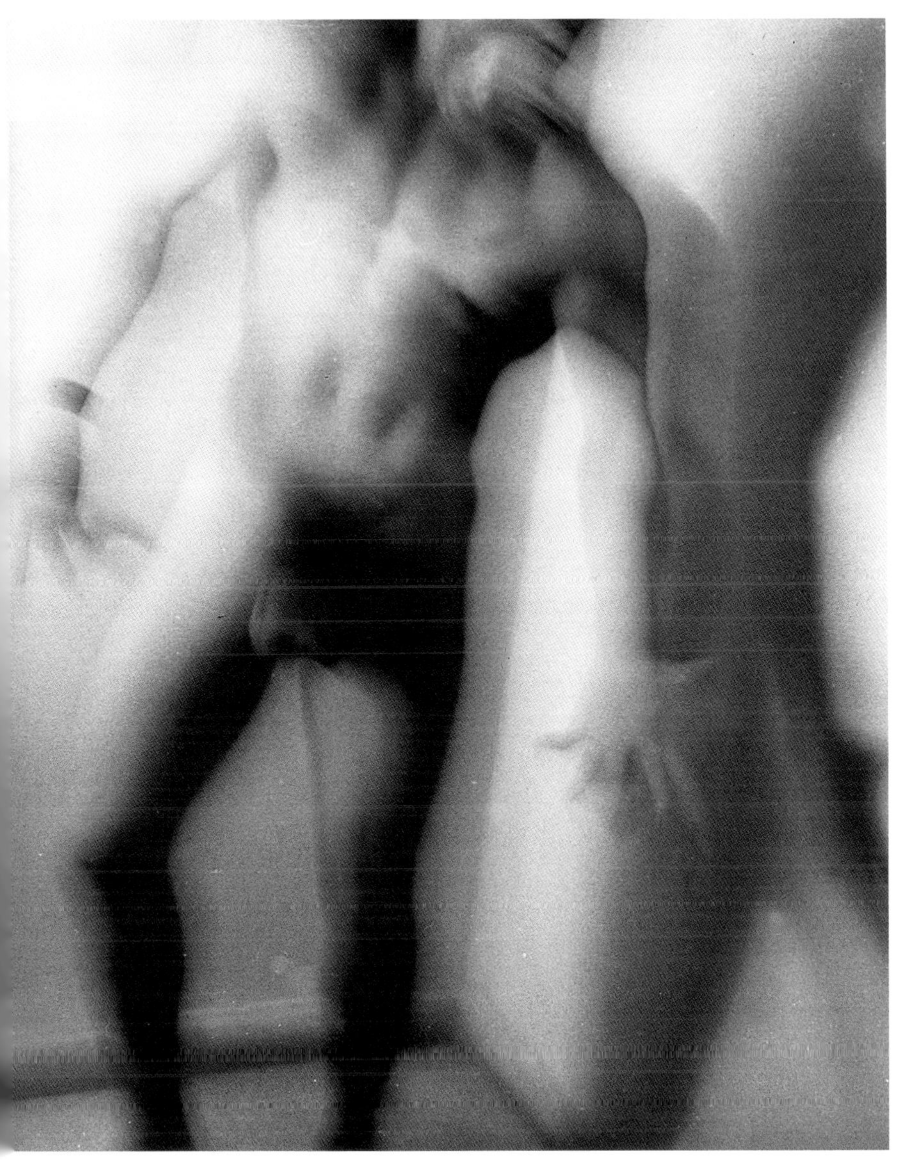

o von Kalckreuth, c. 1955–60

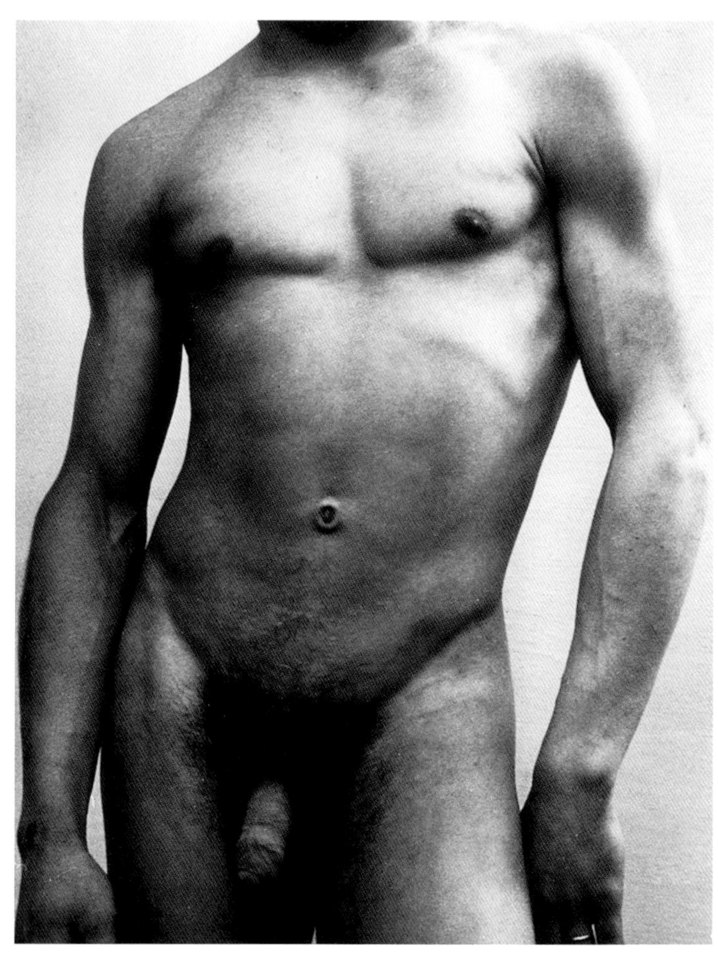

Jo von Kalckreuth, c. 1955–60

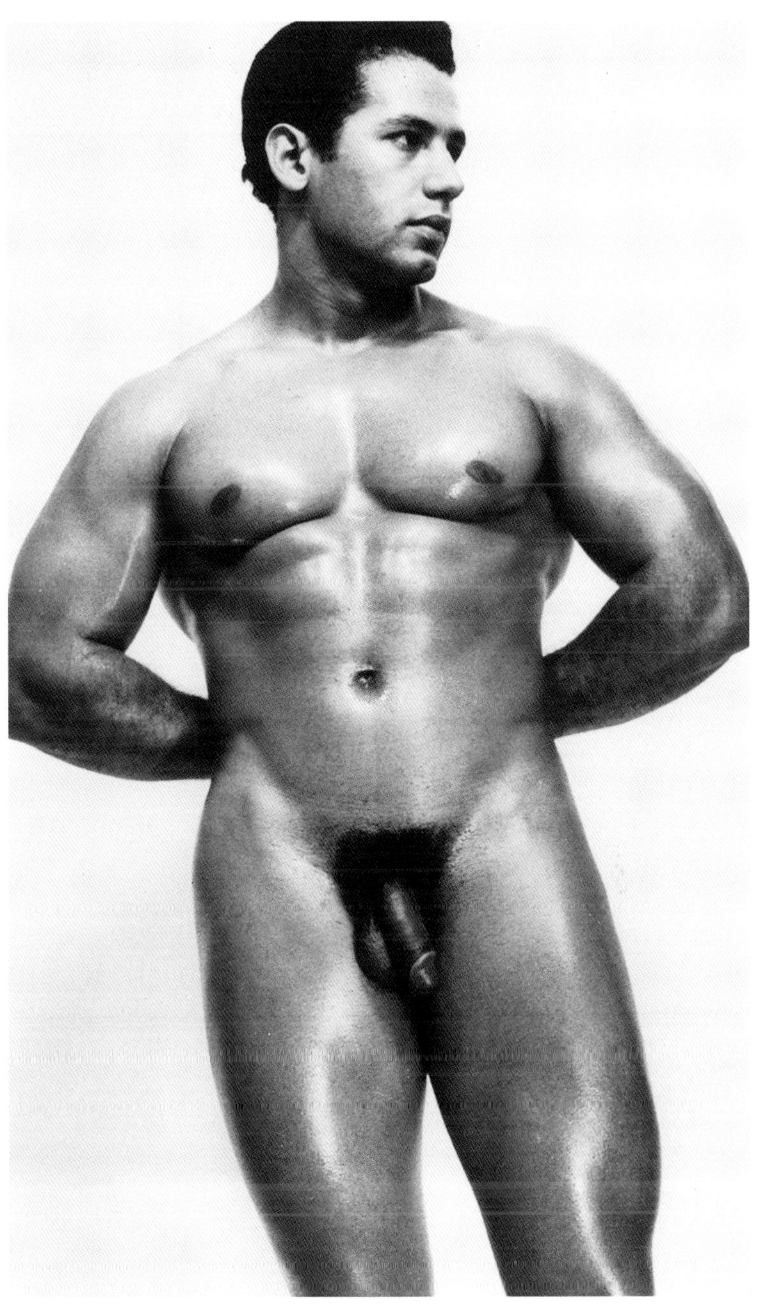

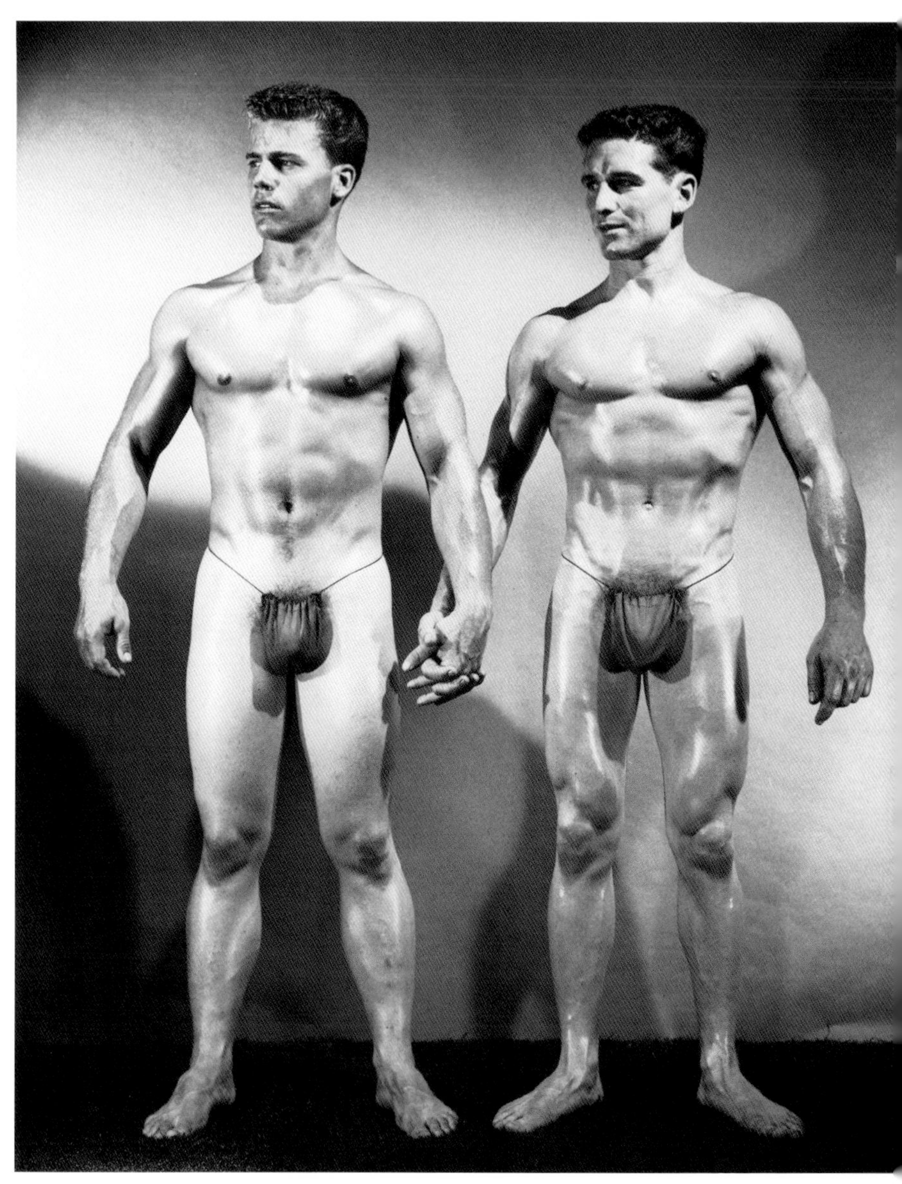

Bruce of Los Angeles, 1950s

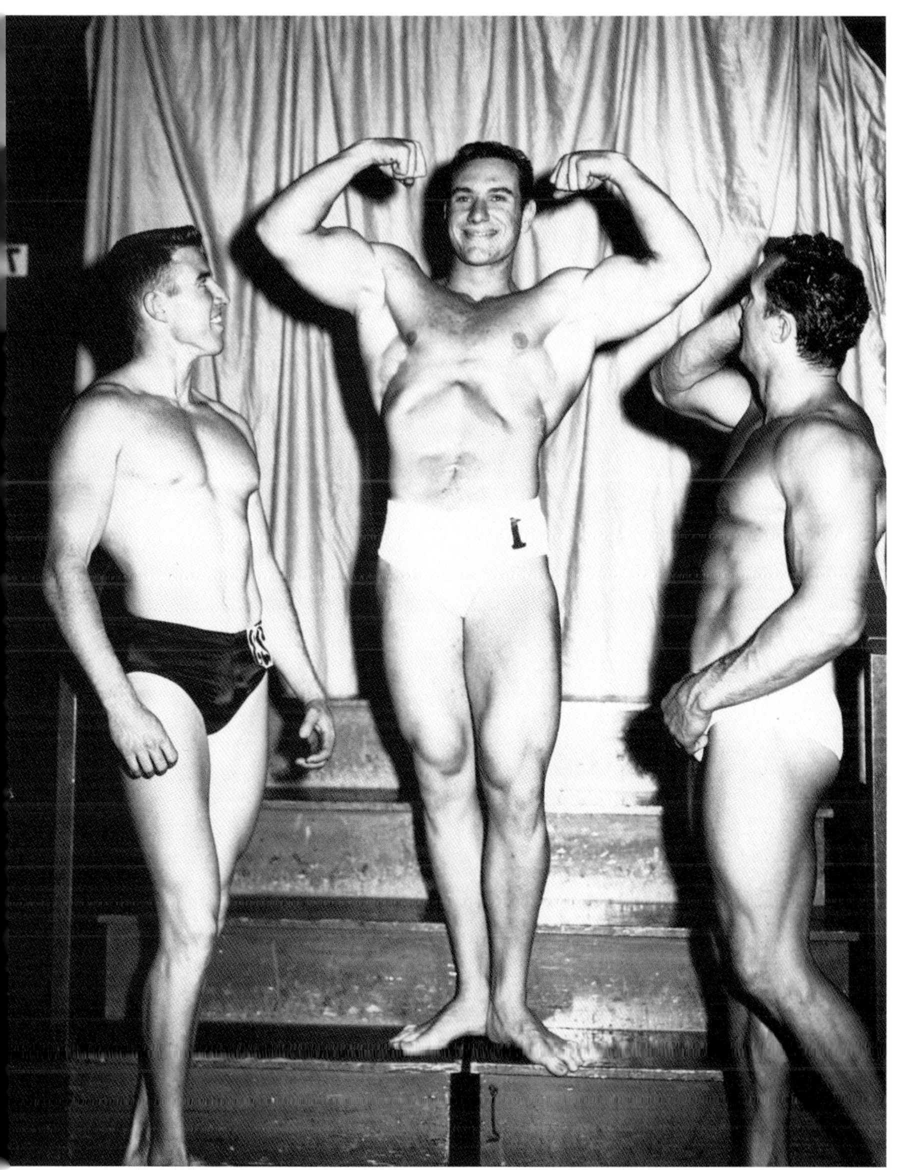

Bruce of Los Angeles, late 1940s

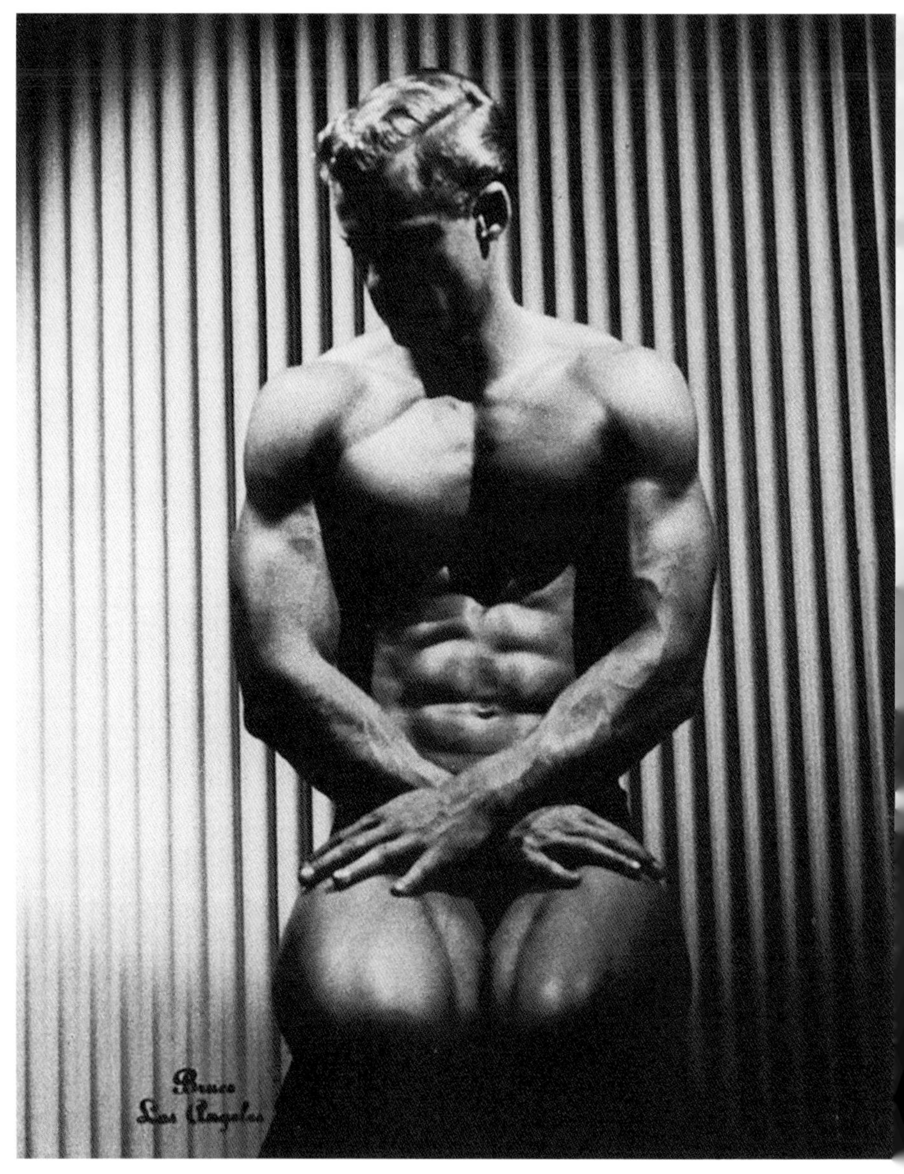

Bruce of Los Angeles, Gordon Hanson, c. 1955

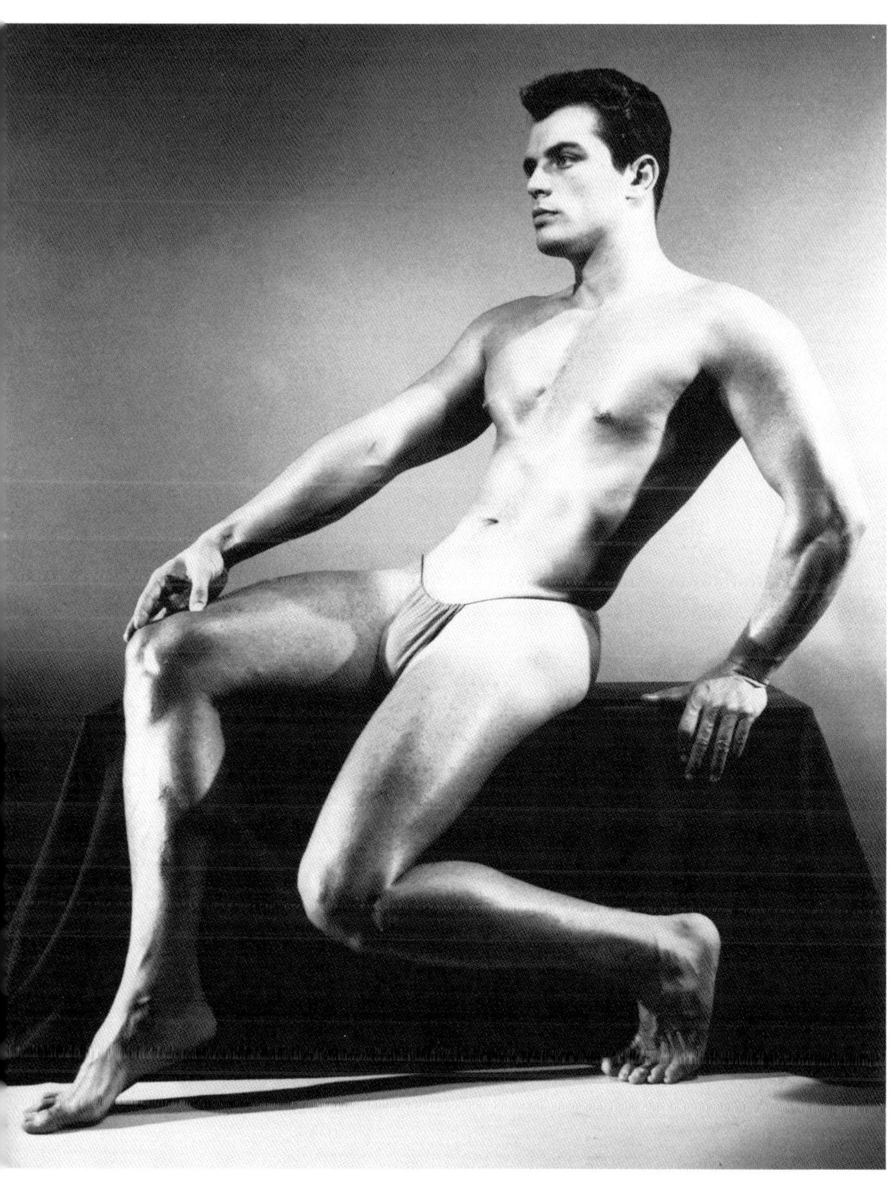

Bruce of Los Angeles, 1950s

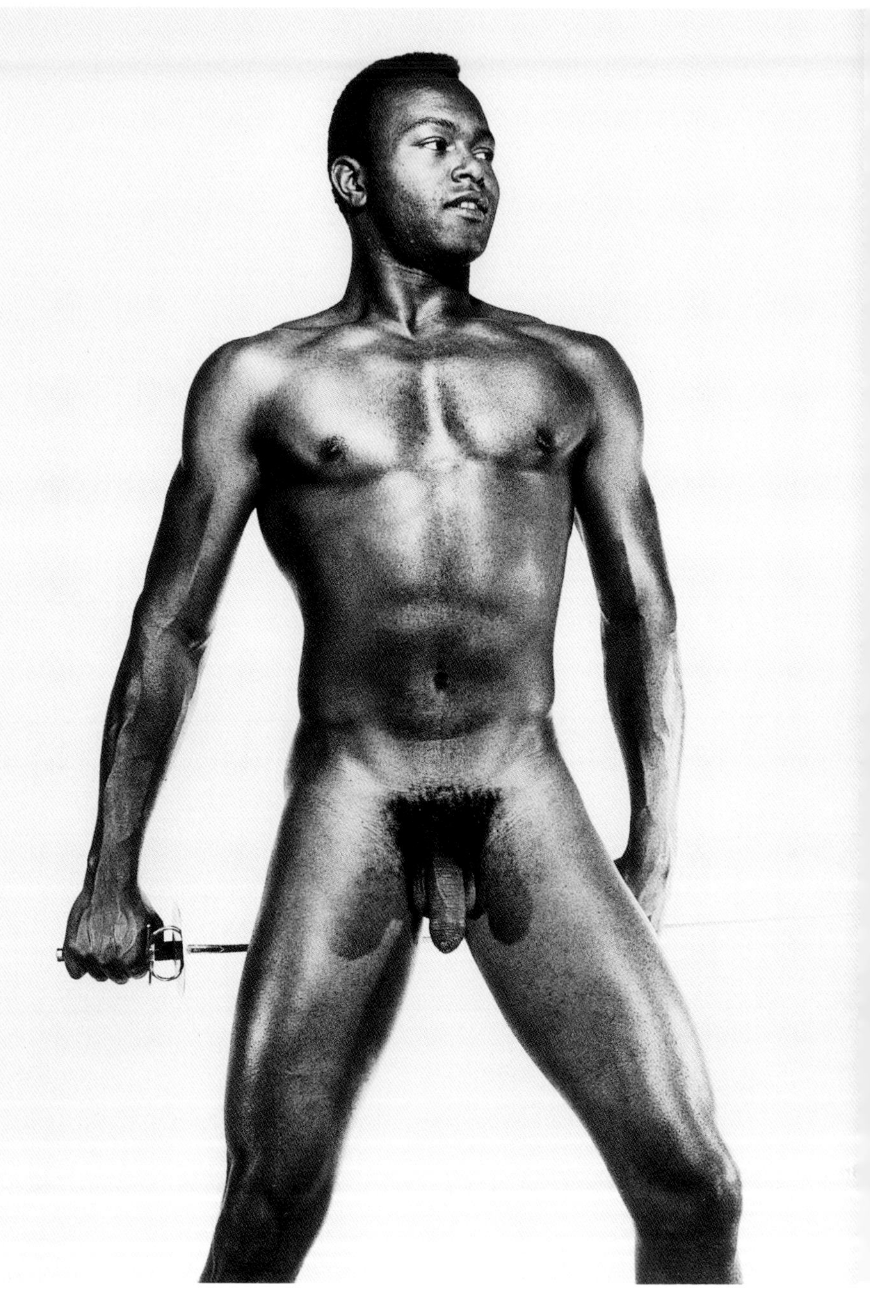

Bruce of Los Angeles, c. 1950

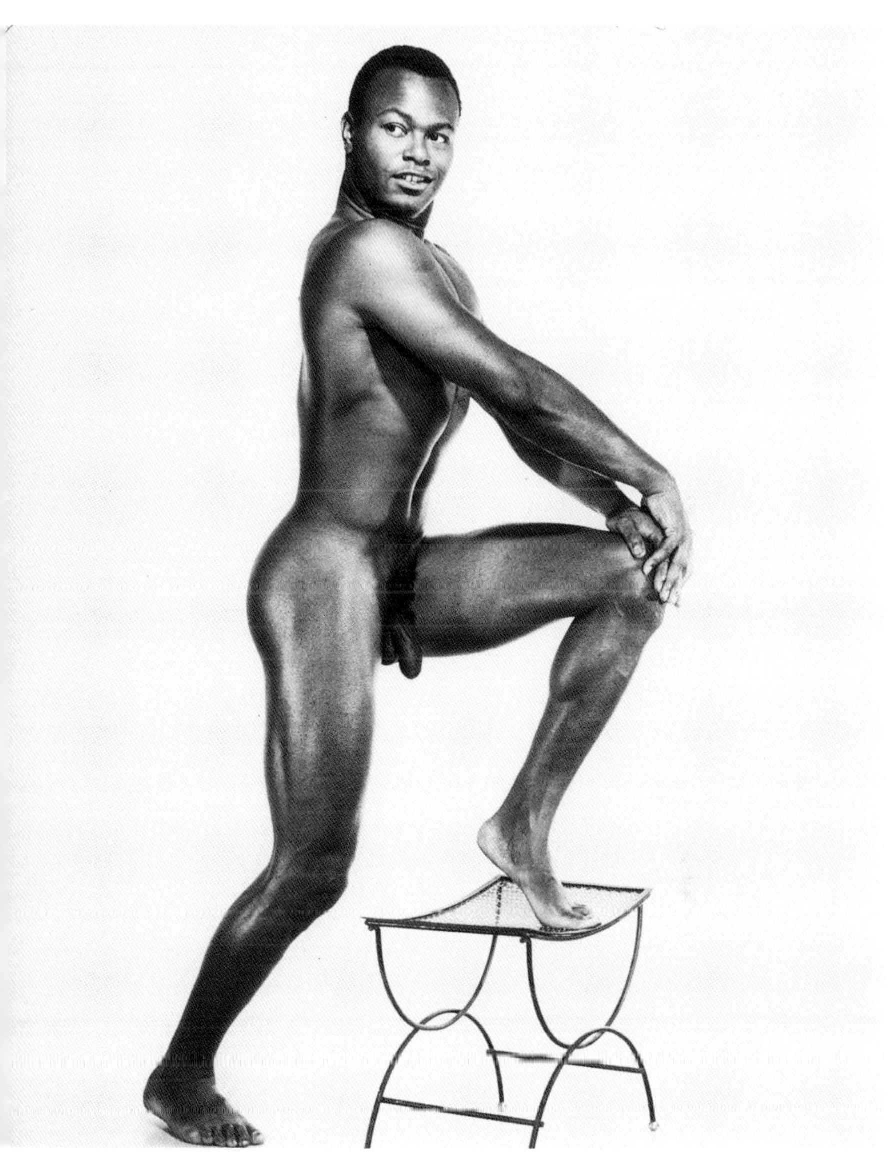

Bruce of Los Angeles, c. 1950

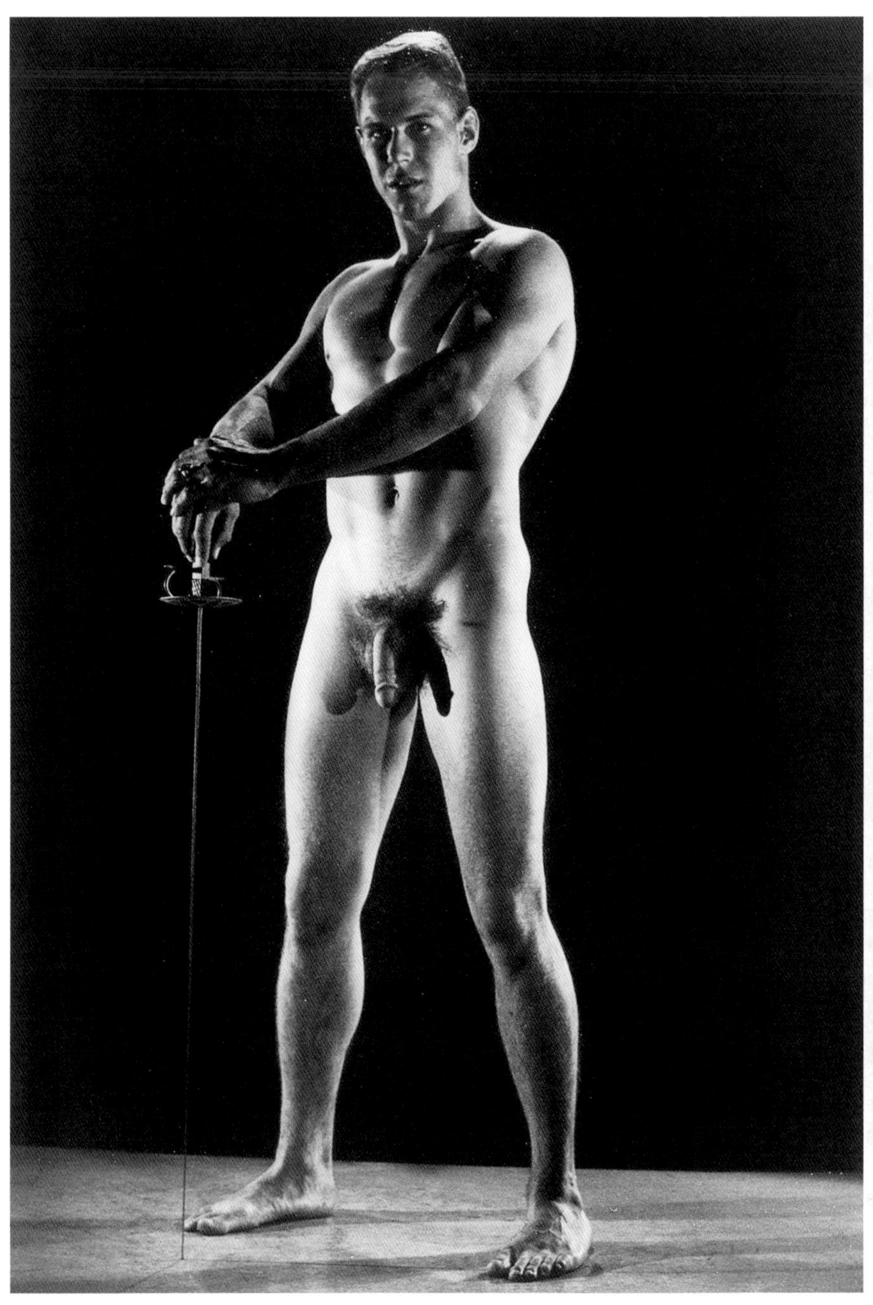

 Bruce of Los Angeles, c. 1950

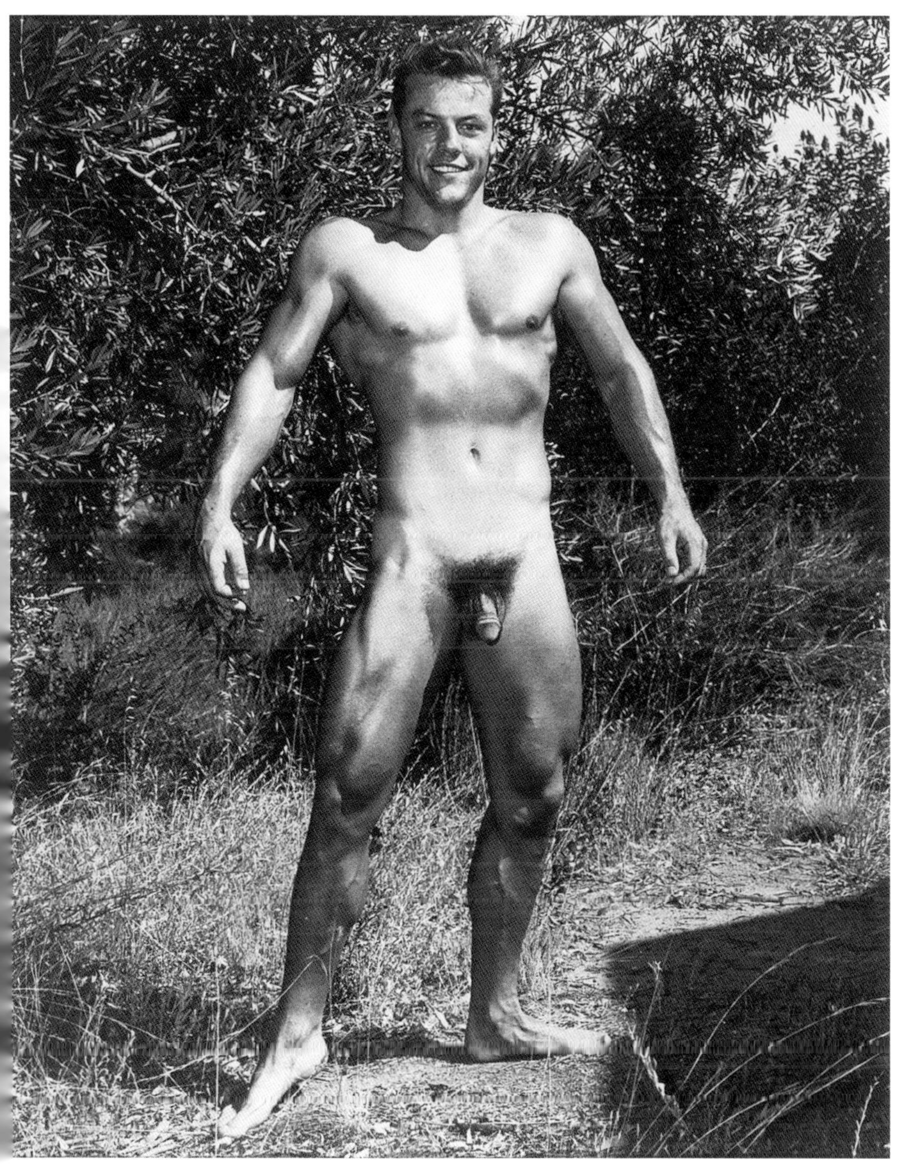

Bruce of Los Angeles, c. 1950

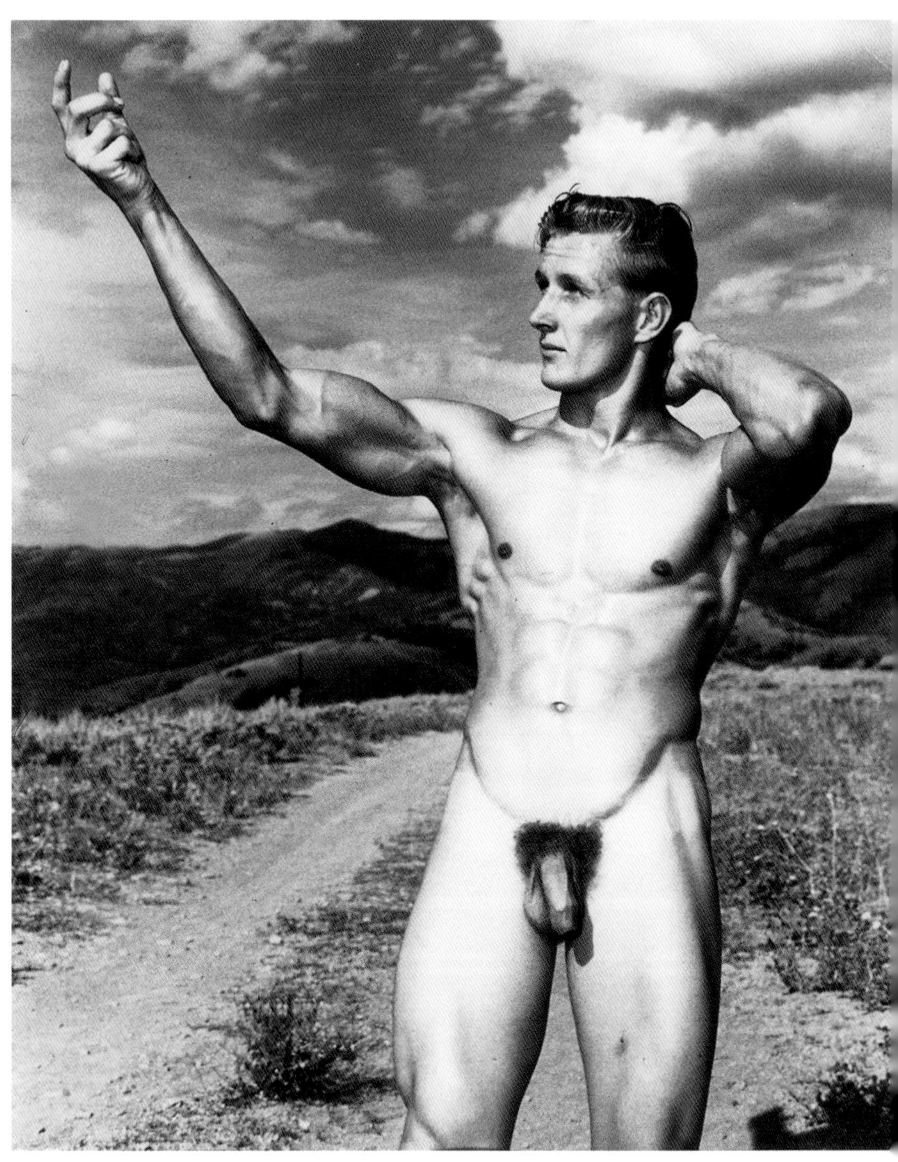

Bruce of Los Angeles, c. 1950

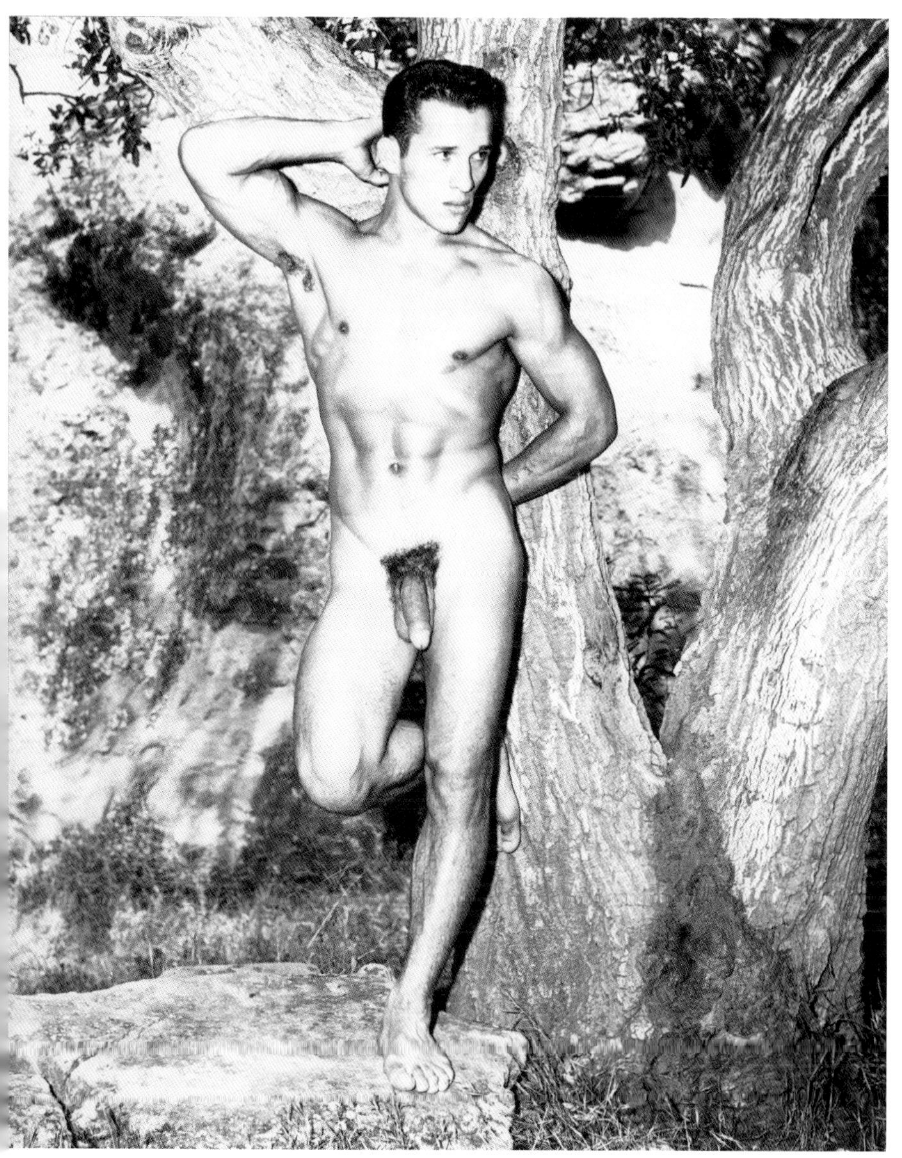

Bruce of Los Angeles, 1950s

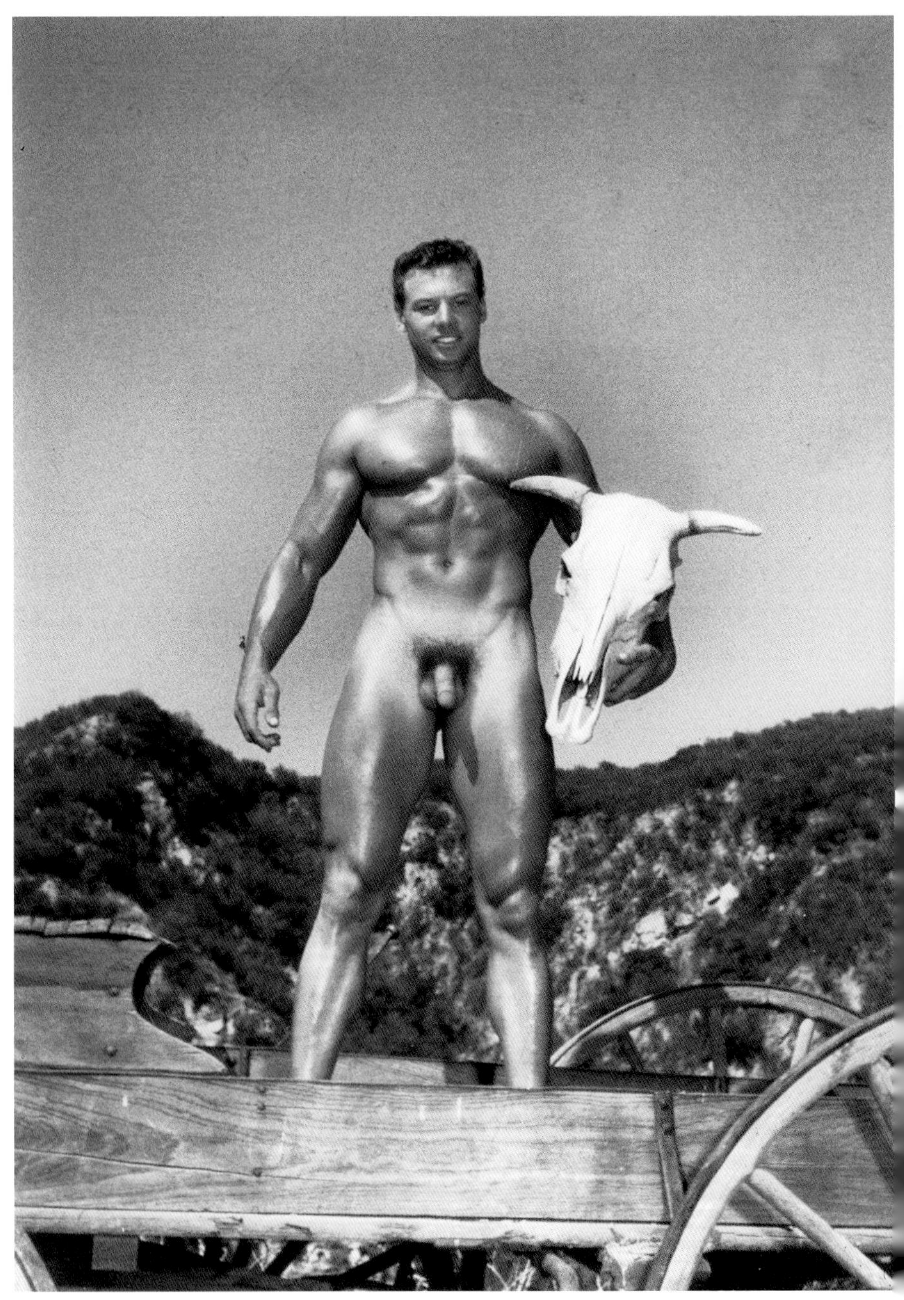

Bruce of Los Angeles, c. 1950

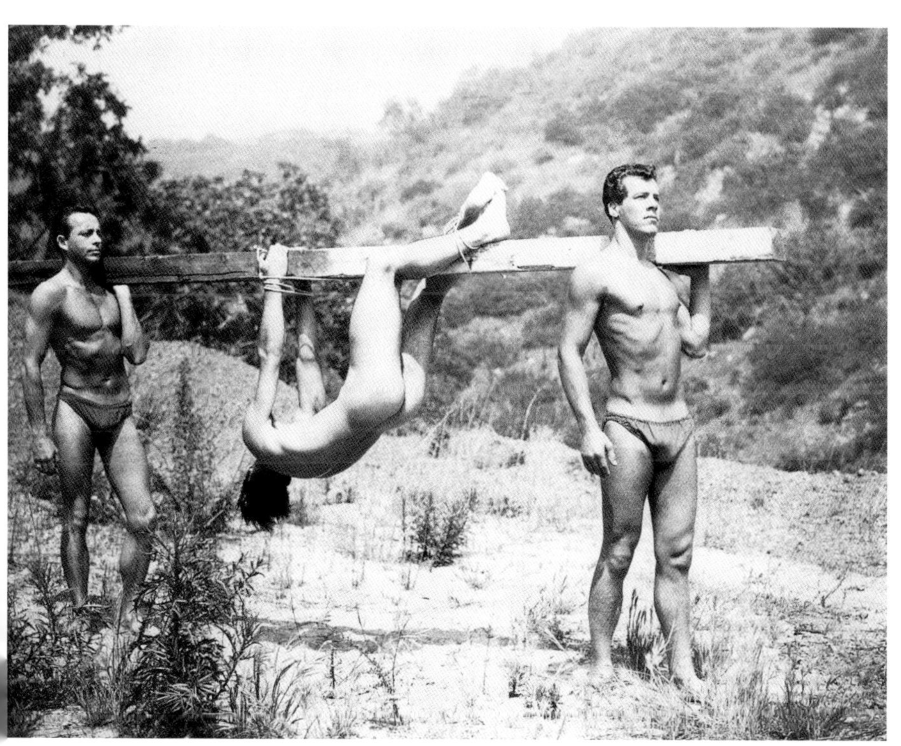

Bruce of Los Angeles, c. 1950

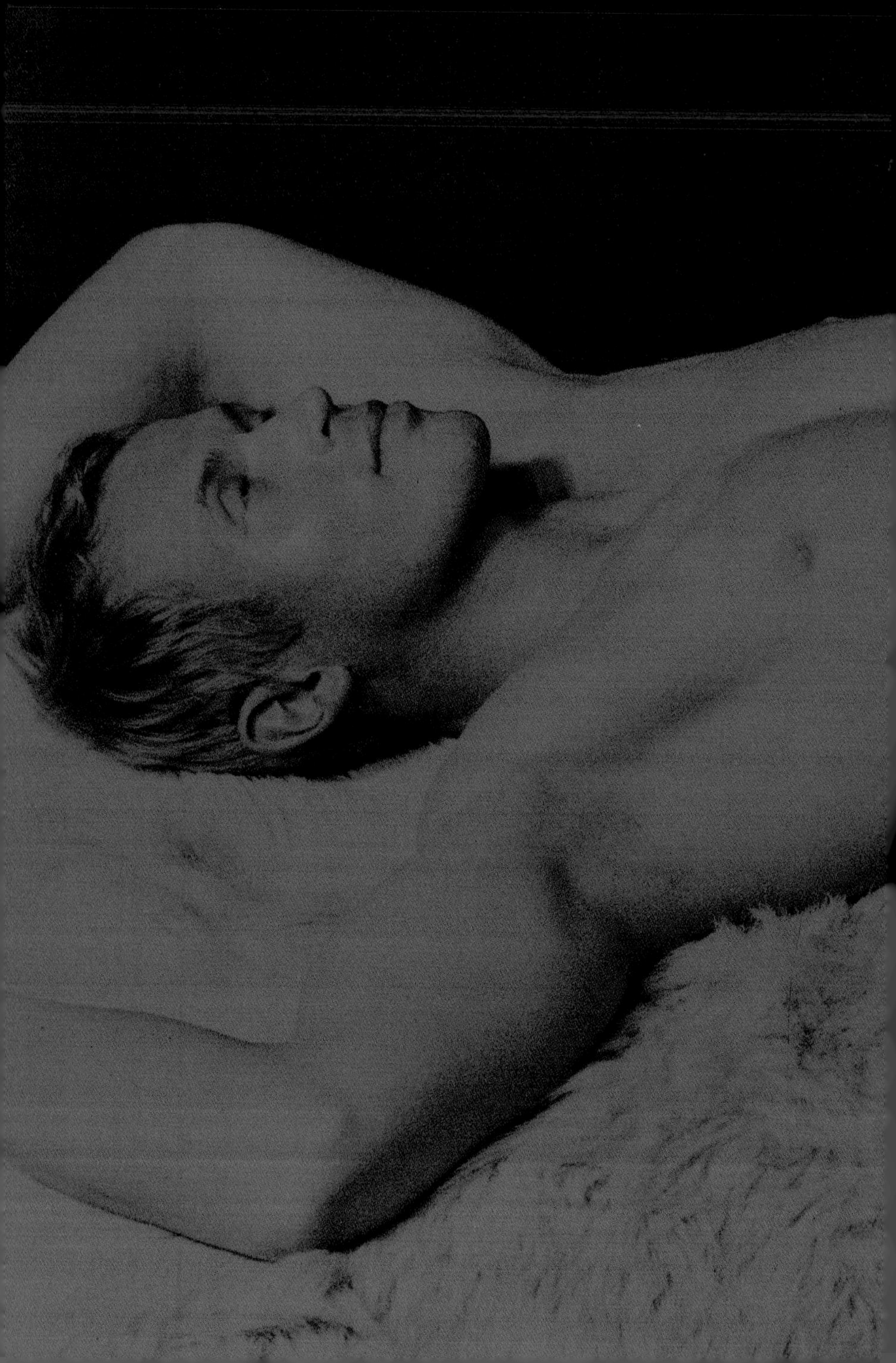

1960–1980

Entering the 1960s, the physique photographers provided the main source of nude male images in the United States and Europe. George Platt Lynes had died at the age of 48 in 1955, and the sort of work he had produced – men with normal proportions and muscles, beautifully lit in the studio – disappeared from the scene.

The 1960s, as they are remembered, did not actually get underway in the U.S. until 1965. Prior to that, little had changed since the 1950s other than Jackie Kennedy's hairdo. There were still no photographs of naked men in the press or magazines. The few seen in the limited circulation "Physique Pictorial" were still wearing posing straps. Full nudes, when bought from suppliers, were turned shyly away from the camera, only their glistening haunches showing. From California through Denver to Chicago and New York, strongly-built young men stared into the camera or into space, displaying their hairless and, for the most part, graceless bodies. It was fun perhaps, but not a lot of fun.

Then the Beatles appeared. In swept rock and roll, drugs, unisex and streaking. The naked male body was suddenly running across sports fields and down city streets, and the newspapers were full of it. This wasn't pornography (for one thing they were running too fast). This was news. Full frontal and all. The barrier had been breached. The world was shocked and loved it.

And a new kind of man, not seen since the Renaissance, made his appearance. Skinny, thick-lipped Mick Jagger came to stand for all that was beautiful. As the famous "Vogue" magazine editor Diana Vreeland said, "Brigitte Bardot's mouth made Mick Jagger possible." Here was androgyny in full force. When Jagger married Bianca somebody, he was only being wed to a female version of himself.

The "happening" became a kind of theater event, and men and women started stripping off everywhere. On Broadway Peter Weiss's play "Marat/Sade" presented its audience with the sight of a man's bare backside as he climbed out of a bathtub. Shock! Soon the musical "Hair" featured naked men (and women) frolicking and singing, albeit in heavy shadow. The new slender, long-haired, boyish, perhaps girlish, silhouettes didn't seem to threaten the public as strong muscled men with large penises had in the past.

The mood was anti-establishment and although the protagonists were mainly wearing velvet trousers, mini-skirts and lots of beads, male nudity had definitely come down off the top shelf. It became the trend for rock stars to wear skin-tight pants and to take their shirts off, a style that is still with us. Jim Morrison even pulled down those skin-tight pants in Florida and was forced to leave the country.

In France, Jean-François Bauret photographed a young Greek model for an underwear ad, except he wasn't wearing any underwear. This was a landmark photograph and a turning point. Soon even Yves Saint-Laurent was posing nude in front of Jeanloup Sieff's camera for his own advertising. Male stars of all kinds wanted to be photographed nude. Mick Jagger undressed for Cecil Beaton. Richard Avedon photographed Rudolf Nureyev dancing without a stitch on.

The art photographer Dianora Niccolini launched her career in the 1970s with the sole aim of photographing nude men. Turning the male body into an object of admiration and lust had previously been categorized as homoerotic. She forced the art community to rethink. Perhaps women liked to photograph men without their clothes on, and to look at the results. For the first time, women and not just homosexuals entered the arena. The fine art photographer Eva Rubinstein shot more abstract but quite beautiful male nudes in the early 1970s too. Don Worth in California and Emerick Bronson in New York were taking poetic and interesting photographs, Worth as early as 1960.

Right at the end of the 1980s the Marcuse Pfeifer Gallery presented a whole exhibition of male nudes – a first for a New York gallery. Ms. Marcuse not only included Dianora Niccolini and the other two major female photographers of men, Imogen Cunningham and Eva Rubinstein, but at least seventeen other women who had photographed men in the buff. From today's point of view it would seem that the gallery had gone to extreme lengths to avoid the accusation that this was an exhibit by homosexuals for homosexuals.

But the critics, all men, would have none of it. They were shocked, offended, and disgusted. The "New York Times" thought it was a feminist attempt to make men look ridiculous and unworthy of respect. Clothes were clearly equated with respectability in the critic's mind. The male critic of "New York Magazine" wrote: "Nude women seem to be in their natural state; men, for some reason, merely look undressed."

Gene Thornton, writing for the "New York Times", summed up the attitude of the time very precisely: "There is especially something to be said for old-fashioned prudery when the unclothed human body is a man's body. No one denies that men's bodies are sexually attractive to most women and also to some men. Nor does anyone deny that the place of the male nude in art is an old and honorable one. Nevertheless, there is something disconcerting about the sight of a man's naked body being presented primarily as a sexual object." Poor Mr. Thornton. He must have gone through hell in the decade that was to follow.

The 1960s freed many people's thinking about nudity. The shame had gone. Acceptance of nudity was considered modern and healthily nonconformist. Witness Woodstock. Modern culture was radically altered by that giant concert. It was hip to be hippie, to smoke dope, and to get your clothes off and wallow in the mud. It was all so refreshing, and among heterosexuals, too!

But those were not the only ideas the hippies brought with them. To be selective about the sex of your bed partner was a form of snobbery. Their ancestors, the Beatniks, had certainly not been particular. The poet Allen Ginsberg had slept with his friends Jack Kerouac and Neal Cassidy. Now the hippies followed suit in their sexual experimentation. The sexual barrier they knocked down brought taboos about male nude photography down with it.

Whomever they might actually choose to sleep with, the public image of rock stars like Mick Jagger, David Bowie, and many others was ambiguous at best. Having long hair and swinging your cute little butt was accepted behavior for any young man. It even came to be expected. These girly-men made for good camera fodder, and soon a number of women photographers began taking nude male photographs. Now the tables were turned. Women were behind the camera and men were in front of it.

Then the young Robert Mapplethorpe emerged to blend many facets of male nude photography from the past into a new style. Strongly influenced by George Platt Lynes, Hoyningen-Huene, Man Ray, and Horst P. Horst, his very well photographed subjects were soon to display more of their maleness than had ever been displayed before.

Photographer George Hester produced a number of books in the early 1970s and managed to include the first full-frontal nude male published for the general public. His beautiful pictures of men, women and children exemplified the new bodily freedom.

Through it all, the physique photographers continued to supply their market with what was now clearly "beefcake." The subterfuges of health, history and art were long forgotten. Strapping young men poured forth, picture after picture, and were clearly there just to be looked at. And now, in the freer climate of the time, they were becoming more obviously erotic. Legs apart, their genitalia were often the center of attraction.

"Beefcake" was put on another level by the imaginative and skilled photographic work of Clifford Baker in California. He displayed his beautiful men outdoors with a new kind of flair and aesthetic quality.

In Europe, Konrad Helbig, Herbert Tobias, Wolfgang von Wangenheim, and Will McBride emerged, each creating his own style of male nude studies. Helbig and von Wangenheim focused on beauty; Tobias and McBride concentrated on a new grittiness and reality. Punk culture was showing its face. All of this photographic activity was the start of a great wave of male nude photography that was to break in the decade that lay ahead.

Im Vergleich zu den 50er Jahren hatte sich, von Jackie Kennedys Haarschnitt abgesehen, kaum etwas verändert. George Platt Lynes war 1955 im Alter von 48 Jahren gestorben, und seine Vorliebe für den gut gebauten, aber nicht übermäßig durchtrainierten Mann, den er gut ausgeleuchtet im Studio aufnahm, verlor in der Szene an Bedeutung.

Anfang der 60er Jahre waren die Physique-Magazine und -Fotografen weiterhin die Hauptlieferanten von Aktaufnahmen in den USA und Europa. In anderen Publikationen war der nackte Mann nach wie vor tabu. Und die Nackten, die man im auflagenschwachen „Physique Pictorial" sah, trugen immer noch einen Lendenschurz. Gänzlich Nackte, wie sie der Versandhandel feilbot, waren verschämt zur Seite gedreht und zeigten der Kamera nur ihre glänzende Kehrseite. Von Kalifornien über Denver bis nach Chicago und New York starrten durchtrainierte junge Männer in die Kamera oder in die Ferne und präsentierten ihre eingeölten und meistens ungeschlachten Körper. Vielleicht machte auch das Spaß, aber keinen besonders großen.

Und dann wurde alles anders. Beatles, Teenager-Hysterie, Drogen, Hippies, Unisex und Flitzer. Plötzlich liefen splitternackte Männer über Sportplätze und durch die Straßen der Städte, und so schaffte es der nackte Mann plötzlich auf alle Titelseiten. Das war keine Pornographie – dafür liefen die Flitzer zu schnell –, aber es war eine Nachricht wert. Splitternackt, oben ohne, unten ohne. Das Tabu war gefallen. Die Öffentlichkeit war geschockt und fand zugleich Gefallen daran.

Und ein neuer Typus Mann war erschienen: Mick Jagger mit seiner schmalen Figur und seinen üppigen Lippen stand für das neue Schönheitsideal. „Brigitte Bardots Mund hat Mick Jagger erst möglich gemacht", befand Diana Vreeland, die Herausgeberin von „Vogue". Androgynität in Reinkultur. Als Mick Jagger Bianca heiratete, nahm er sich lediglich die weibliche Version seiner selbst zur Frau.

Das „Happening" wurde zum Theaterereignis, überall entledigten sich jetzt Männer und Frauen ihrer Kleidung. Am Broadway wurde dem Publikum in einer Aufführung von Peter Weiss' „Marat/Sade" sogar das nackte Gesäß eine Mannes zugemutet, als dieser einer Badewanne entstieg.

Wenig später traten in dem Musical „Hair" übermütige Männer und Frauen auf, die sangen und dabei alles zeigten, wenn auch von schwarzen Schatten verdeckt. Die neue Silhouette des Mannes war schlank, langhaarig und jungenhaft (mädchenhaft?) und wirkte auf die Öffentlichkeit weit weniger bedrohlich als die kräftigen, muskelbepackten Männer.

Die Stimmung richtete sich gegen das Establishment, auch wenn es sich bei den Protagonisten zumeist in Äußerlichkeiten manifestierte. Aktbilder wurden jedenfalls nicht mehr in die obersten Regale oder unter die Ladentheke verbannt.

Rockstars traten in hautengen Hosen auf und ließen sie auch schon mal fallen, wie Jim Morrison in Florida. Jean-François Bauret fotografierte in Frankreich einen jungen Griechen für eine Unterwäscheanzeige – nur hatte er diese Unterwäsche gar nicht an. Das war ein Meilenstein in der Werbefotografie und wirkte wie ein Signal. Wenig später stand Yves Saint-Laurent für eine eigene Werbekampagne nackt vor der Kamera von Jeanloup Sieff. Männliche Stars aus allen Sparten wollten auf einmal nackt abgelichtet werden. Mick Jagger zog sich für die Kamera von Cecil Beaton fast ganz aus, und Richard Avedon fotografierte Rudolf Nurejew splitternackt beim Tanzen.

Die 60er Jahre waren für die Menschen ein Befreiungsschlag. Sie trennten sich von überkommenen Ansichten, die Scham wurde abgelegt. Die sexuellen Schranken waren gefallen, und das Tabu der männlichen Aktfotografie mit ihnen.

In den 70ern trat die Fotografin Dianora Niccolini an, den nackten Mann zu fotografieren. Den männlichen Körper als Objekt der Bewunderung und Lust darzustellen, war bislang immer als homoerotisch eingestuft worden. Niccolini zwang die Kunstszene zum Umdenken. Frauen fotografierten Männer nicht nur nackt, sondern fanden auch ausdrücklich Gefallen an den Bildern.

Auch die bekannte Künstlerin Eva Rubinstein nahm Anfang der 70er Jahre einige abstrakte, aber sehr schöne Männerakte auf. Don Worth in Kalifornien und Emerick Bronson in New York traten mit sehr poetischen Bildern hervor. Worths Werk datiert bis zurück in die 60er.

Ebenfalls Anfang der 70er erschien eine Reihe von Bildbänden des Fotografen George Hester auf dem Markt. Er wagte es zum ersten Mal, einem breiten

Publikum die Frontalansicht eines nackten Mannes zu präsentieren. Seine hervorragenden Bilder von Männern, Frauen und Kindern verdeutlichen die neue Freizügigkeit.

Gegen Ende dieser zwei Jahrzehnte umfassenden Zeitspanne zeigte schließlich die Marcuse Pfeifer Gallery eine Ausstellung männlicher Akte. Das war eine Premiere für die New Yorker Galeriewelt. Marcuse nahm nicht nur Dianora Niccolini und die beiden anderen großen Namen unter den Aktfotografinnen, Imogen Cunningham und Eva Rubinstein, in die Ausstellung auf, sondern noch siebzehn andere Frauen, die Männer im Adamskostüm fotografiert hatten. Von einem Event für Homosexuelle konnte also kaum die Rede sein. Die Kritiker aber, allesamt Männer, zeigten sich schockiert, beleidigt und angewidert. Die „New York Times" wertete die Ausstellung als eine feministische Attacke, als Versuch, den Mann der Lächerlichkeit preiszugeben. Der Kritiker einer anderen New Yorker Zeitschrift schrieb: „Eine nackte Frau scheint uns natürlich, ein nackter Mann hingegen bloß unbekleidet."

Der Kritiker der „New York Times", Gene Thornton, brachte die vorherrschende Meinung auf den Punkt: „Beim Bild des unbekleideten menschlichen Körpers, insbesondere wenn es sich um einen männlichen Körper handelt, hat die althergebrachte Prüderie durchaus etwas für sich. Niemand bestreitet, dass der Körper des Mannes auf die meisten Frauen und auch auf einige Männer sexuell anziehend wirkt. Es bestreitet auch niemand, dass dem nackten Mann in der Kunst ein ehrenwerter Platz gebührt. Dennoch hat der Anblick eines nackten Männerkörpers, der in erster Linie als Lustobjekt gezeigt wird, etwas Beunruhigendes." Armer Mr. Thornton. Das folgende Jahrzehnt sollte ihn noch schwer prüfen.

Es war modern sich nicht anzupassen. Woodstock ist das beste Beispiel. Nach diesem gigantischen Konzertereignis war die Kultur nicht mehr dieselbe. Wer dazugehören wollte, war ein Hippie, rauchte Gras, zog sich aus und wälzte sich im Schlamm. Zudem hatten die Hippies einen neuen Gedanken eingebracht. Allzu wählerisch zu sein bei der Frage, welchem Geschlecht der Partner angehörte, mit dem man ins Bett stieg, galt als Snobismus. Die Vorläufer der Hippies, die Beatniks, waren in der Beziehung auch nicht zimperlich gewesen. Der Dichter

Allen Ginsberg hatte mit seinen Freunden Jack Kerouac und Neal Cassidy ge-
schlafen, und ihnen folgten die Hippies mit ihrer sexuellen Experimentierfreude.

Während all dieser Entwicklungen belieferten auch die Bodybuilder-Foto-
grafen weiterhin ihren Markt mit Bildern, die nun eindeutig „Beefcake" waren.
Die Deckmäntelchen Gesundheit, Historie und Kunst waren längst abgestreift.
In dem neuen, ungezwungenen Klima wurden die Bilder offen erotisch: Die Beine
gespreizt, prangten die Genitalien oft im Mittelpunkt. Die Arbeiten des Kalifor-
niers Clifford Baker zeigten, dass sich auch in diesem Genre durchaus Werke mit
einem gewissen Flair und von ästhetischer Qualität schaffen ließen.

In Europa traten Konrad Helbig, Herbert Tobias, Wolfgang von Wangenheim
und Will McBride in Erscheinung, die alle eigene Richtungen in der Fotografie
des Männeraktes vertraten. Bei Helbig und von Wangenheim stand Schönheit
im Vordergrund, bei Tobias und McBride Realitätsnähe und eine neue Entschlos-
senheit. Die Punkkultur zeigte bereits ihr Gesicht.

In New York betrat der junge Robert Mapplethorpe die Szene. Beeinflusst
von George Platt Lynes, Hoyningen-Huene, Man Ray und Horst P. Horst, griff er
die unterschiedlichen Facetten der Aktfotografie auf und verband sie zu einem
neuen Stil. Diese Einzeltendenzen in der Fotografie sollten im kommenden Jahrzehnt zu einer wahren Flut an Aktfotografie führen.

Au début des années 60, les photographes de culturistes étaient les principaux producteurs de nus masculins en Europe et aux Etats-Unis. George Platt Lynes mourut en 1955 à l'âge de 48 ans, et son goût pour les hommes normalement musclés, superbement éclairés en studio, disparut avec lui.

Avant 1965, aux Etats-Unis, les années 60 ressemblaient en tout point aux années 50, exception faite de la mise en plis de Jackie Kennedy. Il n'y avait toujours pas de photos d'hommes nus dans la presse ni dans les magazines. Ceux qui étaient montrés dans « Physique Pictorial », dont la circulation était limitée, portaient encore des cache-sexe. Les nus intégraux tournaient pudiquement le dos. De la Californie à New York en passant par Denver et Chicago, de jeunes hommes à la musculature imposante regardaient vers l'objectif ou dans le vague, exhibant leur corps imberbes et, souvent, sans grâce.

Puis, soudain, il y a les Beatles, et les vraies années 60 commencèrent. Elles apportèrent avec elles le rock and roll, la drogue, la mode unisexe et le streaking. Des hommes nus traversaient brusquement un terrain de foot ou des rues du centre-ville et les journaux ne parlaient plus que de ça. Ce n'était pas de la pornographie (de toutes façons, ils couraient trop vite), c'était de l'information. Frontale et intégrale. La barrière avait été franchie. Le monde était choqué et ravi.

Un type d'homme tel qu'on en n'avait pas vu depuis la Renaissance réapparut : maigre et lippu, Mick Jagger devint l'incarnation de la beauté masculine. La célèbre rédactrice de « Vogue », Diana Vreeland, déclara : « C'est la bouche de Brigitte Bardot qui a rendu Mick Jagger possible. » L'androgynie était de rigueur. Lorsque Mick Jagger épousa Bianca machin chose, il ne faisait qu'épouser une version féminine de lui-même. On ne savait plus trop qui était qui. Le « happening » devint une sorte d'événement théâtral, des hommes et des femmes se déshabillaient dans tous les coins. Lors de la présentation de la pièce « Marat/Sade » à Broadway, le public vit les fesses nues d'un homme sortant d'une baignoire. Chocking ! Bientôt la comédie musicale « Hair » révéla des hommes (et des femmes) batifolant nus sur scène, quoique sous un éclairage bien étudié. Cette nouvelle silhouette svelte, chevelue, adolescente et androgyne ne semblait pas menacer le public autant que les hommes musclés et bien membrés l'avaient fait par le passé.

L'humeur était à l'anti-establishment et, dans les kiosques, la nudité masculine n'était plus perchée sur un rayon inaccessible au consommateur. Il devint
coutumier pour les rock-stars de monter sur scène torse nu avec un pantalon
moulant, un style qui perdure encore de nos jours. Jim Morrison alla même jusqu'à baisser ce pantalon moulant sur une scène de Floride… et dut quitter le pays.

En France, Jean-François Bauret photographia un jeune modèle grec pour
une publicité de sous-vêtement, mais celui-ci ne portait pas de sous-vêtement.
Cette photo devait rester dans les annales de la photographie, marquant un tournant dans l'histoire du nu masculin. Peu de temps après, Yves Saint-Laurent
posait nu devant l'objectif de Jeanloup Sieff pour ses propres publicités. Bientôt, toutes les vedettes masculines voulurent être photographiées nues. Mick
Jagger fit un strip-tease devant Cecil Beaton et Richard Avedon photographia
Rudolf Noureïev dans le plus simple appareil.

La photographe d'art Dianora Niccolini entama sa carrière dans les années 70
dans le seul but de photographier des hommes nus. Sa capacité à faire du corps
masculin un objet d'admiration, et même de désir, lui aurait autrefois valu l'éti-
quette « d'homoérotisme ». Elle força la communauté artistique à réfléchir. Si
des femmes aimaient photographier des hommes nus, peut-être y avait-il également des femmes qui aimaient les regarder.

Au début des années 70, la photographe d'art Eva Rubinstein réalisa, elle
aussi, des nus masculins plus abstraits mais très beaux. Don Worth en Californie
et Emerick Bronson à New York faisaient tous les deux des photos poétiques et
intéressantes, Worth ayant commencé dès 1960.

A la fin de ces deux décennies, la Marcuse Pfeifer Gallery organisa une
exposition de nus masculins, une première pour une galerie d'art new-yorkaise.
L'exposition incluait, outre le travail de Dianora Niccolini et de deux autres
grandes dames de la photographie, Imogen Cunningham et Eva Rubinstein, les
œuvres d'au moins dix-sept femmes ayant photographié des hommes dans leur
intimité. Avec le recul, il semble que la galerie n'ait pas lésiné sur les moyens
pour éviter d'être accusée de promouvoir l'homosexualité.

Mais les critiques, tous des hommes, n'apprécièrent pas. Ils étaient cho-
qués, offensés et dégoûtés. Le « New York Times » accusa l'exposition d'être une

manœuvre féministe visant à ridiculiser et à rabaisser la gent masculine. Dans leur esprit, le vêtement était indissociable du respect. Le critique d'une revue new-yorkaise déclara : « Nues, les femmes paraissent dans leur élément naturel. Les hommes, eux, pour une raison étrange, ont simplement l'air dévêtu. »

Gene Thornton, critique au « New York Times », exprima exactement le point de vue de l'époque : « Lorsque le corps dévêtu est celui d'un homme, on comprend mieux l'intérêt de notre bonne vieille pudeur. On ne peut nier que le corps de l'homme puisse être sexuellement attirant pour une femme, ainsi que pour quelques hommes. On ne peut nier non plus que le nu masculin occupe une place traditionnelle et honorable dans l'histoire de l'art. Néanmoins, il y a quelque chose de déconcertant dans la vue d'un corps d'homme présenté comme un objet sexuel. »

Les années 60 devaient modifier l'opinion de beaucoup de gens sur la nudité. Elle n'était plus honteuse. Elle était même devenue le symbole de la modernité et du désir de chacun d'être dans le vent. Il n'y a qu'à voir Woodstock. Après ce méga-concert, la culture ne fut plus tout à fait pareille. Pour être branché, il fallait être hippie, fumer de l'herbe, ôter ses vêtements et se rouler dans la boue. Tout ceci était si rafraîchissant ! Bien entendu, il s'agissait d'une nudité très hétérosexuelle.

Mais les hippies apportèrent avec eux un nouveau concept: se montrer trop tatillon sur le sexe de son partenaire sexuel était une forme de snobisme. De fait, leurs ancêtres les beatniks ne s'étaient pas montrés trop stricts sur le sujet. Le poète Allen Ginsberg avait entraîné ses amis Jack Kerouac et Neal Cassidy dans son lit. A présent, les hippies leur emboîtaient le pas avec leurs expériences sexuelles en tout genre. Cette dernière barrière entraîna le tabou du nu masculin dans sa chute.

Qu'ils couchent avec des hommes ou des femmes, l'image de rock-stars tels que Mick Jagger, David Bowie et bien d'autres encore, était plus qu'ambiguë. En outre, ces hommes féminins étaient exhibitionnistes et, bientôt, une armée de femmes photographes se lancèrent dans le nu masculin. Les rôles étaient inversés. Les femmes se retrouvaient derrière la caméra et les hommes, devant l'objectif.

C'est alors que le jeune **Robert Mapplethorpe** fit son entrée, conjuguant différentes facettes du nu classique en un nouveau style. Fortement influencés par **George Platt Lynes, Hoyningen-Huene, Man Ray** et **Horst P. Horst,** ses sujets superbement photographiés dévoilaient plus de masculinité que jamais auparavant.

Au début des années 70, le photographe **George Hester** publia une série de livres et parvint à inclure le premier nu masculin montré de face dans un ouvrage destiné au grand public. Ses belles images raffinées d'hommes, de femmes et d'enfants illustraient la nouvelle liberté du corps.

Pendant tout ce temps, les photographes de culturistes continuèrent à approvisionner leur marché avec des « monsieur muscle ». Les subterfuges de santé, d'histoire et d'art étaient oubliés depuis longtemps. Image après image, ils déversaient leur lot de jeunes mâles n'ayant plus d'autre raison d'être que d'être plaisants à regarder. Du fait de la libération des mœurs, ils devenaient de plus en plus érotiques, leurs organes génitaux étant souvent le principal centre d'intérêt de la photo.

Clifford Baker, qui travaillait en Californie, haussa ces « Beefcake » (les équivalents masculins des pin-up d'antan) à un niveau plus créatif et de meilleure qualité. Ses beaux hommes nus posant dans la nature attestaient d'un sens esthétique plus poussé et avaient d'avantage d'allure.

En Europe, **Konrad Helbig, Herbert Tobias, Wolfgang von Wangenheim** et **Will McBride** entraînèrent chacun le nu masculin dans une nouvelle direction, Helbig et von Wangenheim se concentrant sur la beauté plastique, Tobias et McBride sur un réalisme plus cru. La culture punk pointait son nez. Toute cette nouvelle vague photographique devait se traduire par un déferlement de nus masculins dans la décennie suivante.

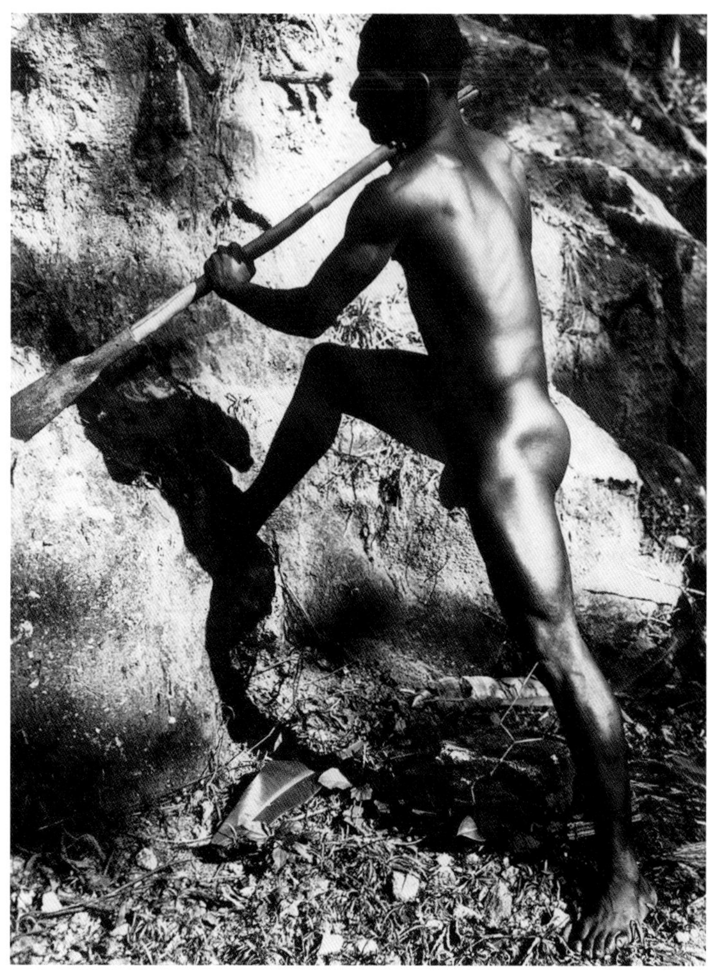

Konrad Helbig, Brazil, 1967/68

Konrad Helbig, c. 1970

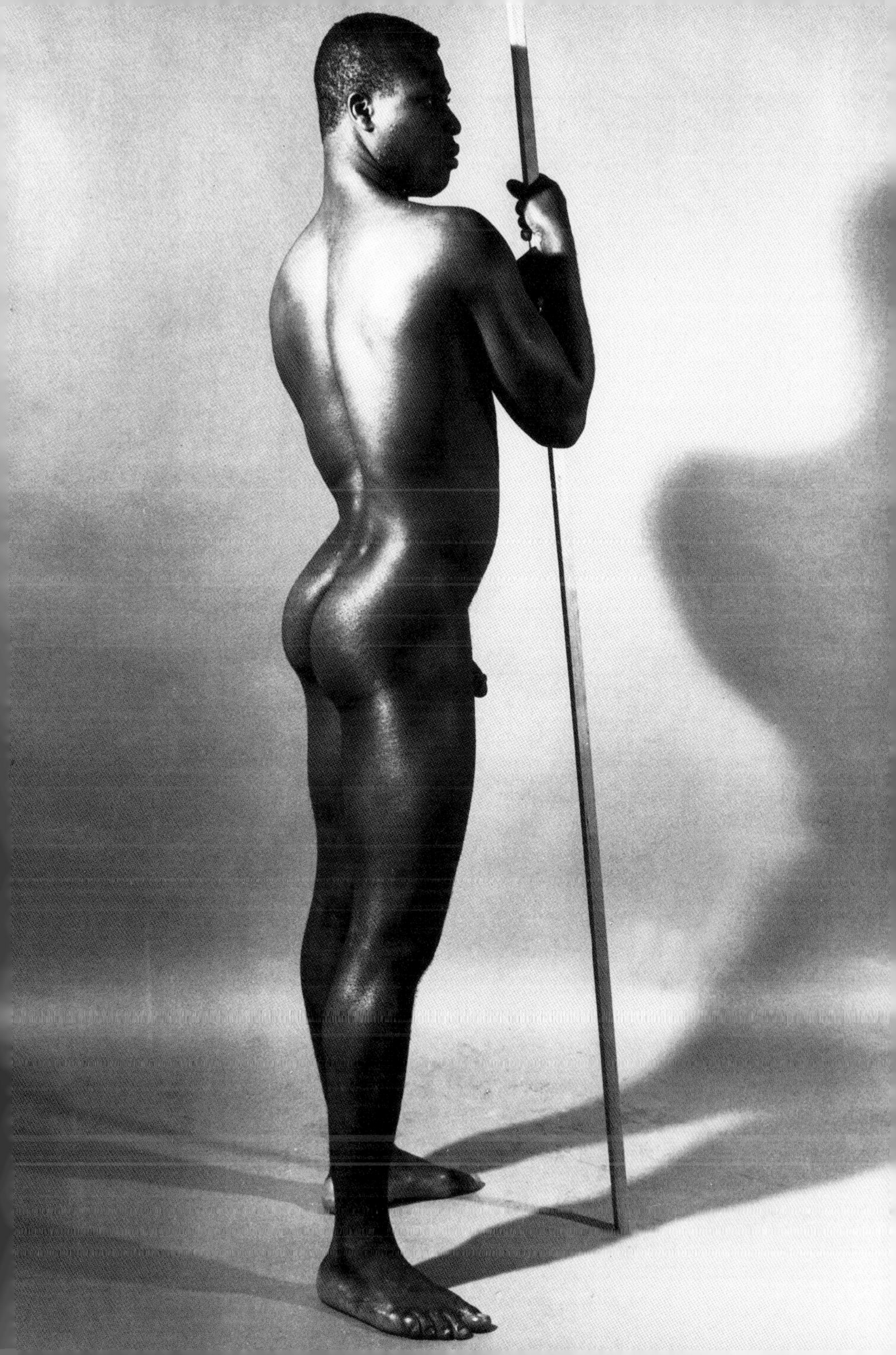

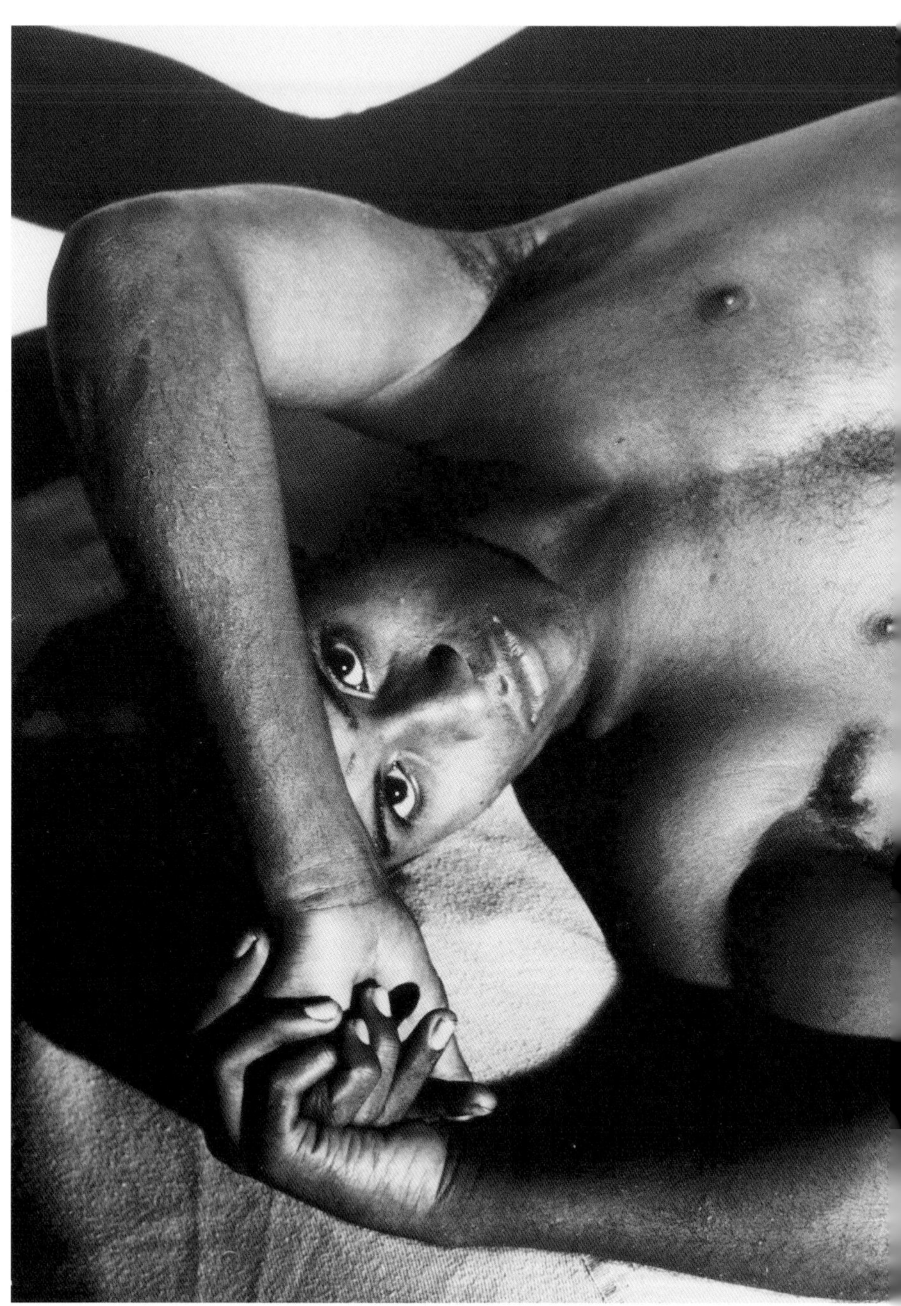

Konrad Helbig, Brazil, c. 1968

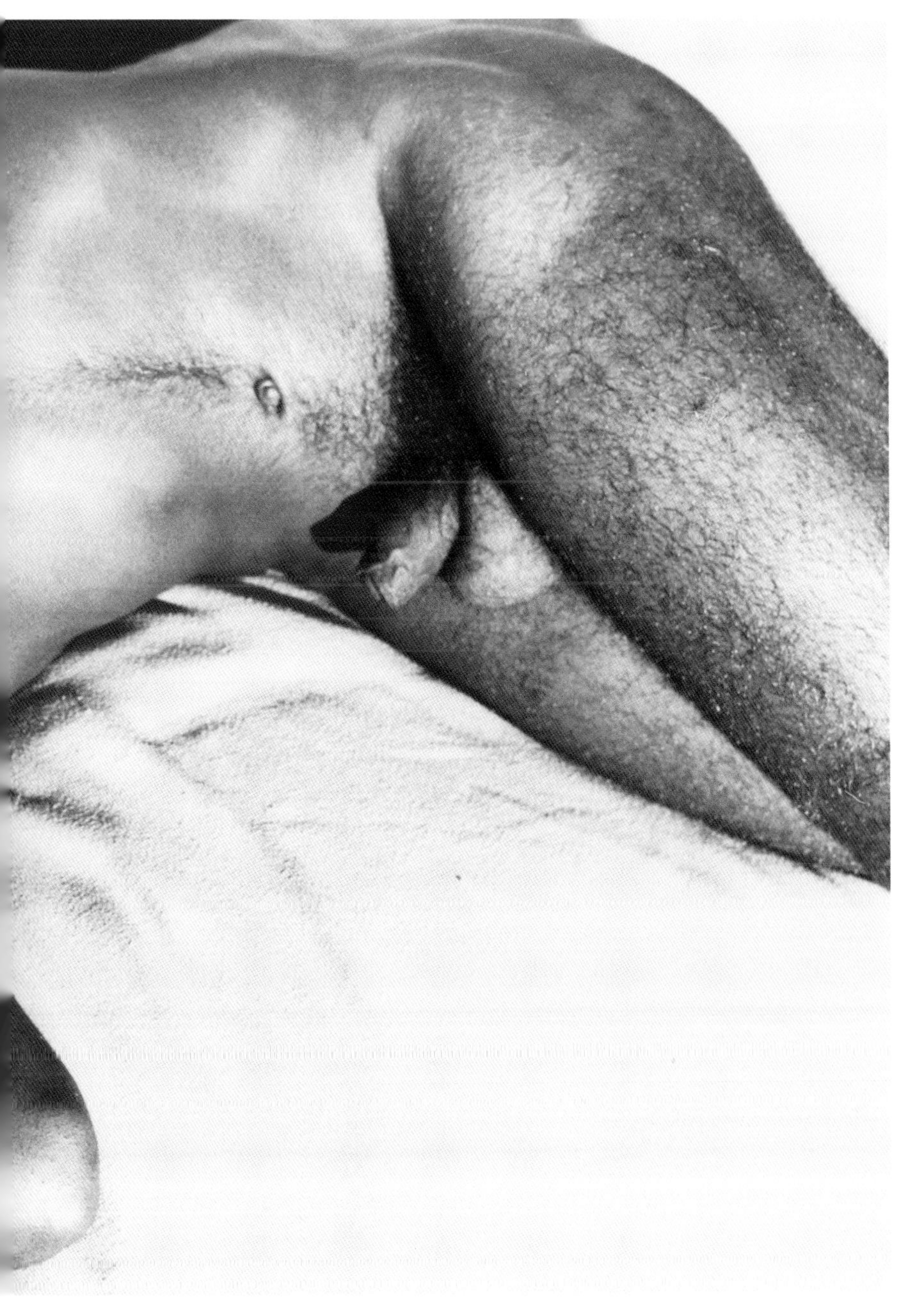

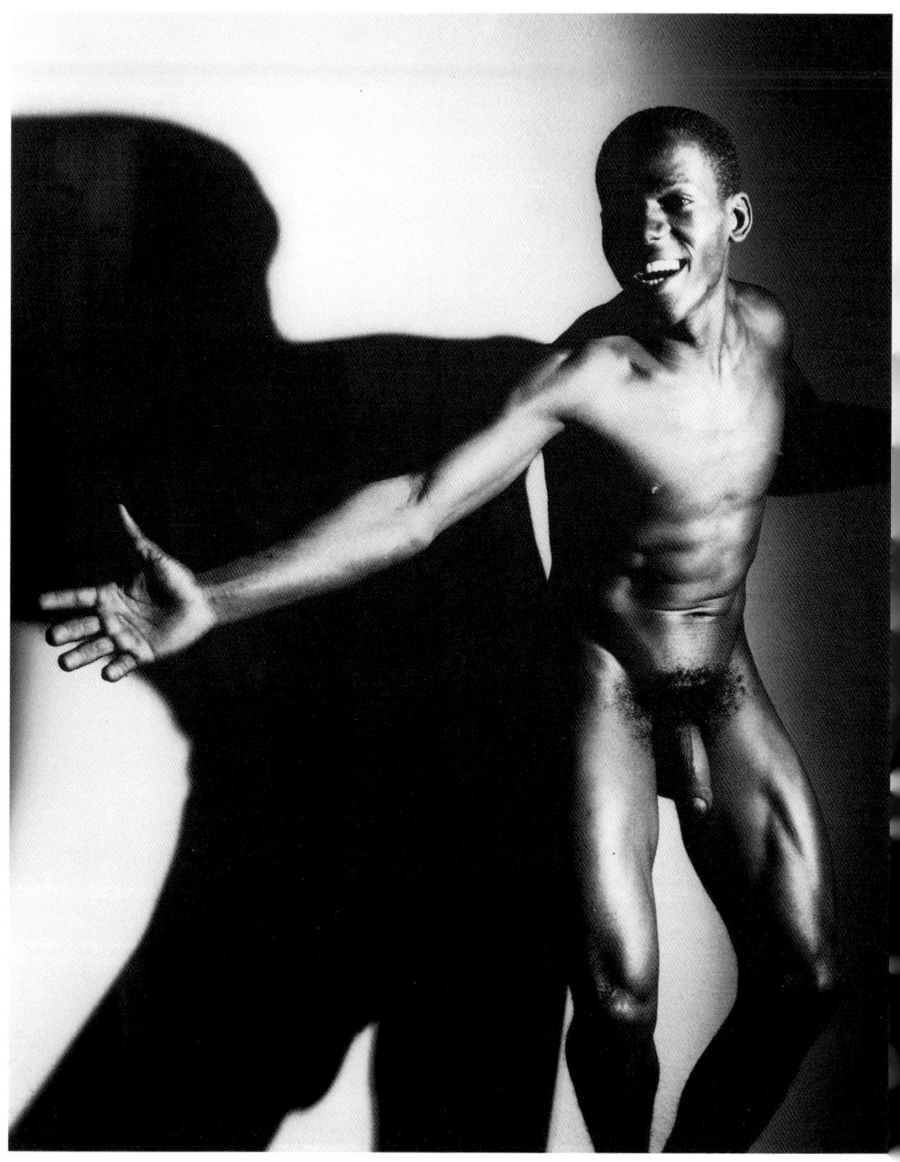

Konrad Helbig, Brazil, c. 1968

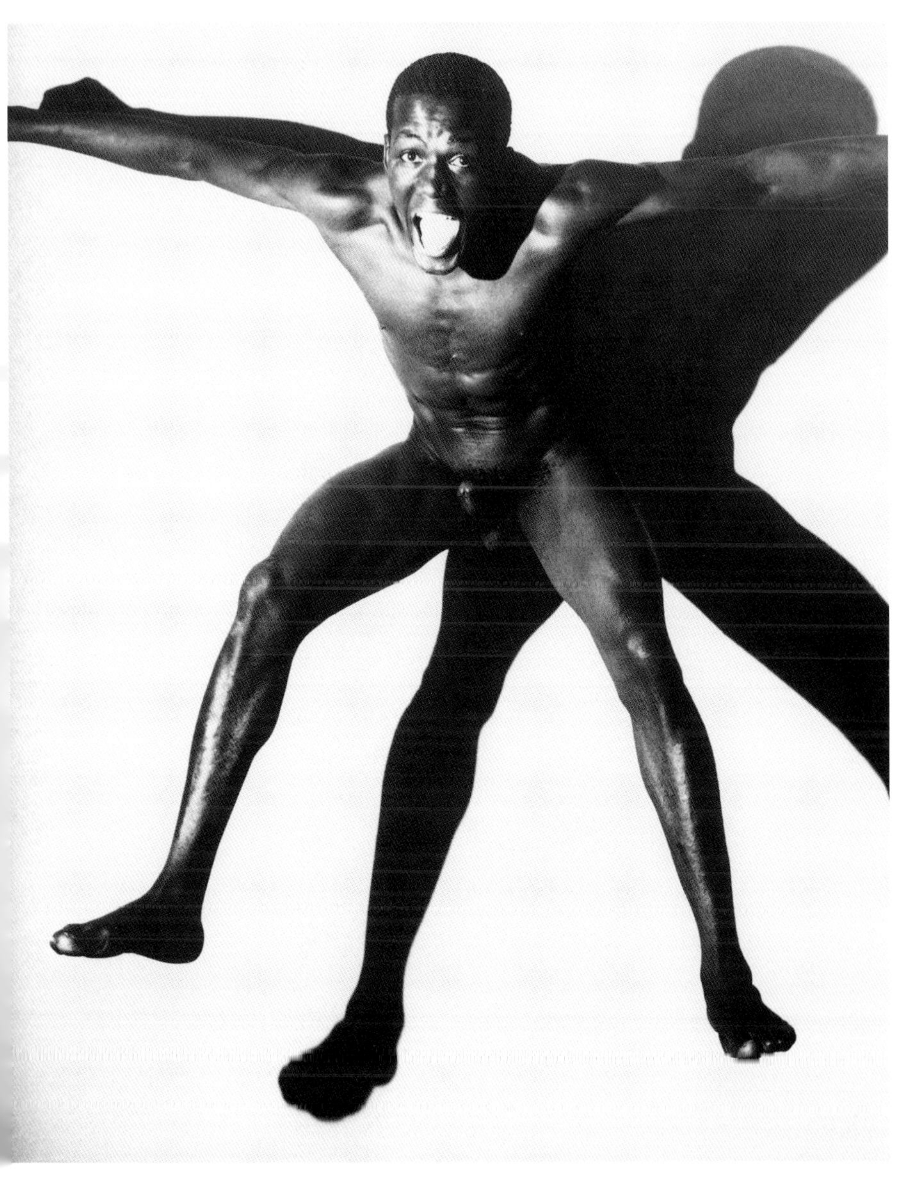

Konrad Helbig, Brazil, c. 1968

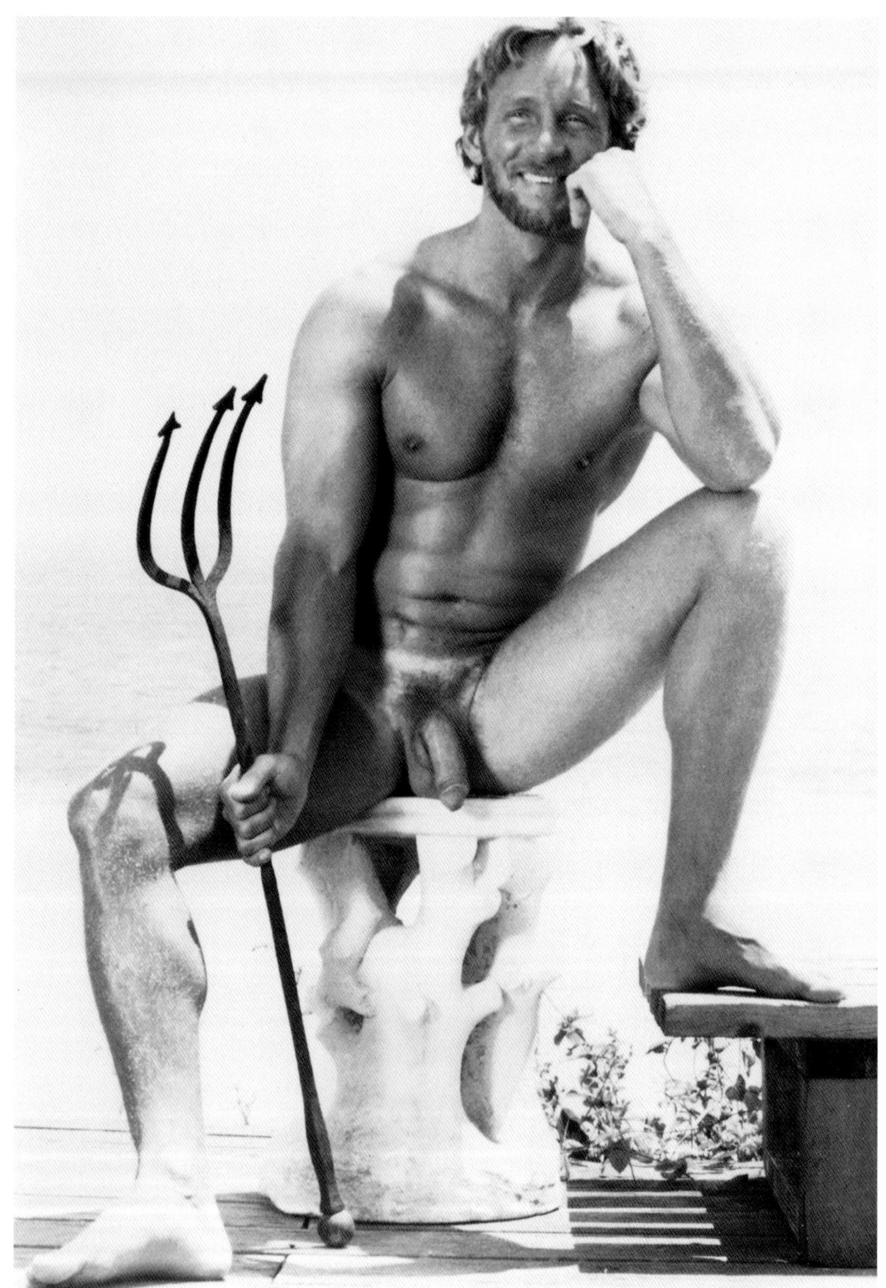

Anonymous, c. 1970

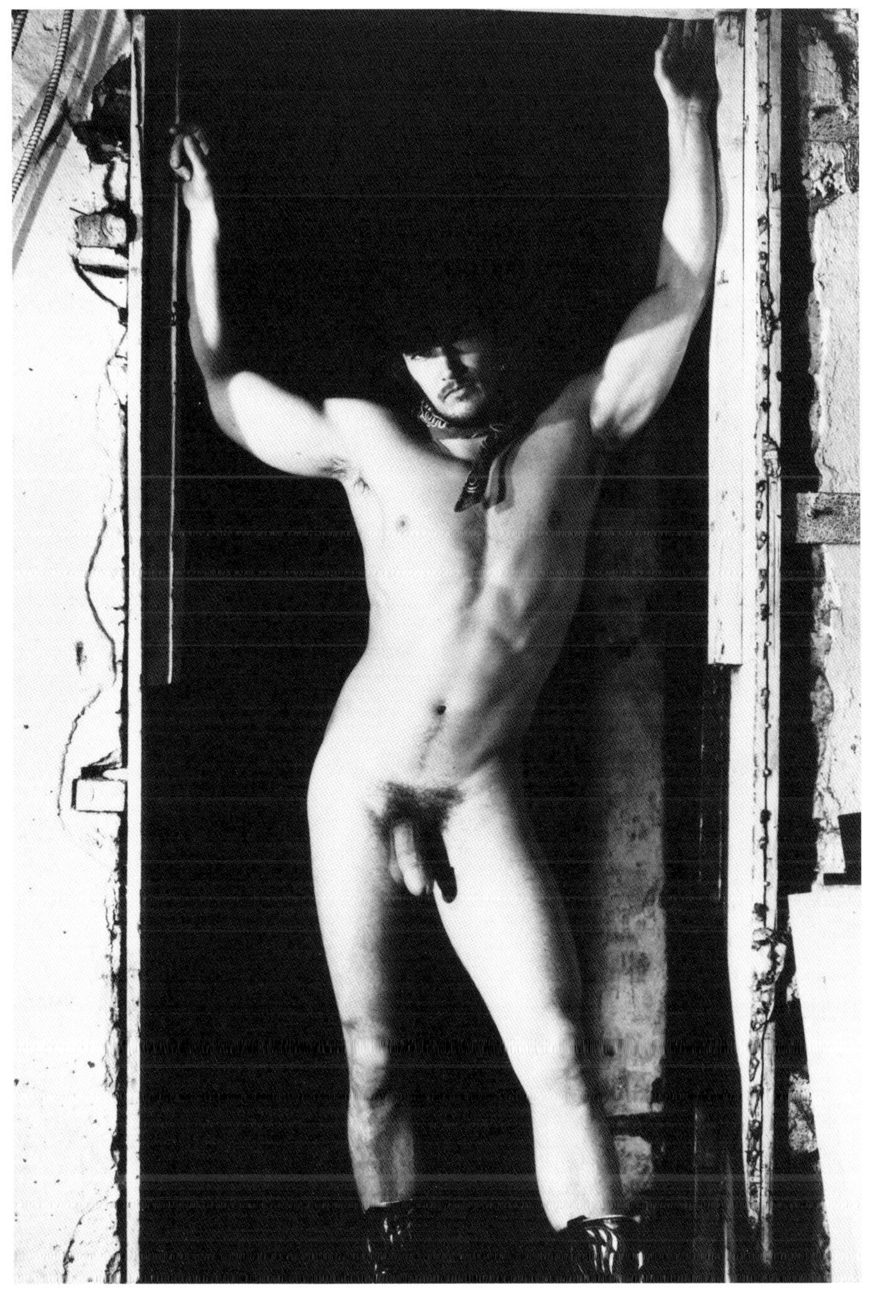

Jim French, c. 1970

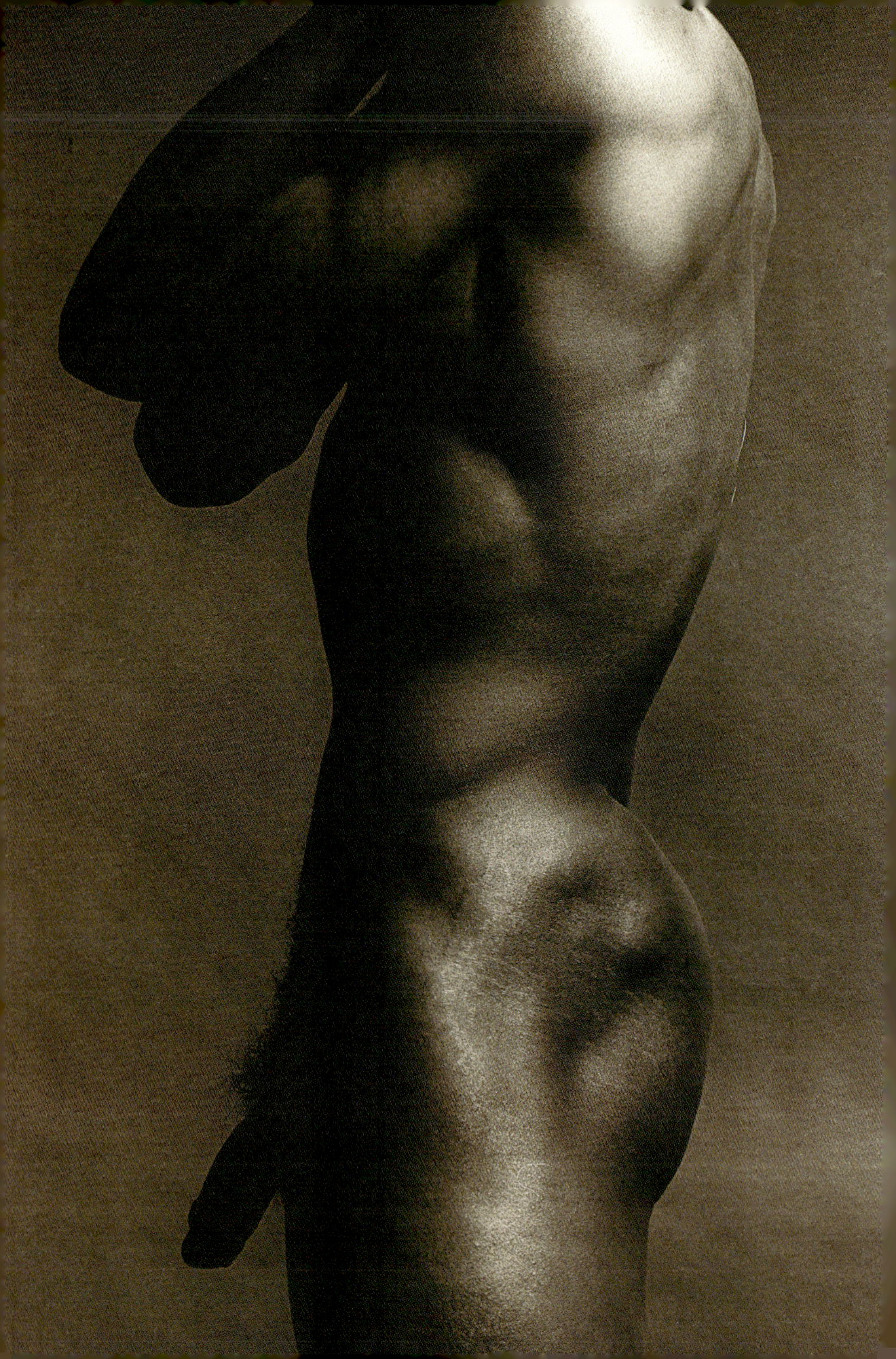

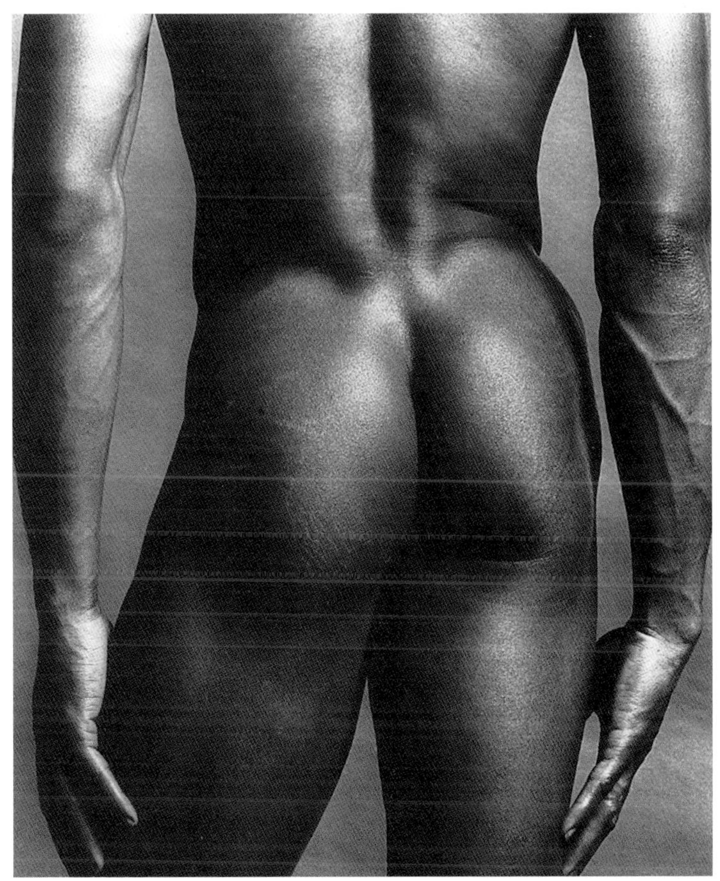

Ken Haak, Black Buttocks and Lower Back, 1968

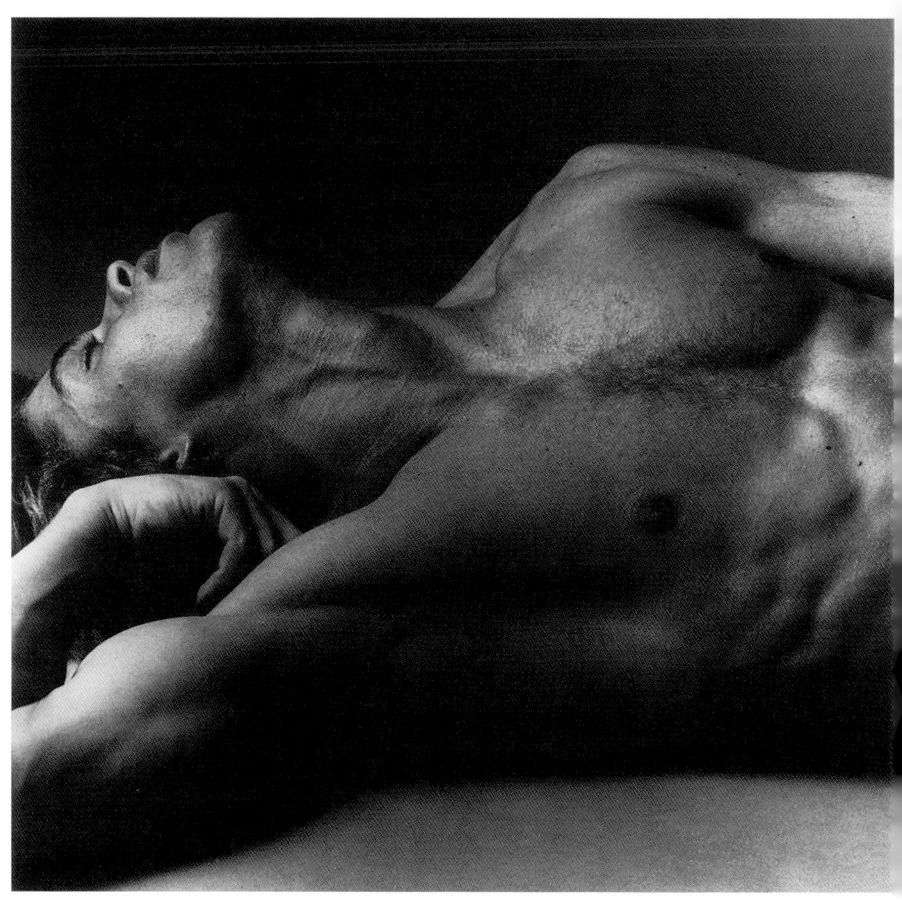

Ken Haak, Recumbent Face and Torso of Young Man, 1973

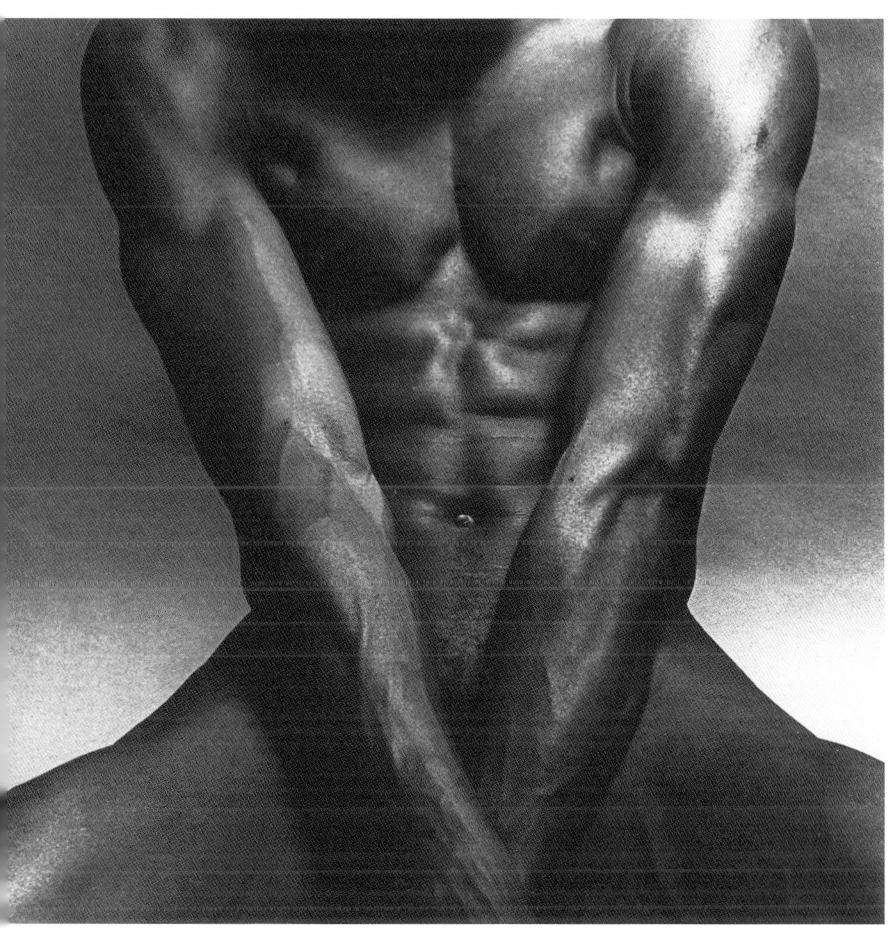

Ken Haak, Muscular Chest with Folded Arms and Splayed Thighs, 1982

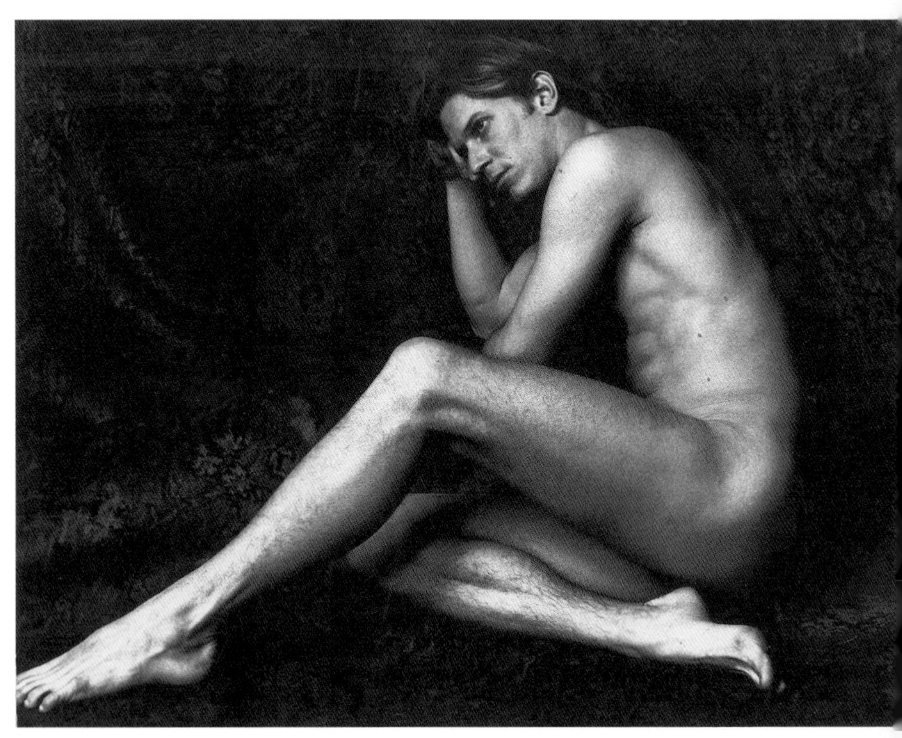

George Hester, c. 1970

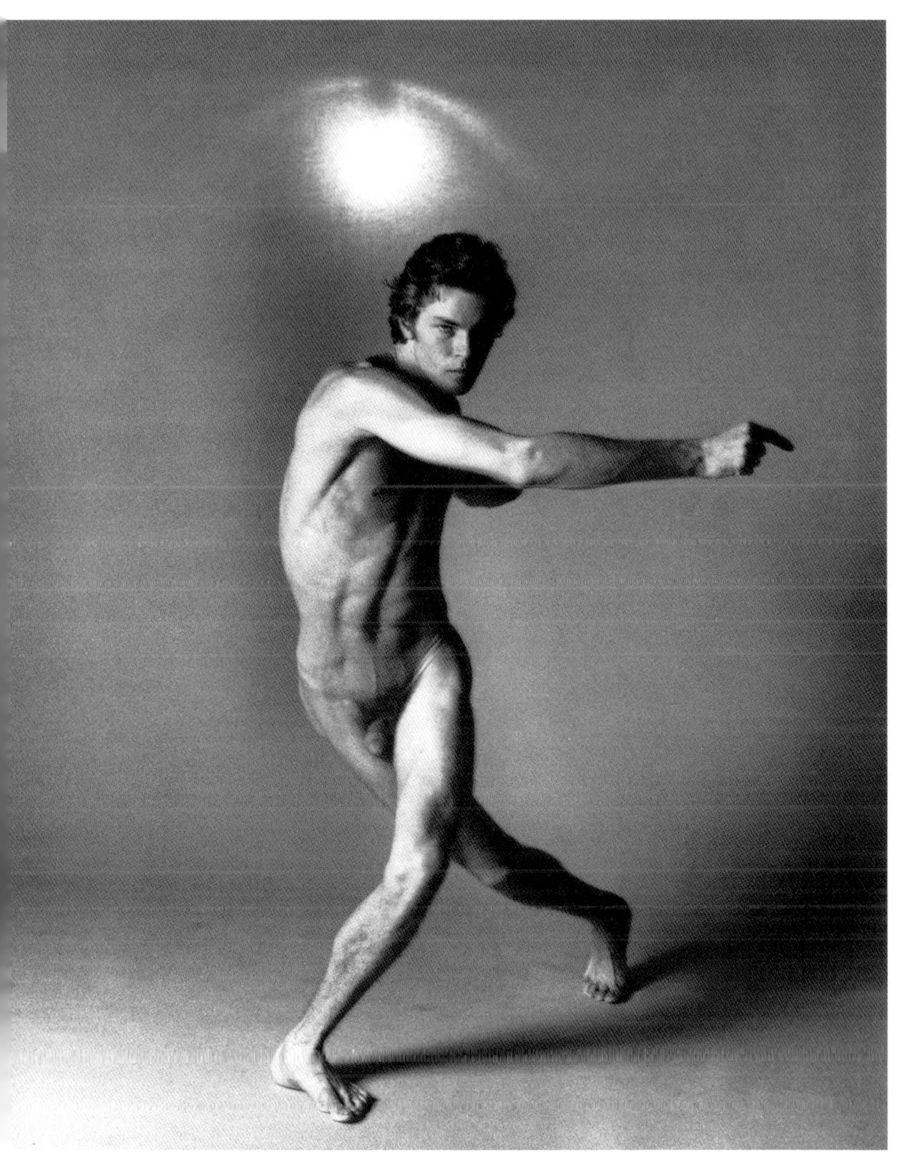

George Hester, c. 1970

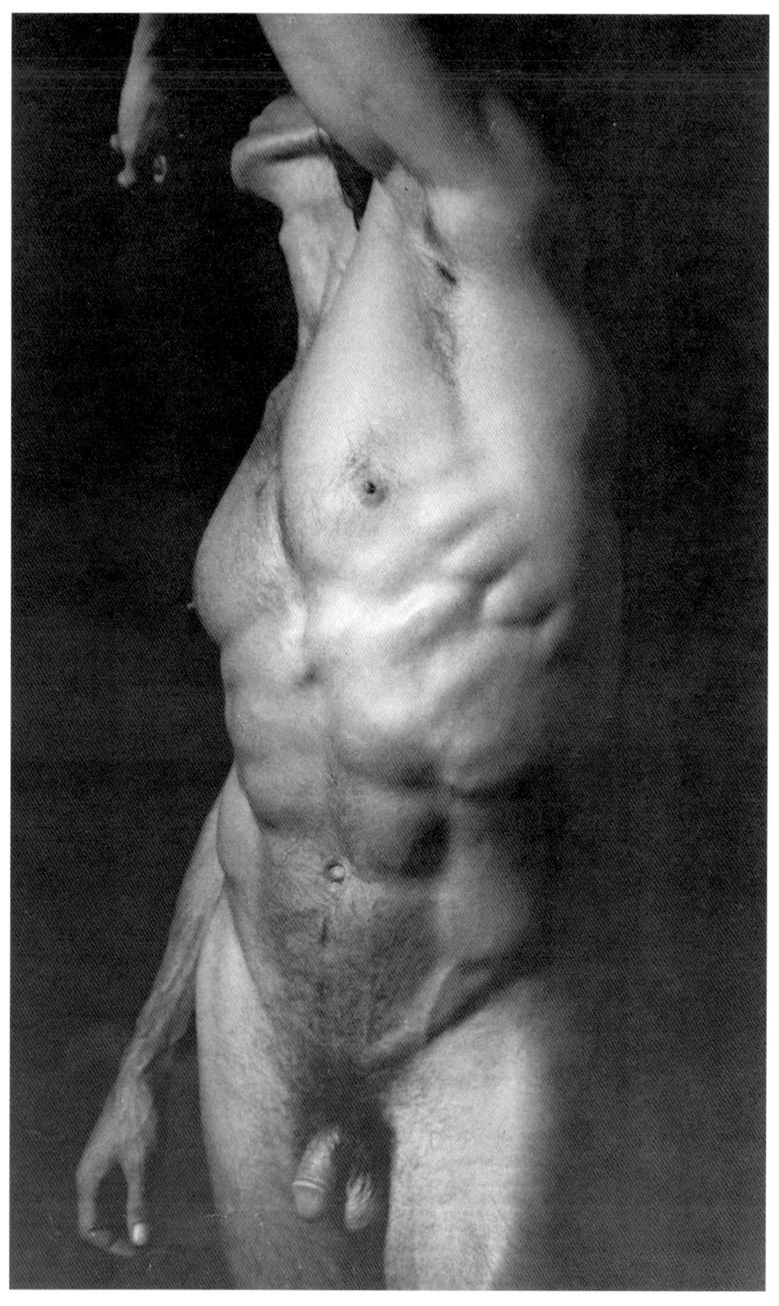

George Hester, c. 1970

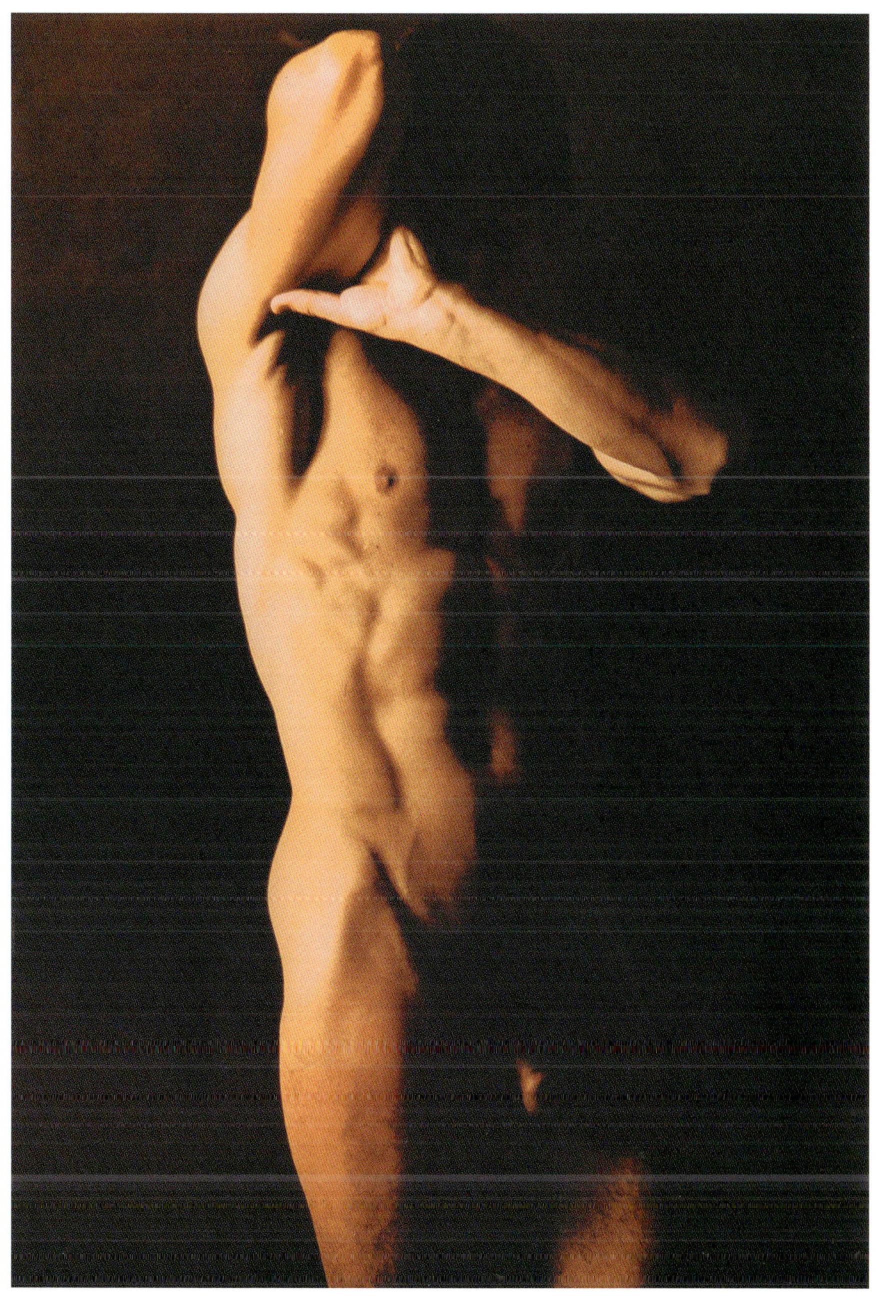

George Hester, c. 1970

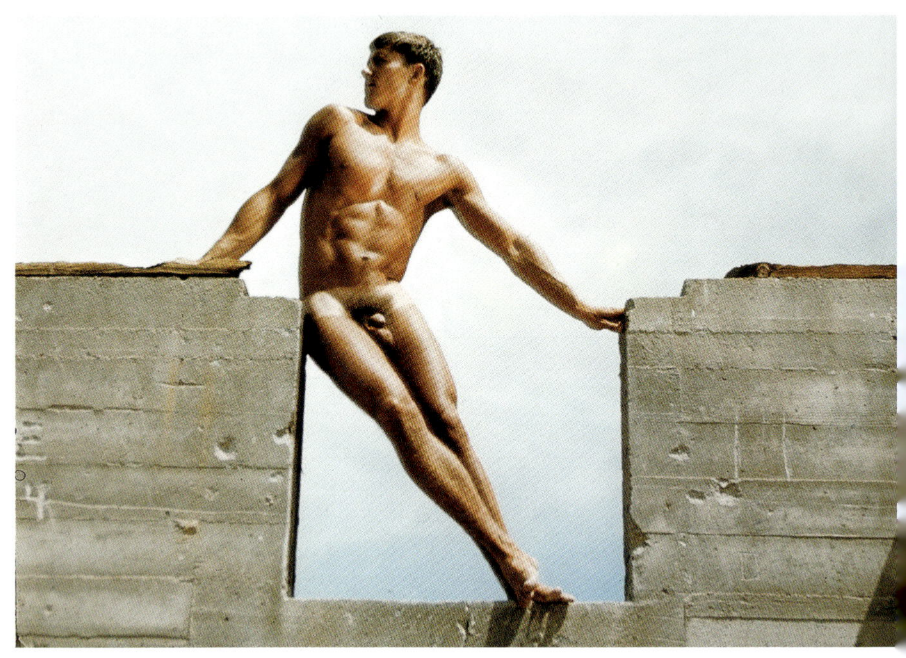
Jim French, 1970s

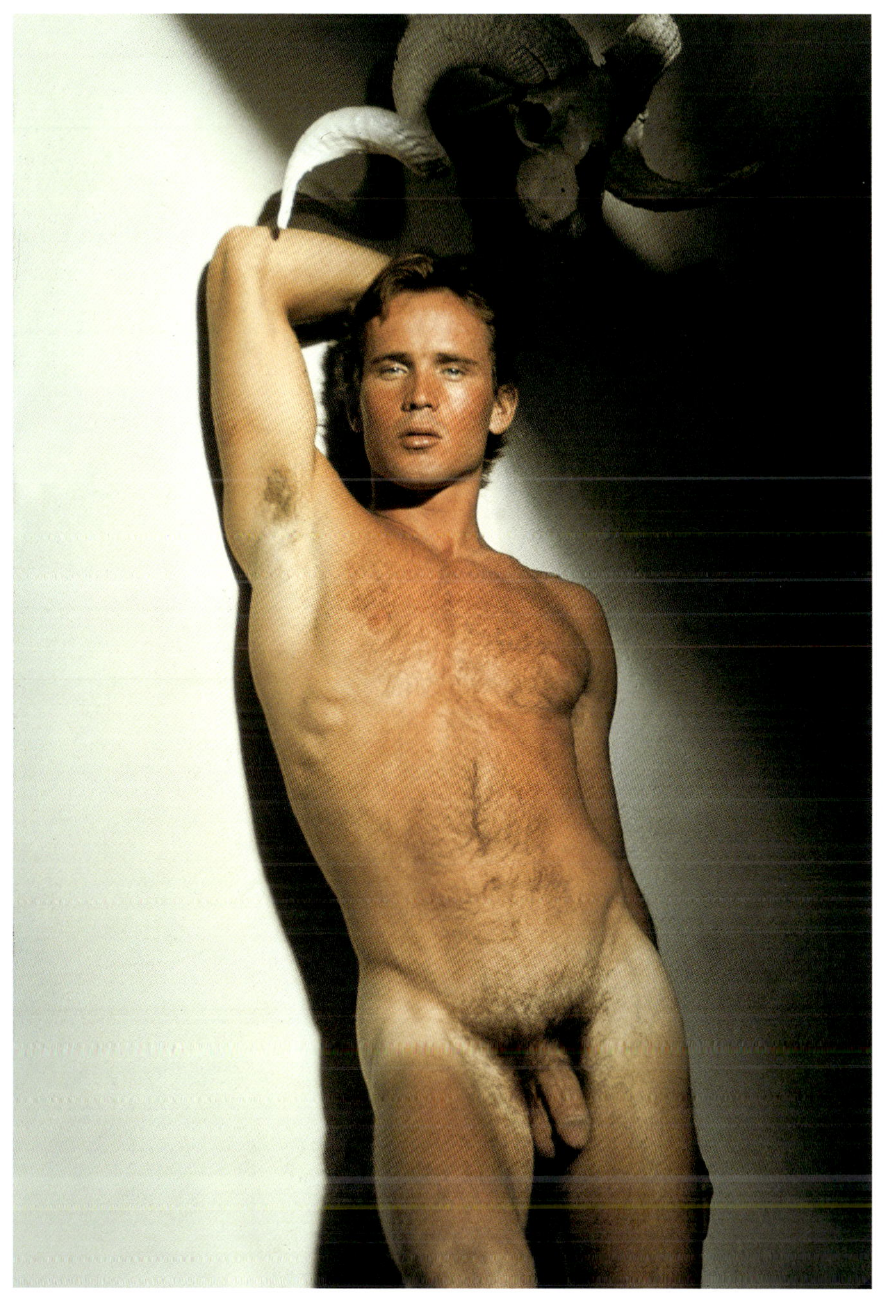

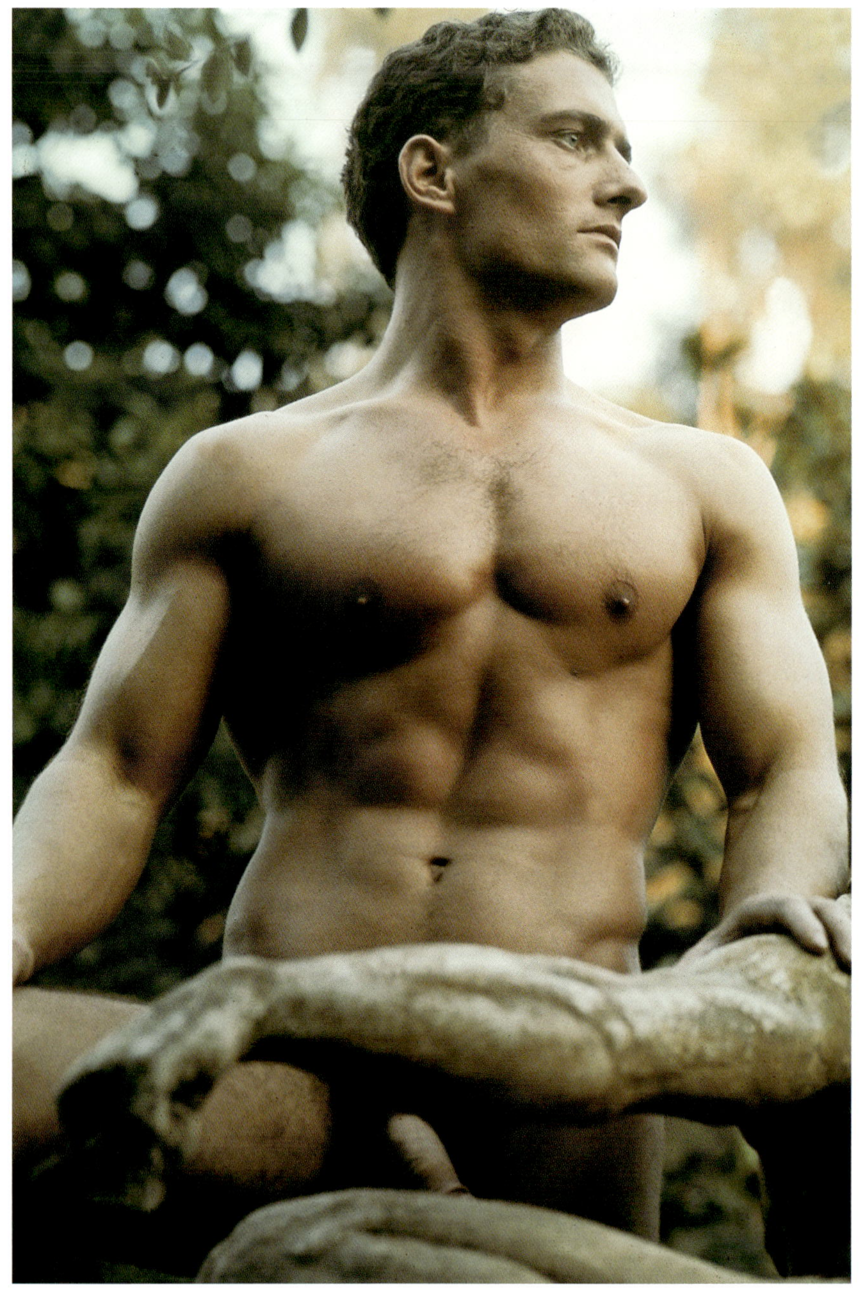

Jim French, 1970s

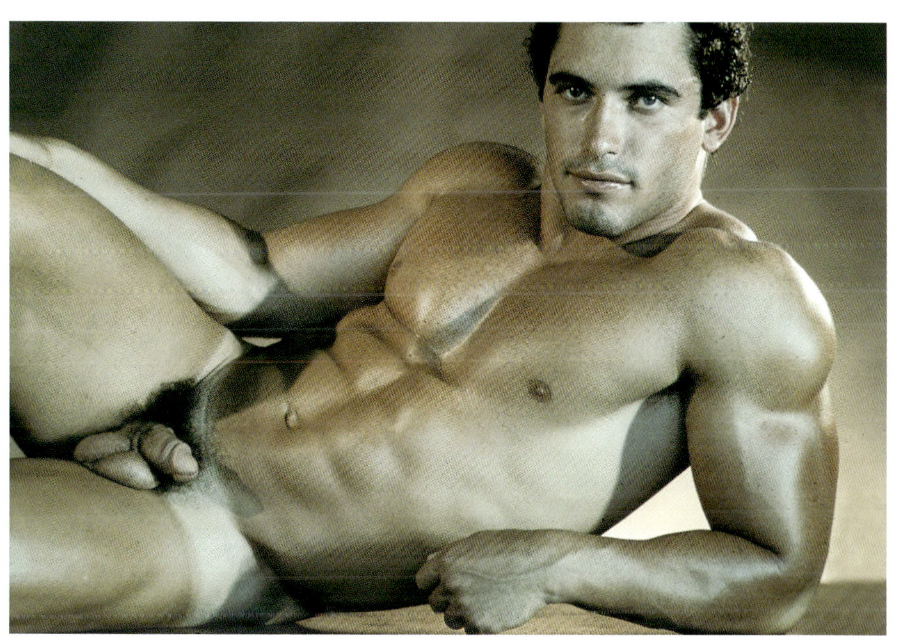

Jim French, 1970s

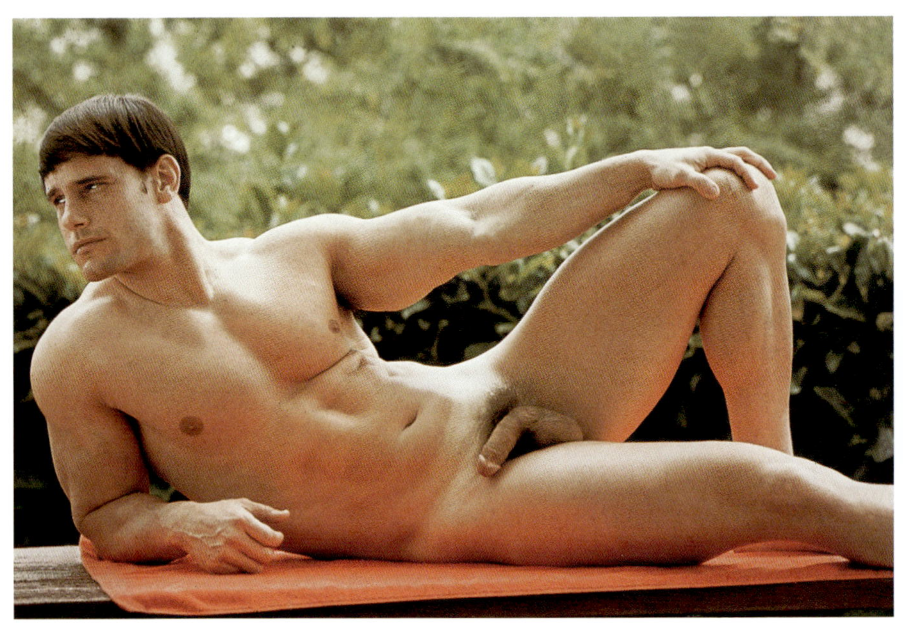

Jim French, 1970s

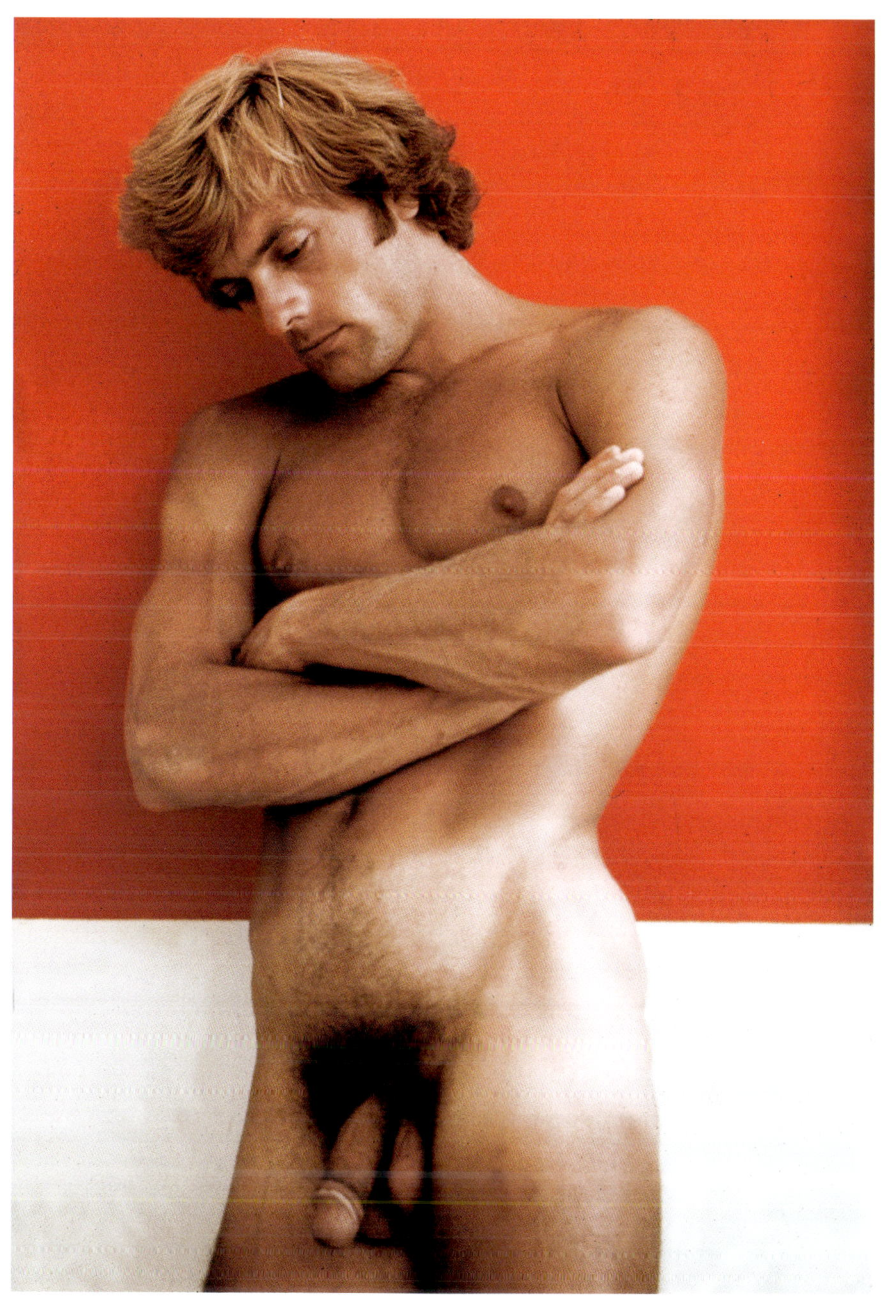

Anonymous, 1970s

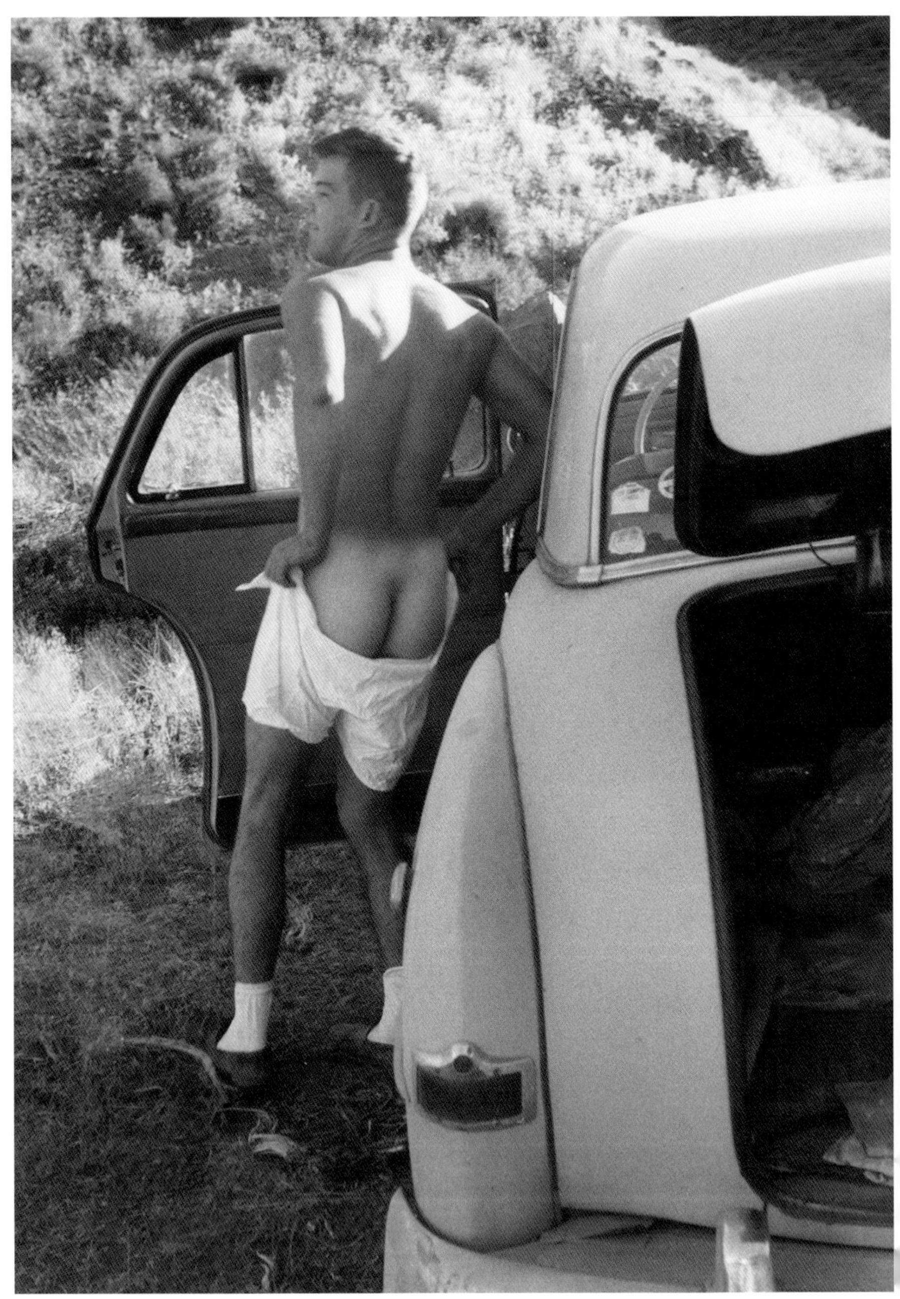

Clifford Baker, Nevada Camping Trip, September 1958

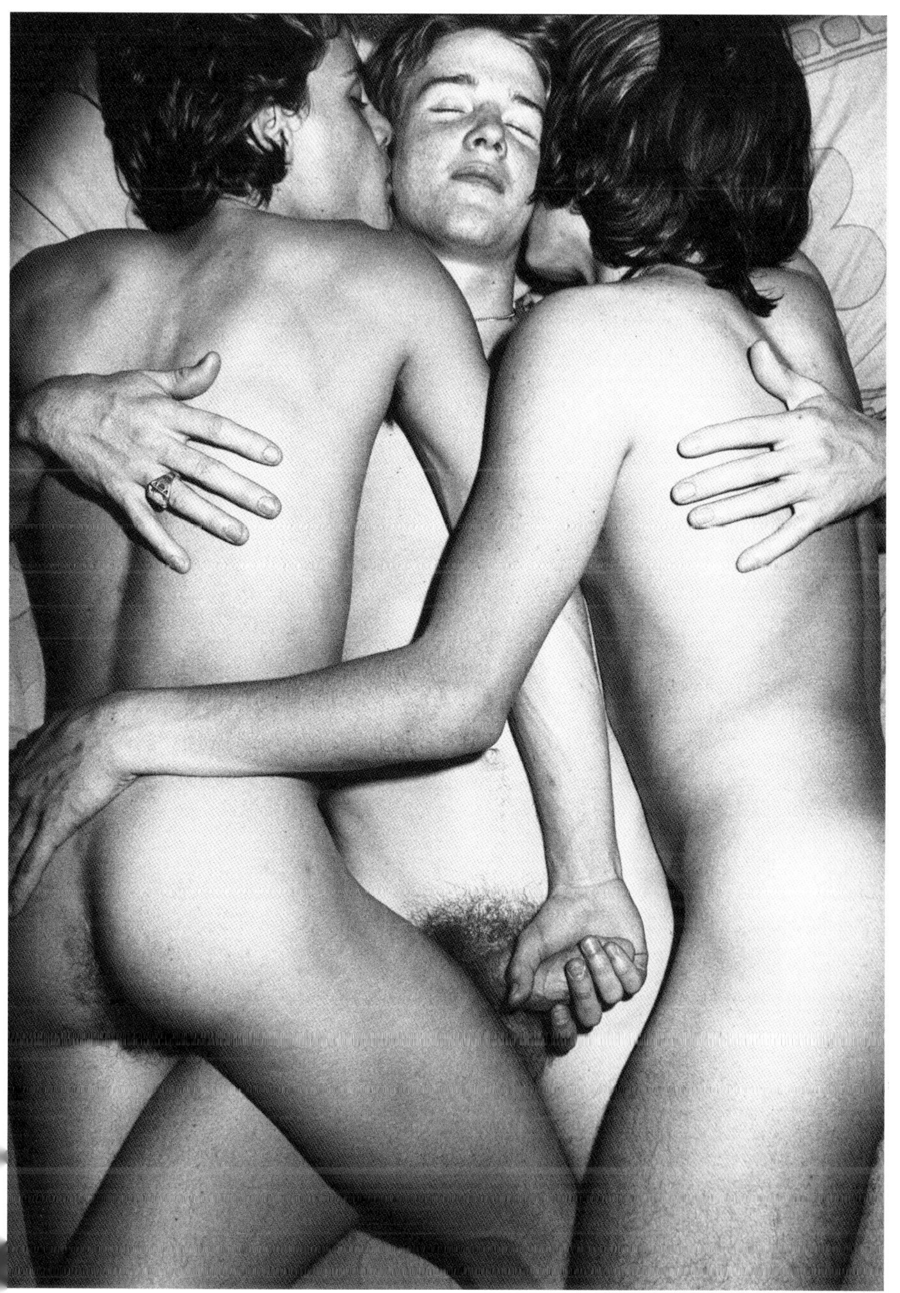

Clifford Baker, Jeff, David and Marty, 1978

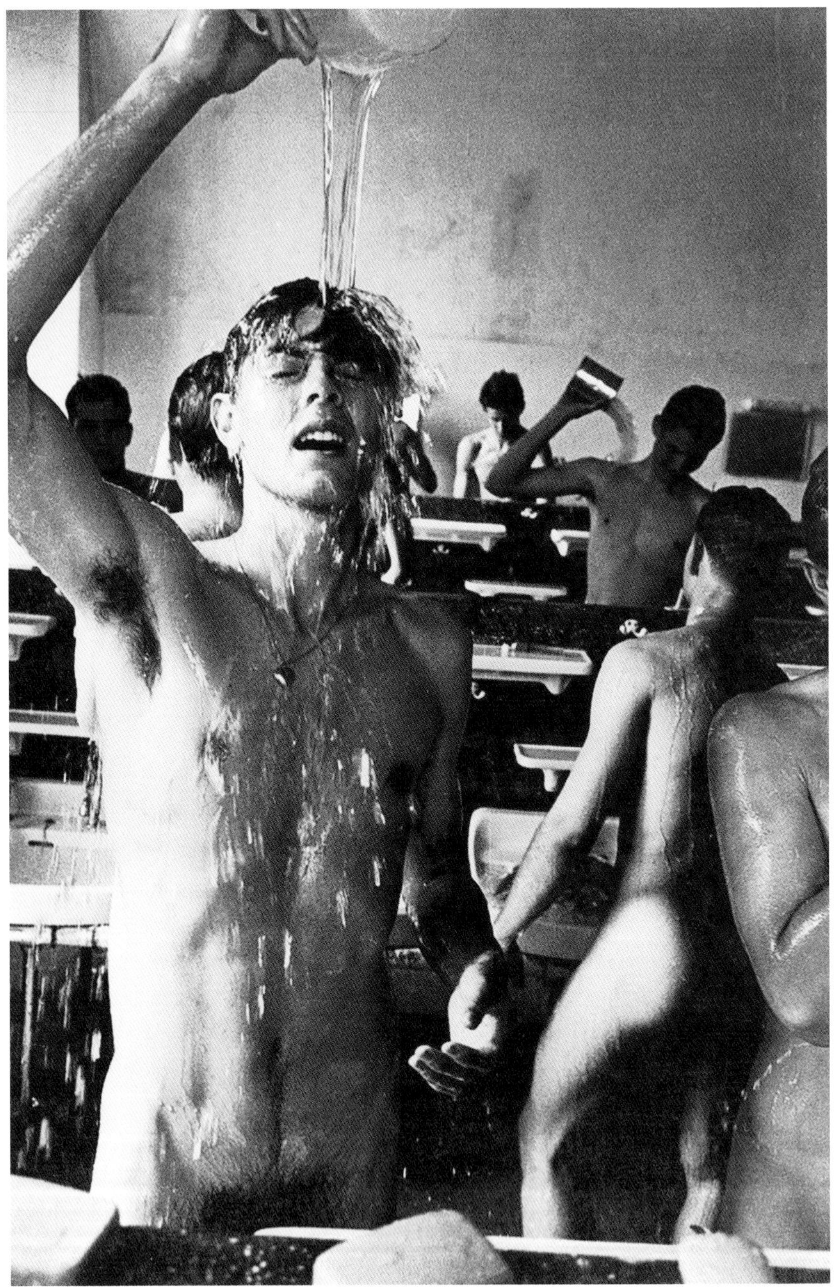

Will McBride, Schloss Salem, Waschung, 1962

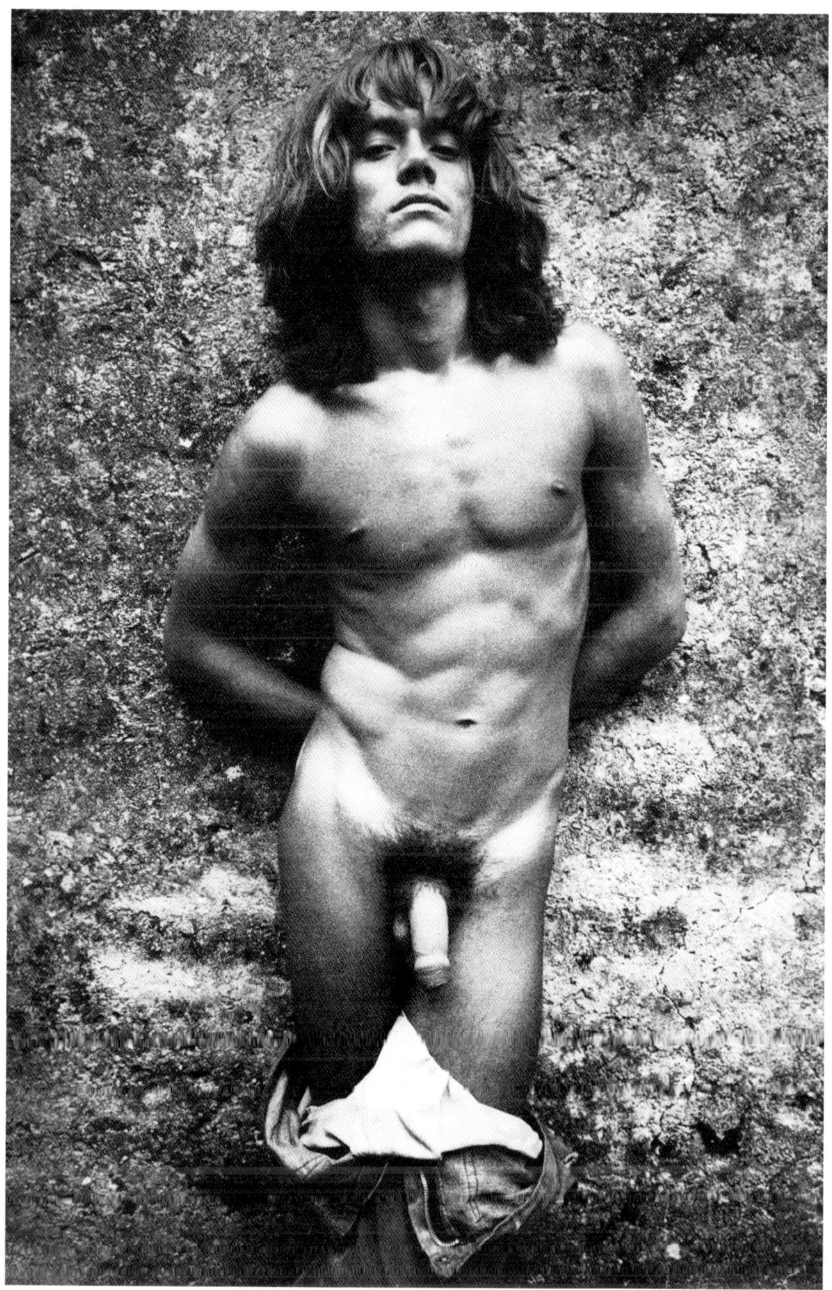

Will McBride, Roland, 1975

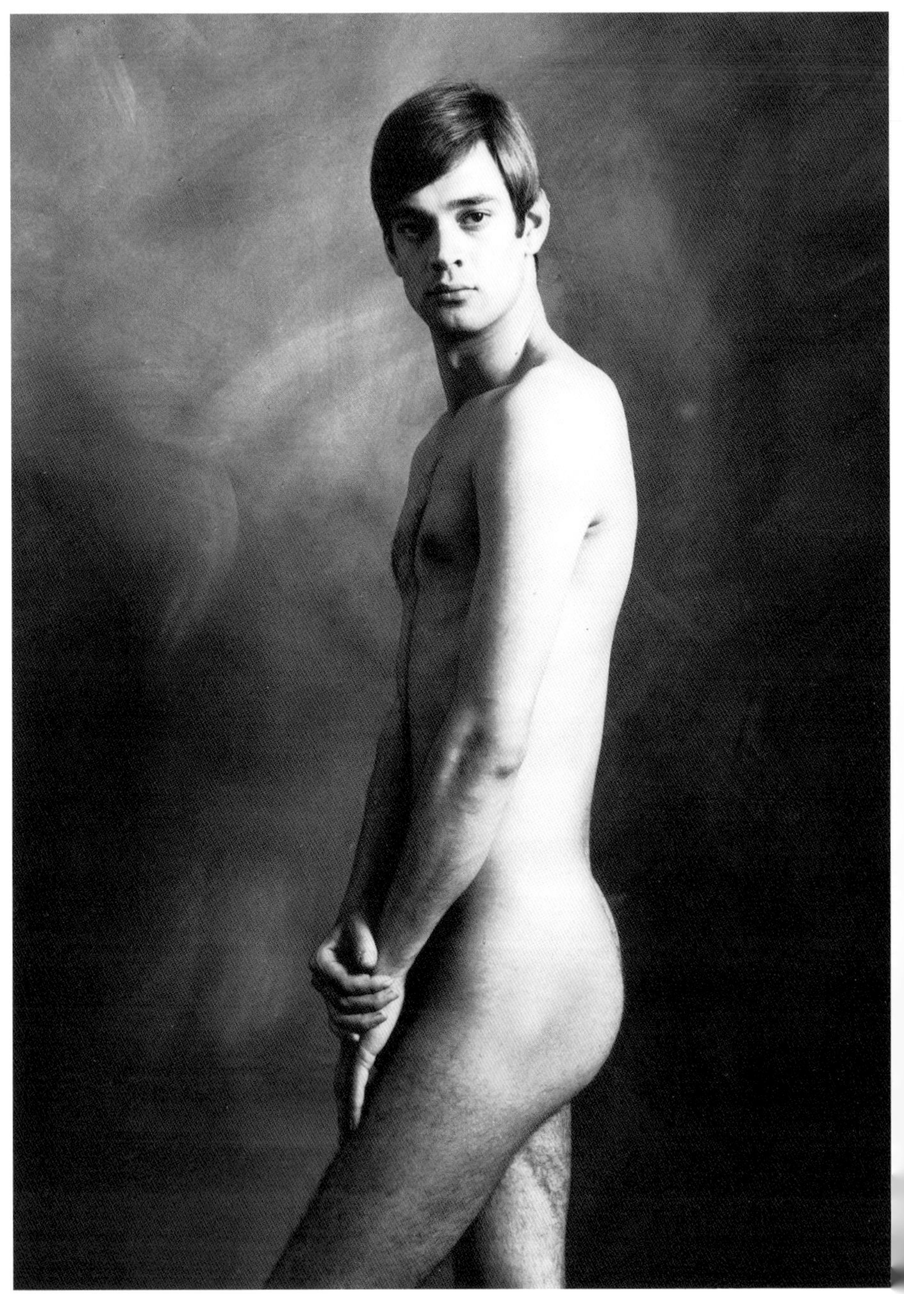

Jean-François Bauret, Selimaille, 1967

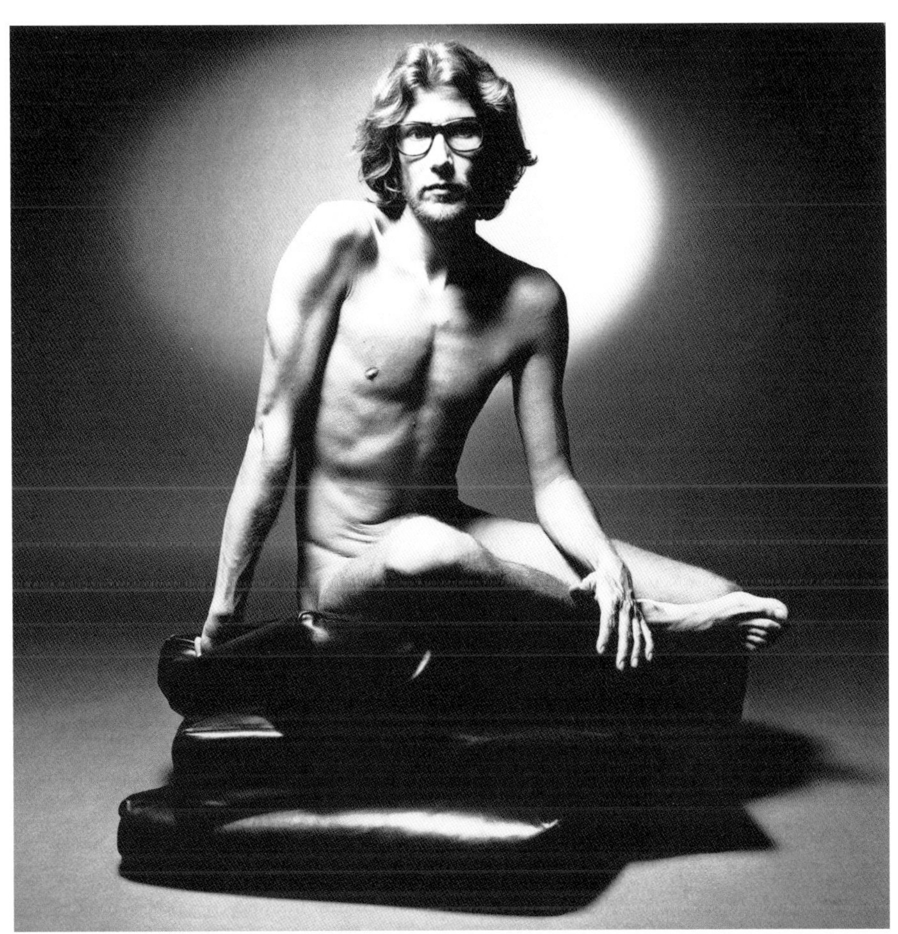

Jeanloup Sieff, Yves Saint-Laurent, 1971

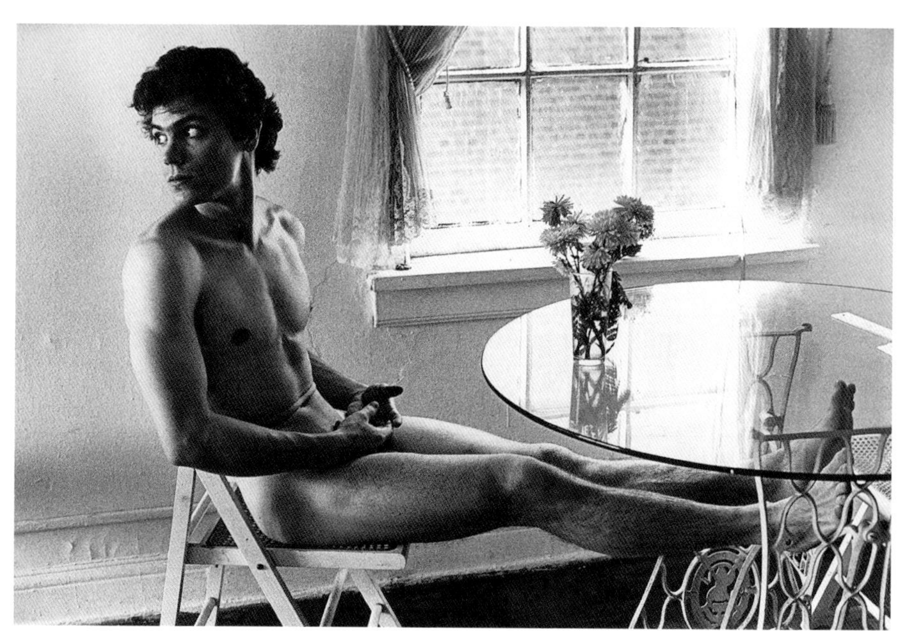

Vivienne Maricevic, Eugene from the Series Naked Men 1979

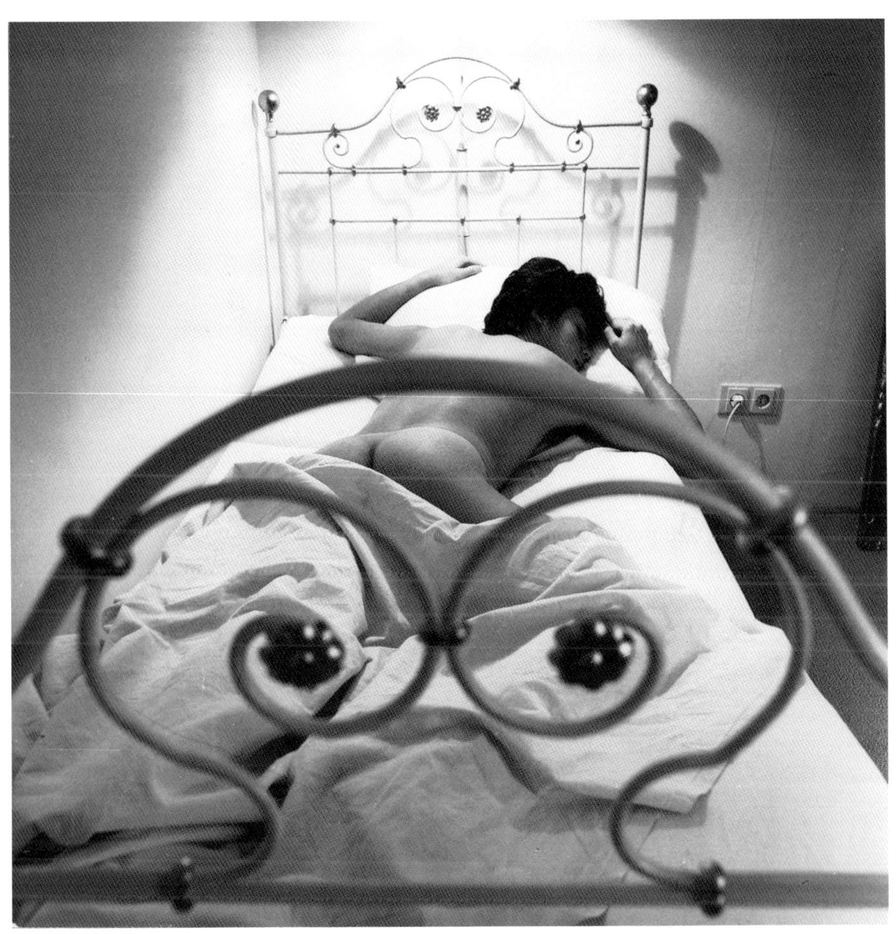

Robert Häusser, Am Morgen, 1978

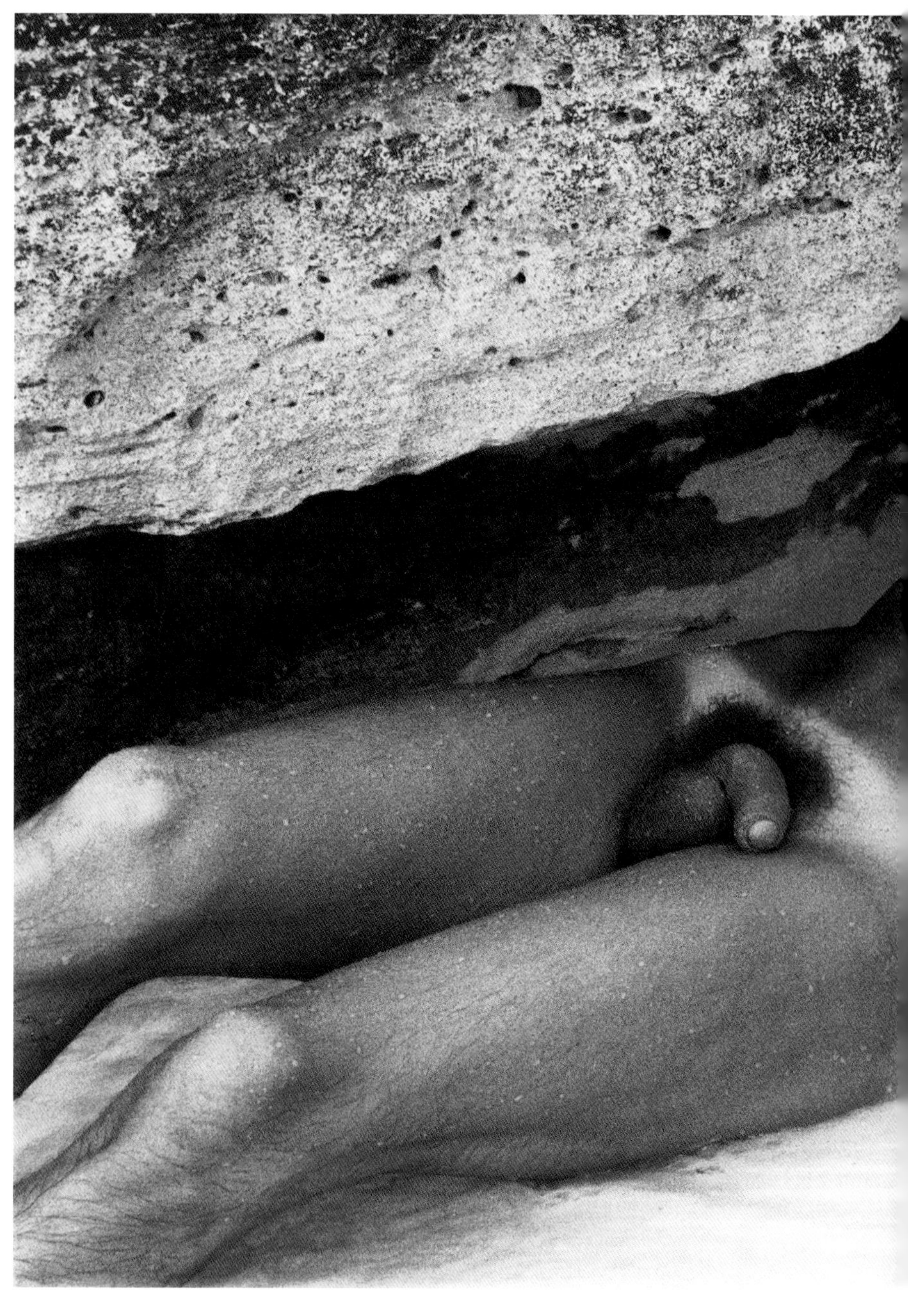

Charlotte March, Nackt am Strand, 1976

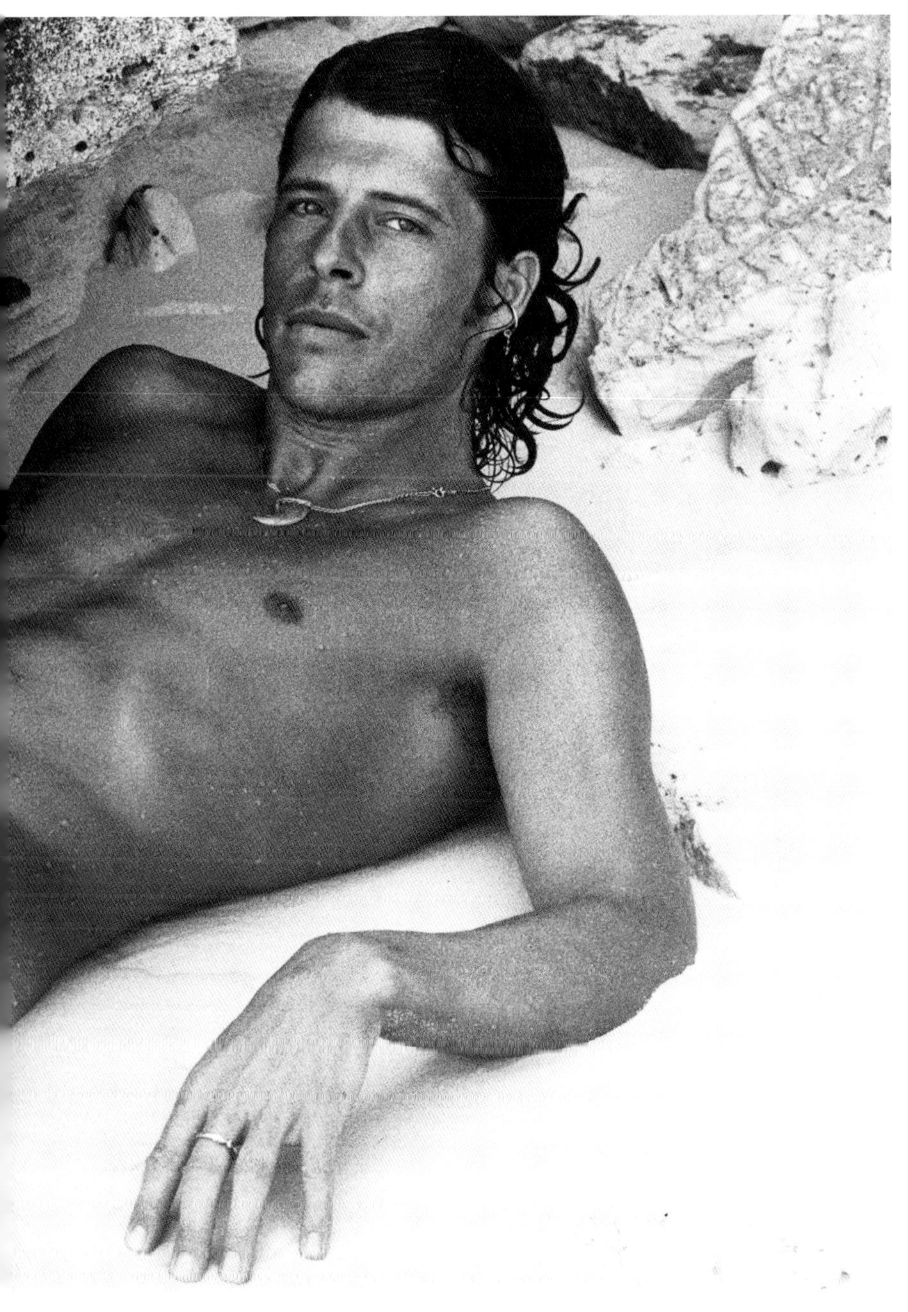

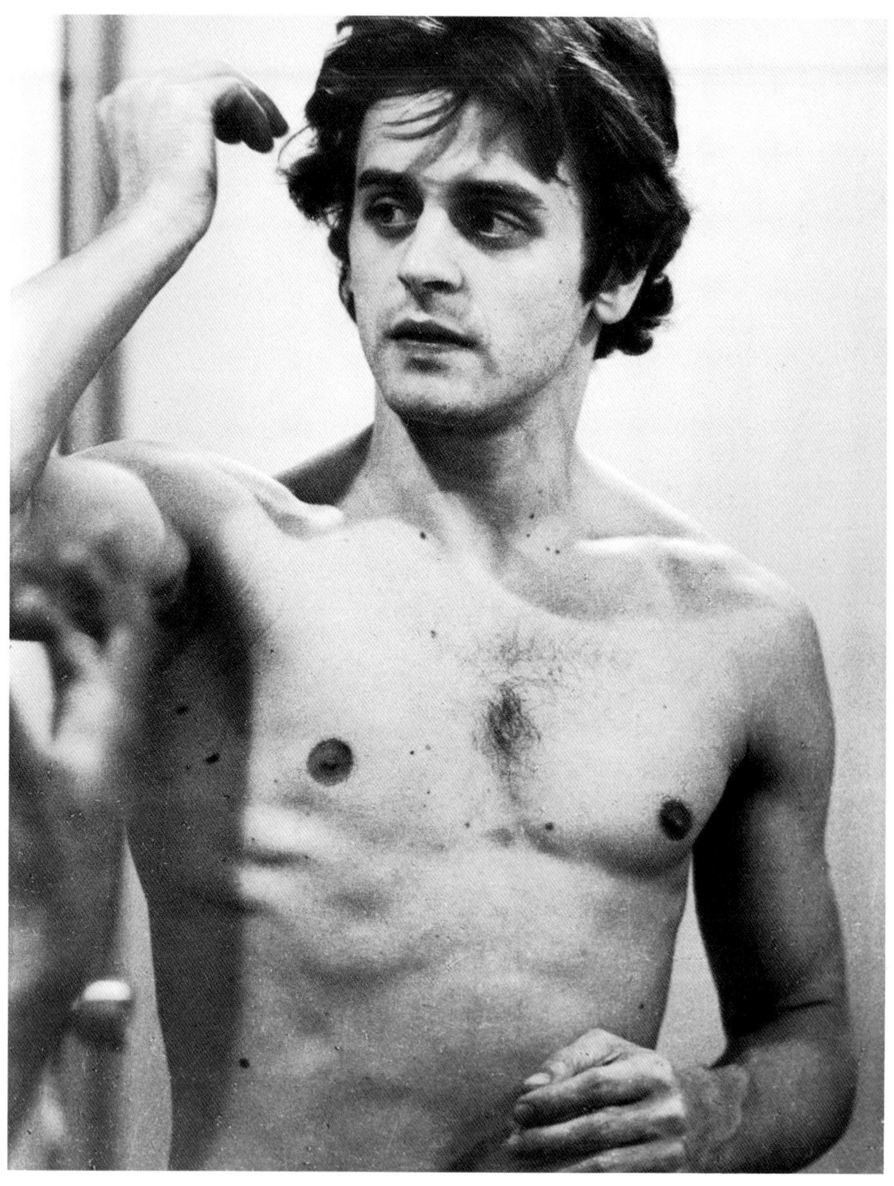

Jon Gilbert Fox, Mikhail Baryshnikov, 1974

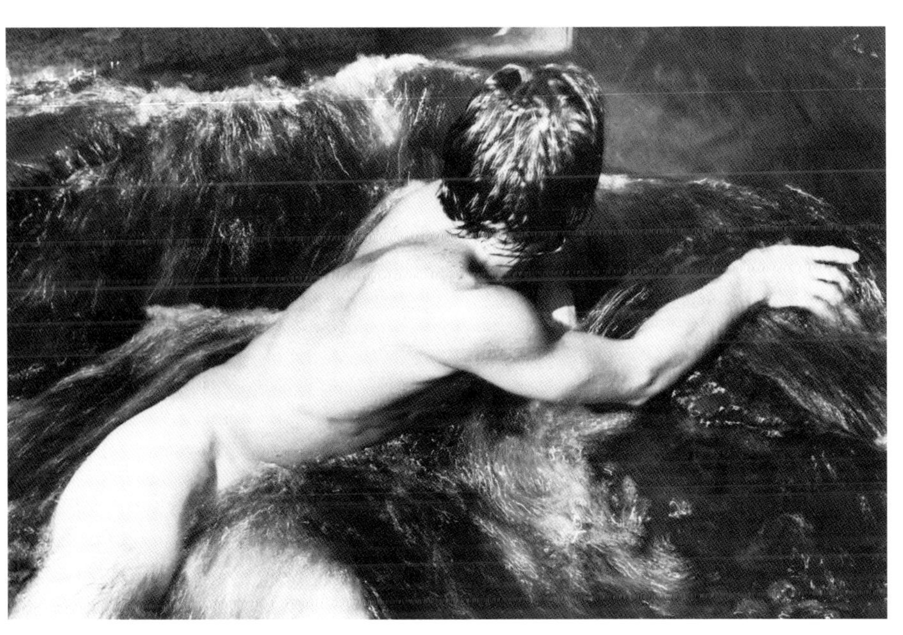

Jon Gilbert Fox, Bull Run, 1973

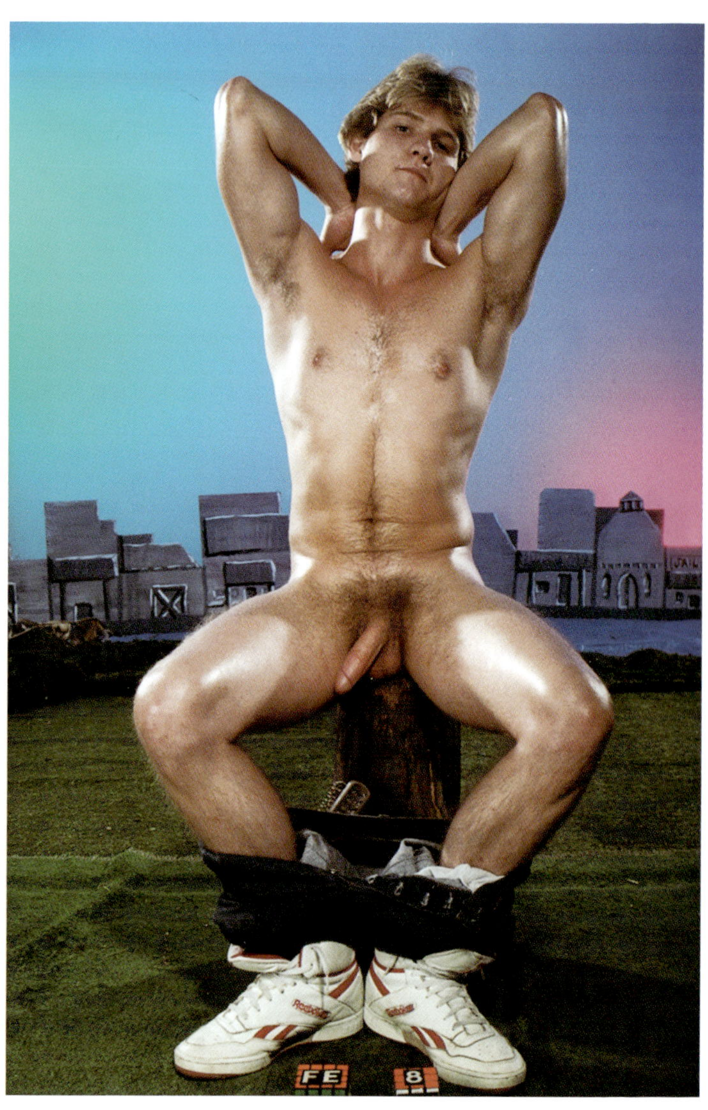

Bob Mizer, c. 1962

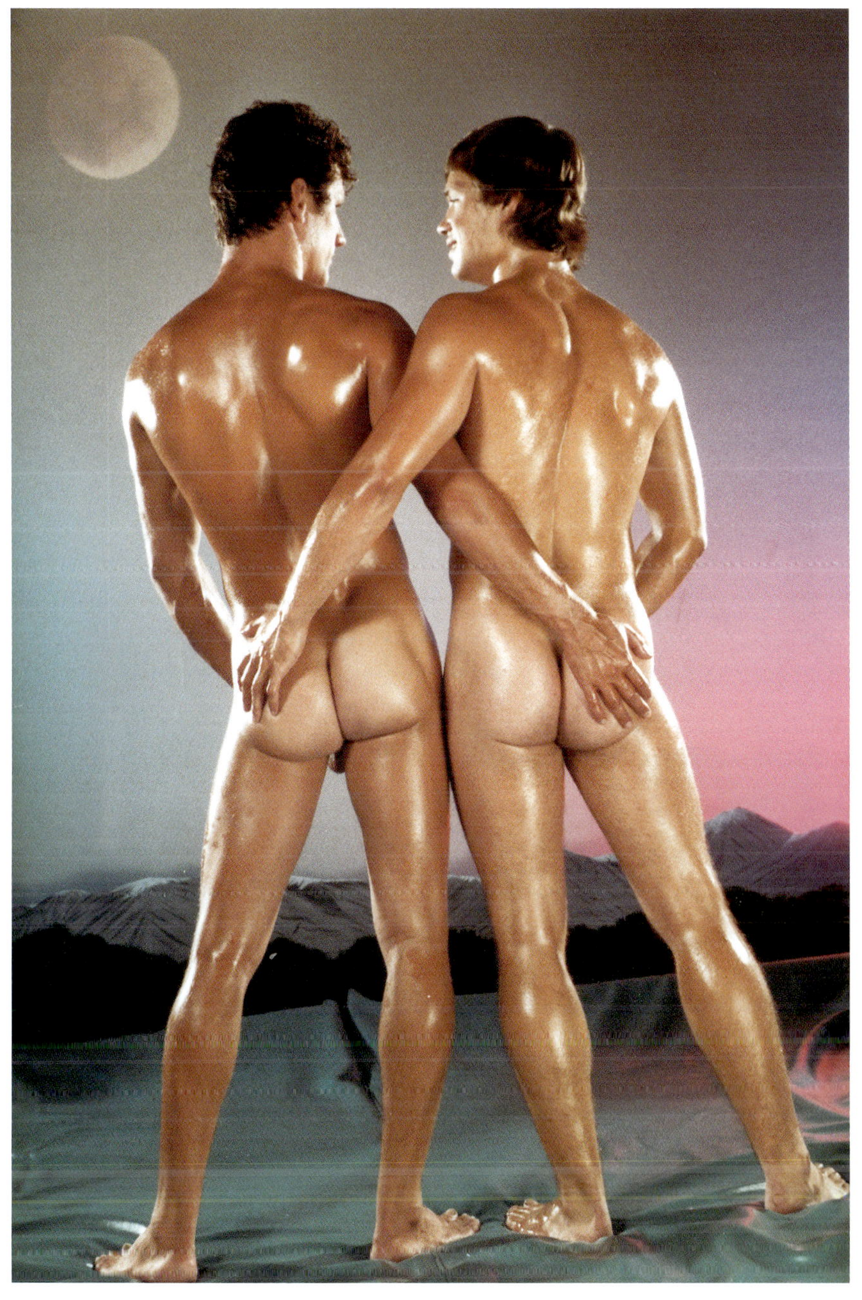

Bob Mizer, c. 1962

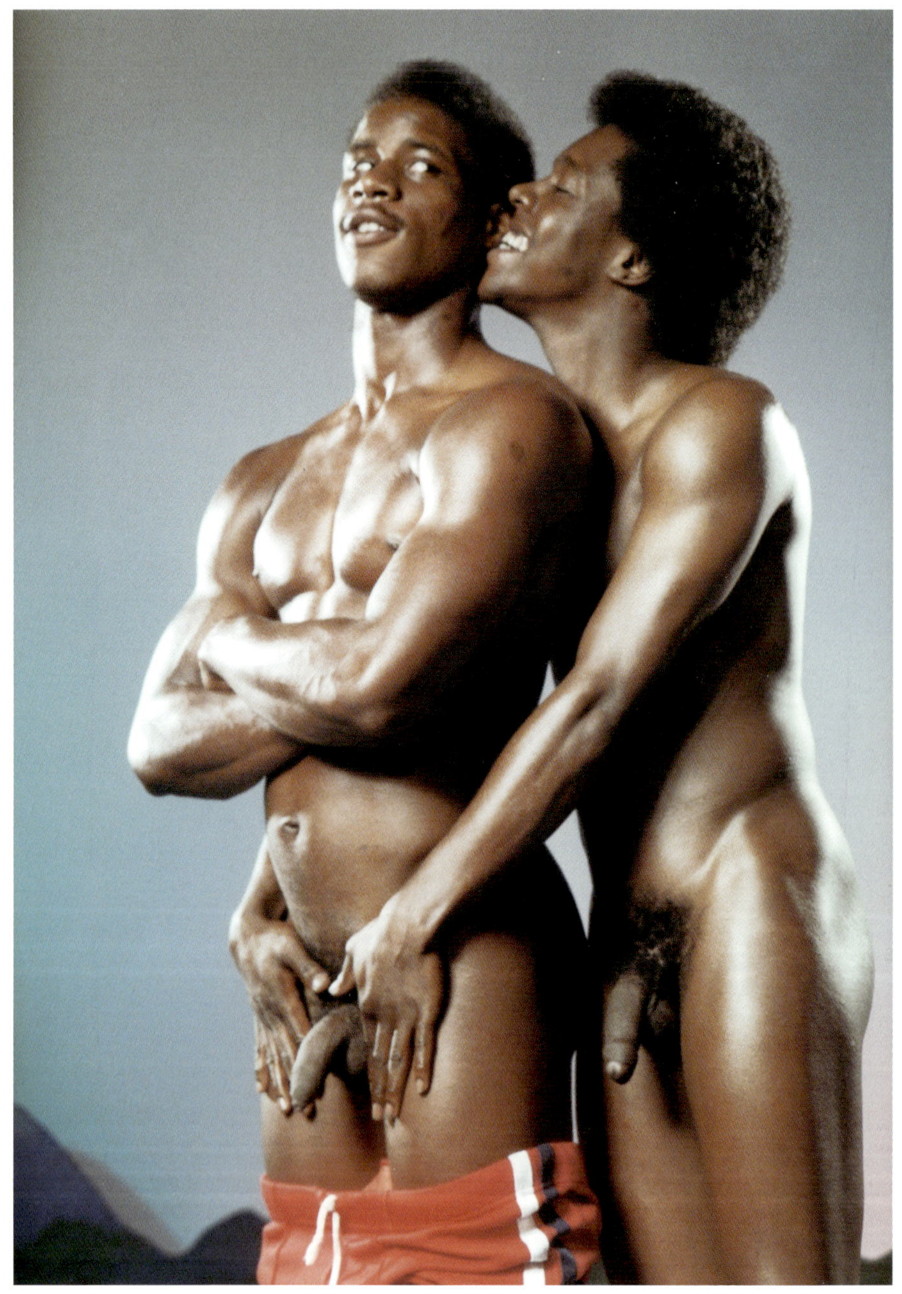

Bob Mizer, c. 1962

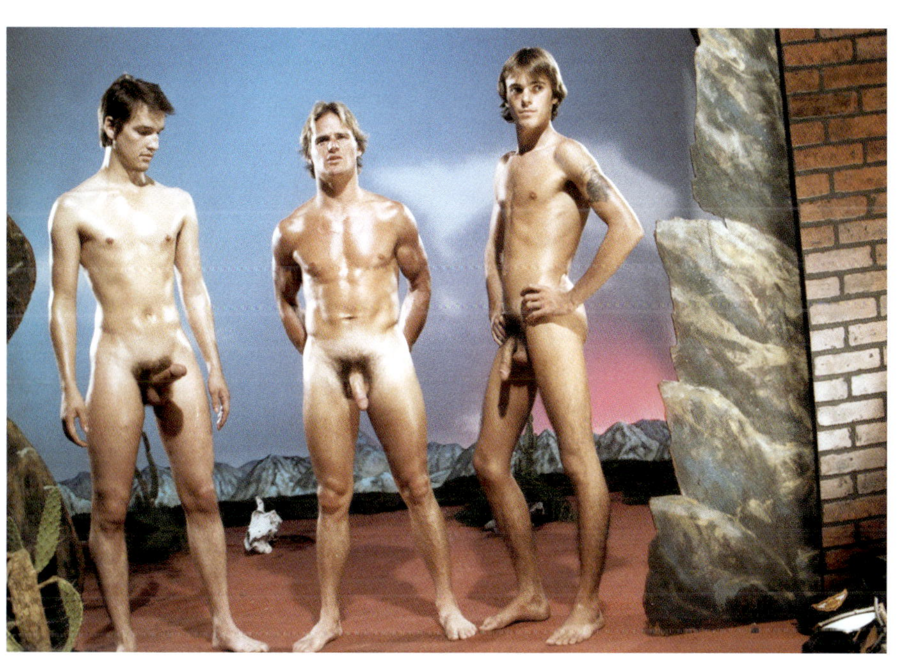

Bob Mizer, c. 1962

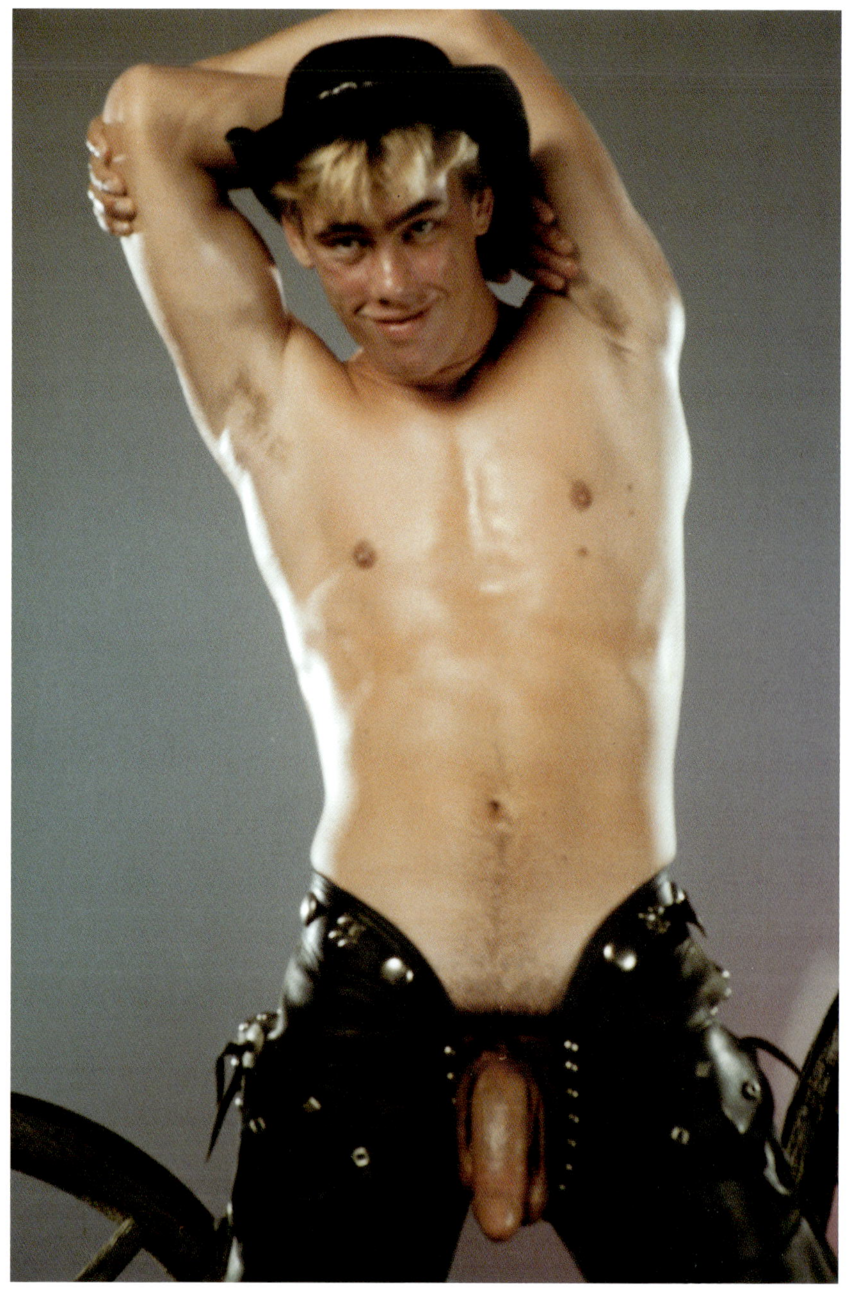

Bob Mizer, c. 1962

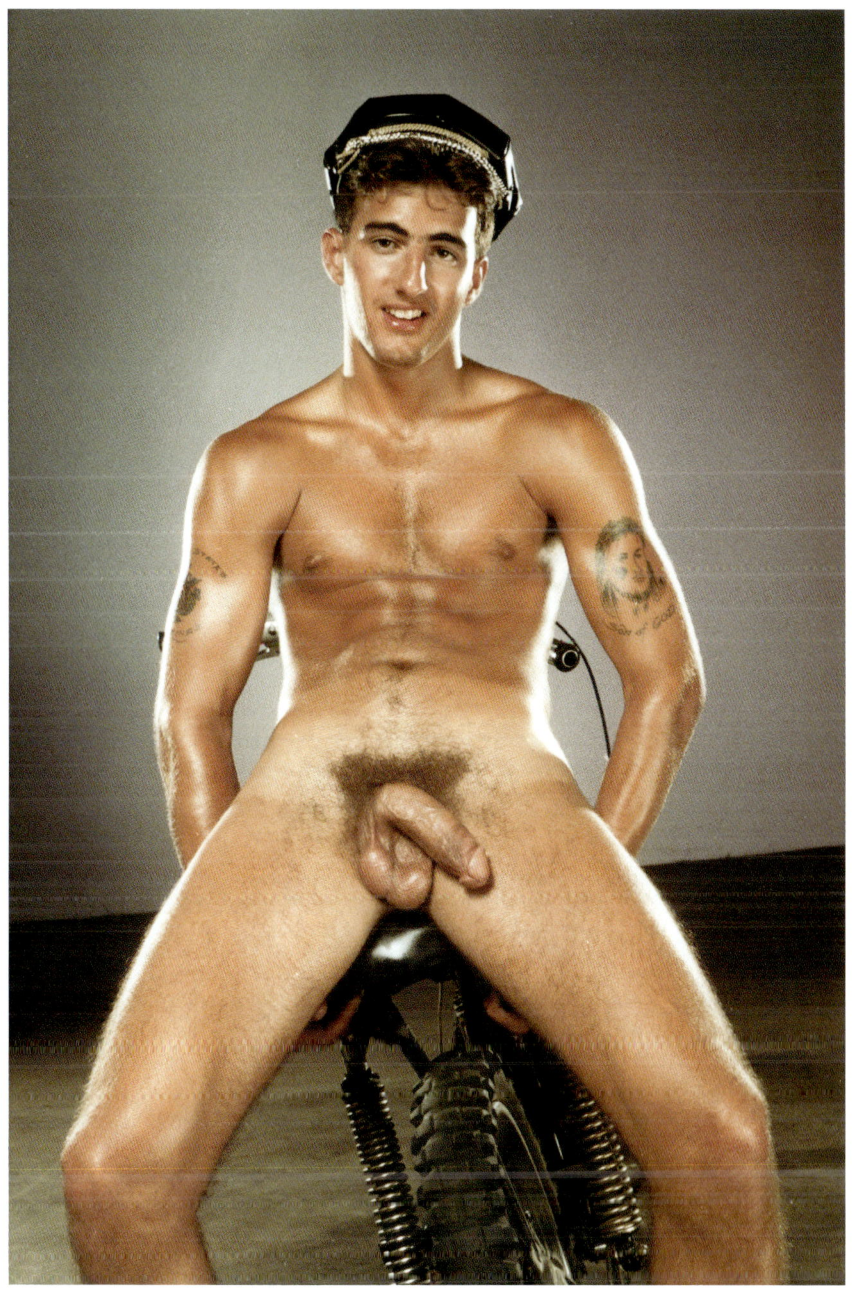

Bob Mizer, c. 1962

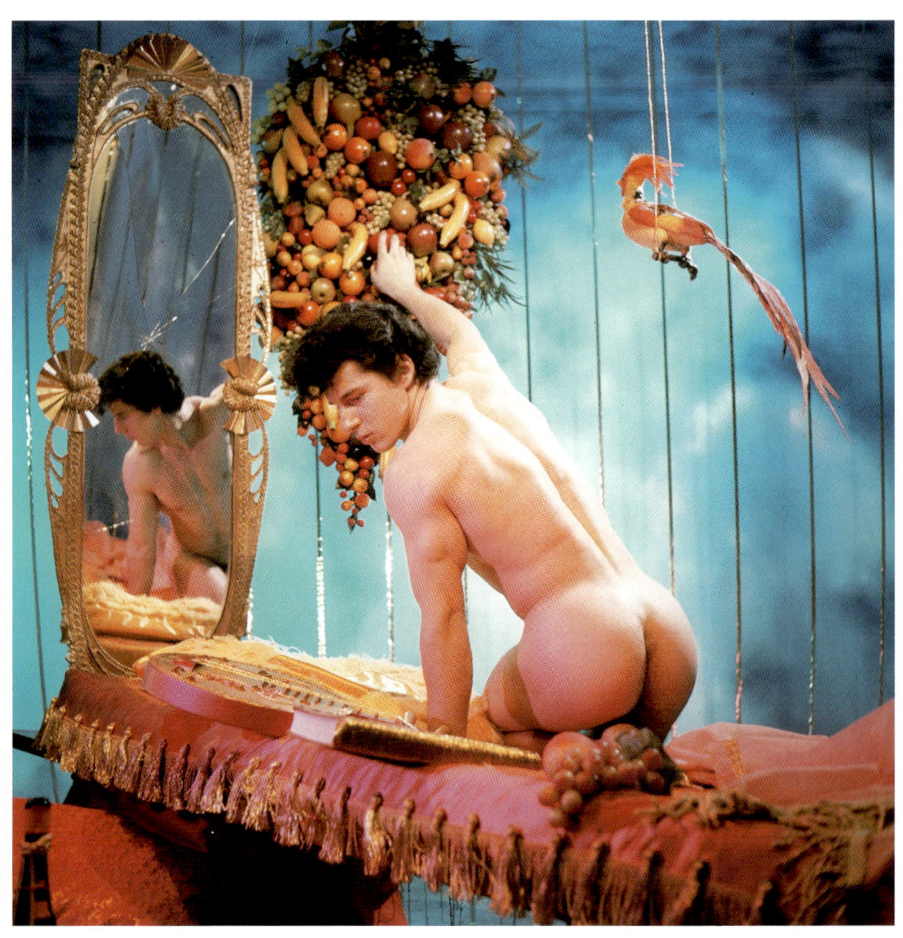

James Bidgood, Gilded Cage Two, 1960s

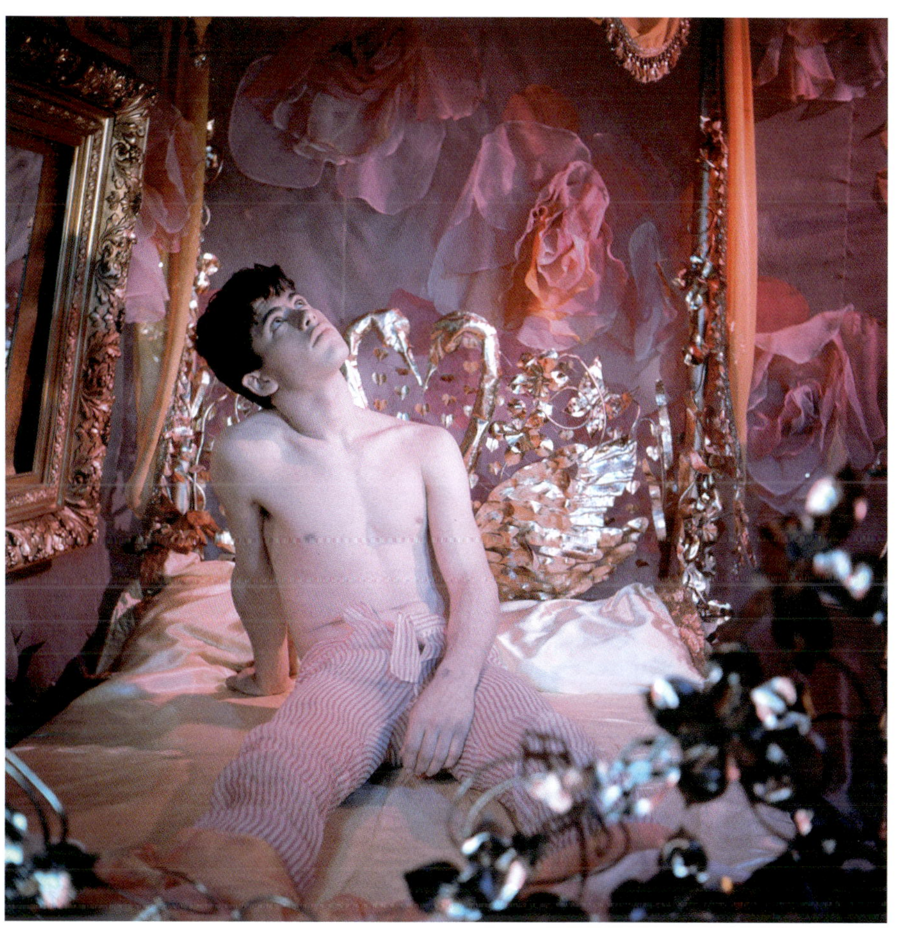

James Bidgood, Bobby Kendall in Pyjamas on Swan Bed (from "Pink Narcissus"), 1960s

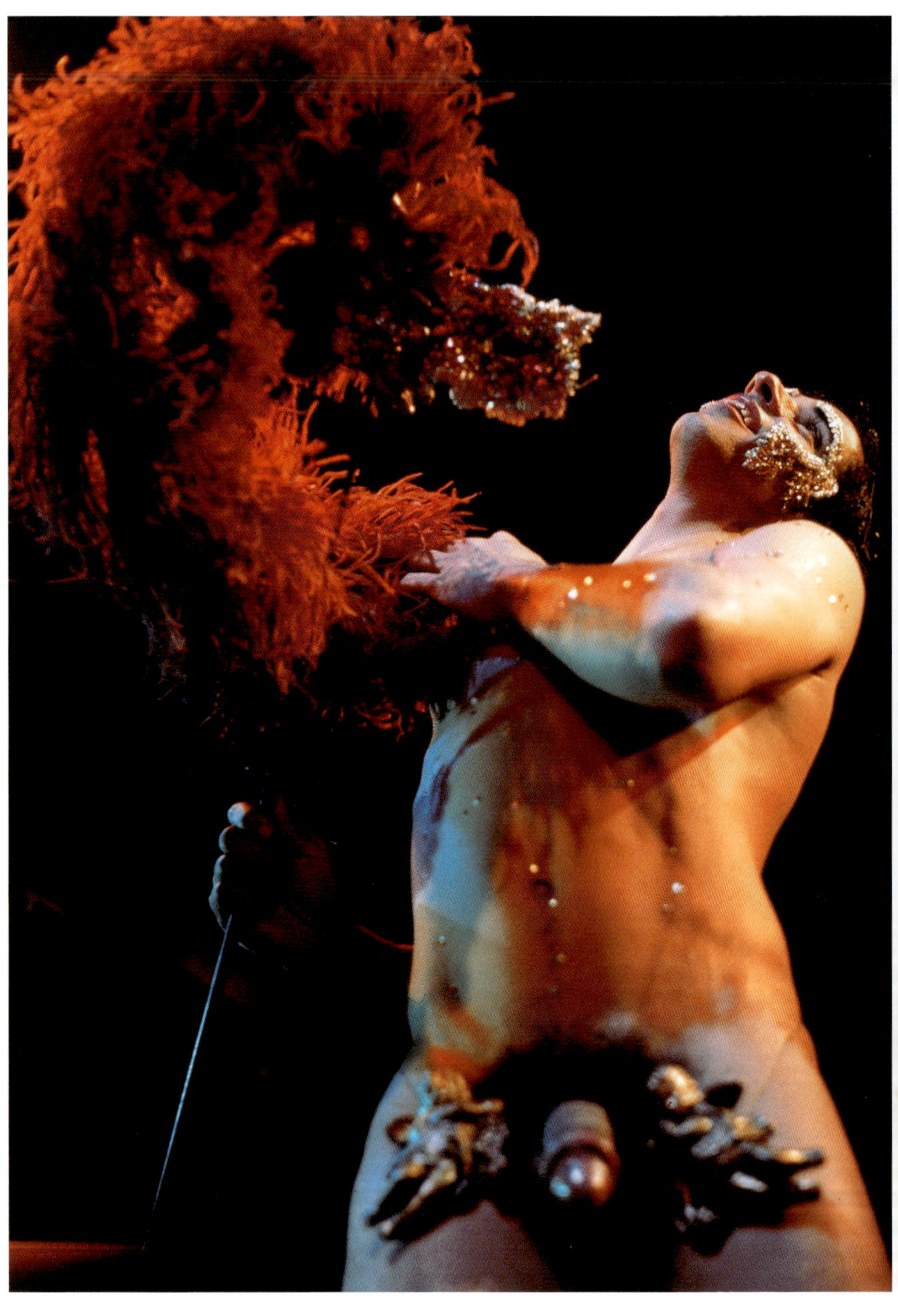

352 **James Bidgood,** Times Square Hustler in Mardi Gras Costume (from "Pink Narcissus"), 1960s

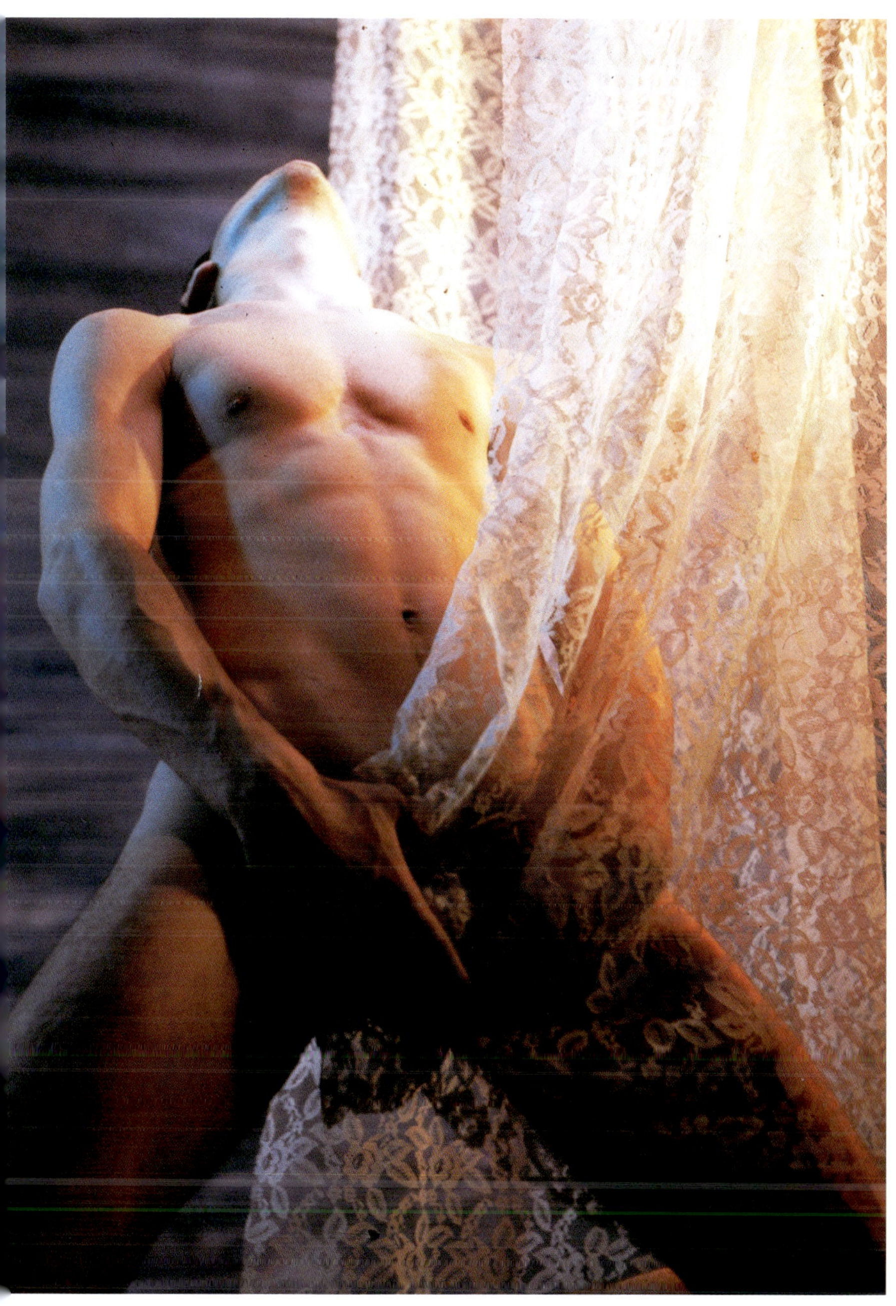

James Bidgood, Bobby Test Five, 1960s

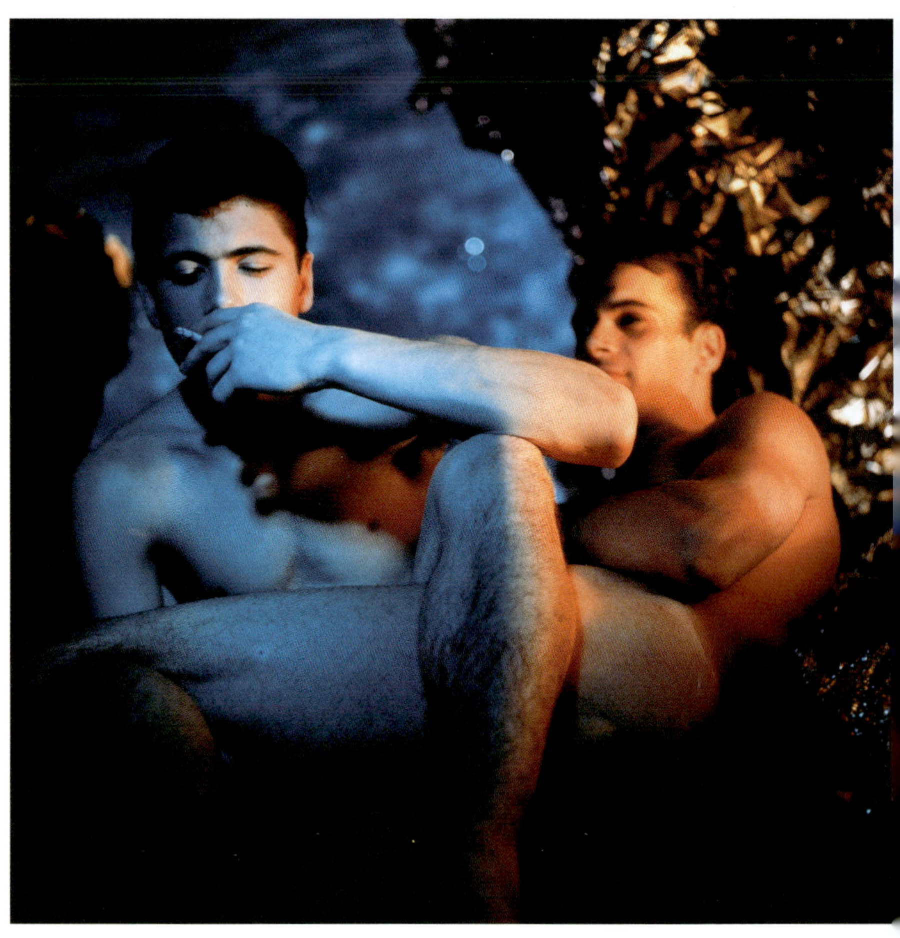

James Bidgood, Sand Castle (Bobby & Jay) One. Fifteen, 1960s

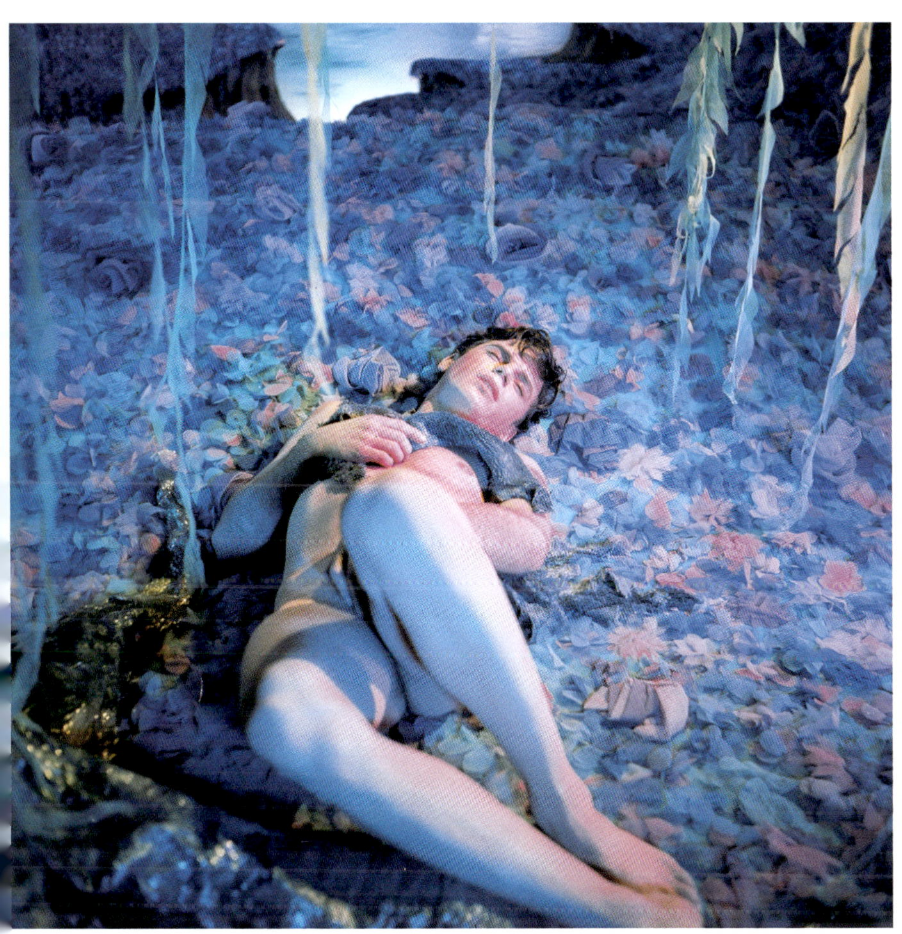

James Bidgood, Willow Tree Three, 1960s

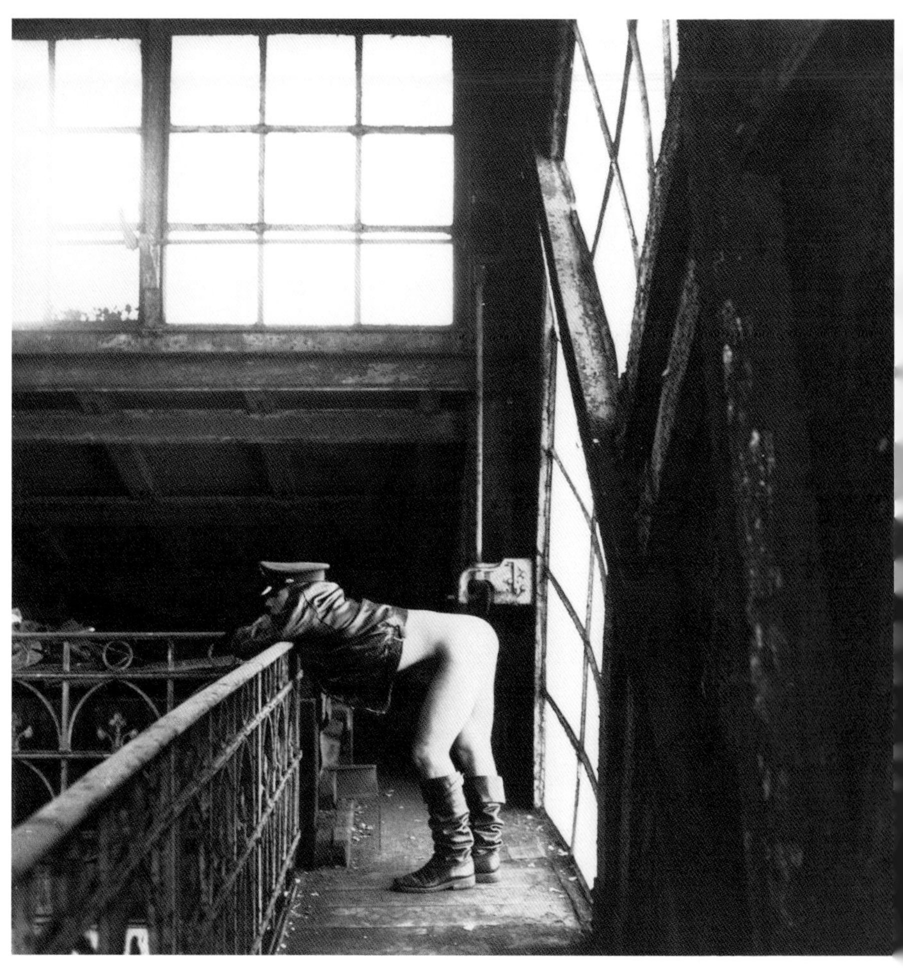

Herbert Tobias, Nach meine Beene is ja janz Berlin verrückt, 1976

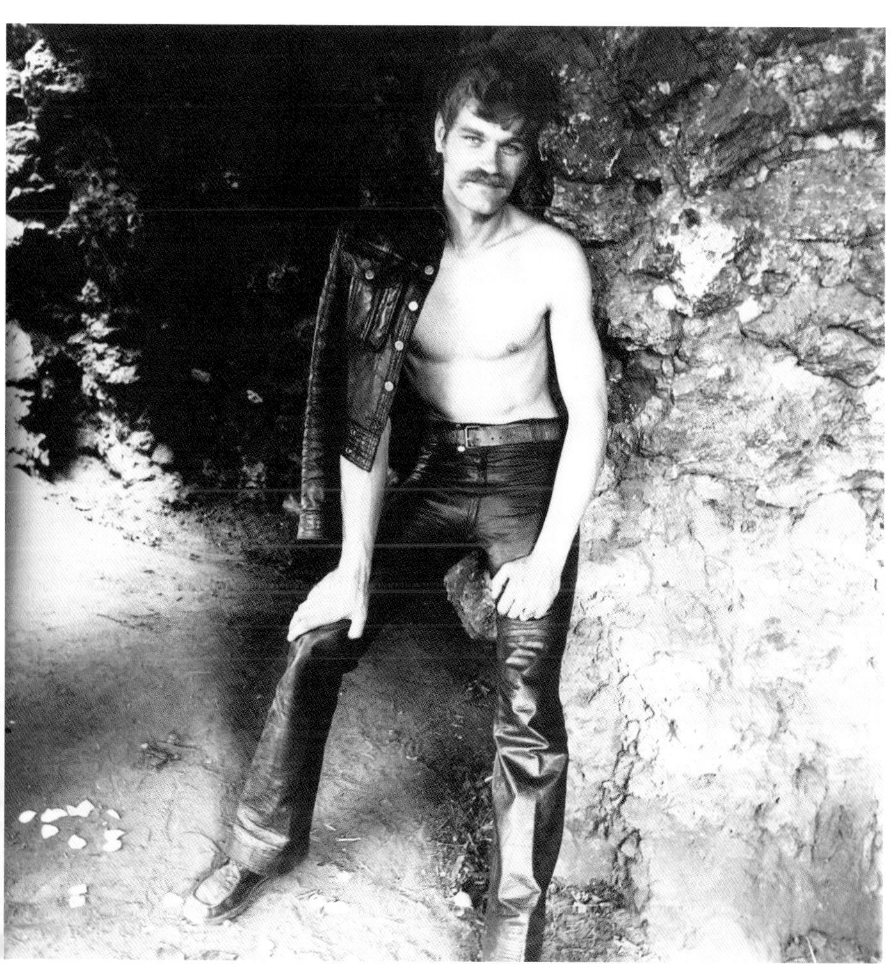

Herbert Tobias, c. 1980

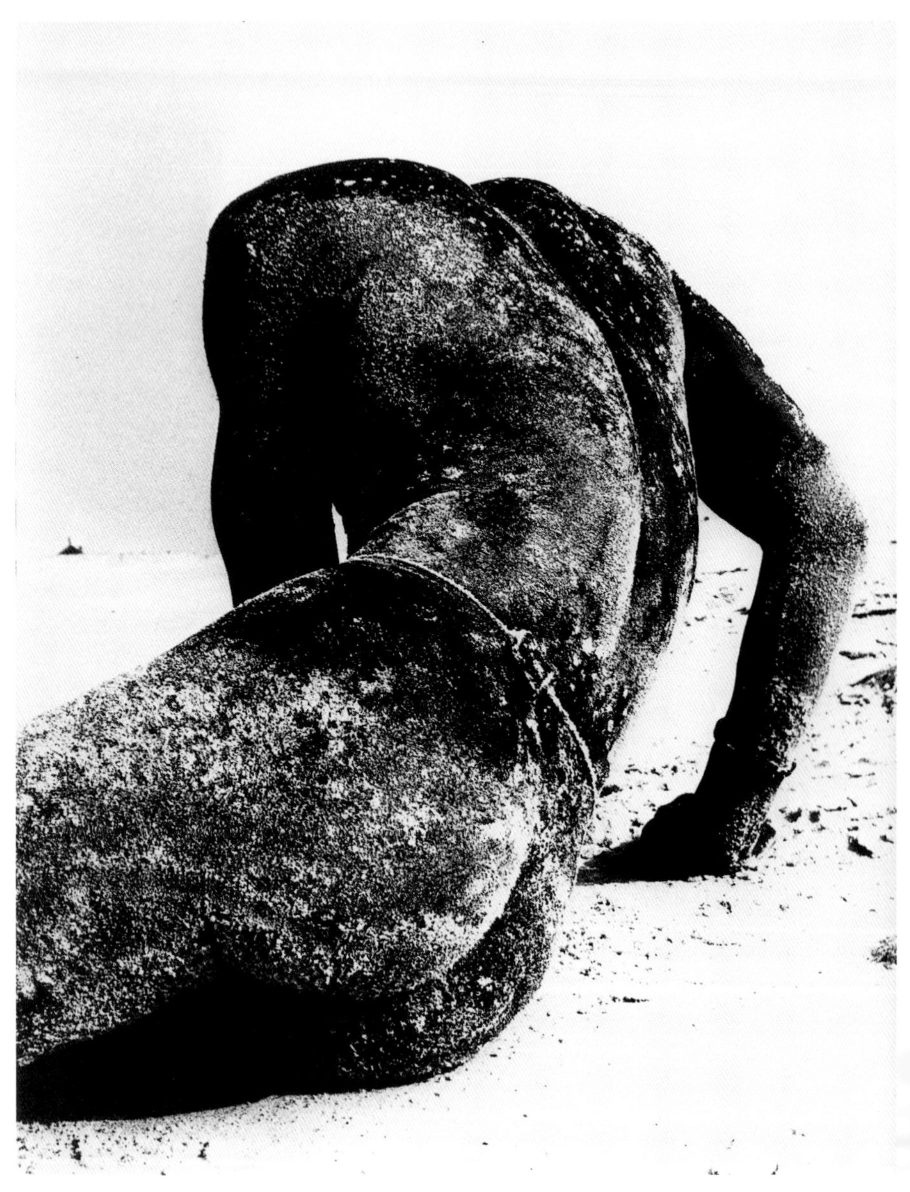

Wolfgang von Wangenheim, Aus der Serie Schwarz, 1976

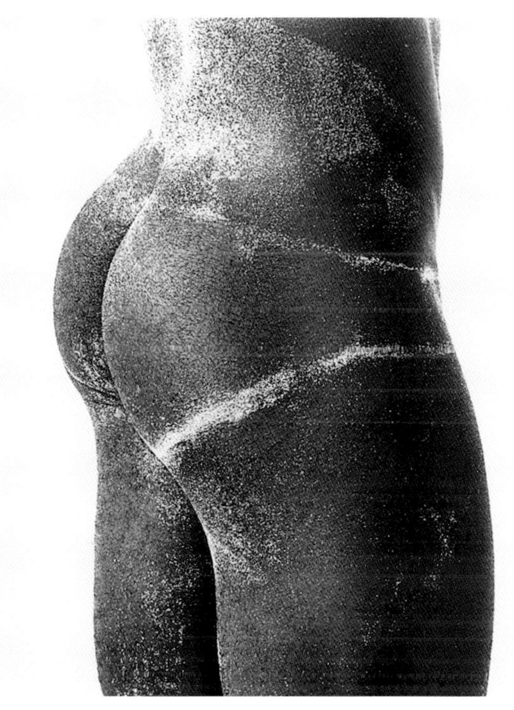

Wolfgang von Wangenheim, Aus der Serie Schwarz, 1976

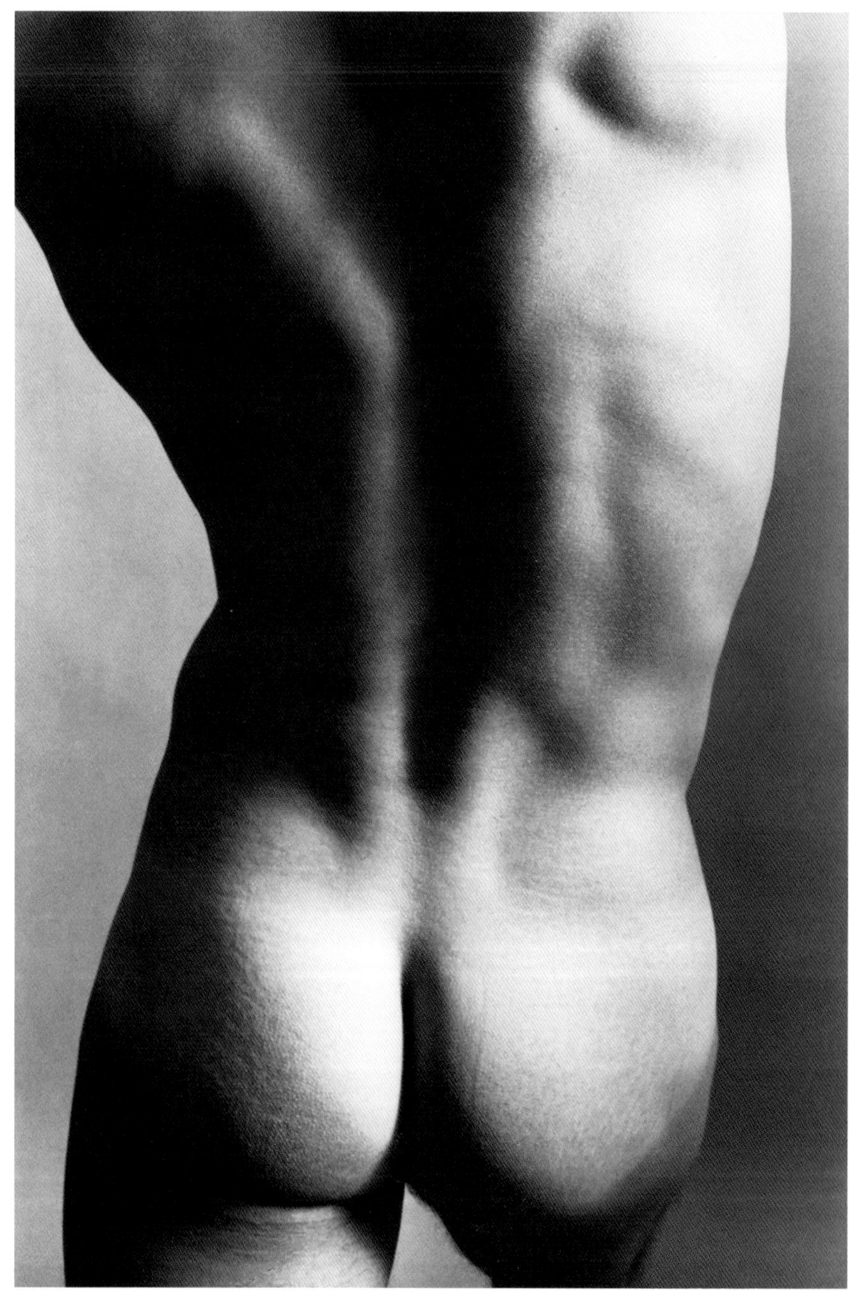

Eva Rubinstein, Man's Nude Back, November 1971

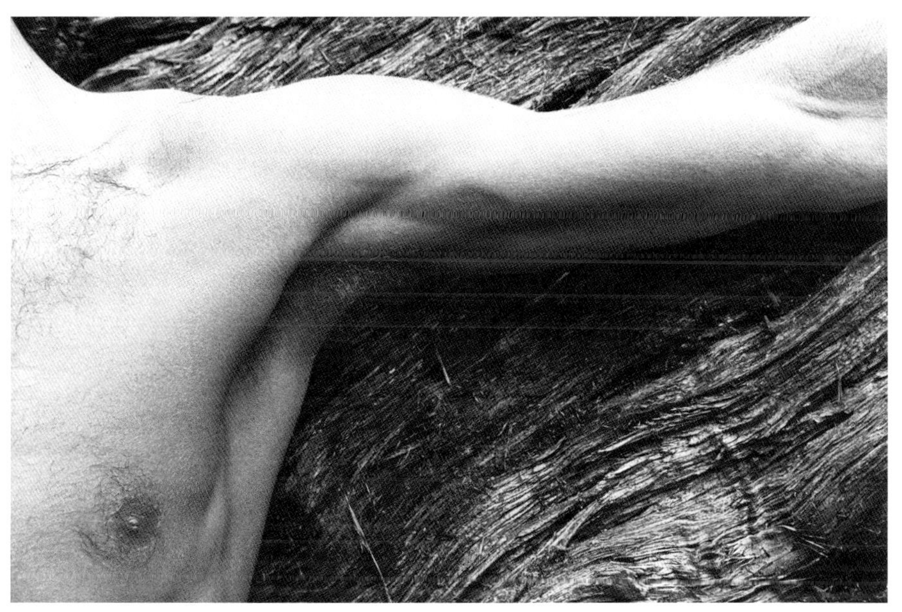

Eva Rubinstein, Arm, Tree Bark, 1974

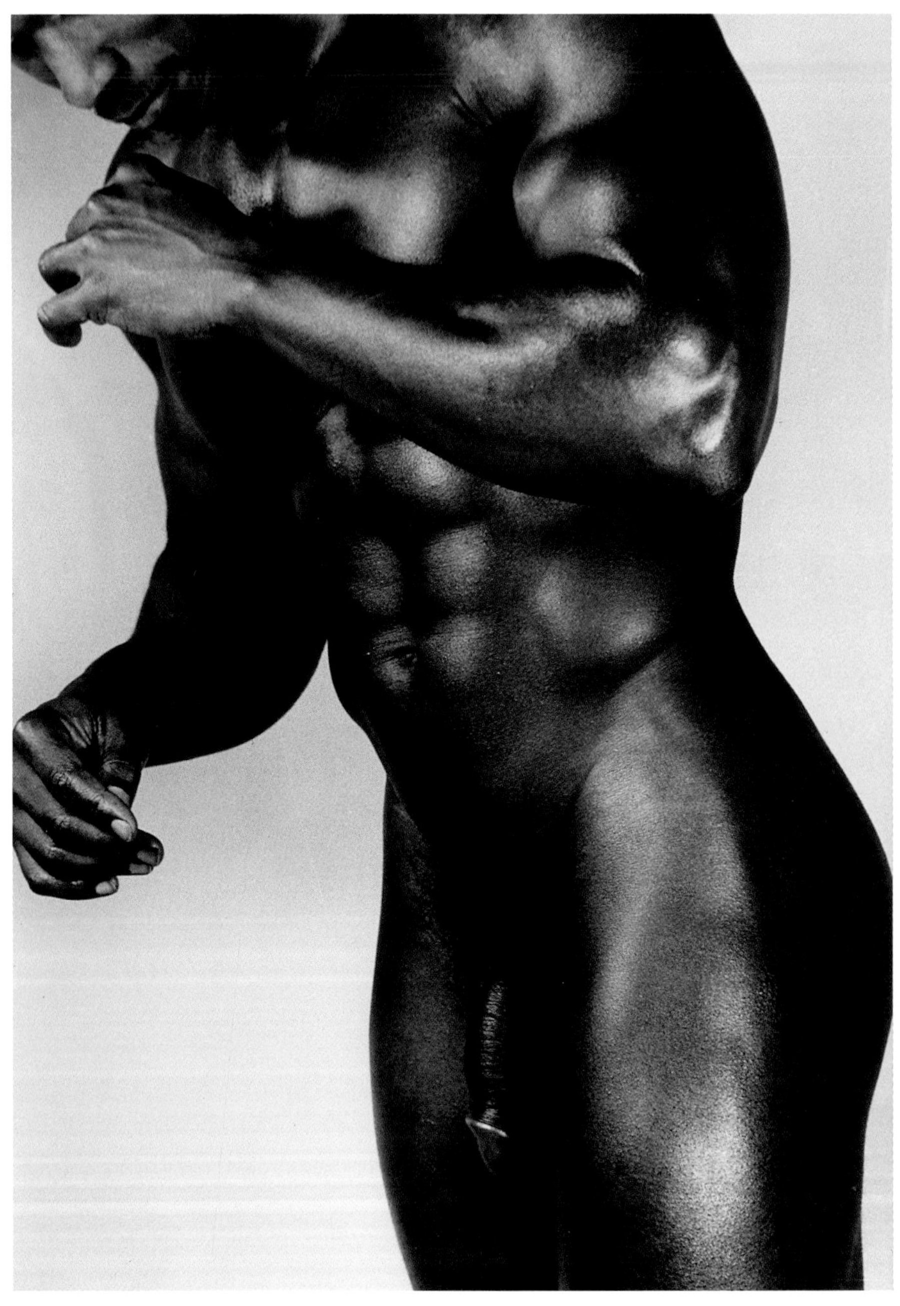

  Dianora Niccolini, "The Bodybuilder", from the Series "Male Nude", 1975

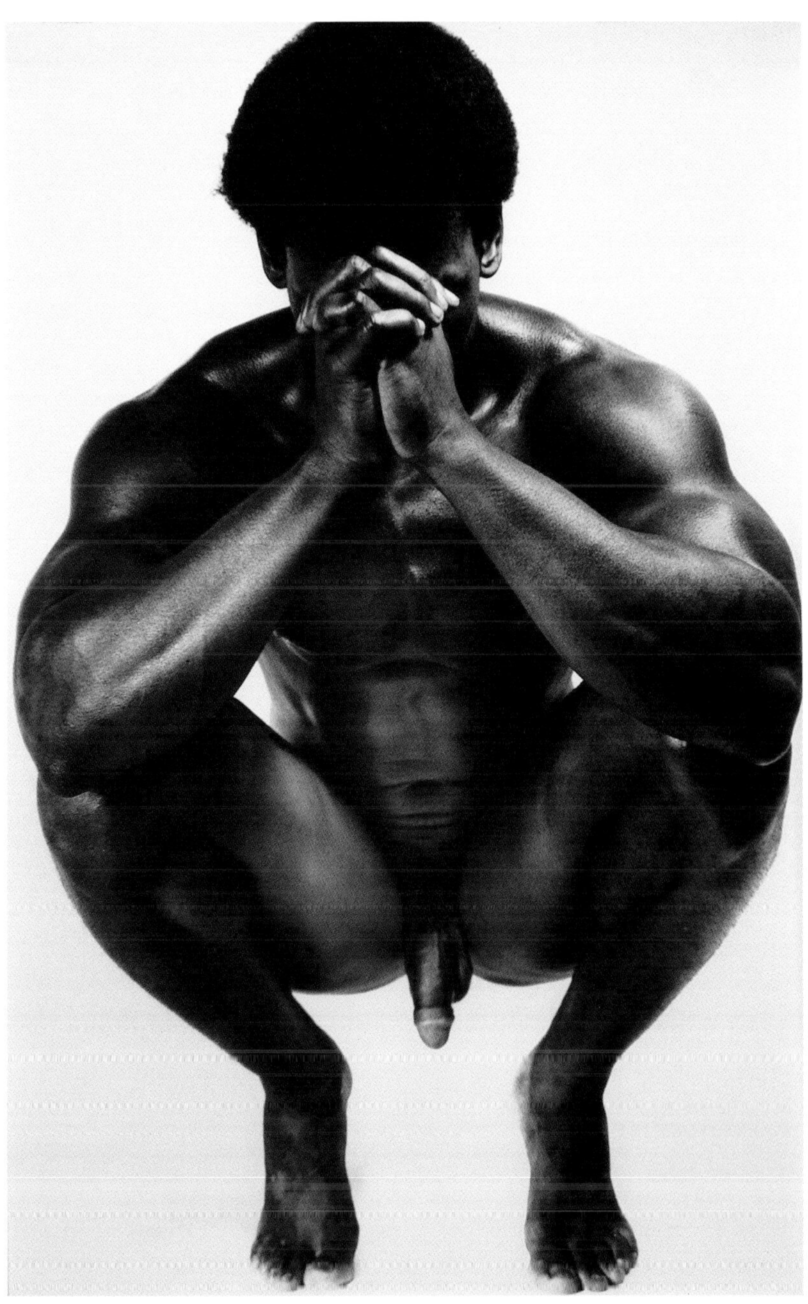

Dianora Niccolini, "The Bodybuilder", from the Series "Male Nude", 1975   **363**

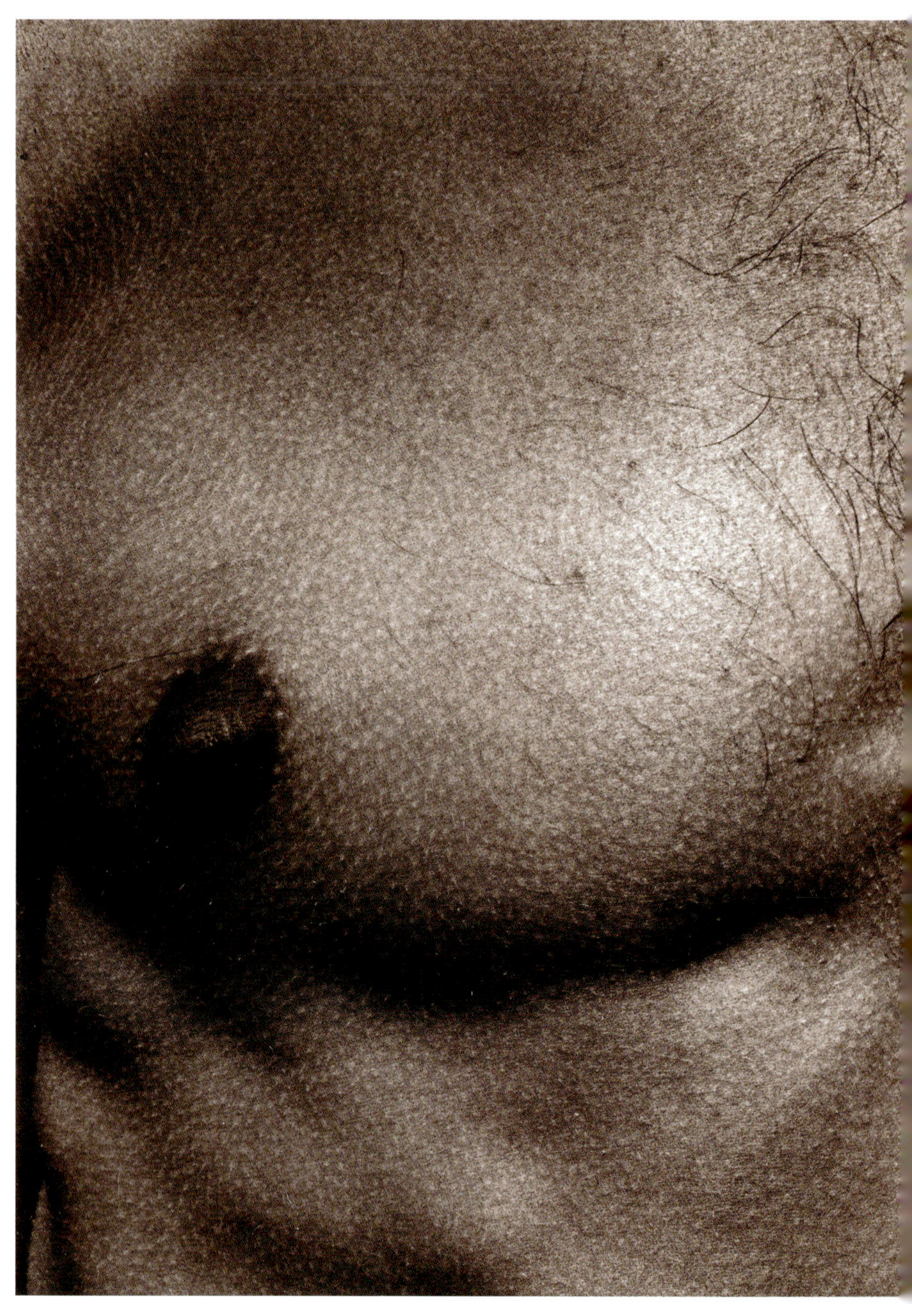

Dianora Niccolini, "The Chest", from the Series "Male Nude", 1975

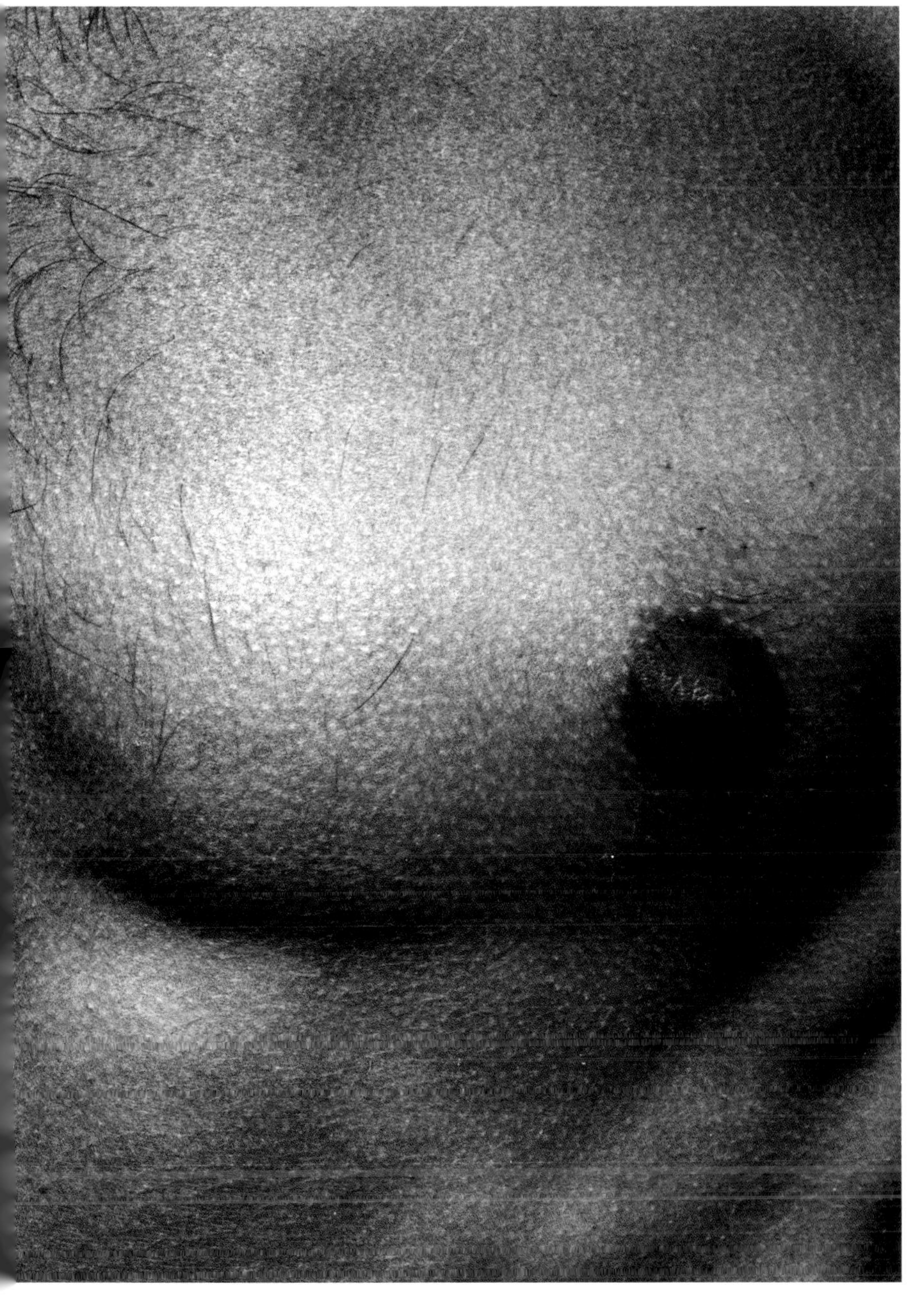

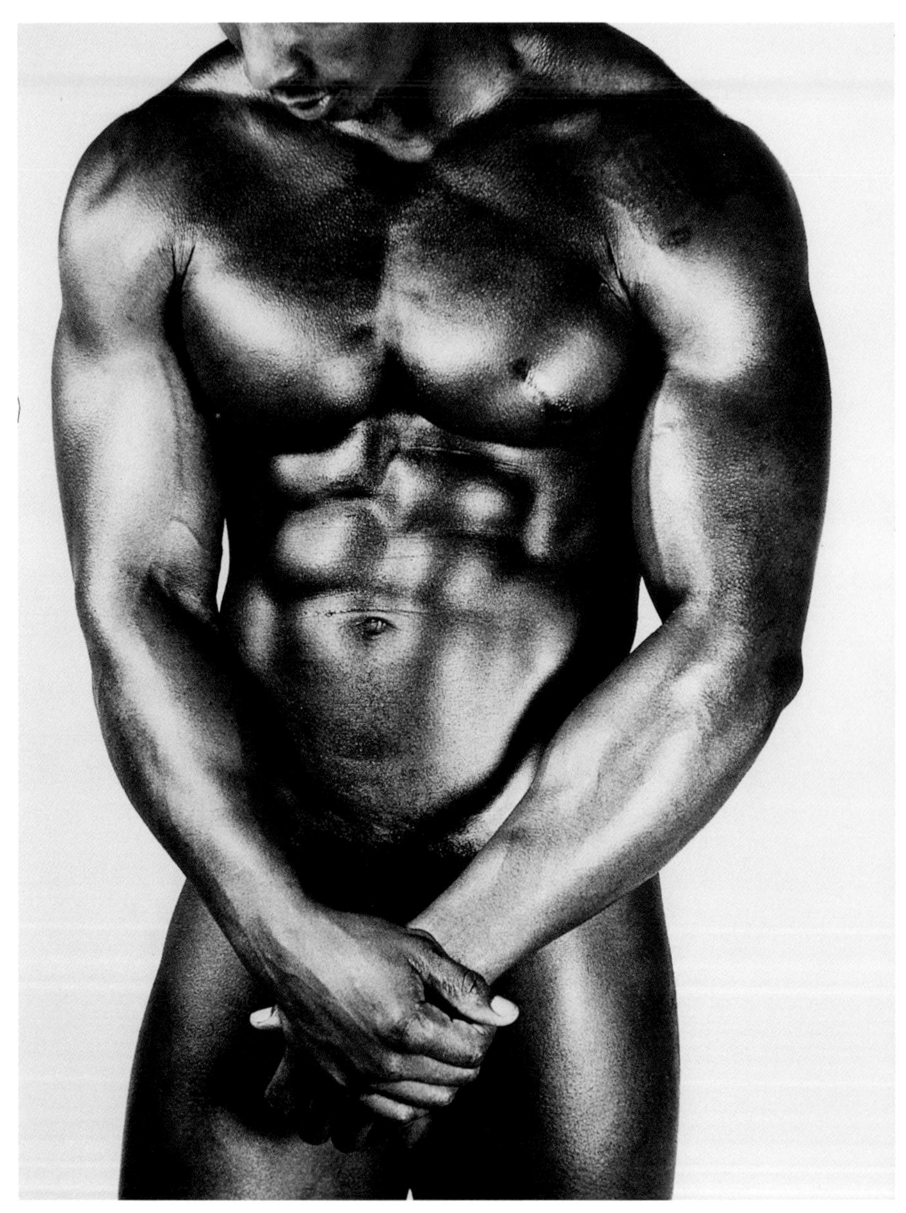

Dianora Niccolini, "The Bodybuilder", from the Series "Male Nude", 1975

366

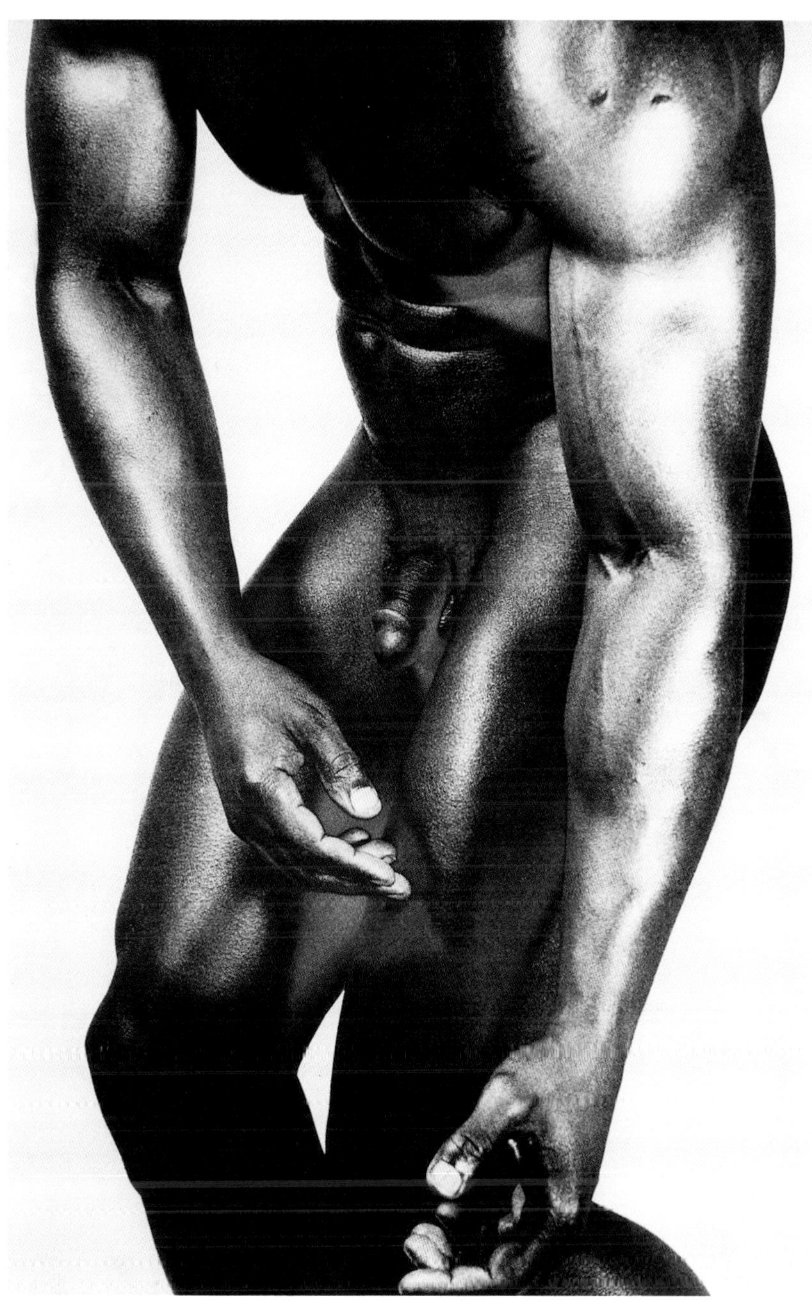

Dianora Niccolini, ``The Bodybuilder'', from the Series ``Male Nude'', 1975   367

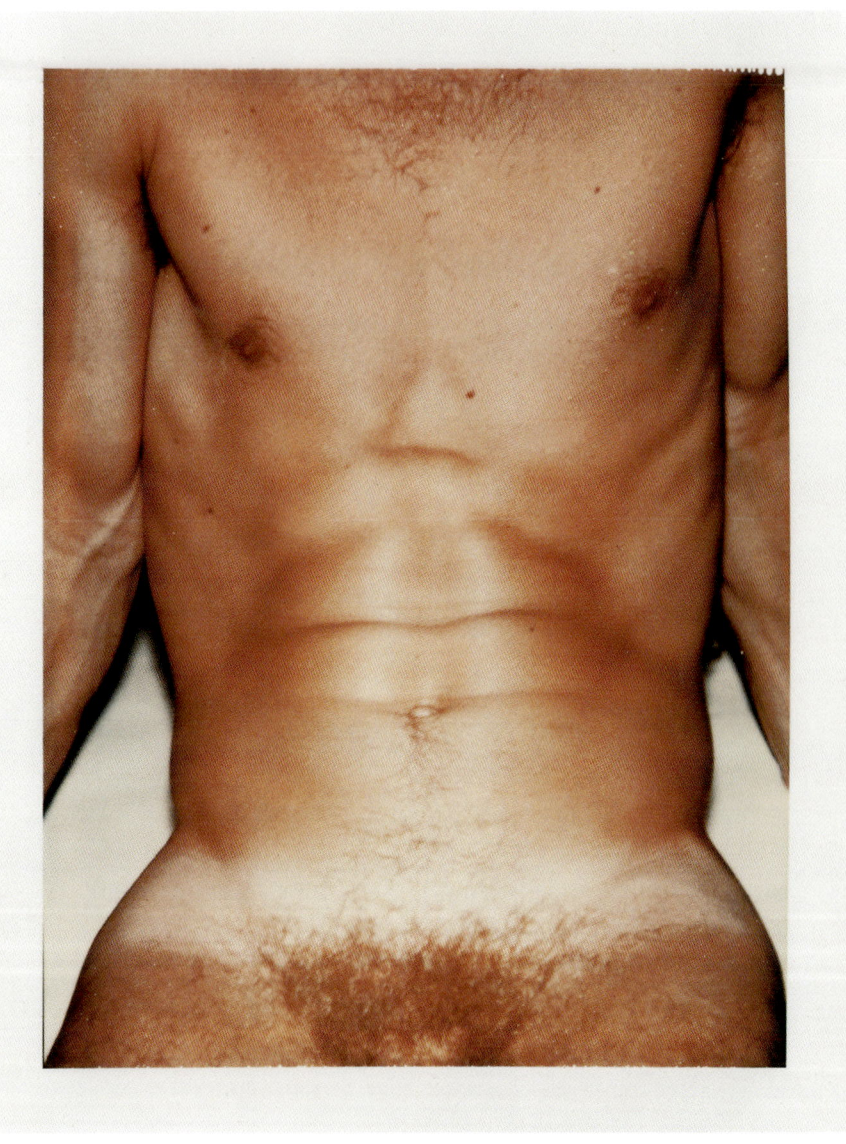

Andy Warhol, Torso, 1977

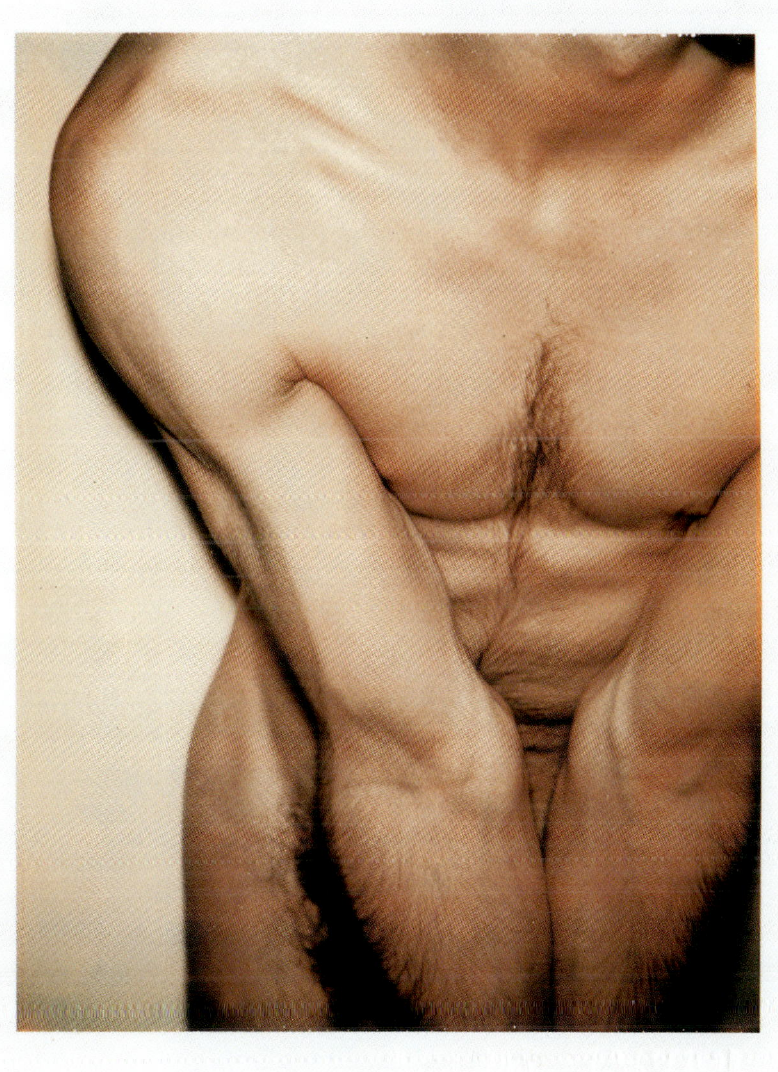

Andy Warhol, Male Nude, 1980

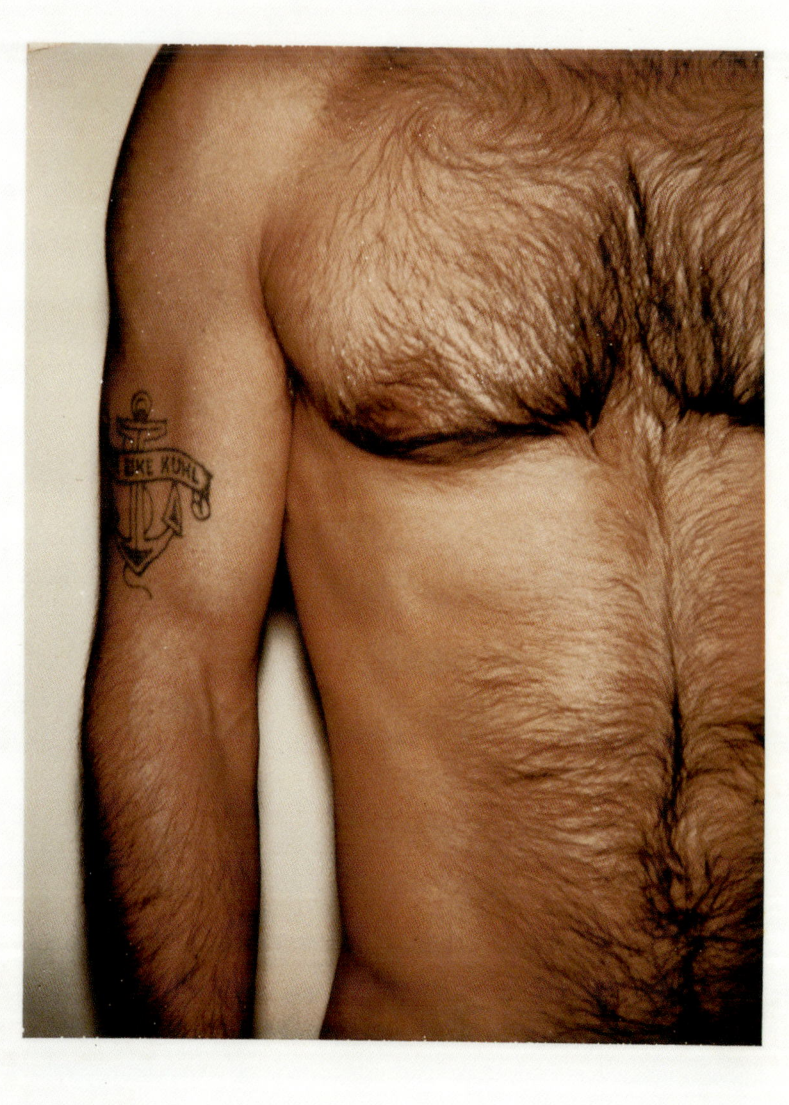

Andy Warhol, Torso, 1977

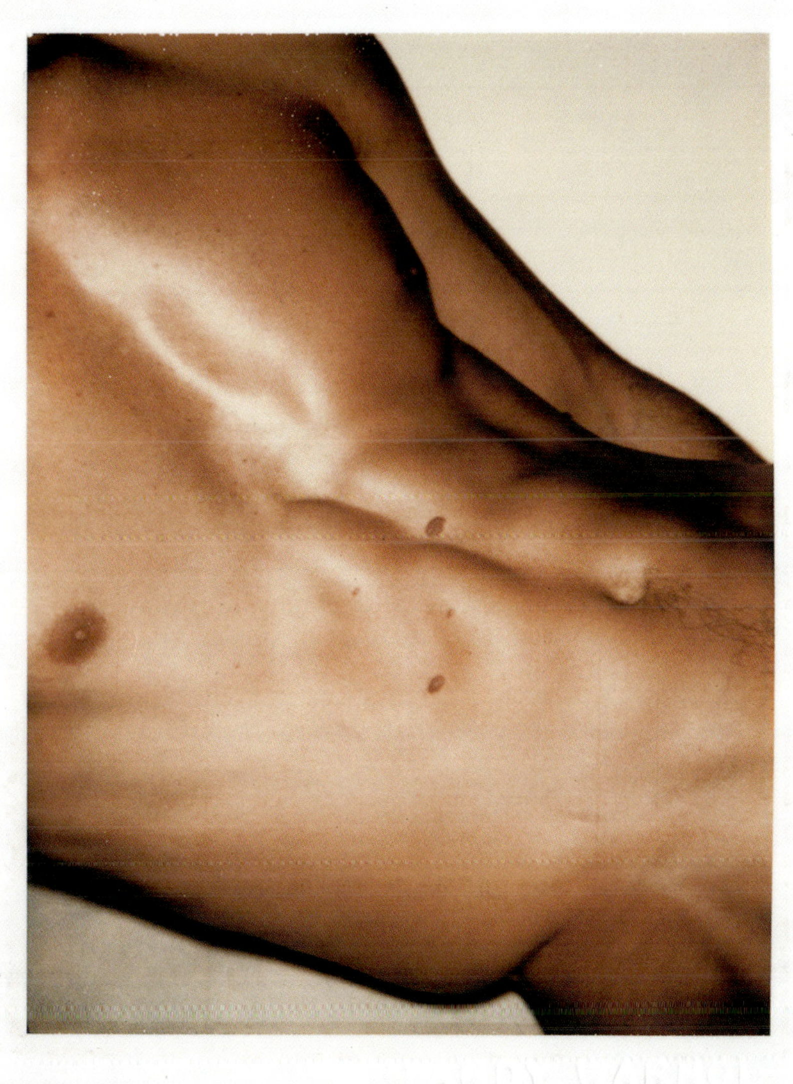

Andy Warhol, Torso, 1977

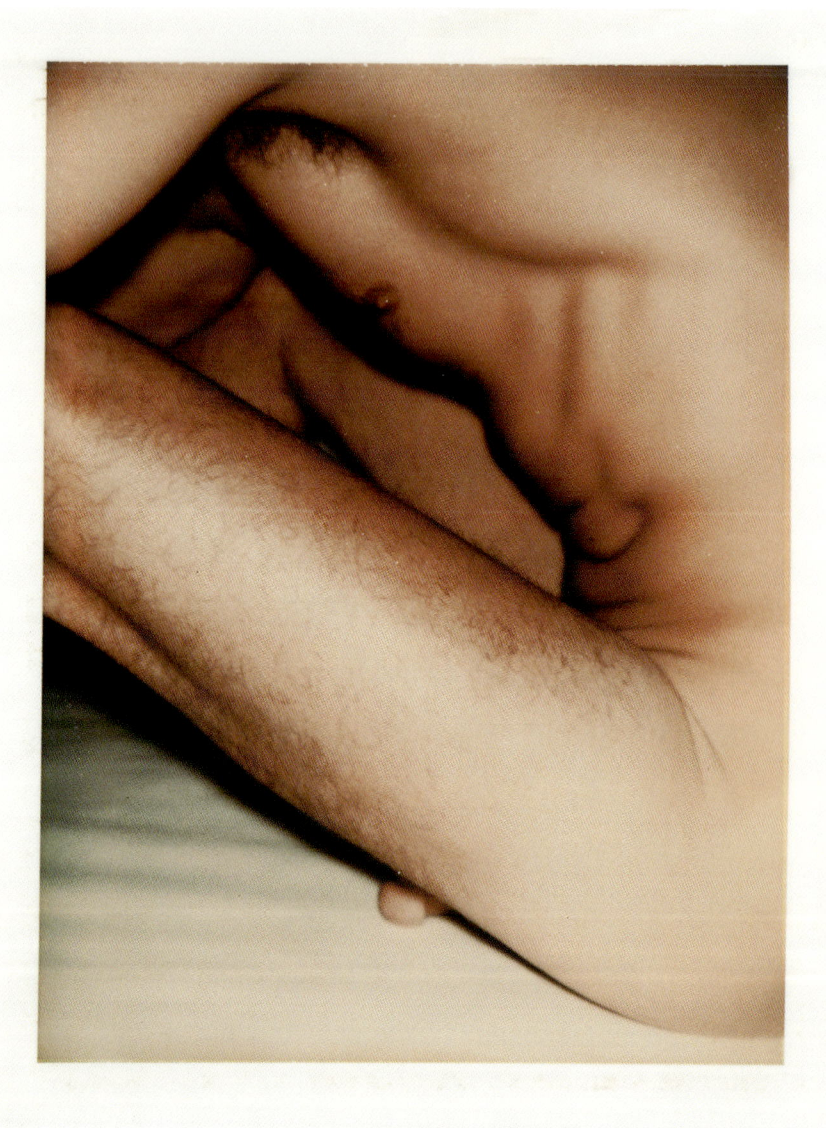

Andy Warhol, Torso, 1977

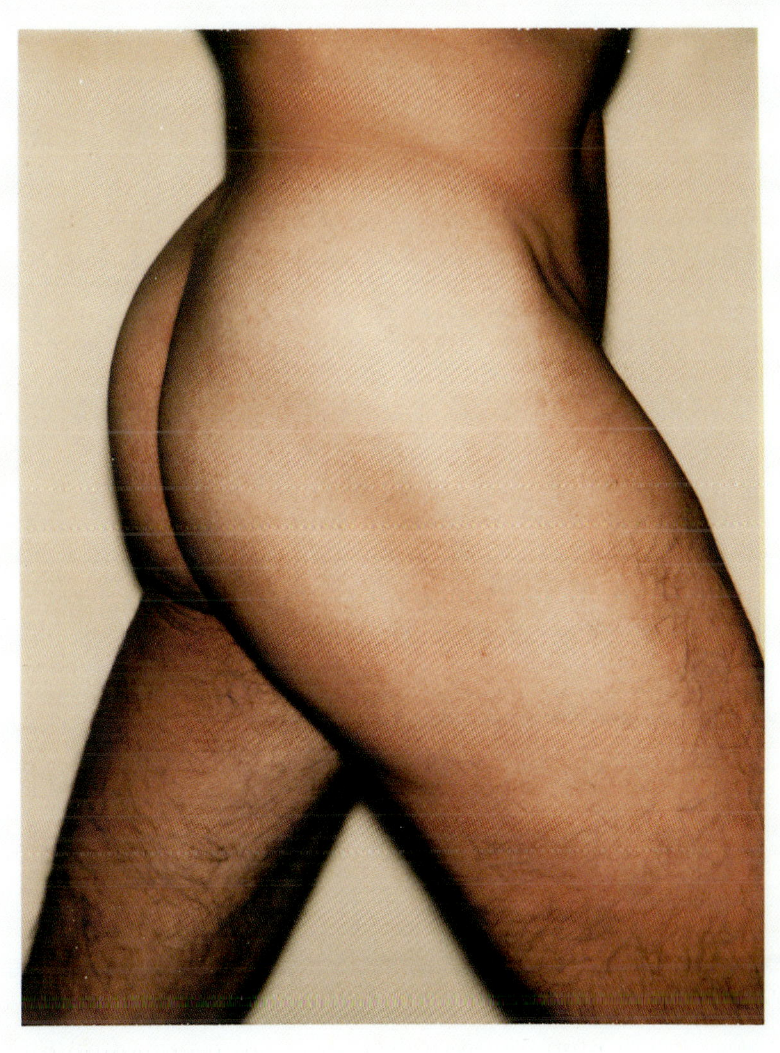

Andy Warhol, Torso, 1977

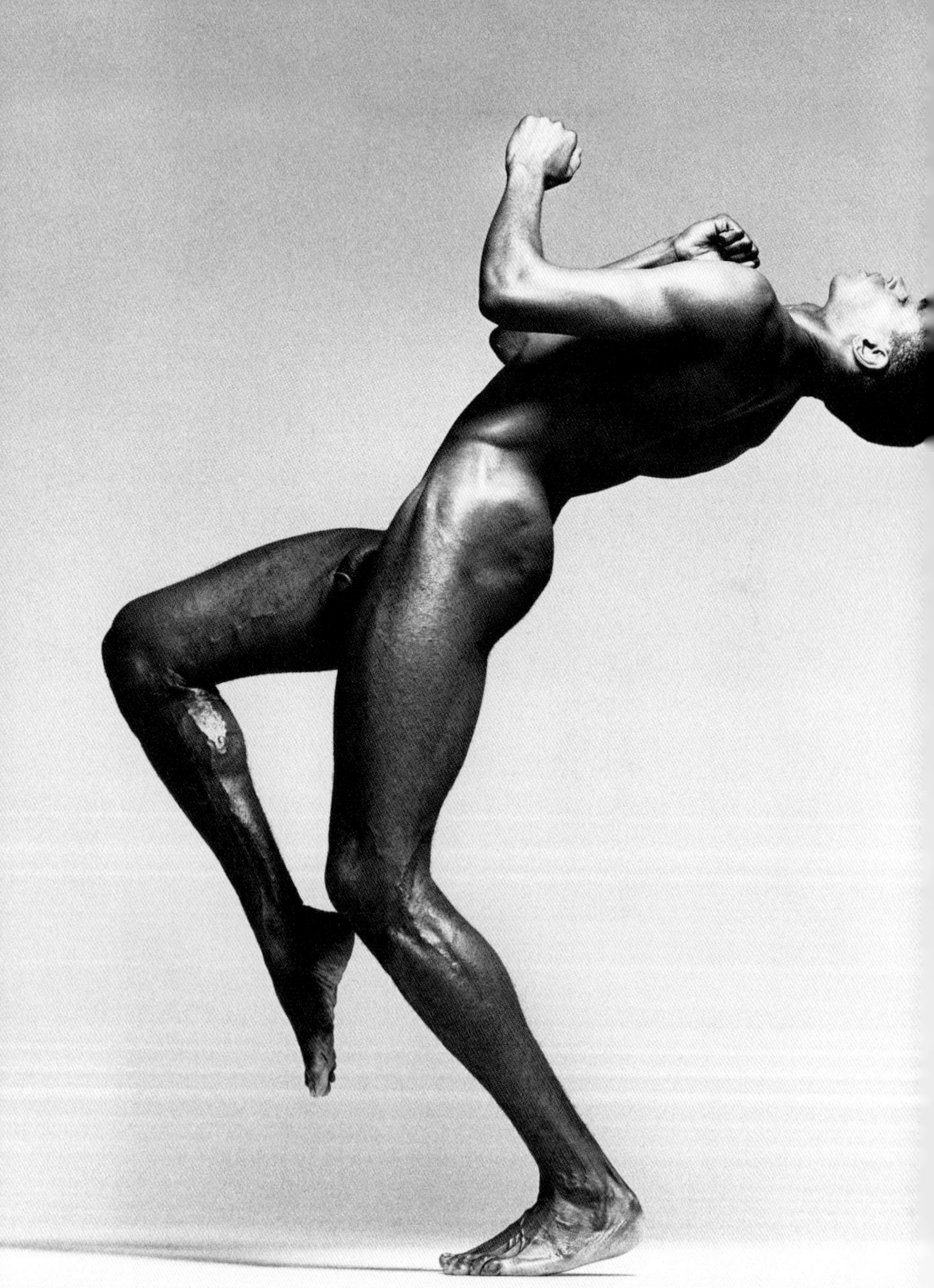

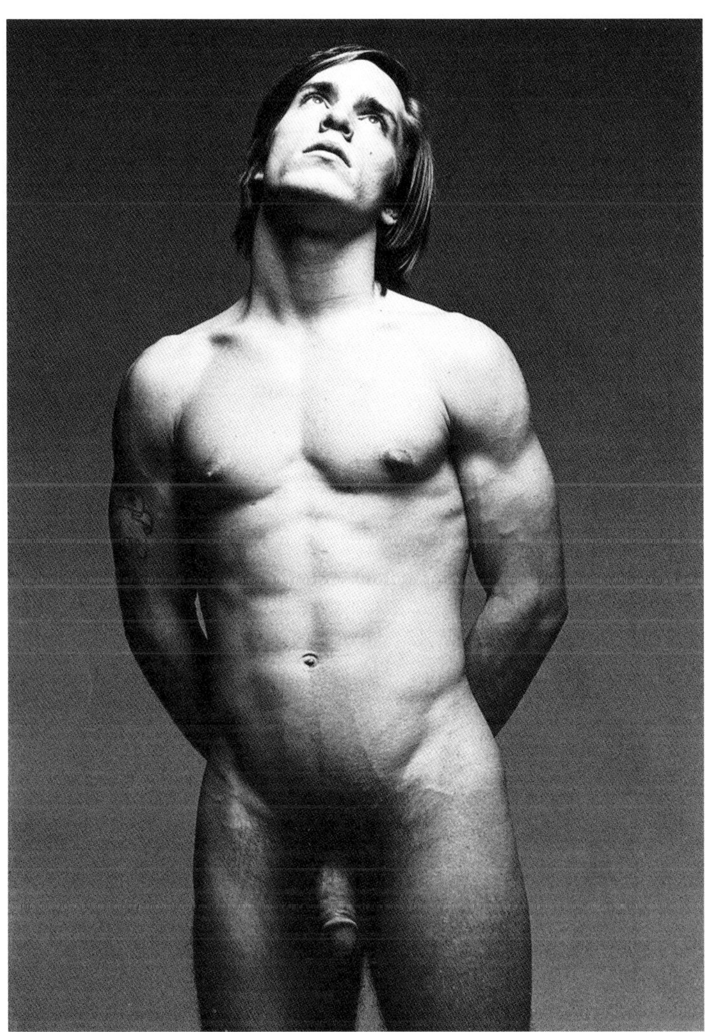

Francesco Scavullo, Joe Dallesandro, 1968

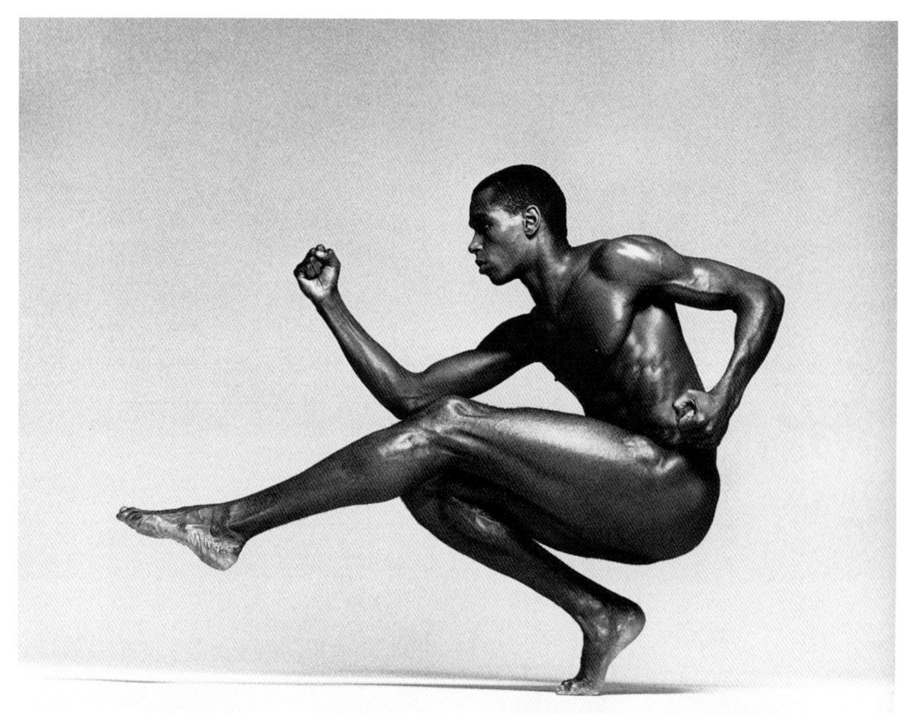

Francesco Scavullo, Sterling Saint Jacques, Portrait, 1978

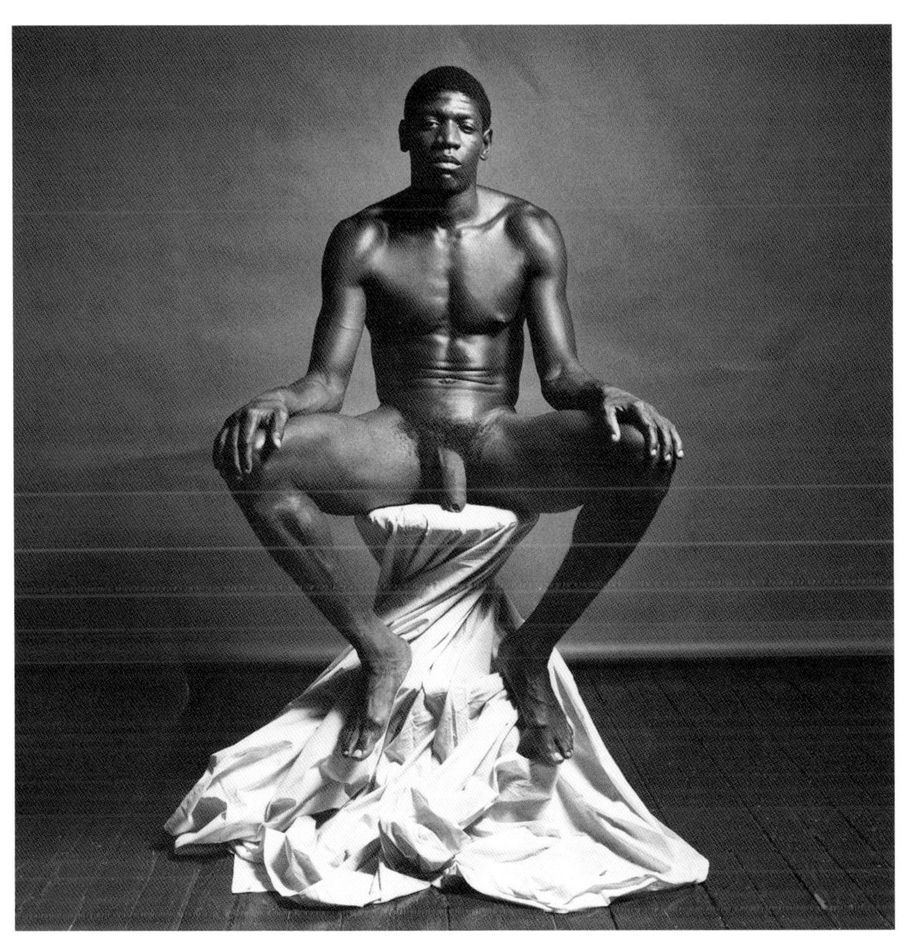

Robert Mapplethorpe, Bob Love, 1979

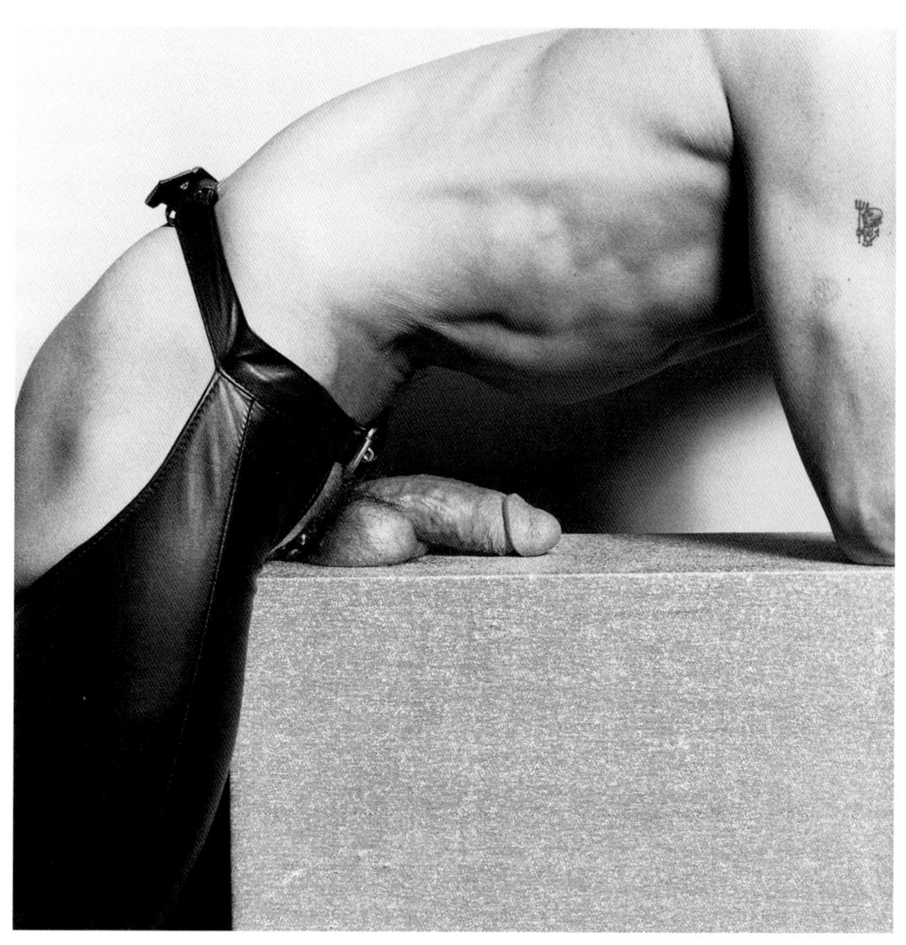

Robert Mapplethorpe, Marc Stevens (Mr. 10 $^1/_2$), 1976

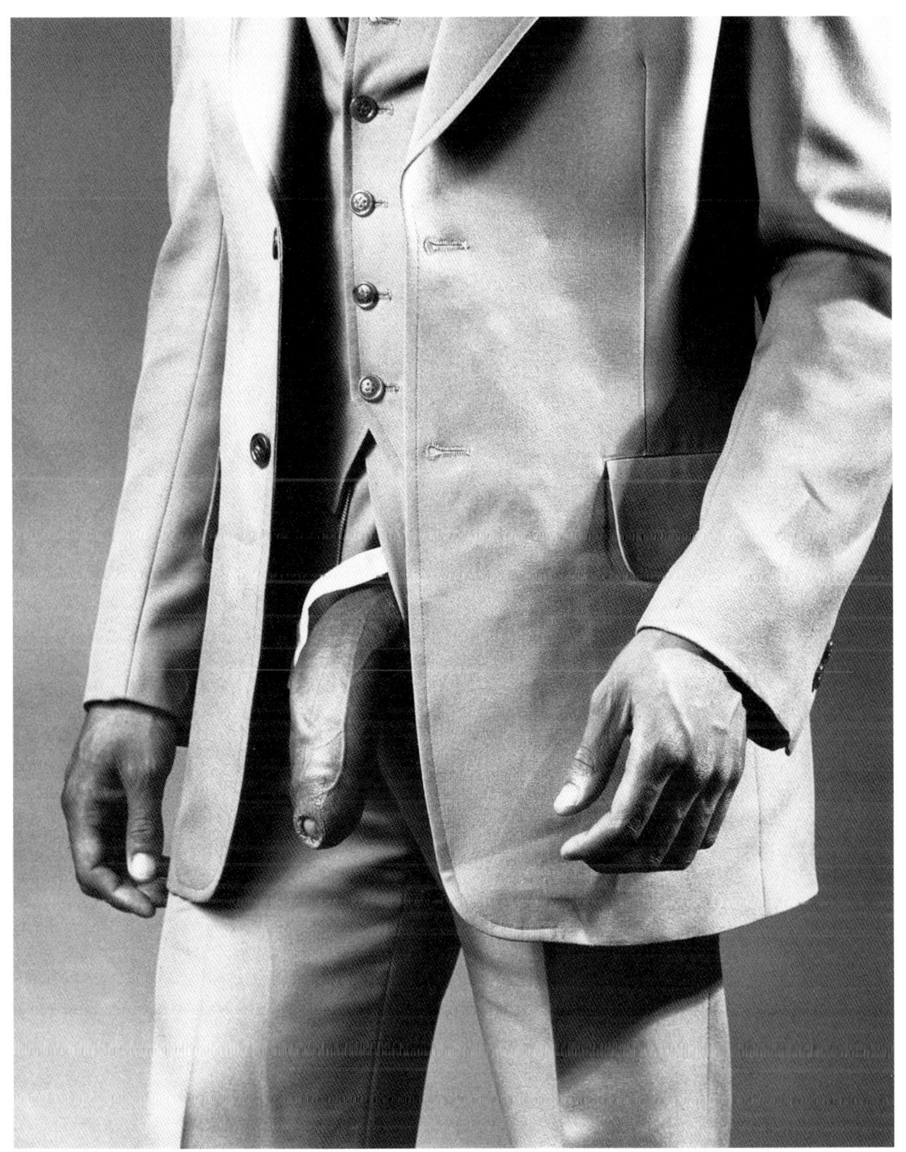

Robert Mapplethorpe, Man in Polyester Suit, 1980

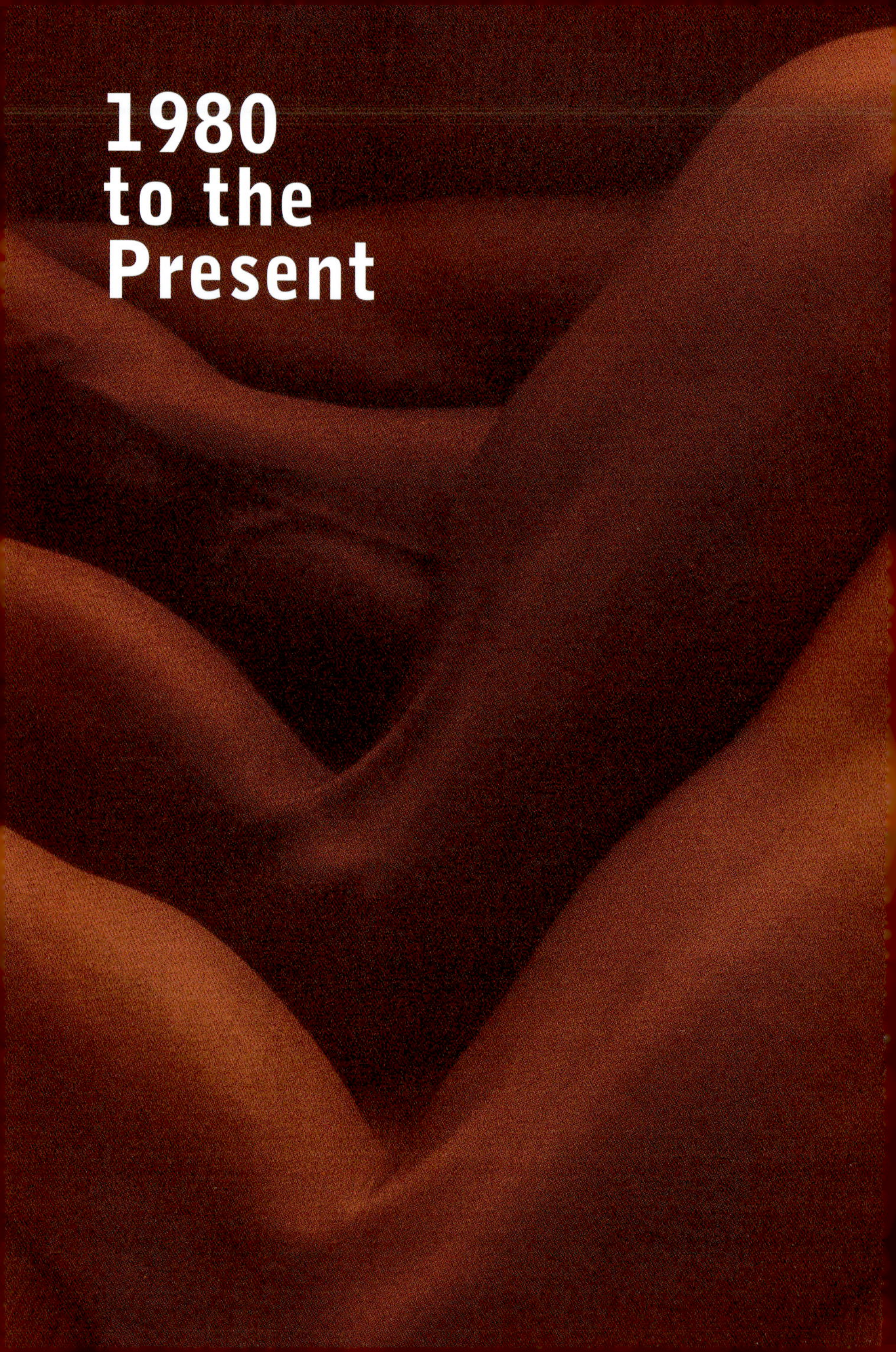
1980
to the
Present

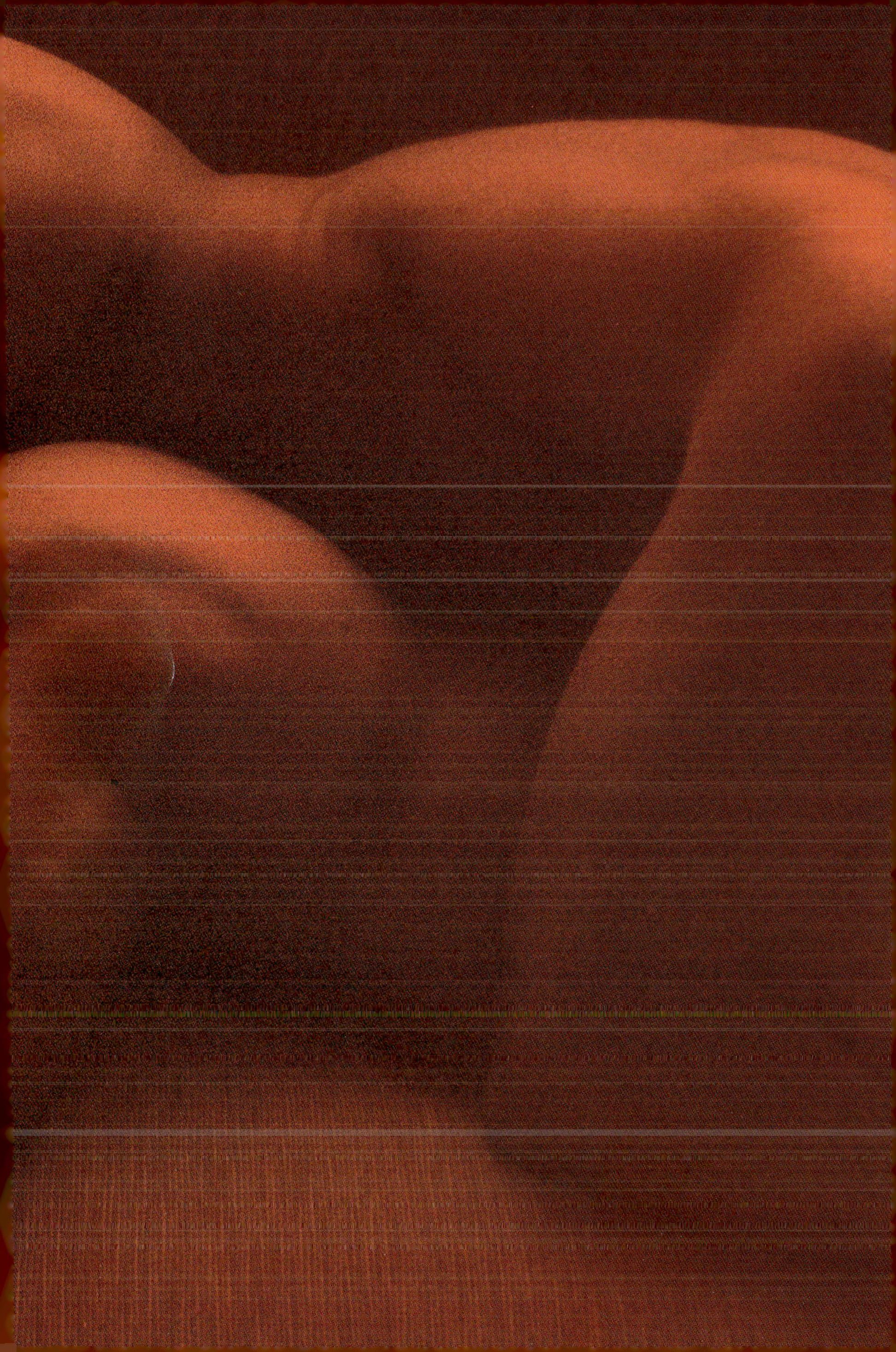

Although the 1960s and 1970s were the years when male nude photography came out of the closet, it was in the '80s that the male nude went public.

In the flush '80s, money was plentiful and much of it was spent on art. The new rich wanted to spend their money on something conspicuous that demonstrated that they (or their wives) had some taste. Photographer Robert Mapplethorpe was ready and waiting. The protégé of wealthy photograph collector Sam Wagstaff, Mapplethorpe was carefully promoted as creating a new kind of valuable art photography. A typical Mapplethorpe exhibit featured delicate children, elegant society ladies, beautiful flowers, and large naked men with equally large sexual equipment.

Sometimes the photographs were of the equipment all by itself. Mapplethorpe's refined technique, so suited to children and flowers, made his graphic sexual pictures even more shocking. And it was the shock that made the difference. Photographic art was heading in a new direction.

When the City of Cincinnati refused to mount the nude photographs in a Mapplethorpe show at their city museum, the photographer became internationally famous. Now displaying the male nude had become a matter of freedom of artistic expression. Soon no photo exhibition was complete without its graphic male nudes. Mapplethorpe also made no bones about his homosexuality, which allowed many other male photographers of naked men to come "out of the closet" and be relaxed about it.

This had an immediate impact upon commercial photography. Bruce Weber made Ralph Lauren clothing famous with his photographs of an imaginary upper-class world, a world replete with young, handsome men with clearcut profiles and plenty of muscles. These young men sailed, partied, swam and sported about, displaying soon-to-be-seen-everywhere bodies.

The same young men also invaded the world of Calvin Klein clothing, via Weber. They then moved on to people the advertising of Gianni Versace and many other prestige clients.

Richard Avedon paired these handsome young guys with the new top female models, coupling fabulous frocks with stark naked men.

Whereas the Bruce Weber men always seemed to be nice boys caught in moments of innocent nakedness, Avedon, Herb Ritts, Greg Gorman, and many others were creating images of undressed men that seemed anything but innocent. Their bodies were often photographed under the inspiration of classical sculpture, but the seductive light and the presentation of face and body were consciously intent upon arousing lust. Lust was the new direction that photography was taking in the 1980s.

Paired off with commercial products, these beautiful nude male bodies not only seemed very desirable but also directly available. Just like the product.

Such photographs quickly became the measure of how gay men wanted to look. Called the "clone" look by gay society itself, buff and built-up bodies were a must, usually accompanied by moustaches, jeans, plaid shirts and heavy boots. Gymnasiums sprang up over every corner grocery. "Straight-looking, straight-acting" was the goal of every homosexual. It was either that or becoming a drag queen. Interestingly, the trend was launched not by men who looked like this, but by the photographs of these ideal men. As Oscar Wilde had remarked almost a century earlier, nature was imitating art.

The look became so associated with homosexuals that when Calvin Klein launched a new look to promote his CK fragrance in 1995, the photography reverted to the androgynous look of the 60s to typify a convincing heterosexual male. Mick Jagger revisited. In the confusion of the last decade of the 20th century, looking like Tarzan or John Wayne indicated you were gay, and looking like Mick or Jim Morrison indicated that you weren't.

Market demand for the male nude image unleashed a flood of new photographers. The leaders like Bruce Weber and Herb Ritts for the most part eschewed frontal nudity. But many inspired by the audacious Robert Mapplethorpe let it all hang out.

On the West Coast Jim French created an empire with his Coll Studio photographs of the humpiest of all humpy men. The Studios offer a range of products, from discreet calendars and appointment books containing no frontal nudity, to lavishly lit studio and exterior photographs of titanic bodies in frontal positions, albeit with no special emphasis on the genitalia. They also produce photo collections of men in singles and duos who are fully aroused. Colt entered the porn film business too, and many photo collections represent scenes from these films. Where once art photography and porn films were at the opposite ends of the nude male image spectrum, now they were approaching one another at rapid speed.

The 1990s have seen the buildup of an entire industry of nude male photography. Books, calendars and postcards are omnipresent. David Sprigle and Jeff Palmer on the West Coast are the industry's leaders. Palmer's highly polished photographs present the male body in a more idealized way. Sprigle with his sorties into South America for fresh models and ideas tends to have a more spontaneous and journalistic flare, but his work is of excellent emotional and photographic quality.

In Miami, Ali and David Morgan have carved out their own male nude worlds. Ali produces highly erotic studio work in black and white. Morgan presents his models in a more athletic and romantic manner.

Tom Bianchi in Los Angeles has created a completely homosexual environment where for the most part groups of perfectly built men cavort at swimming pools or on the seashore. He has also photographed lesbians enjoying themselves in the same kind of environments. There is a feeling of sexual camaraderie in his work which may be Californian. It cannot be called romantic in a traditional sense.

Arthur Tress contrasts strong bodies against a setting of slums and deserted warehouses. E. B. White once wrote that beautiful girls were the flowers of the city; perhaps the Tress men are the beautiful part of what he sees as an increasingly violated world.

Blake Little, a recent arrival on the scene, places his stalwart men in an atmosphere that seems empty and futuristic, as though our way of relating to beautiful men has robbed them of their relevance.

David Armstrong is less concerned with idealized beauty, and photographs the world he sees around him. Mark Morrisroe also reveals his men in a harsh, realistic way.

In the area of true art photography, Andy Warhol's experiments with personally created pornography were little seen by the public until after his death. He shot close-ups of genitalia and intercourse, which left him pale and breathless (according to his assistants). He then painted them over and elevated them to something more artistic.

Duane Michals' many books that combine a poetic sensibility and a gentle appreciation of nude male beauty create a refined eroticism and spirituality that is this artist's own.

Among women photographers, Dianora Niccolini holds the preeminent position in her ability to present the male body as both erotic and ideal. The more journalistic Annie Leibovitz has displayed Sylvester Stallone's highly worked-over body to good advantage. Fashion photographer and film director Rebecca Blake shows a stylish appreciation of masculine beauty when given the opportunity.

Nan Goldin presents her view of a brutal world with no reservations – a world inhabited by numerous naked men.

Ken Probst's remarkable and refined work on porn film sets is hard to place. If any photographer has set out to state that pornography is just another aspect of beauty, it is Probst.

New and interesting photographers of the male nude are cropping up all over the U.S. You have Connie Imboden and Jason Lee in Baltimore, and Clifford Clark with his outdoor studies in California, Klaus Gerhart and Ed Freeman are also doing interesting photography in Los Angeles and Andy Devine has recently relocated there. Chuck Smith in Minneapolis and Mark Lynch in Austin, Texas, are newcomers bringing a fresh approach to photographing the male nude, as are Adrian Jones in Brooklyn, and Richard Kern in New York. Steve Vaccariello's exciting new pictures are shot in New York too.

In France, the great photographer of the male nude, who began in the mid-'70s, is Patrick Sarfati. He alone in Europe presents the powerful male body as a beautiful and idealized presence. He frequently creates a Mediterranean atmosphere forging a link with the classical past, but makes no excuses for his erotic gods. His work in color is probably the finest produced by any contemporary photographer of the male nude.

Sarfati was an early supporter of Pierre et Gilles, who include male nudes in their world of painted and gaudy kitsch. Their male nudes retouched into '50s commercial art are not only erotic and beautiful, but have much to say about our consumer society.

In England, Tony Butcher's photography of black models is both sexy and sensual. The Dutch choreographer Hans van Manen has shown equal talent in photographing male nudes. Many of his subjects are dancers, whose finely tuned physiques and powerful legs have offered him excellent subjects. His country-man Paul Blanca, in contrast, uses his own nude body as a subject for pictures that are sometimes frightening and sometimes very beautiful. His is a strange and underground talent. Erwin Olaf is Holland's contribution to male nude photography of a more commercial nature.

Gian Paolo Barbieri's recent work fuses reportage and magnificent male nudes. Jo Brunenberg brings abstraction and links to the Renaissance into his highly individual work. Germany is home to the photographers Andreas Bitesnich and Baly Hinter Wipflinger, both shooting strong and original nudes. Herlinde Koelbl and Evelyn Krull are there too.

South African Herb Klein finds interesting subjects in Johannesburg. Almond Chu is doing innovative photography of the male in Hong Kong, China. Daniel Hernández presents sensual material and models from Colombia and Miami. And in the Czech Republic, Michael Macků explores the male body with his camera. Bruno Benini in Sydney, Australia, has contributed outstanding studies, many of them of dancers.

Nowadays, it is clear that photographing the male nude is a thriving business. The pressing need to throw off the maschismo attitudes and restraints of the Victorian era has won through. Although freedom to publicly display male nude images has been granted grudgingly, and progress has had its ups and downs, society has gradually moved forward from decade to decade.

The recognition of the male body as a sex object in this century links us strongly to the Renaissance and further back to antiquity.

Whether it heralds a new equality between men and women, whether it predicts a new kind of polymorphous sexuality, or whether it is just a momentary breath of pagan refreshment before another wave of repression and conservatism, is hard to say. But for the male body to break free of the wrappings of centuries has been an impressive achievement, an achievement of photography alone. Those men and women who through their talent, perseverance, courage, and perhaps obsession brought this about, deserve much credit. No doubt it will be accorded to them in time.

Hatte die männliche Aktfotografie in den 60ern und 70ern die ersten zaghaften Schritte aus dem Verborgenen gewagt, so trat sie in den 80ern selbstbewusst an die Öffentlichkeit.

In den rauschenden 80ern feierte sich eine neue Schicht junger Reicher und war nur allzu willig, mit dem Geld der Boomjahre auch Kunstsinn zu beweisen. Als Protegé des wohlhabenden Kunstmäzens Sam Wagstaff wurde der Fotograf Robert Mapplethorpe mit Bedacht als jemand aufgebaut, dessen Kunst Sammlerwert hatte. Eine typische Mapplethorpe-Ausstellung zeigte Bilder von zarten Kindern, eleganten Damen der High-Society, wunderschönen Blumen und großen, nackten Männern mit gleichfalls großen Geschlechtsorganen.

Manchmal waren auf den Bildern auch nur Geschlechtsteile zu sehen. Seine ausgefeilte Technik, die sich so gut für Kinder- und Blumenbilder eignete, machte die drastische Wirkung der Genitalfotos um so anstößiger. Und darauf kam es an.

Robert Mapplethorpe erlangte internationale Berühmtheit, als sich die Stadt Cincinnati weigerte, in einer Einzelausstellung des Fotografen im städtischen Museum auch Aktfotos zu zeigen. Männliche Akte auszustellen, wurde zu einer Frage künstlerischer Ausdrucksfreiheit schlechthin. Plötzlich durften in keiner Ausstellung Fotos von nackten Männern fehlen. Zudem bekannte sich Mapplethorpe offen zu seiner Homosexualität, was es vielen gleichgesinnten Fotografen ermöglichte, sich zu outen.

Die Wirkung auf die Werbefotografie blieb nicht aus. Mit Fotos eines Upper-Class-Paradieses, bevölkert von hübschen jungen Männern mit markanten Profilen und vielen Muskeln, machte Bruce Weber die Mode von Ralph Lauren berühmt. Der Typus Mann, den er bei sportlichen Freizeitvergnügen porträtierte, sollte bald allgegenwärtig werden.

Via Weber eroberten dieselben jungen Schönheiten auch die Welt von Calvin Klein. Anschließend übernahmen sie den Werbeetat von Gianni Versace und vielen anderen Kunden.

Richard Avedon blieb der Moderne treu, er rückte seine hübschen Jungs an die Seite berühmter Topmodels und verband so die Haute Couture mit dem nackten Mann. Doch während Bruce Webers Männer wie nette Jungs wirken, die er im Moment nackter Unschuld überrascht hatte, sind die Bilder von Richard Avedon, Herb Ritts, Greg Gorman und anderen keineswegs unschuldig. Die Künstler ließen sich beim Fotografieren der Modelle häufig von klassischen Standbildern inspirieren, aber die laszive Beleuchtung und die Präsentation von Gesicht und Körper sollten bewusst aufreizend und lustbetont wirken. Es war diese offene Zurschaustellung von Lust, die die neue Fotografie von jener der 80er Jahre unterschied.

In Verbindung mit dem Produkt erschienen diese wunderbaren nackten männlichen Körper nicht nur begehrenswert, sondern, genau wie das Produkt, auch verfügbar.

Diese Fotos wurden bald zum Maßstab, wie der schwule Mann auszusehen habe. In der Szene als „Klon-Look" bezeichnet, wurden nackte Haut und durchtrainierte Körper zu einem Muss. Hinzu kamen Schnurrbart, kariertes Hemd und Springerstiefel. An jeder Straßenecke machte ein Fitnessstudio auf. „Straight looking, straight acting" war das Ziel der Homosexuellen, aussehen und sich verhalten wie Heterosexuelle. Als Alternative blieb die Drag Queen. Interessanterweise wurde dieser Trend nicht von Männern begründet, die bereits dem propagierten neuen Stil entsprachen, sondern von den Fotografen. Das Leben imitierte wieder einmal die Kunst.

Bald wurde dieses Aussehen so stark mit Homosexuellen assoziiert, dass die Fotografie wie in der Kampagne für Calvin Kleins CK-Parfüm 1995 wieder zur Androgynität als dem erstrebenswerten Look für Heterosexuelle umschwenkte. Das letzte Jahrzehnt des 20. Jahrhunderts sorgte für reichlich Verwirrung: Auszusehen wie John Wayne oder Tarzan signalisierte Homosexualität, auszusehen wie Mick Jagger oder Jim Morrison das Gegenteil.

Die große Nachfrage nach Männerakten gab den jungen Fotografen eine Chance. Etablierte Fotografen wie Bruce Weber und Herb Ritts scheuten sich noch, nackte Männer von vorn zu zeigen, doch viele ihrer jungen Kollegen ließen, beeinflusst von Robert Mapplethorpe, alle Hemmungen fallen.

An der Westküste schuf sich Jim French mit seinem Colt Studio ein kleines Imperium. Die Colt Studios bieten eine breite Produktpalette an. Sie reicht von

dezenten Kalendern und Terminkalendern, auf denen keine Vorderansichten von
Nackten zu sehen sind, bis zu verschwenderisch ausgeleuchteten Studio- und
Außenaufnahmen riesenhafter Männerkörper in Vorderansicht, allerdings ohne
besondere Betonung der Genitalien. Sie produzieren aber auch Fotoserien von
Männern oder Männerpaaren, die sexuell erregt sind. Colt war auch ins Porno-
geschäft eingestiegen, und viele seiner Fotoserien sind Standfotos aus seinen
Filmen. Standen in dem breiten Spektrum der bildlichen Darstellung des männlichen Aktes die Fotokunst und der Pornofilm einst im schroffen Gegensatz,
so nähern sie sich heute immer stärker einander an.

Heute, zu Beginn des 21. Jahrhunderts, ist die männliche Aktfotografie
ein florierender Wirtschaftszweig. Bücher, Kalender und Postkarten sind allgegenwärtig. Marktführer hierbei sind David Sprigle und Jeff Palmer. Palmers
Hochglanzfotos sind eher idealisierte Darstellungen des männlichen Körpers,
während Sprigle mit seinen Reisen nach Südamerika, um Modelle und Inspira-
tionen zu finden, einen spontanen und eher journalistischen Ansatz in seine
Arbeit einbringt.

Ali und David Morgan haben sich in Miami ihre eigene Welt der nackten
Männer aufgebaut. Ali produziert ausgesprochen erotische Studioaufnahmen
in schwarz-weiß. Morgan präsentiert seine Modelle in einem eher sportlichen
und romantischen Ambiente.

Tom Bianchi hat in seinen Bildern eine rein homosexuelle Welt erschaffen,
in der sich Männer mit perfekten Körpern am Strand oder Swimmingpool rekeln.
Er fotografierte auch Lesben in ähnlicher Szenerie. In seinen Bildern scheint
eine gewisse sexuelle Kameradschaft auf, die vielleicht typisch für Kalifornien
ist. Jedenfalls ist sie nicht romantisch im traditionellen Sinne.

Die kräftigen Körper auf den Bildern von Arthur Tress stehen im Kontrast
zu der kranken Umwelt, den verseuchten Geländen und Industriebrachen, in die
er sie platziert. So wie E.B. White einst notierte, hübsche Mädchen seien die
Blumen einer Stadt, so sind diese Männer vielleicht der schönste Teil einer Welt,
die Tress als zunehmend geschändeten Ort wahrnimmt.

Blake Little, erst seit kurzem in der Szene, lässt seine robusten Kerle in
einer inhaltsleeren, futuristischen Kulisse auftreten, als hätte der Lebensstil,

den wir einst mit schönen Männern in Verbindung brachten, längst an Bedeutung verloren.

David Armstrong beschäftigt sich ebenfalls nicht mit idealisierter Schönheit und fotografiert die ihn umgebende Alltagswelt. Auch Mark Morrisroe stellt seine Modelle auf sehr realistische Weise dar.

Andy Warhols Experimente mit pornographischen Darstellungen waren vor seinem Tod in der Öffentlichkeit kaum bekannt. Er war bleich und außer Atem, berichten seine Assistenten, wenn er Großaufnahmen von Genitalien und Geschlechtsakten aufgenommen hatte. Die Bilder übermalte er anschließend und verlieh ihnen dadurch etwas Künstlerisches.

In zahlreichen Fotobänden vereint Duane Michals poetische Sensibilität mit einem feinen Gespür für die Schönheit des nackten Mannes und kreiert so auf ganz eigene Art eine überaus kultivierte Erotik und Spiritualität, die zu einem Markenzeichen des Künstlers geworden ist.

Unter den Fotografinnen nimmt Dianora Niccolini mit ihrer Fähigkeit, den männlichen Körper sowohl in idealer als auch erotischer Weise zu präsentieren, eine herausragende Stellung ein. Die eher journalistisch arbeitende Annie Leibovitz zeigt uns Sylvester Stallones hochgezüchteten Körper in vorteilhafter Positur. Auch die Modefotografin und Filmregisseurin Rebecca Blake dokumentiert ein kunstvolles Verständnis für die maskuline Schönheit.

Nan Goldin zeigt uns brutal und vorbehaltlos ihre Sicht der Welt, einer von vielen nackten Männern bevölkerten Welt.

Ken Probsts außergewöhnliche und raffinierte Fotos von Dreharbeiten zu Pornofilmen sind schwer einzuordnen. Aber wenn ein Fotograf mit Recht behaupten kann, Pornographie sei nur ein anderer Aspekt von Schönheit, dann ist es Ken Probst.

Überall in den USA tauchen heute neue und interessante Aktfotografen auf. Connie Imboden und Jason Lee arbeiten in Baltimore. Clifford Clark und Don Worth arbeiten weiter an ihren Außenaufnahmen in Kalifornien. Andy Devine ist kürzlich wieder dorthin gezogen, und Klaus Gerhart und Ed Freeman zählen zu den interessantesten Fotografen in Los Angeles. Chuck Smith und Mark Lynch in Austin, Texas, sind Newcomer, die eine unverbrauchte

Sicht in die Aktfotografie einbringen. Das Gleiche gilt für Adrian Jones in Brooklyn und Richard Kern in New York. Dort entstehen auch die aufregenden neuen Bilder von Steve Vaccariello.

Ein bedeutender Aktfotograf in Frankreich ist Patrick Sarfati, der Mitte der 70er in Erscheinung trat. Er ist der Einzige in Europa, der den starken männlichen Körper als eine wunderbare und idealisierte Erscheinung zeigt. Die häufig mediterrane Umgebung auf seinen Bildern knüpft an die Antike an, aber er bedarf keiner Rechtfertigung mehr für seine Götter des Eros. Seine Farbfotos sind vielleicht die schönsten, die in der gegenwärtigen Aktfotografie zu finden sind.

Sarfati war ein früher Förderer von Pierre et Gilles, die ihre Akte in gemalte, herausgeputzte Kitschszenen integrieren. Ihre in Werbeplakate der 50er hinein-retuschierten Akte sind nicht nur erotisch und schön anzusehen, sie verraten auch einiges über unsere Konsumgesellschaft.

Die Aktfotos von schwarzen Modellen, die Tony Butcher in England auf-nimmt, sind sexy und sinnlich. In Holland hat der Choreograph Hans van Manen bewiesen, dass er auch als Fotograf Talent hat. Sein Thema sind Tänzer, deren feinnervige Körper und kräftigen Beine ihm hervorragendes Material liefern. Sein Landsmann Paul Blanca hat seinen eigenen nackten Körper zum Thema seiner Bilder gemacht, die manchmal erschreckend, manchmal wunderschön sind. Mit seinen verwirrenden Arbeiten zählt er zum Underground. Die Bilder von Erwin Olaf hingegen sind Hollands Beitrag zur kommerziellen Aktfotografie.

Gian Paolo Barbieris Arbeiten verknüpfen Fotoreportage und Aktfotografie. Jo Brunenberg bringt strenge Abstraktion und Verweise auf die Renaissance in seine sehr individualistischen Arbeiten ein. Die Fotografen Andreas Bitesnich und Baly Hinter Wipflinger stammen aus Deutschland und machen kraftvolle und originelle Aktaufnahmen. Herlinde Koelbl und Evelyn Krull kommen ebenfalls aus Deutschland. Herb Klein aus Südafrika findet seine Themen in Johannes-burg. Almond Chus innovative Aktfotografie stammt aus Hongkong, China. Daniel Hernández spürt sein Material und seine sinnlichen Modelle in Kolumbien und Miami auf. Und in der Tschechischen Republik erforscht Michael Mackŭ den männlichen Körper mit der Kamera.

Bruno Benini hat seine hervorragenden Arbeiten, darunter viele Fotostudien von Tänzern, in Sydney geschaffen.

Zu Beginn des 21. Jahrhunderts wird deutlich, dass die Fotografie des Männeraktes ein überaus lebendiger Bestandteil unserer Kultur ist. Die Wahrnehmung und Präsentation des männlichen Körpers als Objekt der Lust und Begierde verbinden uns mit der Renaissance und der Antike. Ob dies nun Vorbote einer neuen Gleichheit von Mann und Frau ist, die Vorwegnahme einer neuen polymorphen Sexualität oder nur eine Atempause vor einer neuerlichen Welle der Unterdrückung und des Konservatismus, wissen wir nicht. Die Befreiung des männlichen Körpers aus jahrhundertealten Fesseln bleibt eine Errungenschaft, die man sich nicht mehr nehmen lassen sollte. Wir verdanken sie der Fotografie und den zahllosen Männern und Frauen, die mit ihrem Talent, ihrer Ausdauer, ihrem Mut und vielleicht auch mit Besessenheit darum gekämpft haben.

Les années 60 et 70 virent la photo de nu masculin sortir du placard. Dans les années 80, elle devait occuper le devant de la scène.

Dans l'euphorie des années 80, on dépensait sans compter, notamment dans le domaine de l'art. Les nouveaux millionnaires et milliardaires voulaient investir leur argent dans quelque chose qui se voie et montrer qu'ils (ou leurs épouses) avaient du goût. Robert Mapplethorpe les attendait au tournant. Protégé de Sam Wagstaff, riche collectionneur de photos, Mapplethorpe fut habilement promu comme le créateur d'un nouveau genre de photographies d'art qui se vendaient cher. Son œuvre incluait de jolis bambins, d'élégantes dames de la bonne société, des fleurs délicates et des hommes nus au physique impressionnant, équipés d'organes tout aussi impressionnants.

Parfois, il ne photographiait que l'organe en question, en gros plan. Sa technique stylisée, si adaptée aux portraits d'enfants et aux fleurs, rendait ces images de sexes encore plus choquantes, et ce choc fut le détonateur. La photographie d'art cherchait sa voie, elle venait de la trouver dans le nu masculin.

Lorsque la ville de Cincinnati refusa de montrer les nus de Mapplethorpe dans son musée, le photographe devint une célébrité mondiale. Désormais, montrer des nus masculins revenait à défendre la liberté d'expression artistique. Bientôt, il n'y eut plus une seule exposition de photo sans nus osés. Mapplethorpe ne cachait pas non plus son homosexualité, ce qui aida de nombreux photographes de nu à afficher la leur sans que cela ne fasse scandale.

La déflagration se répercuta jusque dans le monde de la photo publicitaire. Bruce Weber rendit la mode de Ralph Lauren célèbre grâce à ses images d'une aristocratie imaginaire, un univers peuplé de nombreux beaux jeunes hommes au profil patricien et aux muscles saillants. Ils faisaient de la voile, dansaient, nageaient et couraient sur la plage en exhibant des corps qui allaient bientôt être affichés sur tous les murs.

Ces mêmes jeunes hommes envahirent également le monde de Calvin Klein, via Bruce Weber. Puis ils s'emparèrent du vaste budget publicitaire de Gianni Versace. Et de celui de nombreux autres clients.

Richard Avedon reprit ces mêmes jeunes hommes et les coucha entièrement nus aux pieds des nouveaux top modèles habillées en haute couture.

Si les hommes de Bruce Weber semblaient toujours être de gentils garçons surpris dans un moment de nudité ingénue, ceux de Richard Avedon, Herb Ritts, Greg Gorman et bien d'autres encore, n'avaient rien d'innocent. Leurs corps étaient souvent photographiés dans des poses inspirées des sculptures antiques, mais sous des éclairages séducteurs où leur expression et leur posture étaient clairement destinées à éveiller le désir. C'était surtout ce désir qui distingua la photographie des années 80.

Associés à des produits commerciaux, ces superbes corps nus ne semblaient pas uniquement très désirables, mais également très accessibles, à l'instar des produits qu'ils vantaient.

Ces photos établirent rapidement les nouveaux critères de beauté des gays. Se qualifiant eux-mêmes de «clones», les gays se mirent à exhiber leur corps bodybuildé, en le parant de préférence de moustaches, de jeans, de chemises de bûcheron et de Rangers. Des clubs de gym apparurent à tous les coins de rue. L'objectif de tout homosexuel qui se respectait était d'avoir l'air d'un dur. La seule autre alternative était de devenir drag queen. Fait intéressant, cette mode ne fut pas lancée par des hommes qui présentaient cet aspect si désirable, mais par des photos de créatures de rêve qui n'existaient que dans les fantasmes des photographes. Comme l'avait constaté Oscar Wilde un siècle plus tôt, une fois de plus, la nature imitait l'art.

Cette «super-virilité» devint tellement associée à la communauté homosexuelle que, lorsque Calvin Klein lança une nouvelle campagne publicitaire pour son parfum CK Fragrance en 1995, le photographe dut se rabattre sur l'androgynie des années 60 pour trouver un look hétérosexuel convaincant. Du Mick Jagger revu et corrigé. Dans la confusion de la dernière décennie du XXᵉ siècle, ressembler à Tarzan ou à John Wayne signifie que vous êtes gay, avoir l'air de Mick Jagger ou de Jim Morrison, que vous ne l'êtes pas.

La grande demande de nus masculins propulsa des hordes de nouveaux photographes sur le marché. Les chefs de file tels que Bruce Weber ou Herb Ritts évitaient généralement la nudité frontale, mais beaucoup d'autres, inspirés par l'audacieux Robert Mapplethorpe, déballèrent carrément le paquet.

Sur la côte ouest, Jim French a bâti un véritable empire avec ses studios Colt où il photographie les plus baraqués d'entre les baraqués. Ses éditions proposent une vaste gamme de produits allant des calendriers et des agendas les plus softs, sans nudité frontale, aux photos somptueusement éclairées, en studio et en extérieur, présentant des corps sculpturaux vus de face, mais sans que l'accent soit mis particulièrement sur les organes génitaux, et jusqu'aux photos d'hommes en érection, seuls ou en groupe. Colt ayant également fait son entrée dans l'industrie du porno, bon nombre de ses albums contiennent des arrêts sur images de ses films. La photographie d'art et la pornographie, qui se situaient autrefois aux deux extrêmes du nu masculin, se rapprochent à présent, et plus rapidement qu'on ne le croit.

Dans les années 90, le nu masculin est devenu une industrie florissante. Les livres, les calendriers et les cartes postales se renouvellent sans cesse. En Californie, David Sprigle et Jeff Palmer mènent la danse. Les photos de Palmer, très sophistiquées, présentent le corps masculin d'une manière plus idéalisée. Sprigle, qui cherche ses modèles et son inspiration en Amérique du Sud, réalise des images plus spontanées et documentaires, mais d'une excellente qualité photographique et émotionnelle.

A Miami, Ali et David Morgan ont créé leur propre univers de nus masculins, Ali avec des photos de studio très érotiques, marquées par de forts constrates noirs et blancs, Morgan dans un style plus athlétique et fleur bleue.

A Los Angeles, Tom Bianchi s'est inventé un environnement complètement homosexuel où des groupes d'hommes au corps parfait batifolent au bord de piscines ou sur la plage. Il a également, dans le même style, photographié des lesbiennes. Ses images dégagent une atmosphère de camaraderie sexuelle plutôt californienne, mais on ne peut pas franchement parler de « fleur bleue » dans son cas.

Arthur Tress photographie des corps puissants dans des bidonvilles ou des entrepôts abandonnés. E.B. White déclara un jour que les jolies filles étaient les fleurs de la ville. Les hommes de Tress représentent sans doute la part de beauté dans un monde de plus en plus dénaturé.

Nouveau venu, Blake Little place ses vigoureux gaillards dans une atmosphère au dépouillement futuriste, comme si tous les biais par lesquels nous
considérions la beauté masculine autrefois n'avaient plus d'importance.

David Armstrong, moins intéressé par l'idéal de beauté, photographie le
monde tel qu'il le voit. Mark Morrisroe présente, lui aussi, ses hommes sous un
angle cru et réaliste.

Dans le domaine de la photographie purement artistique, les expériences
d'Andy Warhol avec une pornographie faite maison eurent peu d'écho jusqu'après sa mort. Ses gros plans d'organes génitaux et de rapport sexuels,
qui le faisaient ressortir de la salle de bains le teint blême et le souffle court
(d'après ses assistants) furent ensuite repeints et élevés à quelque chose de
plus artistique.

Les nombreux ouvrages de Duane Michals, qui marient la sensibilité poé-
tique à une appréciation subtile de la beauté du corps masculin, dégagent un
érotisme raffiné et une spiritualité qui n'appartiennent qu'à lui.

Parmi les femmes photographes, Dianora Niccolini occupe une position
prééminente par sa faculté de présenter le corps masculin à la fois comme un
objet érotique et un idéal. Plus journalistique, Annie Leibovitz a su mettre en
valeur le corps gonflé à bloc de Sylvester Stallone. Lorsqu'on lui en donne la
possibilité, Rebecca Blake, photographe de mode et réalisatrice, présente une
image racée de la beauté masculine.

Nan Goldin nous offre sa vision d'un monde brutal et sans concessions.
Un monde peuplé de nombreux hommes nus.

Le travail remarquable et raffiné de Ken Probst sur les plateaux de films
porno est difficile à classer. Jamais un photographe n'aura mieux présenté la
pornographie comme l'une des multiples facettes de la beauté.

D'intéressants jeunes photographes de nu masculin surgissent un peu
partout aux Etats-Unis. Connie Imhoden et Jason Lee à Baltimore. Clifford
Clark, qui continue ses photos en extérieur en Californie, tout comme Don
Worth. Andy Devine vient également de s'y installer. Klaus Gerhart et Ed
Freeman font un travail passionnant à Los Angeles. Chuck Smith, à Minnea-
polis, et Mark Lynch, à Austin, Texas, apportent une vision fraîche du nu

masculin. Tout comme Adrian Jones à Brooklyn et Richard Kern à New York, où Steve Vaccariello réalise également ses images excitantes.

En France, le grand photographe de nu masculin est sans conteste Patrick Sarfati. Apparu dans les années 70, il est le seul en Europe à présenter des corps puissants à la fois beaux et idéalisés. Ses images baignent souvent dans une atmosphère méditerranéenne qui les relie à un passé classique, mais il n'offre aucun prétexte pour ses dieux mythiques. Son travail en couleur est sans doute ce qui se fait de mieux aujourd'hui en matière de nu masculin. Il fut l'un des premiers défenseurs de Pierre et Gilles, dont l'univers bigarré et kitsch inclut des hommes dévêtus. Leurs nus masculins retouchés dans le style des publicités des années 50 sont, non seulement érotiques et beaux, mais également révélateurs sur notre société de consommation.

En Angleterre, Tony Butcher réalise des images sensuelles et sexuelles de modèles noirs.

En Hollande, le chorégraphe Hans van Manen sait photographier le nu masculin avec talent. Bon nombre de ses modèles sont des danseurs, dont les corps fermes et les cuisses musclées lui ont été d'excellentes sources d'inspiration. Son compatriote Paul Blanca se sert de son propre corps nu pour réaliser des images tantôt effrayantes, tantôt d'une grande beauté. Erwin Olaf, lui, est la contribution de la Hollande à la photographie de nus publicitaires.

Le travail récent de Gian Paolo Barbieri mêle le reportage à de magnifiques nus masculins. L'œuvre très personnelle de Jo Brunenberg converge vers l'abstraction et les allusions à la Renaissance. En Allemagne, Andreas Bitesnich et Baly Hinter Wipflinger réalisent tous deux des nus puissants et originaux. Parmi les autres photographes allemands intéressants, on ne saurait oublier Herlinde Koelbl et Evelyn Krull.

En Afrique du Sud, Herb Klein ne cesse de découvrir d'intéressants modèles à Johannesburg. Almond Chu réalise des images innovatrices d'hommes nus à Hong Kong, Chine. Daniel Hernández trouve des thèmes et des modèles sensuels à Miami et en Colombie. En République tchèque, Michael Macku explore le corps masculin avec son objectif. A Sidney, Bruno Benini crée de remarquables études, souvent de danseurs.

Au début du XXIe siècle, il est évident que la photographie de nu masculin se porte bien. Le besoin urgent de rejeter les contraintes étouffantes de l'ère victorienne et les attitudes machistes l'a emporté. Bien que la libération des images de l'homme nu ait connu des hauts et des bas au cours de ce siècle, elles n'ont jamais cessé de se multiplier.

La transformation du corps de l'homme en objet sexuel nous relie fortement à la Renaissance et, plus loin encore, à l'Antiquité. Il est difficile de dire si elle traduit l'égalité entre les hommes et les femmes, si elle annonce une nouvelle forme de sexualité polymorphe ou si elle constitue une simple bouffée de paganisme rafraîchissante avant une nouvelle vague de répression et de conservatisme. Une chose est sûre, la libération du corps masculin ne s'est faite que grâce à la photographie. Les hommes et les femmes qui l'ont rendue possible par leur talent, leur persévérance, leur courage et, parfois, leurs fantasmes, méritent tout notre respect. Le temps continuera probablement à leur donner raison.

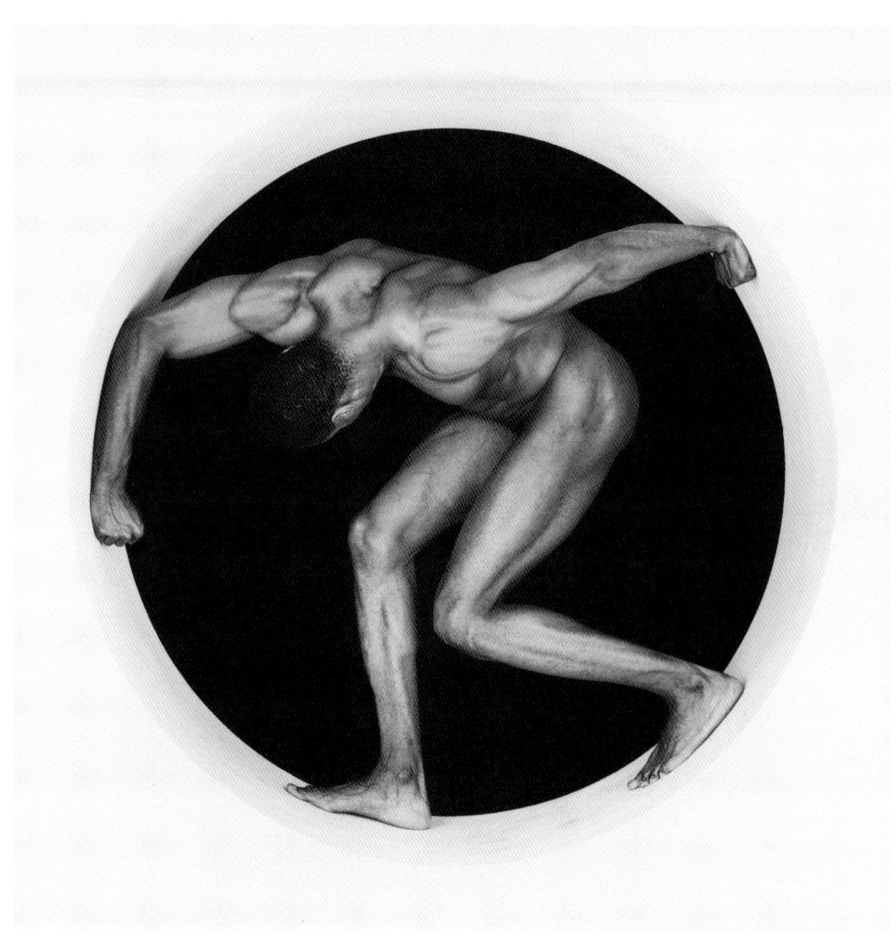

Robert Mapplethorpe, Thomas, 1987

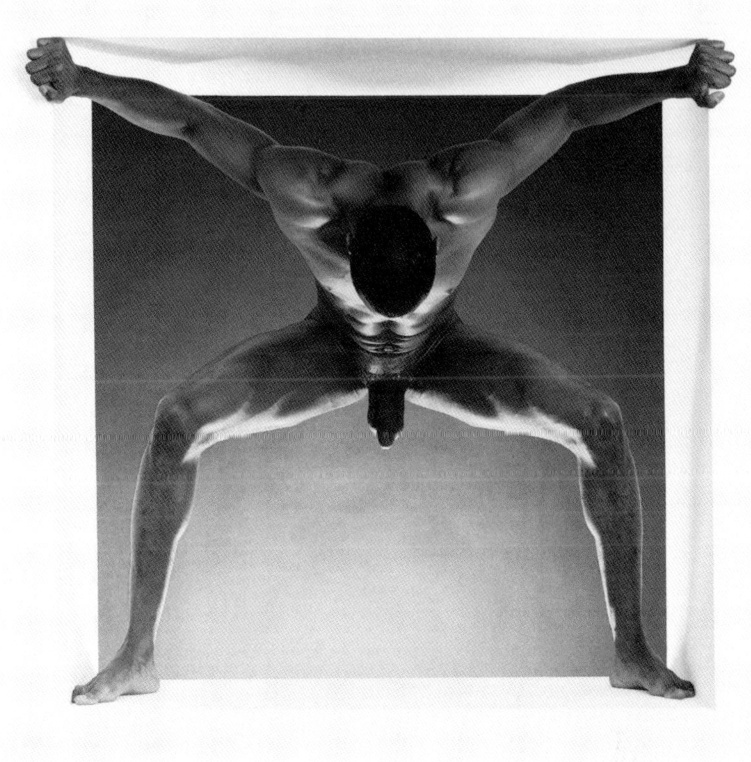

Robert Mapplethorpe, Thomas, 1986

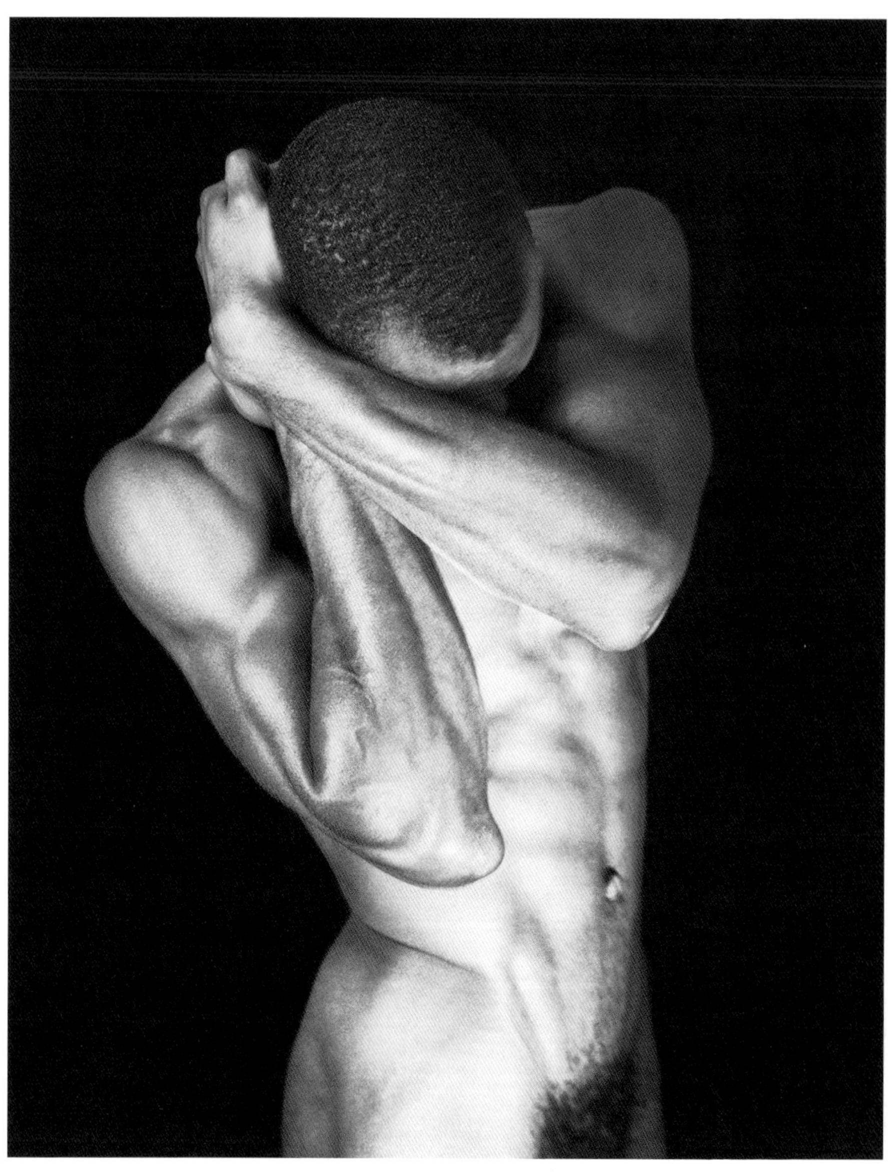

Robert Mapplethorpe, Thomas, 1986

402

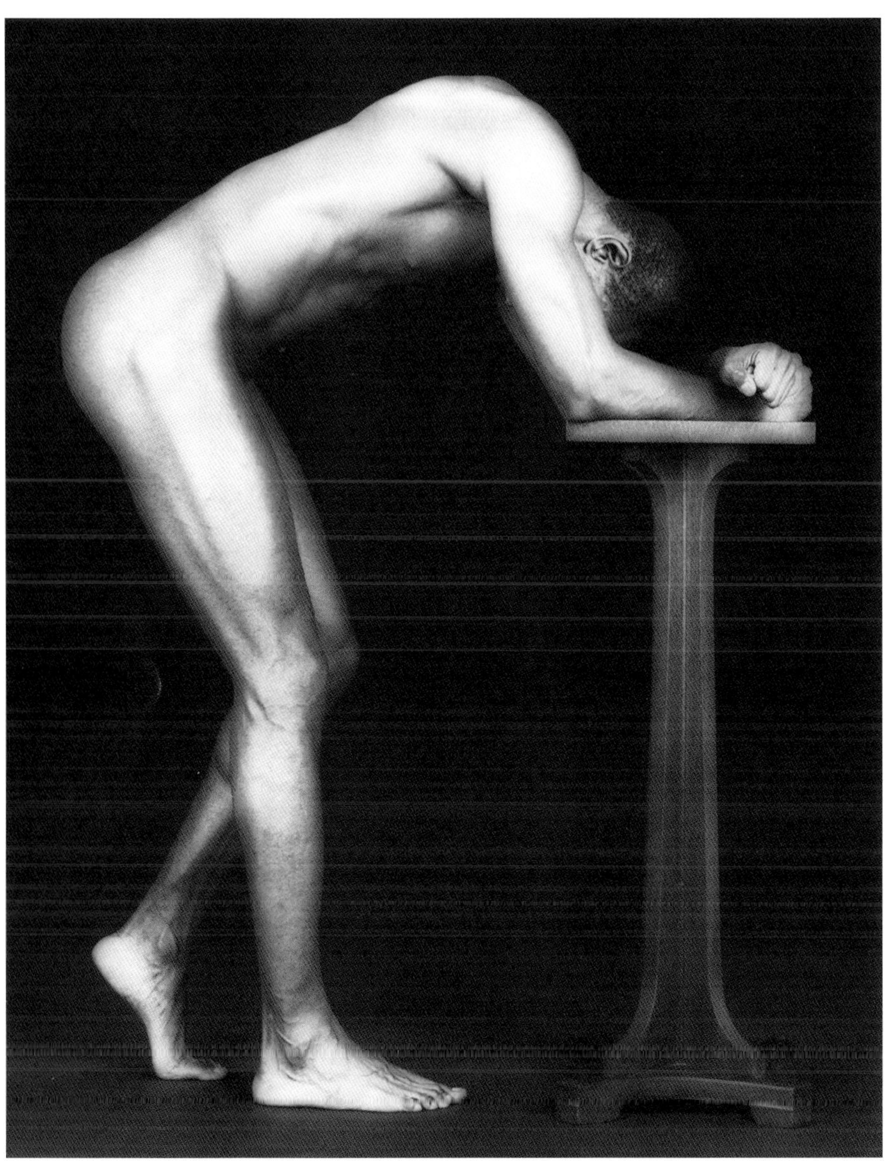

Robert Mapplethorpe, Thomas, 1986

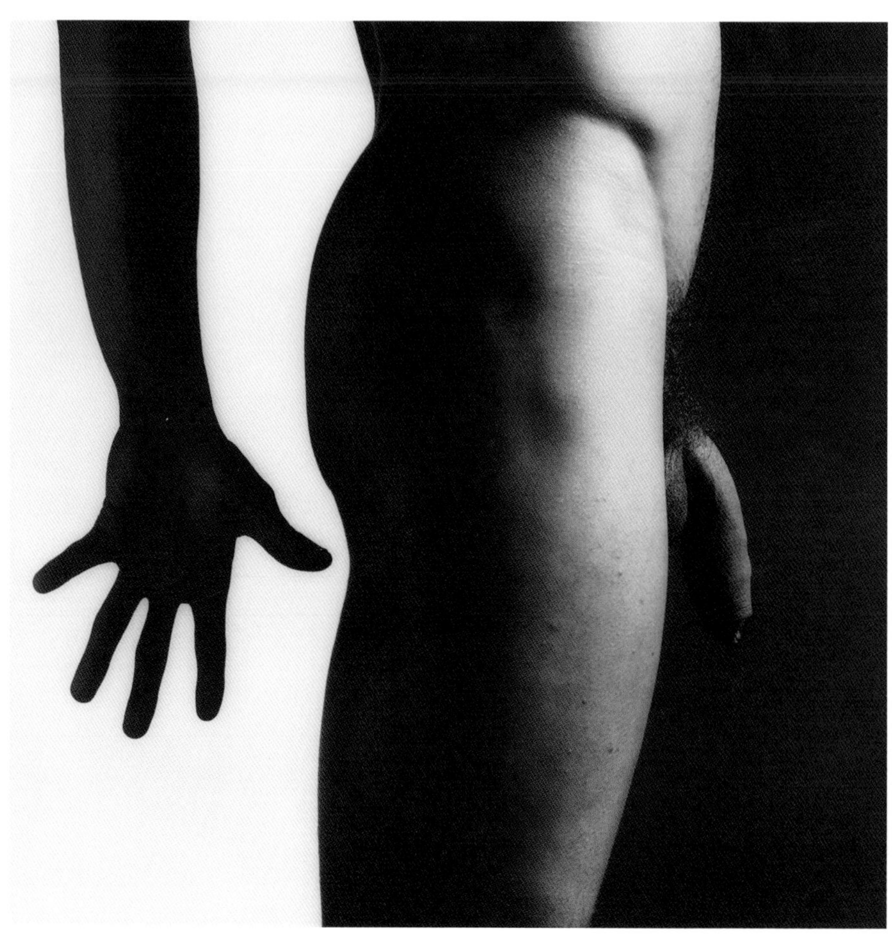

Robert Mapplethorpe, Untitled, 1981

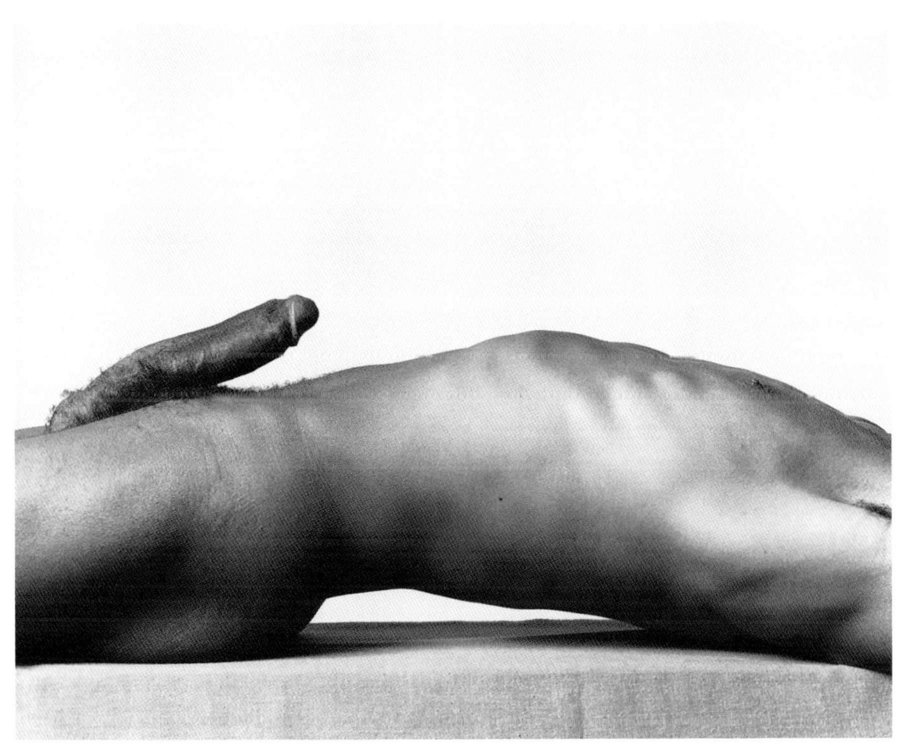

Robert Mapplethorpe, Christopher Holly, 1980

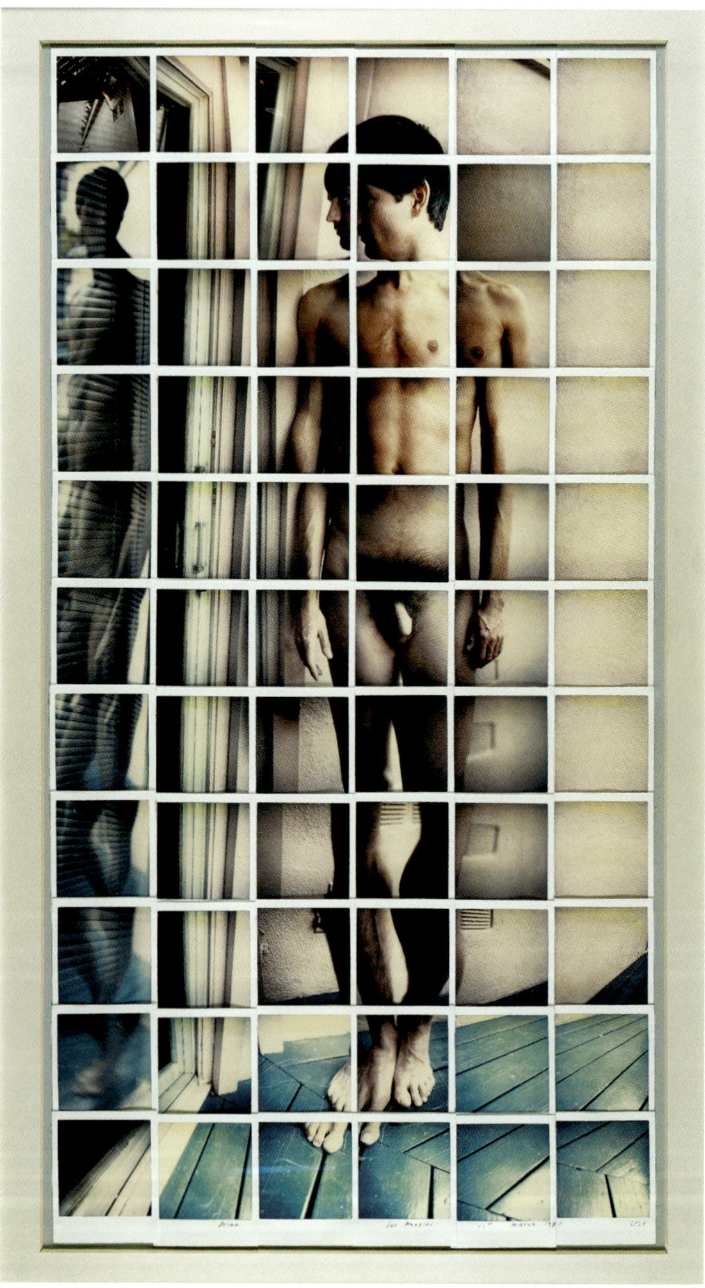

  David Hockney, Brian, Los Angeles, 21st March 1982

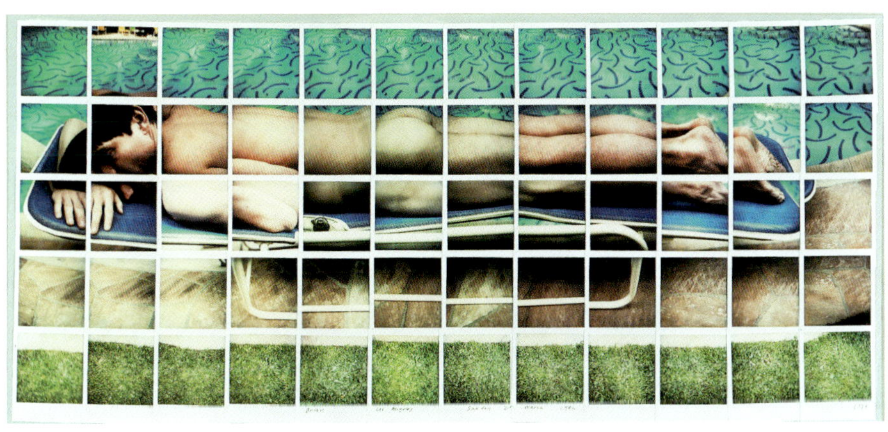

David Hockney, Brian, Los Angeles, Sunday 21st March 1982

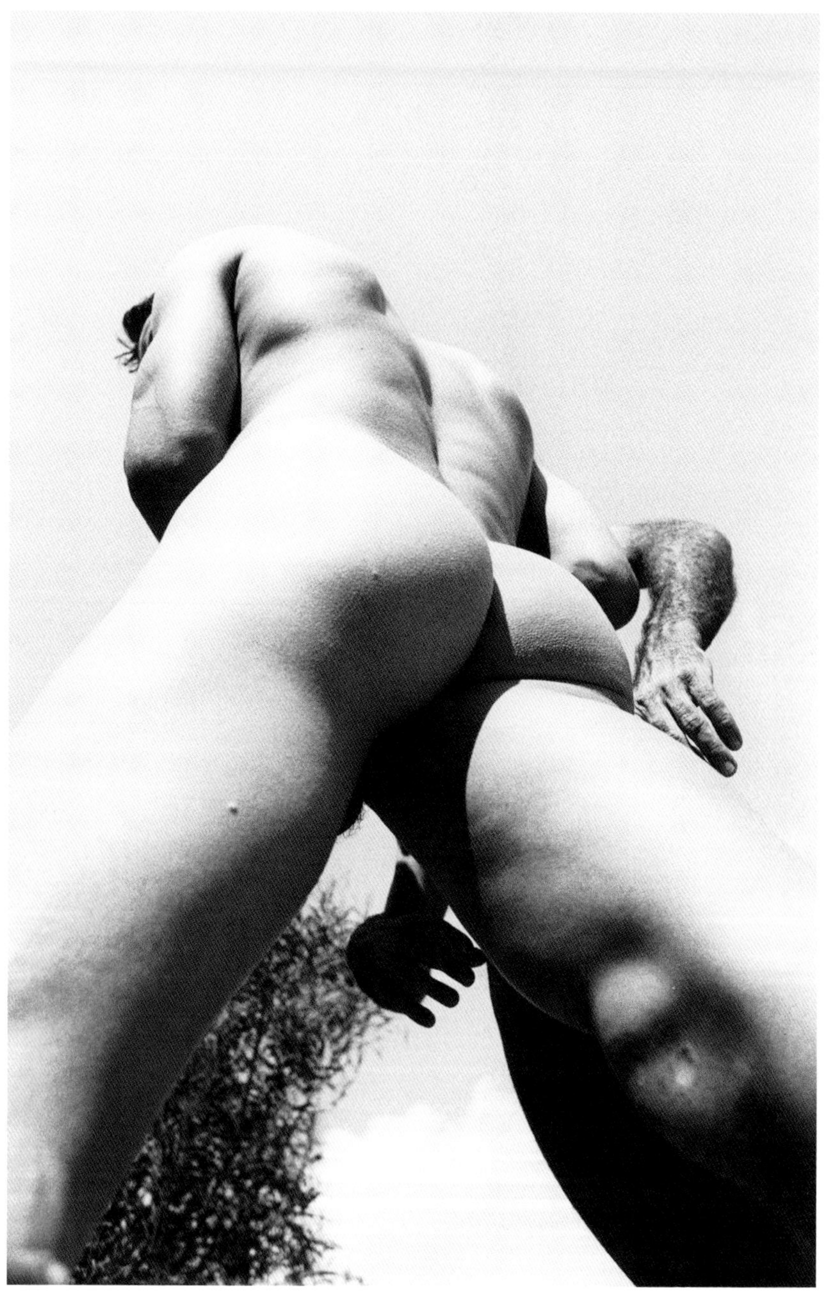

Ernestine Ruben, Hunks, 1989

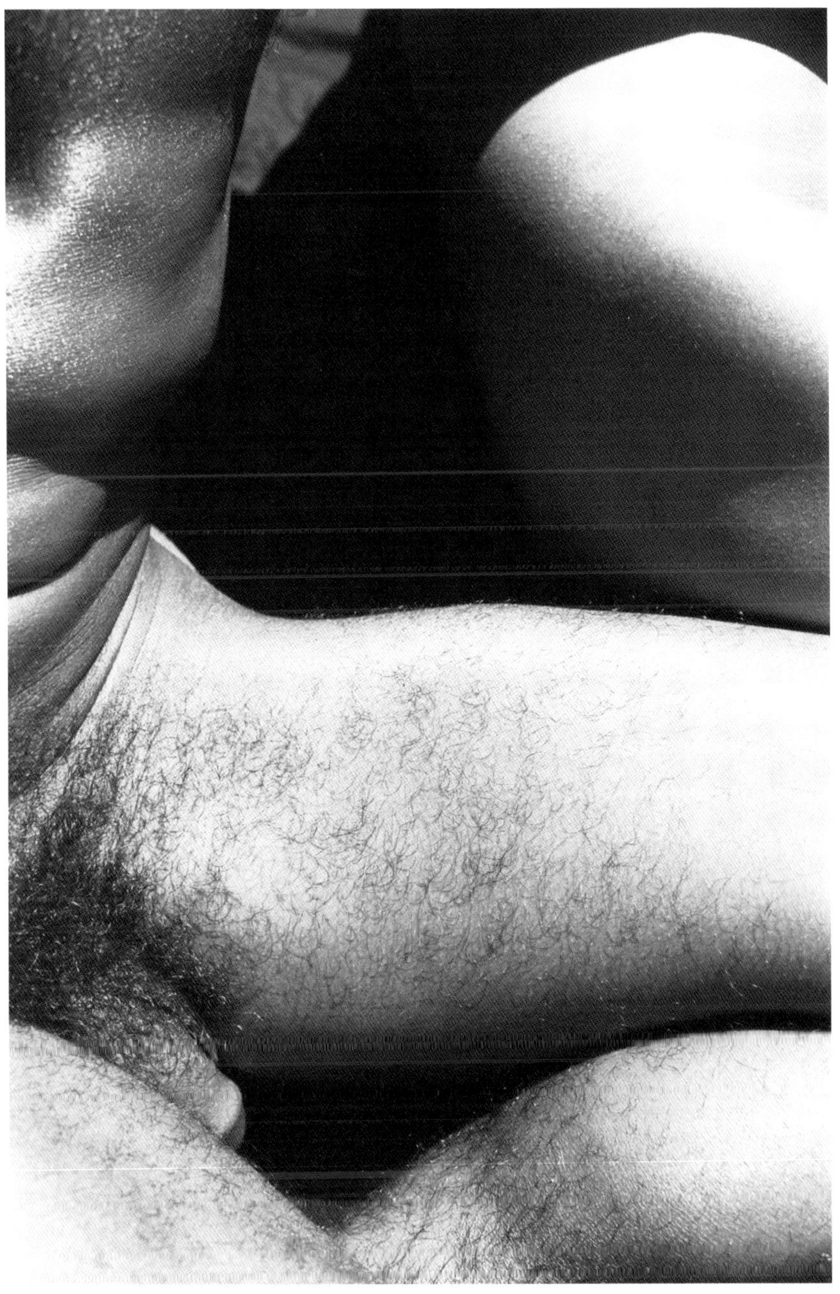

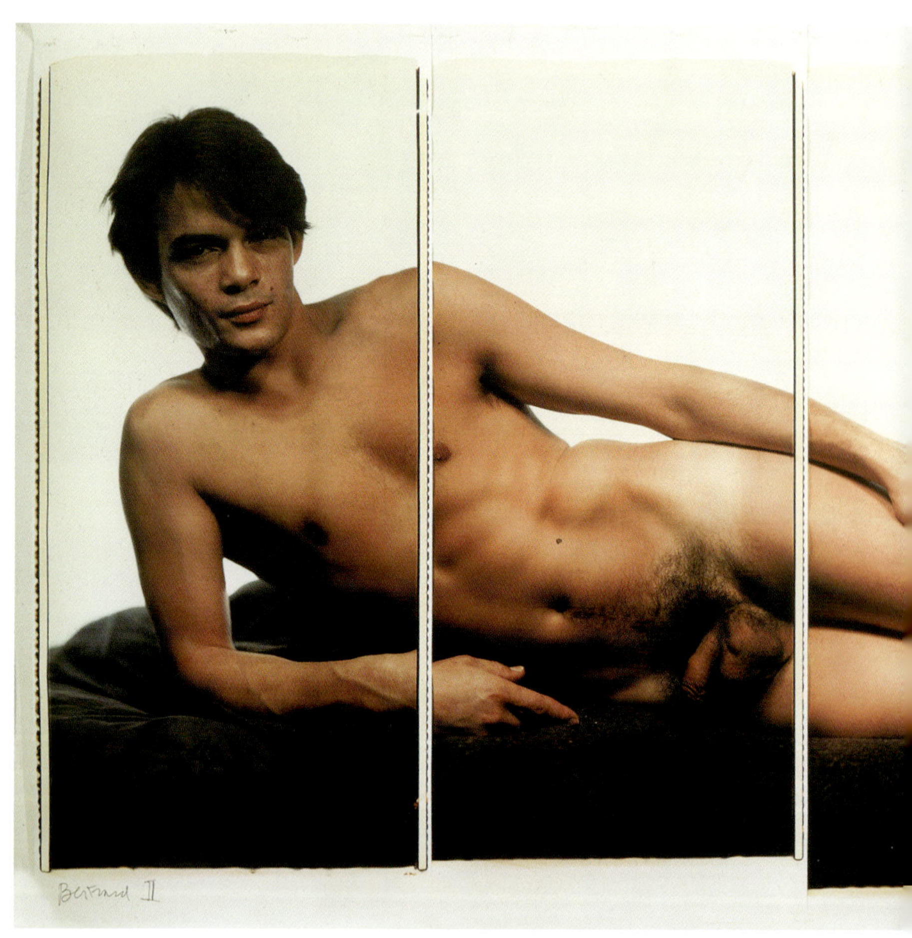

Chuck Close, Bertrand 2, 1984

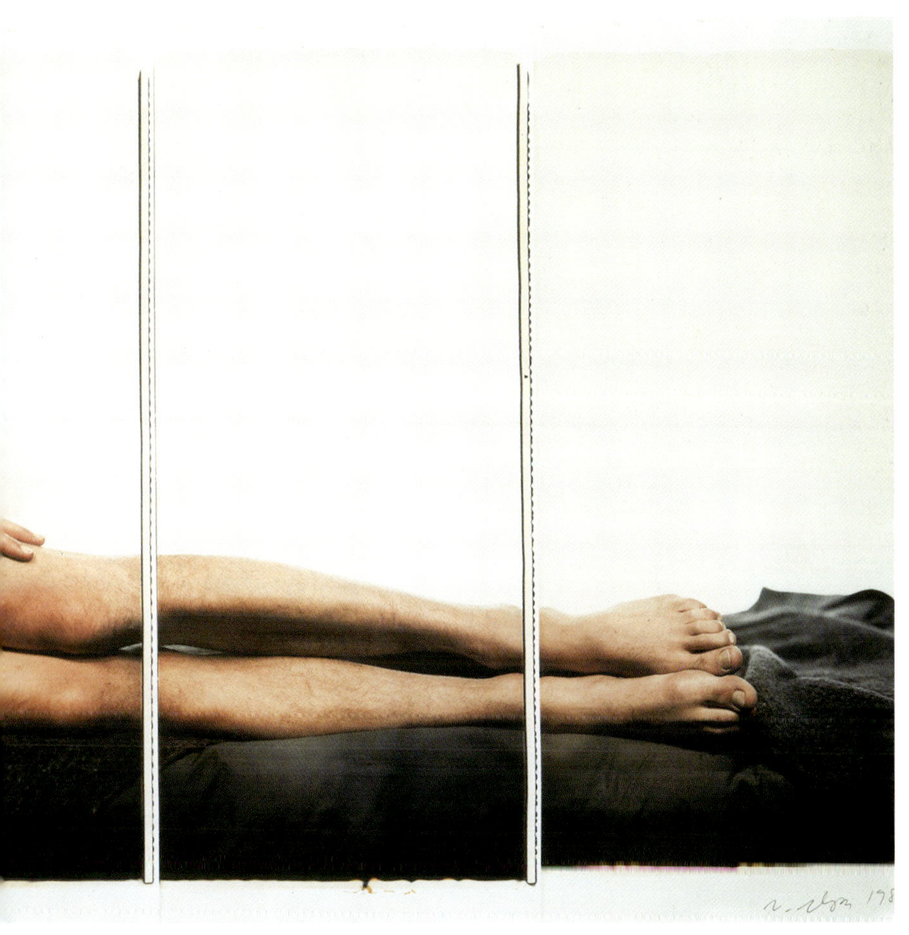

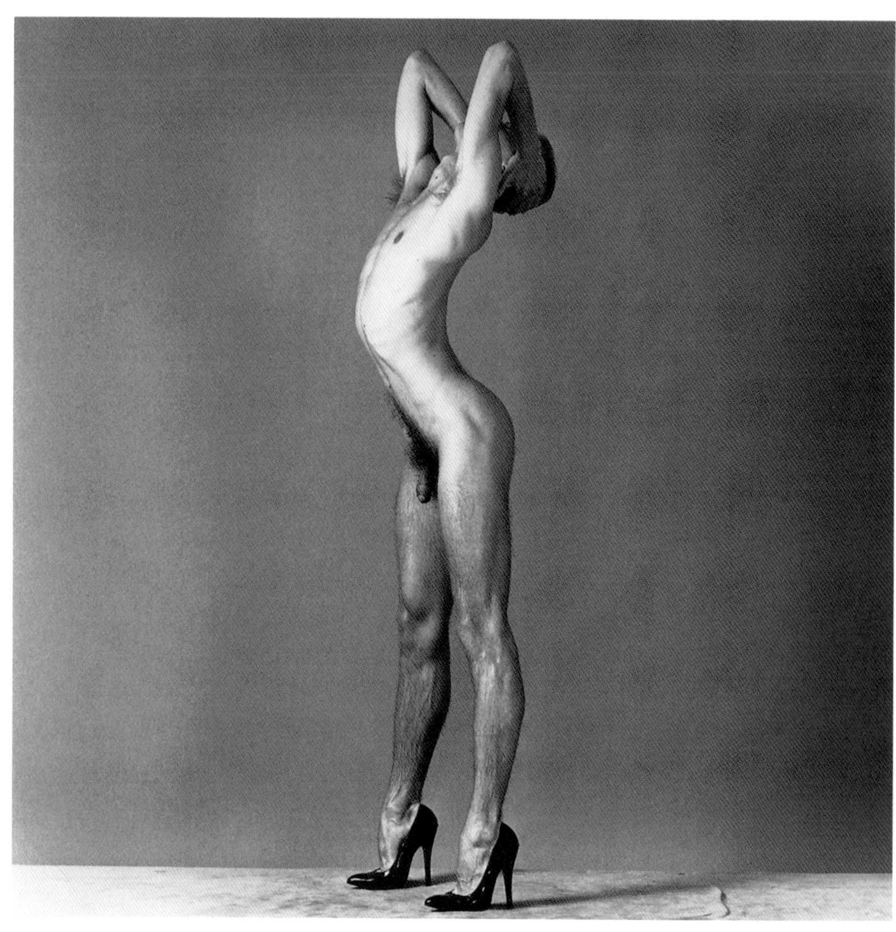

Hans van Manen, Hans van der Heijden, 1986

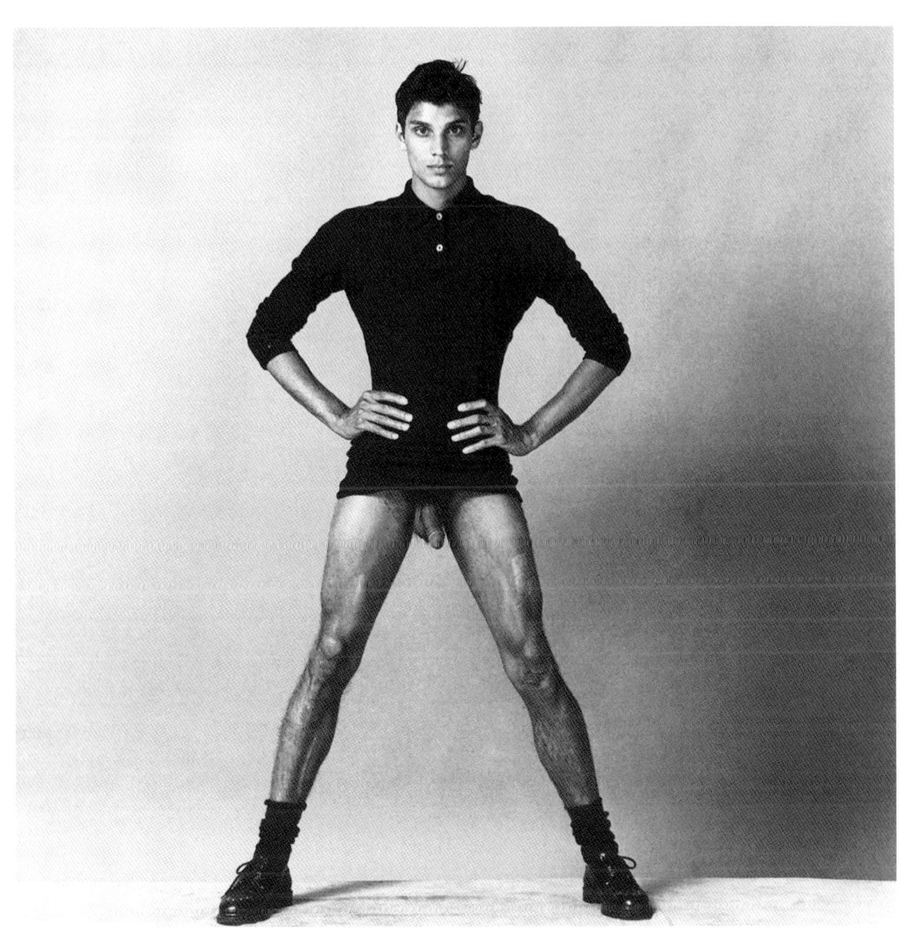

Hans van Manen, Vinoodh Matadin, 1986

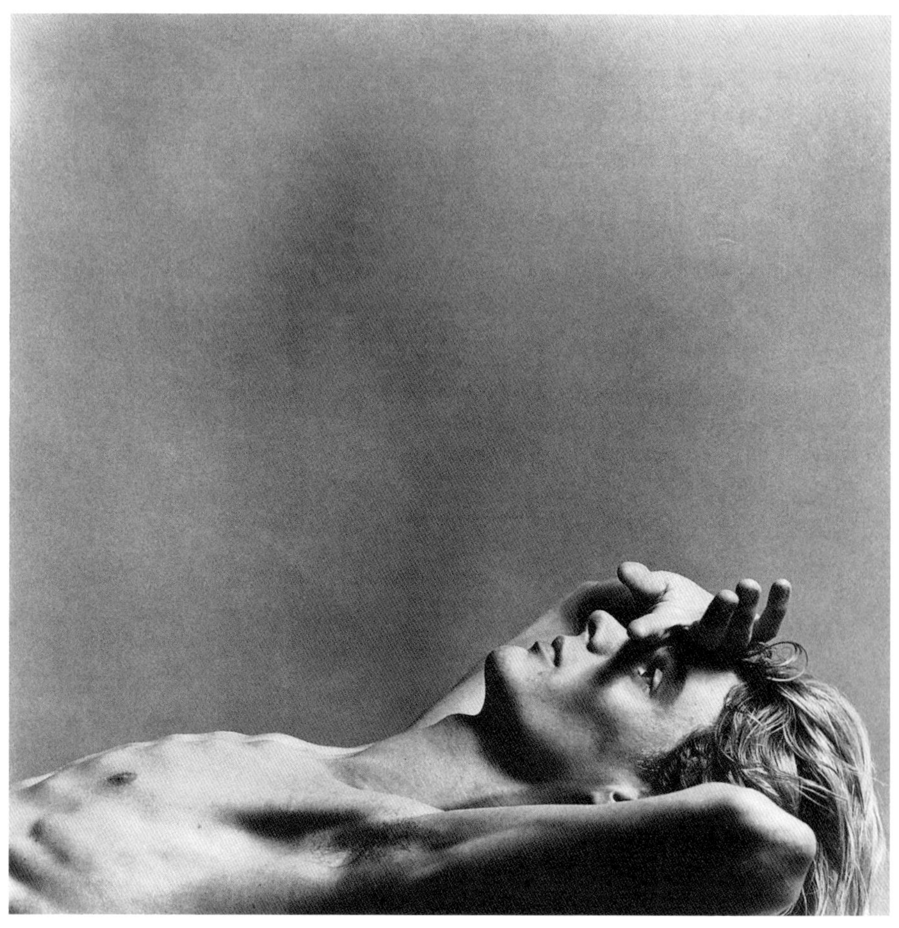

Hans van Manen, Albert Jan van der Stel, 1983

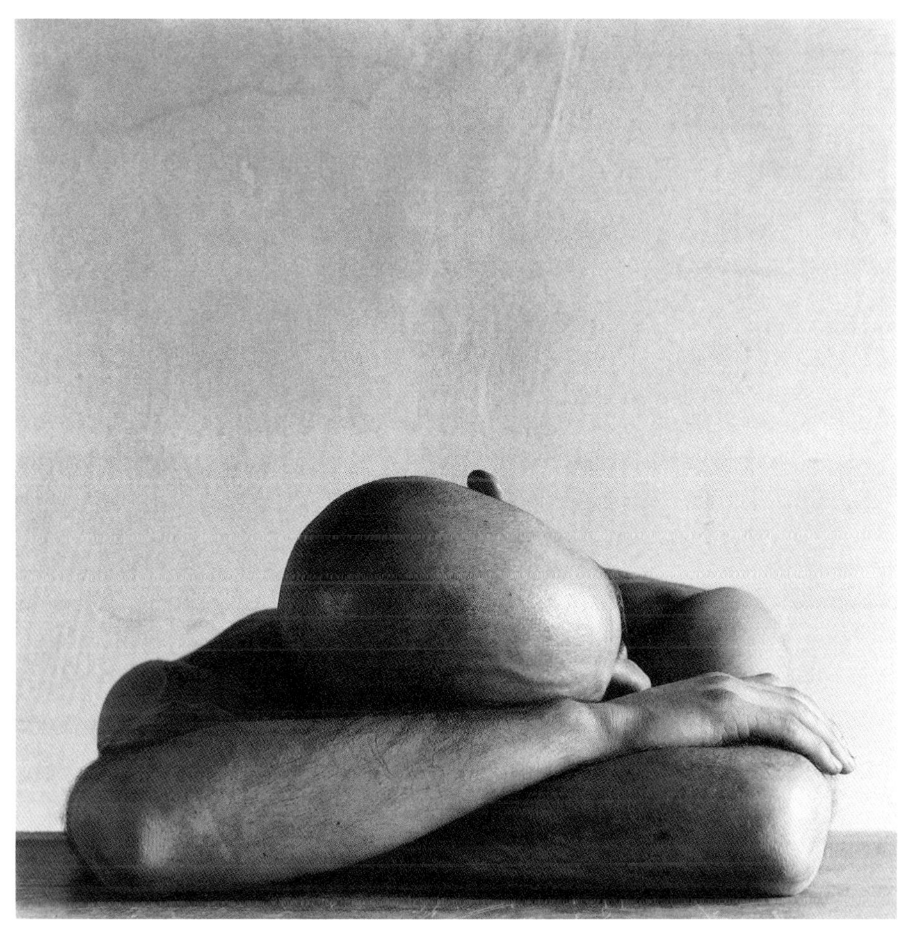

Hans van Manen, Tony Westwood, 1983

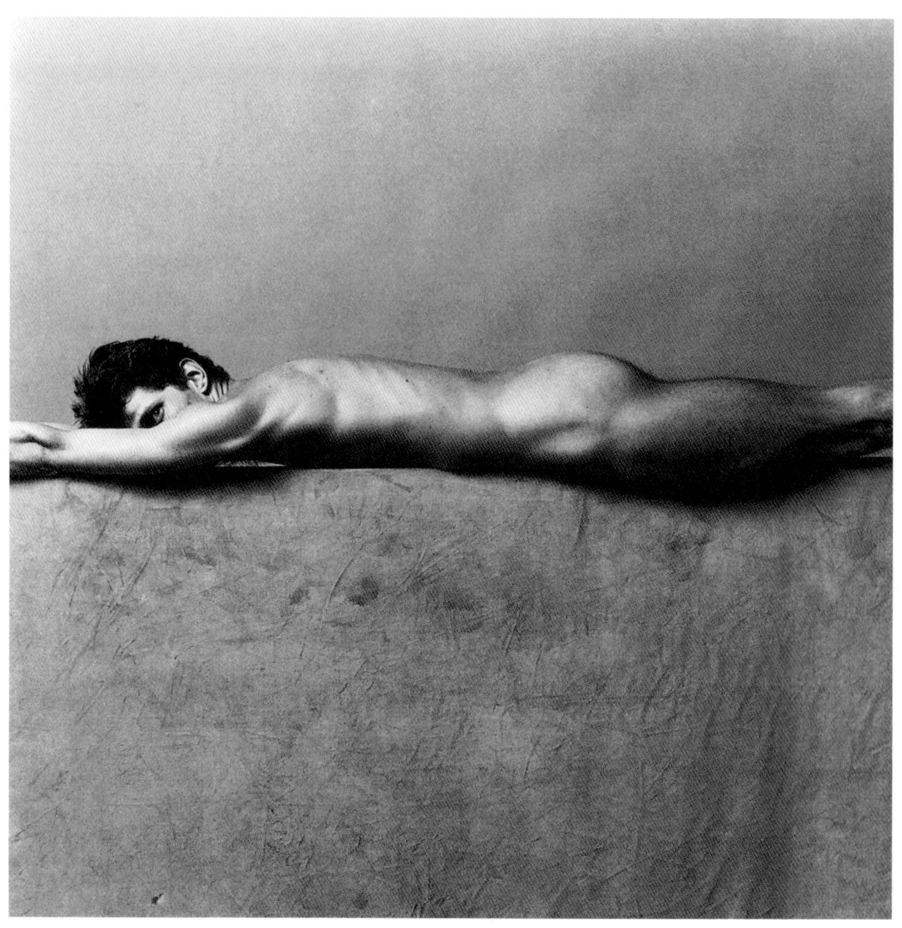

Hans van Manen, Erwin Olaf, 1984

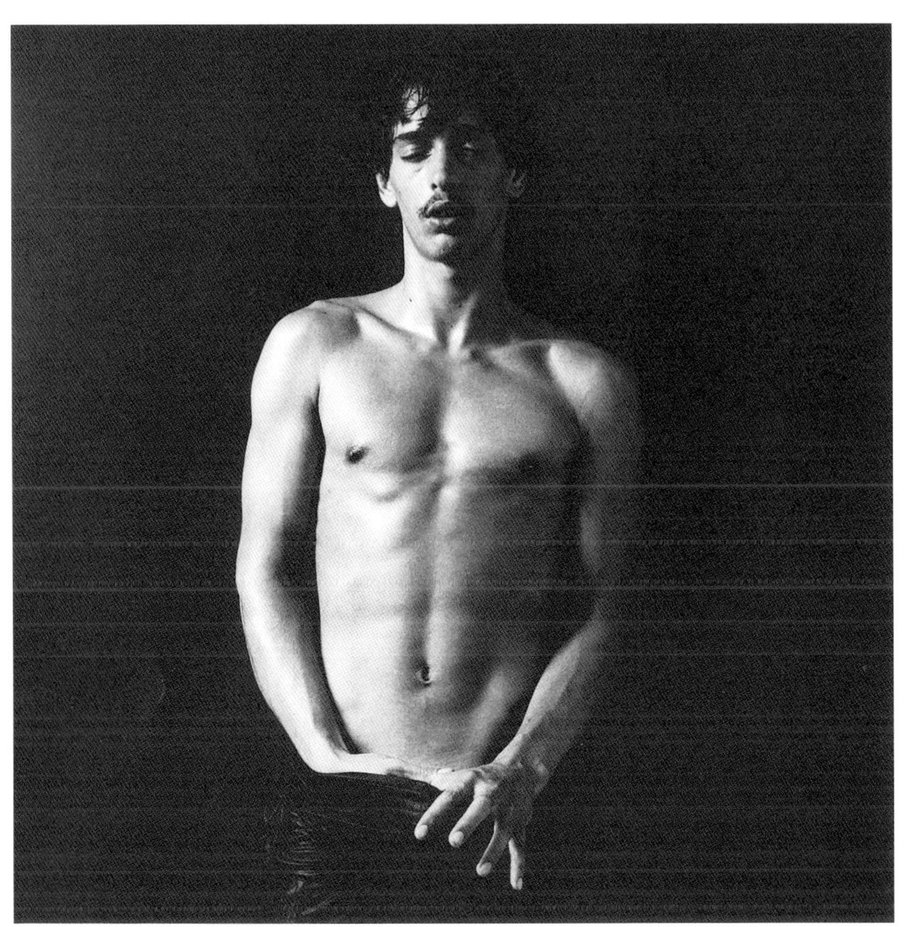

Hans van Manen, Interior – Robbie Smit, 1984

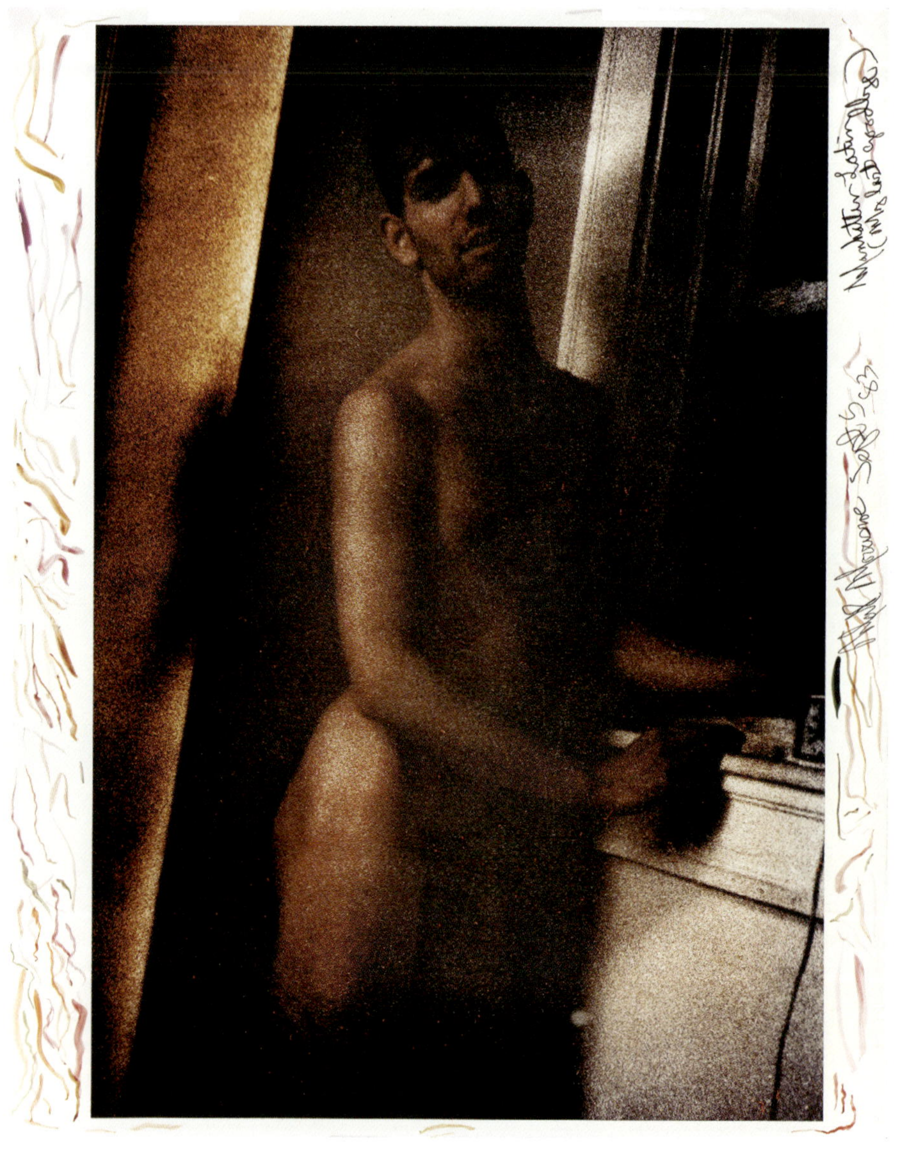

Mark Morrisroe, Manhatten Latin (My Last Goodbye), 1983

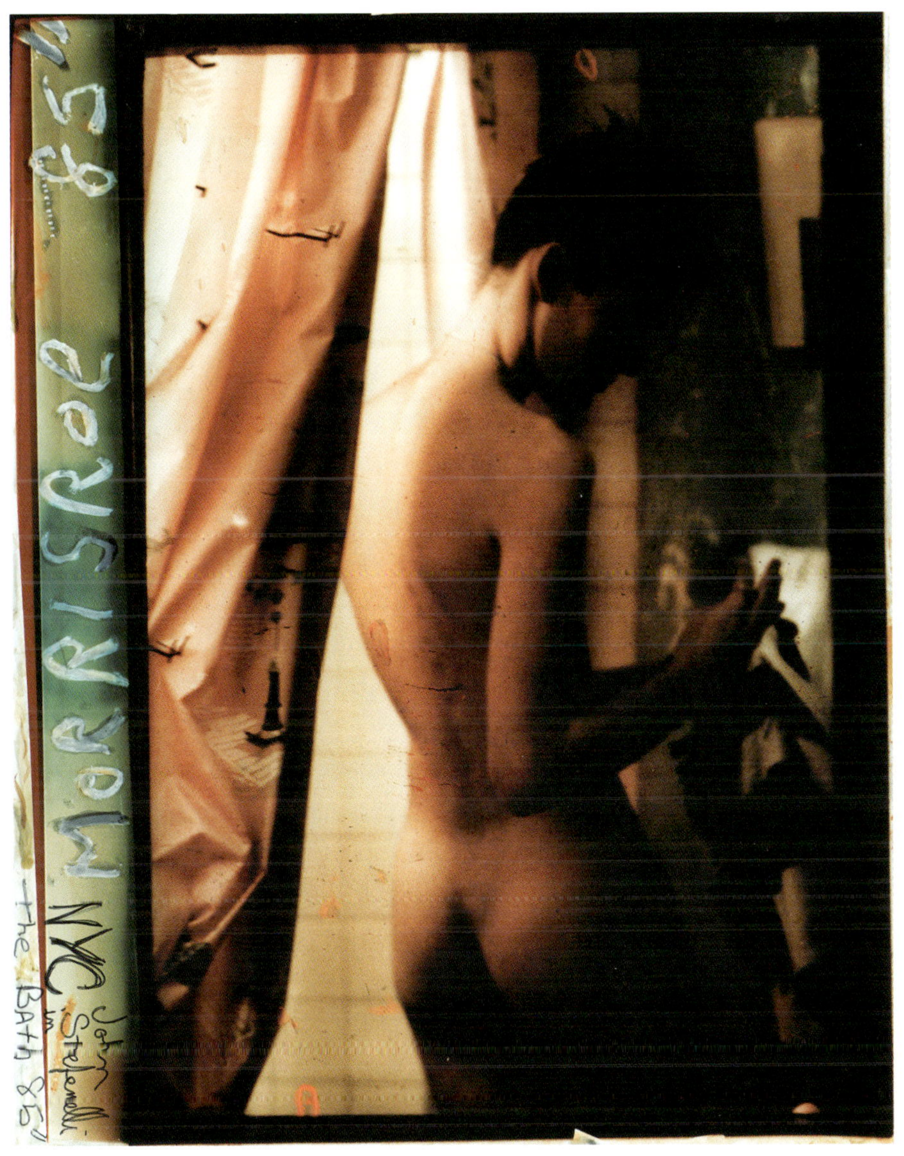

Mark Morrisroe, N.Y.C. John Stefenelli in the Bath, 1985

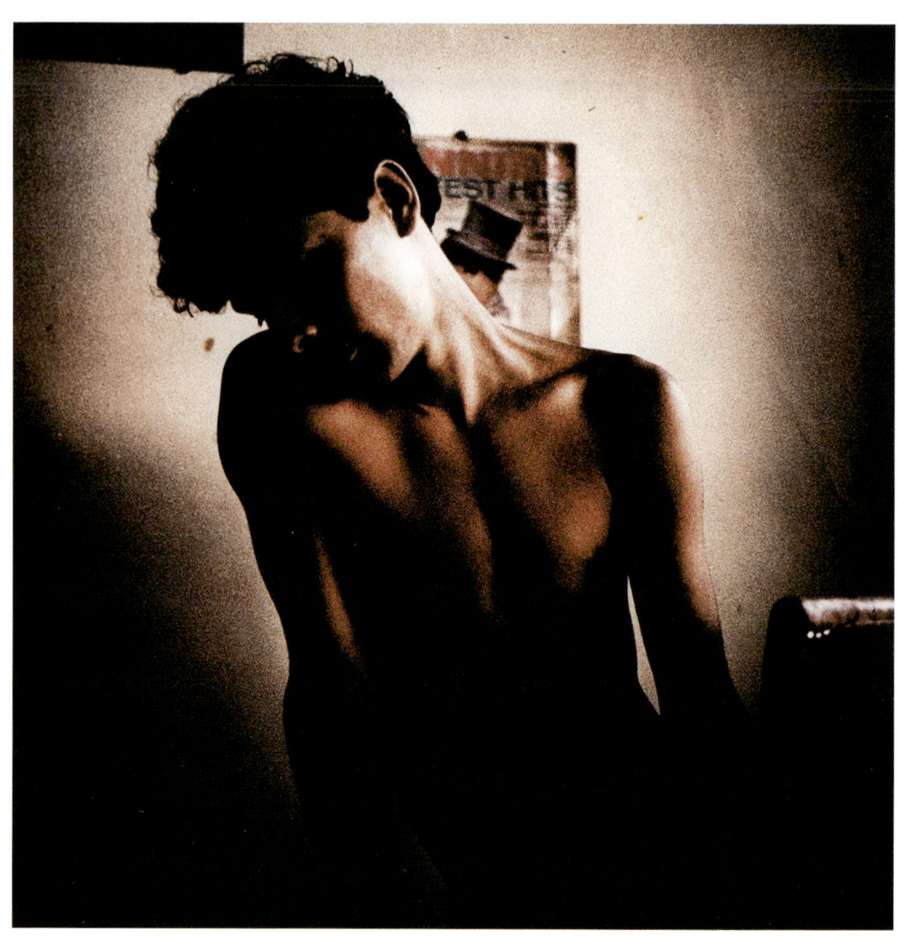

Mark Morrisroe, Untitled, 1982

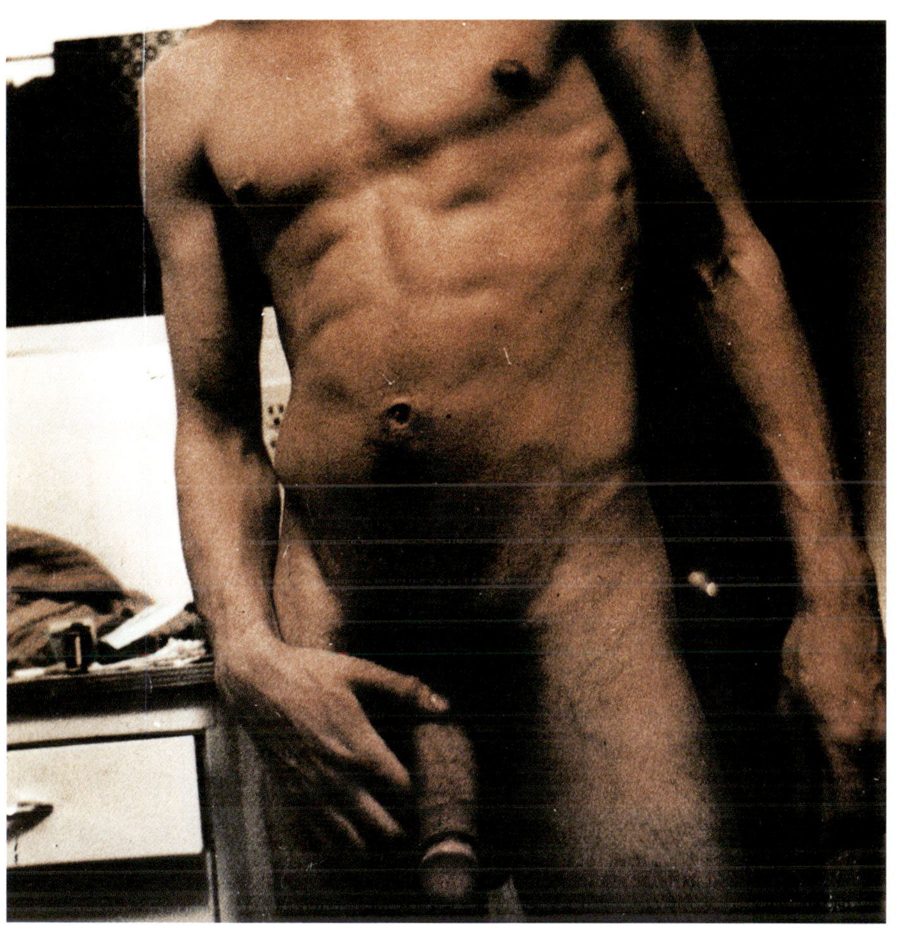

Mark Morrisroe, Untitled, 1982

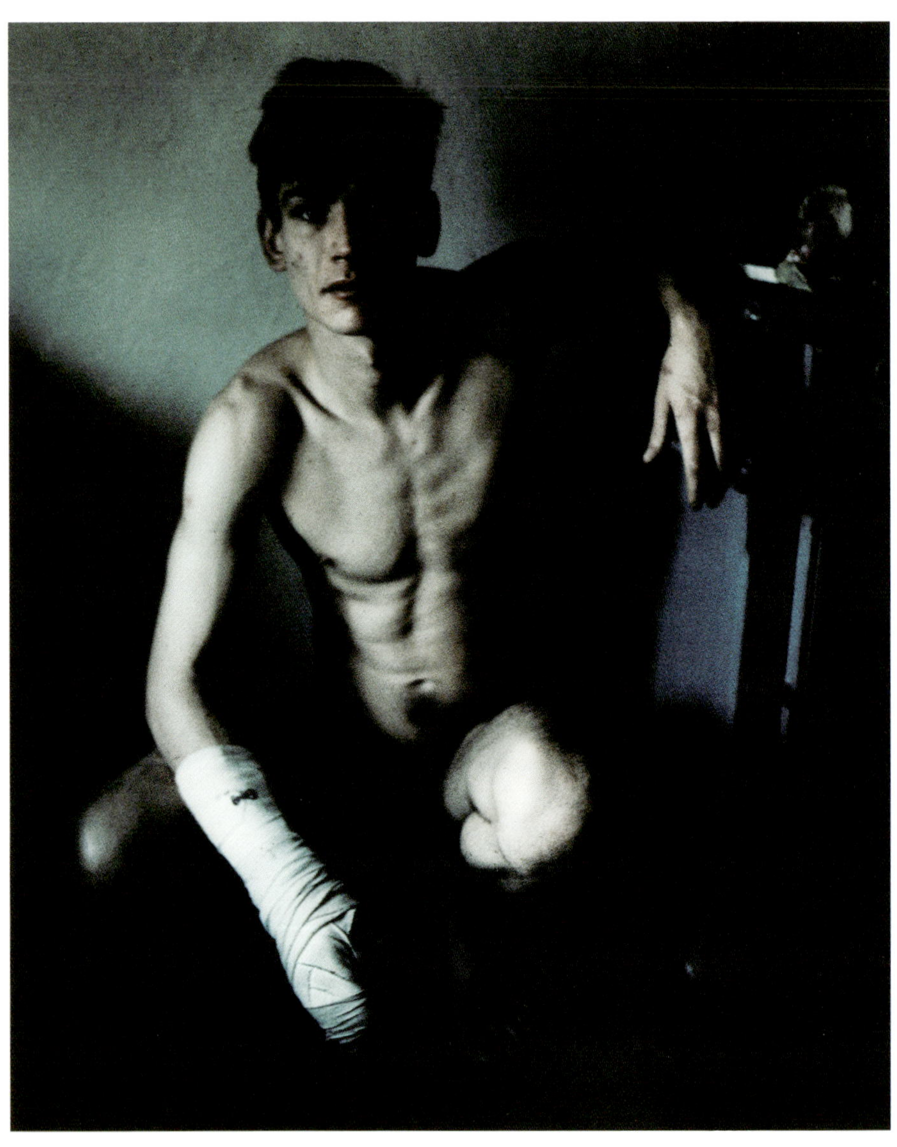

Mark Morrisroe, Untitled, 1984

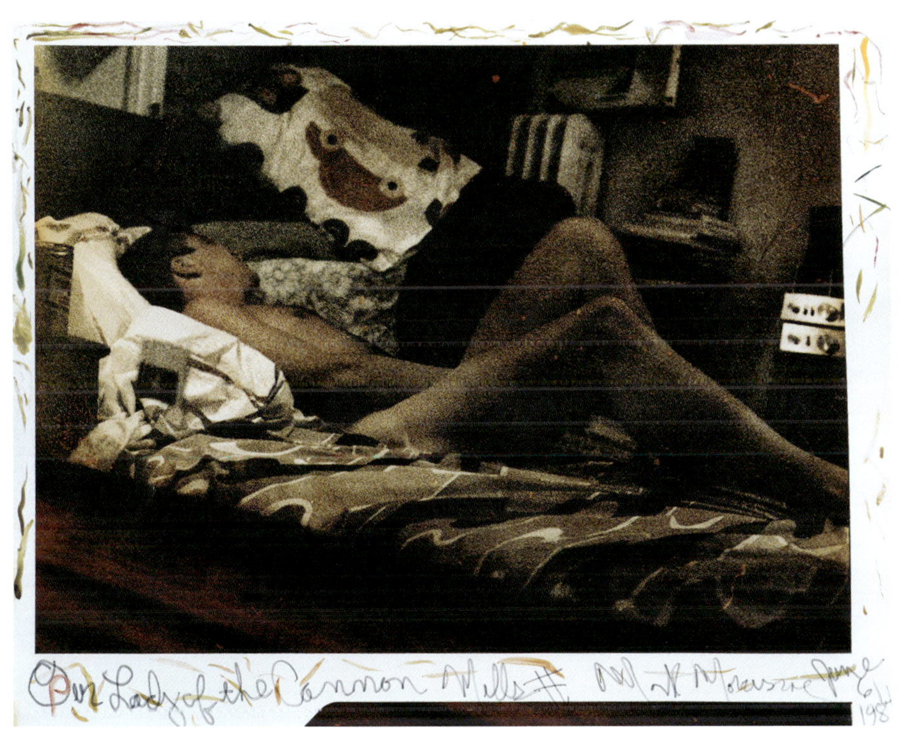

Mark Morrisroe, Our Lady of the Cannon Wells, 1984

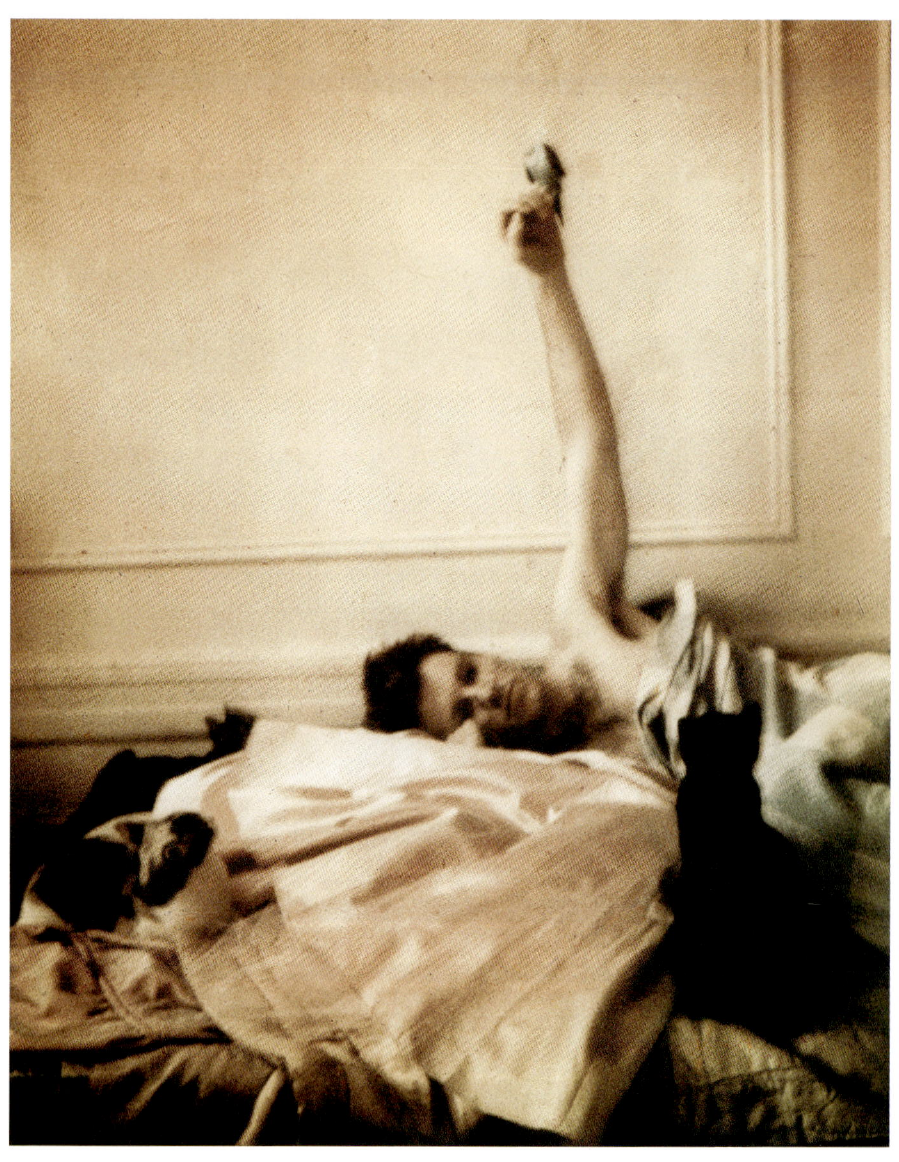

Mark Morrisroe, Fascination 83, 1983

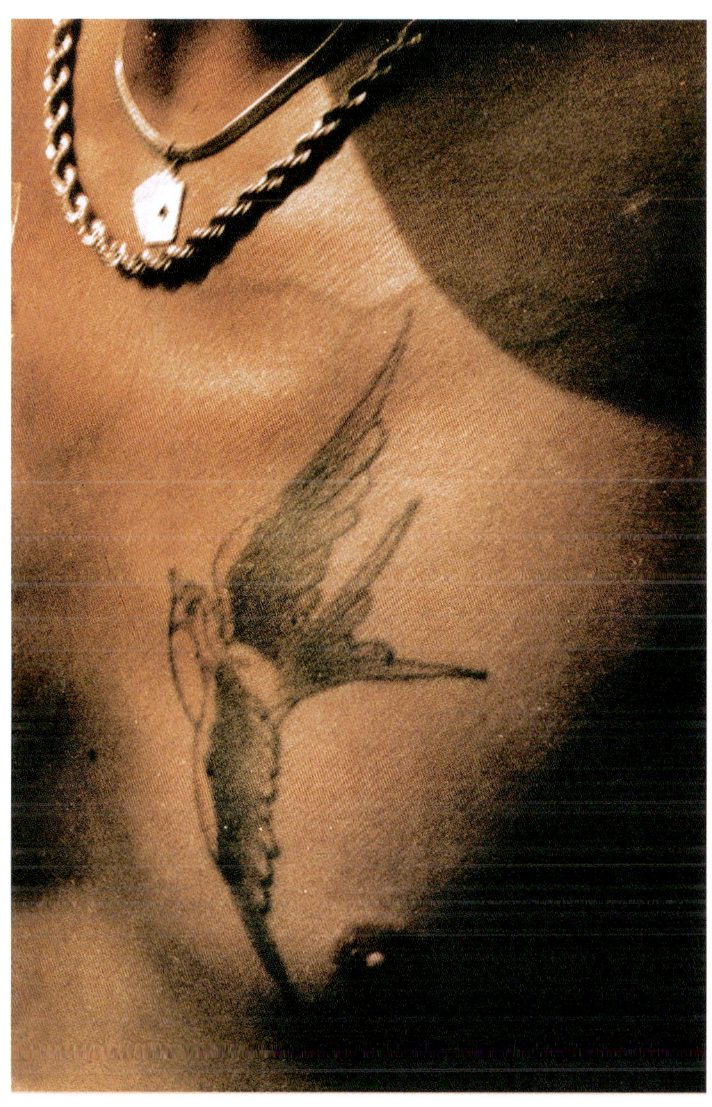

Mark Morrisroe, Untitled, 1988

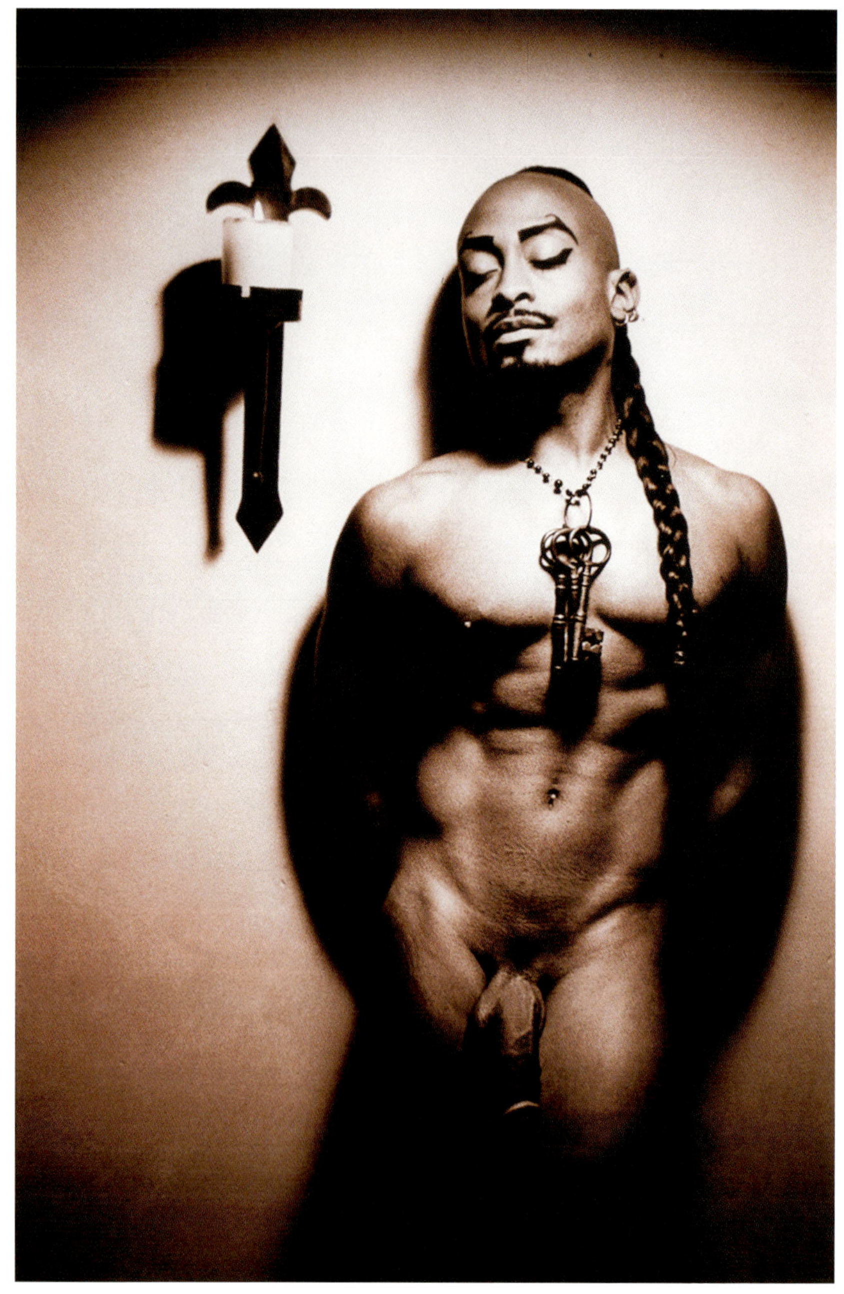

 Stephen John Phillips, "The Keeper of the Keys", from the Series "Harem Pictures", 1996

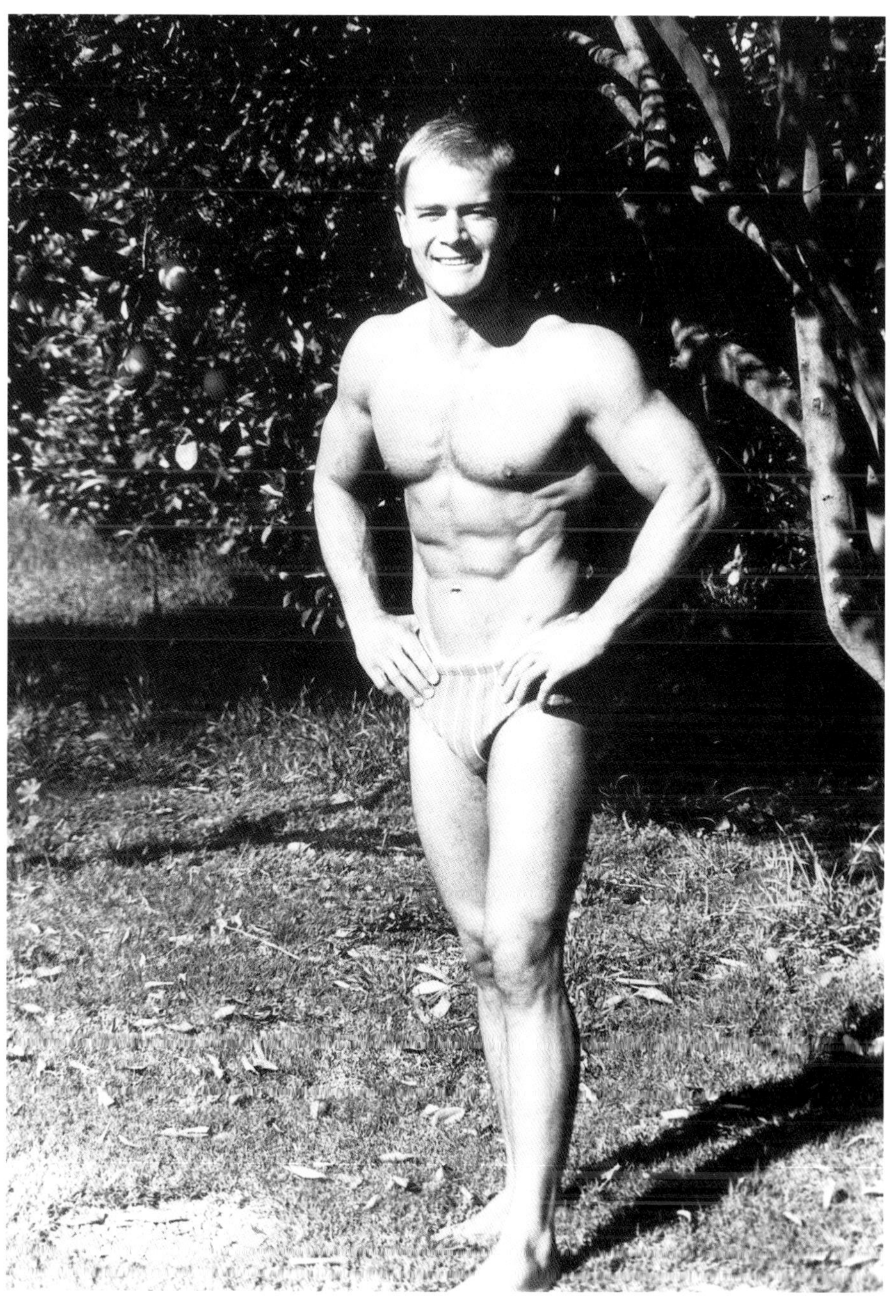

John Pelletier, *Self-Portrait with Mirror,* 1986

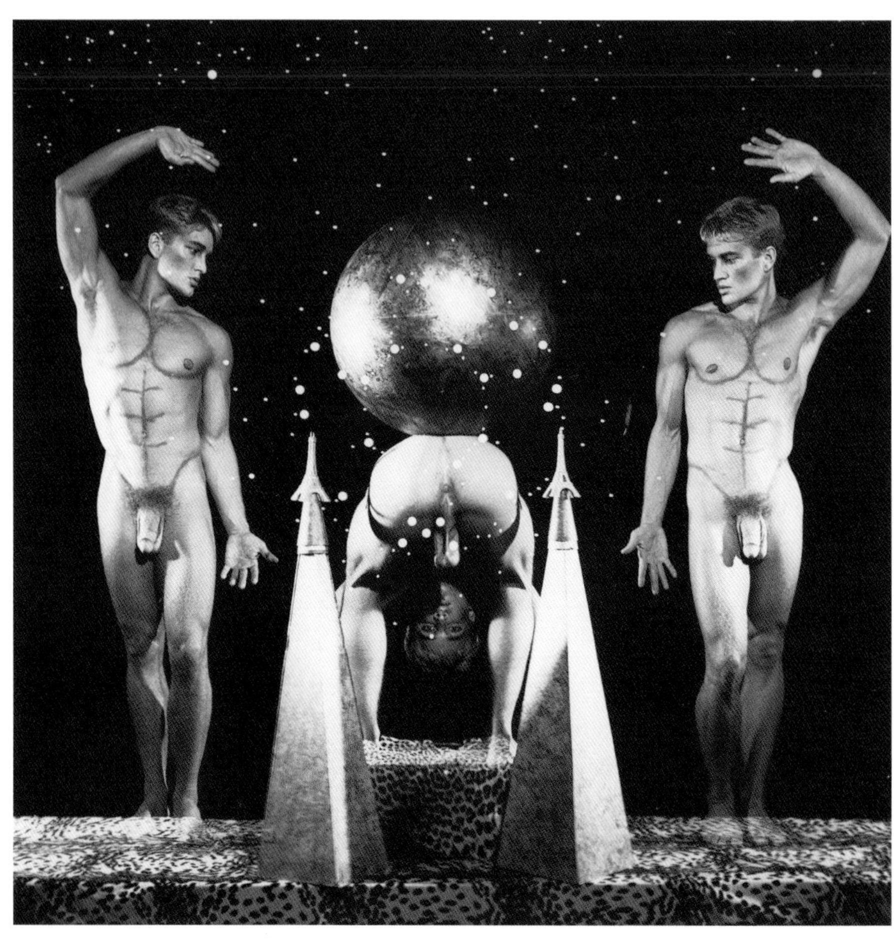

Steven Arnold, Center of the Universe, 1989

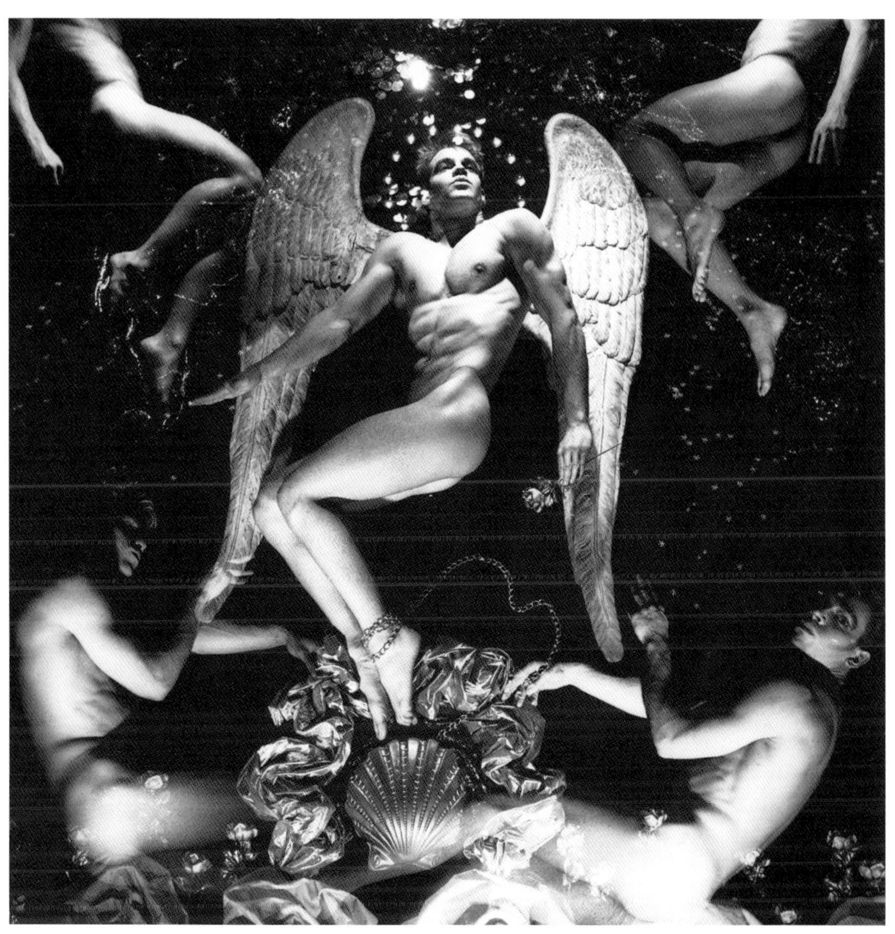

Steven Arnold, Heal-a-zation Swathe'a la Glob Ba, 1981

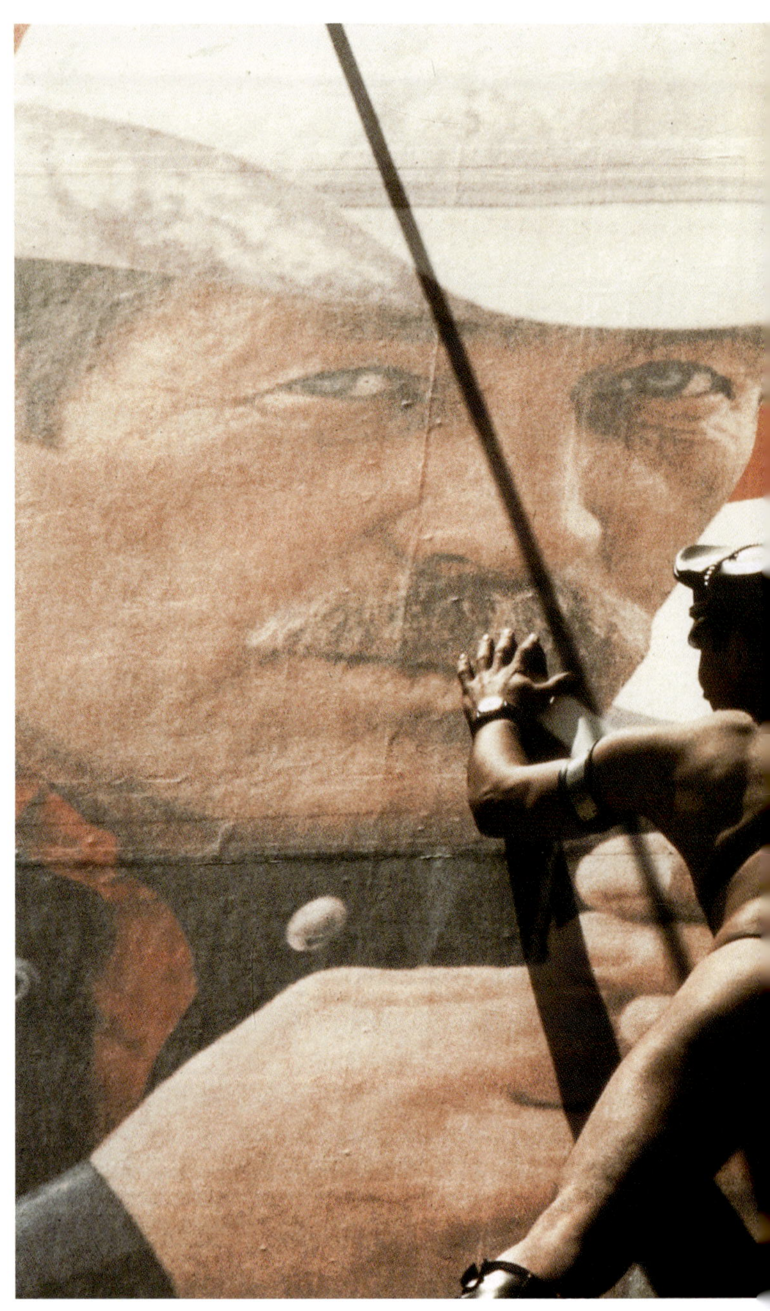

430 **Victor Arimondi,** Macho Man, 1981

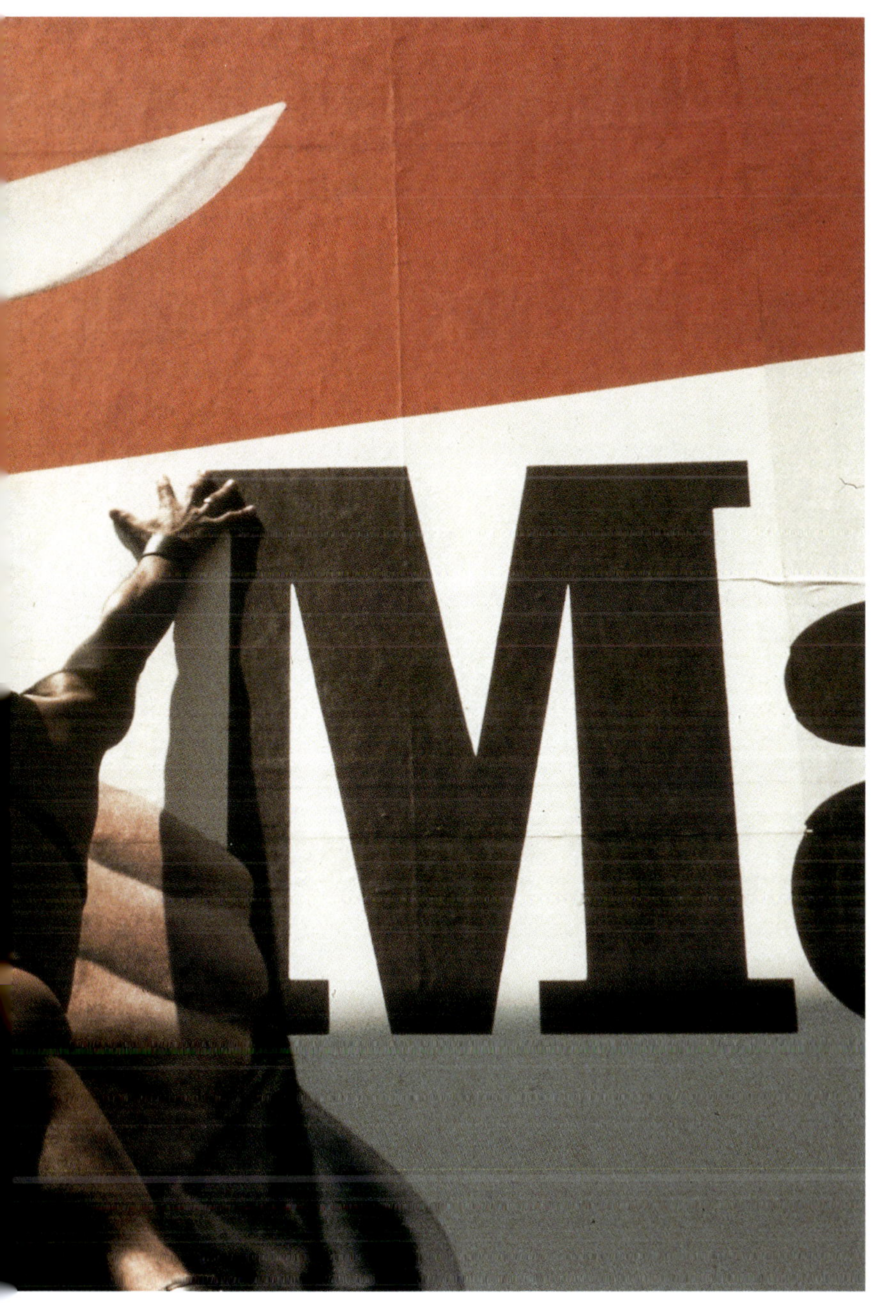

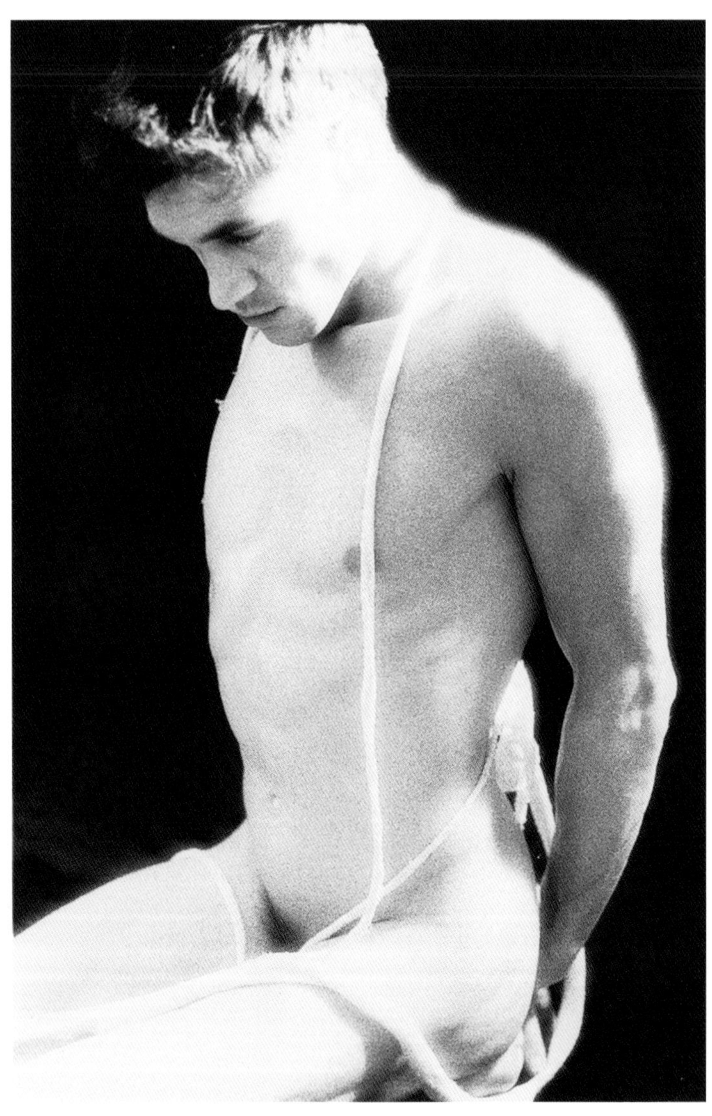

Keith Giles, Johnny, 1987

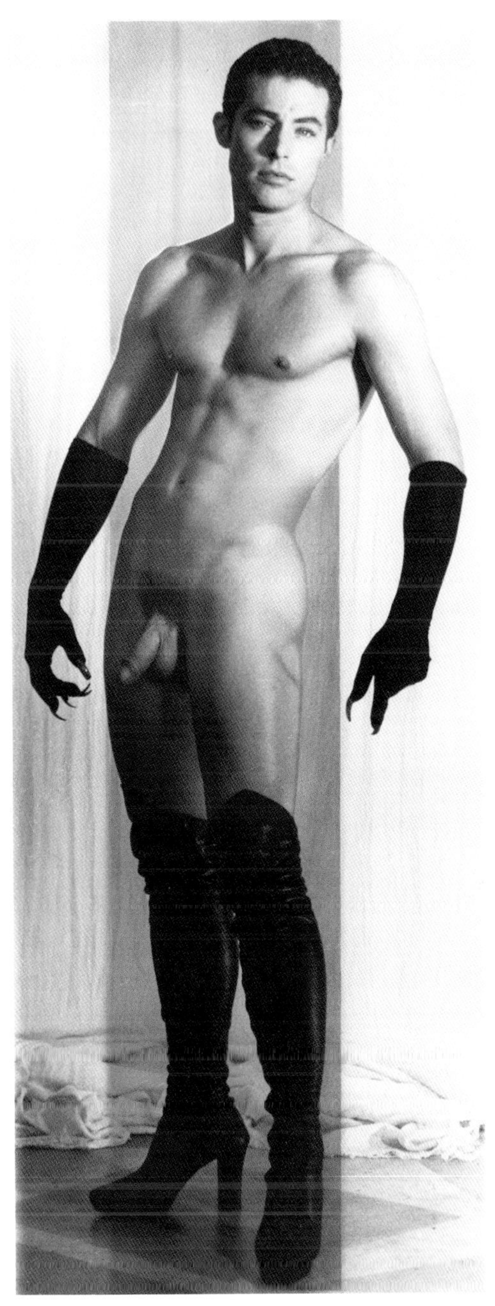

Keith Giles, Chris, 1996

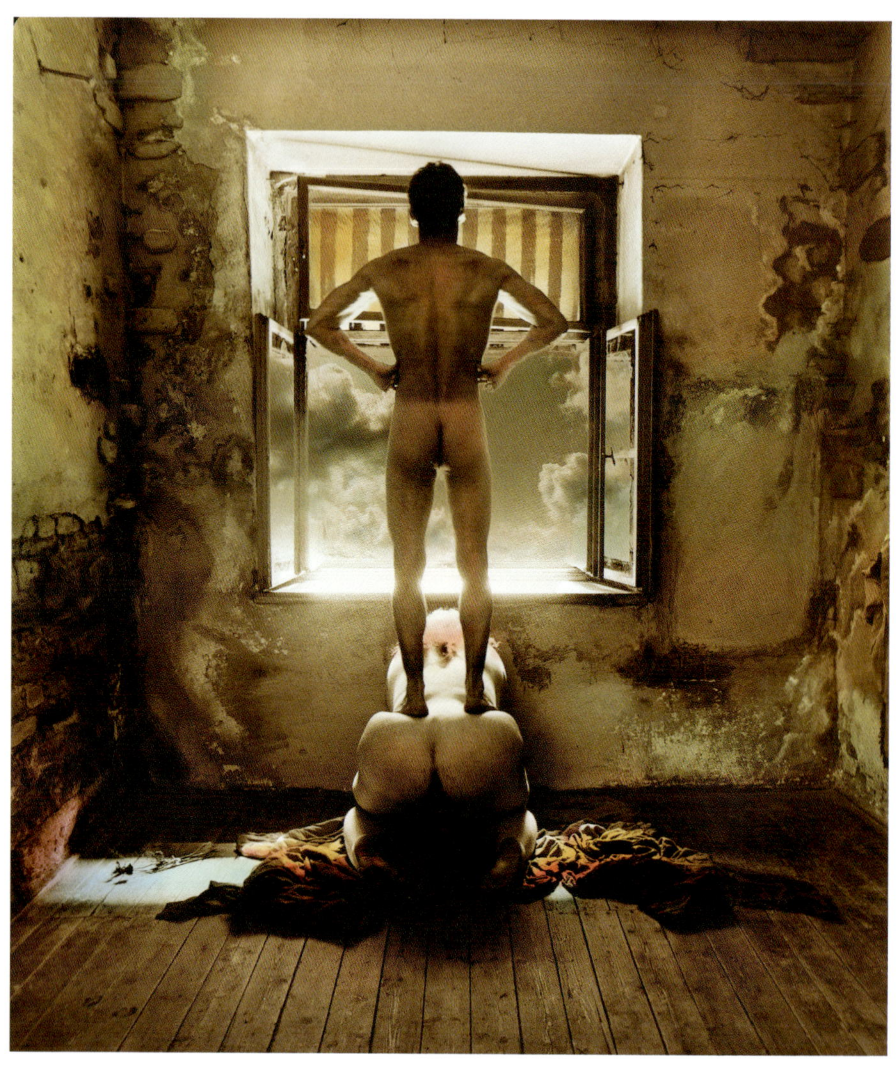

Jan Saudek, The New View from my Window, 1986

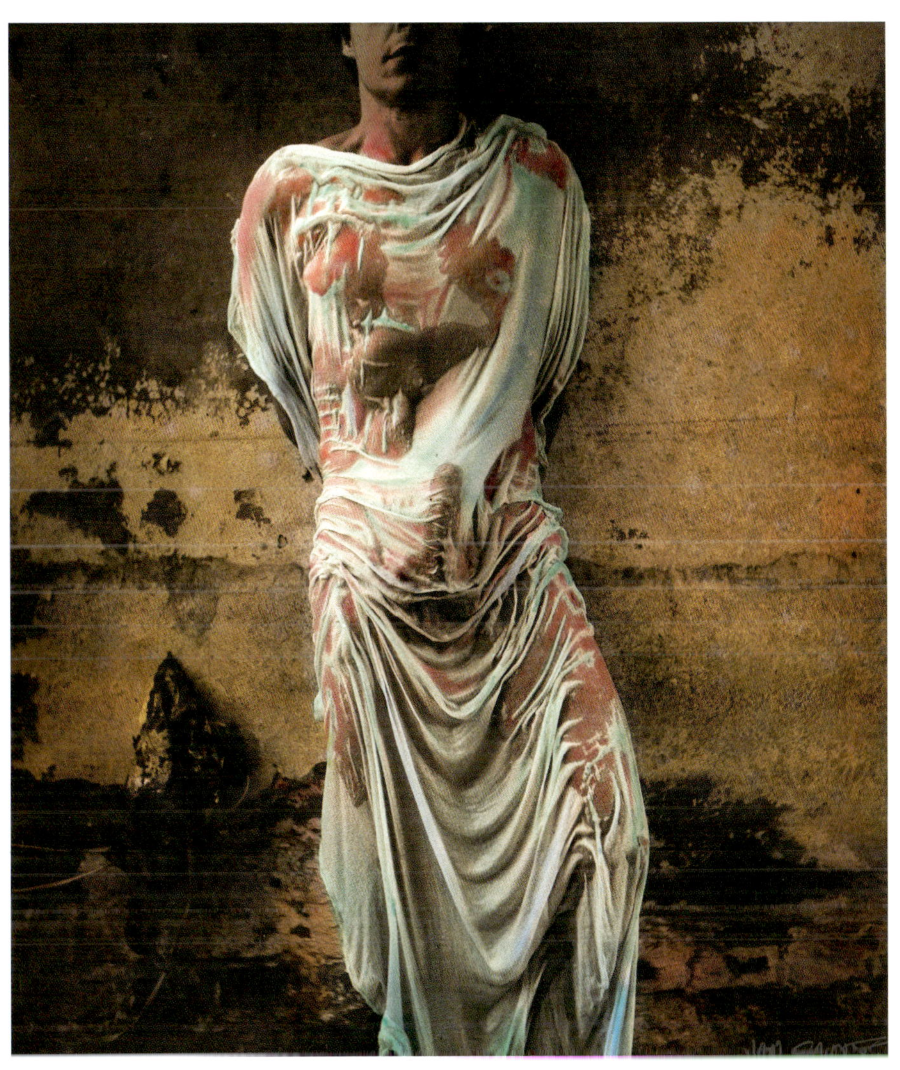

Jan Saudek, Portrait of a Man, 1984

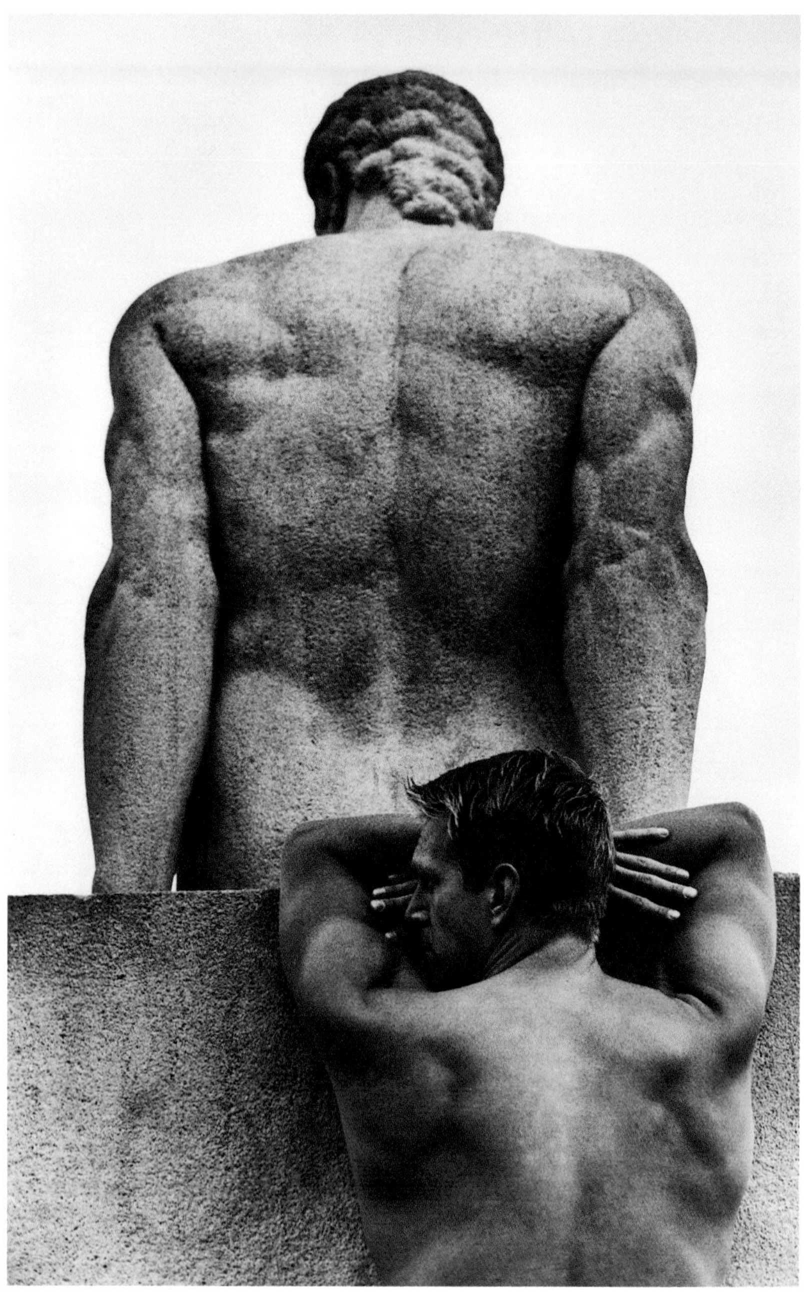

Rebecca Blake, Paris, c. 1990

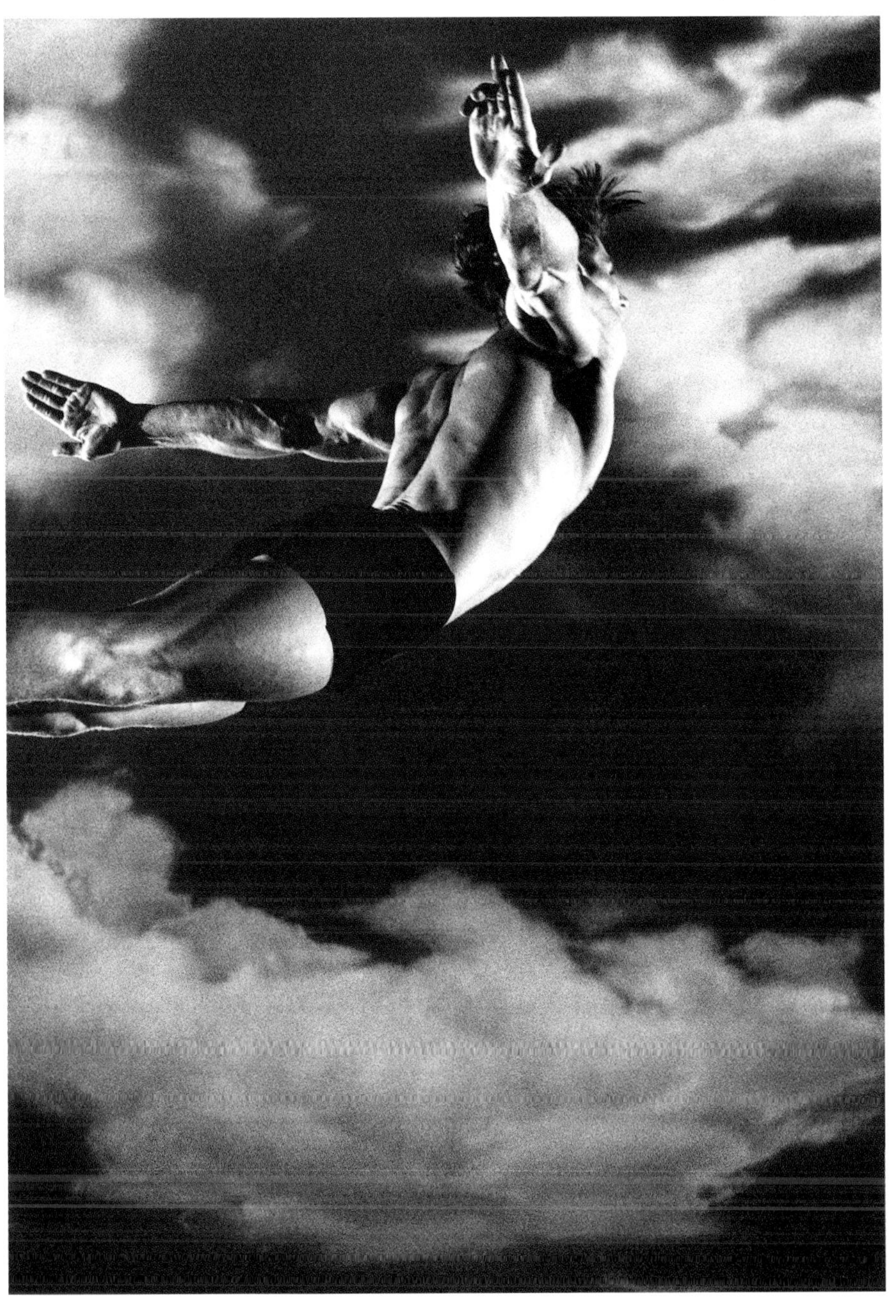

Rebecca Blake, New York, c. 1990

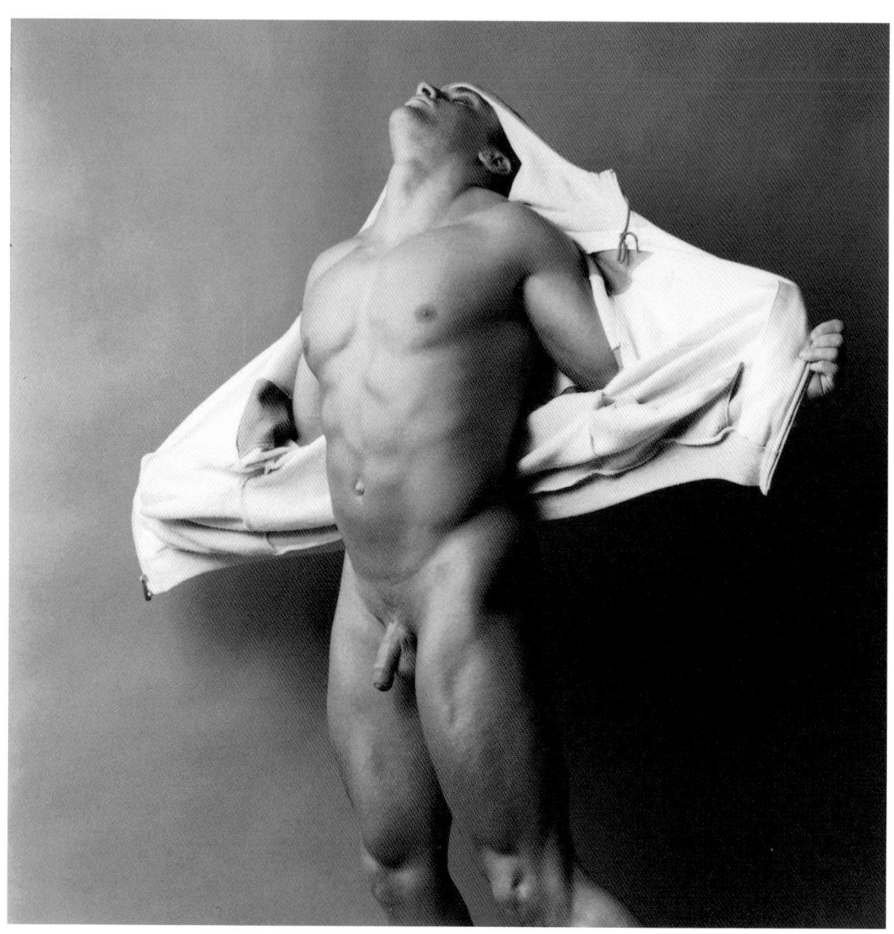

Stanley Stellar, Revelation, 1990

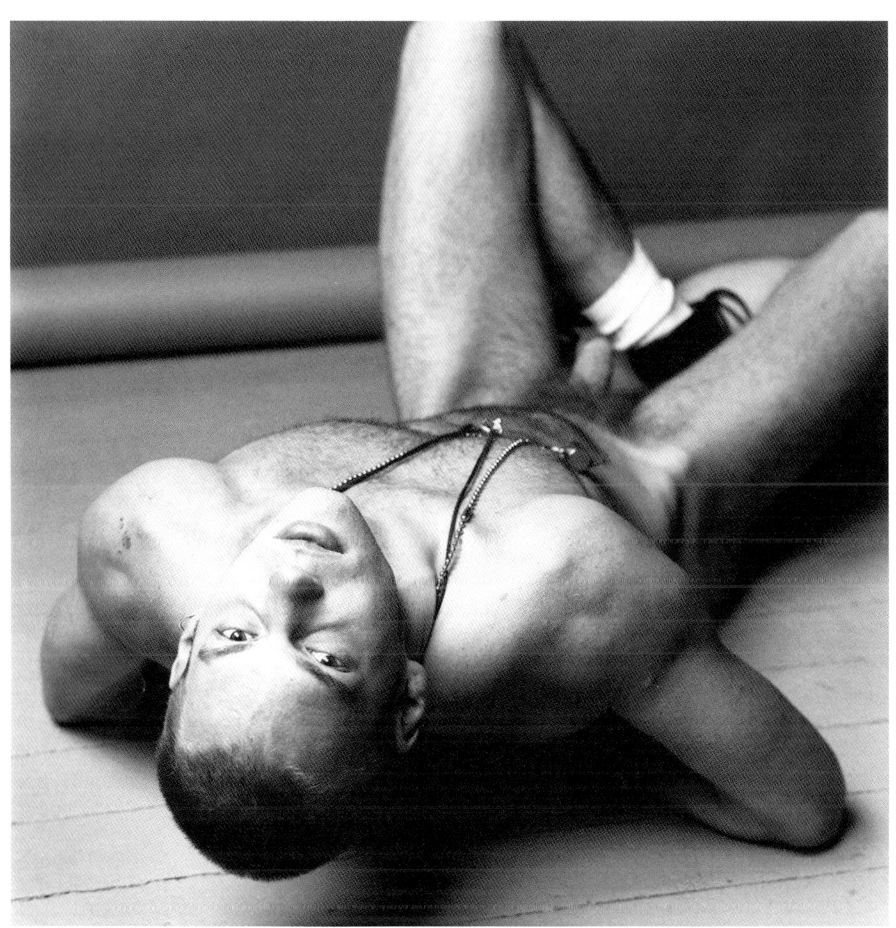

Stanley Stellar, Craig on my Floor, 1990

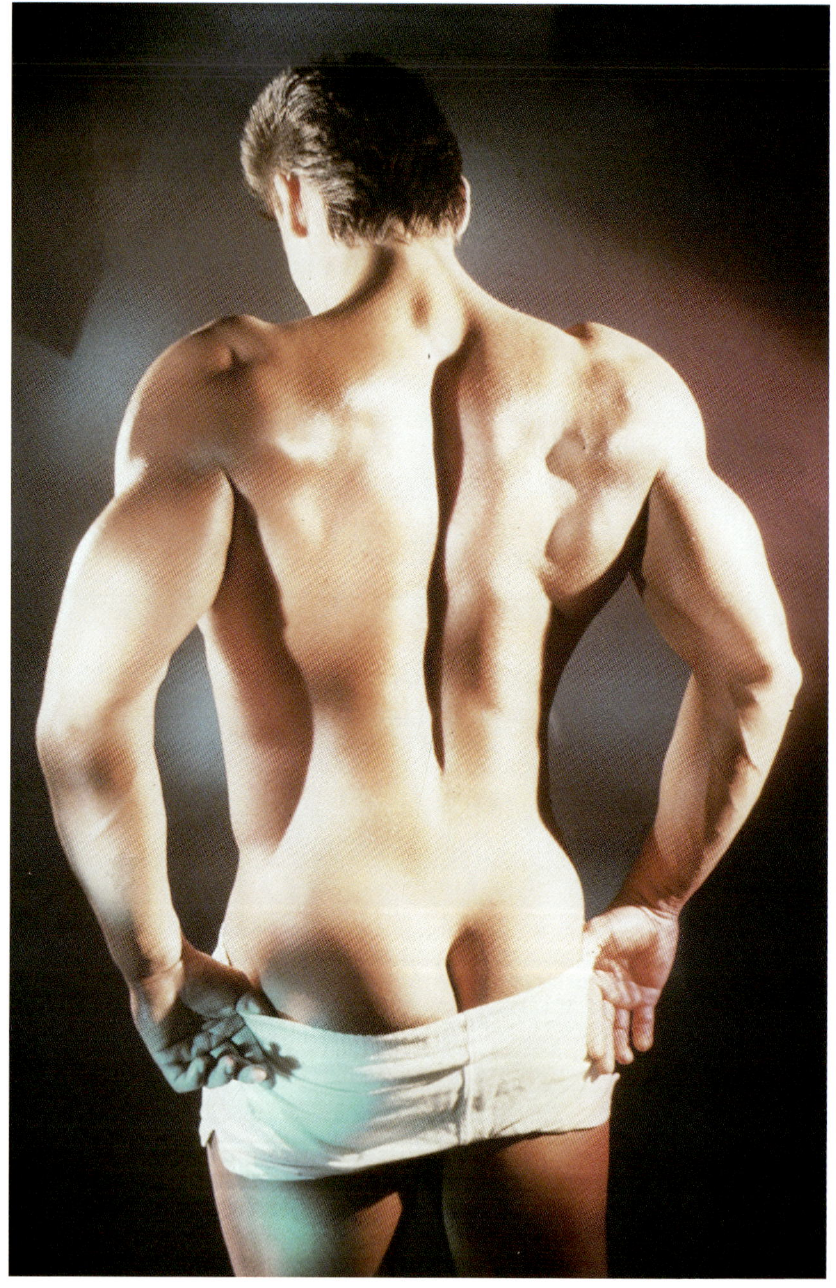

Patrick Sarfati, The Back, 1992

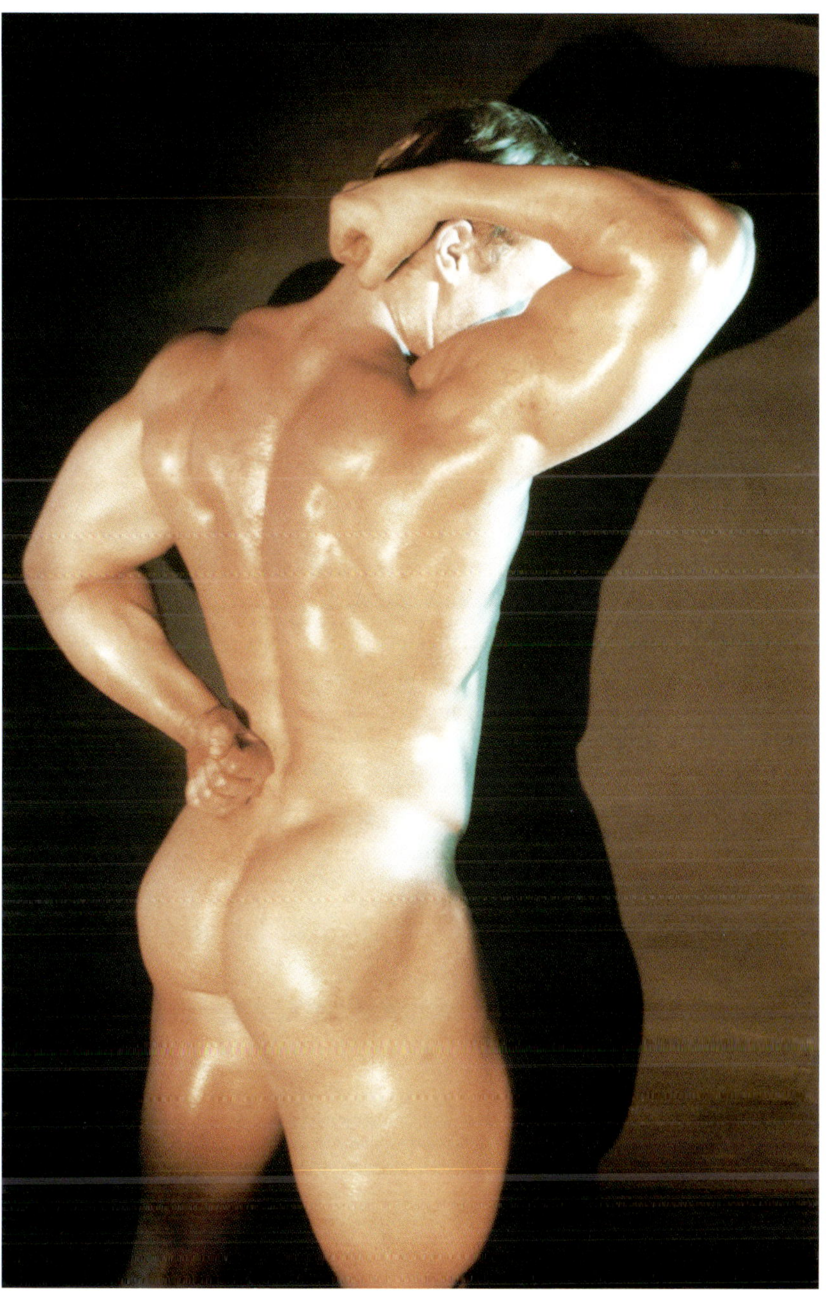

Patrick Sarfati, Plastic, 1992

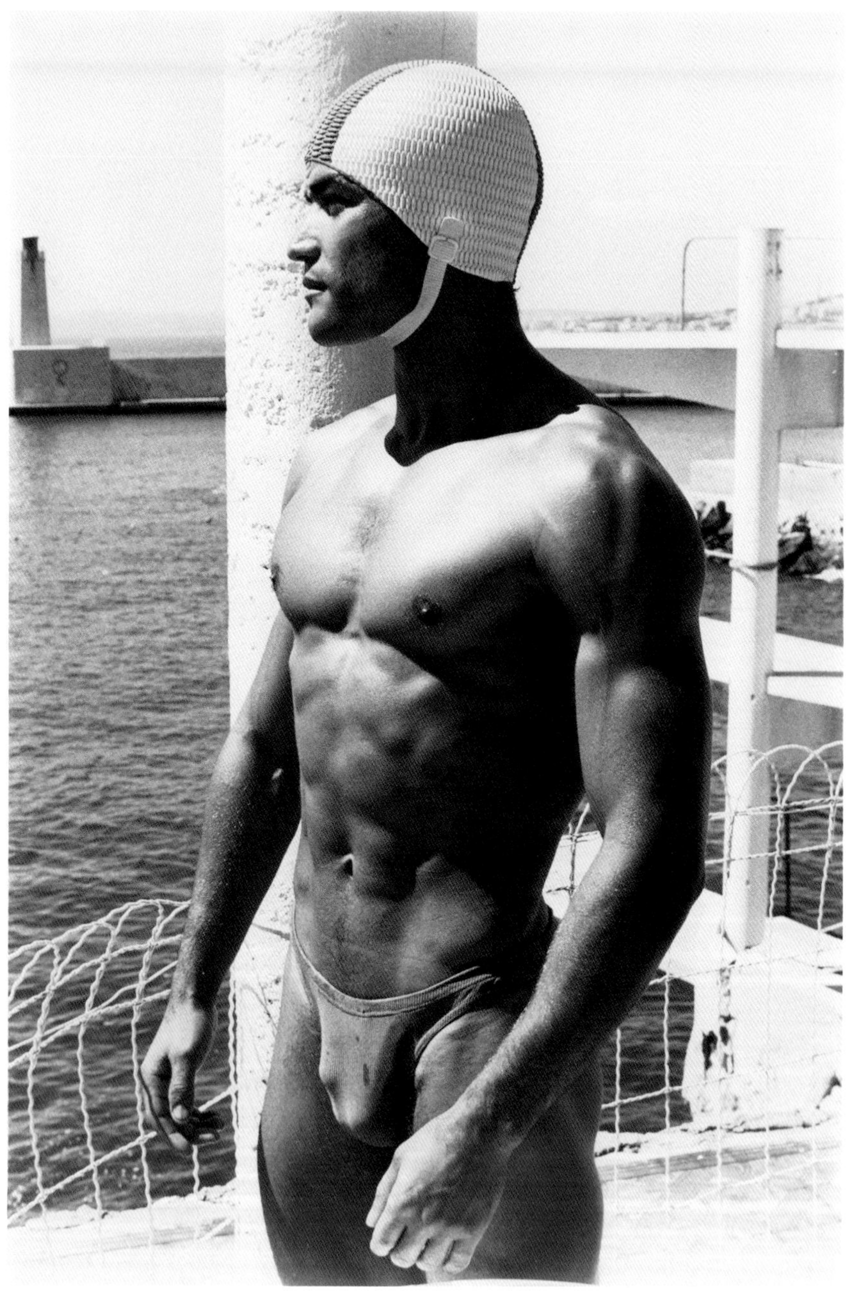

Patrick Sarfati, The Bather, 1990

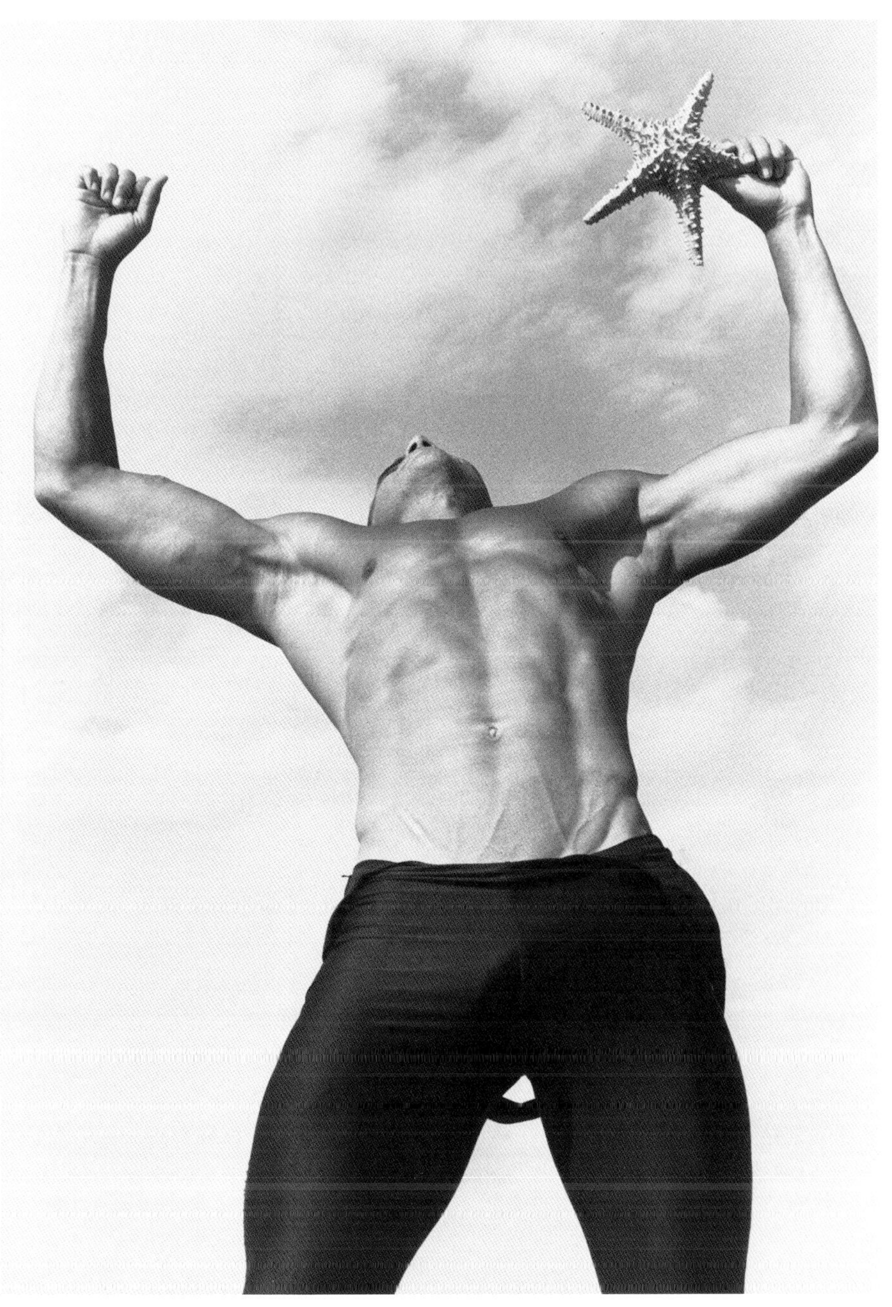

Patrick Sarfati, Starfish, 1990

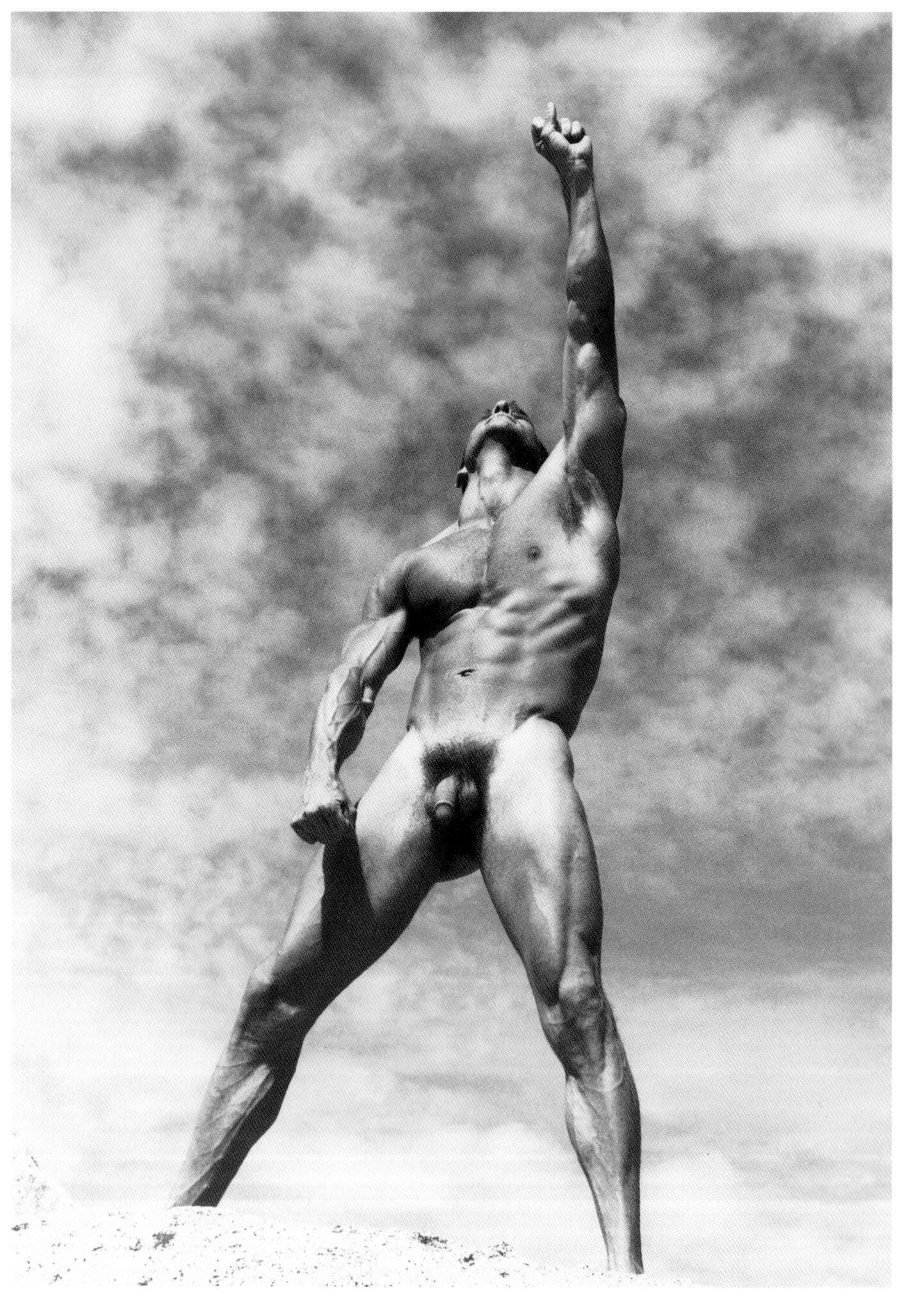

Jeff Palmer, Victory, 1992

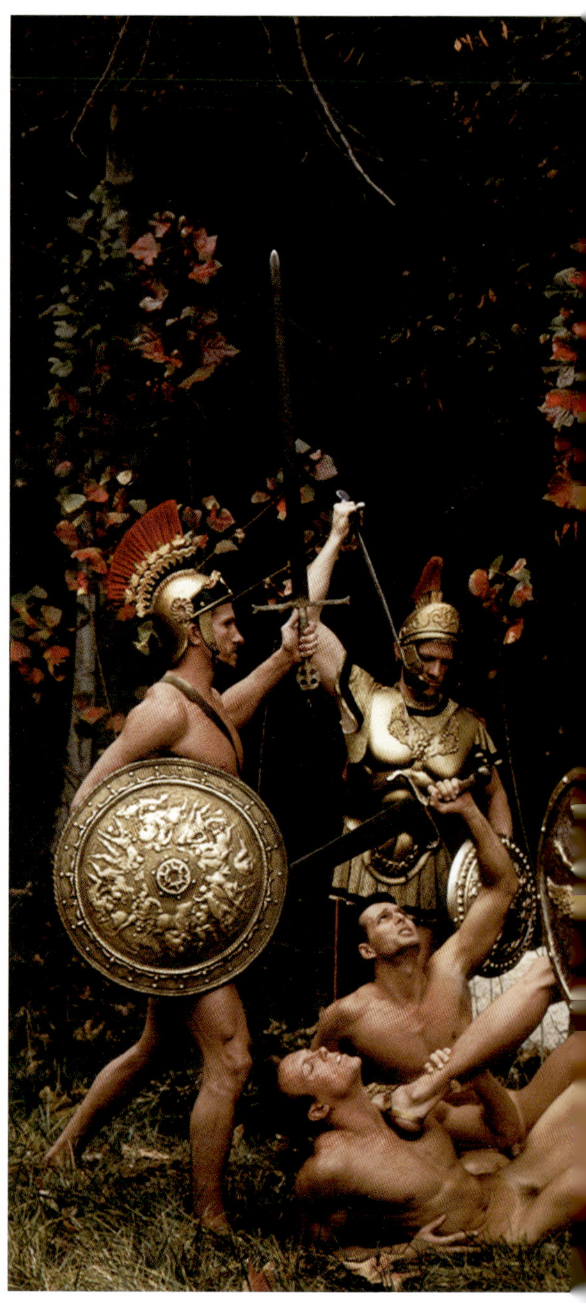

Robert Rausch, Bastards in Battle, 1994

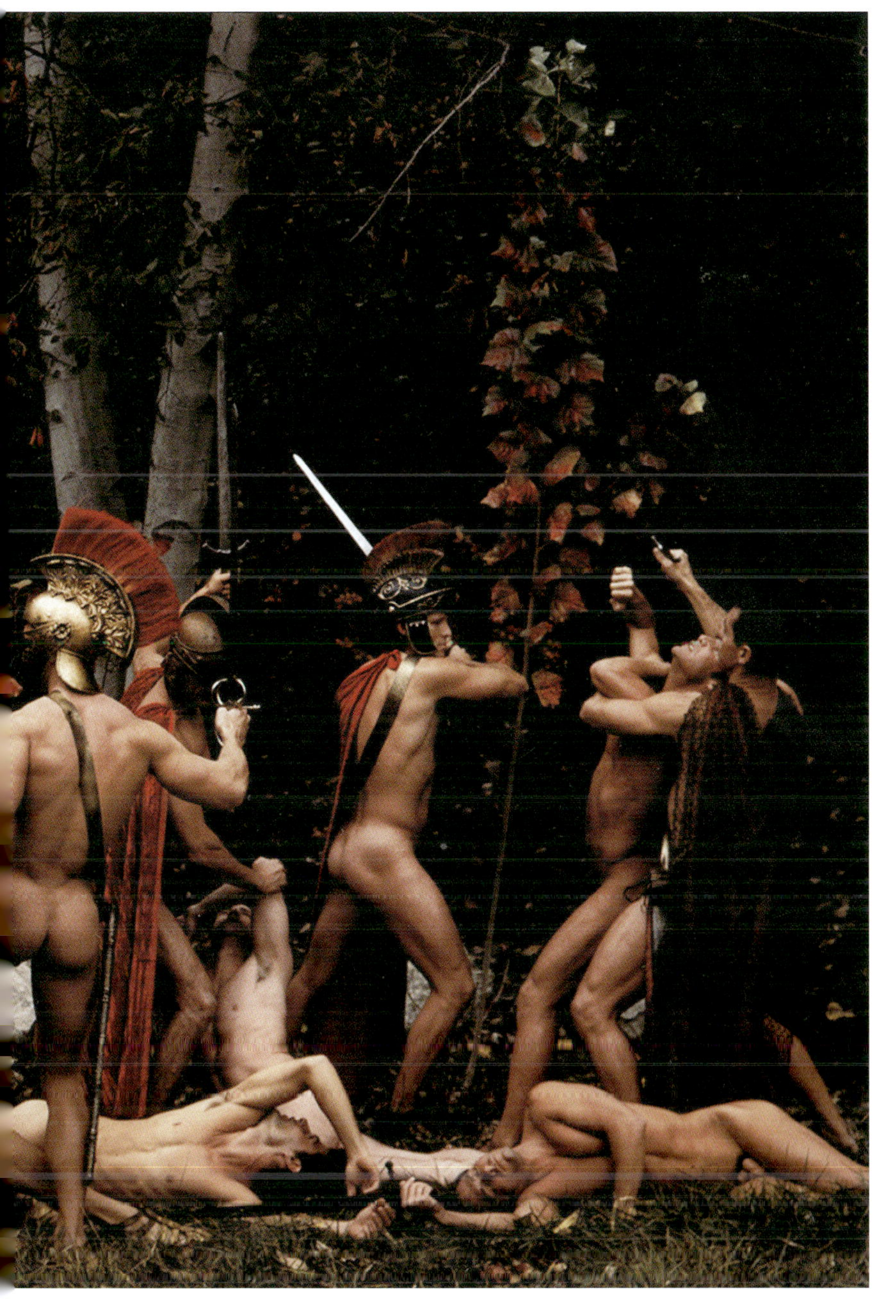

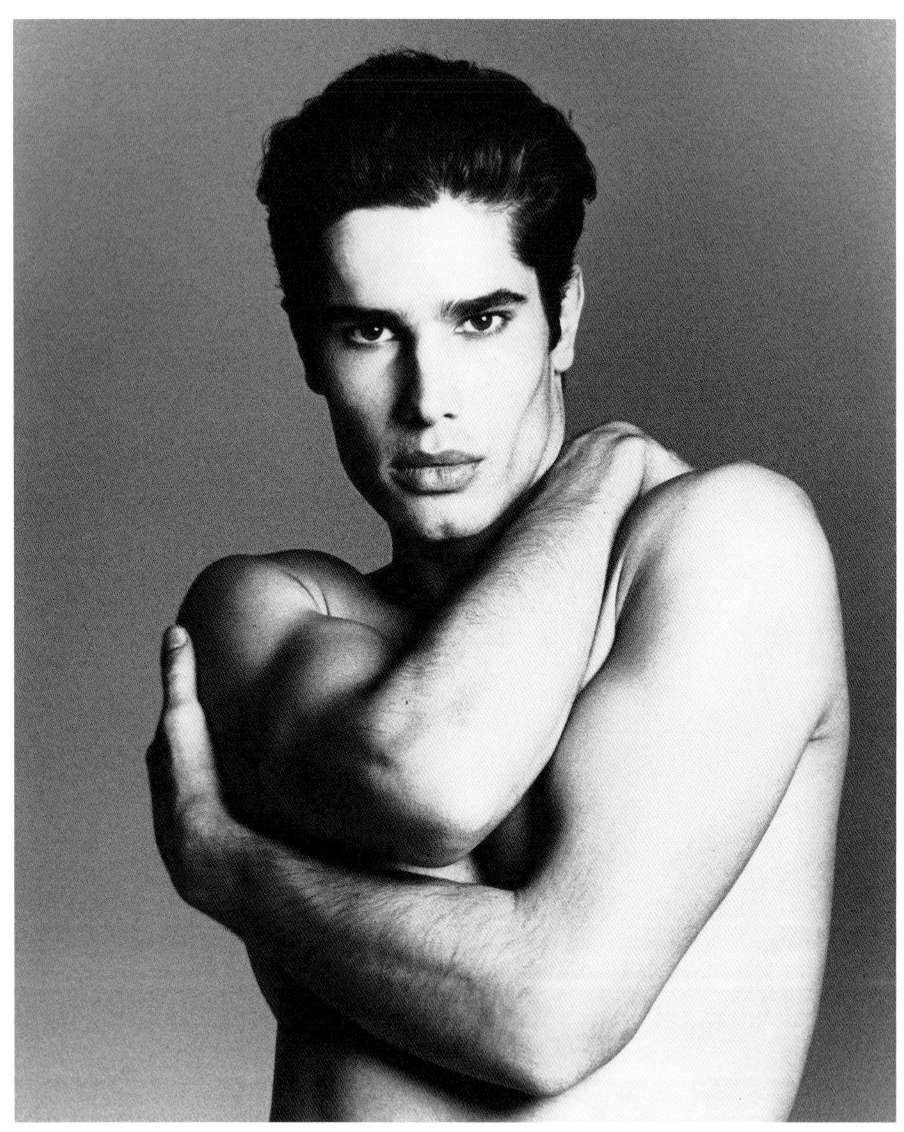

Francesco Scavullo, Cameron, 1991

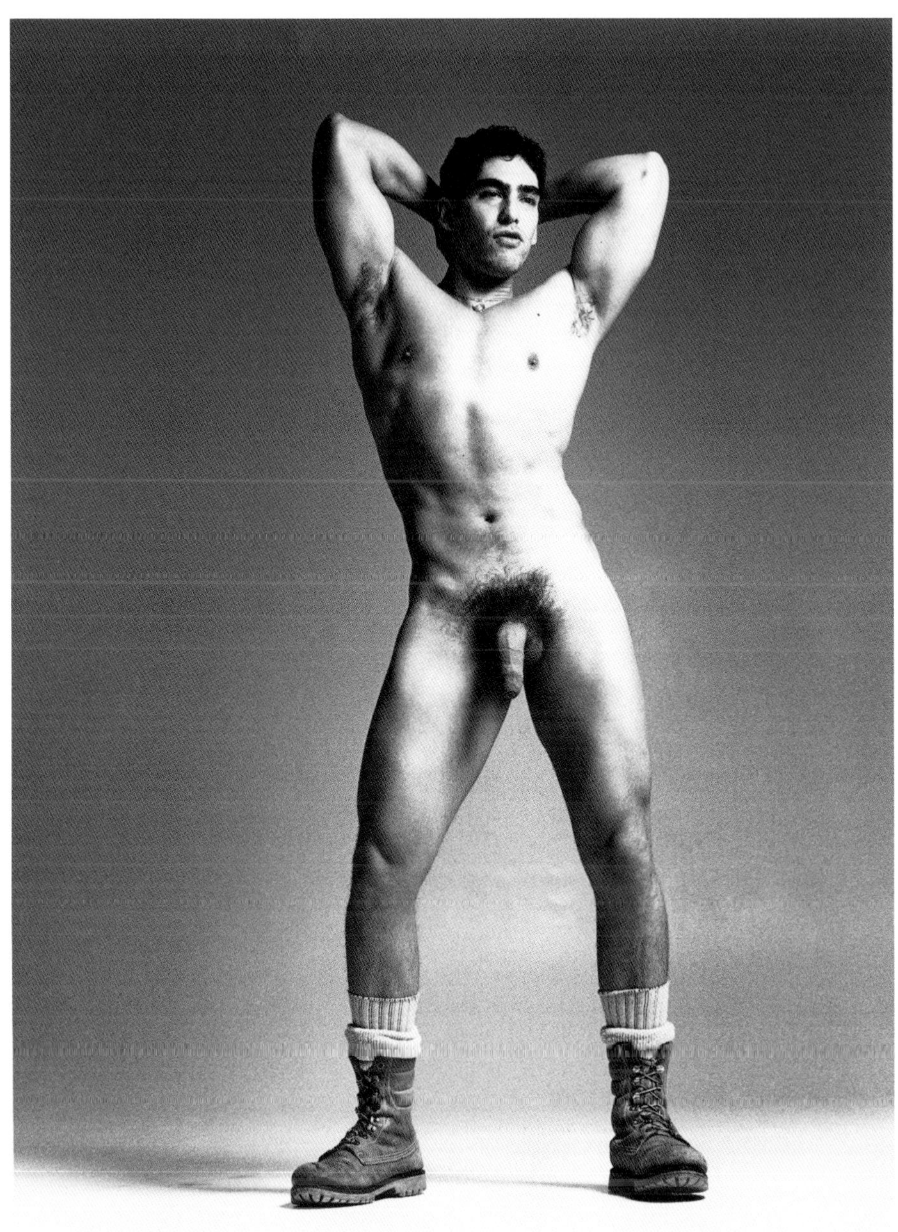

Francesco Scavullo, Rocky, 1993

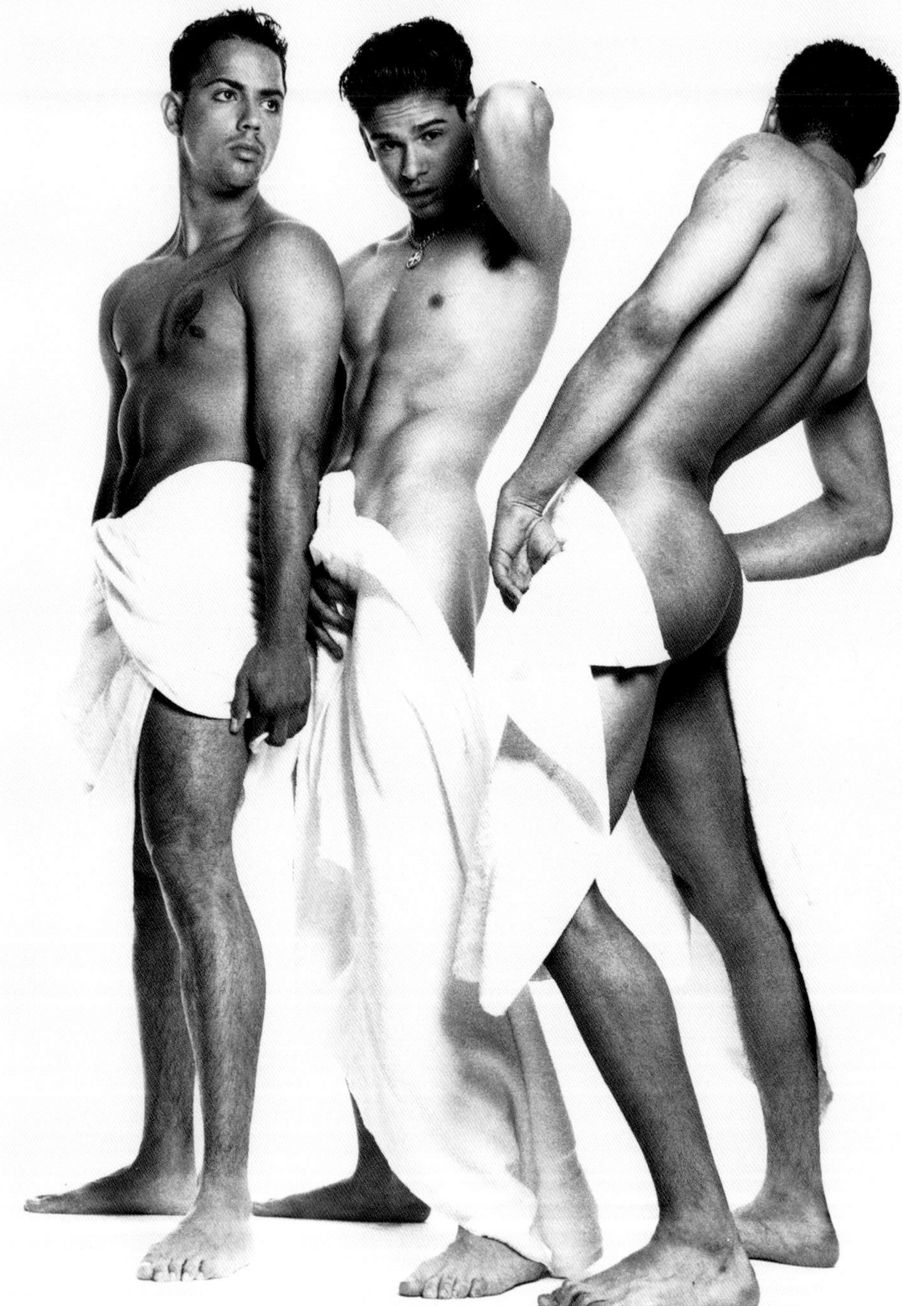

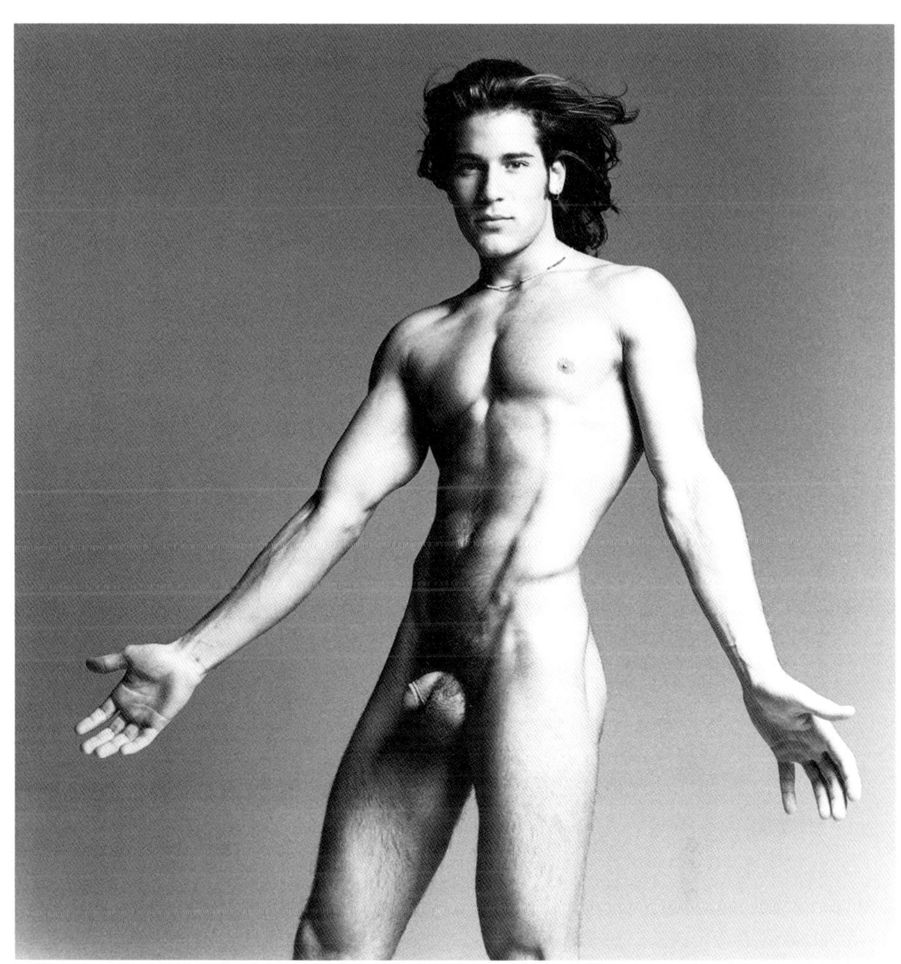

Francesco Scavullo, David, 1993

Francesco Scavullo, Subliminal, 1992

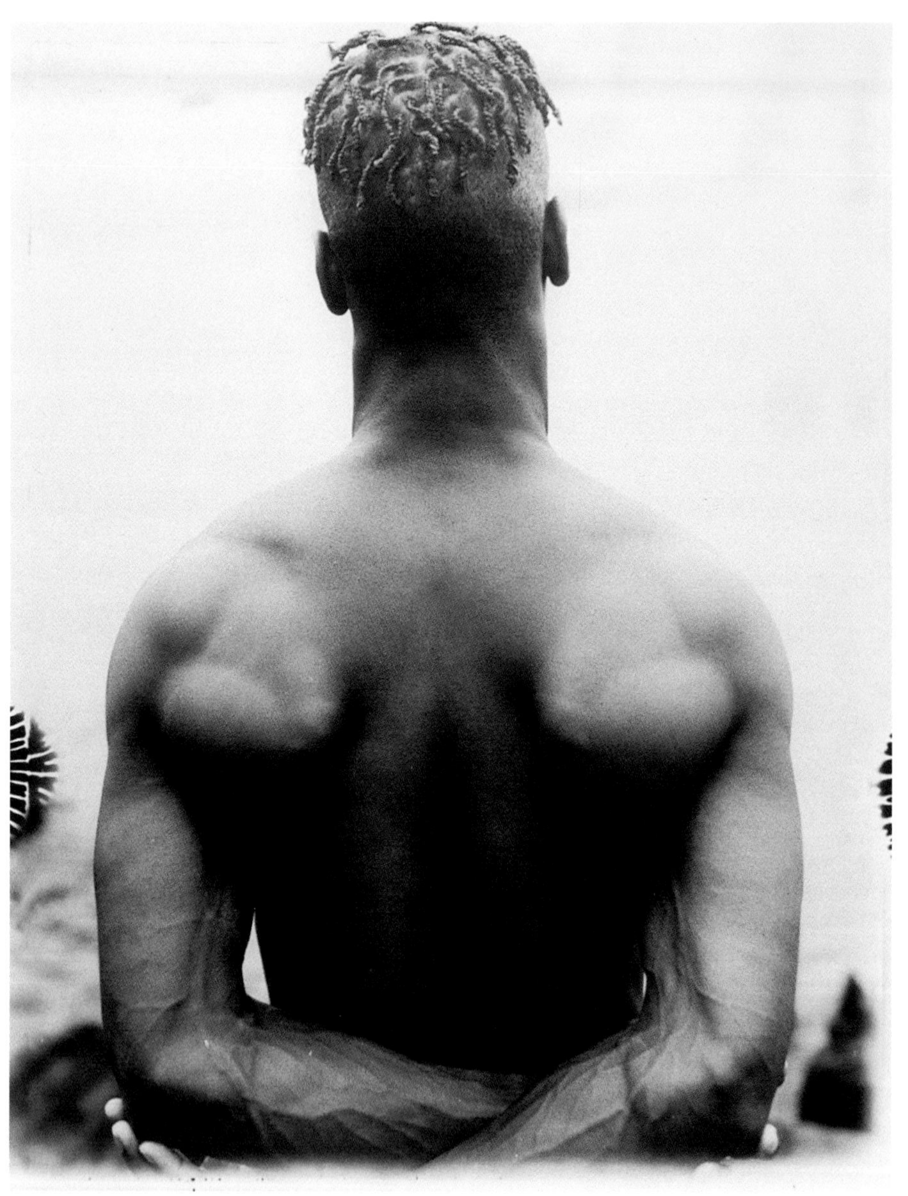

Vincent Cianni, Chris' Back, 1995

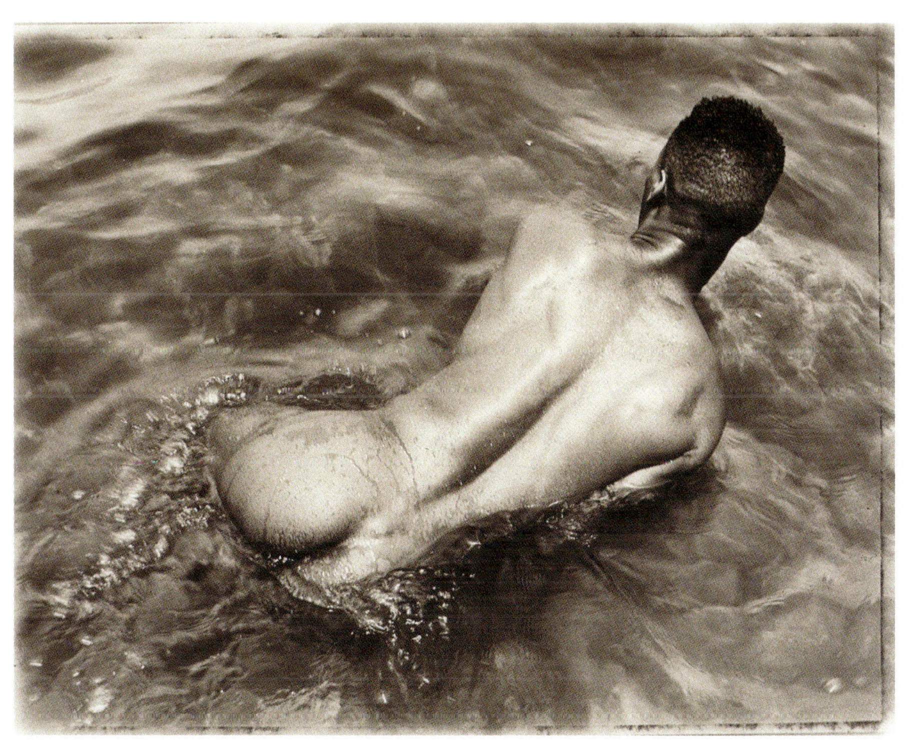

Vincent Cianni, Chris, Shelter Island, 1995

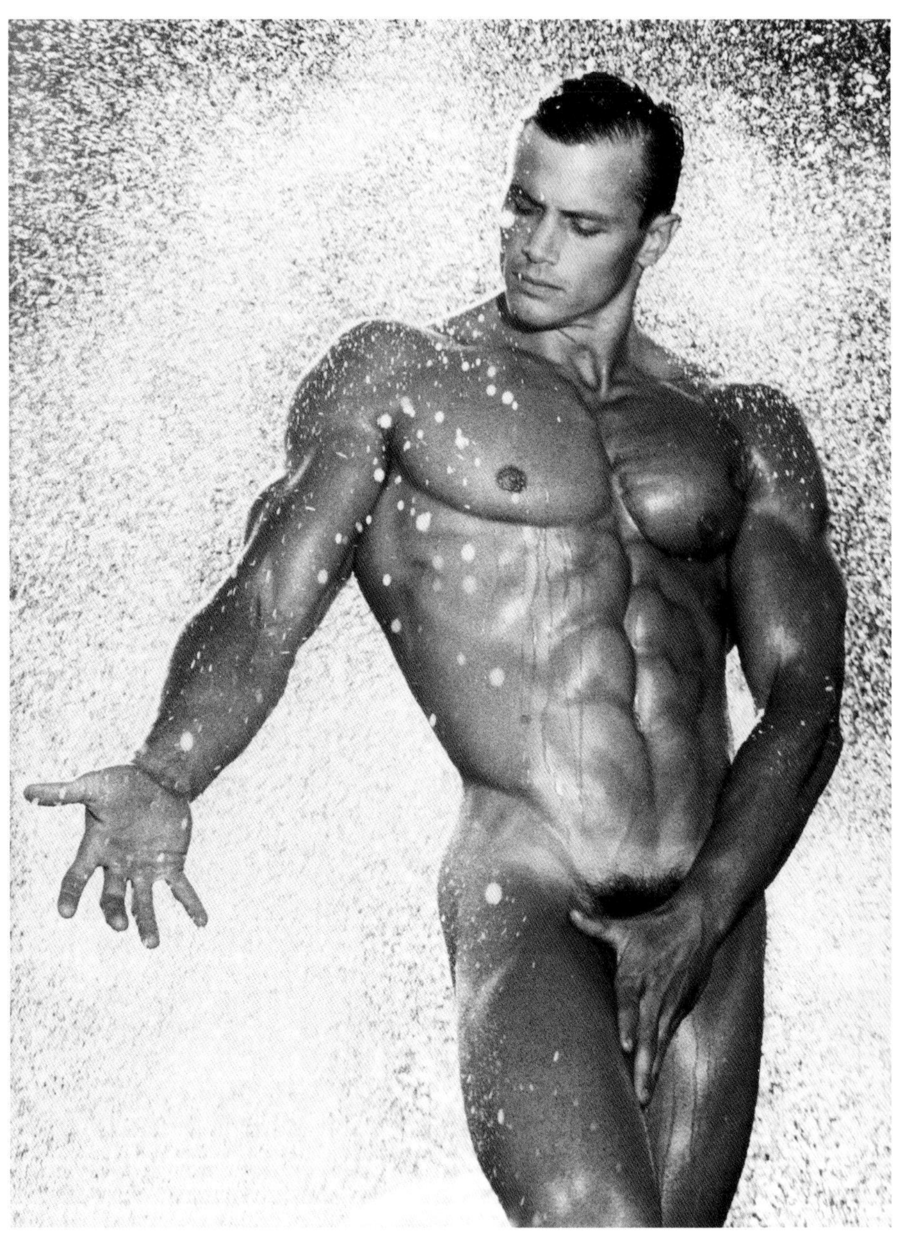

Jim French, John Pruitt, Splash, 1985

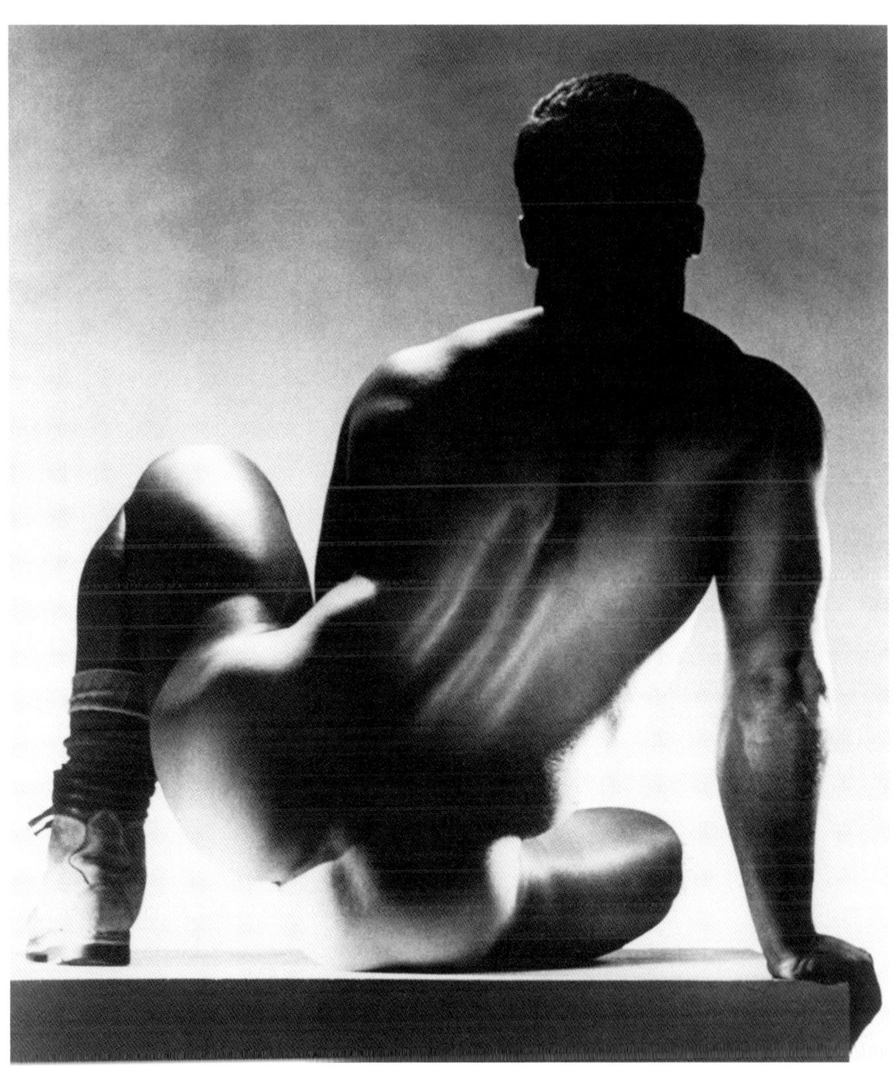

Jim French, Scooter, Studio, 1986

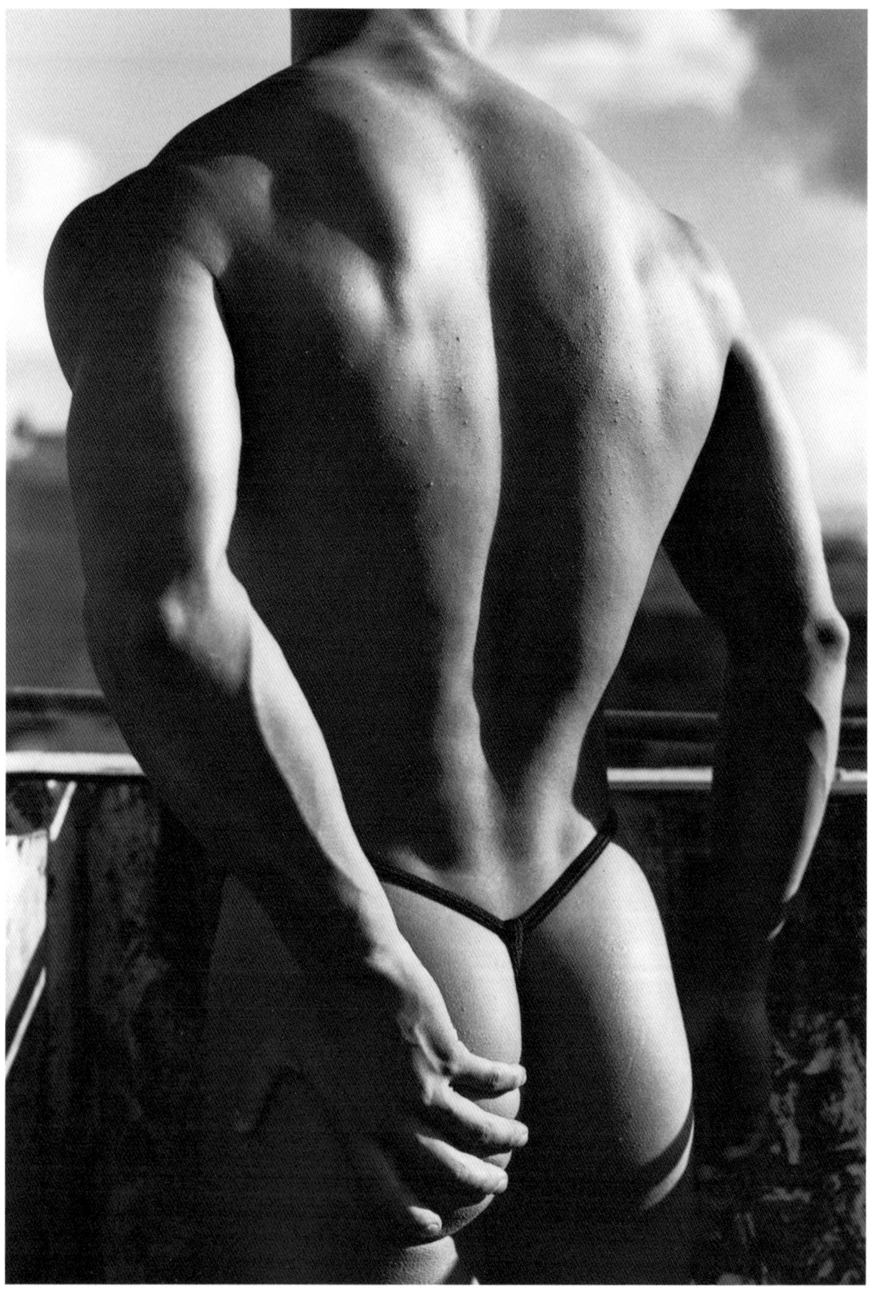

Daniel Hernández, Dorso, 1993

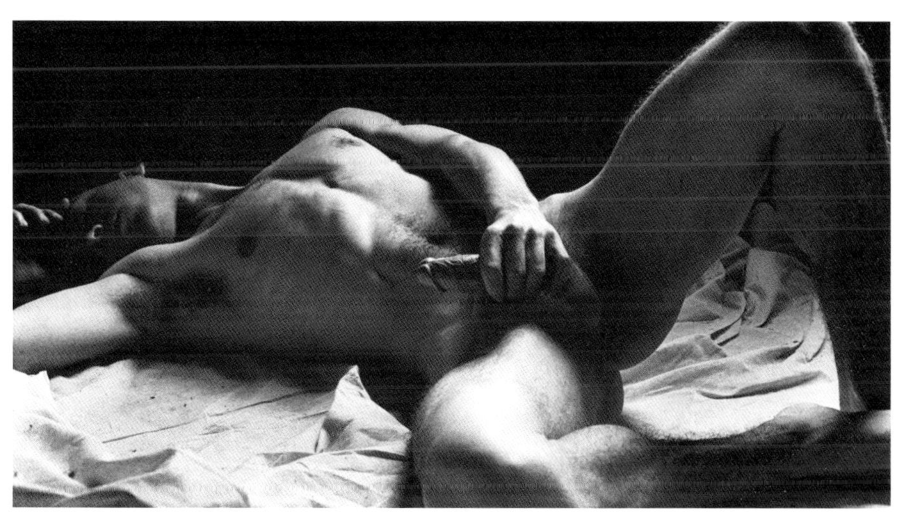

Daniel Hernández, Fuego en la Obscuridad, 1988

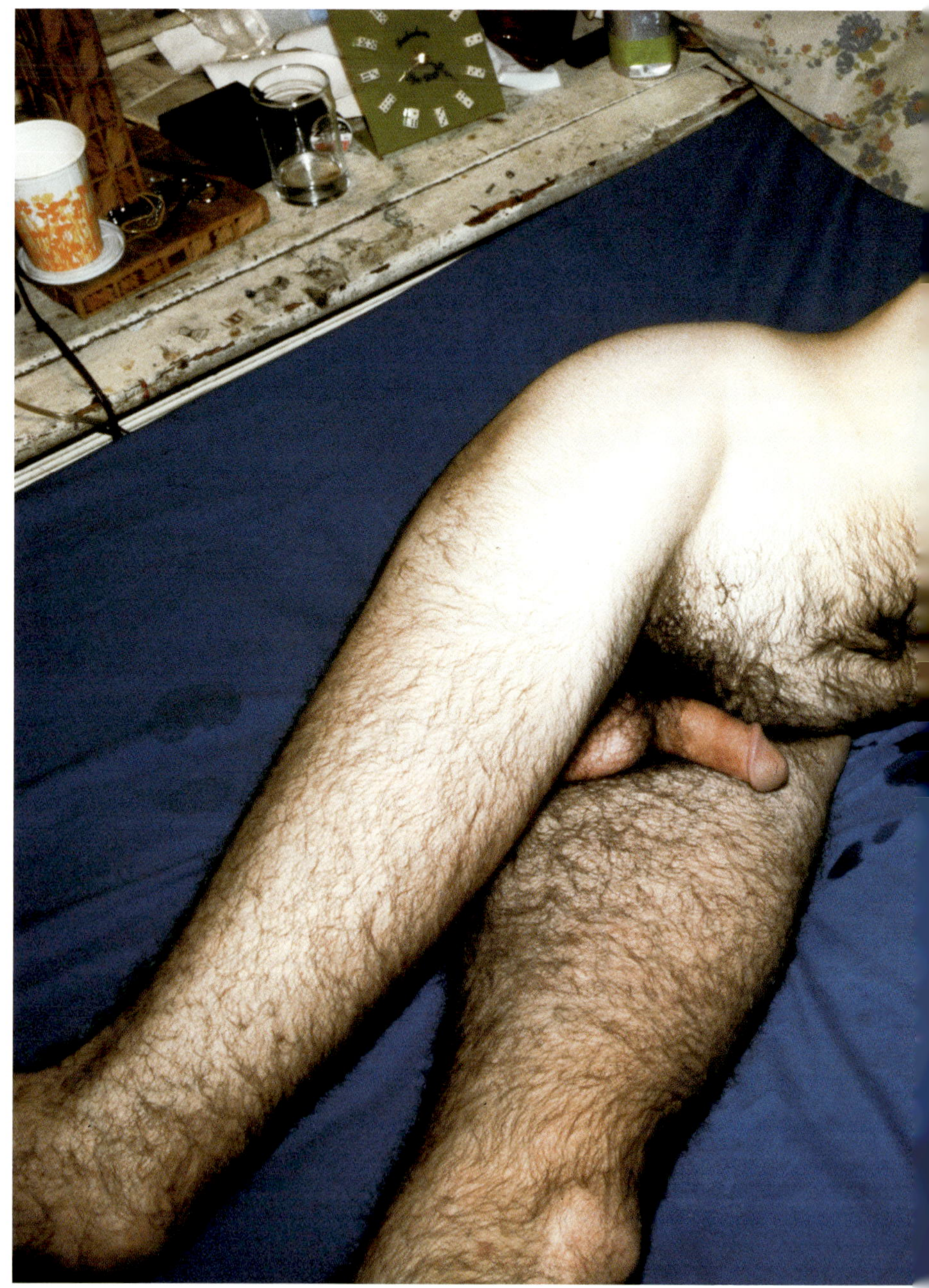

Nan Goldin, Brian after Coming, 1983

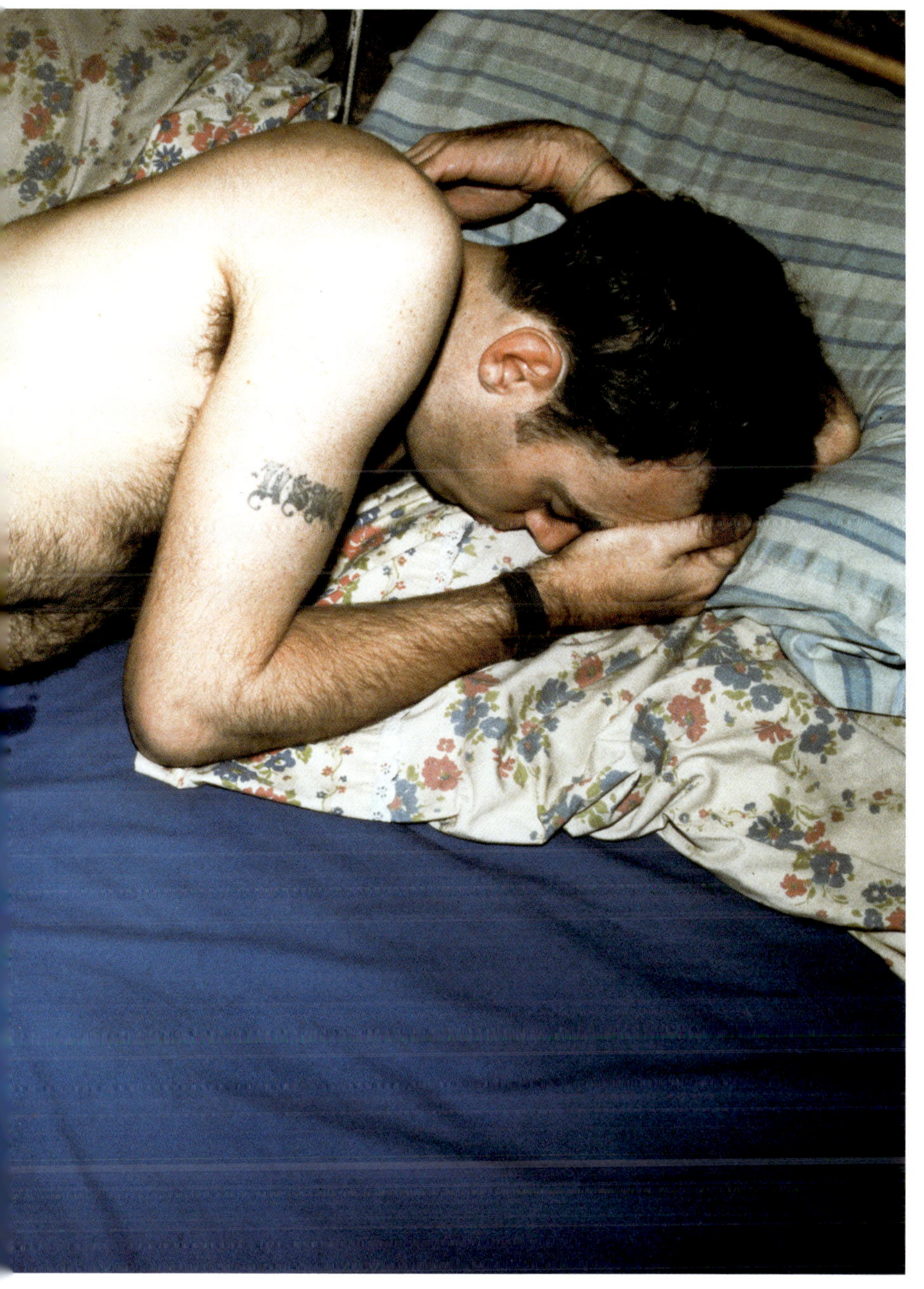

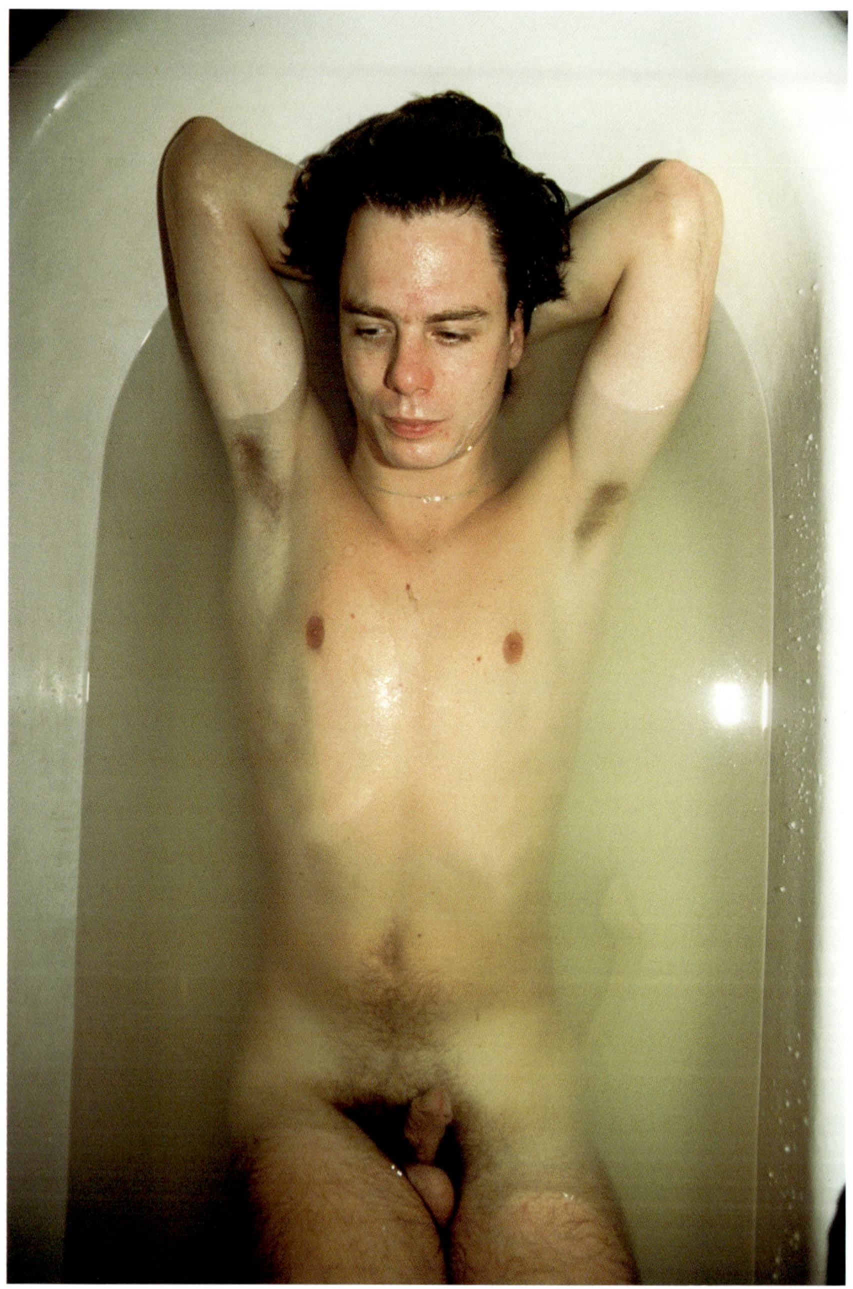

Nan Goldin, *Mull in the Tub*, 1988

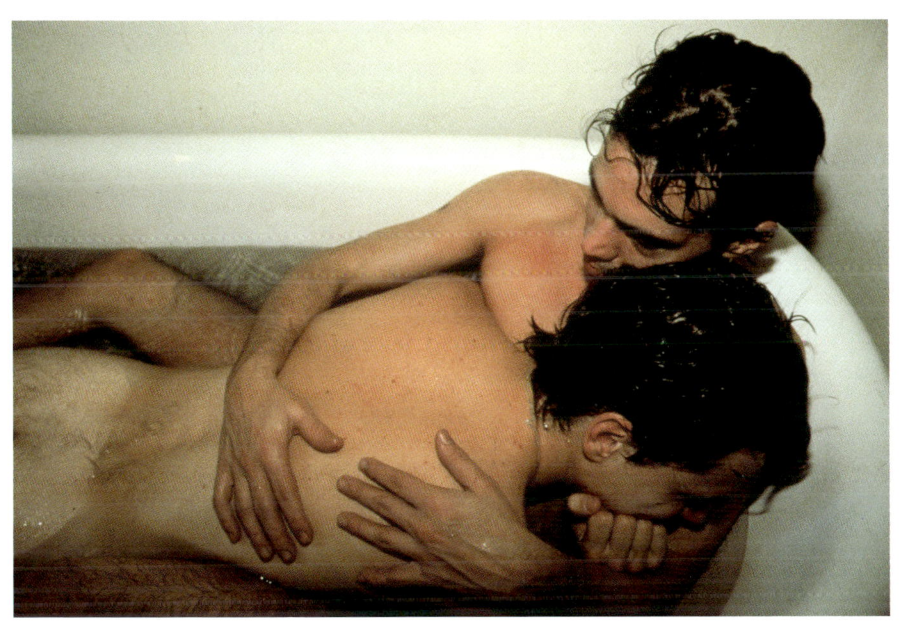

Nan Goldin, Matt and Lewis in the Tub, 1988

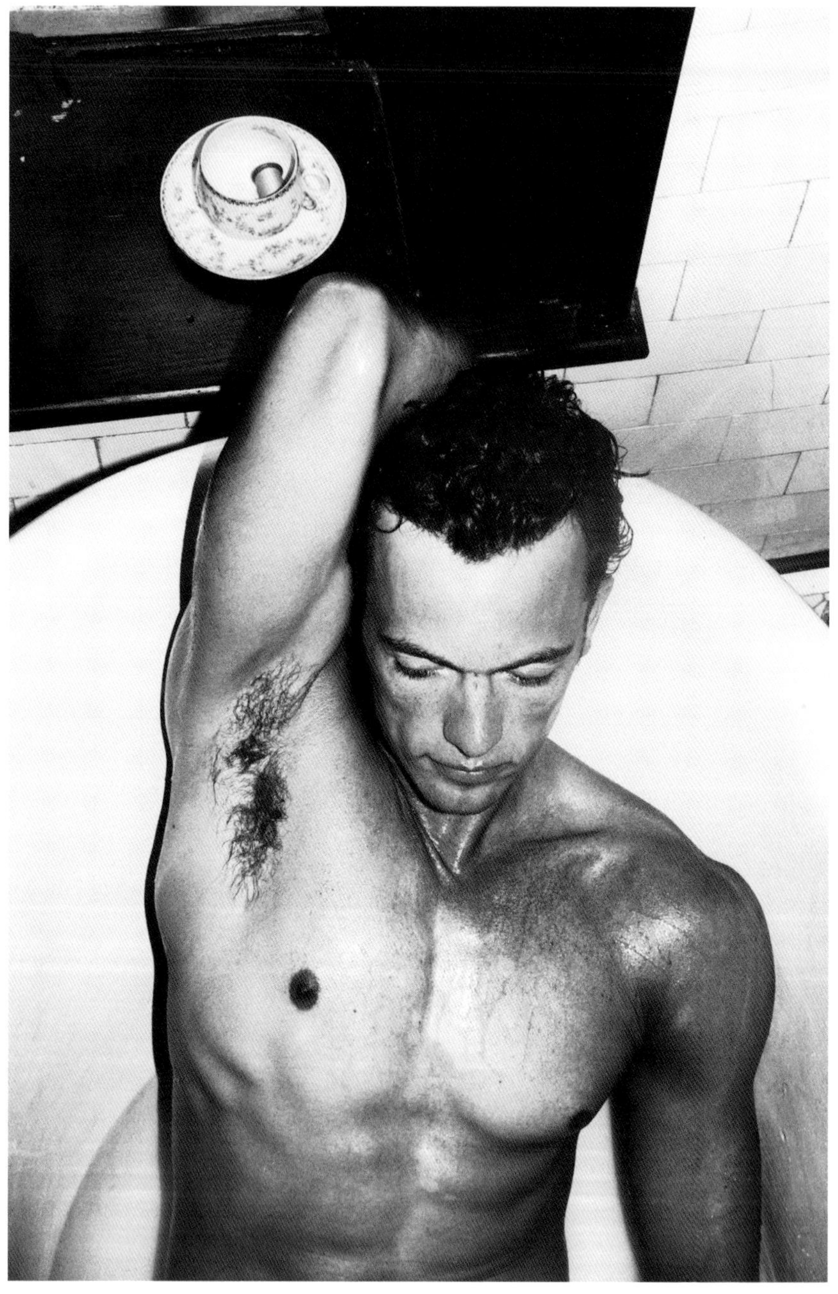

Conrad Hechter, Lane, 1990

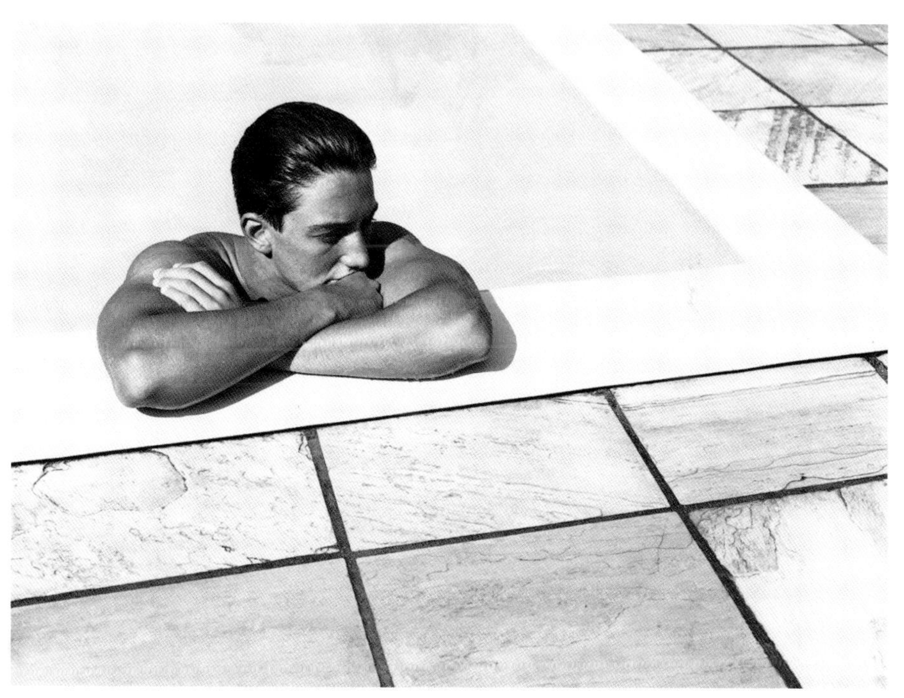

David Sprigle, Luciano, 1993

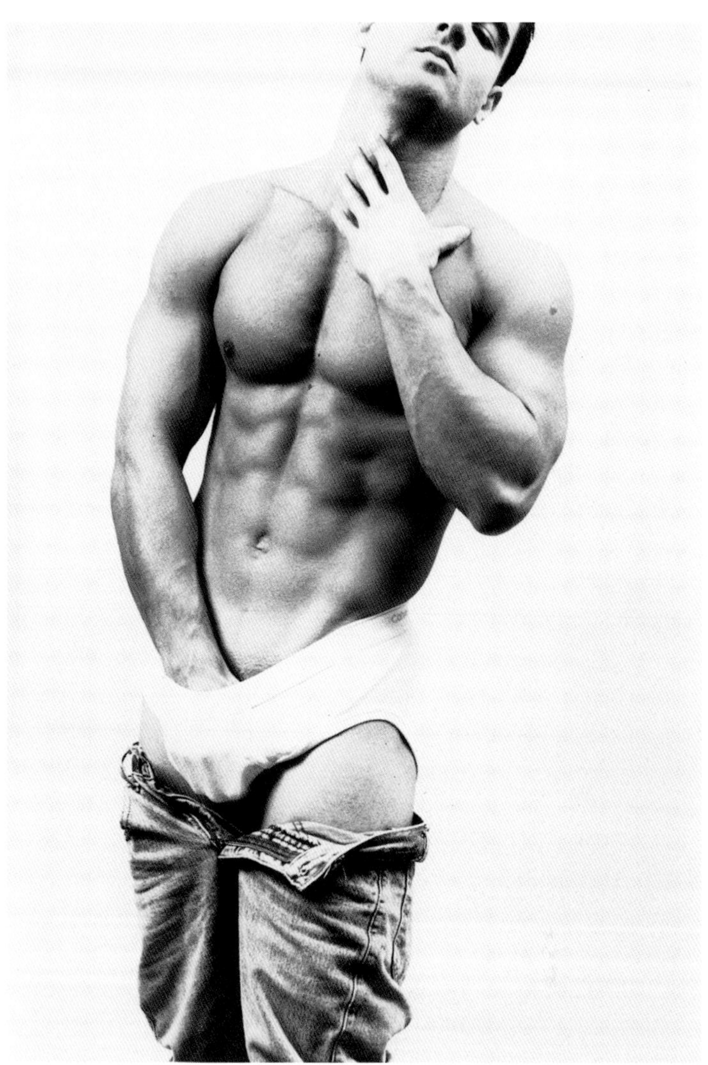

Darryl Strawser, Rey Barbossa, 1993

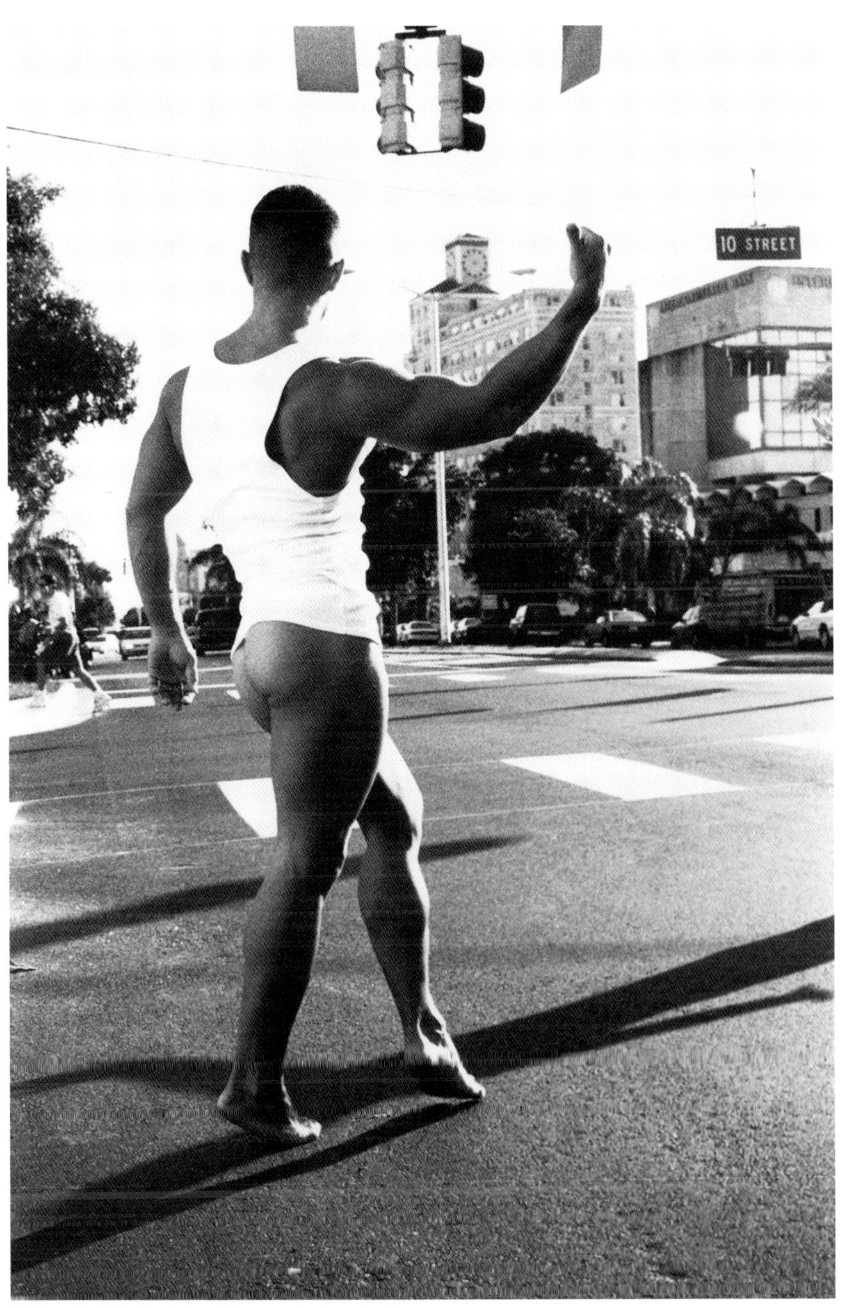

Darryl Strawser, Jojo Odyssey, November 1995   **465**

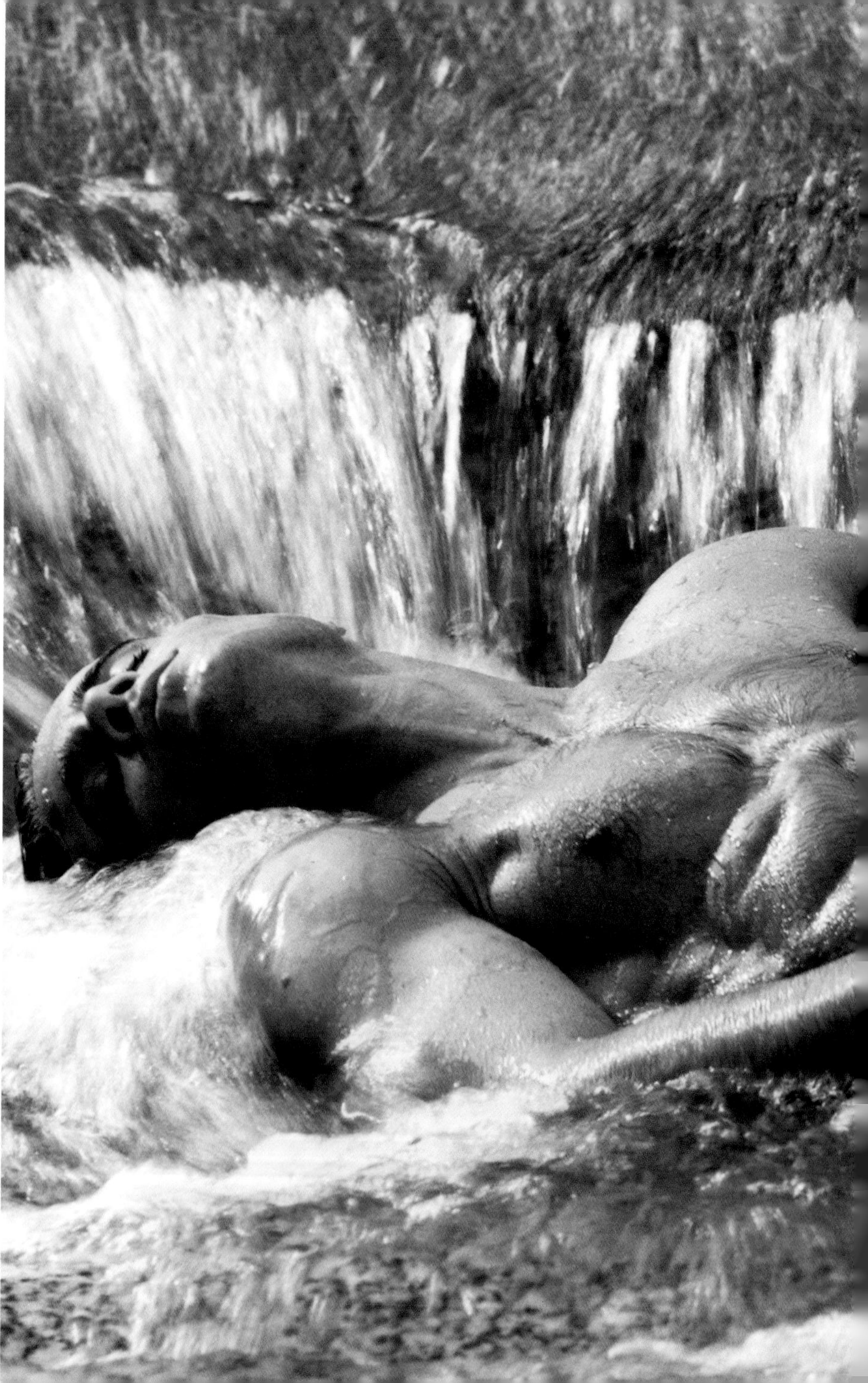

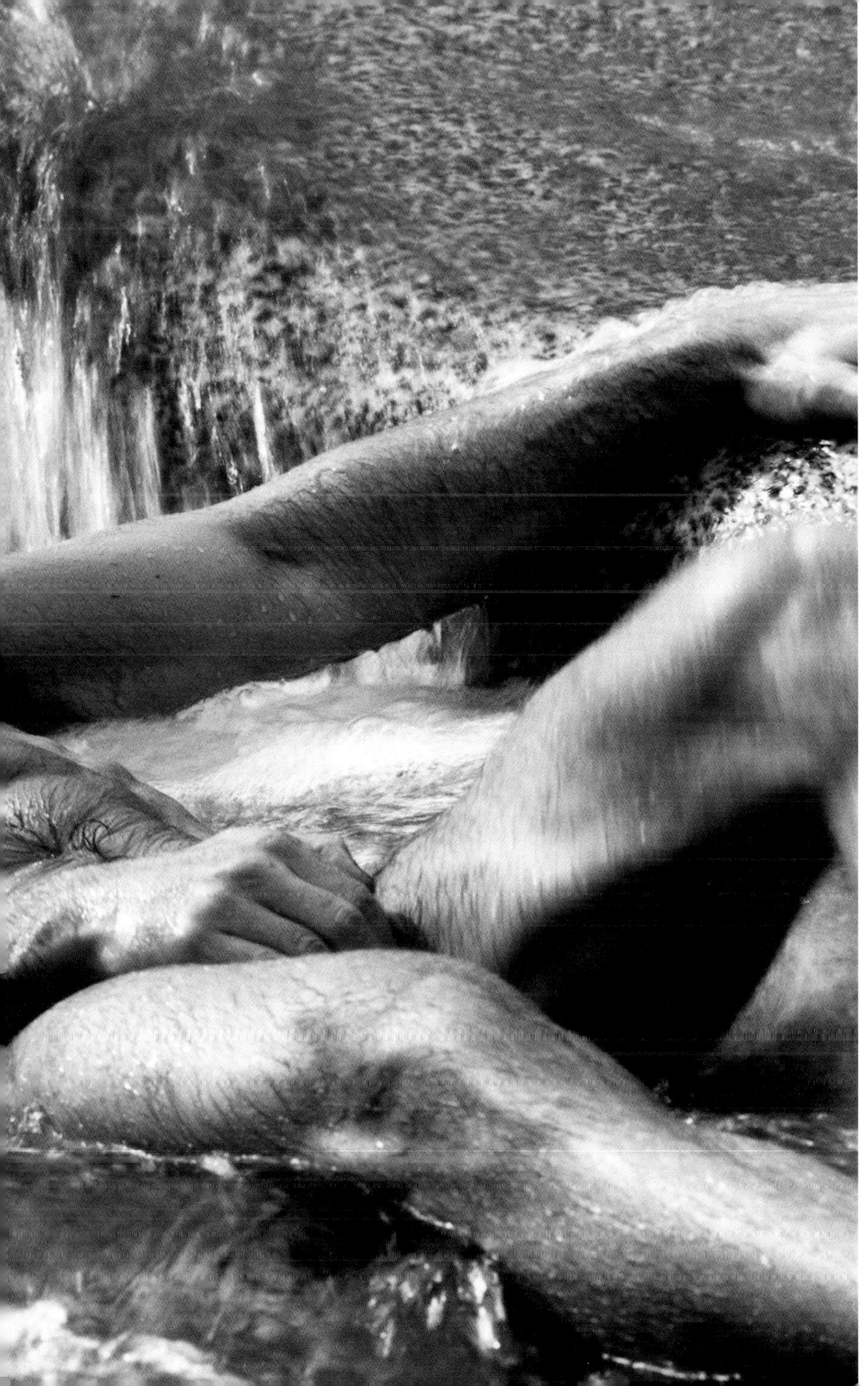

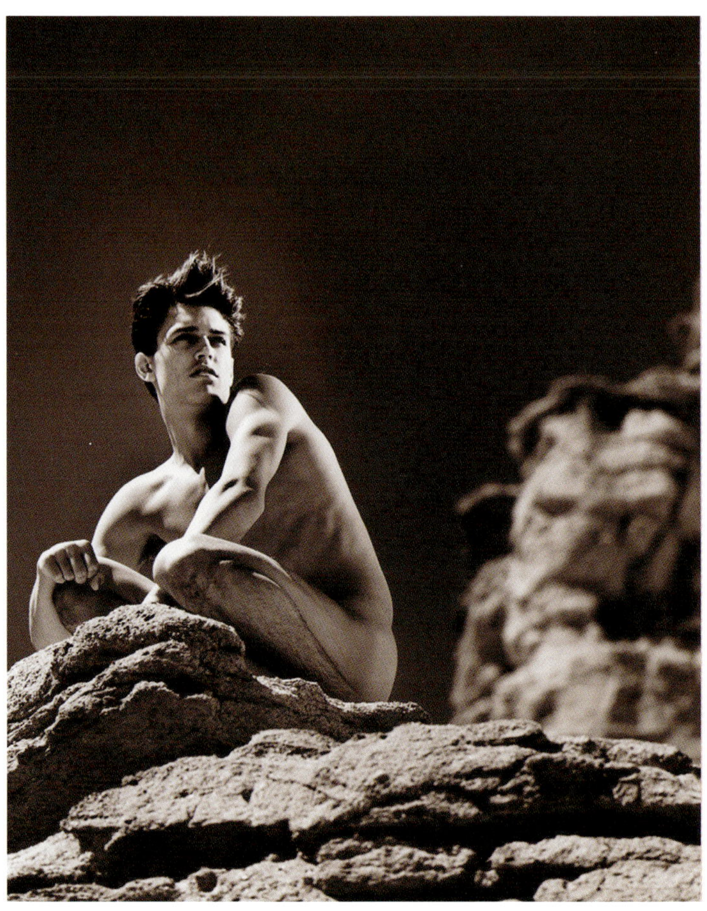

Greg Gorman, Aaron on the Rock, 1991

◄ **Greg Gorman,** Scott in Waterfall, 1990

Greg Gorman, Tony Ward Bent Over, 1988

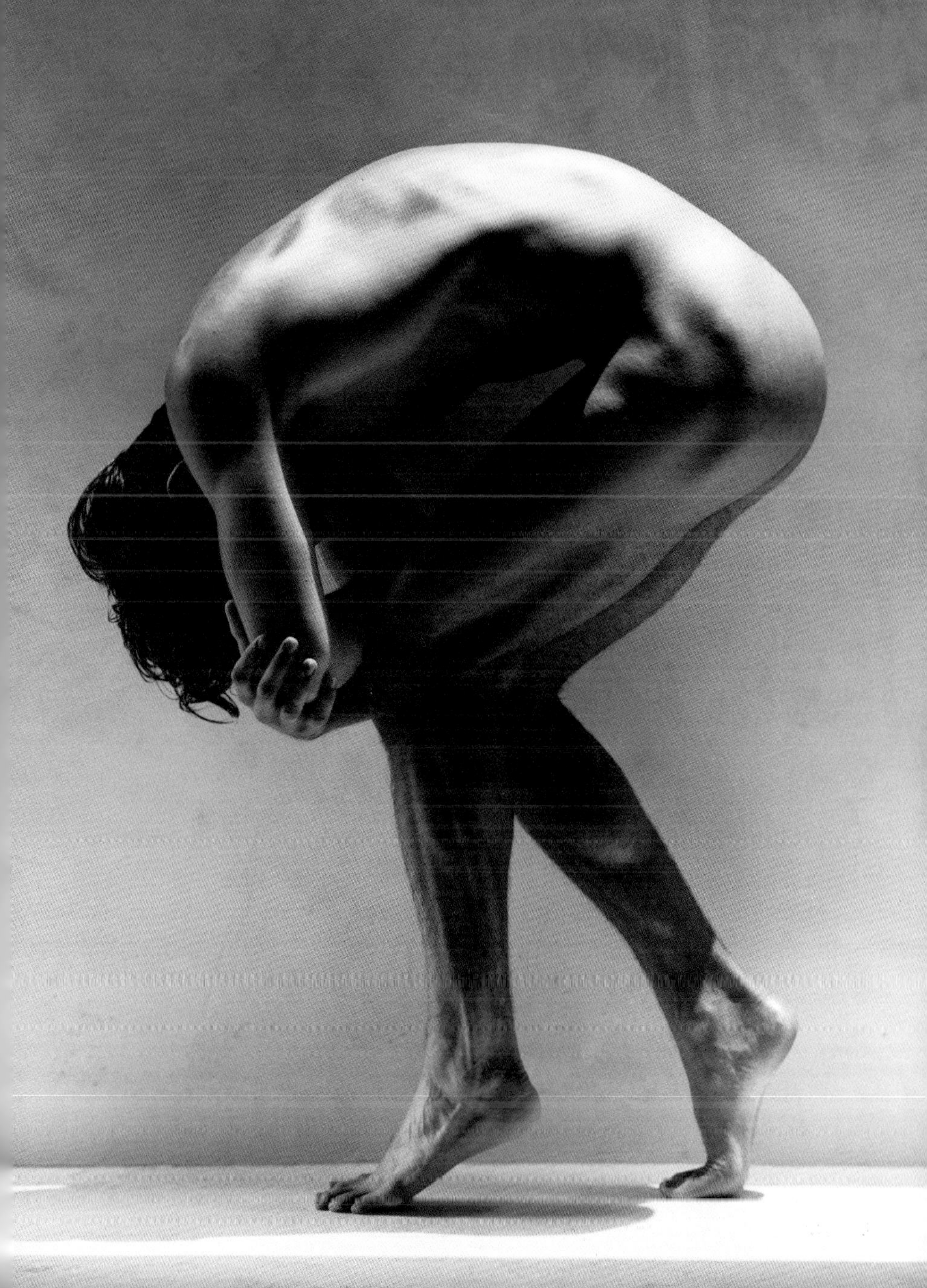

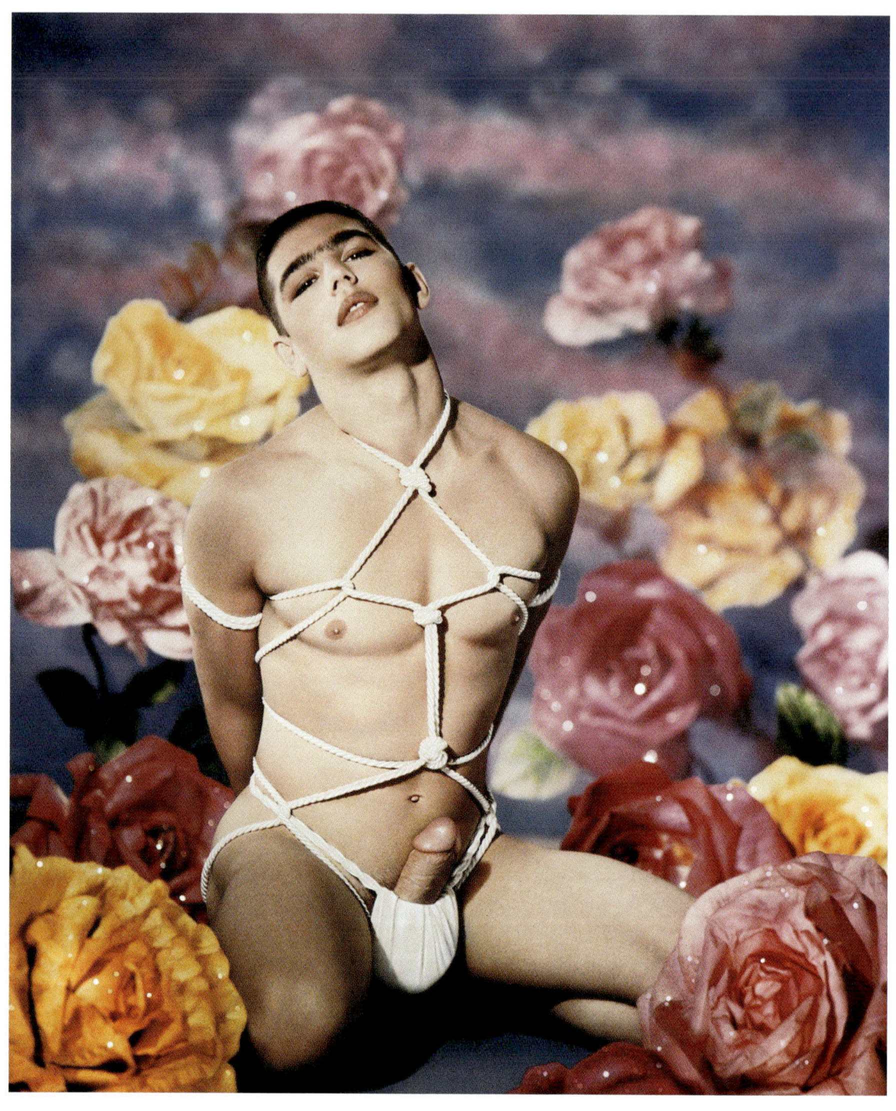

Pierre et Gilles, Le Garçon attaché – Charly, 1993

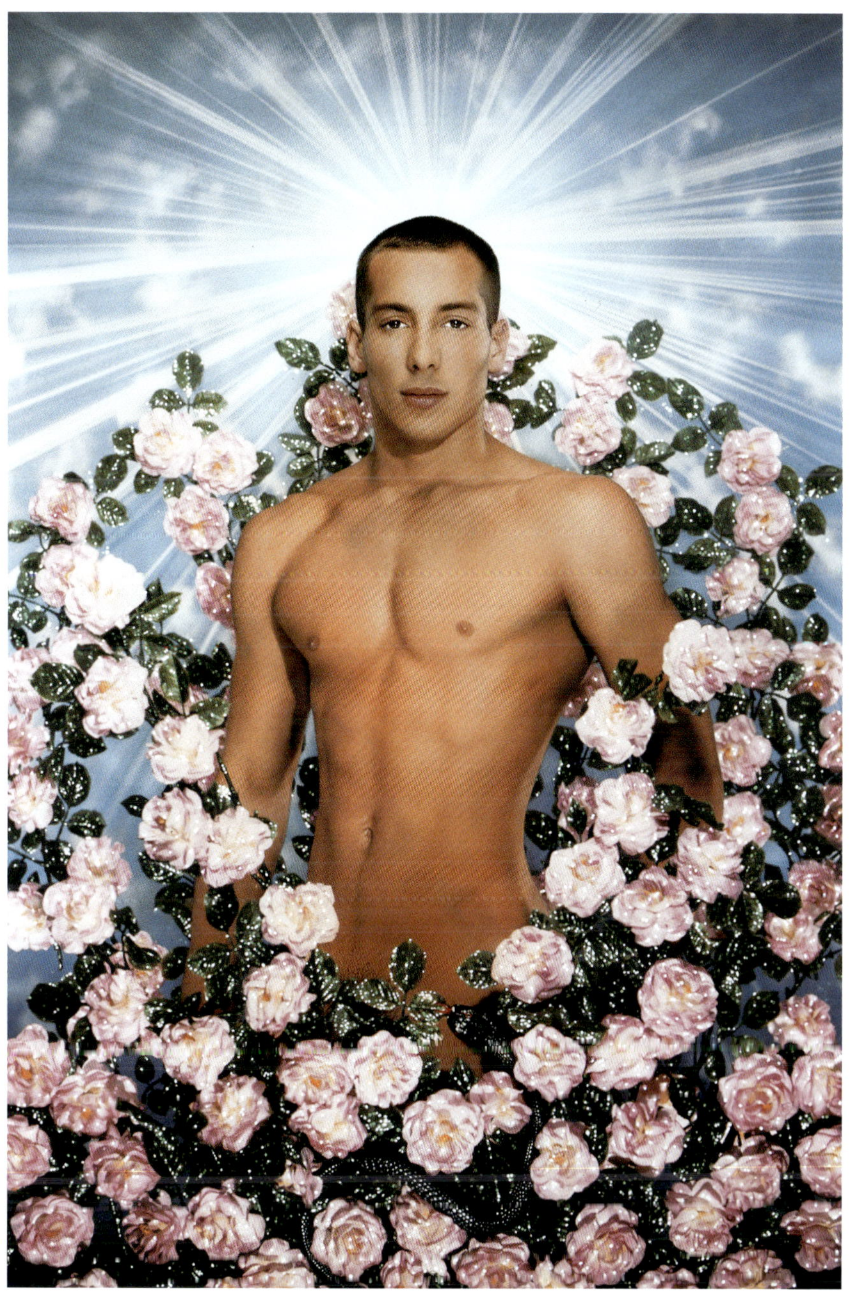

Pierre et Gilles, La Tentation d'Adam – Johan, 1996

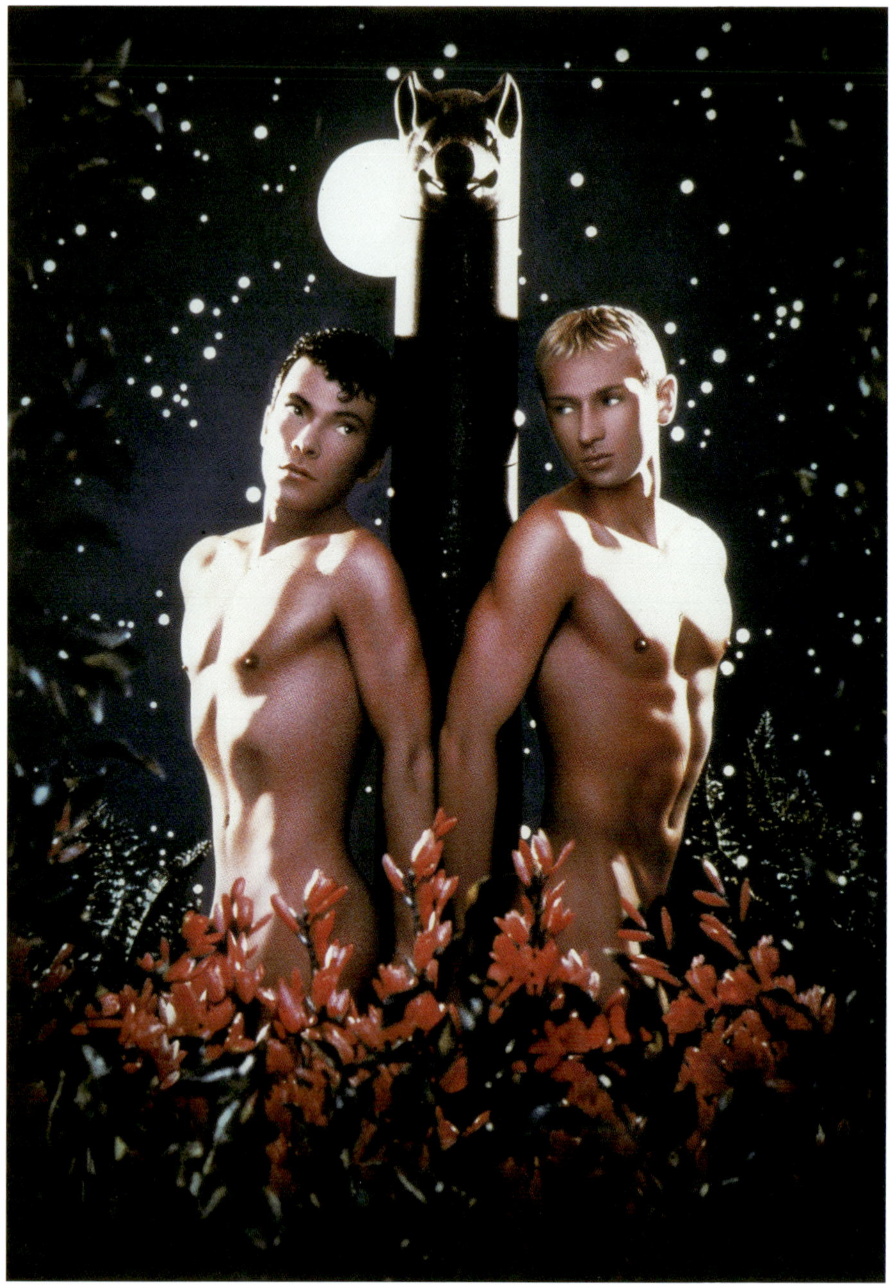

Pierre et Gilles, *Le Totem – Pierre et Gilles, 1993*

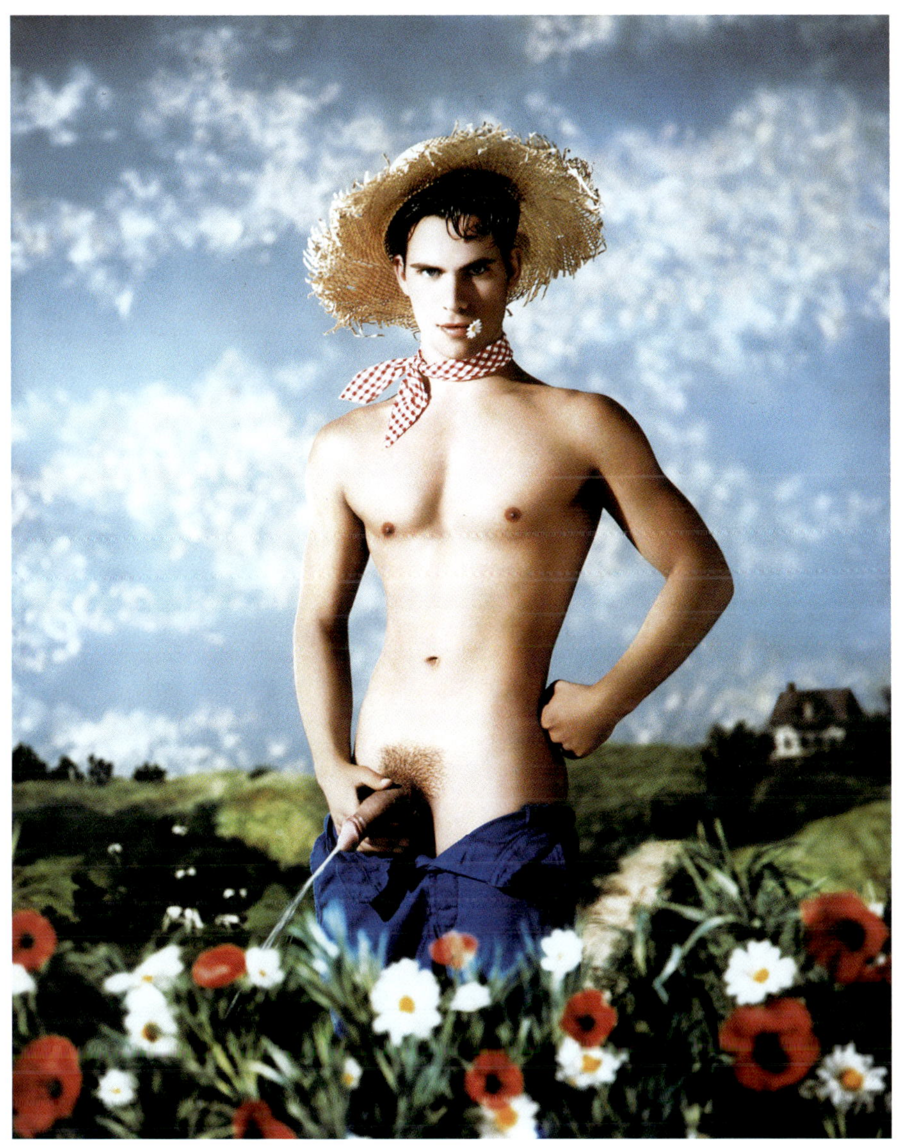

Pierre et Gilles, Le Petit Jardinier – Didier, 1993

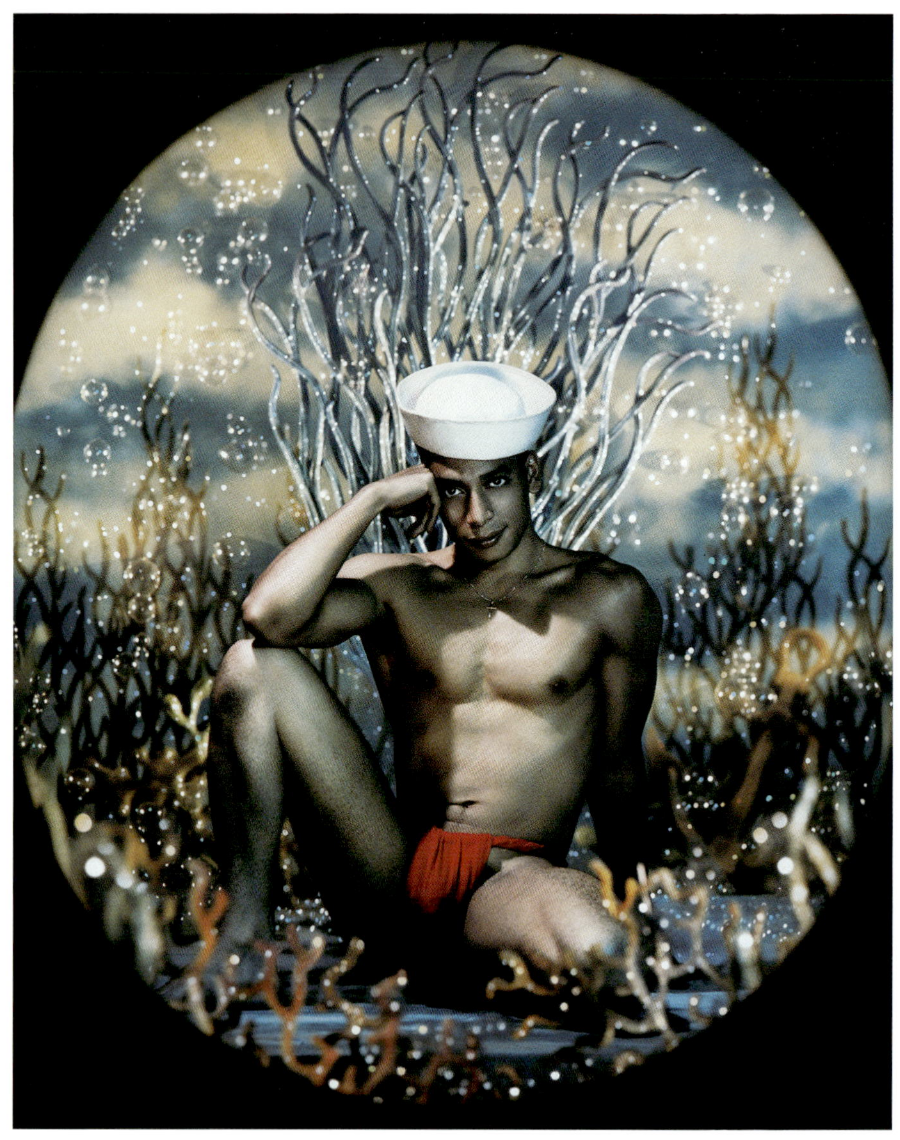

Pierre et Gilles, Le Marin Rêveur – Ken, 1994

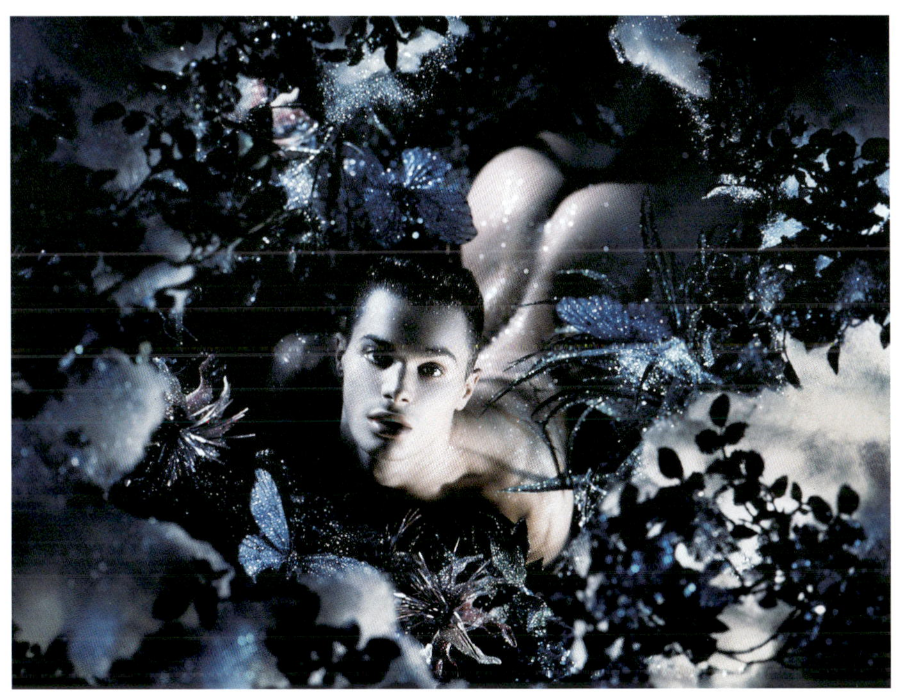

Pierre et Gilles, Enzo, 1992

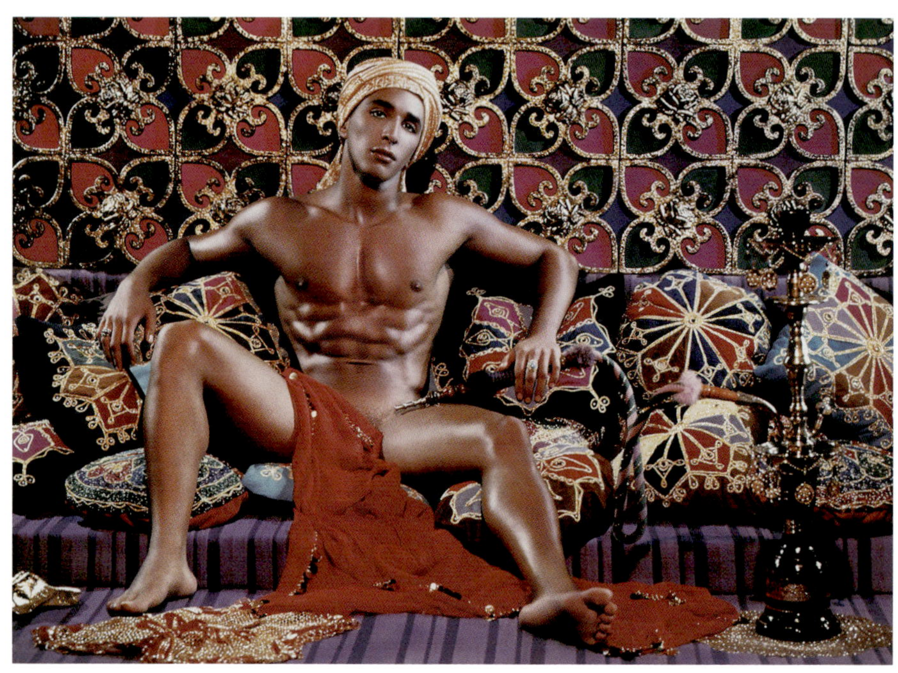

Pierre et Gilles, Le Fumeur de Narguilé – Aziz, 1996

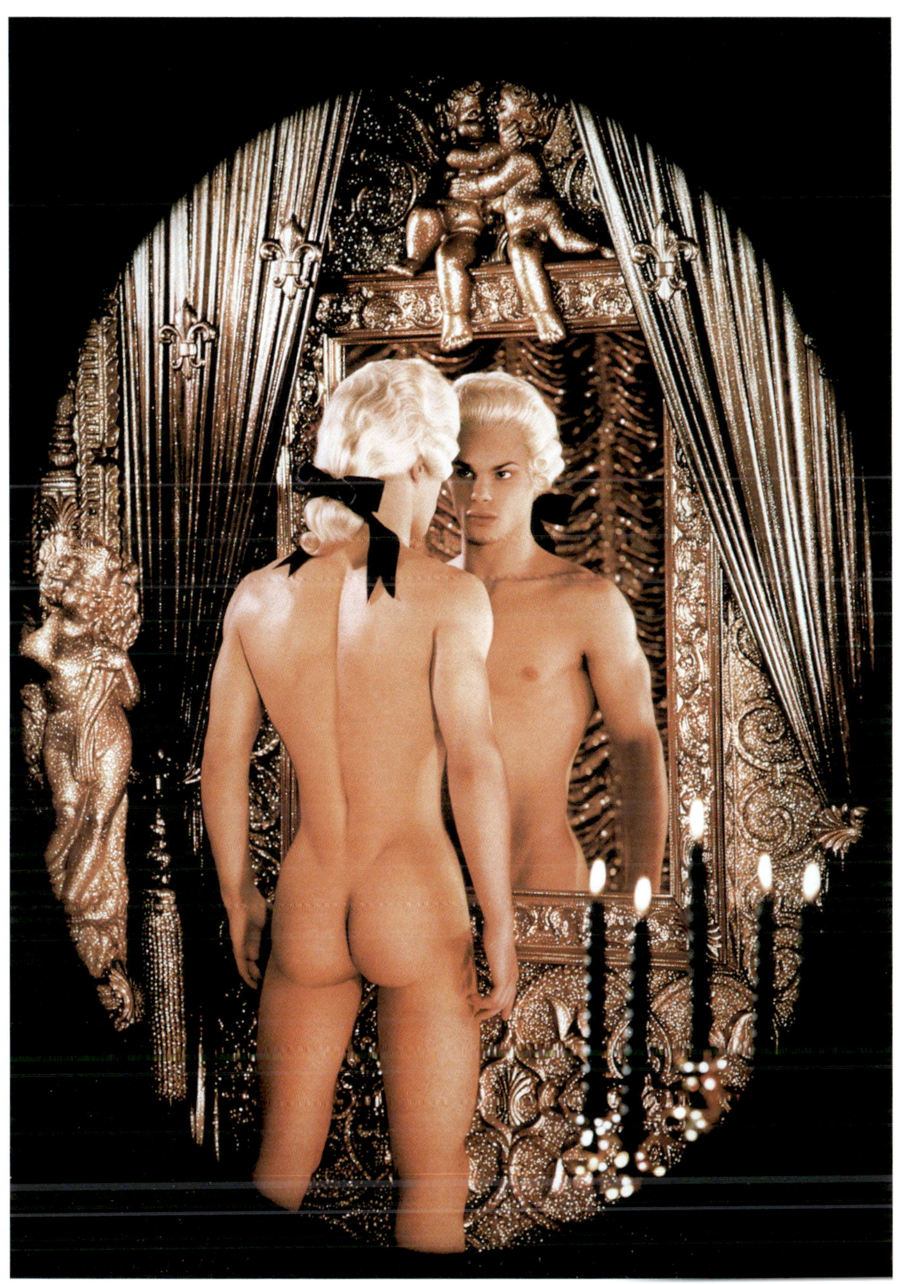

Pierre et Gilles, Casanova – Enzo, 1995

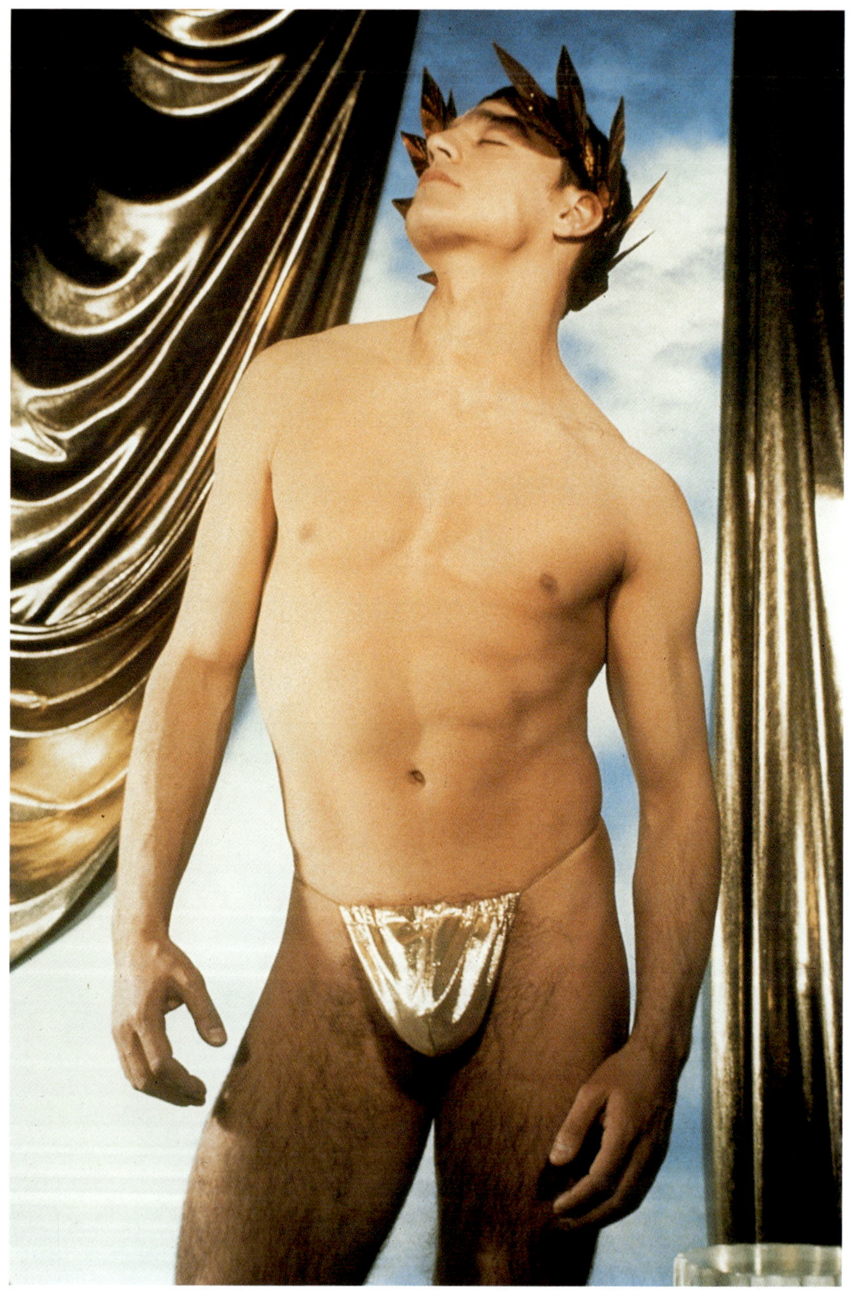

José Villarrubia, Roman, 1990

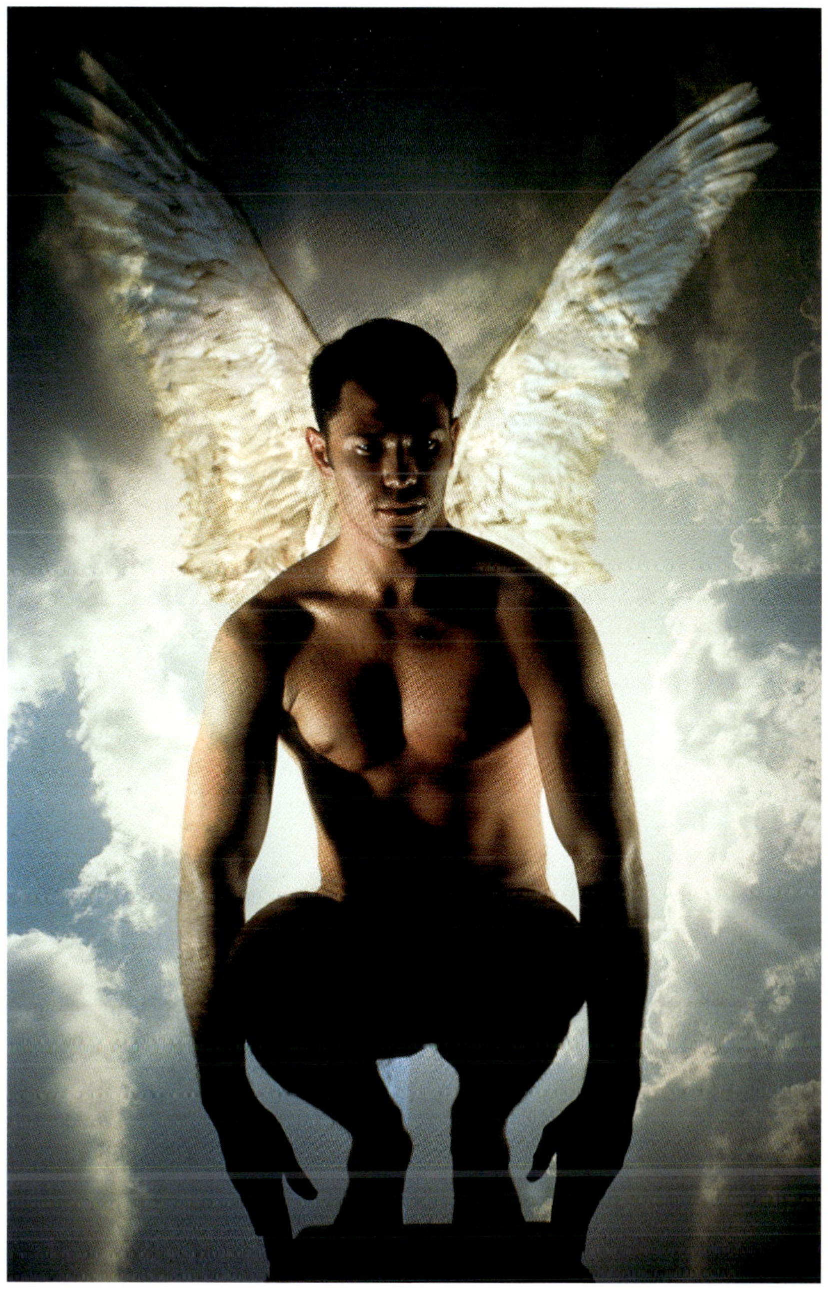

José Villarrubia, Guardian Angel, 1993

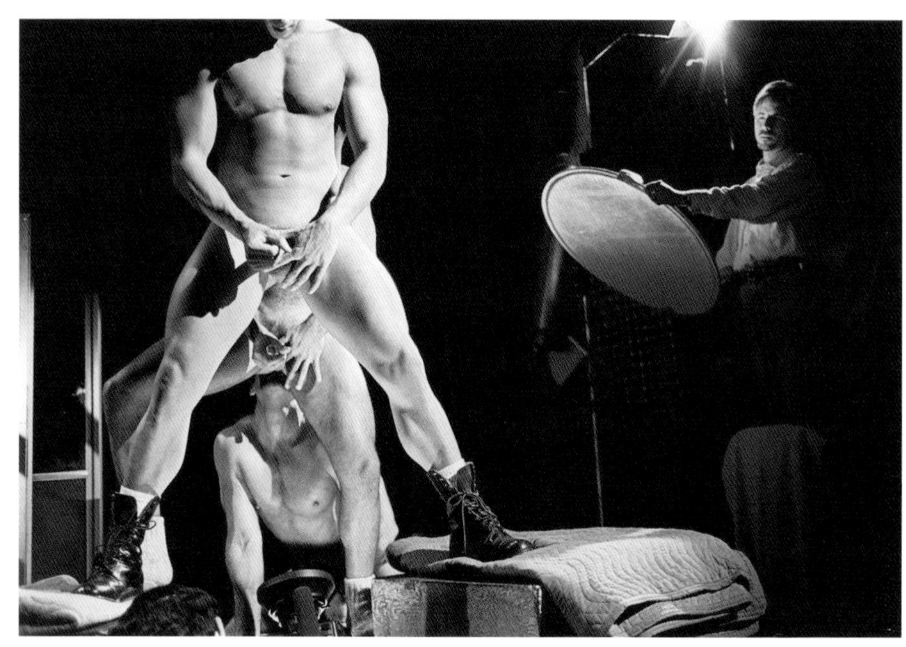

Ken Probst, Homage to George Platt Lynes, 1994

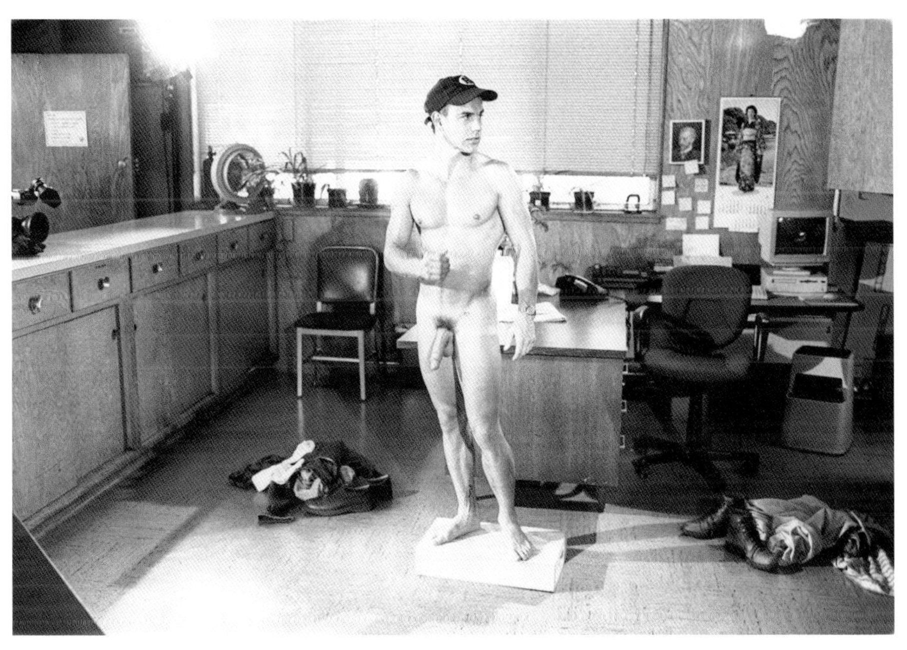

Ken Probst, Brennan, Pint-Sized Adonis, 1996

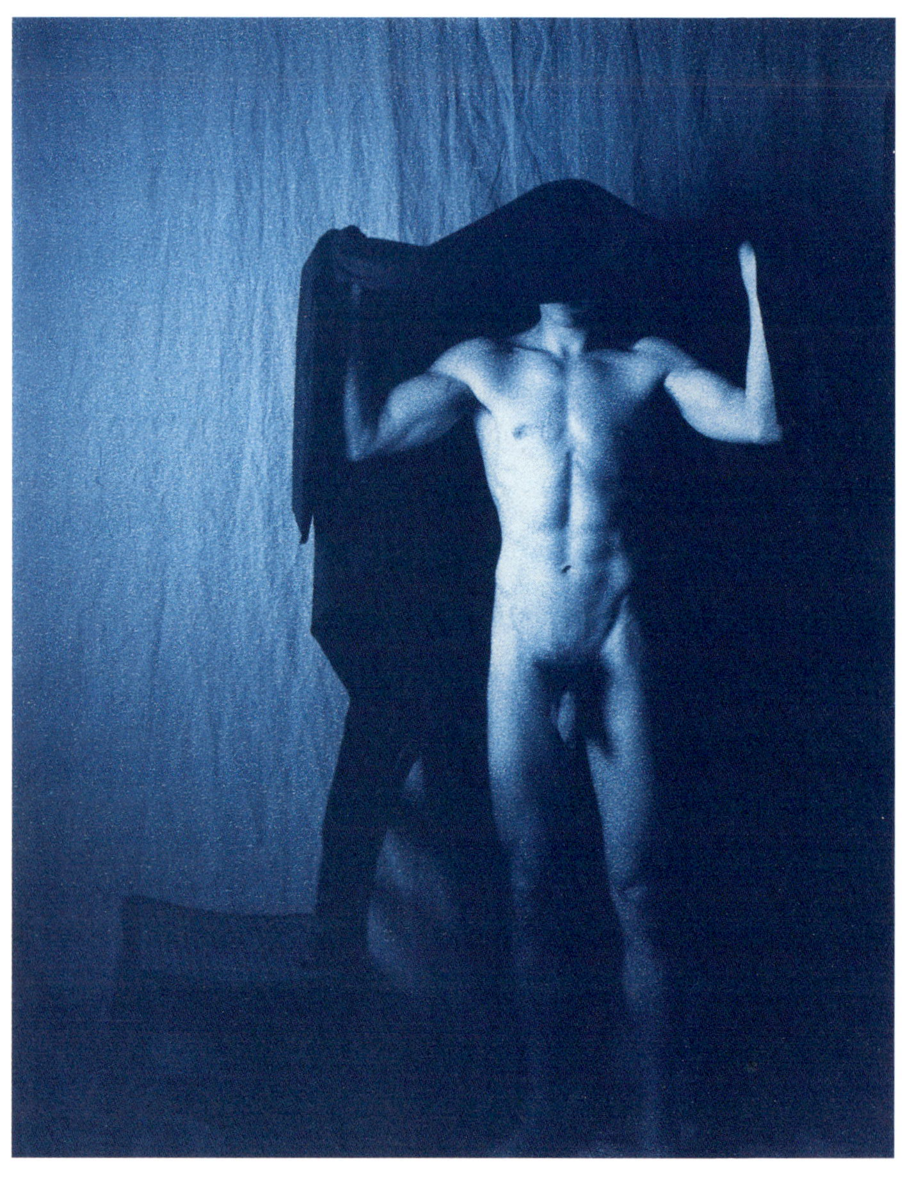

John Dugdale, Focusing Cloth, 1994

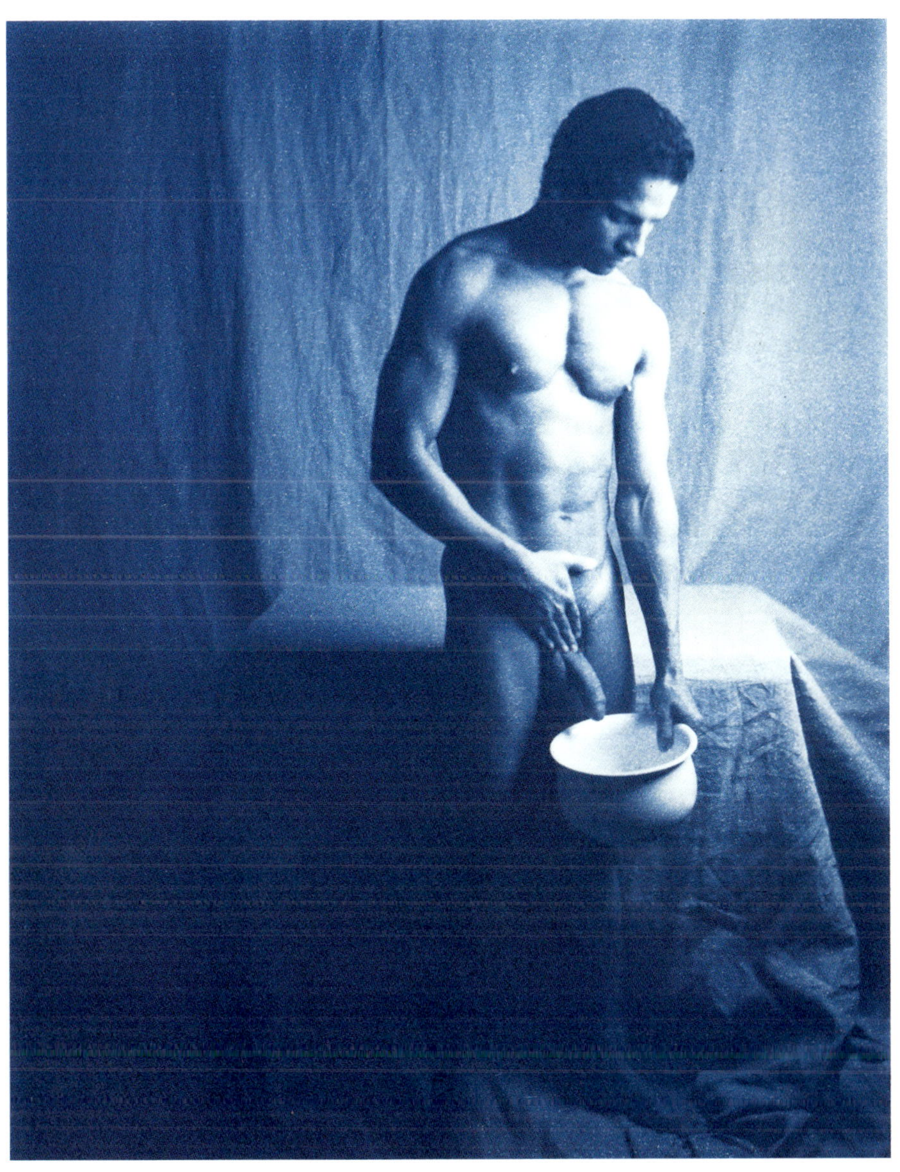

John Dugdale, Giovanni with Chamberpot, 1994

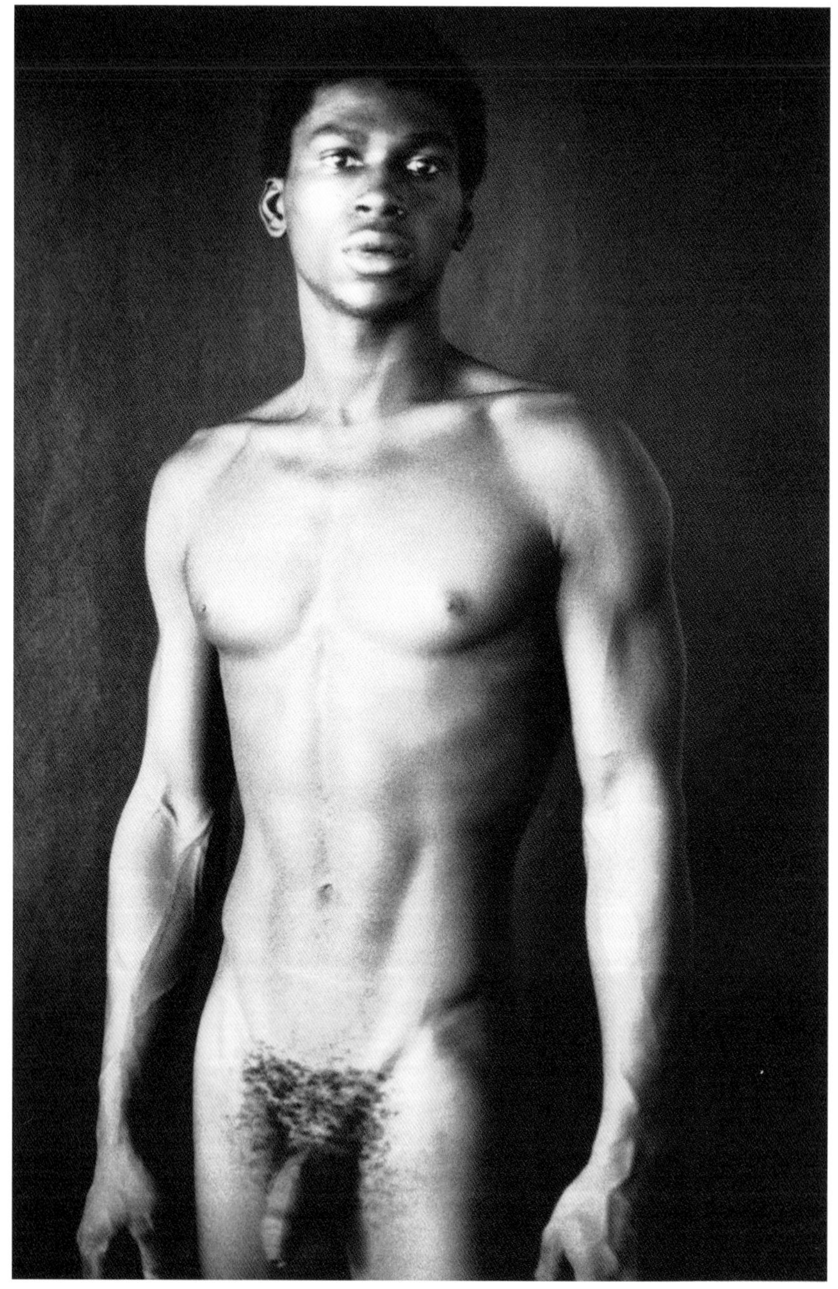

484

Dick Sweet, c. 1990

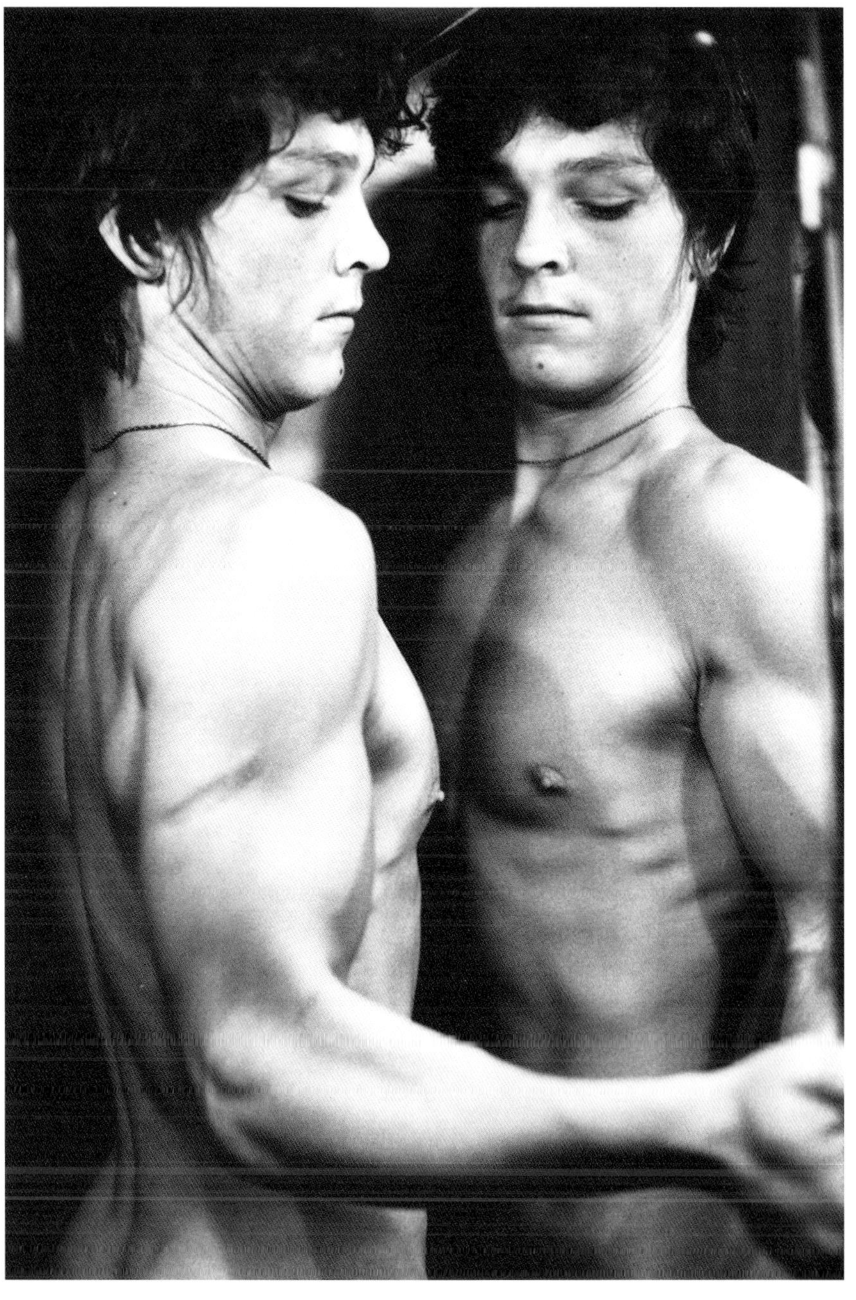

Dick Sweet, c. 1985

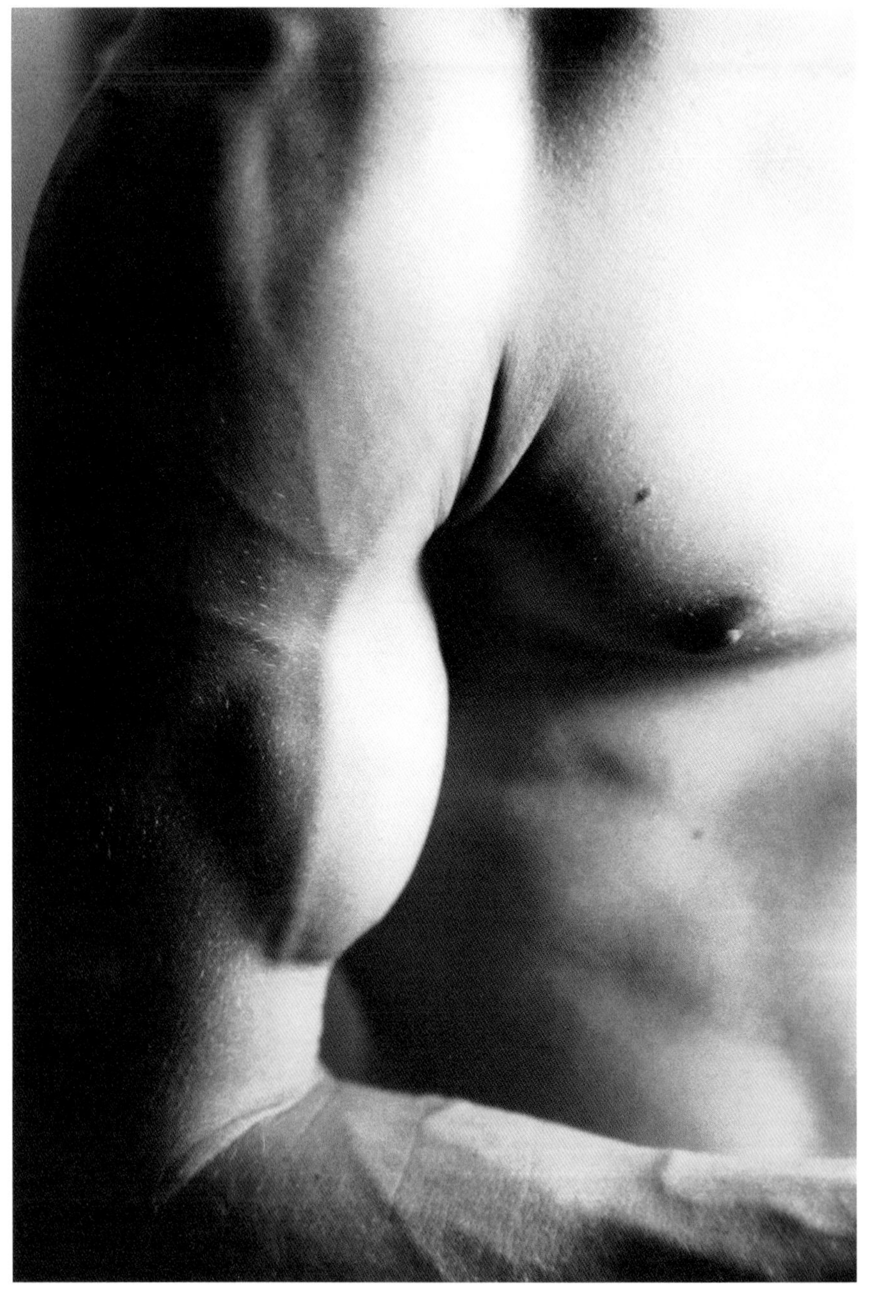

Dick Sweet, c. 1990

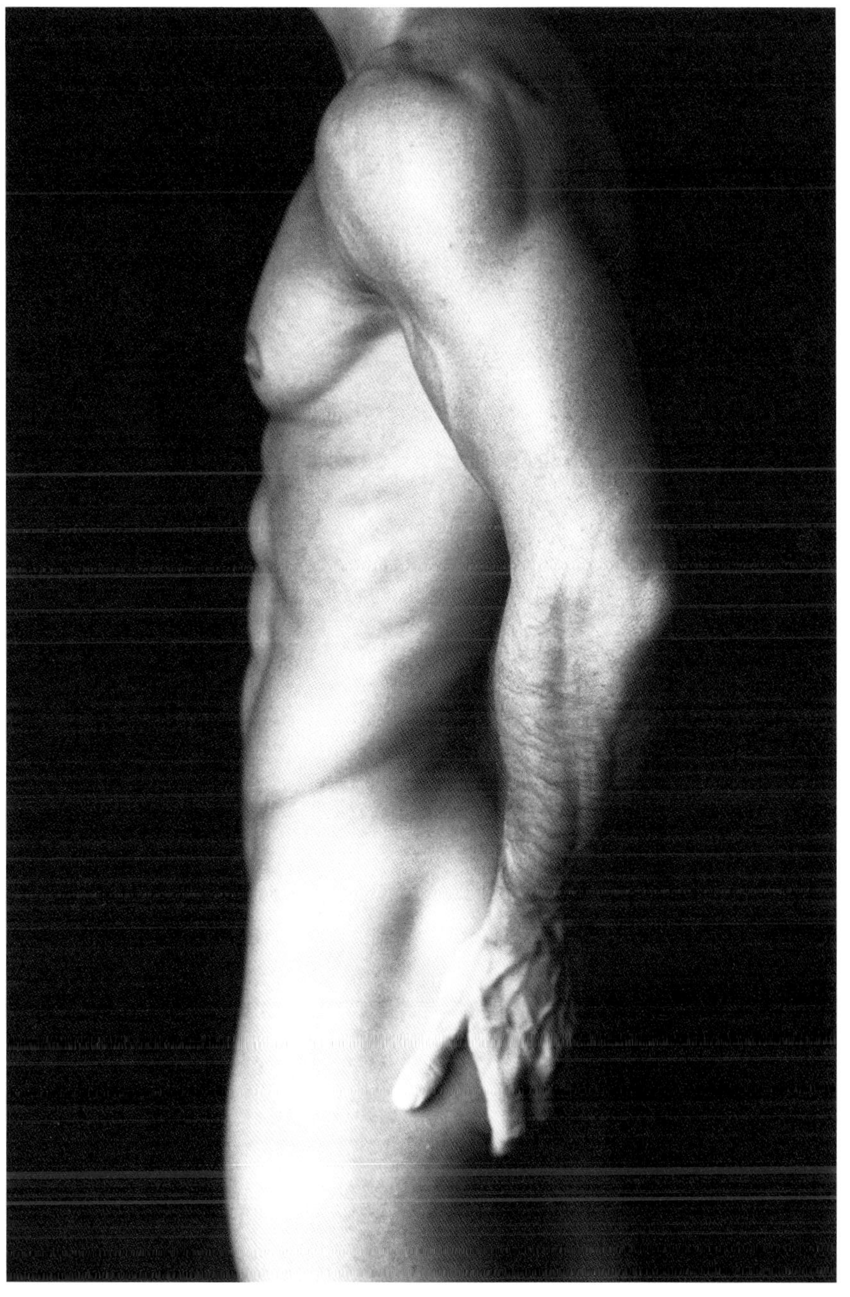

Dick Sweet, 1996

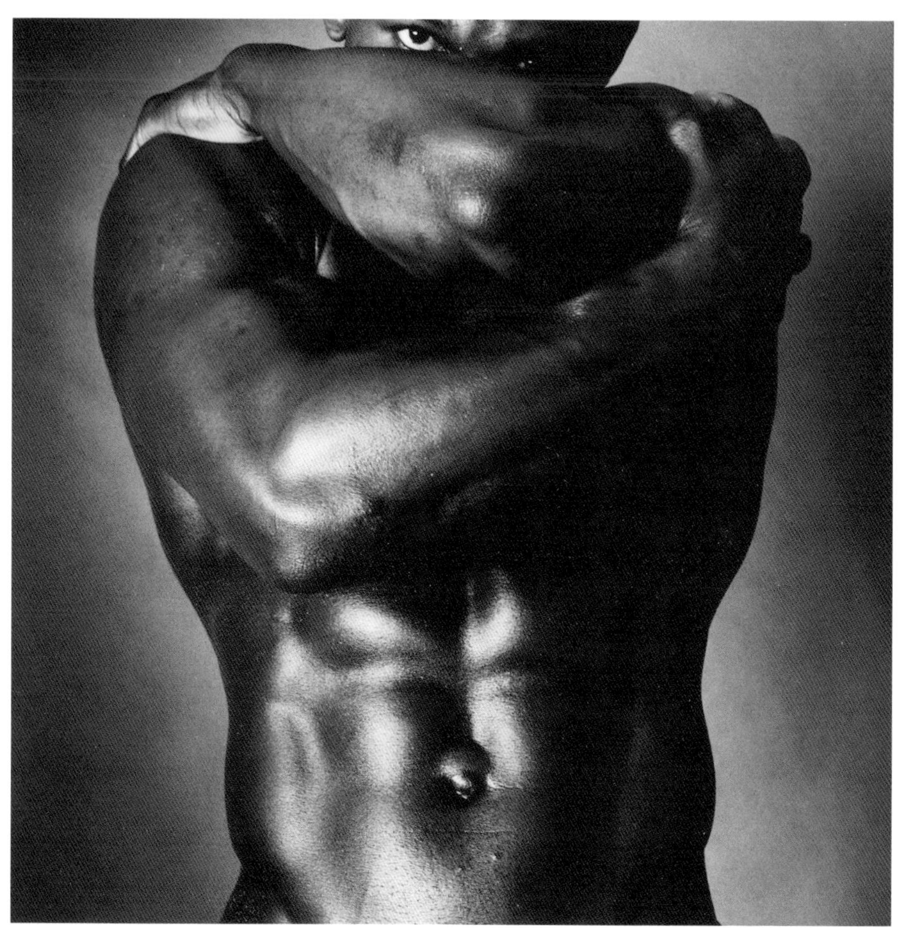

Harriet Leibowitz, Duramus, 1996

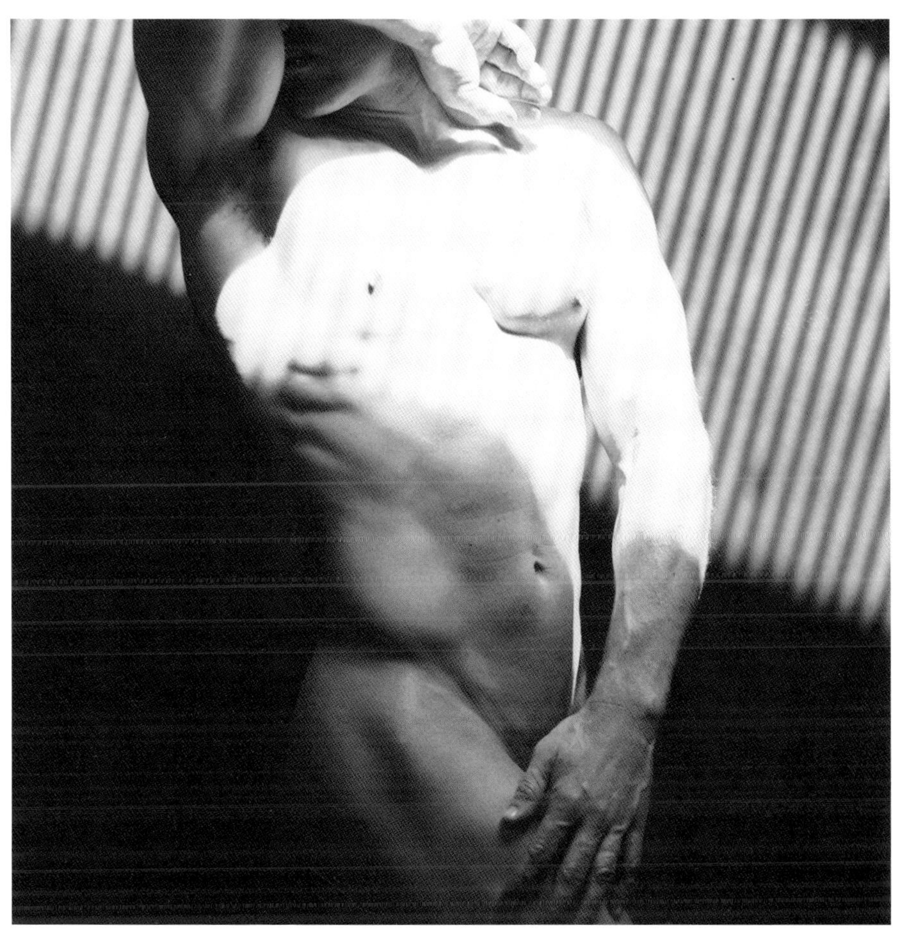

Harriet Leibowitz, Larry, 1996

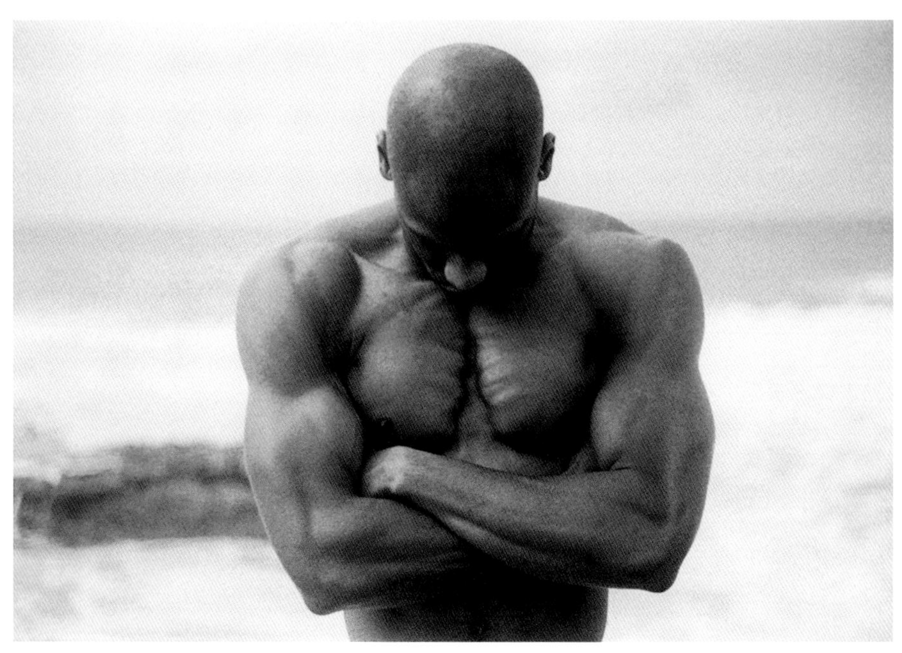

Steve Vaccariello, Marcus, with Arms, 1997

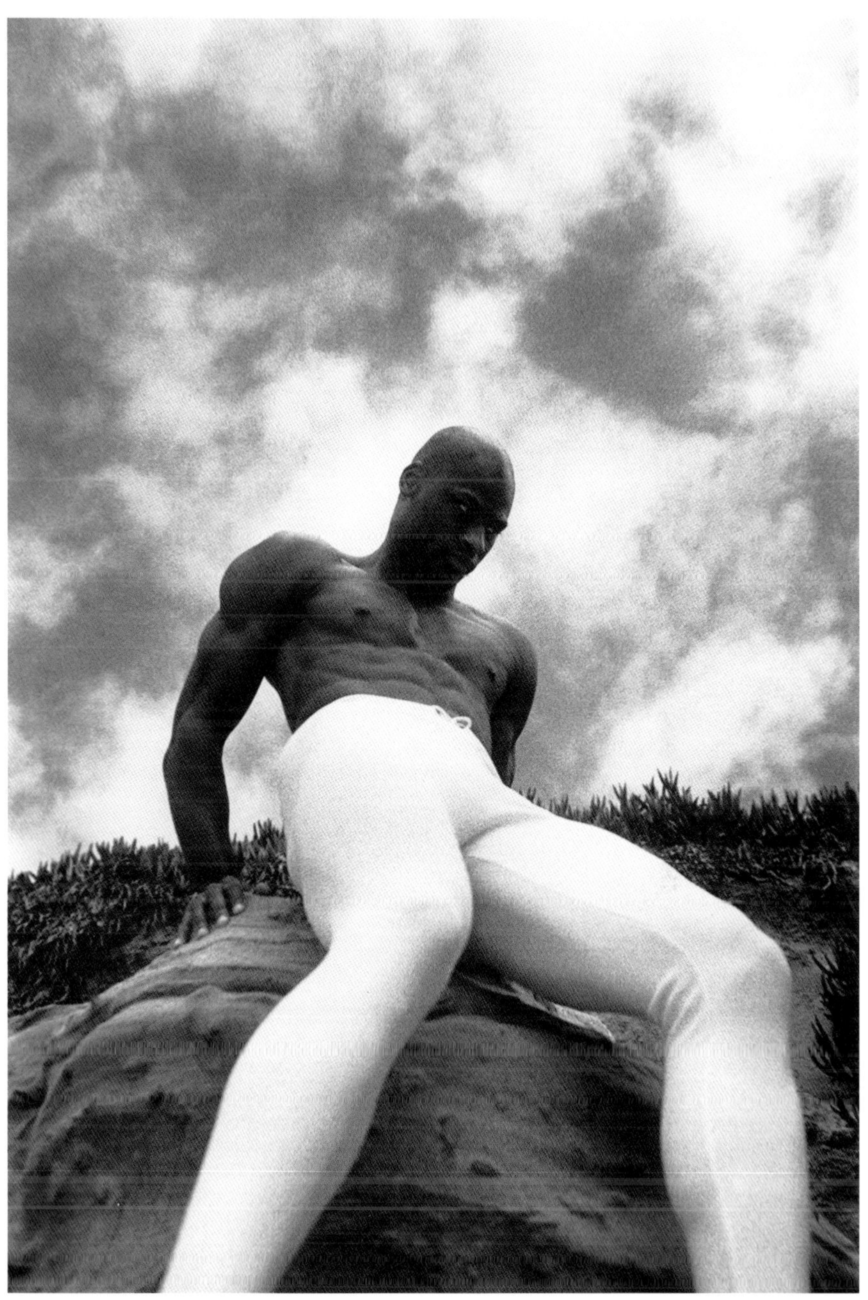

Steve Vaccariello, Marcus, with Tights, 1997

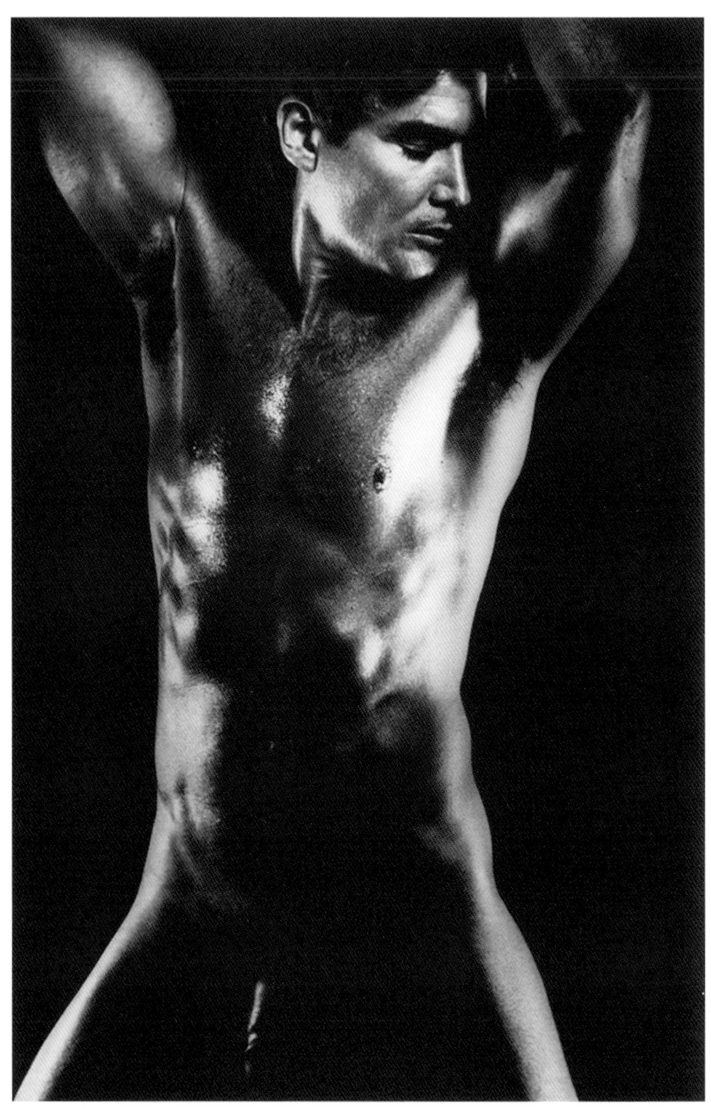

Dianora Niccolini, Robert, 1997

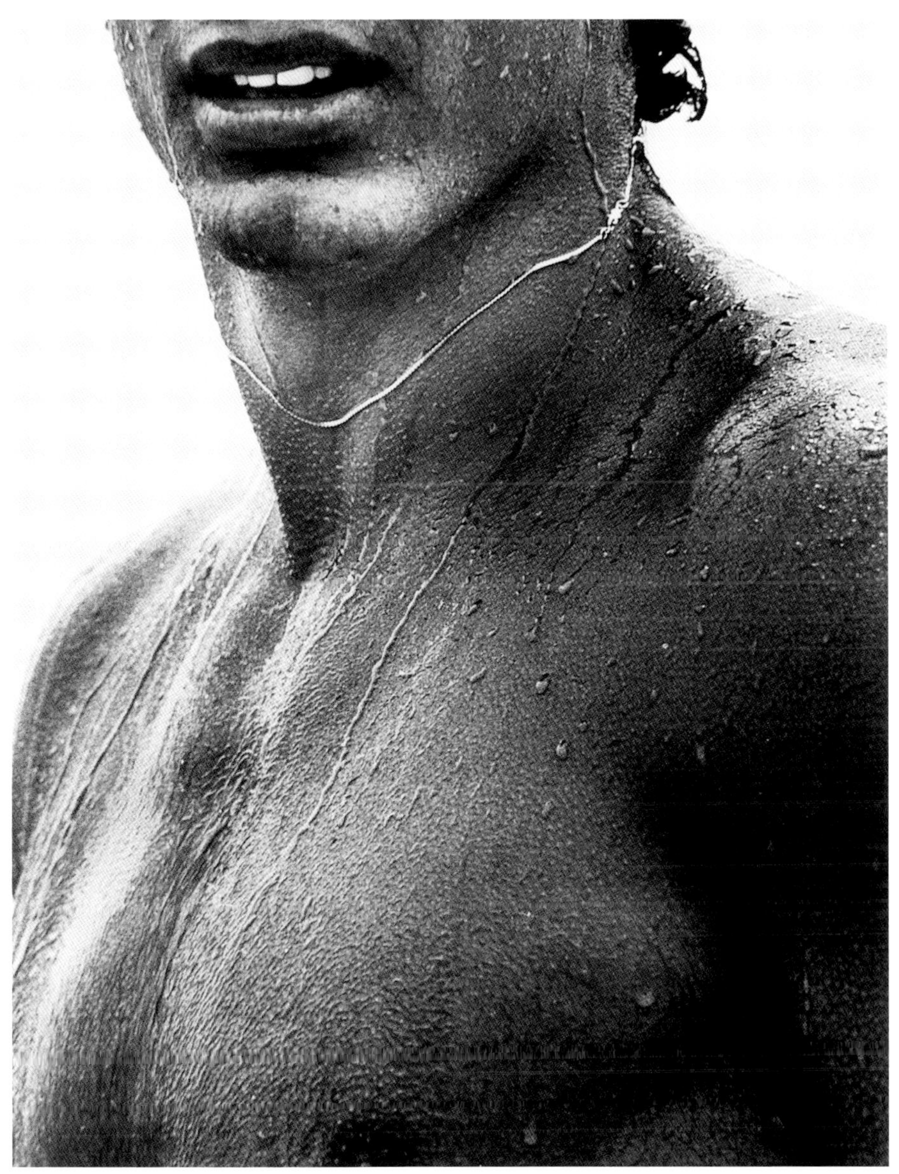

Dianora Niccolini, The Swimmer, 1983

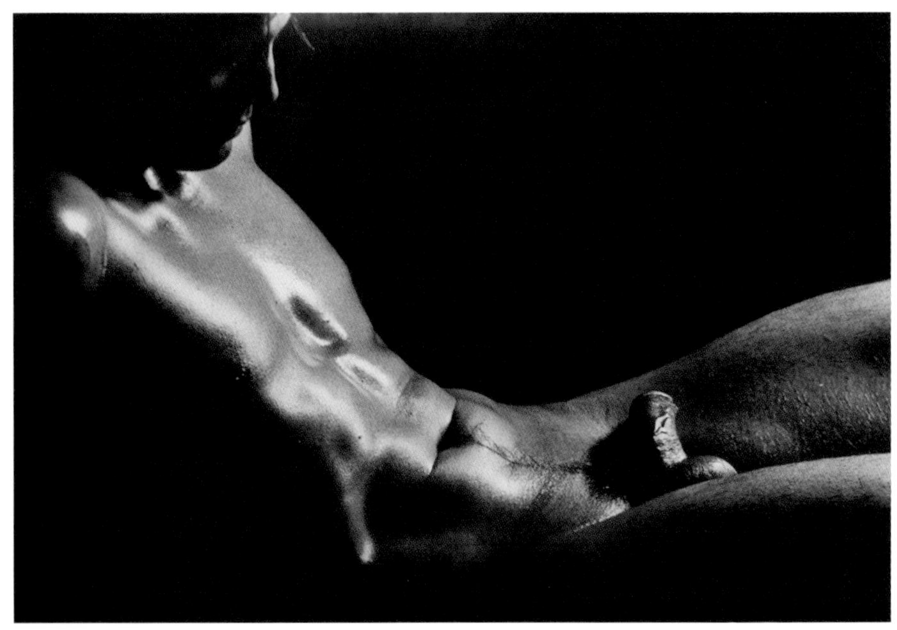

Dianora Niccolini, The Reclining Nude, 1997

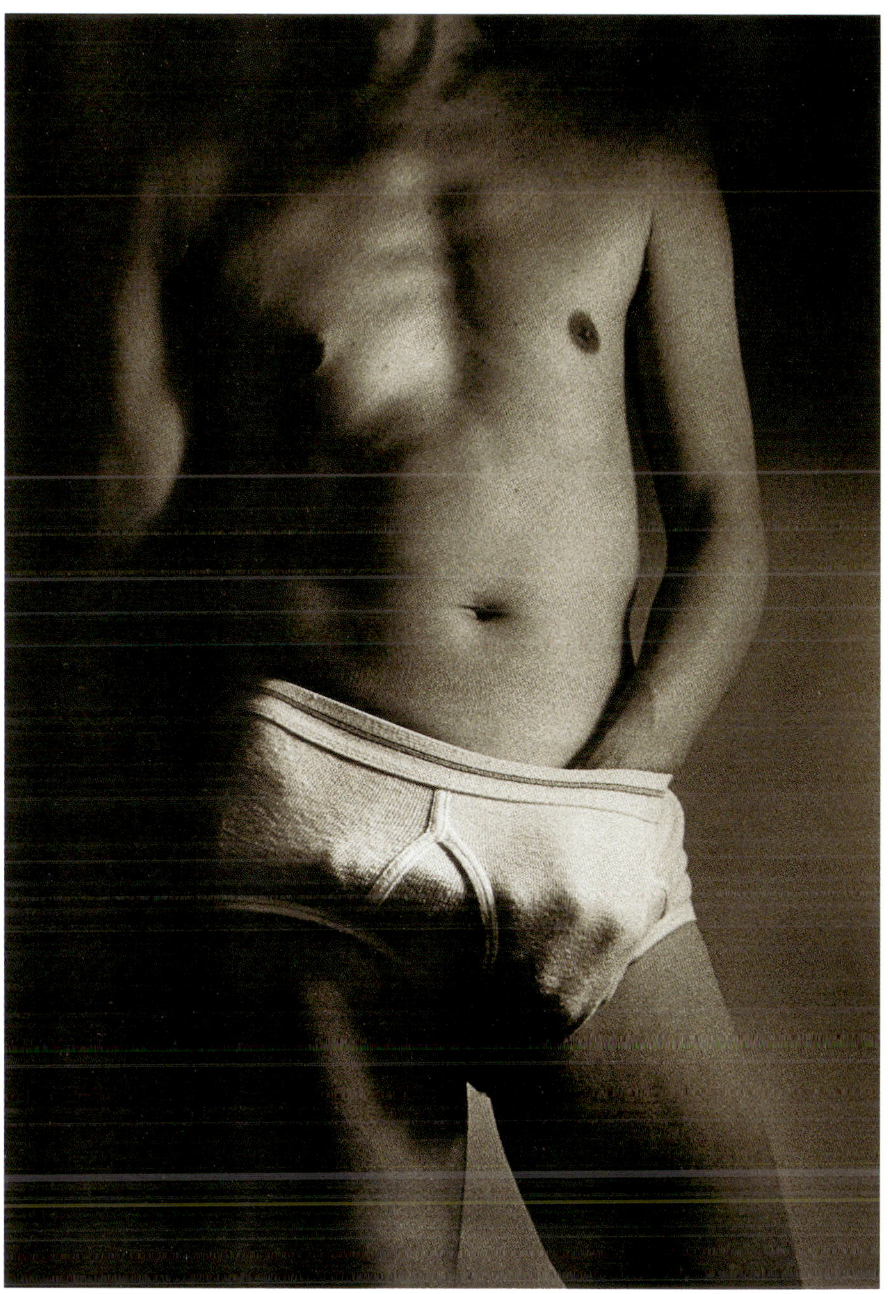

Dianora Niccolini, Self Discovery, 1980

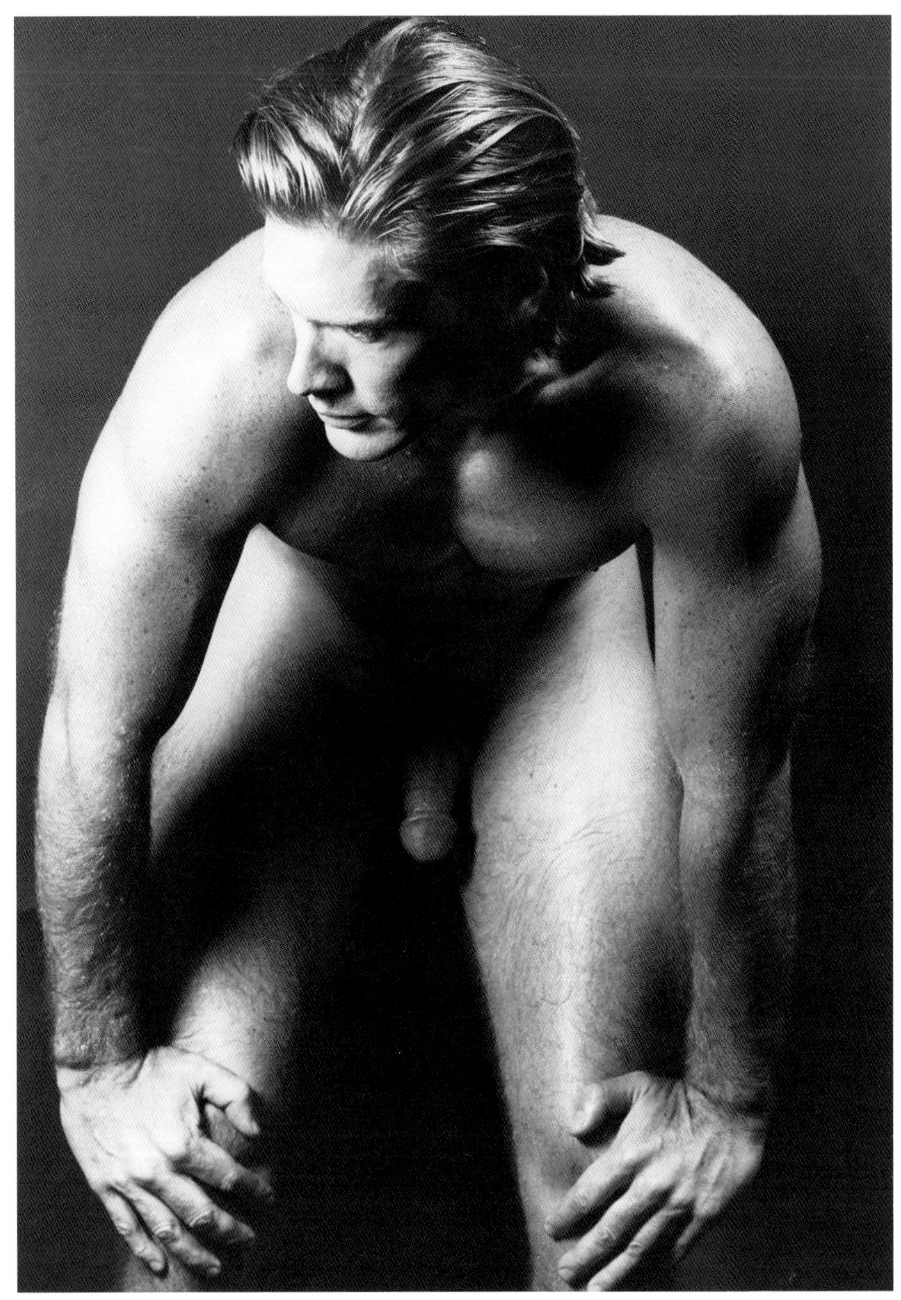

Dianora Niccolini, Stockton, 1997

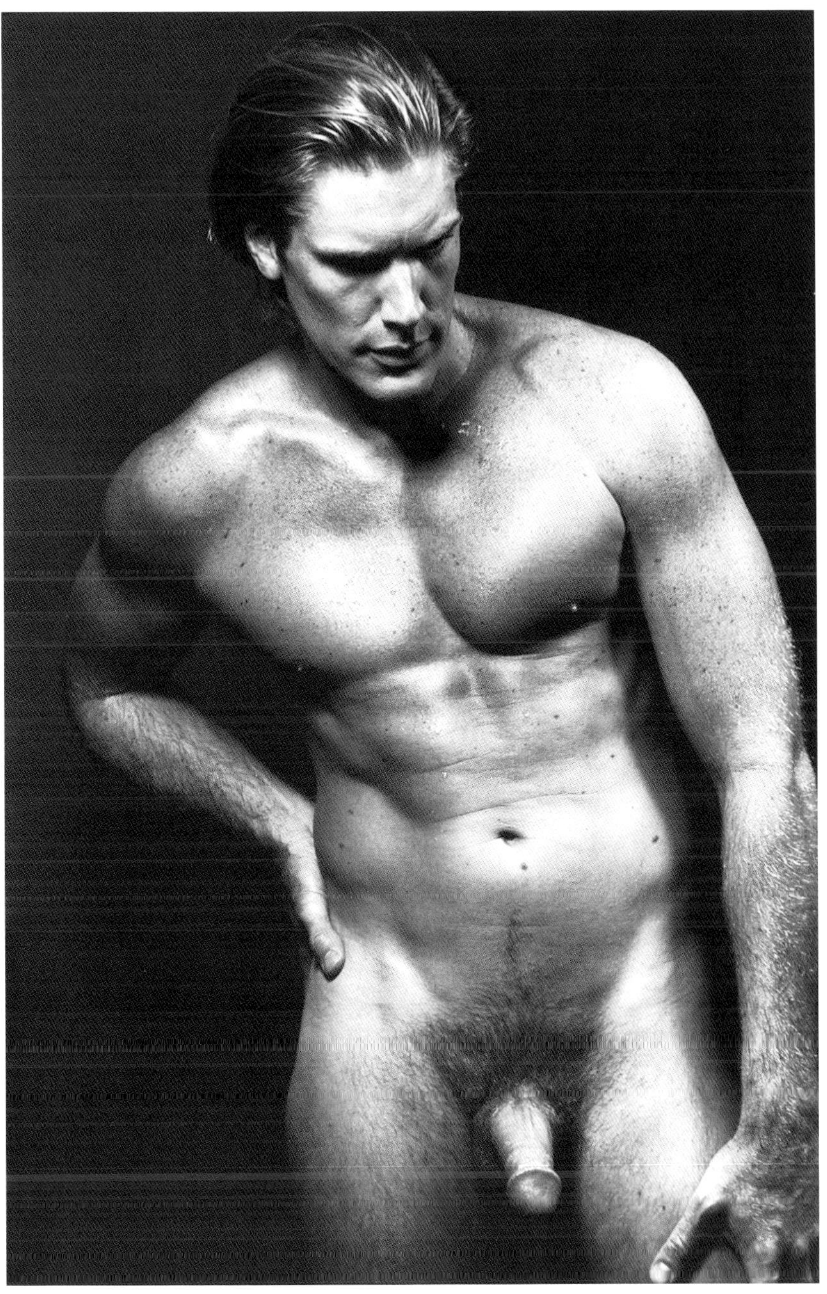

Dianora Niccolini, Stockton, 1997

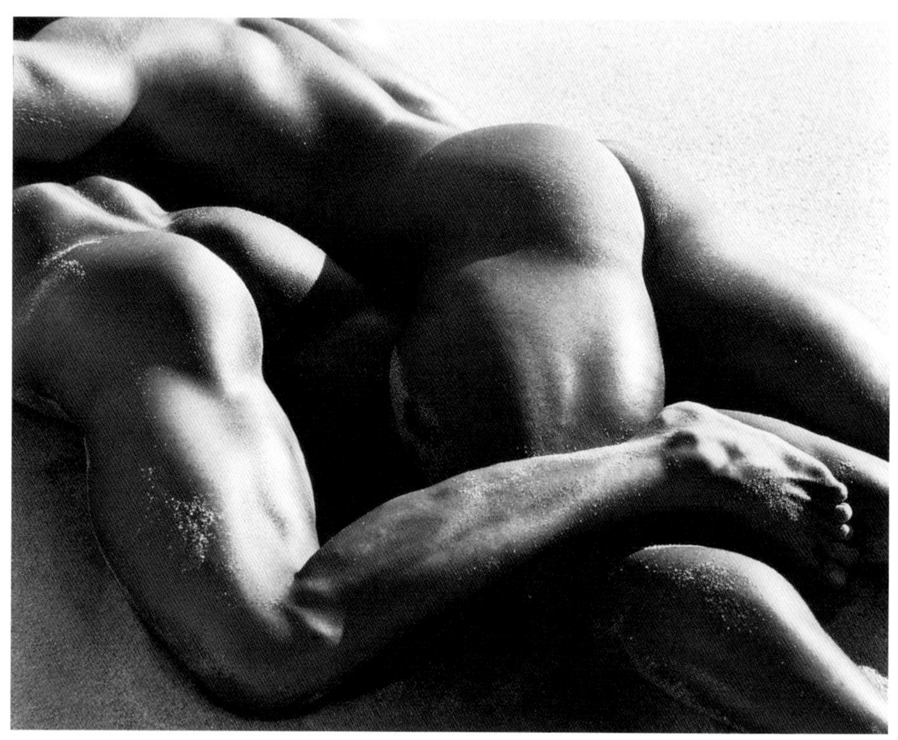

Herb Ritts, Duo IV, 1990

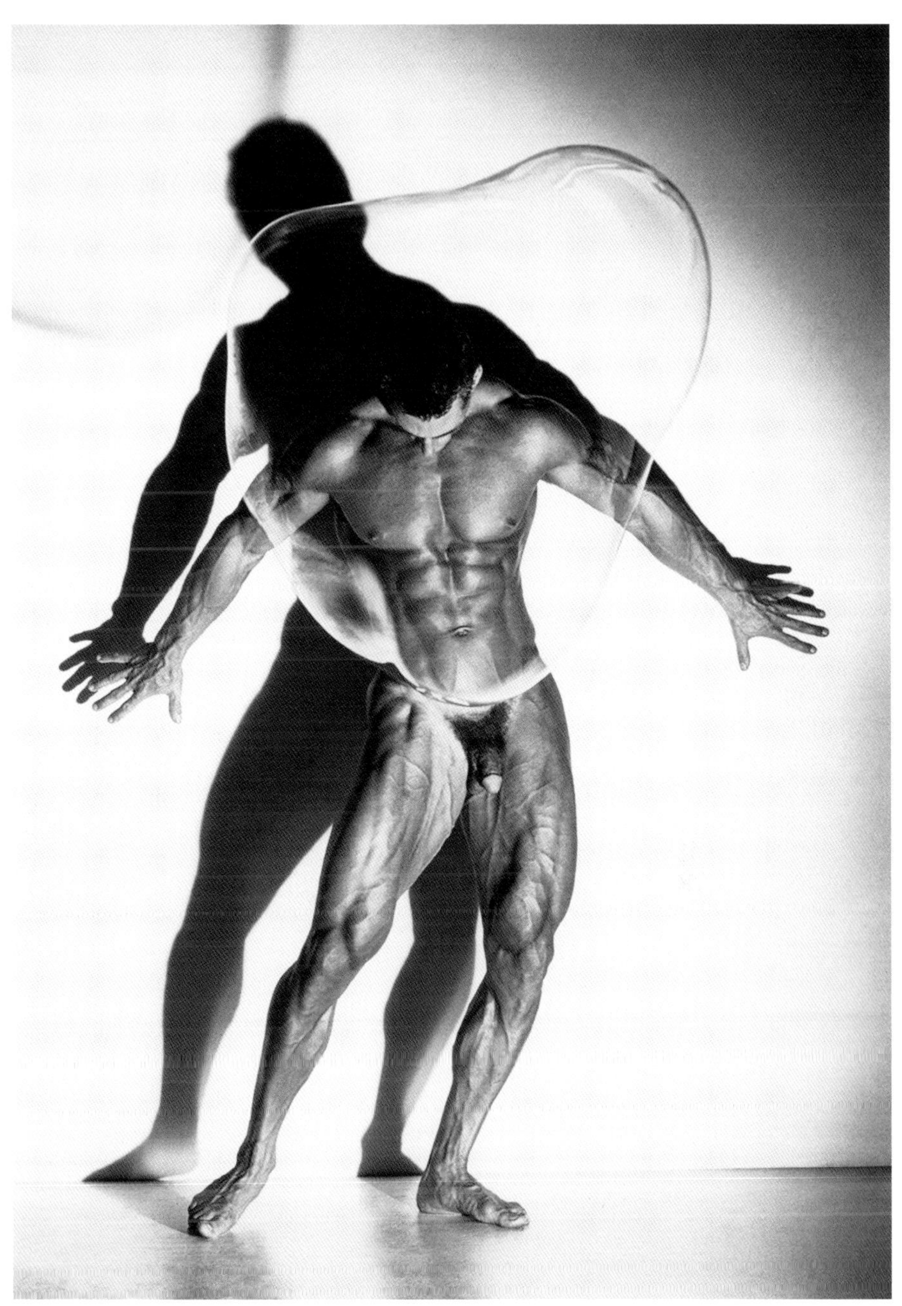

Herb Ritts, Male Nude with Bubble, 1987

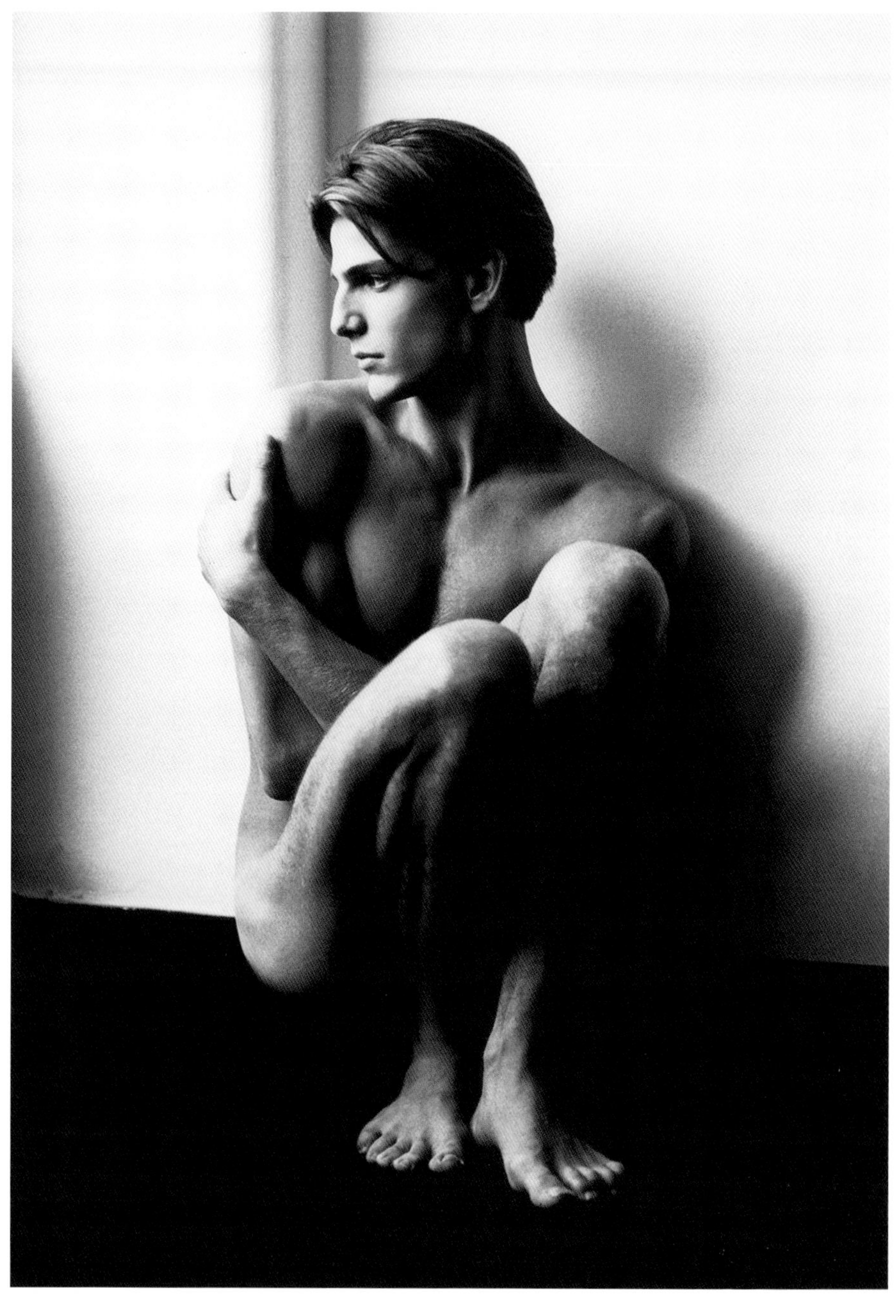

Herb Ritts, Stephano Seated, 1985

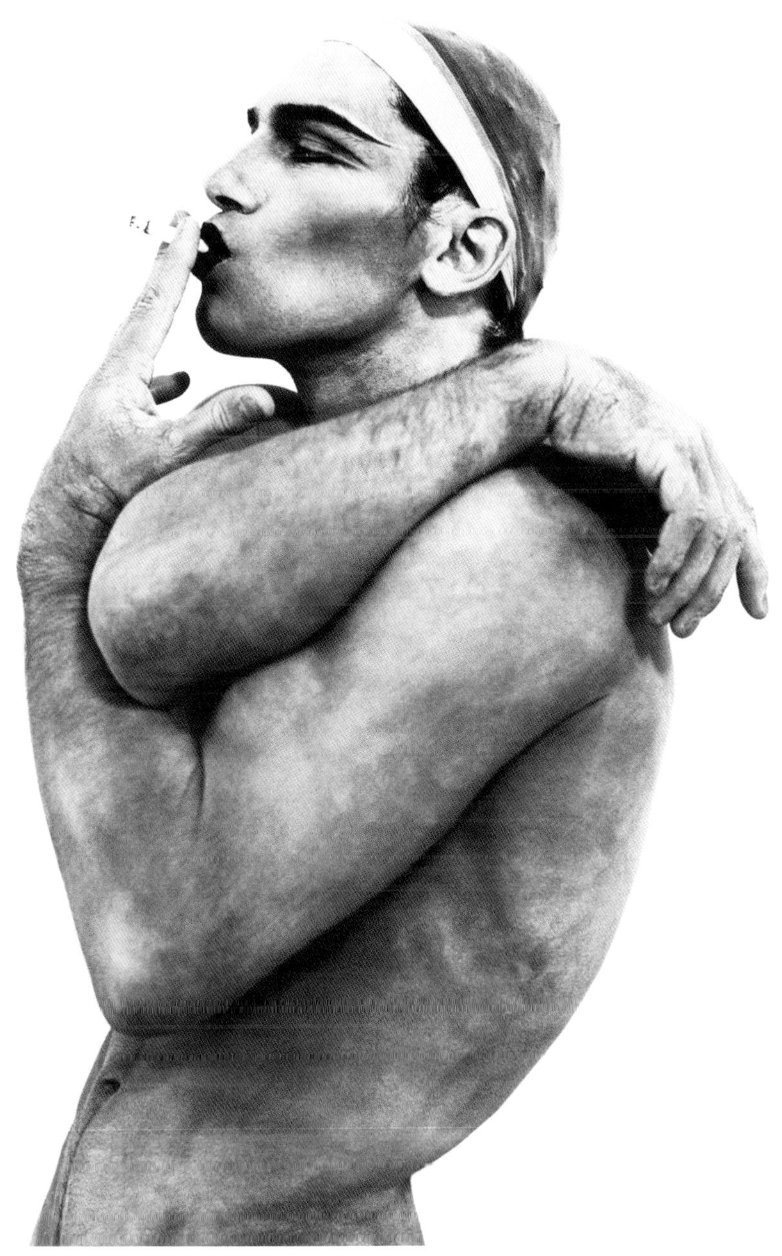

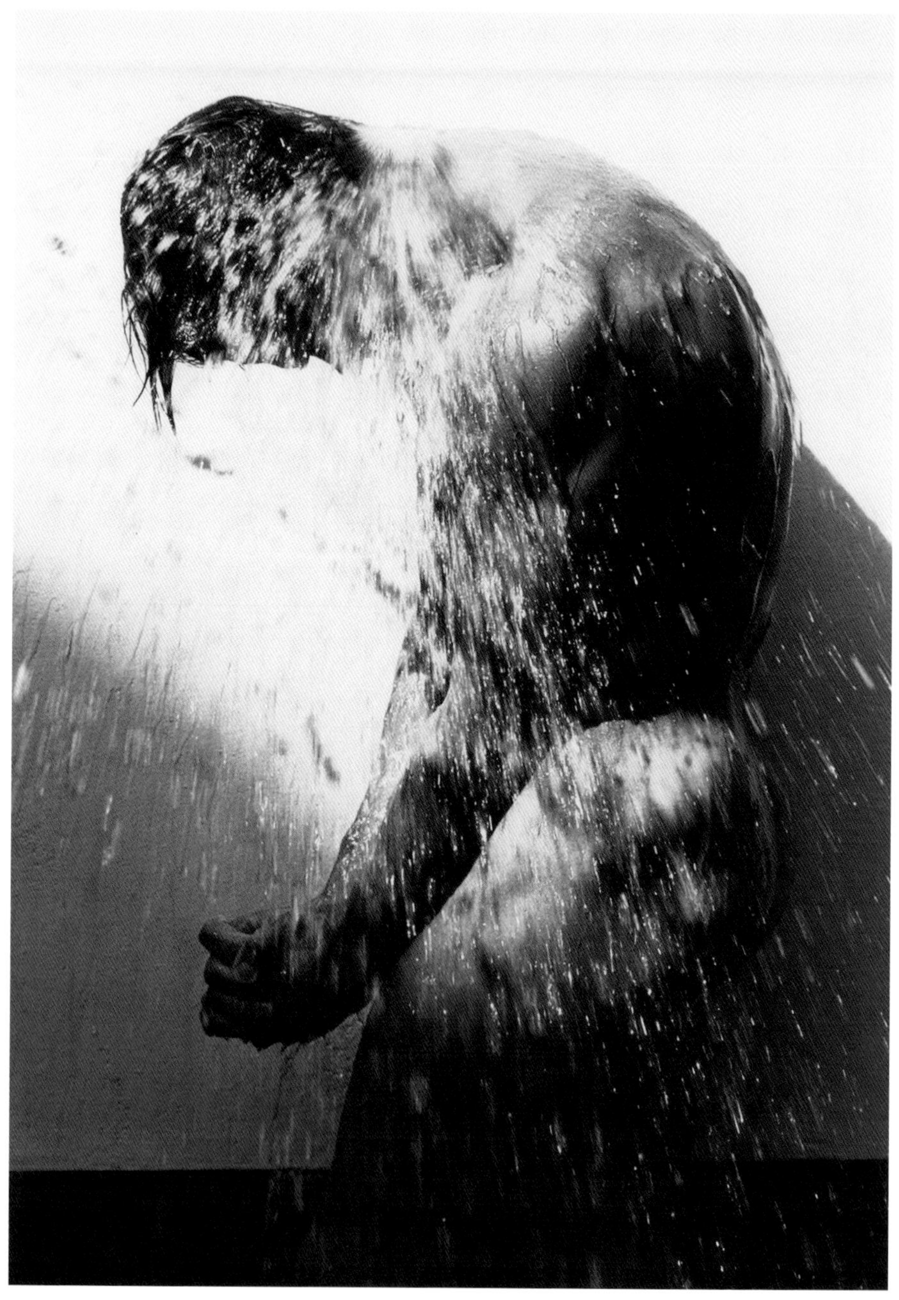

Herb Ritts, Splash, 1989

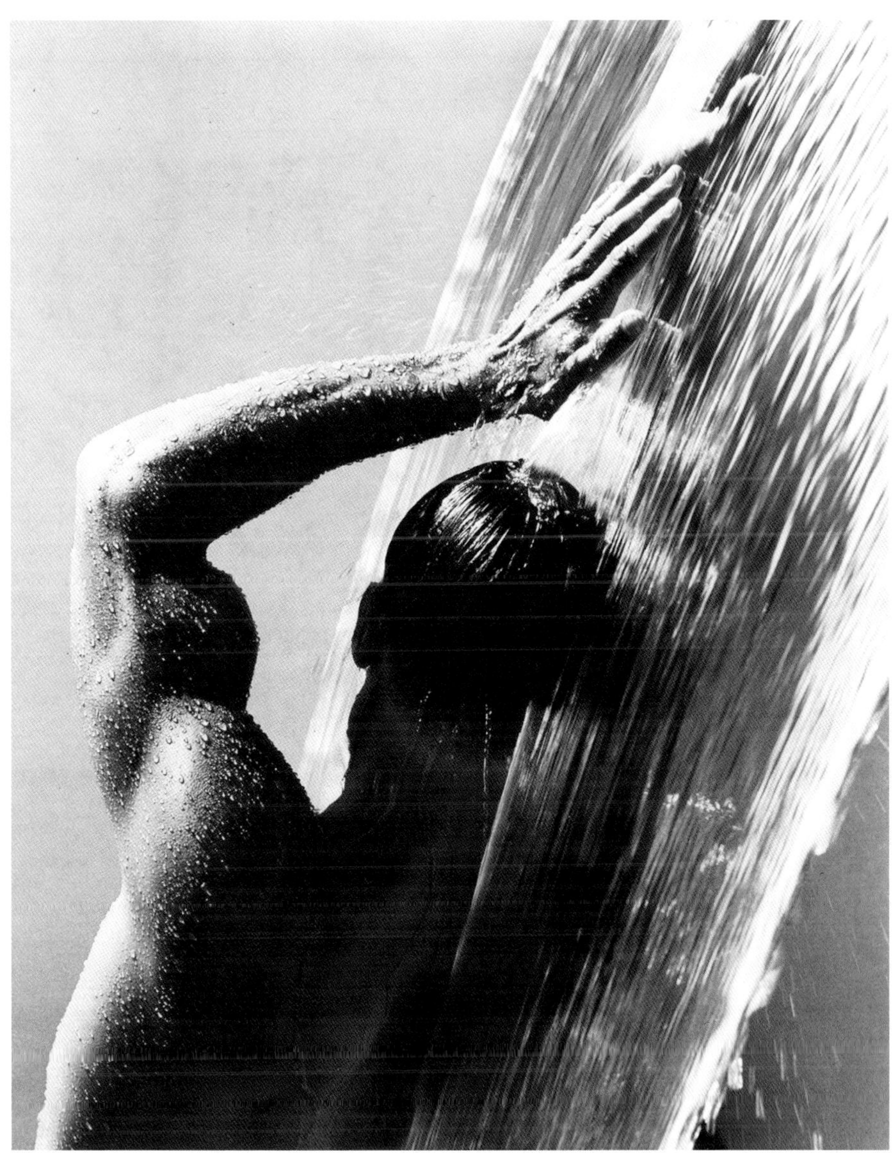

Herb Ritts, Waterfall IV, 1988

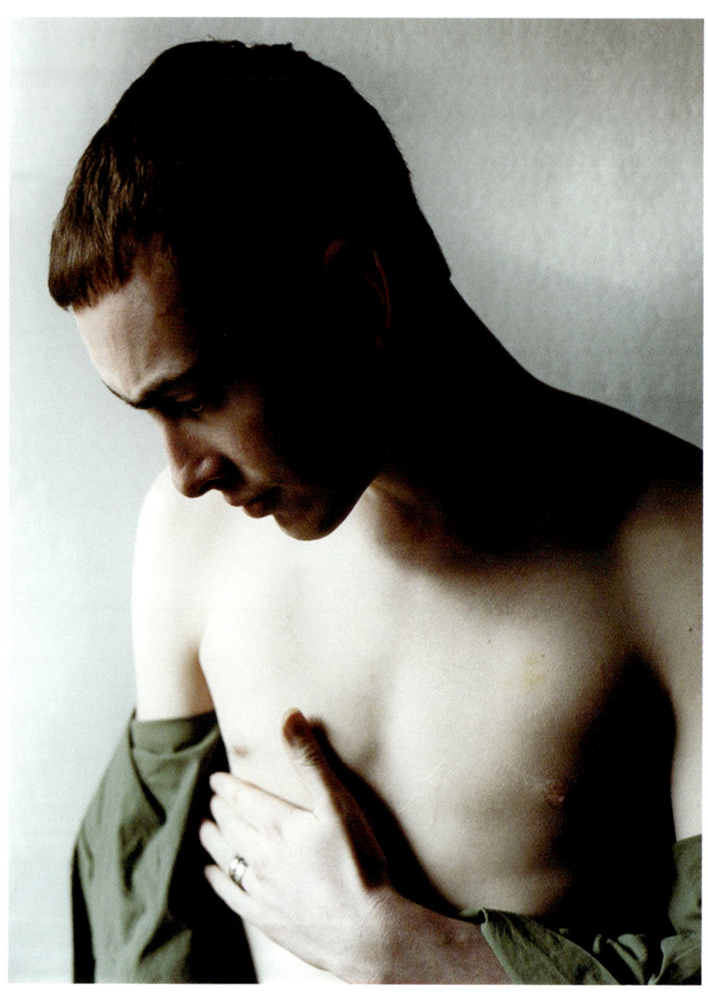

Wolfgang Tillmans, Barnaby, 1991

Wolfgang Tillmans, Palomino, Piss, 1995

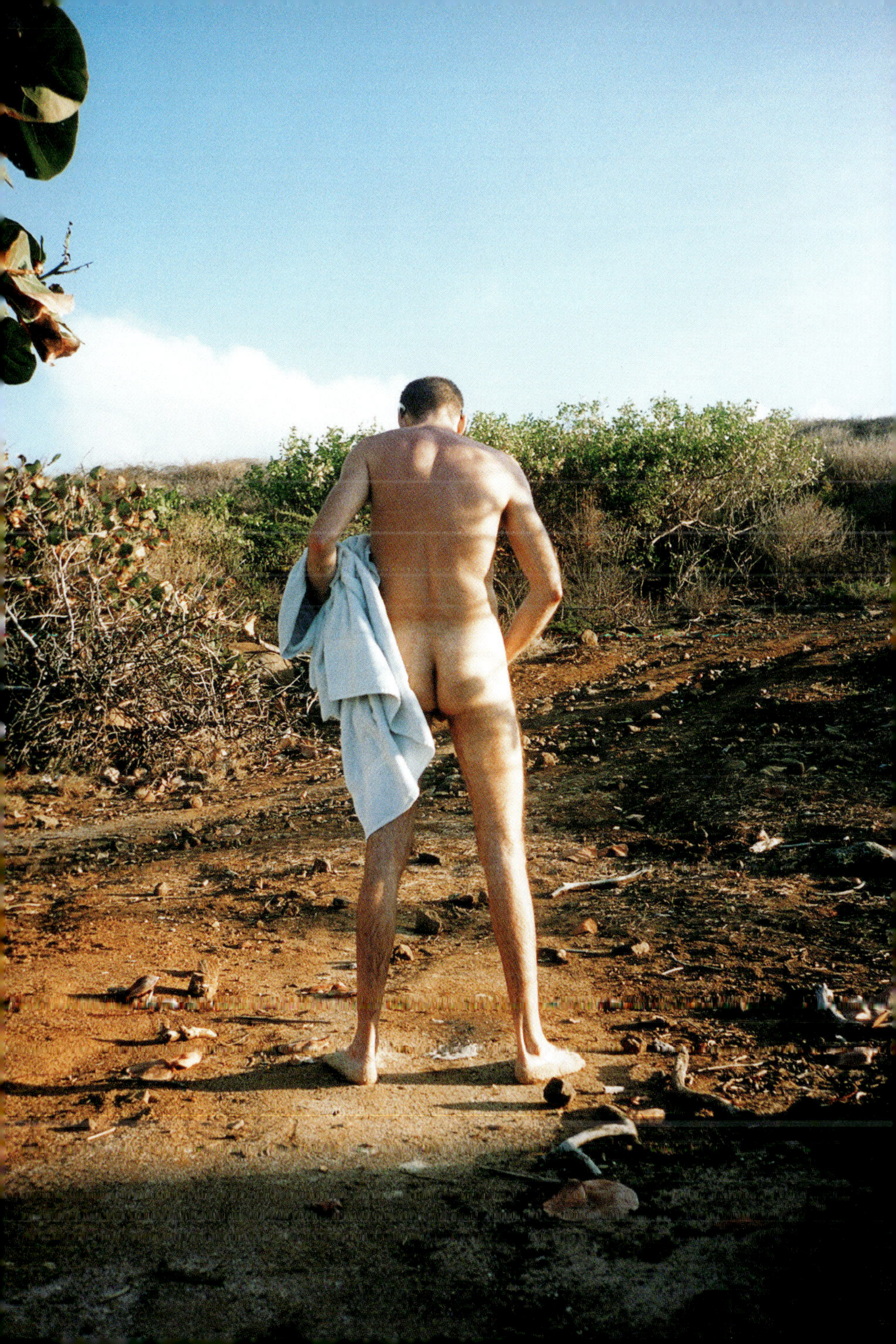

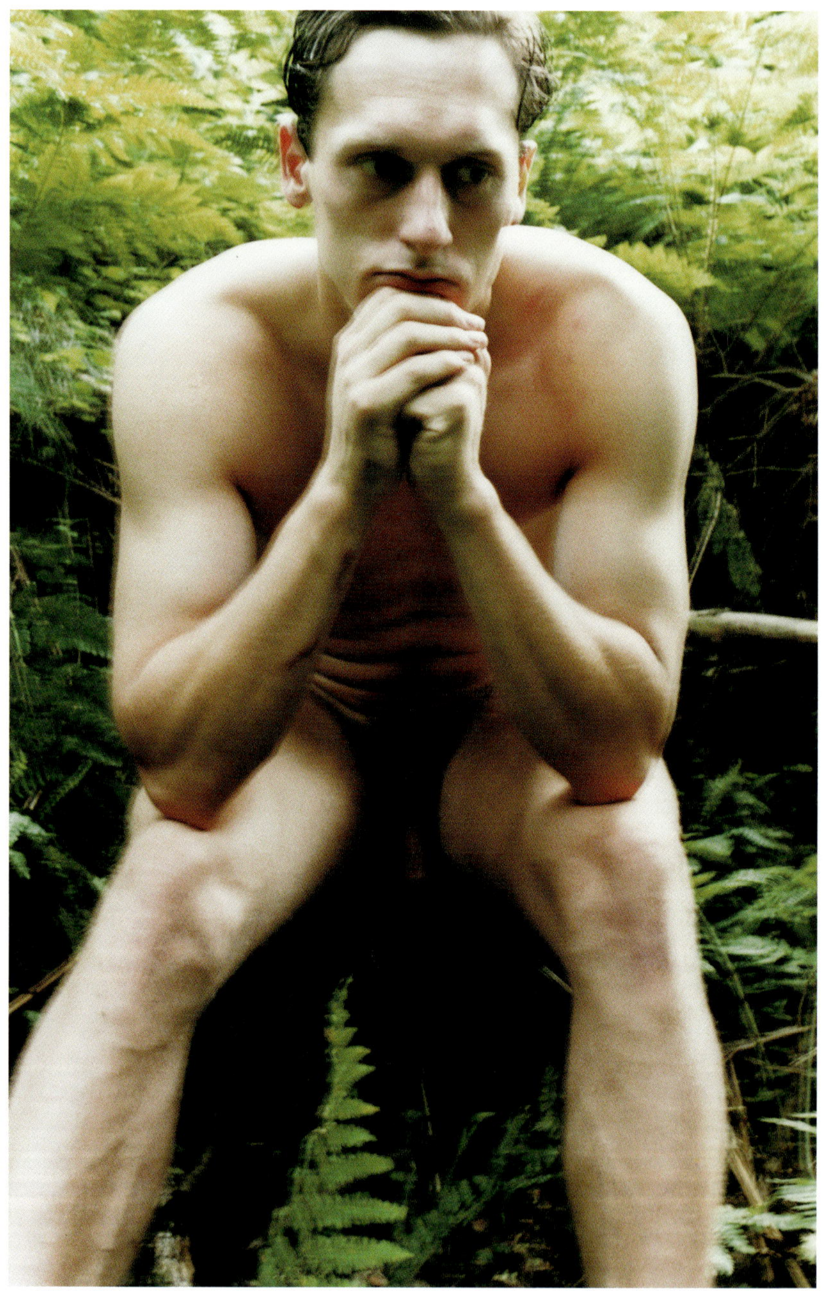

 Wolfgang Tillmans, Arnd, Nude, Sitting, 1991

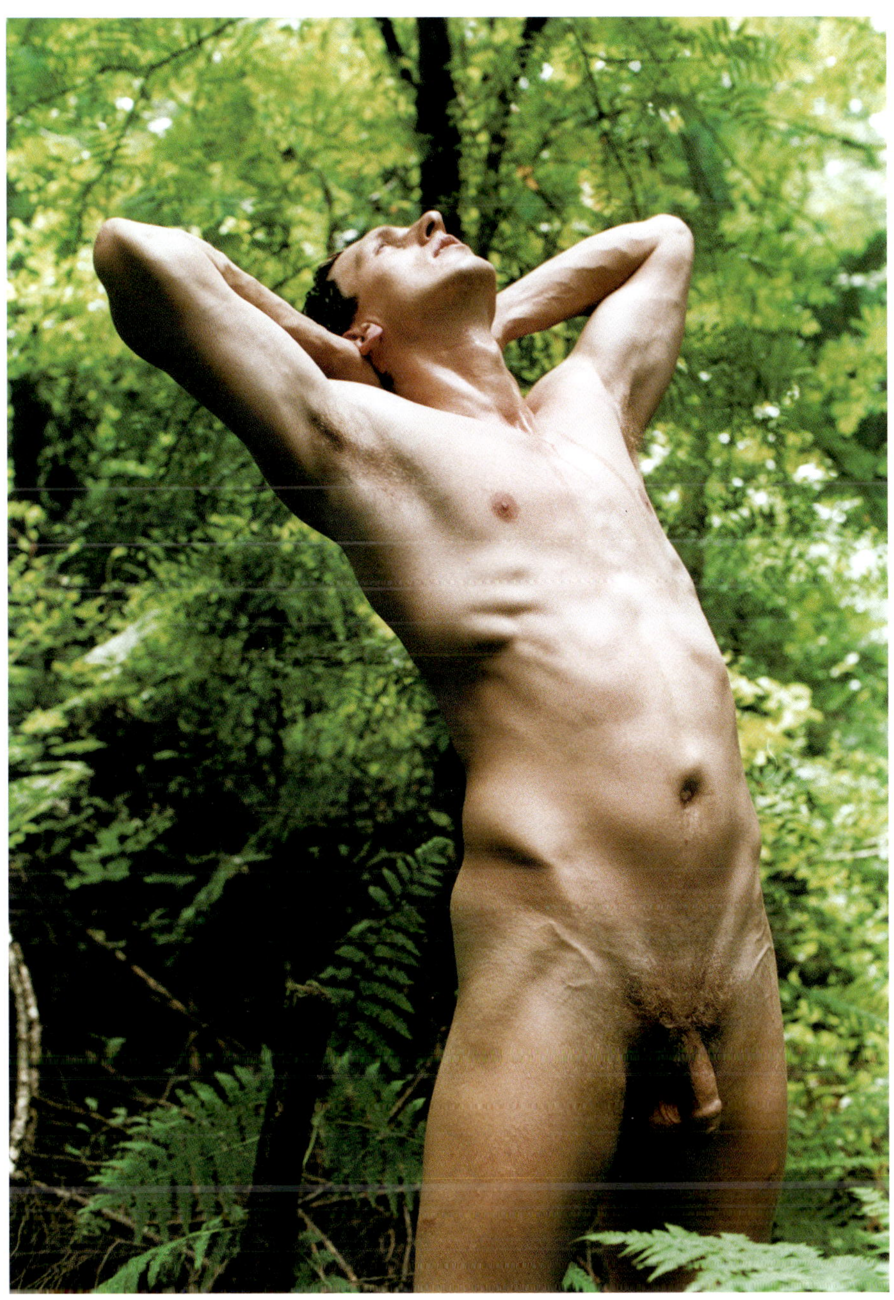

Wolfgang Tillmans, *Arnd, Nude, Stretching, 1991*

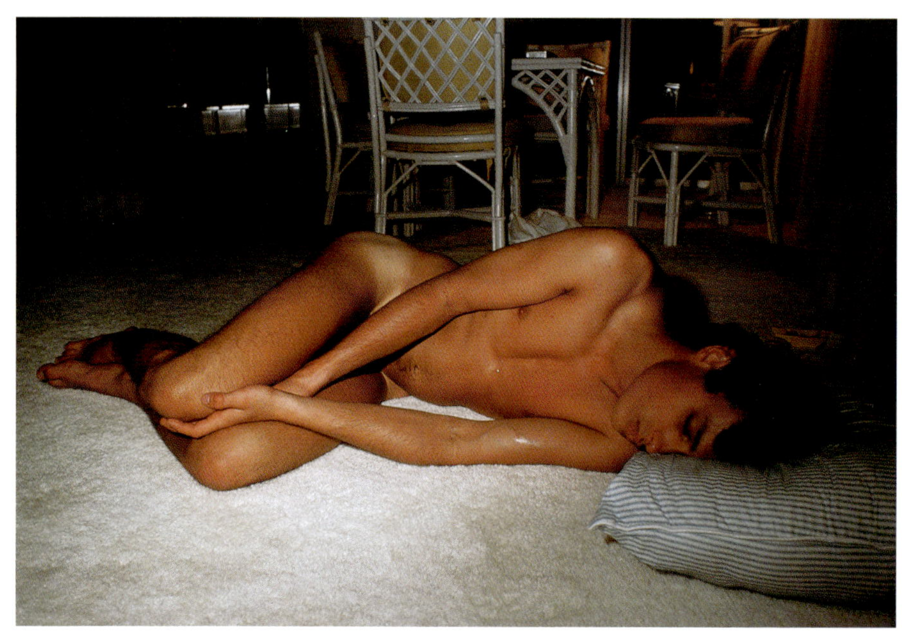

David Armstrong, Kevin, 1977

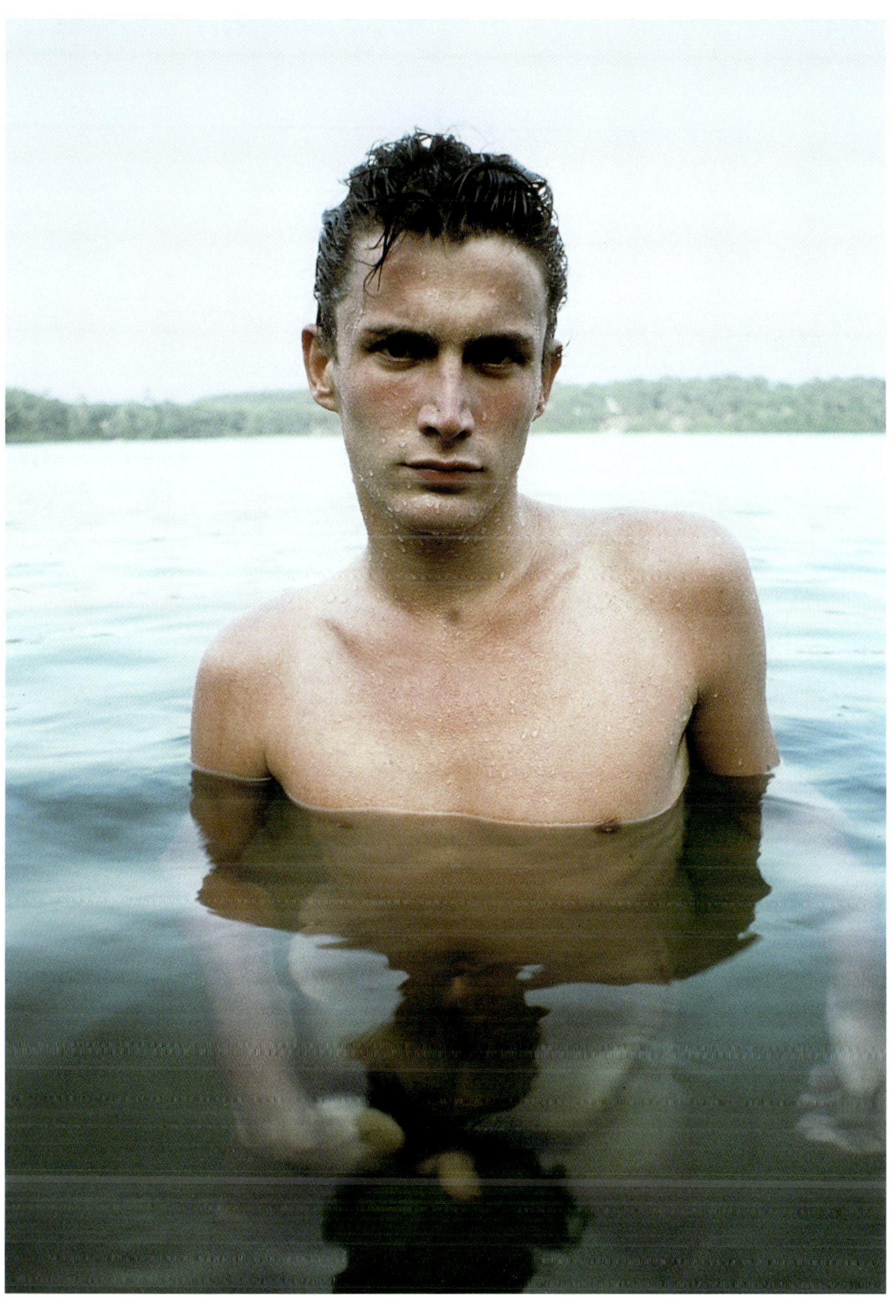

David Armstrong, Chris, 1979

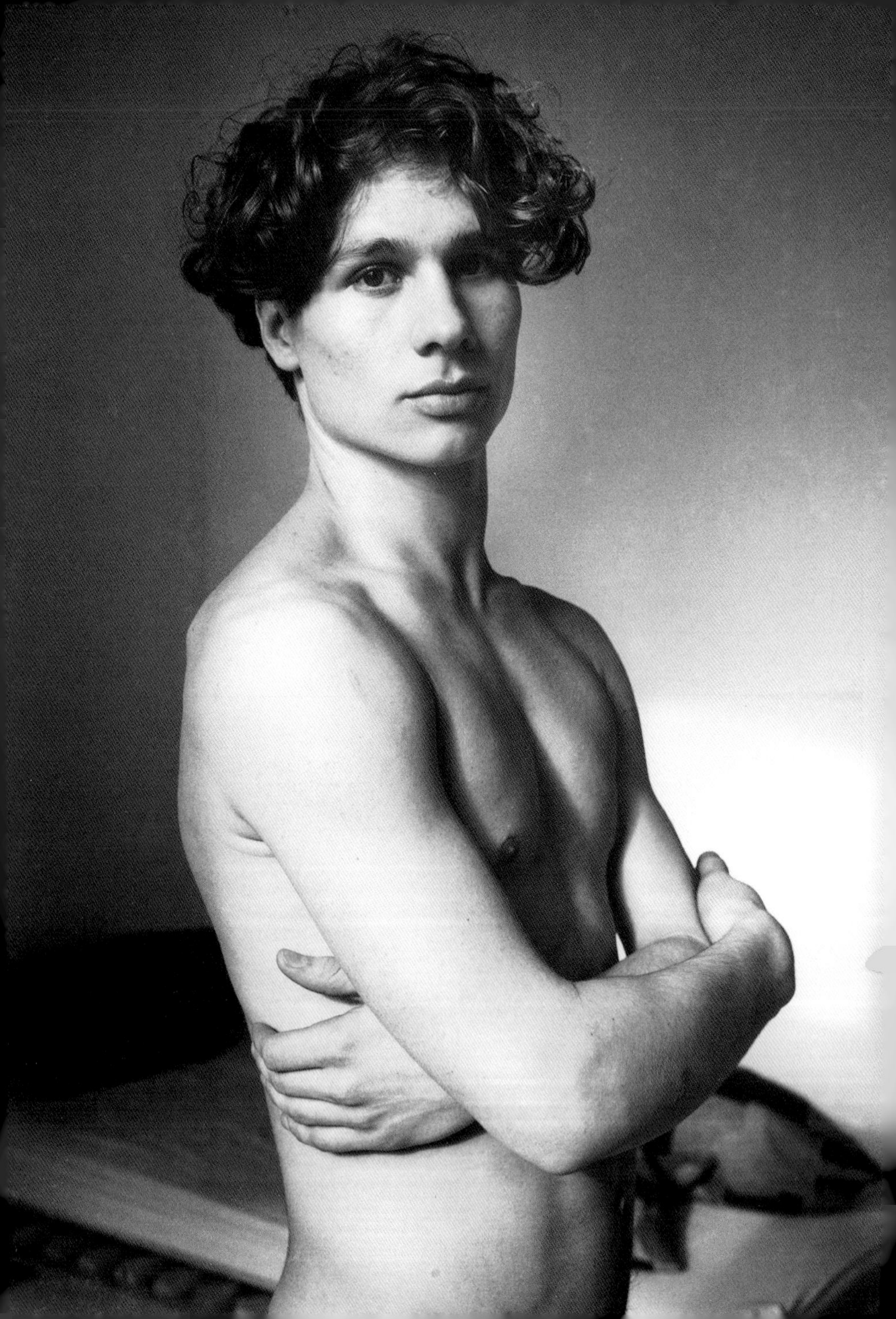

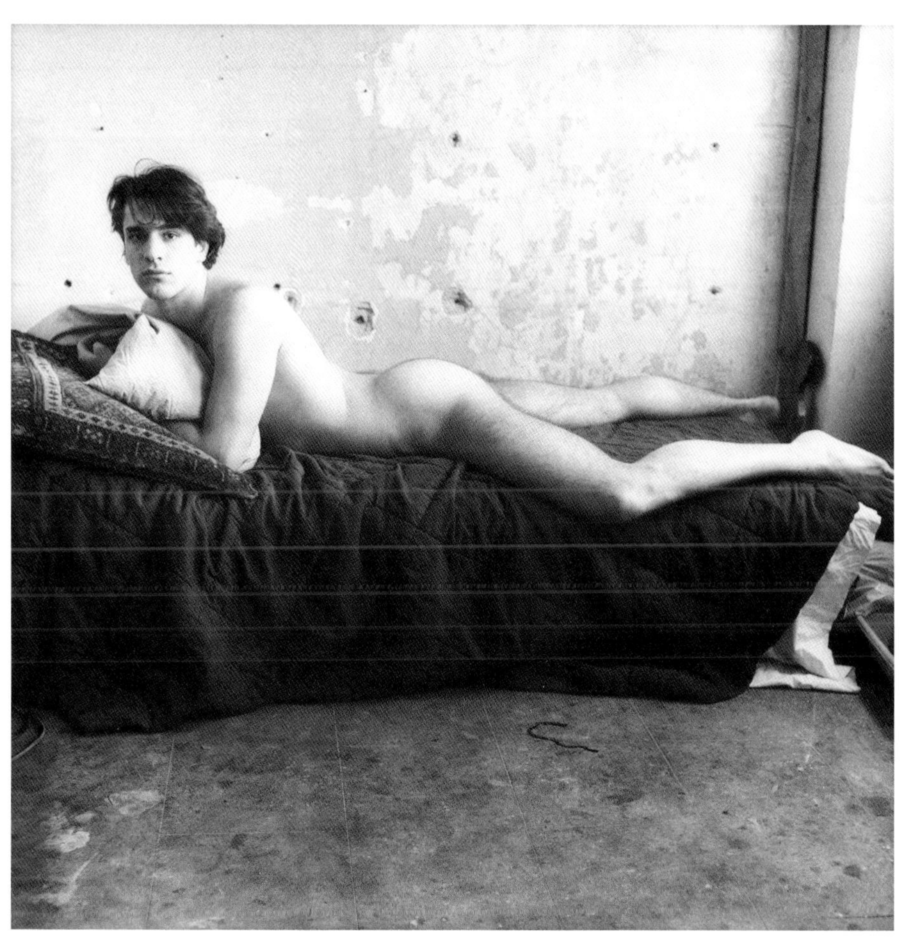

David Armstrong, Brian, 1982

David Armstrong, Thilo in his Bedroom, 1994

▶ **David Armstrong,** Effi on Joey's Bed, 1991

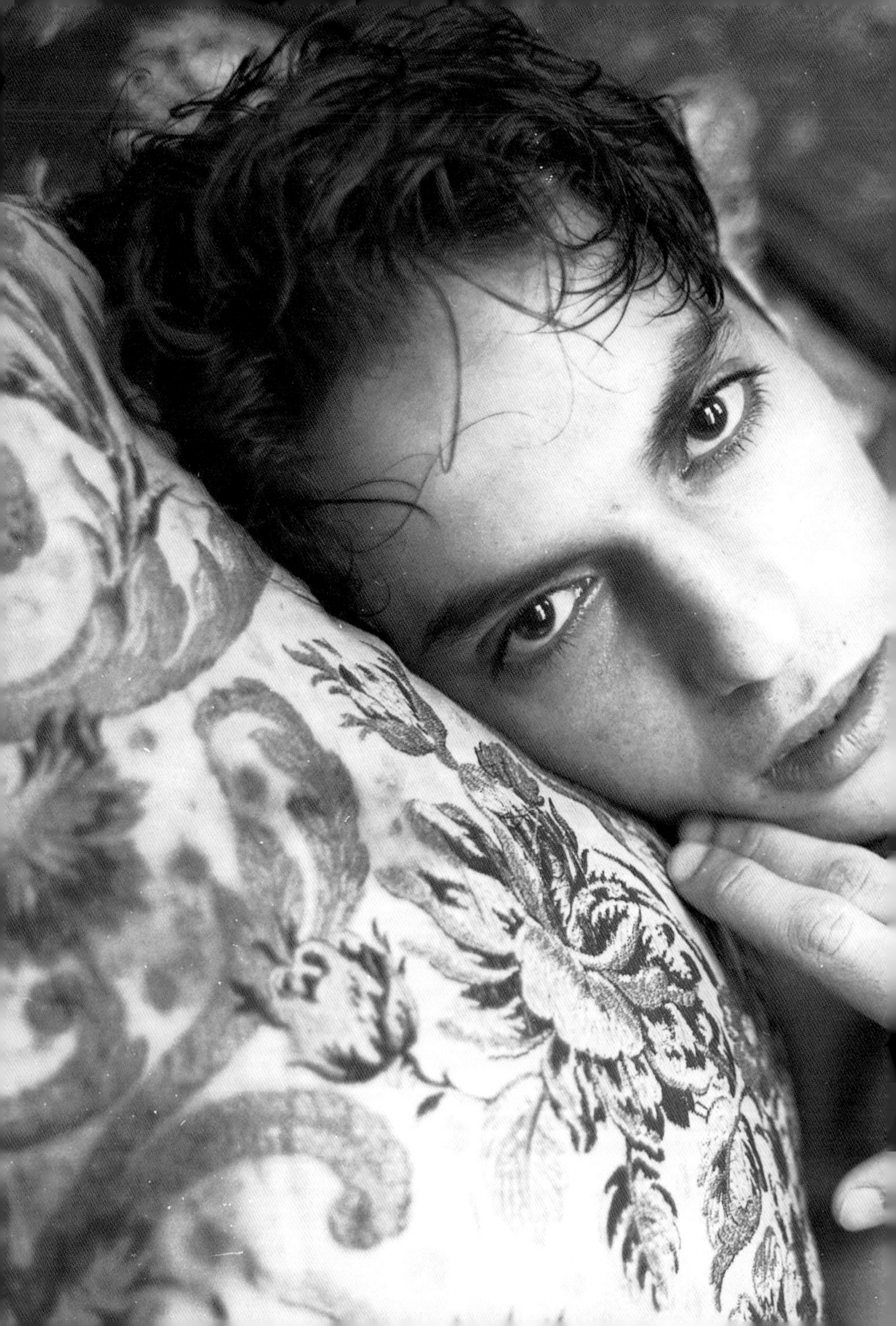

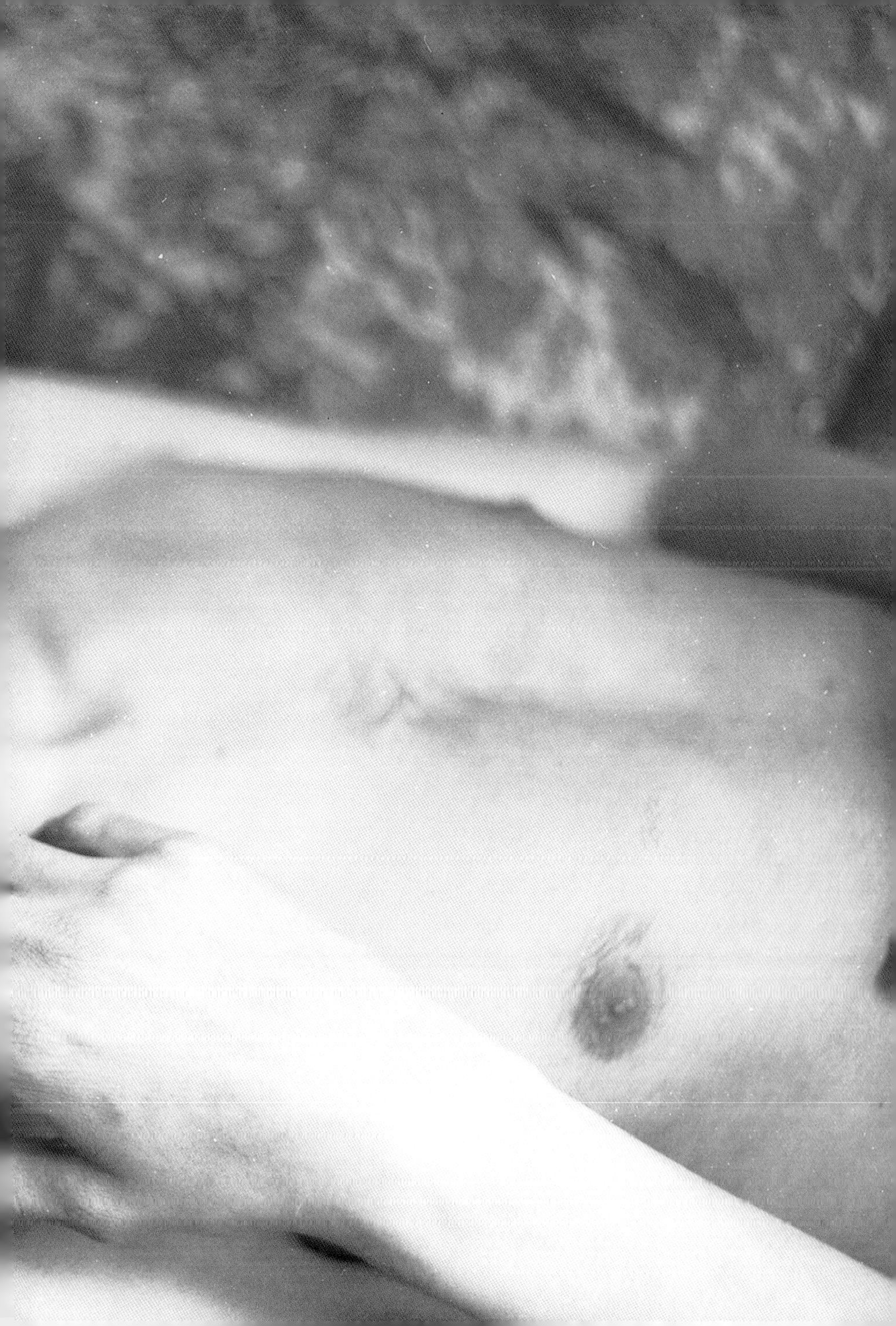

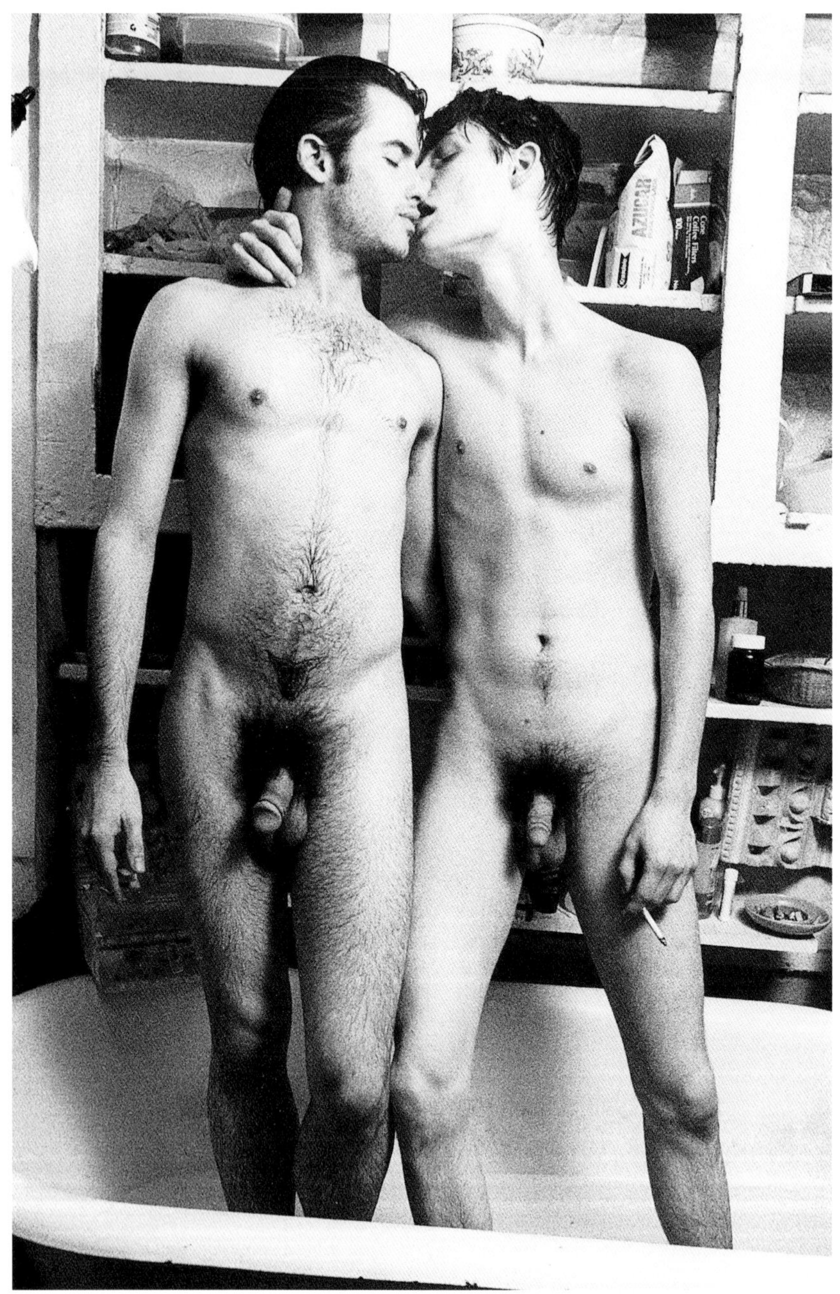

514

Terry Richardson, Brian and Christian in Tub

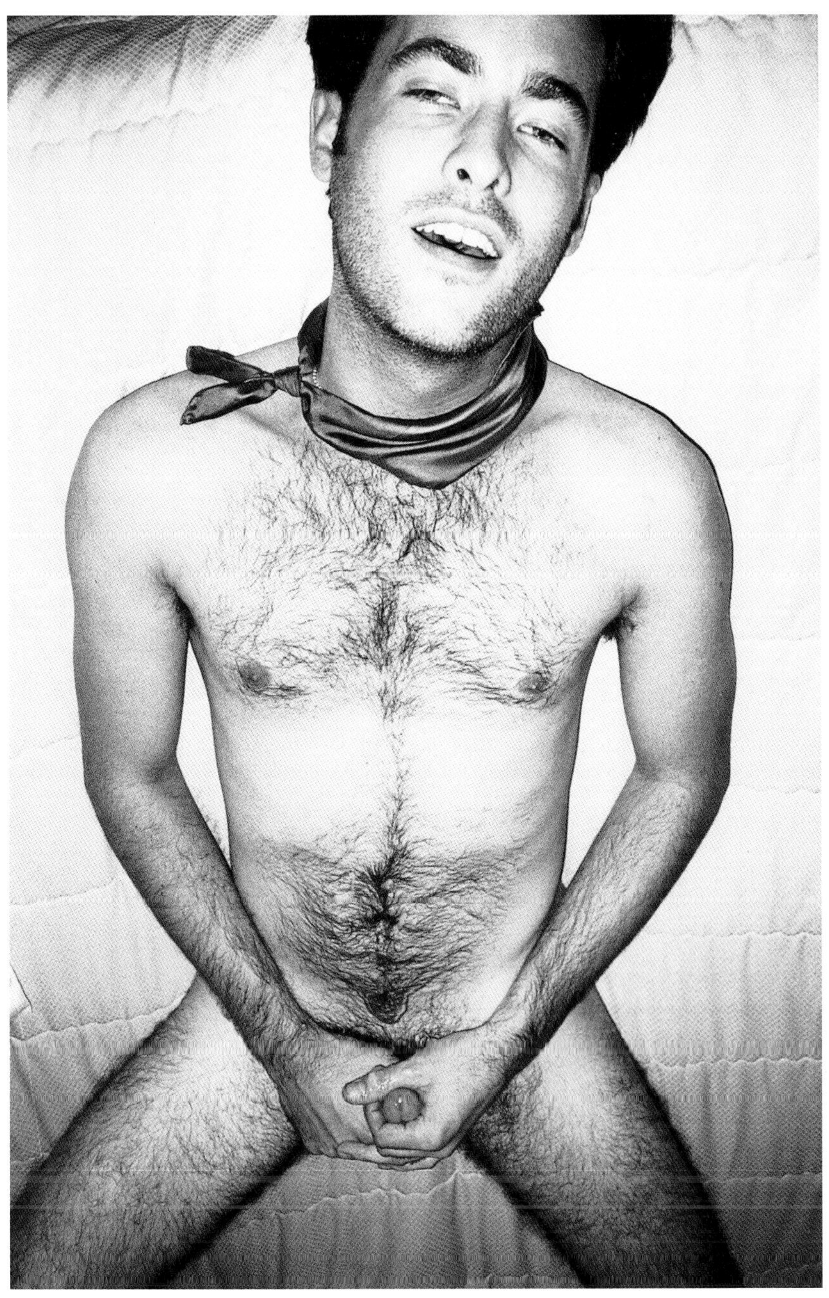

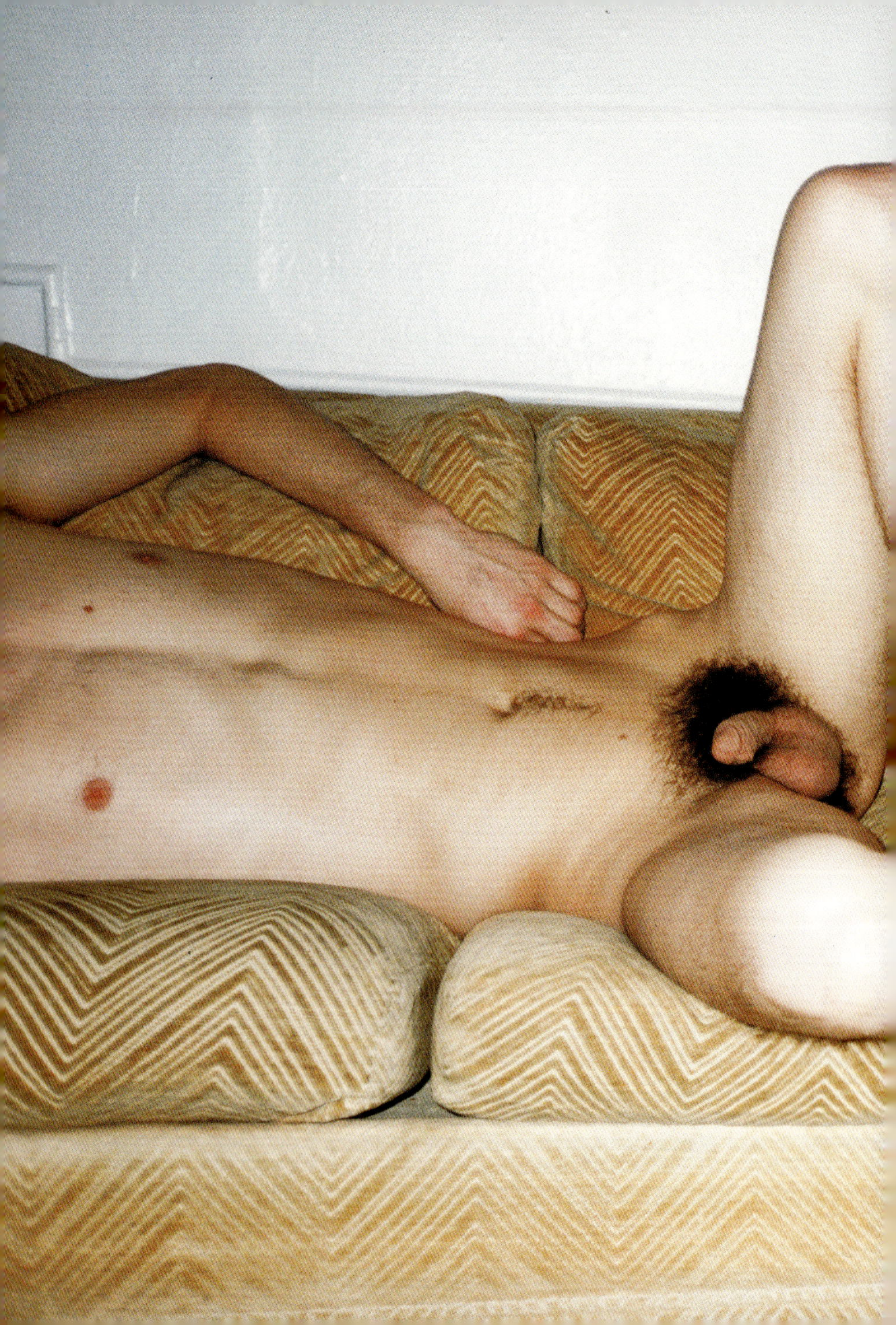

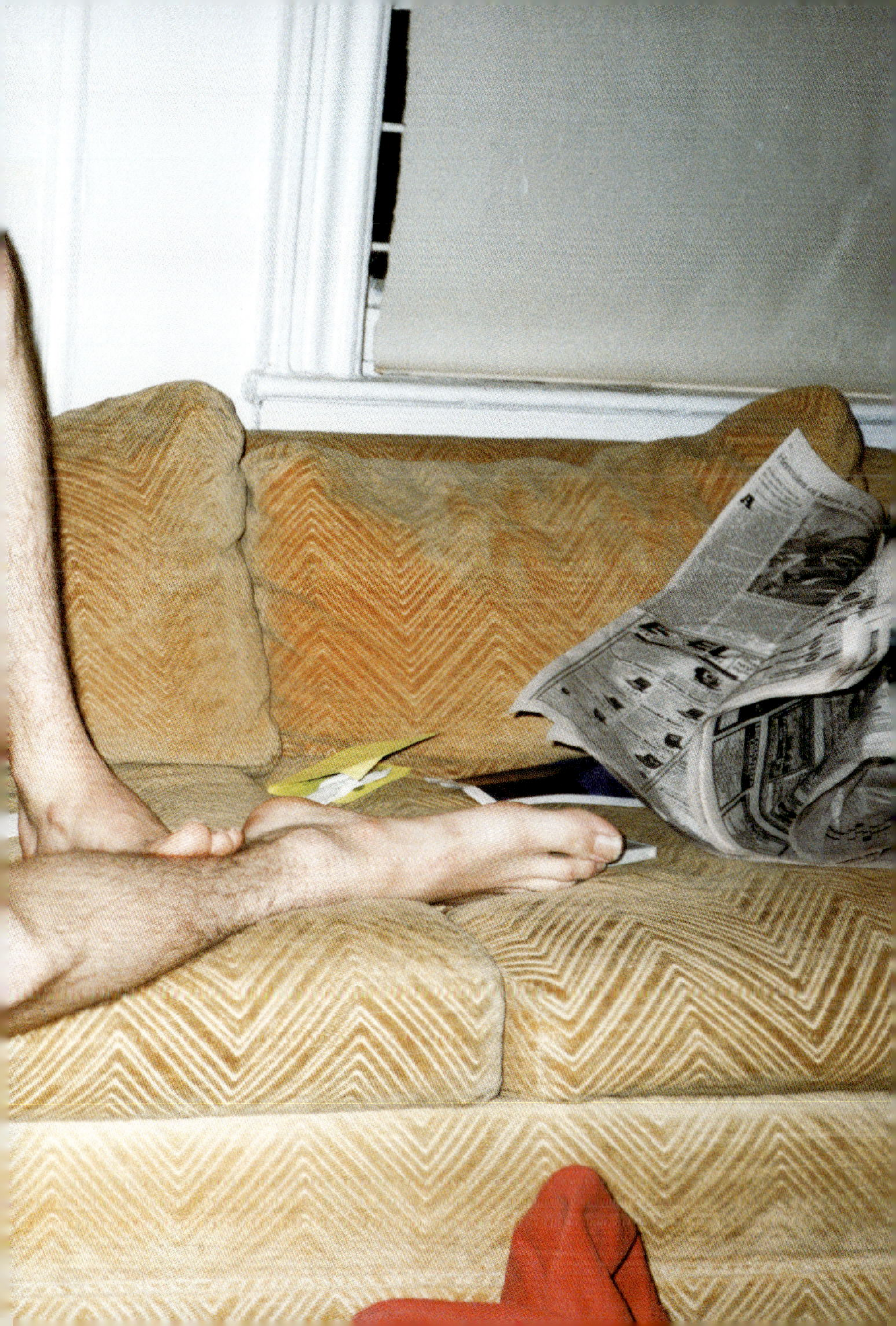

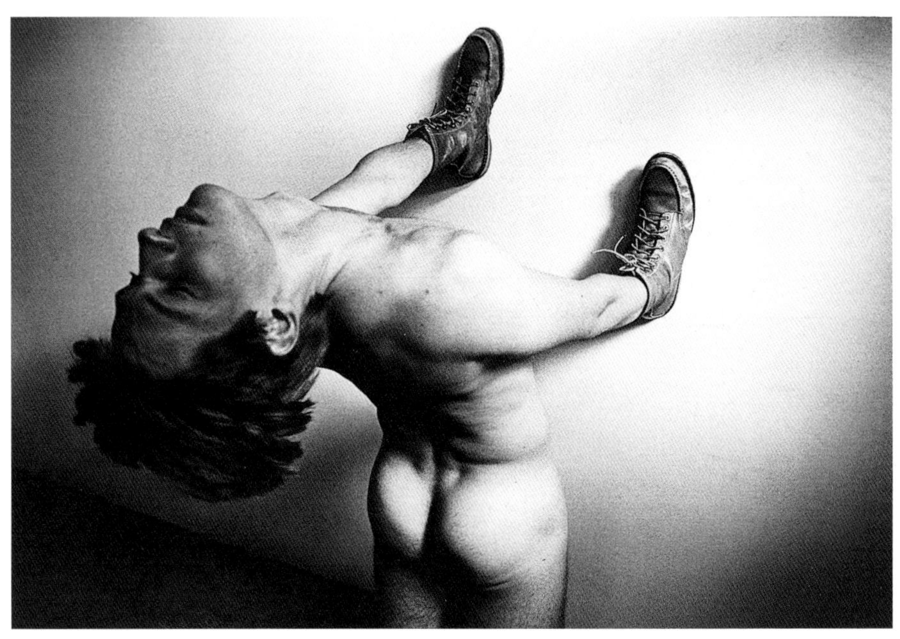

The unfortunate man could not touch the one he loved. It had been forbidden by law. Slowly his fingers became toes and his hands became feet. He ~~wore~~ now began to wear shoes on his hands to disguise his pain. It never occurred to him to break the law.

Duane Michals, 1978

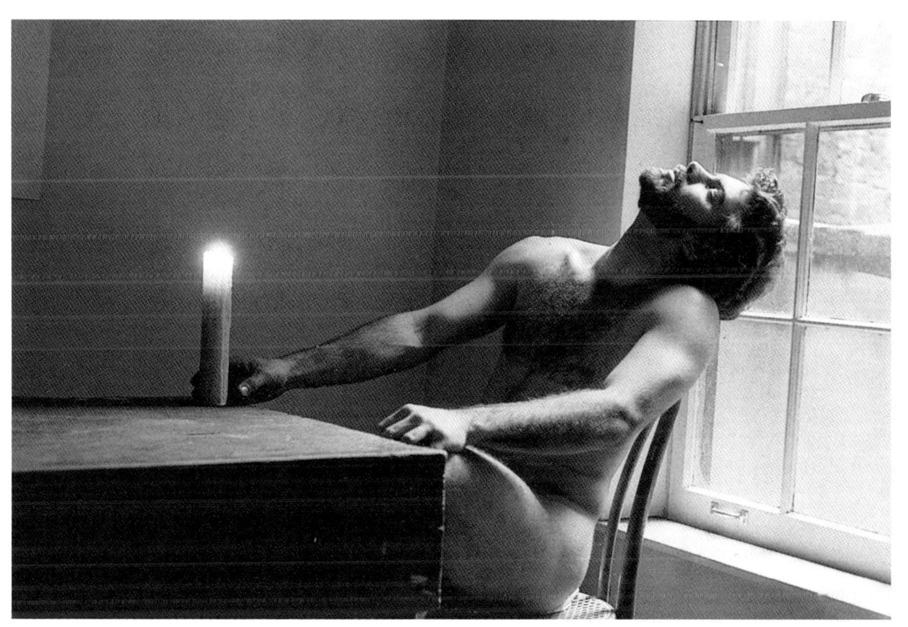

Duane Michals, 1992

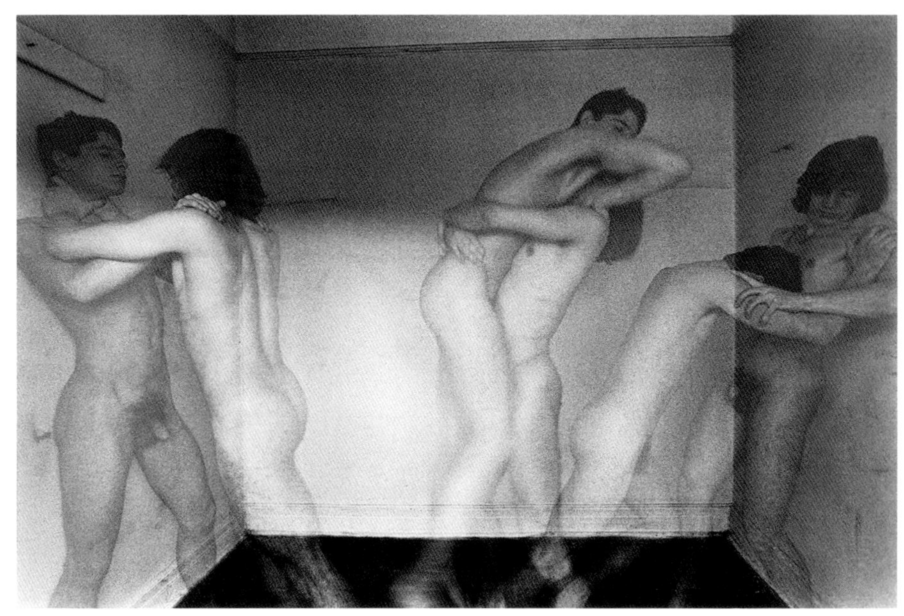

Duane Michals, Violent Men, 1982

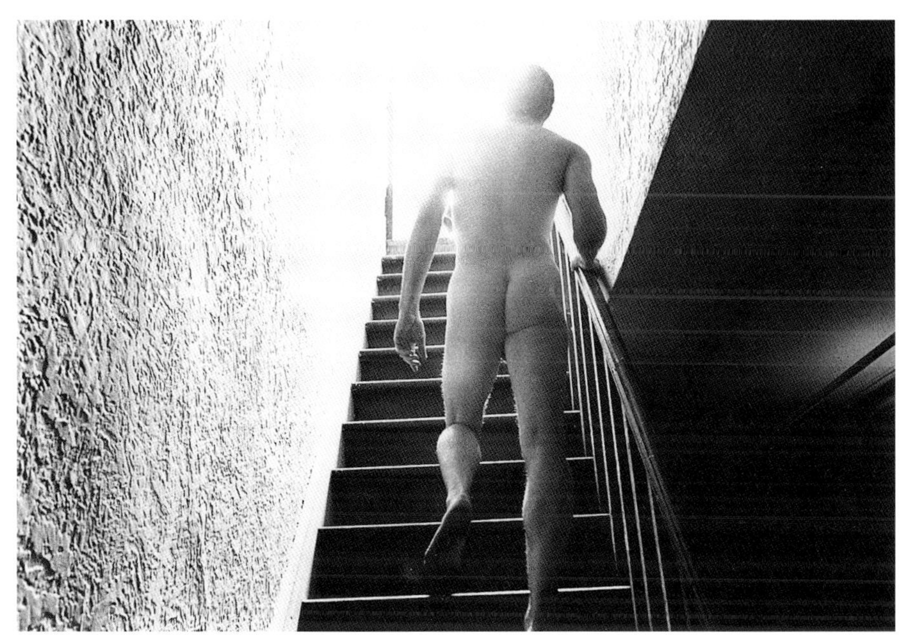

Duane Michals, 1971

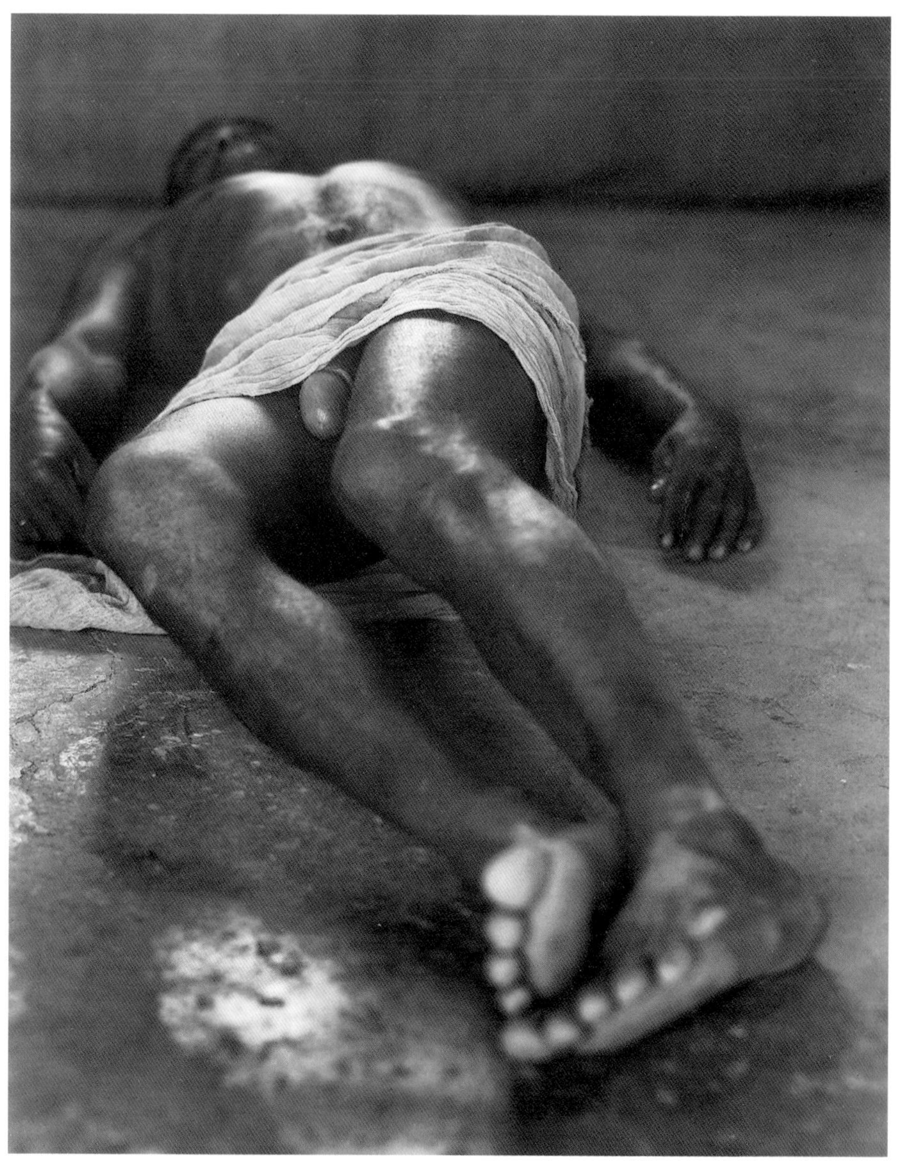

Gian Paolo Barbieri, Vezo Village at Sundown. A Fisherman Resting, 1994

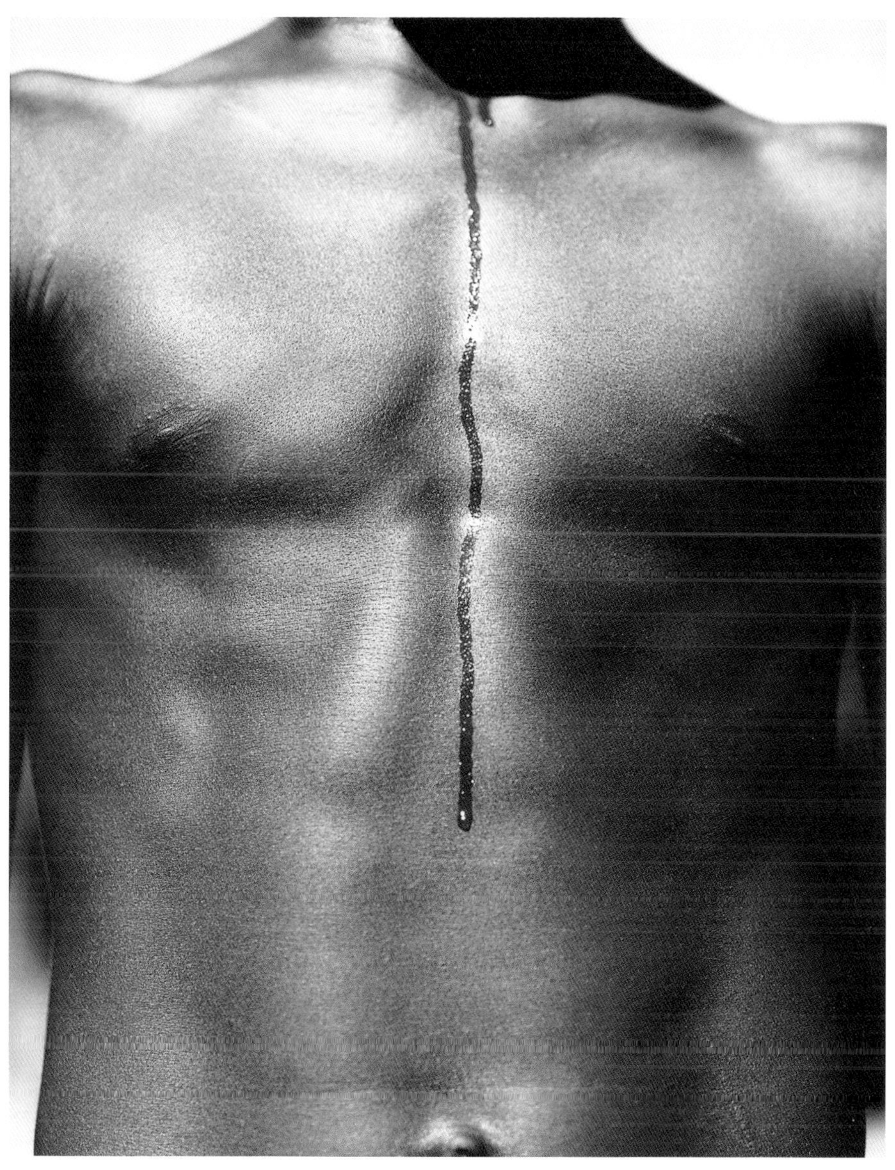

Gian Paolo Barbieri, Noon in the Village of Anakao, 1994

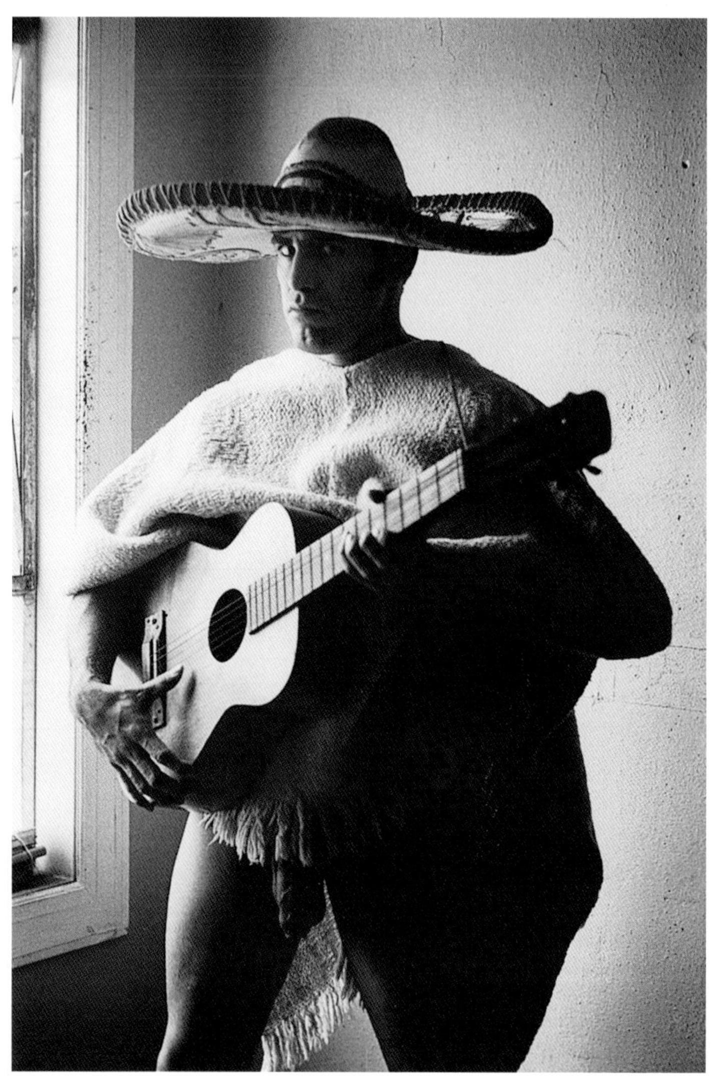

John Sonsini, Louie, 1997

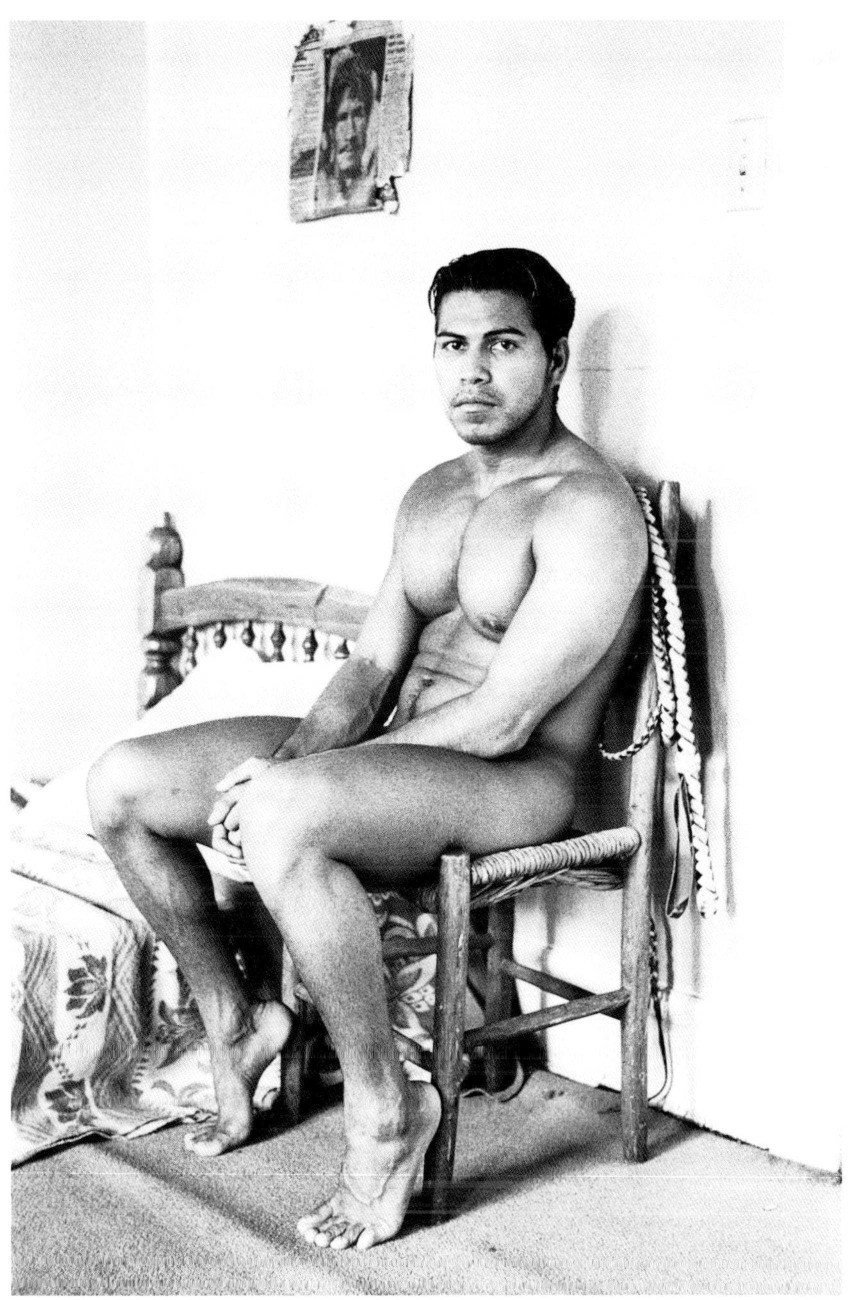

525

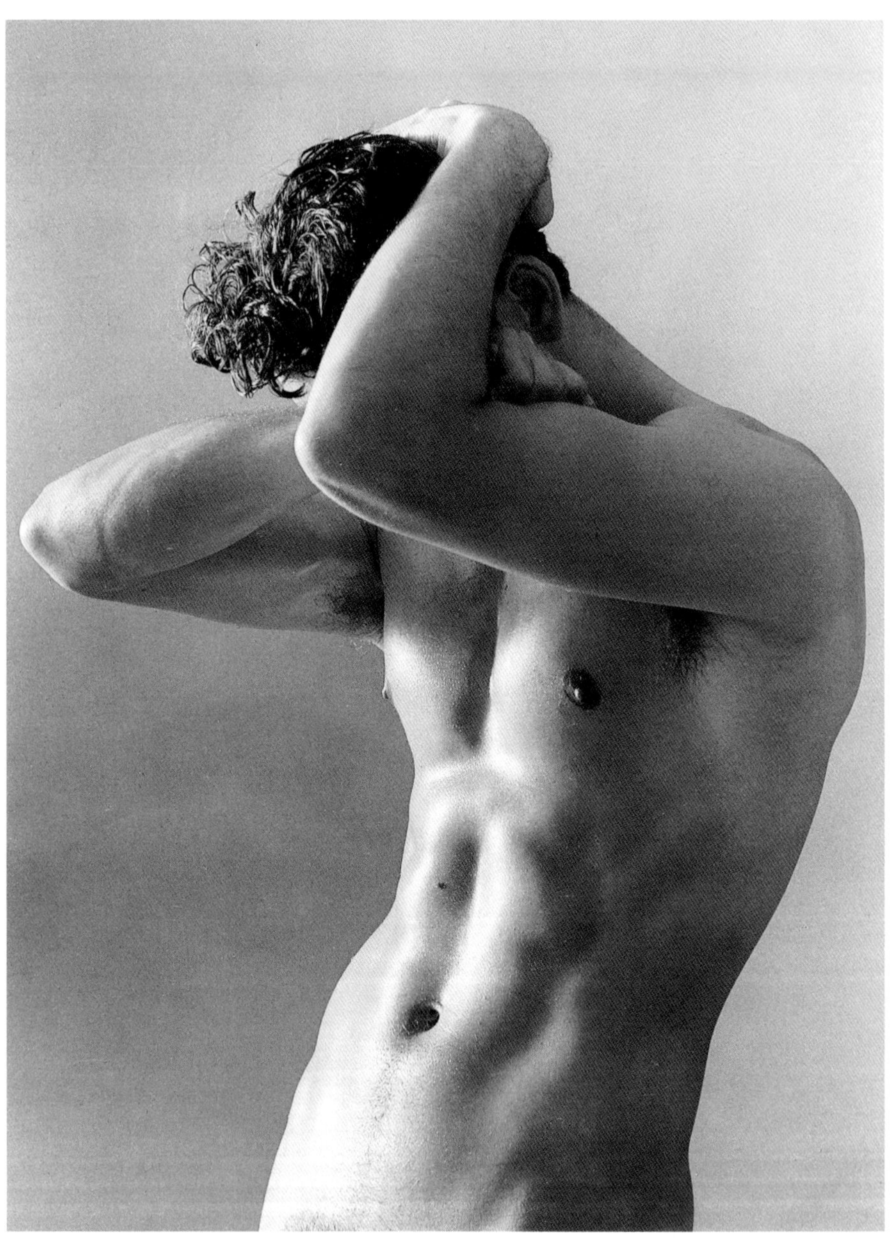

Bruno Benini, Simon, 1994

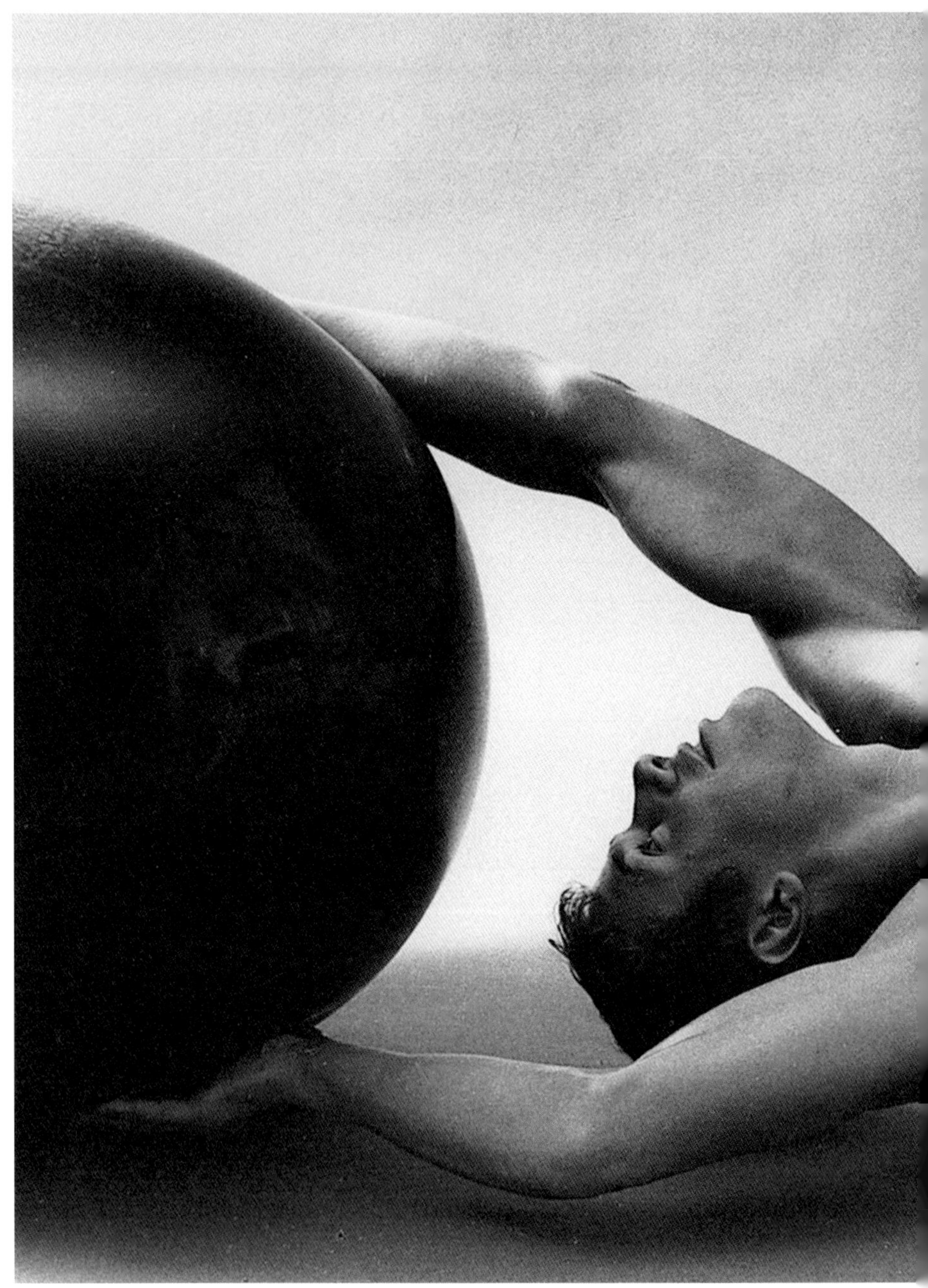

Bruno Benini, Kick, 1994

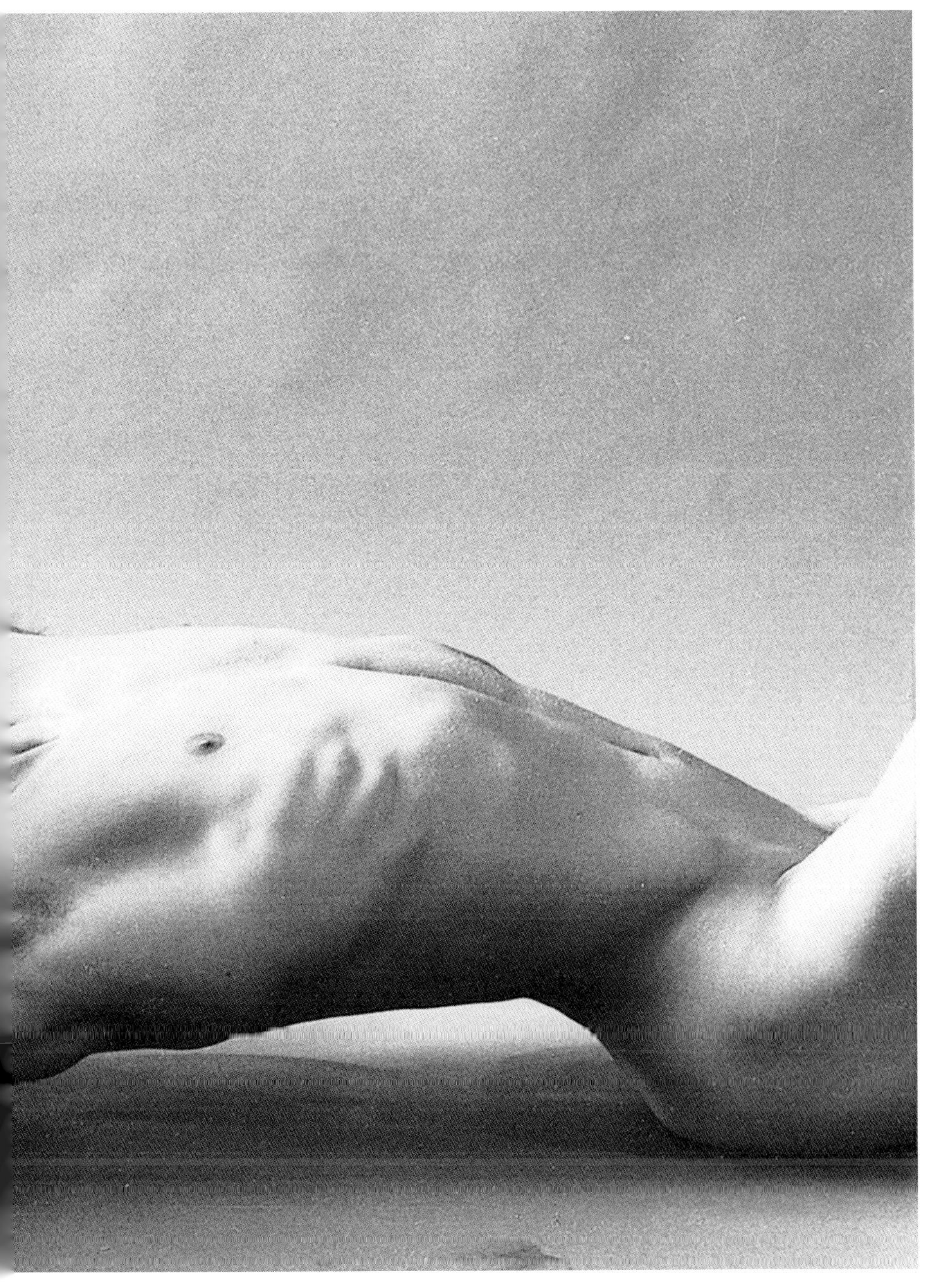

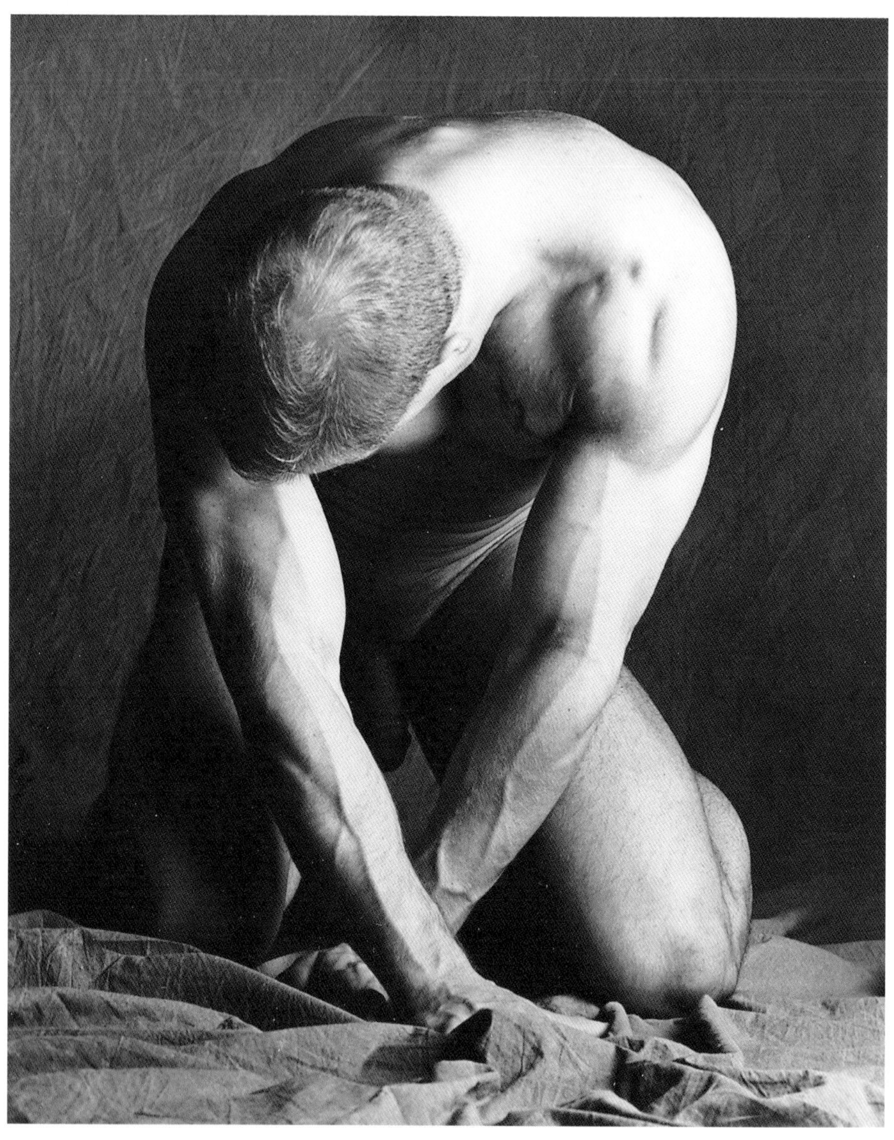

David Morgan, Nick, 1991

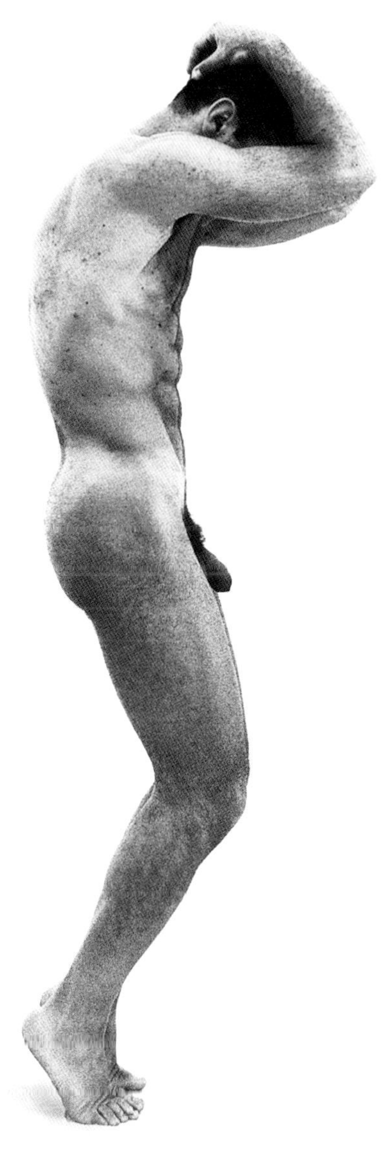

Baly Hinter Wipflinger, Untitled, May 1994

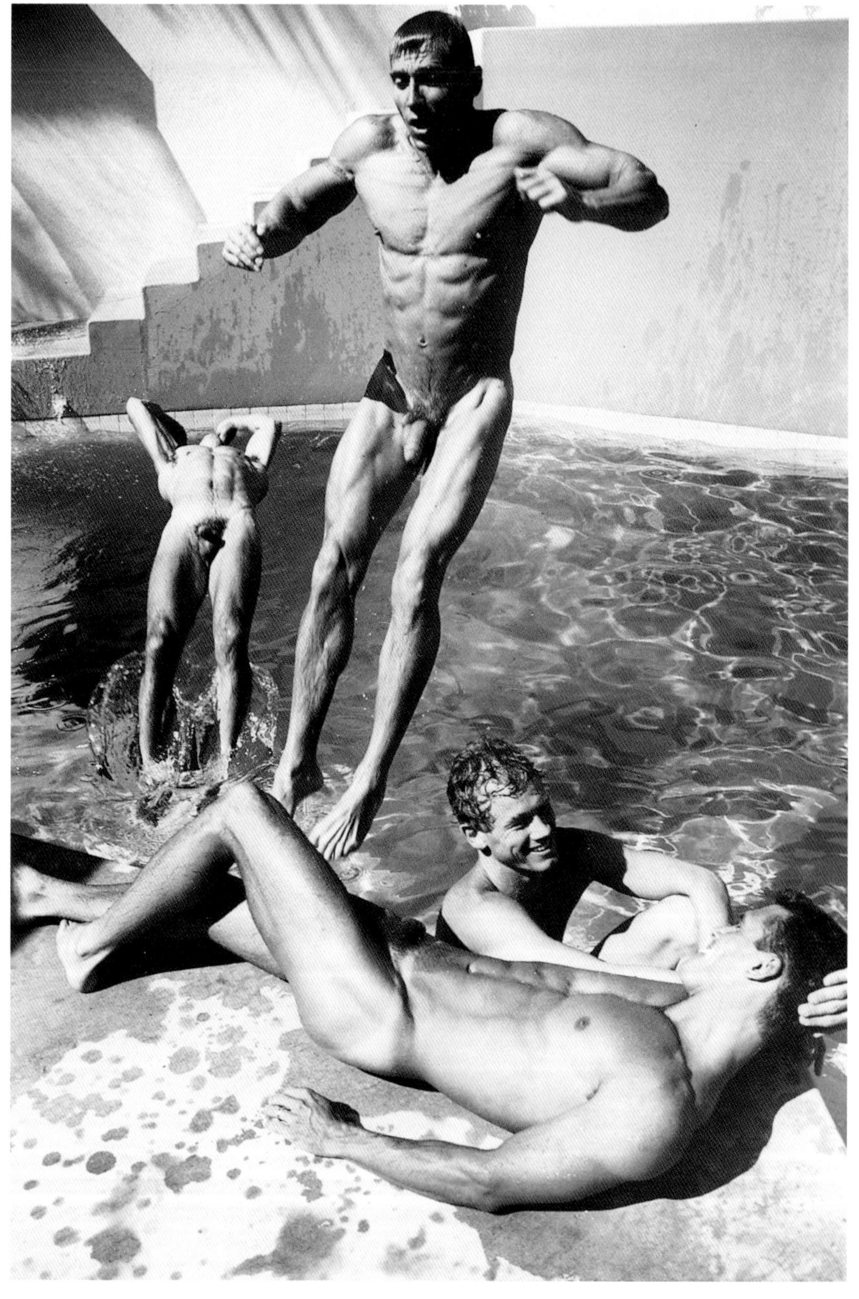

532   **Tom Bianchi,** Victor and Darius in the Air, 1990

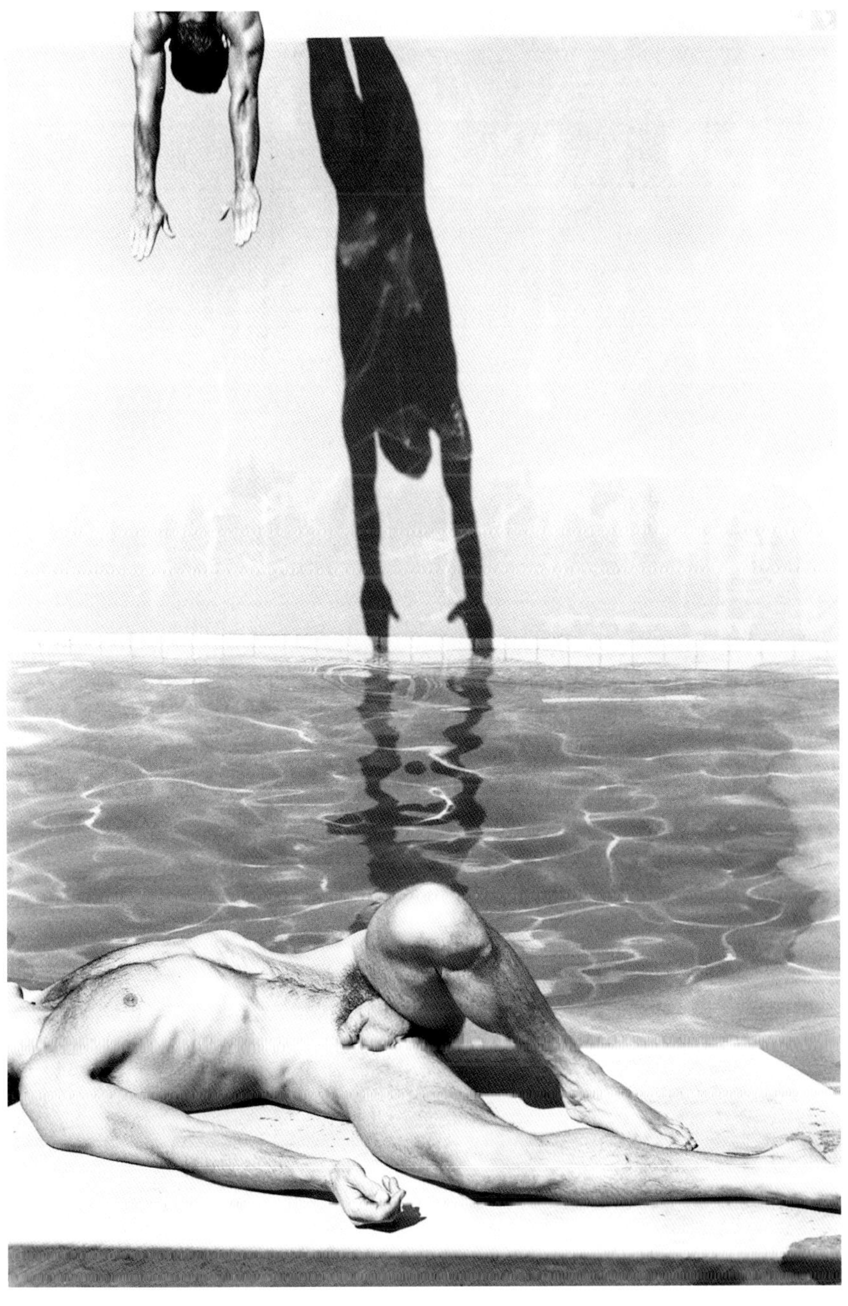

Tom Bianchi, 1990

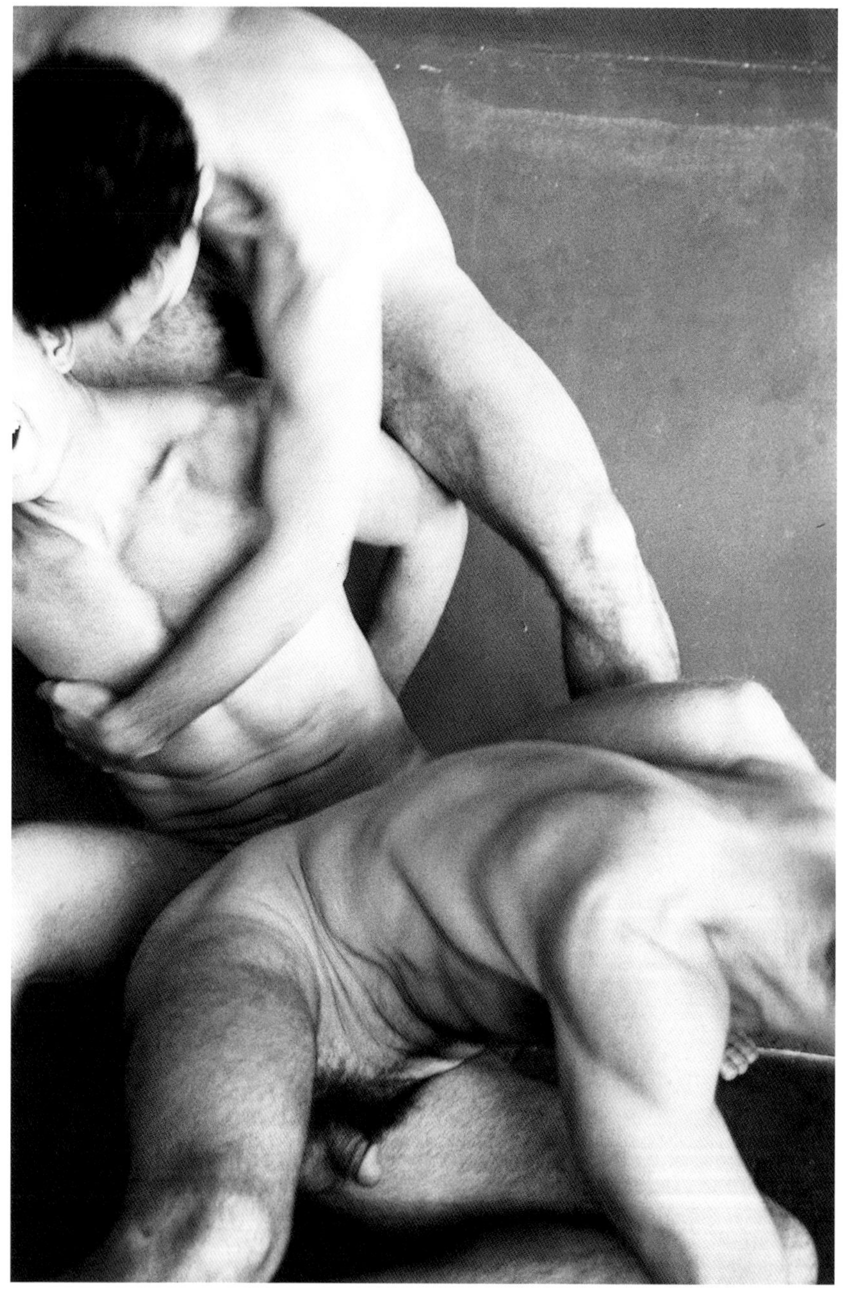

Tom Bianchi, 1991

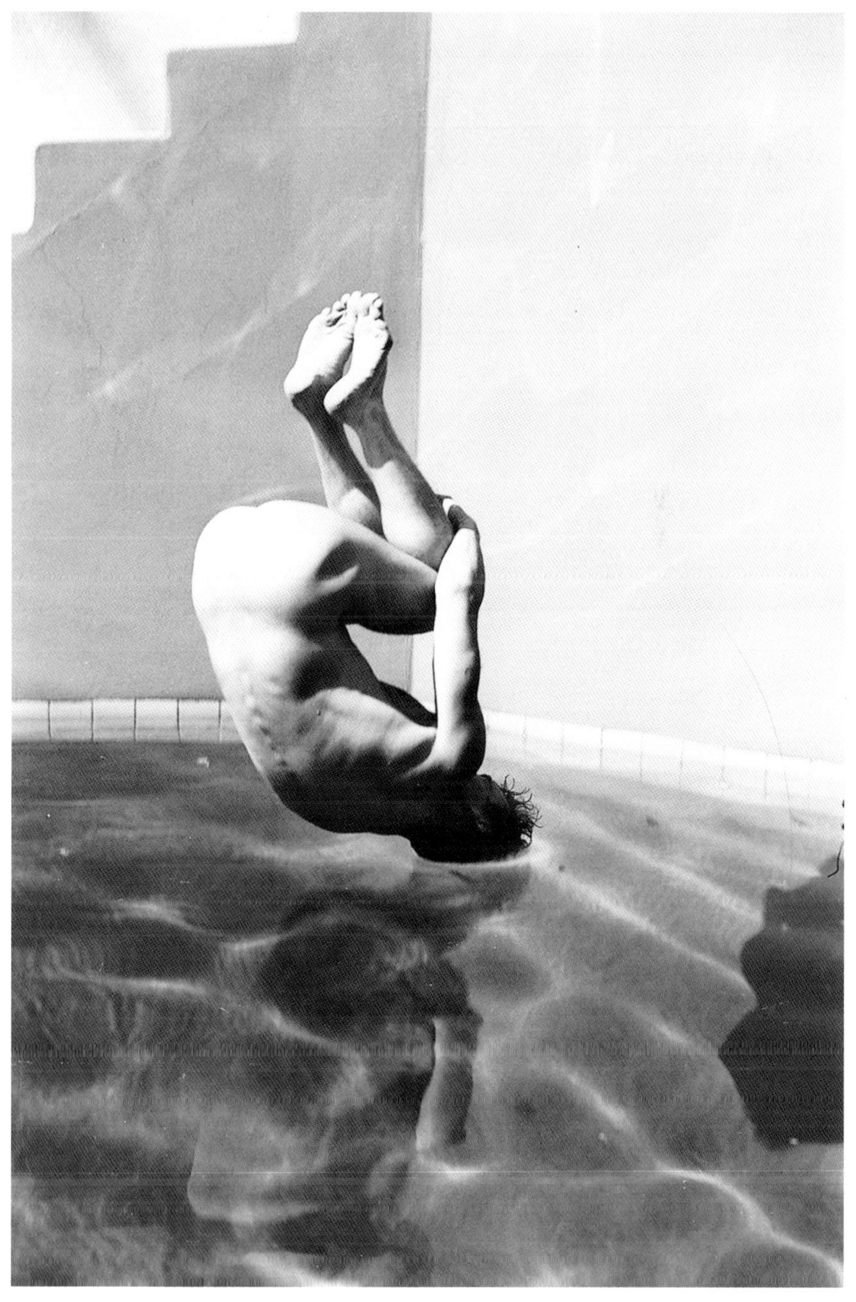

Tom Bianchi, 1988

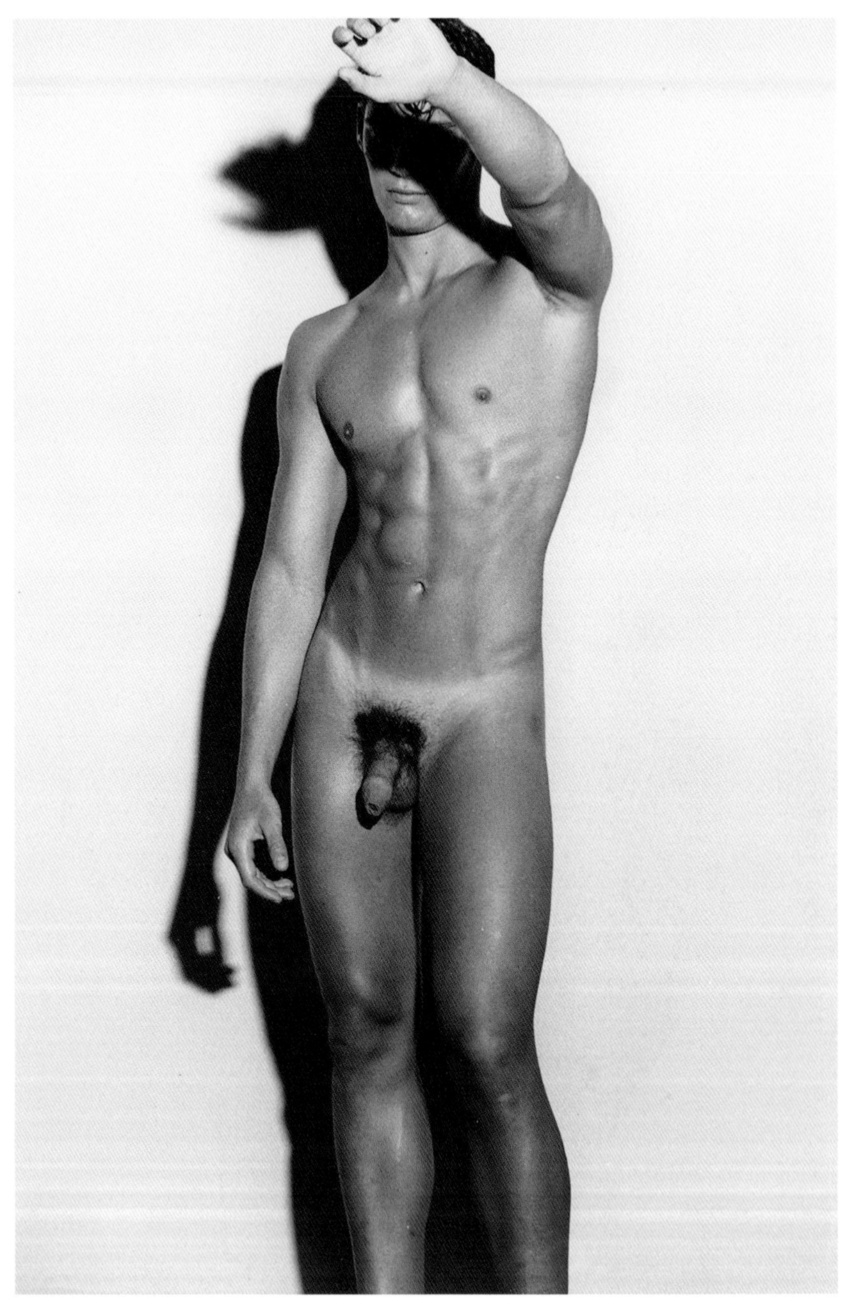

Herb Klein, Charlie, 1993

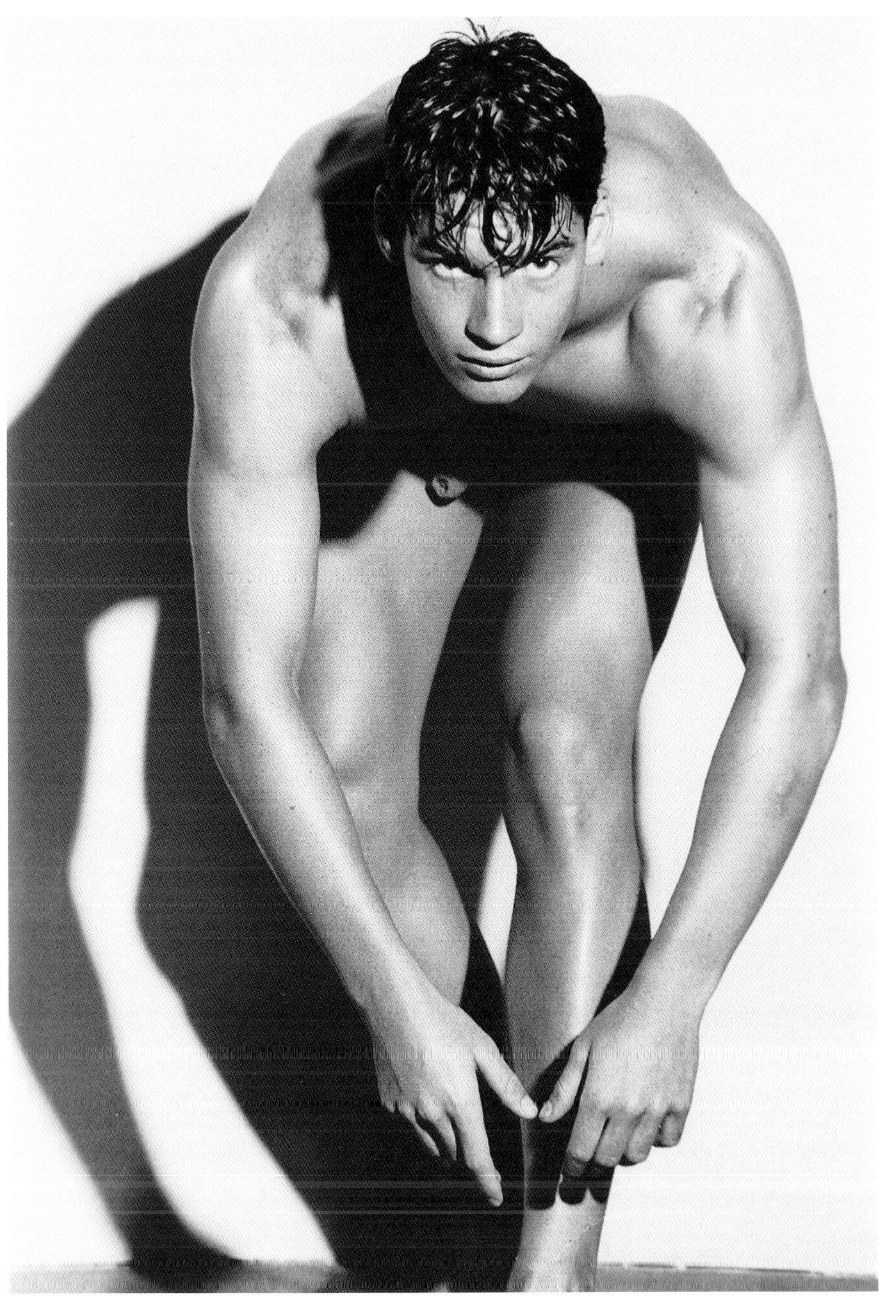

Herb Klein, Charlie, 1993

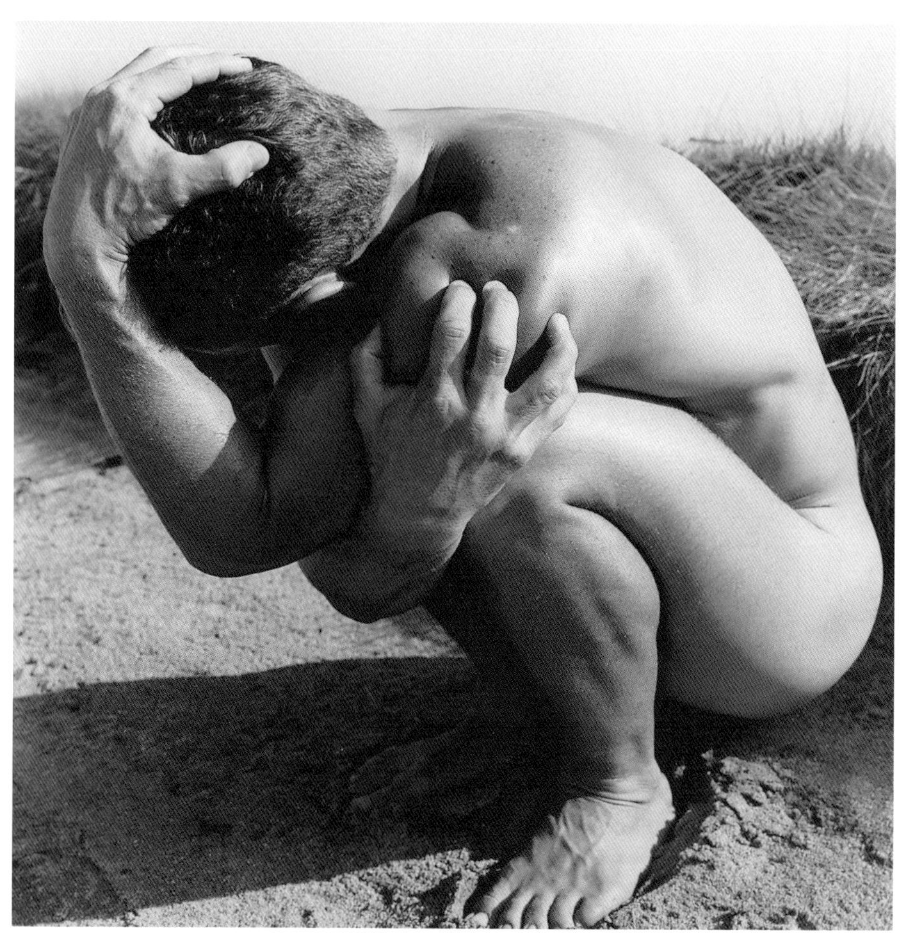

Frank Yamrus, Steve – Atlas, 1994

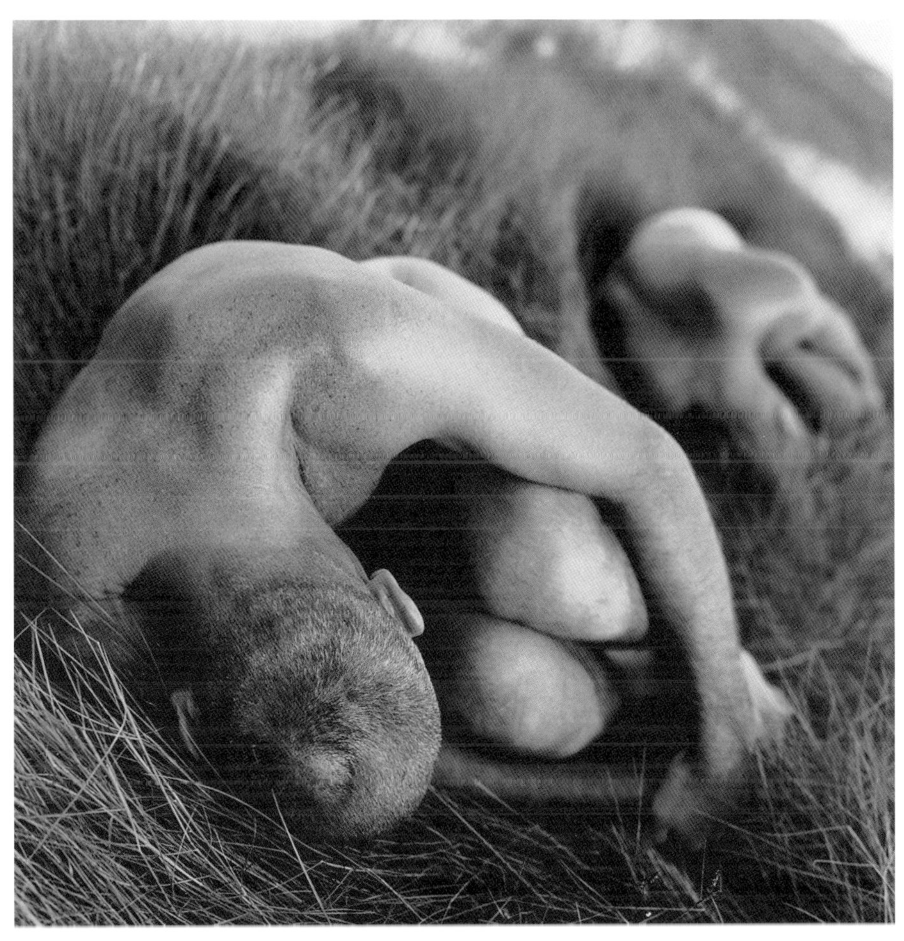

Frank Yamrus, Tommy – Pods, 1994

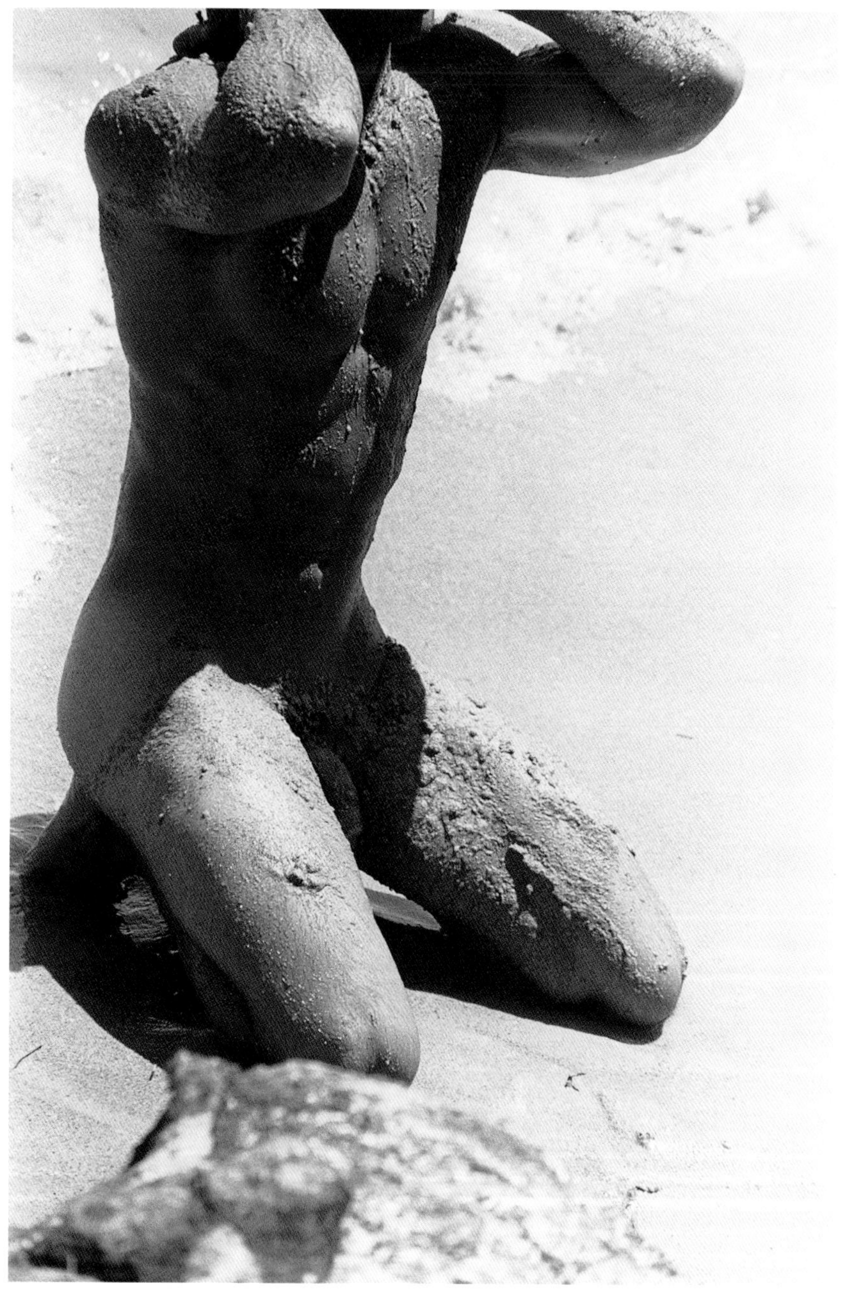

540

Andy Devine, 1996

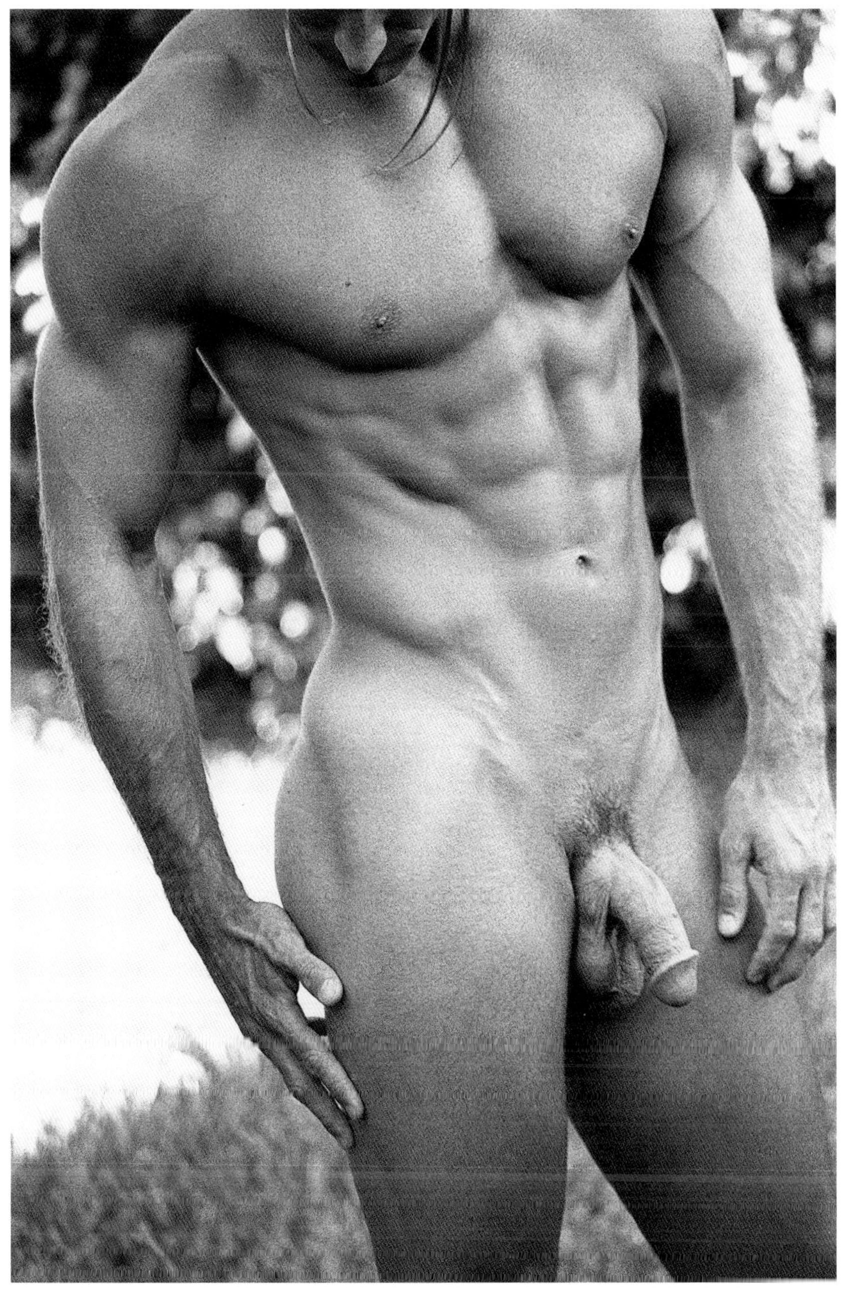

Andy Devine, 1996

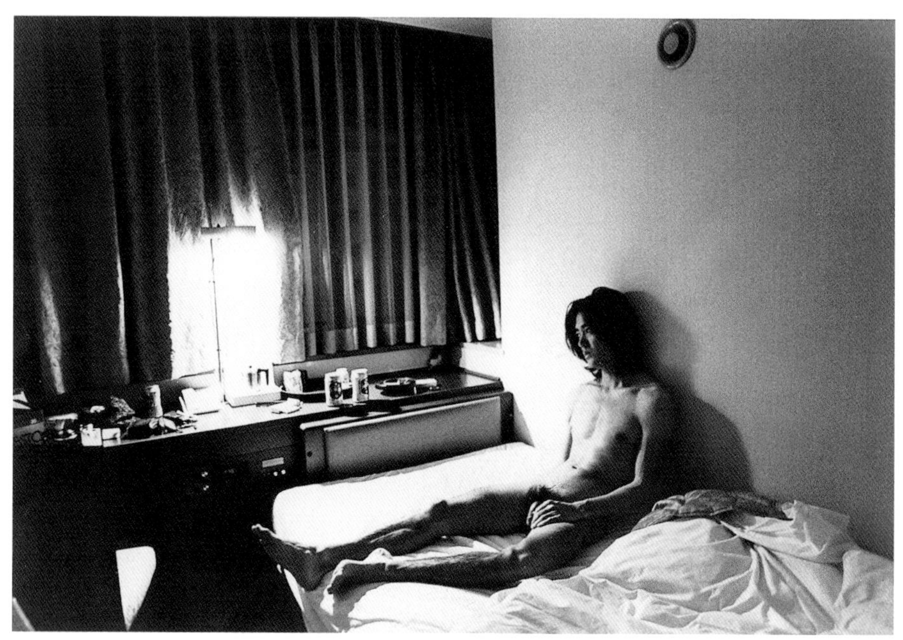

Sakiko Nomura, Untitled, from the Series "Naked Time", 1997

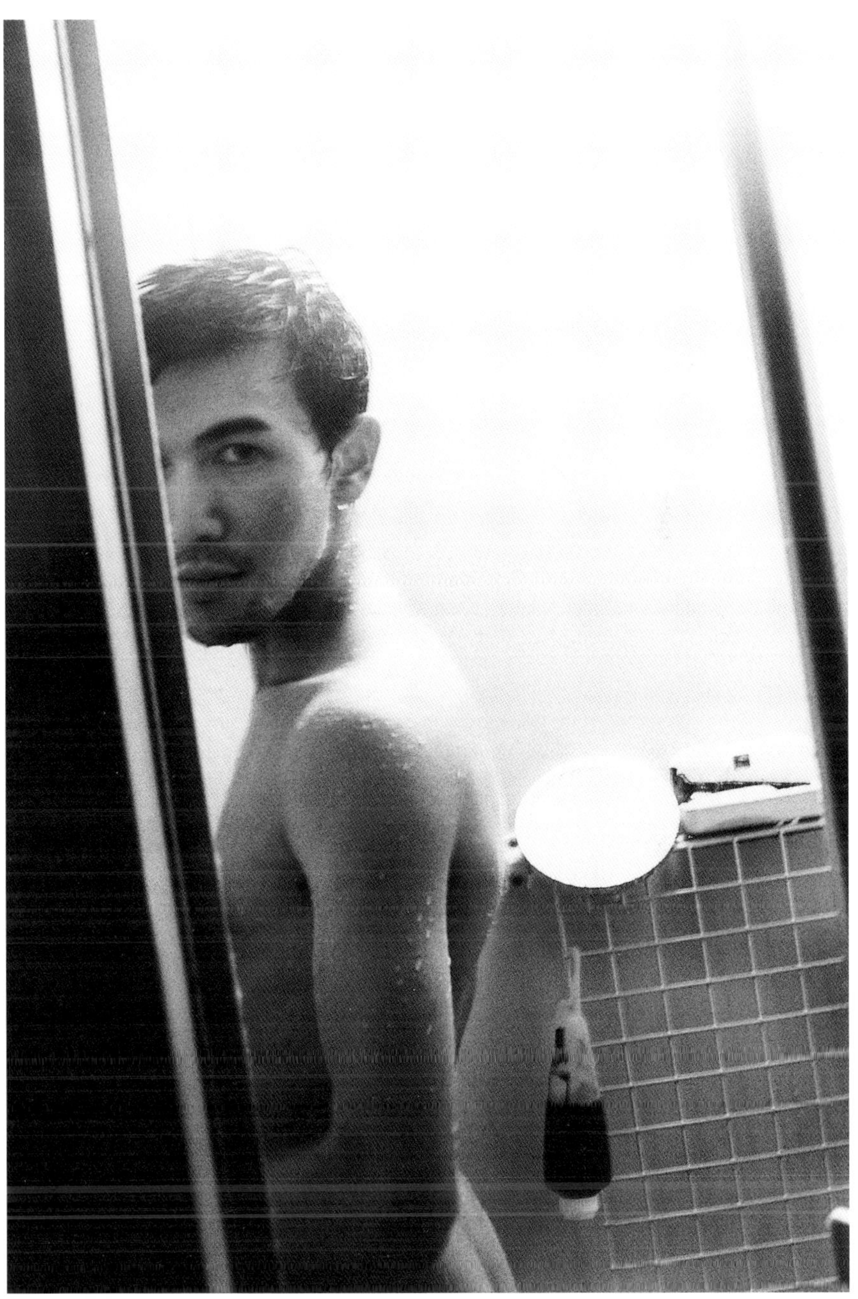

Sakiko Nomura, Untitled, from the Series "Naked Time", 1997

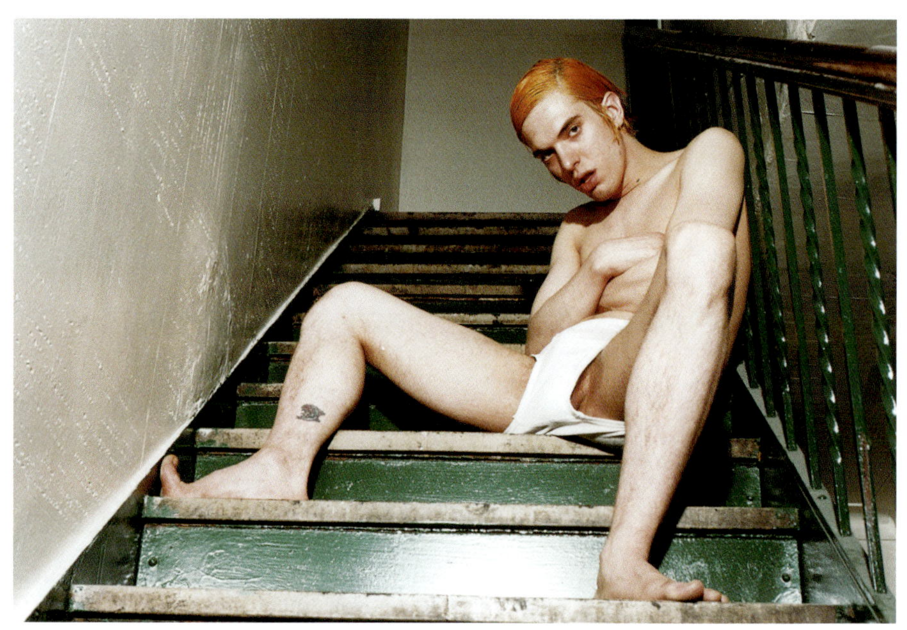

Richard Kern, Lyle Sitting on the Stairs, 1997

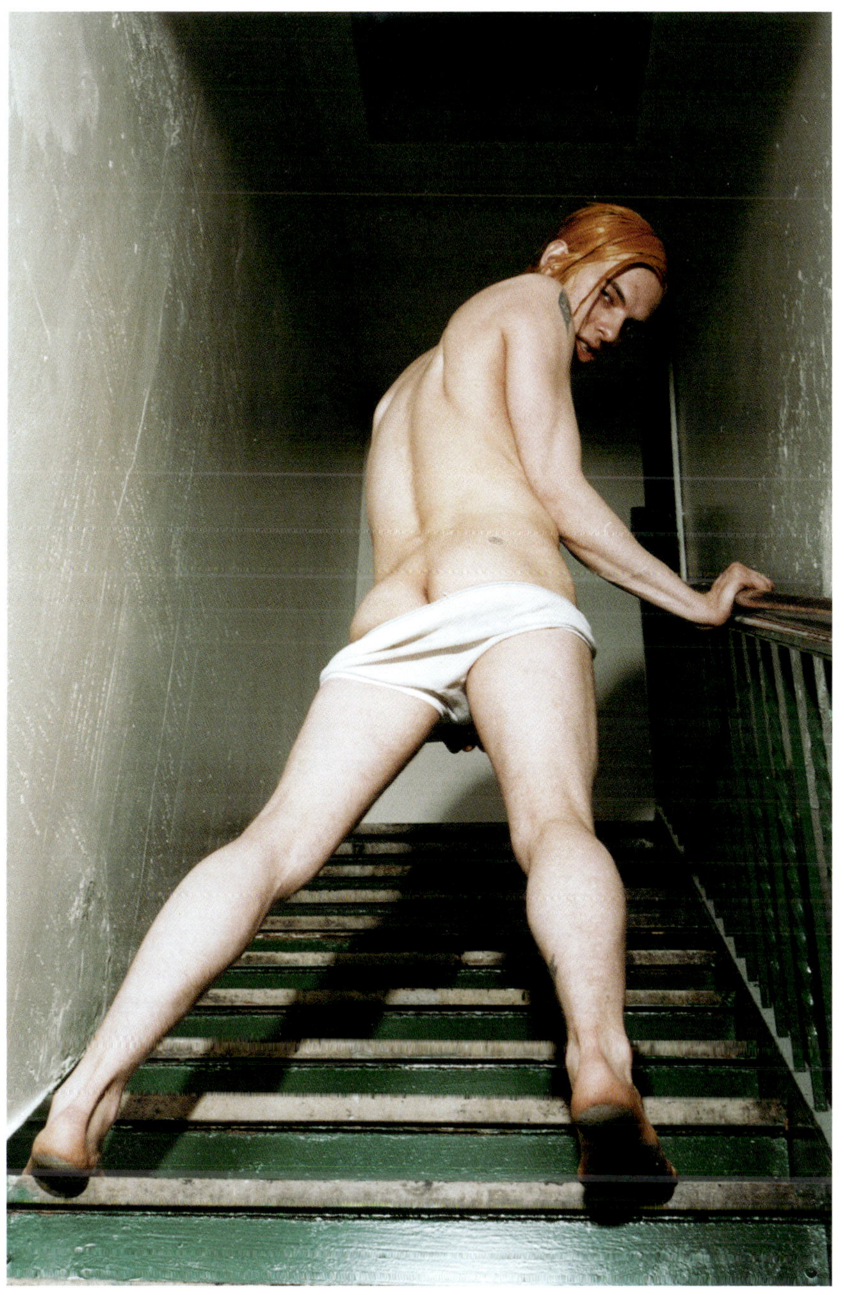

Richard Kern, Lyle Standing on the Stairs, 1997

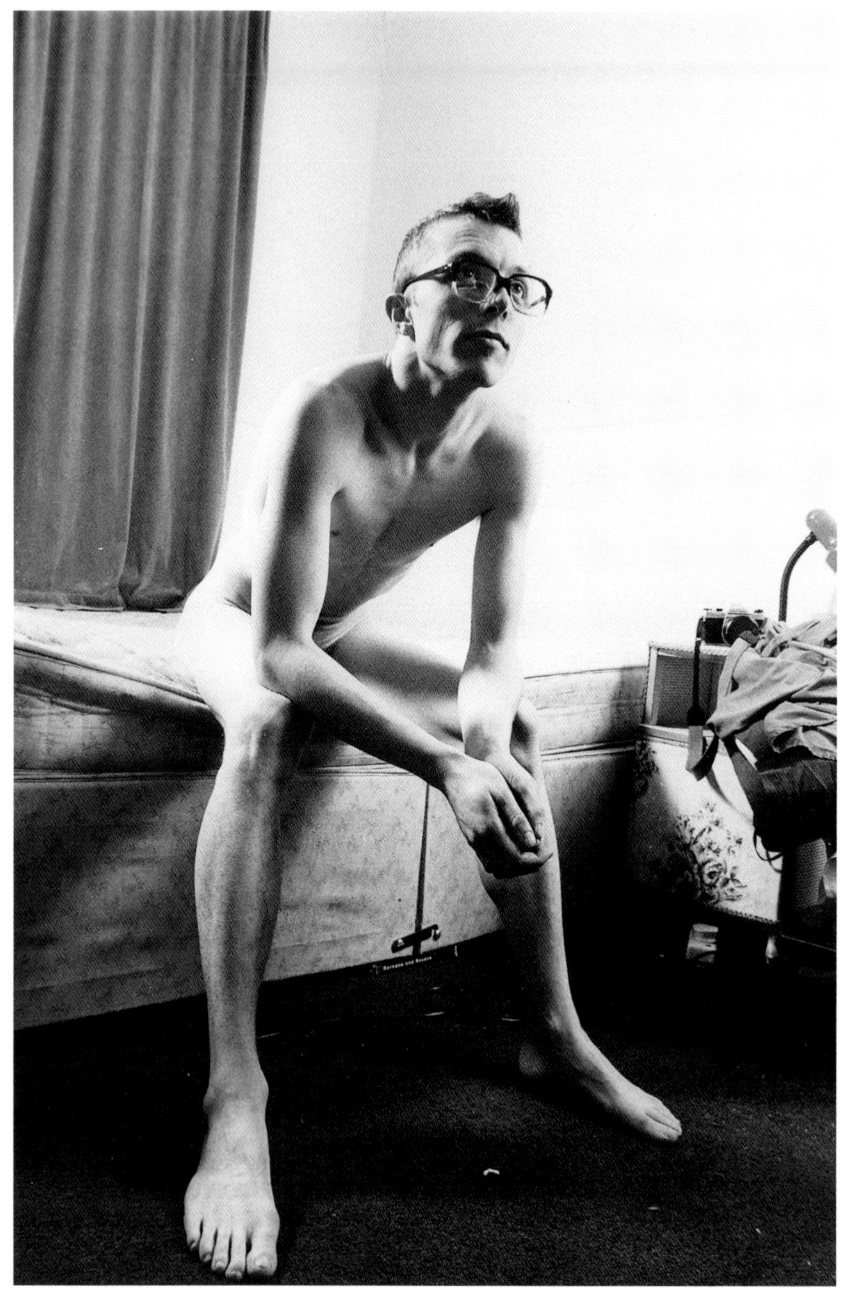

Richard Kern, Jake Sitting on the Bed, 1997

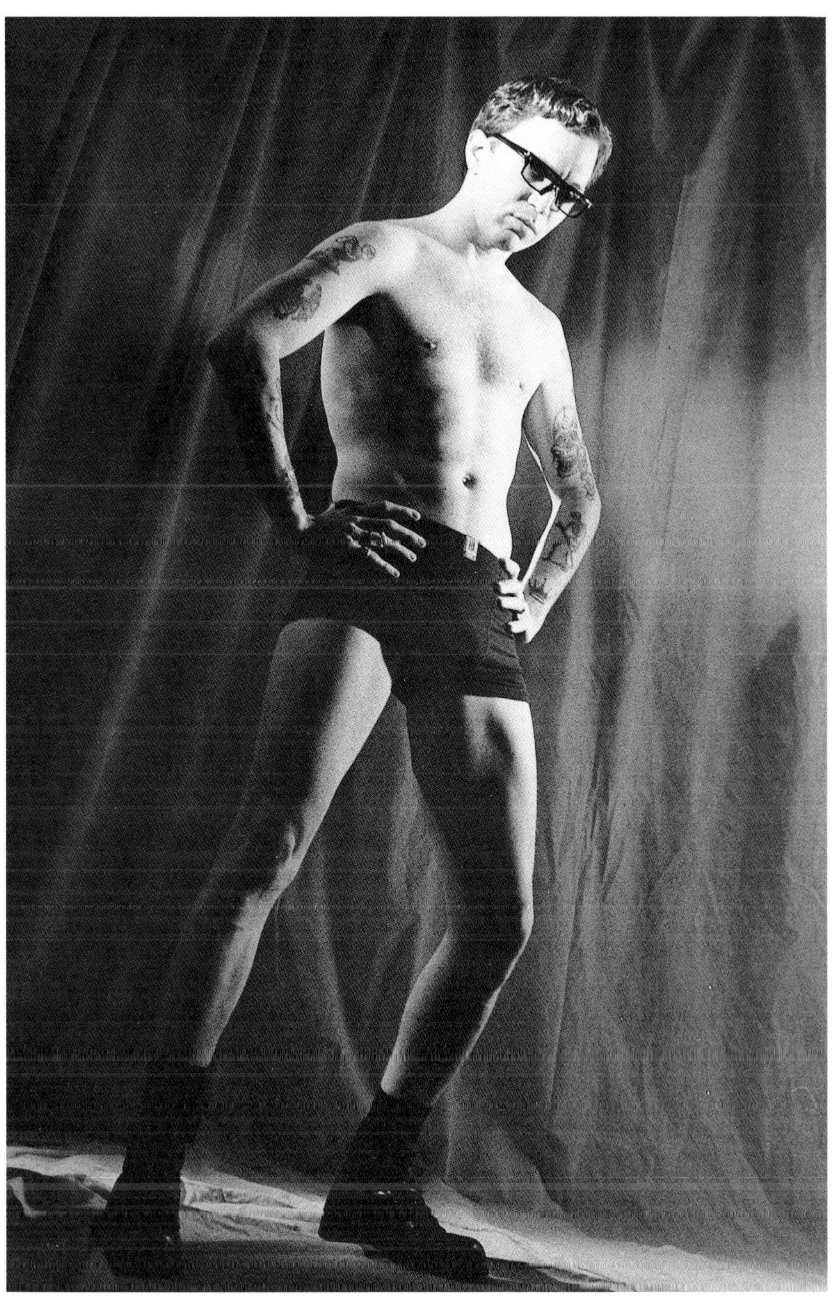

Richard Kern, Bruce La Bruce with his Hands on his Hips, 1994   **547**

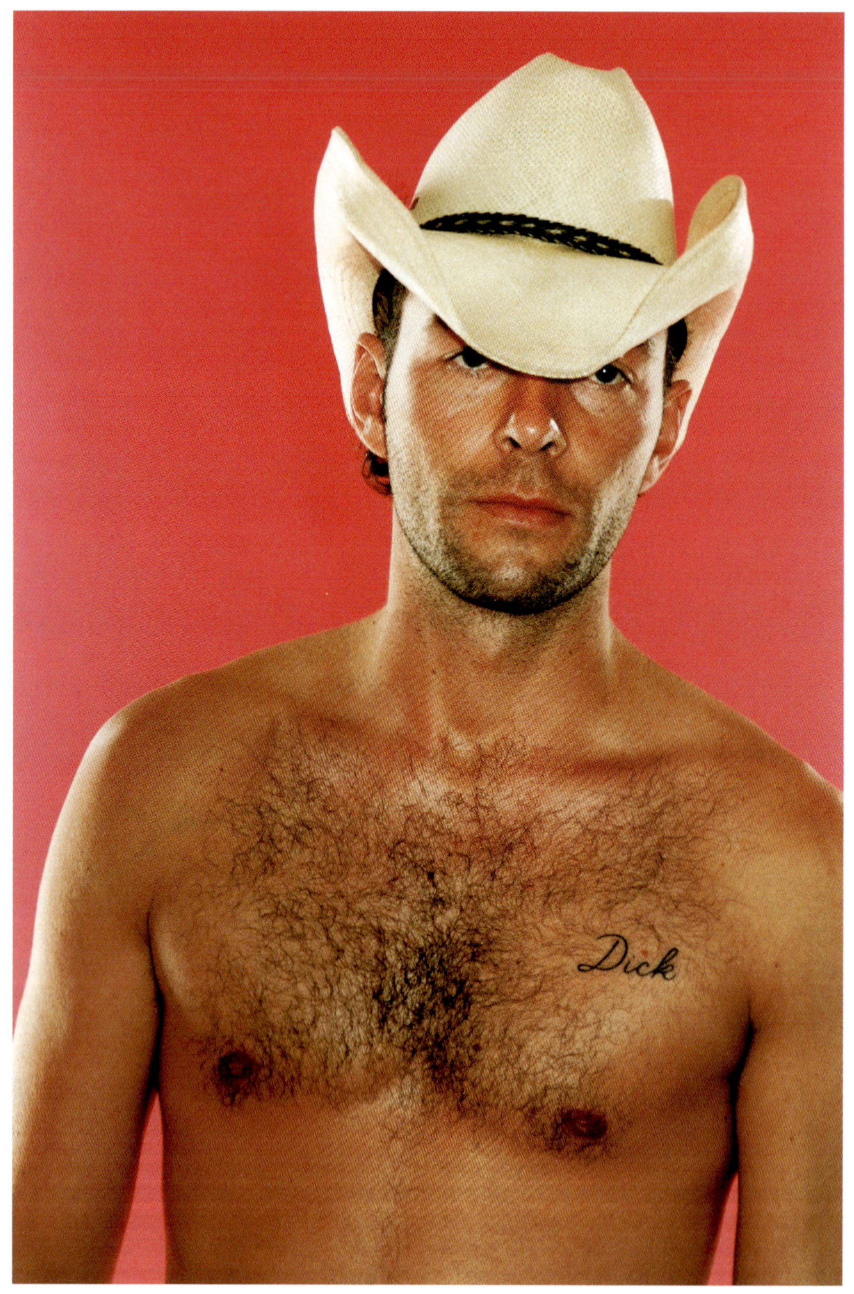

Jürgen Teller, Dick Page, 1996

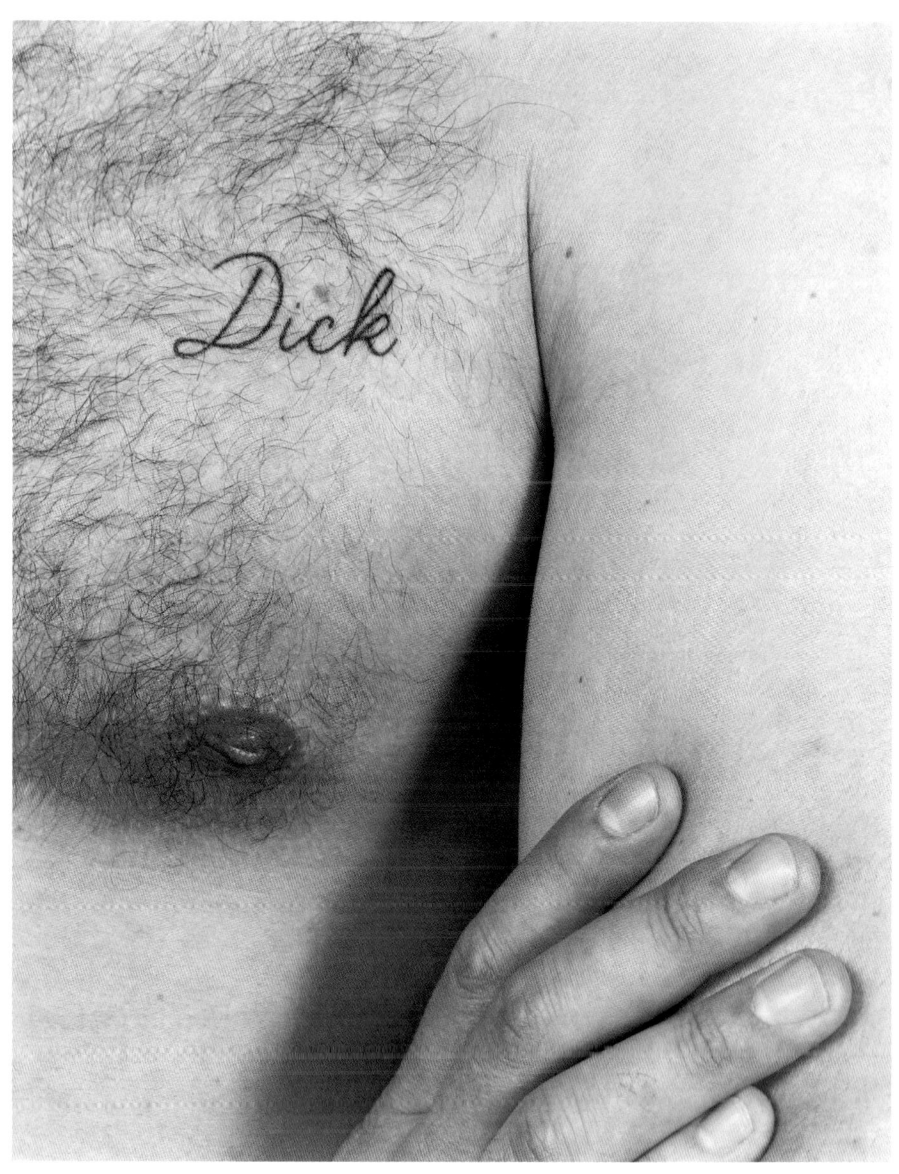

Jürgen Teller, Dick Page, 1996

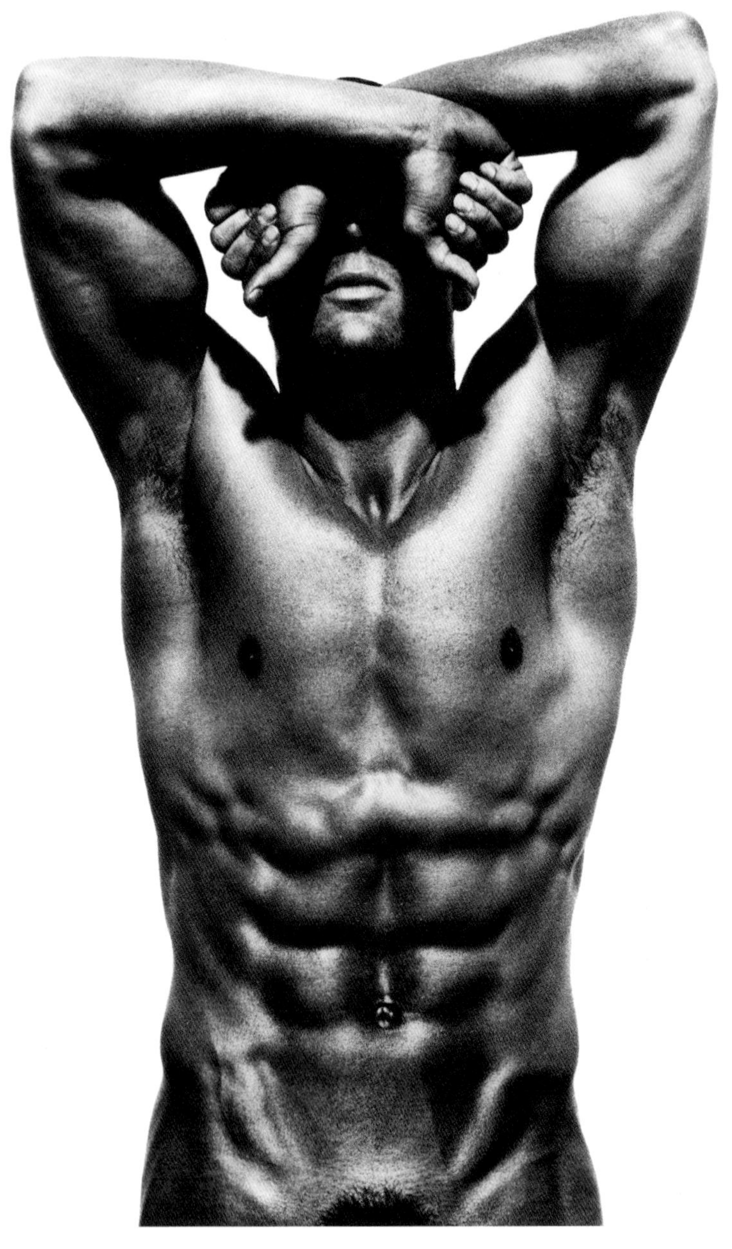

Andreas H. Bitesnich, Ingo # 59, 1994

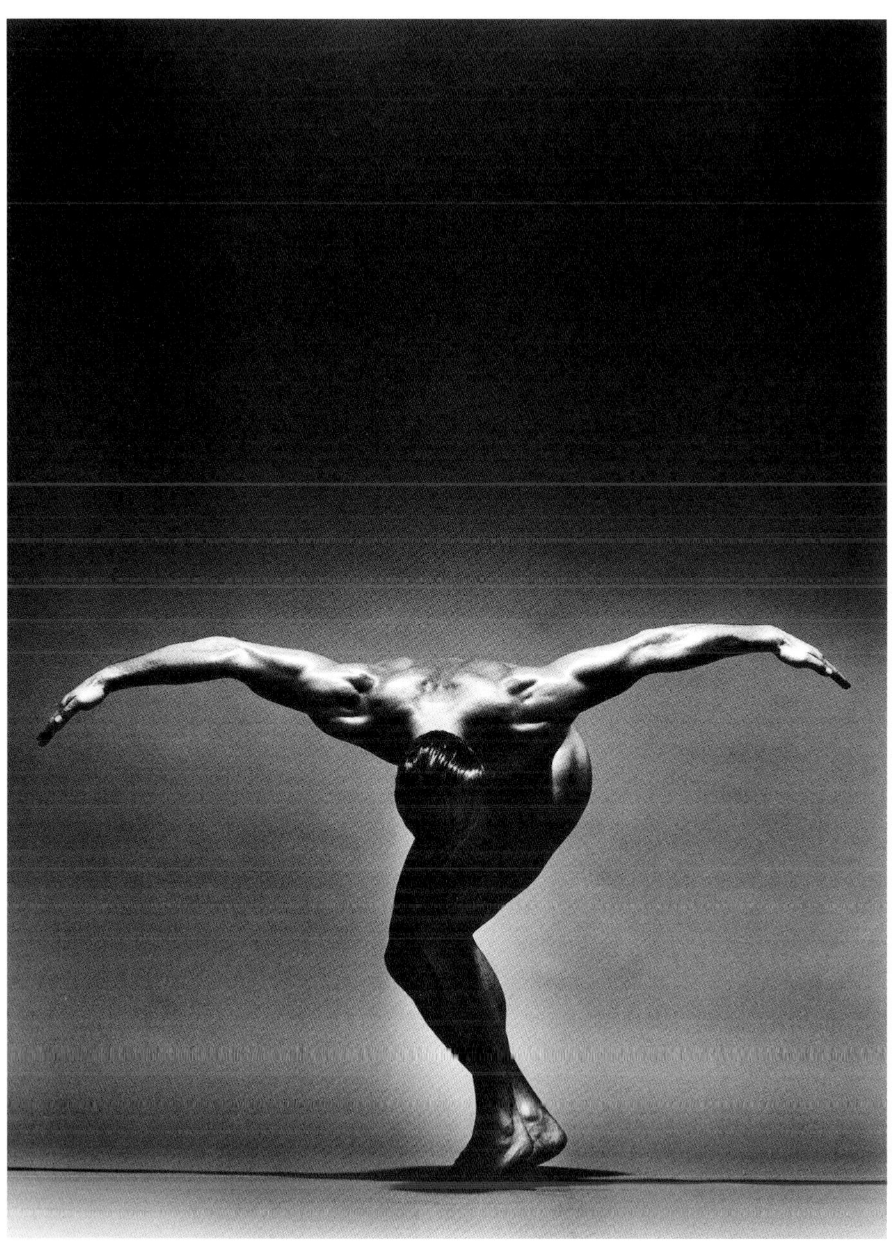

Andreas H. Bitesnich, Anthony "Birdman", 1995

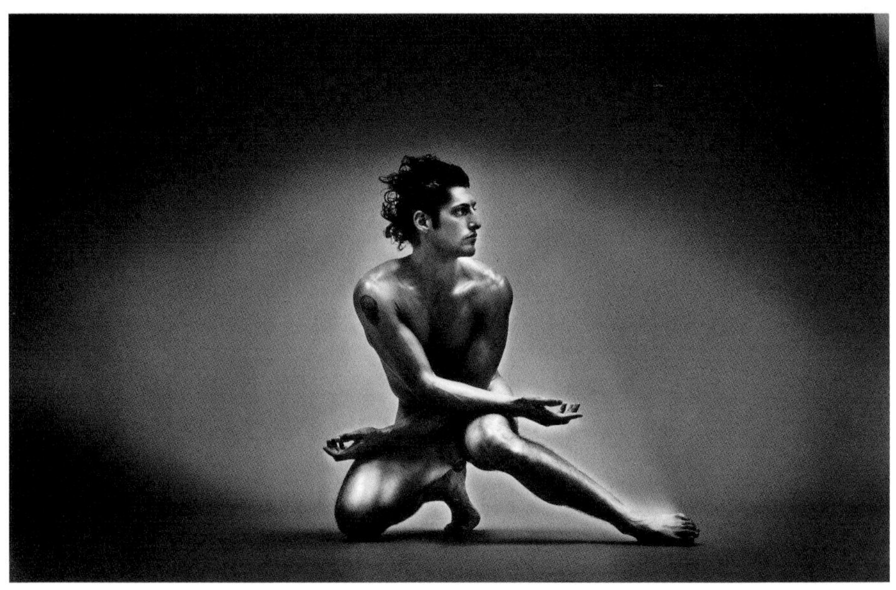

Andreas H. Bitesnich, Tony Ward # 71, 1994

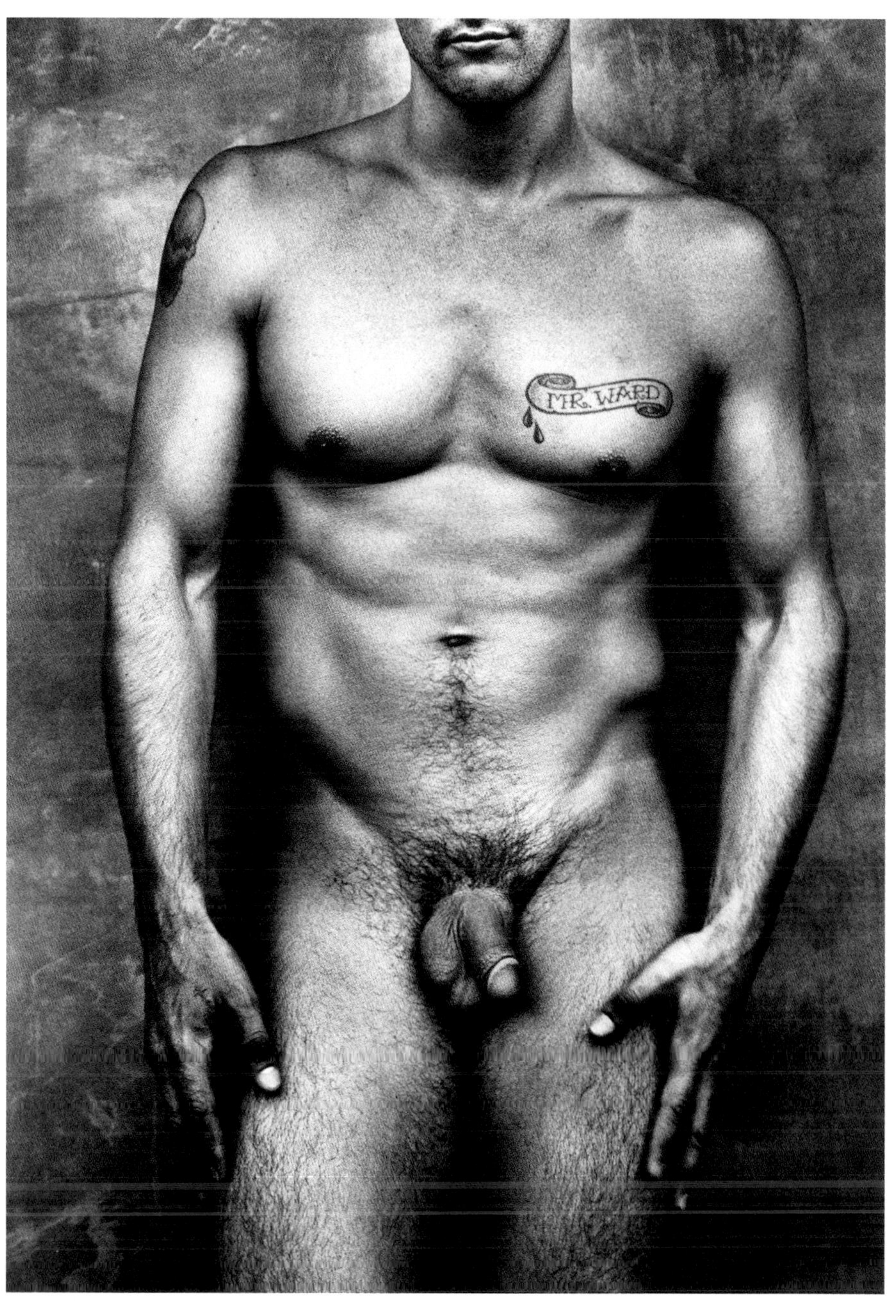

Andreas H. Bitesnich, Tony # 27, 1995

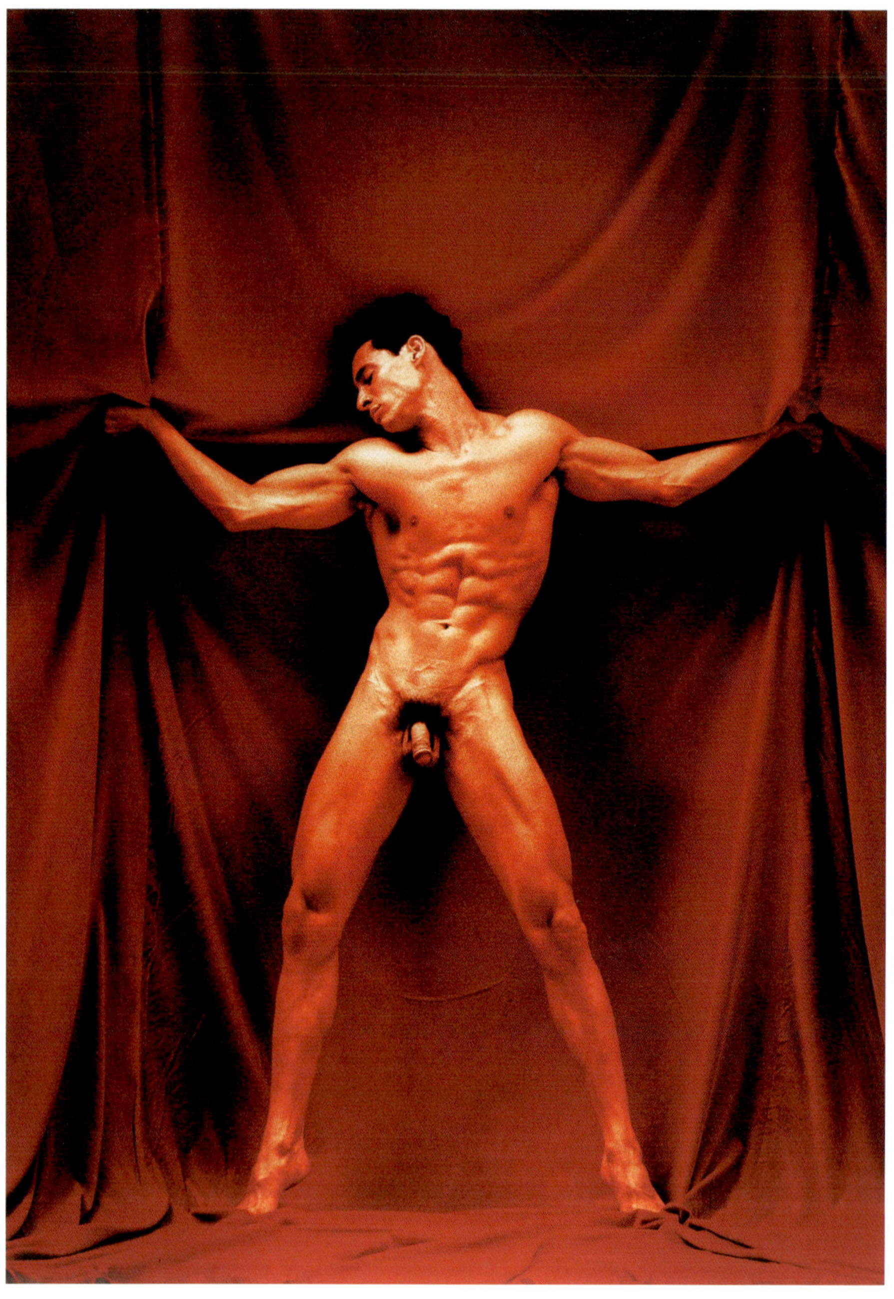

Andreas H. Bitesnich, Shy # 78, 1995

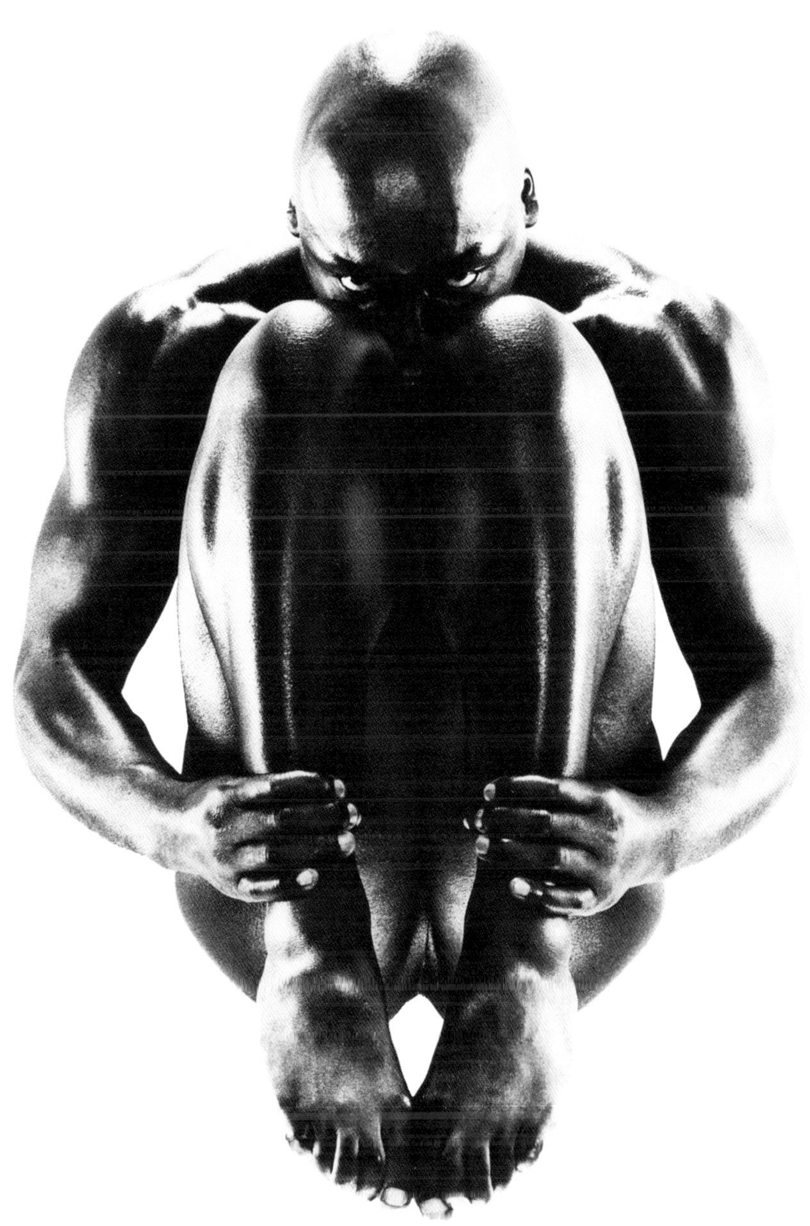

Andreas H. Bitesnich, Roy # 15, 1995

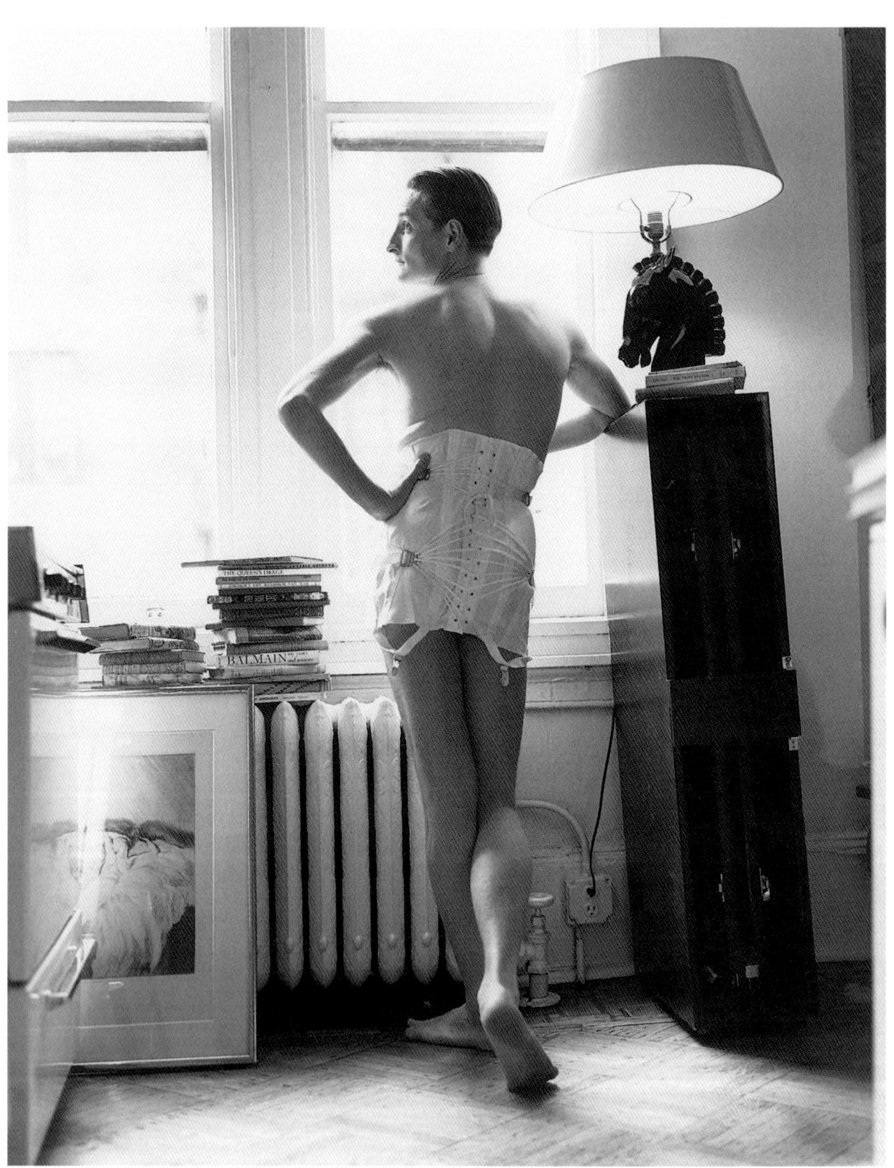

Steven Meisel, Hamish Bowles, 1993

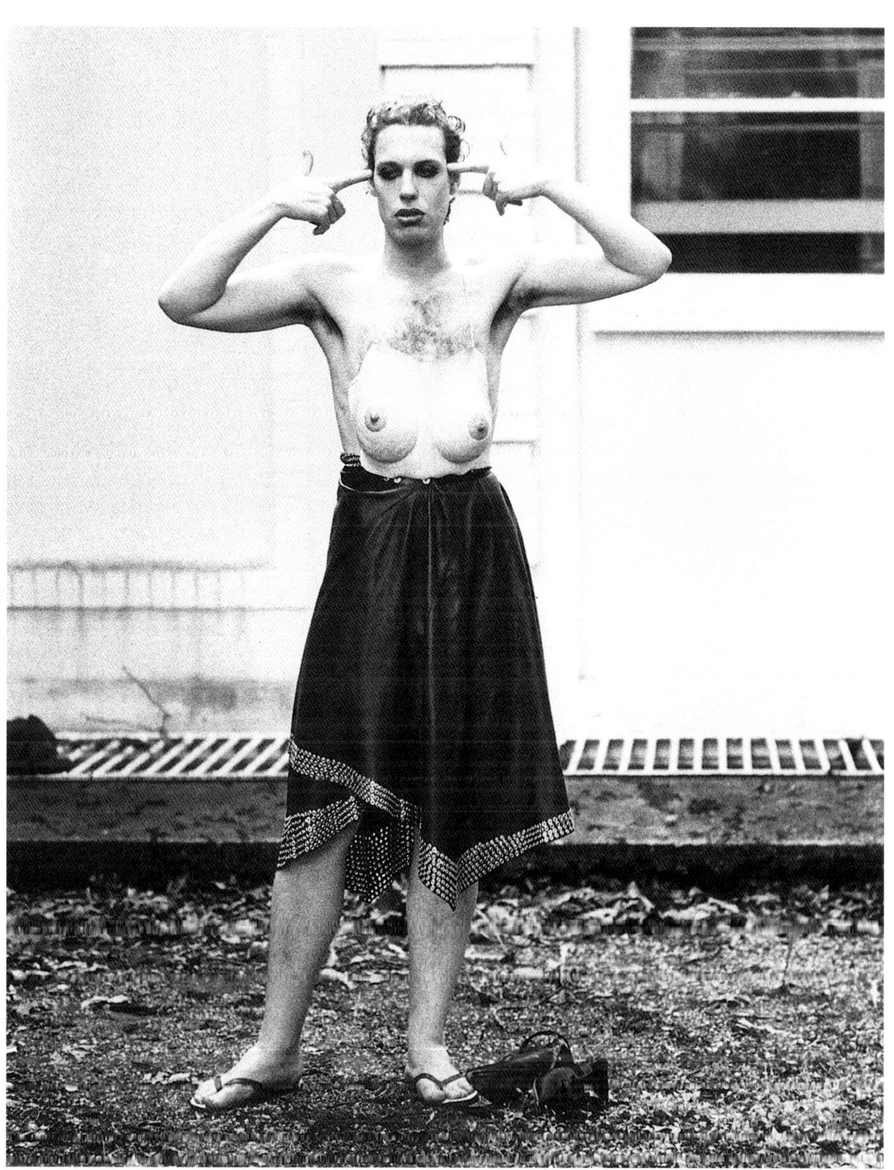

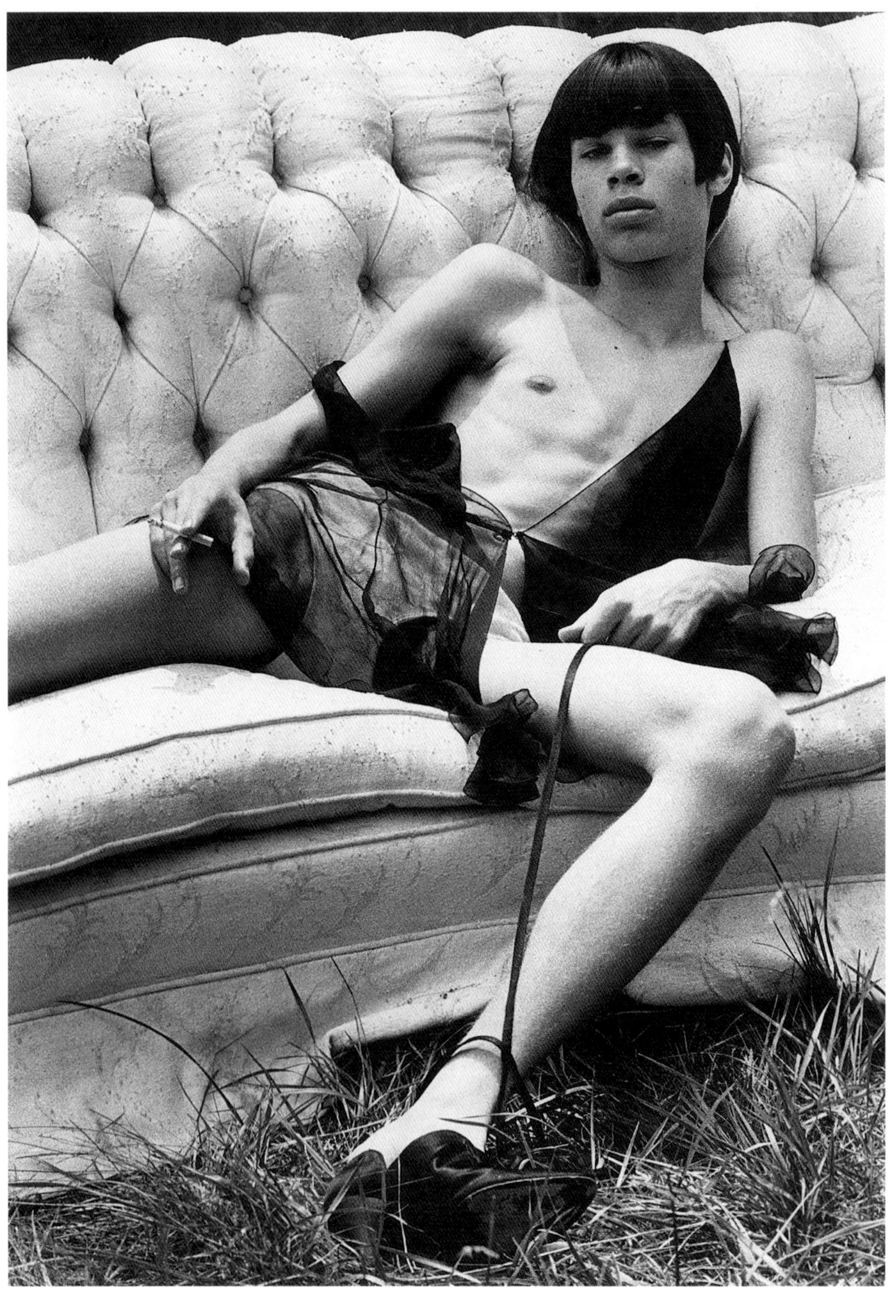

Steven Meisel, Sean, 1987

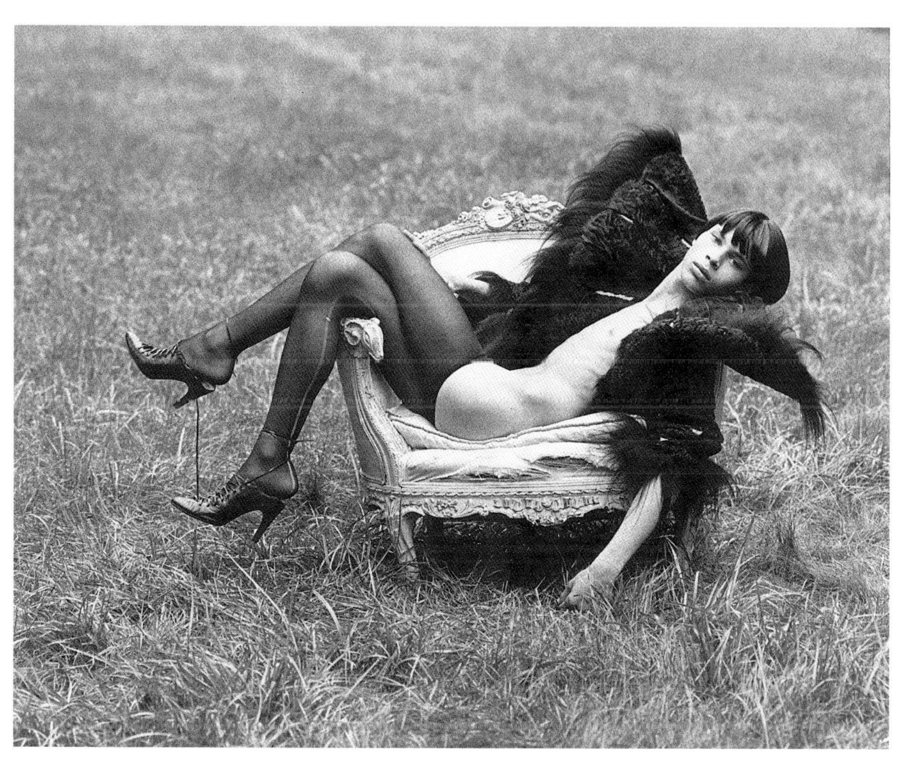

Steven Meisel, Sean, 1987

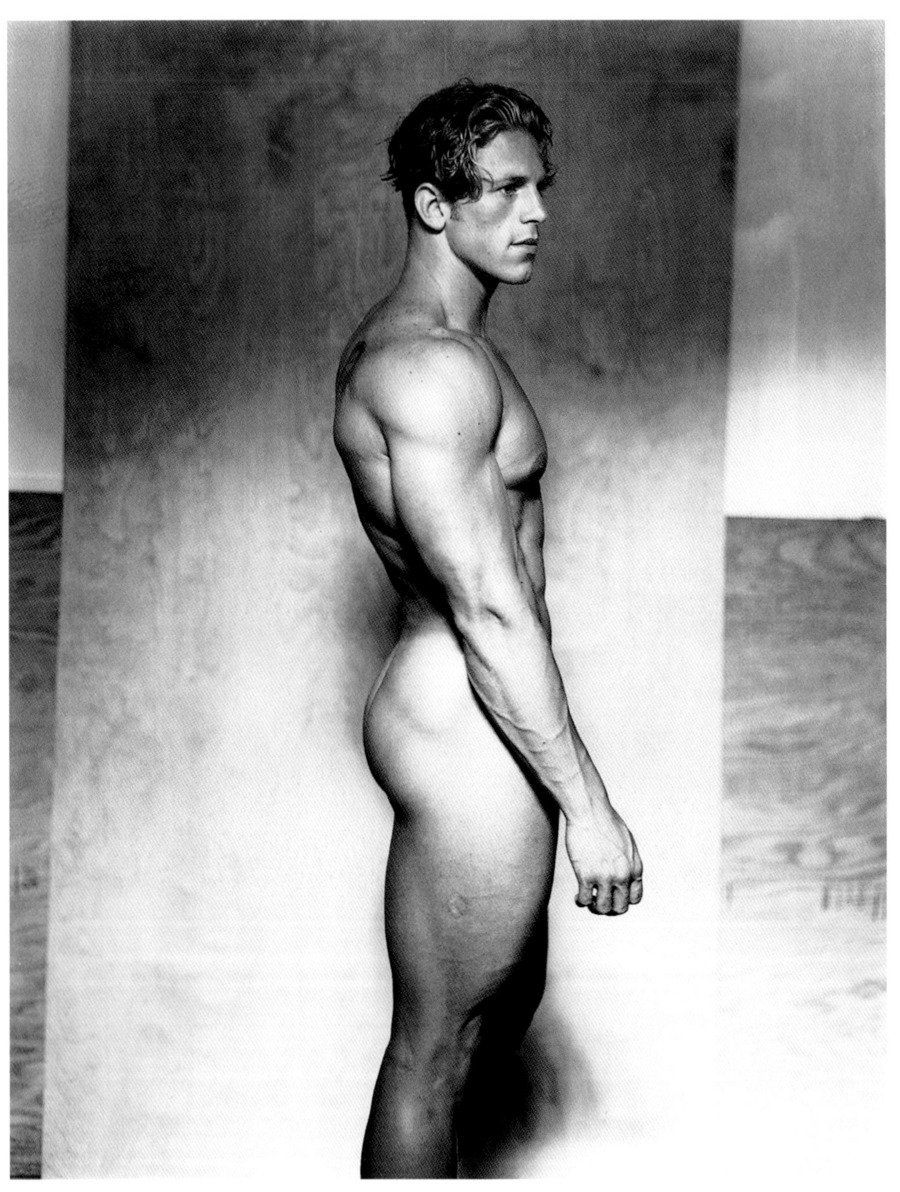

Blake Little, Andrew, Profile, 1995

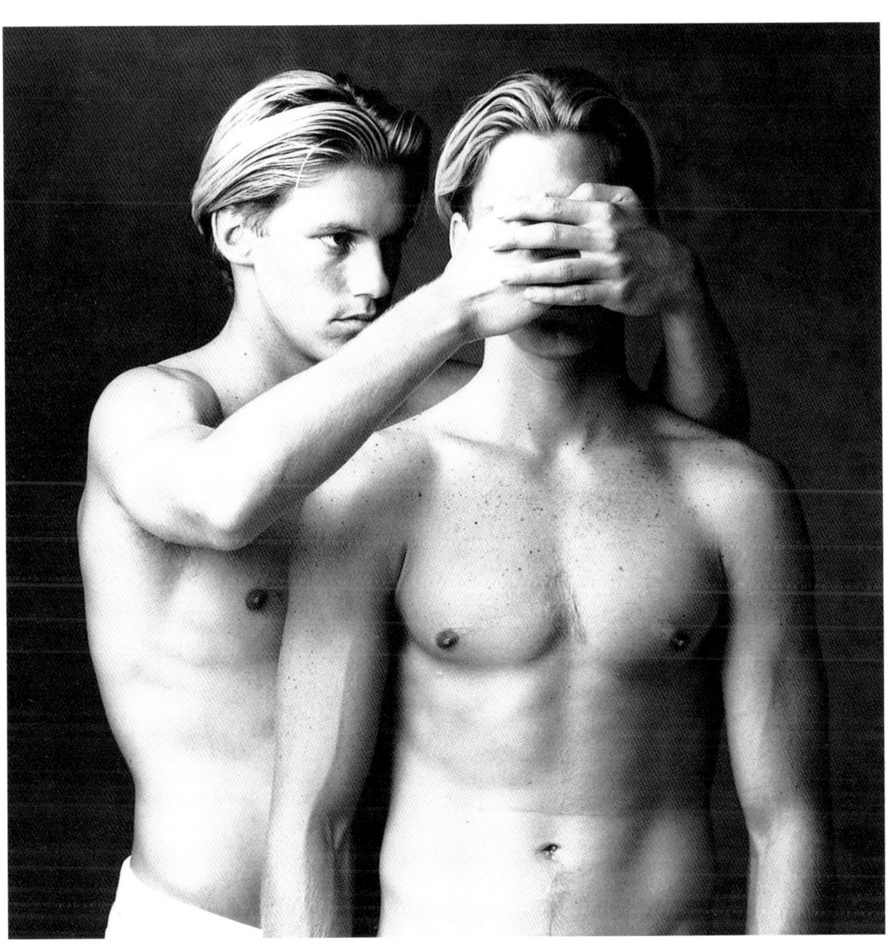

Blake Little, Derek and Keith, 1996

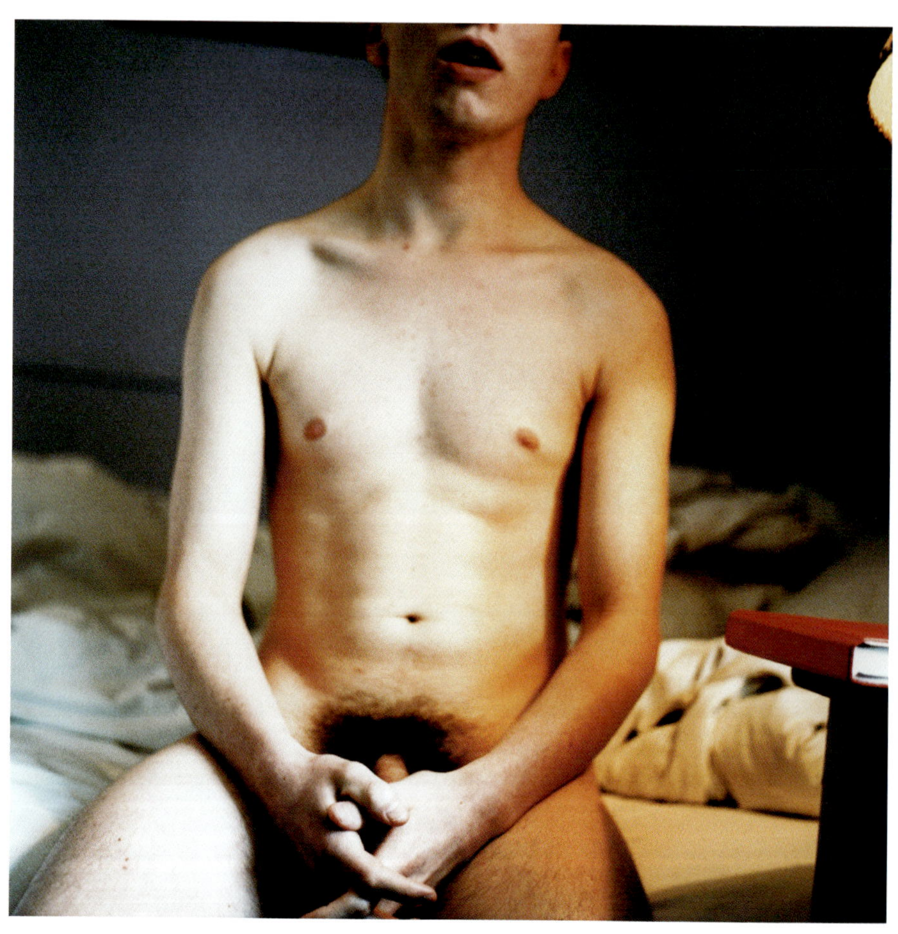

Jack Pierson, Paul Lee, 1997

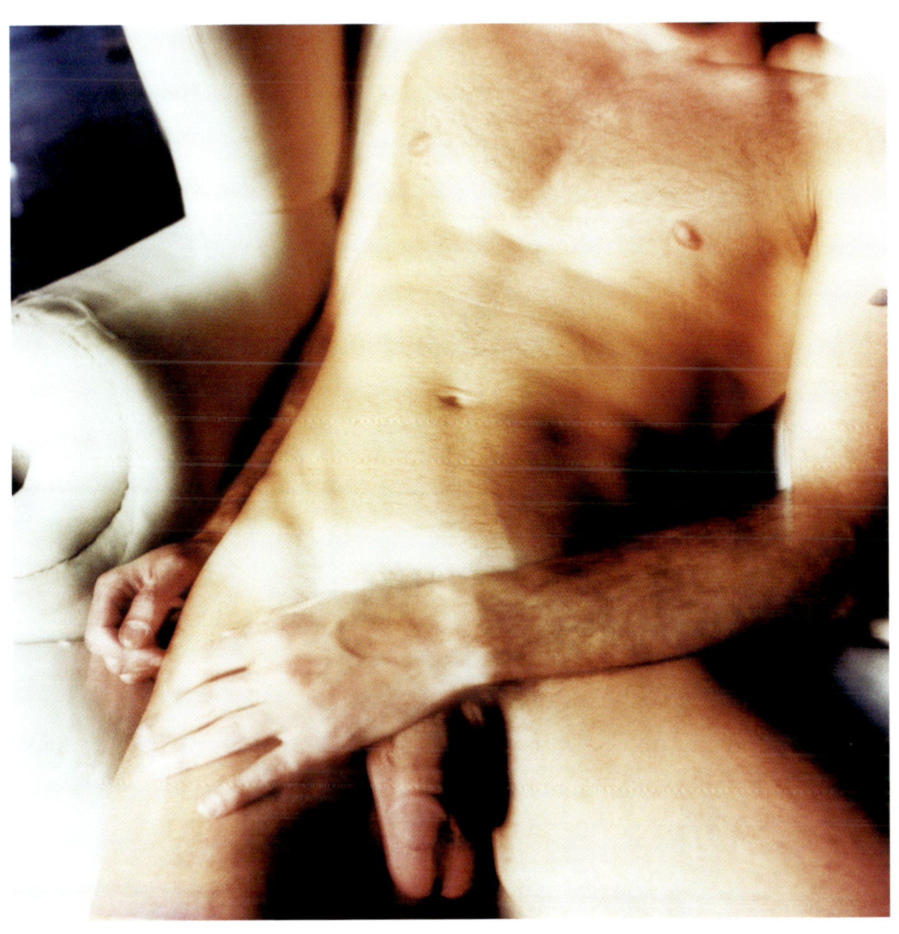

Jack Pierson, J. S. III, 1997

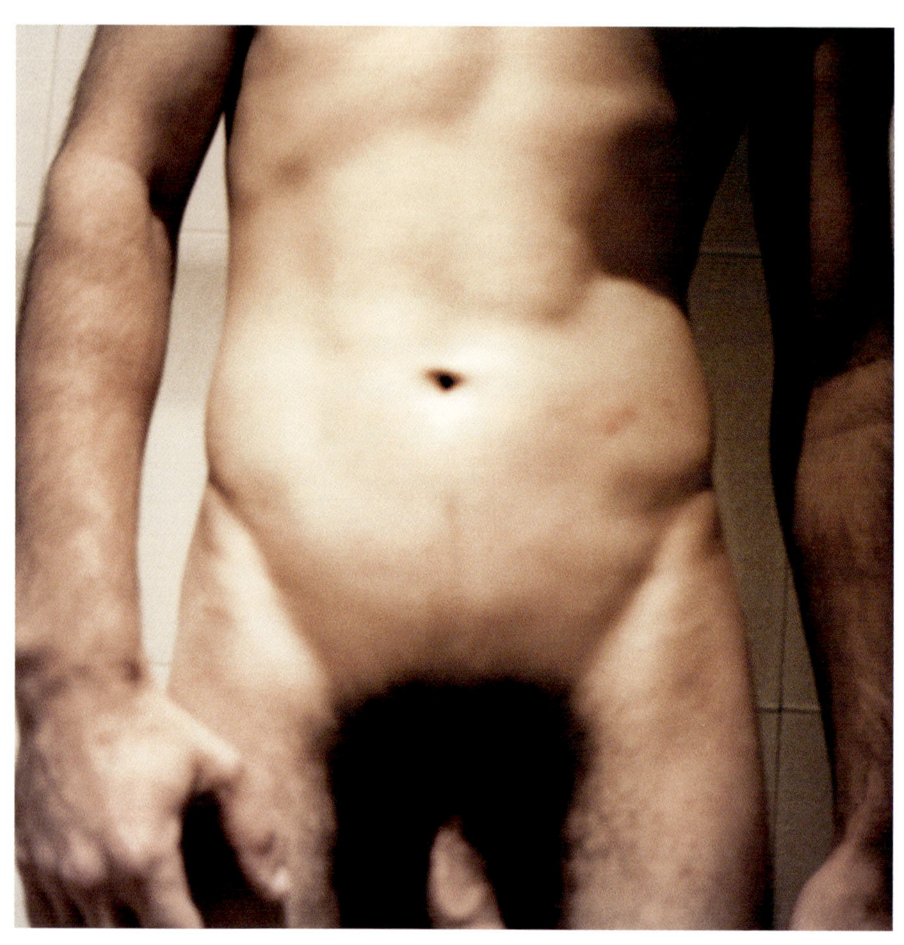

Jack Pierson, Unknown, 1996

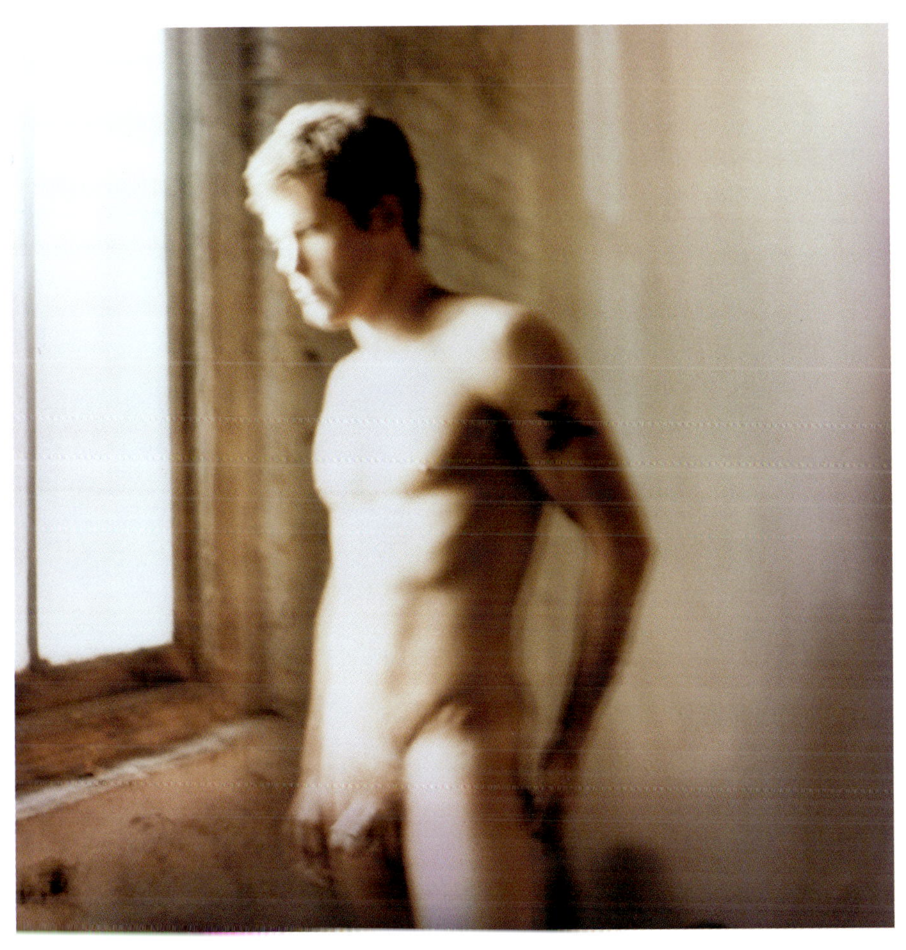

Jack Pierson, John Spencer III, 1997

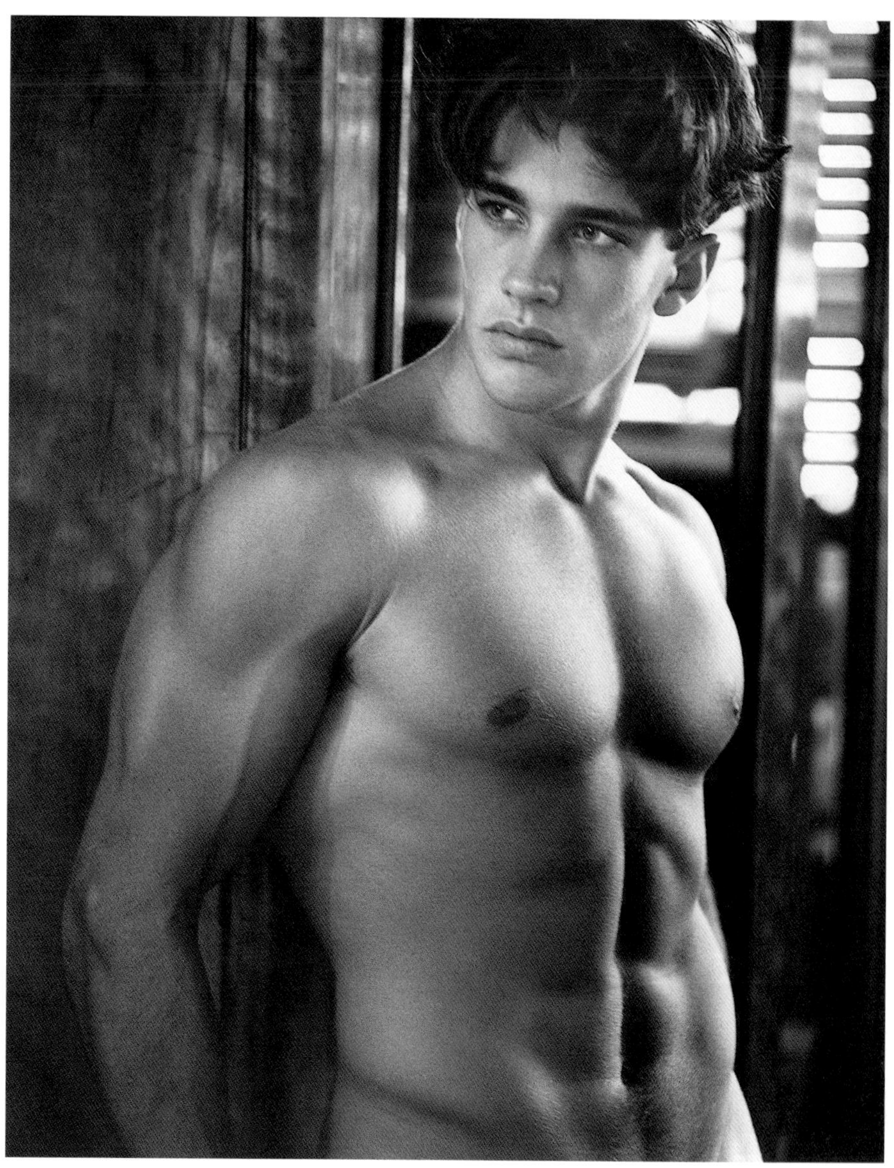

Bruce Weber, Jesse from Brooklyn, 1997

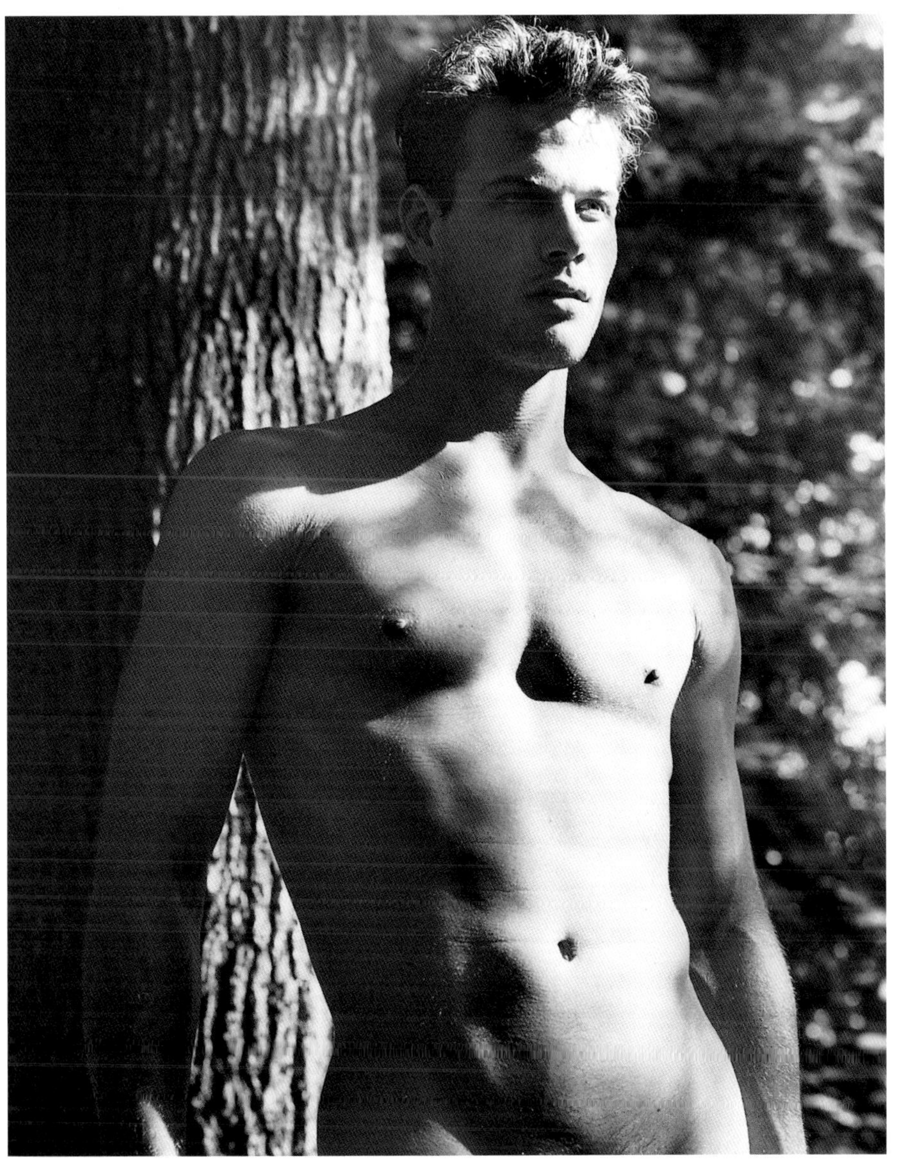

Bruce Weber, Brett – Adirondack Park, 1997

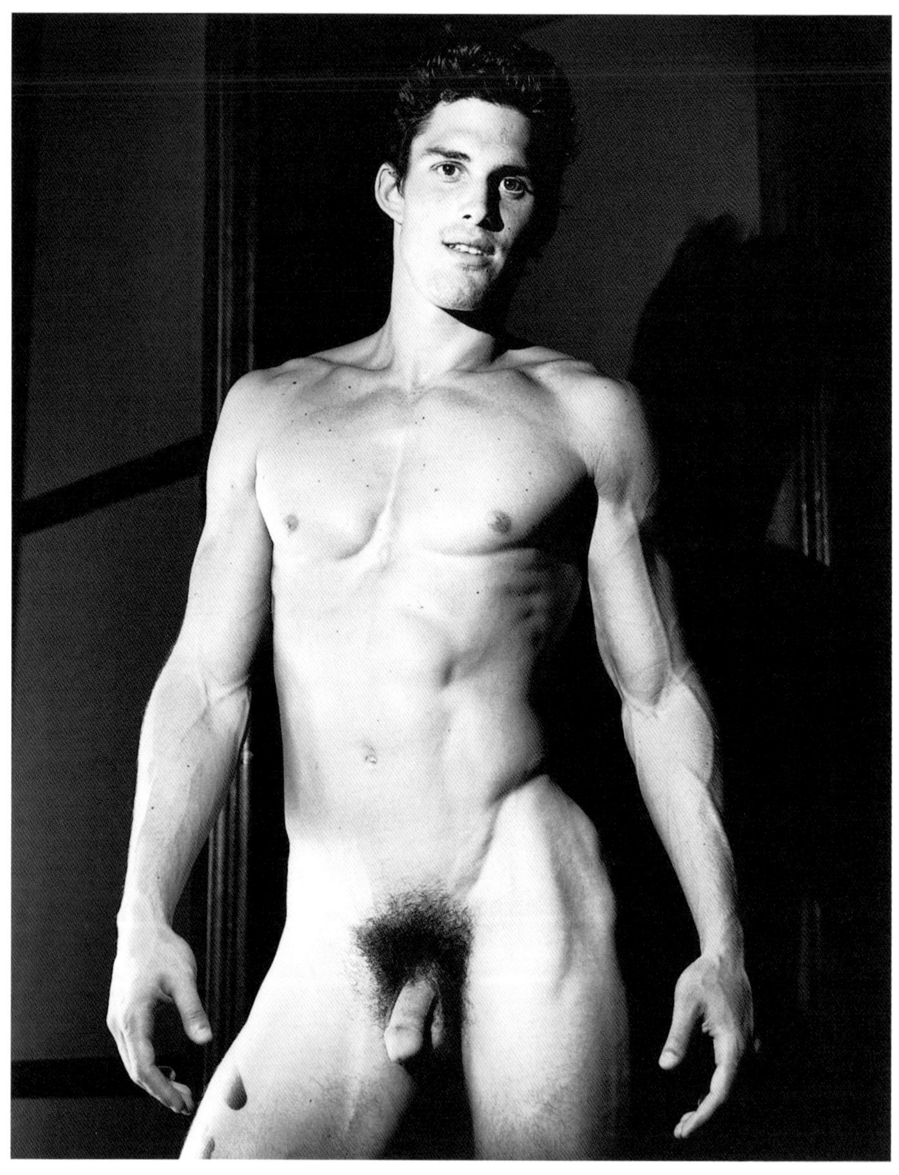

Bruce Weber, Teddy Showing off his New Jersey Muscles #2, 1997

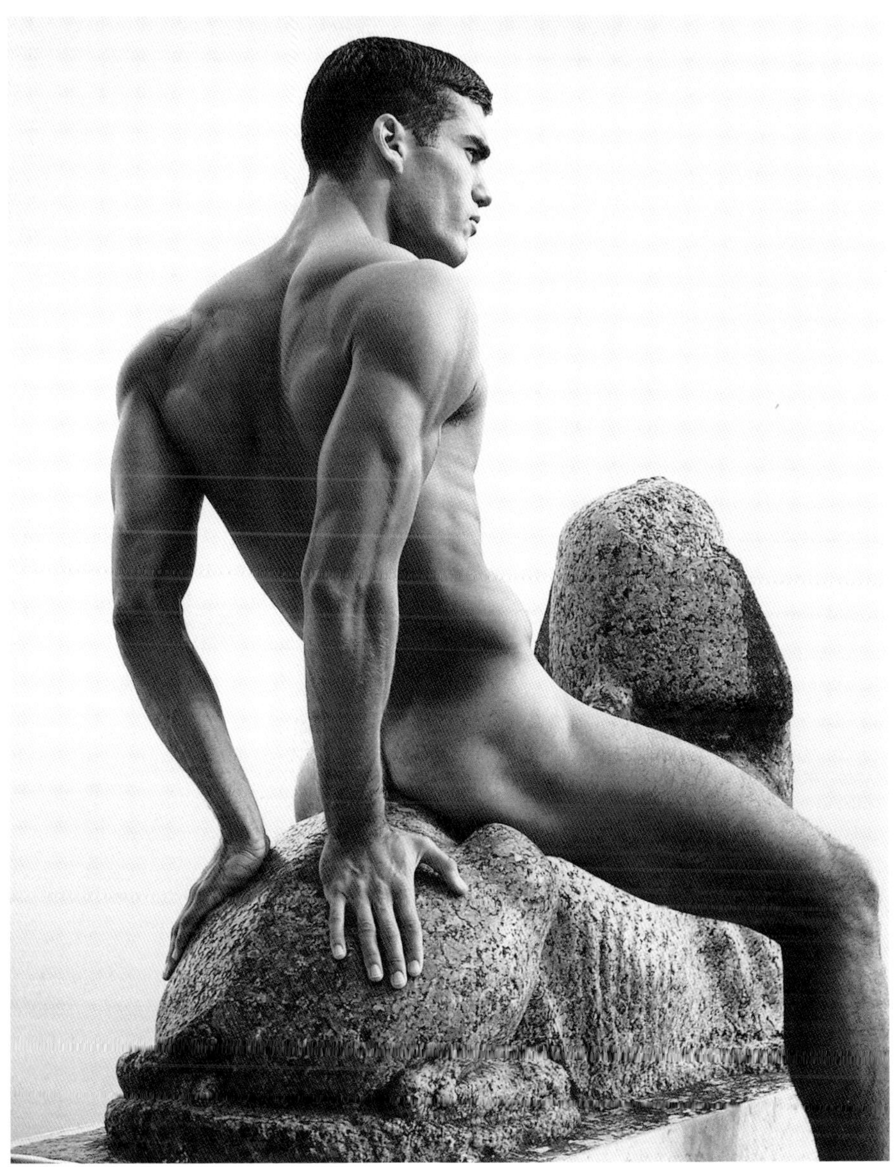

Bruce Weber, Guy from the Navy, 1994

Copyright

Unless otherwise specified, copyright on the works reproduced lies with the respective photographers.

Sonsini Collection, Los Angeles, CA, USA **p. 286:** Bruce of Los Angeles, Courtesy Gordon Hanson, Los Angeles, CA, USA **pp. 287:** Bruce of Los Angeles, John Sonsini Collection, Los Angeles, CA, USA **pp. 290–292:** Bruce of Los Angeles, Courtesy Throckmorton Fine Art, Inc., New York, NY, USA **p. 293:** Bruce of Los Angeles, John Sonsini Collection, Los Angeles, CA, USA **pp. 294/295:** Bruce of Los Angeles, Courtesy Throckmorton Fine Art, Inc., New York, NY, USA **pp. 310/311:** Konrad Helbig, Private Collection, Hamburg, Germany **p. 316:** Anonymous, Author's Collection, Miami Beach, FL, USA **pp. 318–321:** Ken Haak, Courtesy David Carlson, East Hampton, NY, USA **pp. 344–349:** Bob Mizer, Courtesy Athletic Model Guild, P. O. Box 1732, Alameda, CA 94 501, USA, Tel.: (510) 769–1066: Fax: (510) 769–2922 **pp. 356/357:** Herbert Tobias, F. C. Gundlach Collection, Hamburg, Germany **pp. 368–373:** Andy Warhol, Polaroid polacolor print, 10.8 x 8.6 cm. © 2005 Andy Warhol Foundation for the Visual Arts/ARS, New York **p. 377:** Robert Mapplethorpe, © 1979 The Estate of Robert Mapplethorpe, New York, NY, USA **p. 378:** Robert Mapplethorpe, © 1976 The Estate of Robert Mapplethorpe, New York, NY, USA **p. 379:** Robert Mapplethorpe, © 1980 The Estate of Robert Mapplethorpe, New York, NY, USA **p. 400:** Robert Mapplethorpe, © 1987 The Estate of Robert Mapplethorpe, New York, NY, USA **pp. 401–403:** Robert Mapplethorpe, © 1986 The Estate of Robert Mapplethorpe, New York, NY, USA **p. 404:** Robert Mapplethorpe, © 1981 The Estate of Robert Mapplethorpe, New York, NY, USA **p. 405:** Robert Mapplethorpe, © 1980 The Estate of Robert Mapplethorpe, New York, NY, USA **p. 406:** David Hockney, Composite Polaroid, 40» x 18« **p. 407:** David Hockney, Composite Polaroid, 20» x 38 1/2« **pp. 410/411:** Chuck Close, Polacolor II. © Photograph courtesy PaceWildenstein, New York, NY, USA **pp. 418–425:** Mark Morrisroe, F. C. Gundlach Collection, Hamburg, Germany. Courtesy Pat Hearn Gallery, New York, NY, USA **pp. 428/429:** Steven Arnold, © Steven Arnold Charitable Foundation, Los Angeles, CA, USA **p. 462:** Conrad Hechter, Courtesy of FotoFactory Press, Santa Monica, CA, USA **p. 463:** David Sprigle, Courtesy of FotoFactory Press, Santa Monica, CA, USA **pp. 480/481:** Ken Probst, Courtesy of Vance Martin Photography and Fine Art, San Francisco, CA, USA **pp. 482/483:** John Dugdale, Courtesy of Wessel + O'Connor Gallery, New York, NY, USA **pp. 498–503:** Herb Ritts, © Herb Ritts, Courtesy Fahey/Klein Gallery, Los Angeles, CA, USA **pp. 504–507:** Wolfgang Tillmans, Courtesy Daniel Buchholz, Cologne, Germany/ Andrea Rosen Gallery, New York, NY, USA **p. 531:** Baly Hinter Wipflinger, From the book »Album Privato«, © 1995 Babilonia Edizioni, Milan, Italy **pp. 536/537:** Herb Klein, Courtesy of FotoFactory Press, Santa Monica, CA, USA **pp. 560/561:** Blake Little, Courtesy of Wessel + O'Connor Gallery, New York, NY, USA **pp. 562–565:** Jack Pierson, Courtesy Galerie Aurel Scheibler, Cologne, Germany **pp. 566–569:** Bruce Weber, © Bruce Weber and property of Bruce Weber/Little Bear, Inc., New York, NY, USA

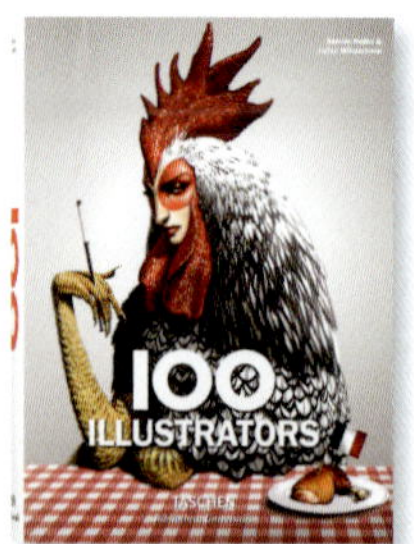

100 Illustrators

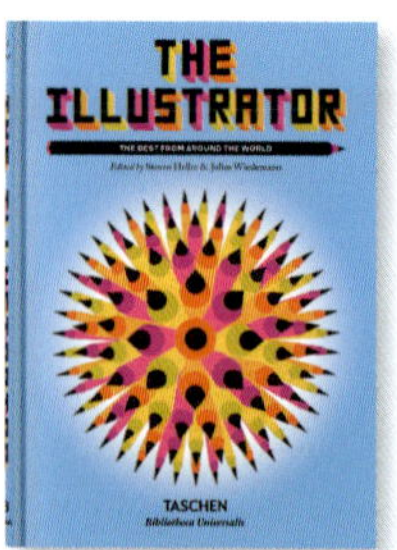

The Illustrator

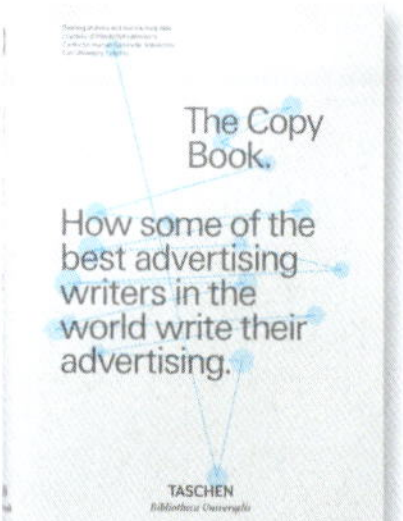

D&AD.
The Copy Book

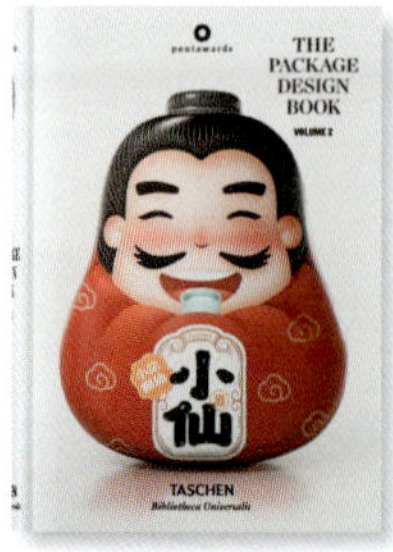

The Package Design
Book. Volume 2

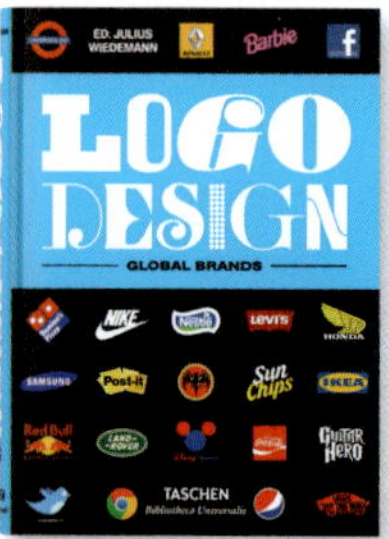

Logo Design.
Global Brands

Bookworm's delight:
never bore, always excite!

TASCHEN
Bibliotheca Universalis

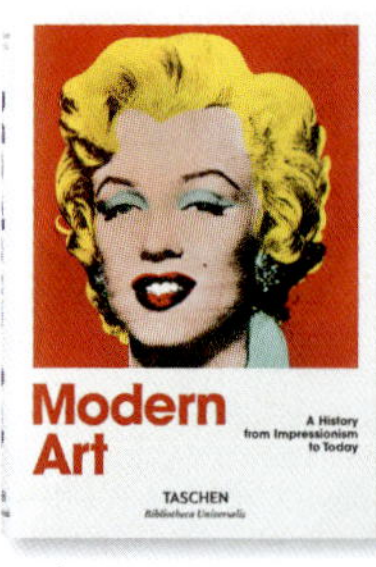

Modern Art

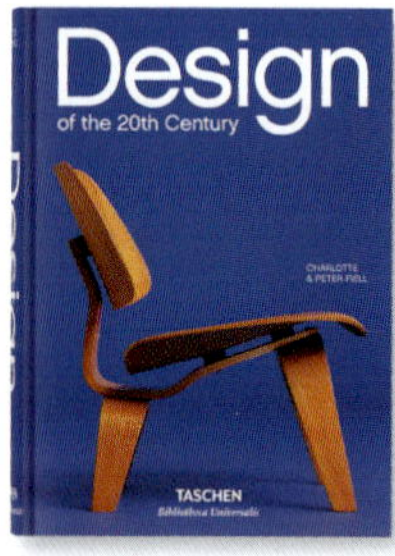

Design of the 20th Century

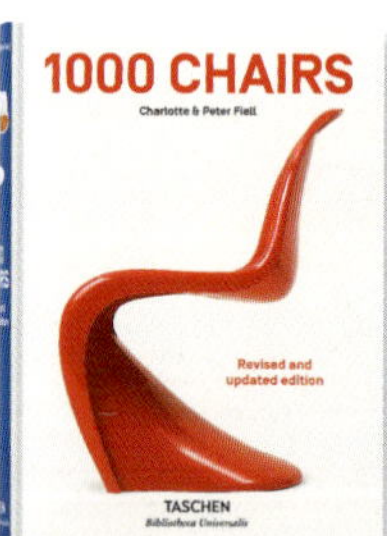

1000 Chairs

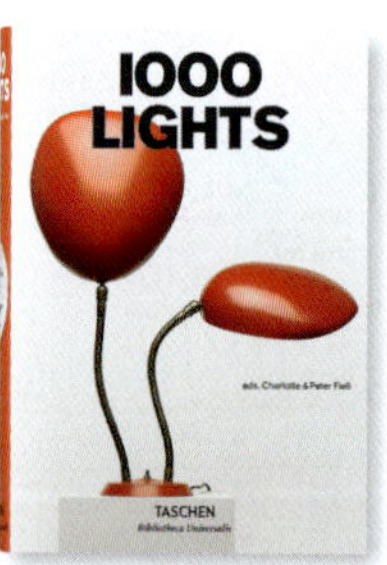

1000 Lights

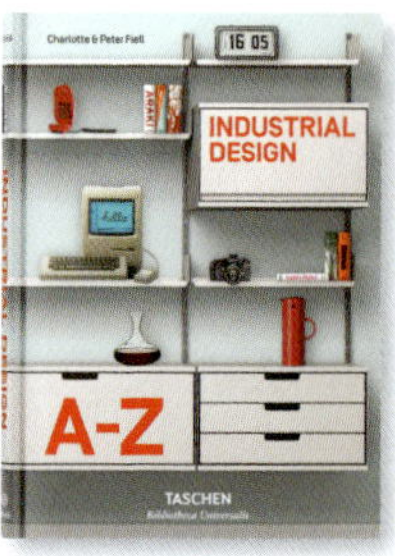

Industrial Design A–Z

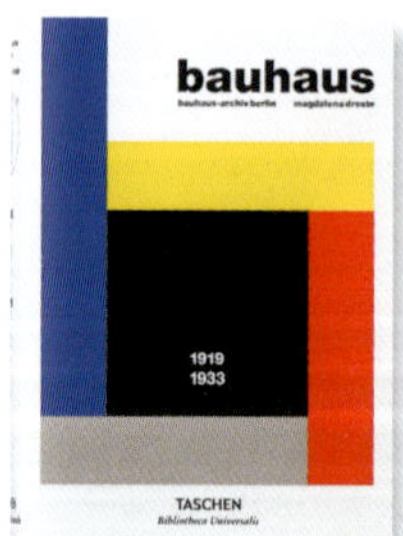

Bauhaus

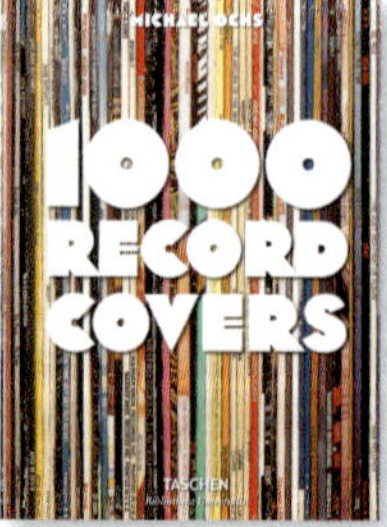

1000 Record Covers

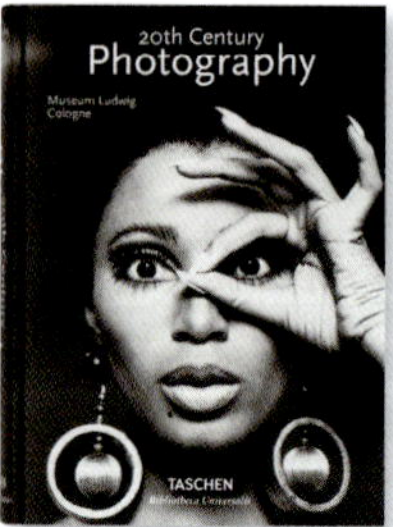

20th Century Photography

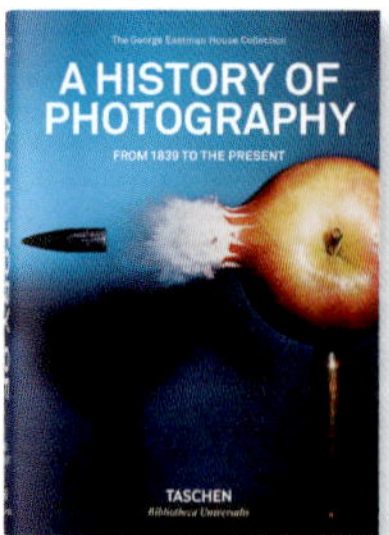

A History of Photography

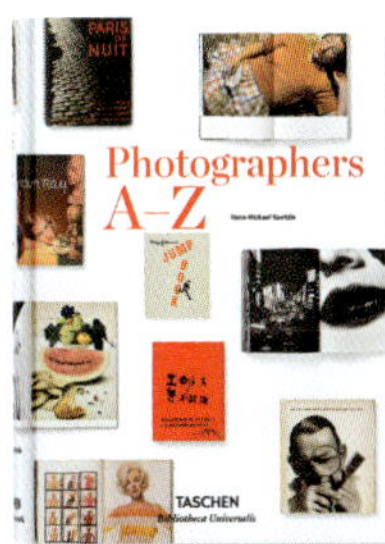

Photographers A–Z

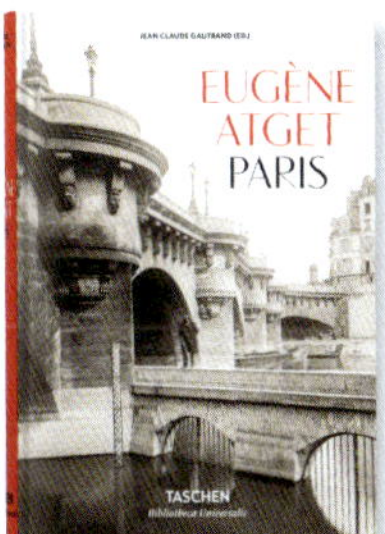

Eugène Atget. Paris

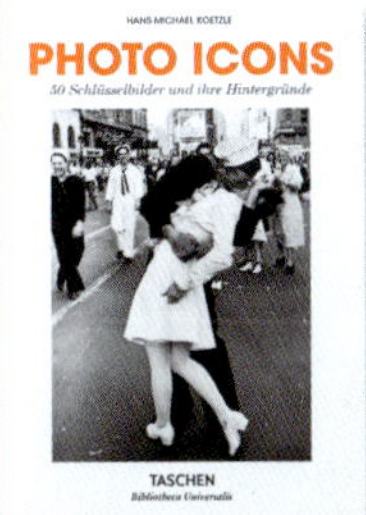

Photo Icons

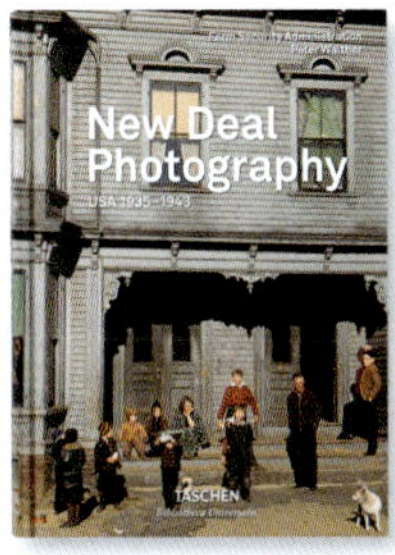

New Deal Photography

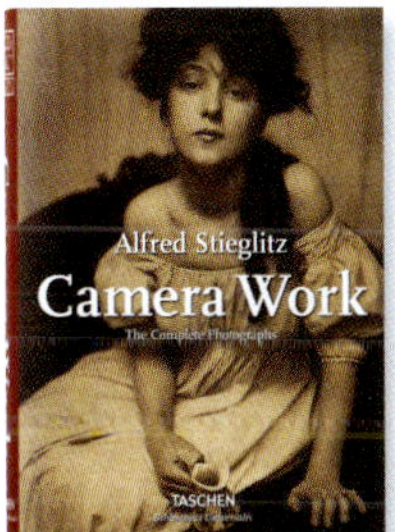

Stieglitz.
Camera Work

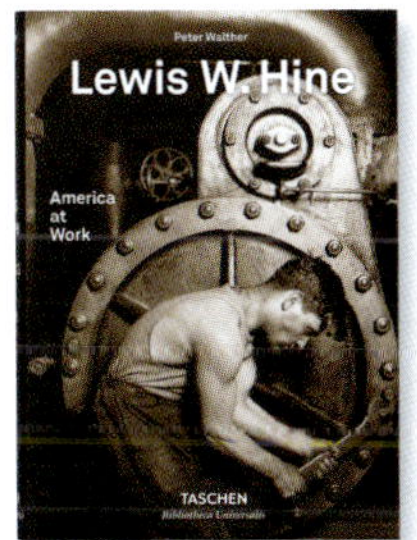

Lewis W. Hine

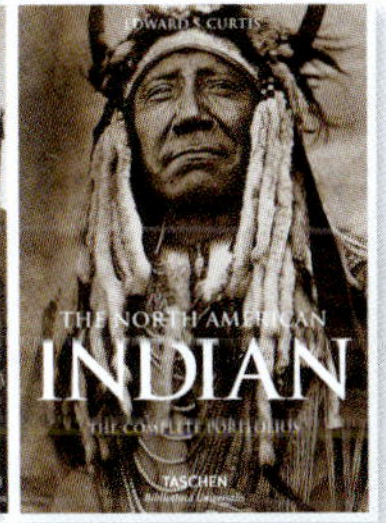

Curtis. The North
American Indian

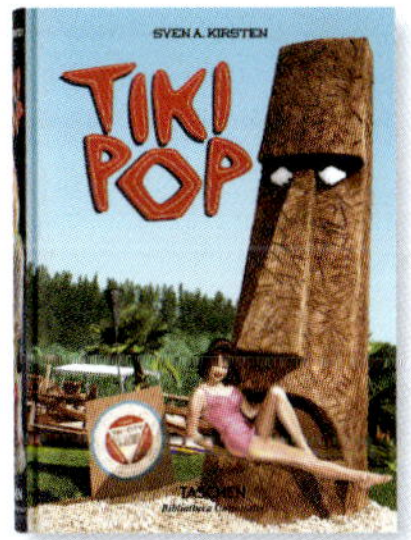

Tiki Pop

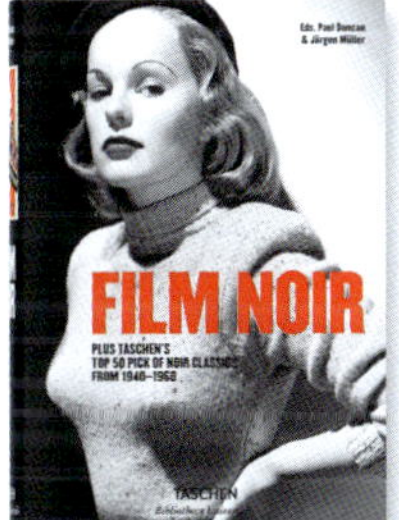

Film Noir

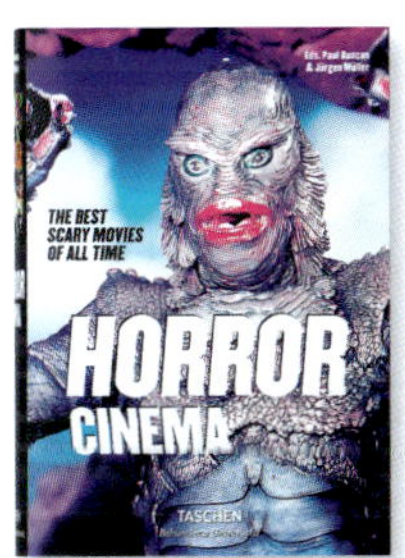

Horror Cinema

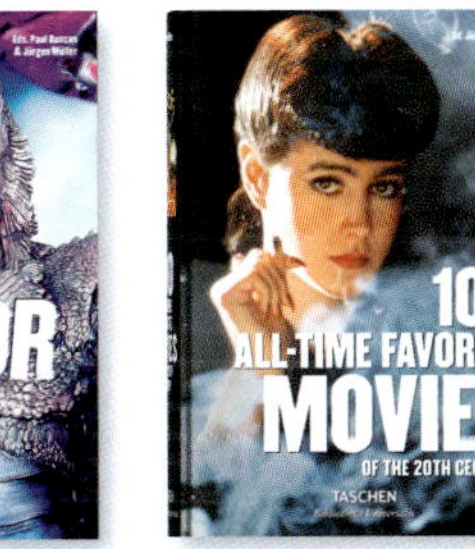

100 All-Time
Favorite Movies

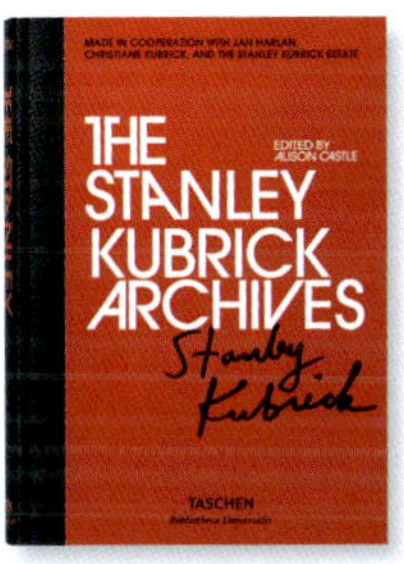

The Stanley Kubrick
Archives

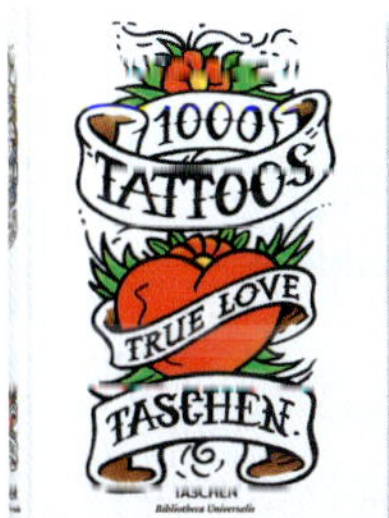

1000 Tattoos

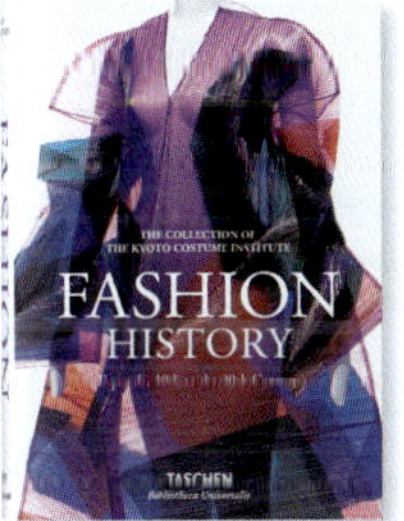

Fashion History

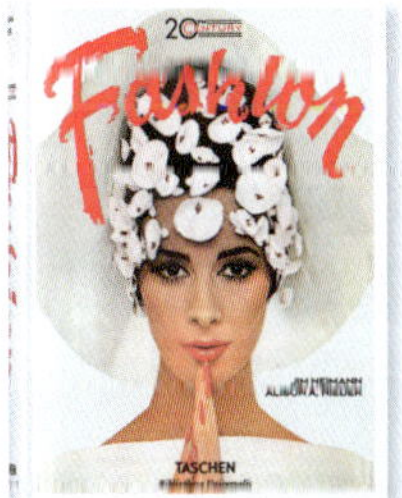

20th Century Fashion

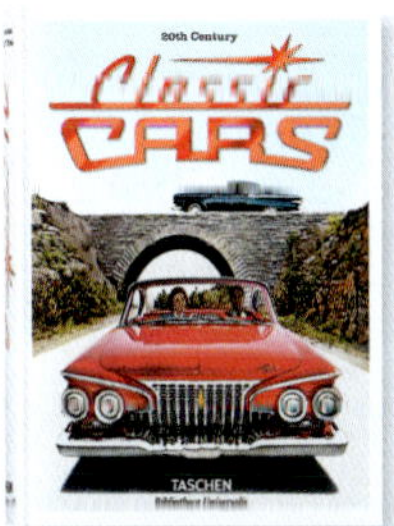

20th Century Classic Cars

Dedication
To Kevin Voelcker

Acknowledgements
David Leddick would like to thank:
All the photographers and their staffs, dealers, collectors and friends
from all points of the globe who so willingly provided the photographs
that make up this book. To list them all would be as many names as are
in the text. I made no contacts who did not wish to participate in this
project and made great efforts to provide materials as quickly as they
could. To all of you there is no way to thank you enough. This has been
a vast undertaking and you made it possible to do it right.

Front cover: **Dianora Niccolini**, The Swimmer, 1983
Back cover: **Ken Haak**, Black Buttocks and Lower Back, 1968
pp. 30/31: **Gaudenzio Marconi**, Homme nu dans la position
de la création d'Adam de Michel-Ange, 1870
Cliché Bibliothèque Nationale de France, Paris
pp. 66/67: **Wilhelm von Gloeden**, c.1900
pp. 128/129: **George Platt Lynes**, Monroe Wheeler, 1935
Anatole Pohorilenko Collection, New York, NY, USA
pp. 204/205: **Herbert List**, Nach dem Bad, 1955
© Herbert List Nachlass – Max Scheler, Hamburg, Germany
pp. 296/297: **Anonymous**, 1960s
pp. 380/381: **Jeff Palmer**, The Grey Couple, 1993

EACH AND EVERY TASCHEN BOOK PLANTS A SEED!
Each year, we offset our annual carbon emissions with carbon credits
at the Instituto Terra, a reforestation program in Minas Gerais, Brazil,
founded by Lélia and Sebastião Salgado. To find out more about this
ecological partnership, please check: www.taschen.com/institutoterra
Inspiration: unlimited. Carbon footprint: (almost) zero.

Want to see more? Visit taschen.com to view our current publications,
browse our latest magazine, and subscribe to our newsletter.